HISTORY

OF THE

5th ROYAL GURKHA RIFLES

(FRONTIER FORCE)

1858 TO 1928

The Naval & Military Press Ltd

Published by
The Naval & Military Press Ltd
5 Riverside, Brambleside, Bellbrook
Industrial Estate, Uckfield, East Sussex,
TN22 1QQ England
Tel: +44 (0) 1825 749494
Fax: +44 (0) 1825 765701
www.naval-military-press.com

In reprinting in facsimile from the original, any imperfections are inevitably reproduced and the quality may fall short of modern type and cartographic standards.

HISTORY OF THE FIFTH ROYAL GURKHA RIFLES (FRONTIER FORCE), 1858 TO 1928

Field-Marshal the Hon. F. S. Earl Roberts of Kandahar, V.C., K.G., K.P., G.C.B., O.M., G.C.S.I., G.C.I.E., Colonel of the Regiment.

For Private Circulation Only.

HISTORY

of the

5TH ROYAL GURKHA RIFLES

(FRONTIER FORCE)

1858 TO 1928

Dedicated
TO
COUNTESS ROBERTS, D.B.E.,
IN MEMORY OF HER FATHER,
FIELD-MARSHAL EARL ROBERTS, V.C.,
K.G., K.P., P.C., G.C.B., G.C.S.I., G.C.I.E., O.M.,
FIRST COLONEL OF THE FIFTH GURKHAS,
UNDER WHOM THE REGIMENT GAINED MANY OF ITS
EARLY AND GREAT DISTINCTIONS

ADDENDA.

In addition to those officers mentioned in the Preface, the Regiment is indebted to Major R. C. Duncan, M.V.O., O.B.E., Captain R. A. Briggs and Captain A. T. Cornwall-Jones for the assistance given by them in the compilation of this History.

PREFACE

WHEN it was decided some years ago to produce a history of the Regiment, nothing more ambitious was aimed at than a chronicle of the activities of the 5th Gurkhas during the Great War. Later, Colonel H. E. Weekes, O.B.E., initiated the project of a complete history to deal with the period 1858 to 1928. Various serving officers were deputed to undertake the task in their spare time, among whom may be mentioned Lieutenant-Colonel H. T. Molloy, D.S.O., Brevet Lieutenant-Colonel H. R. C. Lane, D.S.O., O.B.E., Major K. C. S. Erskine, M.C., Captain J. L. Johanson, and Captain N. Macdonald. Others have helped in the production of maps and photographs, and in this connection valuable work has been done by Captain R. T. Cameron, Captain R. G. Leonard, Captain P. R. Broadway, Lieutenant G. W. S. Burton, and Major K. C. S. Erskine, M.C.

A number of retired officers were asked to write reminiscences or to assist by unearthing old photographs, and of these the Regiment is indebted to Major-General Sir J. M. Stewart, K.C.B., K.C.M.G., Major-General Sir Ivor Philipps, K.C.B., Major-General H. J. P. Browne, C.B., Major-General M. R. W. Nightingale, C.B., C.M.G., C.S.I., D.S.O., Brigadier-General the Honourable C. G. Bruce, C.B., M.V.O., Brigadier-General W. D. Villiers-Stuart, C.B.E., D.S.O., and Colonel F. W. Evatt.

The special thanks of the Regiment are due to General Sir Ian Hamilton, G.C.B., for his spirited foreword.

The courtesy of the following publishers and owners of copyright is gratefully acknowledged :—

> Messrs. Sampson Low, Marston & Co., 100, Southwark Street, London, S.E.1, for permission to make use of three copyright maps, viz.: The Paiwar Kotal, Charasia and the Country round Kabul, and the Action at Kandahar, included in "The Afghan Campaigns of 1878–1880," by Sydney H. Shadbolt.

Messrs. John Murray, 50a, Albemarle Street, W.1, for permission to make use of the copyright map of Palosin Camp published in Nevill's " Campaigns of the North-West Frontier."

The Controller of H.M. Stationery Office for permission to make use of four maps published in " The Campaign in Mesopotamia," compiled under the auspices of the Historical Section, Committee of Imperial Defence, viz. : Map No. VI of Vol. I, Map of Lower Mesopotamia from Vol. II, and Maps of Ramadi and Khan Baghdadi from Vol. IV.

Messrs. Holmes, photographers of Peshawar, and Messrs. Melaram, photographers of Nowshera, for permission to reproduce those copyright photographs which bear their names.

CONTENTS

PART I

THE REGIMENT BEFORE THE GREAT WAR

CHAP.		PAGE
I.	1858 to 1863	3
II.	1863 to 1878	13
III.	The Second Afghan War: November, 1878, to December, 1879	33
IV.	The Second Afghan War (continued): October, 1879, to the Conclusion of Hostilities	52
V.	Peace and War, 1881 to 1892	76
VI.	A Record of Changing Conditions	118
VII.	Kagan, Waziristan, and Tirah, 1893 to 1898	131
VIII.	1898 to 1914	154
IX.	The 2nd Battalion, 1886 to 1914	173

PART II

THE FIRST BATTALION IN THE GREAT WAR

CHAP.		
I.	Events from August 4th, 1914, to May 30th, 1915	203
II.	The Battle of June 4th, and Subsequent Events to June 27th, 1915	217
III.	Battle of June 28th, and Subsequent Events to August 5th, 1915	232
IV.	Battle of August 6th–10th, and Subsequent Events to August 20th, 1915	246
V.	Battle of August 21st, 1915, and Subsequent Events to the Evacuation	258
VI.	India—Arrival in Mesopotamia	272
VII.	Mesopotamia: The Battle of Ramadi	283
VIII.	The Battle of Khan Baghdadi and the End of the War	295

PART III

THE SECOND BATTALION IN THE GREAT WAR

CHAP.		
I.	Outbreak of the War—British Officers in France—Events of Summer, 1915—Drafts for the Front—"C" Company in Gallipoli	305
II.	1915—Epidemic of Malaria—Mohmand Unrest—1916 and Orders for Overseas—Departure from India and Arrival in Mesopotamia—Operations on Euphrates Front	318
III.	Departure from Nasiriyeh—Baghdad—Ramadi—Hit and Khan Baghdadi—Garrison Duty in Iraq—Return to India	328

PART IV

THE THIRD BATTALION

CHAP.		PAGE
I.	November 28th, 1916, to May 15th, 1919	347
II.	Third Afghan War—The Battalion in Mardan. May, 1919, to September, 1920	353
III.	The Arab Rising—Disbandment. September, 1920, to July, 1921	862

PART V

THE REGIMENT AFTER THE GREAT WAR

CHAP.		PAGE
I.	The 1st Battalion, 1919 to 1928	383
II.	The 2nd Battalion, 1919 to 1928	413
	Epilogue	445

APPENDICES

NO.		PAGE
I.	Relating to the Raising of the Regiment	449
II.	Honours and Awards	450
III.	Casualties sustained by 5th Royal Gurkha Rifles, F.F., arranged by Campaigns	466
IV.	List of Officers who served with the Regiment, 1858 to Present Day	471
V.	List of Officers attached during the Great War, 1914–18	478
VI.	Commandants, 5th Royal Gurkhas, F.F.	480
VII.	Brief Records of Services of Officers of the Regiment on Staff or other Extra-Regimental Employment and of Retired Officers during the Great War	481
VIII.	The Work of the Depots during the Great War	487

LIST OF ILLUSTRATIONS

FIELD-MARSHAL THE HON. F. S. EARL ROBERTS OF KANDAHAR, V.C., K.G., K.P., G.C.B., O.M., G.C.S.I., G.C.I.E., COLONEL OF THE REGIMENT ... *Frontispiece*

	FACING PAGE
BT.-MAJOR H. F. M. BOISRAGON	3
TWO VIEWS OF ABBOTTABAD, 1864	8
KIT WORN ABOUT 1865 AND 1882	26
THE CAPTURE OF THE SPINGAWAI KOTAL, DECEMBER 2ND, 1878	38
THE BALA HISSAR, KABUL, 1879	60
KABUL, 1880	60
GROUPS OF OFFICERS, 1865 AND 1880	70
THE NILT POSITION	108
THREE WHO GAINED THE VICTORIA CROSS	114
SUBADAR-MAJOR PARSU KHATTRI, I.O.M., SARDAR BAHADUR, 1859 TO 1900	148
ORDER OF MERIT MEN, 1899	158
THE K.C.B. CUP, PRESENTED BY FOUR EX-COMMANDANTS OF THE REGIMENT IN 1911	162
1/5TH GUARD, BOER PRISONERS' CAMP, ABBOTTABAD, 1902	168
RECRUITS BRIDGE-BUILDING, ABBOTTABAD, 1906	168
COLONEL E. MOLLOY, C.B.	173
PART OF THE NUCLEUS OF THE 2ND BATTALION, WITH E. VANSITTART, ADJUTANT	178
2/5TH ON THE RANGE: OLD STYLE "VOLLEY FIRING"	178
BEGINNING OF WEEK-END WAR, 1908: 2/5TH DIGGING IN ON REACHING WALAI	194
END OF WEEK-END WAR: ZAKKA TRIBESMEN BRINGING IN RIFLES	194
BRITISH OFFICERS OF THE REGIMENT, TAKEN IN ABBOTTABAD SHORTLY AFTER THE OUTBREAK OF THE GREAT WAR, 1914	203
EARLY DAYS IN 1915: EEL FISHING ON THE BANKS OF THE SUEZ CANAL; MORE FISHING ON THE CANAL; 1/5TH MACHINE GUN MOUNTED AGAINST SUBMARINES ON THE S.S. "ANNABERG" EN ROUTE TO GALLIPOLI	208
LANCASHIRE LANDING ("W" BEACH) FROM CAPE HELLES END	220
"V" BEACH AND SEDD-UL-BAHR FROM CAPE HELLES	220
LOOKING NORTH ALONG THE COAST FROM CAPE TEKKE	224
GULLY BEACH (LOOKING SOUTH)	224
PANORAMA OF THE SUVLA POSITION, FROM THE TURKISH POSITION ON KOJA CHEMEN TEPE	240
PANORAMA OF "V" BEACH, TAKEN FROM THE END OF THE PIER BUILT OUT TO THE "RIVER CLYDE"	240
OFFICERS' DUG-OUTS, ANZAC; ANZAC, LOOKING SOUTH ALONG COAST; ANZAC FRONT: QUINN'S POST TO LONE PINE	246
PANORAMA LOOKING SOUTH-EAST FROM CHOCOLATE HILL	264
"WHAT MIGHT HAVE BEEN": THE NARROWS FROM KOJA CHEMEN TEPE	266

LIST OF ILLUSTRATIONS

	FACING PAGE
Men of the 1/5th at Damakjelik Bair	266
Digging Madhij Position, November, 1917; Route March: 1/5th crossing Dam at Habbaniyeh Escape; Ramadi Memorial on Ramadi Ridge; Proclamation of Armistice by General Brooking at Ramadi	290
Shergat (Tigris): Ancient Asshur. Entraining at Dhibban en route for India. "Gott Strafe England": A German Drawing on a Wall of the Wrecked Wireless Station at Baghdad. The Residency, Baghdad: Used as G.H.Q.	300
The Great War Memorials	305
At Battalion Headquarters, Damakjelik Bair: Inspection before taking over Trenches	312
2/5th Men in a Fire Trench beyond Damakjelik Bair	312
2/5th Lewis Guns at Ramadi, Mesopotamia, 1917: Preparing to Advance: in Action	332
Sections of 2/5th in Battle Formation, Ramadi, Mesopotamia, 1917	336
A Runner, 2/5th, Mesopotamia, 1917	336
2/5th marching to Docks from Rest Camp, Basra, to embark for India. 2/5th embarking at Basra for Karachi on s.s. "Bankora," May 23rd, 1919	342
Kacha Garhi, 1919: Corner of 3/5th Camp. Relief of Samawa: Samcol on the March with Armoured Construction Train	358
Lining Bank of Euphrates: Action at Khidhr	366
The Defence Vessel F2, near Khidhr	366
Samcol Headquarters at First Action of Imam Abdulla	376
Railway Bridge at Imam Abdulla, destroyed by the Arabs	376
Darsamand Camp, 1920: Part of 1/5th Perimeter Wall	386
Parachinar Fort, 1922	386
Clearing after a Duststorm	390
Razmak (Old) Camp: 1/5th Perimeter after the Blizzard, February 7th, 1923	394
1/5th on Convoy Escort Duty, closing on Razmak (Old) Camp	394
1/5th Advance Guard opening out on Right Bank of the Tauda China	398
Camel Convoy in Tauda China passing Liaison Point between Old and New Razmak	398
The 1/5th Quarterguard over the Main Gate, Fort Lockhart, 1924	404
The Unveiling of the Frontier Force Memorial, Kohat, October, 1924	404
Field-Marshal Sir Arthur Barrett, G.C.B., G.C.S.I., K.C.V.O.	410
"Flathead Left" from Asa Khan Camp	418
Makin	418
The Blizzard at Kaniguram	430
"Jirga" discussing Peace Terms, Kaniguram	430
Battalion Aid Post at Giga Khel	432
General Lucas bidding Farewell to the 2/5th on its leaving "Skeencol"	432
Malakand from "Guides Piquet," 1925	440
Chief Commissioner's Durbar, Chakdara, 1926: "A" Company, 2/5th, Guard of Honour	440
Abbottabad, 1928, Looking North from Sarban; The View from the Terrace, Officers' Mess	442
Kit and Small Arms Armament, 5th Royal Gurkha Rifles (Frontier Force)	446

LIST OF MAPS

	FACING PAGE
Palosin Camp, April 23rd, 1860	12
Position on the Ambela Pass, October 20th—December 16th, 1863	24
Paiwar Kotal and Spingawai Pass	40
Sketch Map of Kandahar and Neighbourhood	72
Samana	104
View of Nilt Ravine from Maiun, looking South	116
Suez Canal	216
Action of Gully Ravine	244
Sketch illustrating 29th Indian Infantry Brigade trenches in the Hill 60 Area, August—December, 1915	268
Sketch Map of Gallipoli	270
Ramadi	334
Sketch Map of Khan Baghdadi	340
The Khyber Pass and Bazar Valley	360
Sketch Map showing Operations near Dabbus, October 29th and 30th, 1920	374
Sketch Map illustrating Action of Imam Abdullah, November 11th, 1920	378
Mesopotamia	380
Sketch Map of the Area, Sora Rogha—Ahnai Tangi, January 14th, 1920	420
The Anzac Position, Gallipoli	Pocket at end
Map of Kabul and Surrounding Country	Pocket at end
Black Mountain	Pocket at end
Gilgit, Kashmir and North-West Frontier	Pocket at end
Afghanistan, Baluchistan and North-West Frontier	Pocket at end

Gaiety, simplicity, bravery and loyalty,
  These the gifts they bring from out their homes among the hills,
Vigour and stout-heartedness, and pride be-fitting royalty,
  And love of high achievement and the strength that love instils.

FOREWORD

By General Sir Ian Hamilton.

During the year 1874 the mud fort at Dera Ismail Khan was held by "A" Company of the 92nd Gordon Highlanders. They were the only British troops serving trans-Indus and the "Piffers"—as we used to call the officers of the Punjab Frontier Force—were very kind to the young subaltern who, after the sudden death of his Captain, found himself alone with his Highlanders in their midst. At that time Brigadier-General Sir Charles Keyes was in command of the Force. He was the hero of both sides of the border; father of a hero-to-be (Admiral Sir Roger Keyes of Dardanelles and Zeebrugge fame), and where all were kind, he was kindest. He invited me to gallop for him at field days; he initiated me gently into the horrors of inspections; he even took me with him for a glorious ten days' trip along the debatable marches of the Indian North-West Frontier, during which we had so ticklish an interview with a body of tribesmen from over the way that for about the space of two minutes it was touch and go whether the two-year old Sir Roger would not become an orphan.

Sir Charles had lost the fingers of his left hand as the result of having been first man over the top at the recapture of the Crag Piquet during the Umbeyla Campaign. At the action of the Barari Gorge, during the Mahsud Waziri Campaign of 1860, he had fought in single combat with the enemy chief and killed him, thereby winning the campaign. On his own he had done it, just as Sir Roger would have won the Dardanelles Campaign on his own had he been a free agent instead of a loyal Chief of Staff. Here is the story as it came to me on the Frontier in 1873: The battle was going badly for us. The Waziris were pressing back the British. Each of them well ahead of his men, the two champions ran together, sword in hand. As they closed in mortal combat the firing died away. Fascinated by the rapid cut and thrust of the sword-play, troops and tribesmen stood as still as stones. The battle had turned into a duel. The gallant Wazir fell. Forthwith the whole 7,000 of his followers took to their heels and disappeared into the folds of the mountains. The Hazara Gurkha Battalion, afterwards called the 5th Gurkhas, were the only formed body of troops remaining on the battlefield at this moment, they being close up in reserve. Every man of them saw the encounter, and the yell with which they greeted the result gave wings to the flight of the foe.

If the Gurkhas watched Keyes, Keyes had his eye upon the 5th Gurkhas. I know how he valued the element they contributed to the Punjab Frontier Force. Whether he was actually in camp that night I cannot remember, but I do remember, as if it were yesterday, his telling me the story of the baptism of fire of the Hazara Battalion at Palosin, thus enabling me to realize more vividly than most history readers the tremendous scrimmage which took place at grey dawn on April 23rd, 1860, when 3,000 Mahsuds rushed the camp and it was sword versus bayonet for fifteen terrible minutes. He told me, too, the tale of the dandy subaltern who was buttoning on his shirt collar in his tent during this hand-to-hand struggle between two mobs in the half light. When his bearer appeared with that peculiar greeny-yellow look on his face, which in an Indian of a non-fighting class betokens the approach of imminent danger, whether it take the form of a tiger or a tribesman—when this servant appeared and cried out to him in a lamentable voice: "*Sahib, sahib! Waziri log agya!*"[1] he replied without turning a hair: "*Bolo darwaza band hai!*"[2] The battle ended on a note of triumph for the newly raised Gurkhas. The Guides formed line across the camp and managed to keep one half of it intact while they gradually *saf karoed*, or cleaned out, the remainder. Major Rothney, commanding the Gurkhas, taking with him the 4th Sikhs, then sallied forth and stormed the ridge above the camp from which the enemy were still pouring down, and pursued them many miles.

A good opening this, to the career of a regiment which was to become famous. For during the second Afghan War it would hardly be too much to say that the 5th Gurkhas played the leading part. Whenever Lord Roberts spoke of "the Gurkhas" he was usually thinking of the 5th Gurkhas. Every officer became known to me in my capacity as A.D.C. to Brigadier-General "Redan" Massy, commanding the Cavalry, but Neville Chamberlain, A.D.C. to Lord Roberts, knew them better still. My brother, Vereker Hamilton, an artist, came out to India in 1886, and asked Lord Roberts what he considered the most dramatic, and at the same time most paintable, incident of the campaign of 1878–81. He sent him to Captain Neville Chamberlain, who told him that the incident which should, of all others, be put on to canvas was the storming of the Afghan stockade in the deodar forest at Spingawai Kotal by the 5th Gurkhas at grey dawn on December 2nd, 1878. Lord Roberts not only agreed, but afterwards bought the picture.

The Battle of Charasia, on September 6th, 1879, furnished history with one of those spectacles which adorn the galleries of a soldier's

---

[1] "My lord, my lord! The Waziris are upon us!"
[2] "Tell them the door is shut!" (The Indian equivalent of an English lady's "Say I am not at home.")

retrospect and make him feel that it is better to have lived and fought than never to have fought at all. When he closes his eyes and saunters down those galleries of memory he would be more than human if he did not experience a feeling of superiority to those mild creatures of the future who may have to content themselves with unconvincing Hollywood encounters. For a long time I had been watching the turning movement of the 72nd Highlanders, the 5th Gurkhas, and the 5th Punjab Infantry against the right flank of the Afghan Army, having indeed been sent there on that express duty by my Chief, General Massy, for we still believed then in pursuit of men armed with breech-loaders by men armed with lances and swords. During two very anxious hours the attack hung fire. The heights were steep, the defence was stout, and neither gun nor rifle-fire seemed to make any impression. All at once, in a long line of scattered groups, our infantry left the cover of their rocks and began to scramble up the last 150 yards or so of the ridge. There was a lull in the firing. The smoke-cloud lifted and down came the Afghan Regulars! Right on to the top of the Gurkhas they charged. My heart came into my mouth. Our lives—everyone's life—hung upon the conduct of this battalion. They stood firm. Fitzhugh, John Cook, and the gallant 5th never faltered, but stood their ground like bricks and shot the Afghan counter-attack to pieces. Enormous was the relief. If those Gurkhas had given way not one of us (in my opinion) would have got back to India. Lord Roberts himself always said that this battle was the most touch-and-go affair of his career. The tops of the high mountains overlooking Charasia were literally white with masses of armed tribesmen watching to see which way the struggle would turn. Compared with our battles on the Dardanelles the casualties seem trifling, but the penalty of defeat, or even of a repulse, would have been annihilation.

The British Raj came into collision with the tribesmen from Kohistan in the north on December 10th, 1879, when Brigadier-General Macpherson took seven of their standards. Eclipsed by the heavier fighting round Sherpur cantonments, this action was classed at the time as a side-show. Historically, however, it possesses a special interest as the Kohistanis were a distinct lot, and I think the 5th Gurkhas would like to hear from one of the few eyewitnesses living, how their regiment acquitted itself at the engagement of Mir Karez. Young Neville Chamberlain was looking on, and I repeat the account of old Neville Chamberlain as nearly as may be in his own words. After some preliminary skirmishing Mir Butcha and his Kohistanis fell back upon a conical hill, where they determined to stand and fight it out. The 3rd Sikhs and the 5th Gurkhas formed up in columns, with Morgan's mountain guns in support, and moved on in a stately manner against the enemy, marching in step as if on inspection parade.

As the front ranks touched the base of the hill the whole mass broke into a charge. Up they went, the officers well in front. "It reminded me," said Sir Neville, "of a favourite picture of mine in the Galleries of Versailles, 'The Assault on the Mamelon Vert'; the surge onwards of a mass of men which looked, and was, irresistible."

After the Afghan War the late Field-Marshal Earl Roberts had to select supporters for his arms. He chose:—

"Dexter—A Highlander of the 72nd Regiment.
"Sinister—A Gurkha.
"Both habited and holding in their exterior hands a rifle."

* * * * *

Inheriting this distinction from the finest commander of troops in action and under fire the British Army has known since the days of Marlborough, the 5th Gurkhas entered upon the Great War. They sailed right into the maw of that monster which, with its mechanized jaws, munched up impartially whatever was presented to it—north, south, east, west; heroes, horses, houses, gold; plough-boys, poets, musicians, ne'er-do-weels; fine food for powder, all of them. But there were just a few hours always in each campaign when the old soldierly virtues, some inherited, some acquired, still carried their full weight. These were the few hours before barbed wire and trenches tied up the artistry of war. The 5th Gurkhas should have landed with the Anzacs, whose headlong valour needed just that counterpoise which would have been afforded to them by a small reserve of regulars possessing perfect discipline and an instinctive, inherited knowledge of woodcraft and how to work their way up over rocky cliffs or round about them, cutting pathways with their accustomed marvellous swiftness through thickets of scrub jungle. In a rough-and-tumble struggle through and over so strange a battlefield, my experiences in Afghanistan, Burma, in the Relief of Chitral, in Tirah, and in South Africa, had taught me that the white man fights at a disadvantage unless it is his own particular sort of bush. He is apt to become bewildered and lose his bearings. But that is the Gurkhas' opportunity. Upon such a field as that of Anzac before it had been mapped out by trenches, even the Afridi himself must have played second fiddle to the Gurkha.

As for the Turks, in that blind man's buff fight amidst the scrub, rocks, and precipices of the Sari Bair Ridge on April 25th, 1915, at Anzac, the 5th Gurkhas, had they only been there, would have had them at their mercy. They would have worked round their flank or penetrated their line through the most impenetrable jungle, and cut off their heads with their *kukris* almost before they knew they had lost them. But once trenches had been dug, and once the cruel web of barbed wire had spread its meshes far and wide across no-man's land, the Gurkha had been robbed of his special, almost superhuman virtue in woodcraft and hill-climbing. In a trench he remained a brave soldier, and he could handle rifle and bomb with the best of them. But there were many other brave soldiers eager to do or die upon that peninsula which was the Achilles heel of the Central European Powers. The supreme chance for the Gurkha had been allowed to slip away. Why were there no Gurkhas on Gallipoli during that critical first twenty-four hours when empires hung in the balance? The day of the landing was their moment.

Hurried as had been my inspection of the landscape from the decks of H.M.S. *Phaeton* on March 18th, I had already made up my mind pretty definitely on two points: First, Bulair was out of the picture; secondly, the picture needed Gurkhas in the foreground. So, although Lord Kitchener had given me most clearly to understand I was not to embarrass him by asking for more troops, I hardened my heart, and on March 22nd, directly it was decided that the landing must take place, I cabled him asking for a brigade of Gurkhas. There were Gurkhas sitting idle within two days' sail of us, and anyway there was still time before the landing to collect most of the Gurkha soldiers in our service and send them to the Dardanelles. Not satisfied with this cable, three days later I reinforced it with a letter from which the following is an extract:—

MARCH 25th, 1915.

" . . . I am very anxious, if possible, to get a brigade of Gurkhas, so as to complete the New Zealand Divisional Organization with a type of man who will, I am certain, be most valuable on the Gallipoli Peninsula. The scrubby hill-sides on the south-west face of the plateau are just the sort of terrain where these little fellows are at their brilliant best. There is already a small Indian commissariat attached to the mountain batteries, so there would be no trouble on the score of supply.

" As you may imagine, I have no wish to ask for anything, the giving of which would seriously weaken our hold on Egypt, but you will remember that four mounted brigades belonging to Birdwood's force are being left behind to look after the land of the Pharaohs, and a mounted brigade for a battalion seems a fair exchange. Egypt, in fact, so far as I can make out, seems stiff with troops, and each little ' Gurkh ' might be worth his full weight in gold at Gallipoli. . . ."

What answer did I get to these appeals? None. As the 5th Gurkhas remember, they landed on June 2nd. Thank God for that.

But for them, as for us, it was too late. This is no grouse. Mistakes are always the order of the day when England goes to war. But I have rubbed in this mistake, here—firstly, because it was one of those errors which make or unmake empires; secondly, because it has been put about with cruel iteration that at the Dardanelles we got everything we asked for; thirdly, because my quotation from a letter which exists is proof positive that I am not now cracking up the Gurkhas through politeness.

As to the heroic work of the 5th at Gallipoli and afterwards, it needs no embroidery in a foreword. Their deeds are enshrined not only in the body of this work, but in the hearts of the Indian and British nations. Their sufferings, losses, and ultimate triumph will become a legend. The fame of the noble 5th Gurkhas will never die, and if any politician of the hereafter dreams of disbanding their cadre, or changing their number, or of any other like atrocity, may the perusal of this volume paralyse his sacrilegious hand.

Ian Hamilton

PART I

THE REGIMENT BEFORE THE GREAT WAR

Bt.-Major H. F. M. Boisragon.
Raised the Hazara Goorkha Battalion, 1858.

THE HISTORY OF
THE 5TH ROYAL GURKHA RIFLES
(FRONTIER FORCE)

CHAPTER I

1858 TO 1868

Origin and Constitution, 1858.

For the beginnings of the Regiment whose two battalions now go proudly under the title of the 5th Royal Gurkha Rifles (Frontier Force) we cast back across the years to the time of the Mutiny. As the 25th Regiment of Punjab Infantry, or the Hazara Goorkha Battalion, it was raised under orders bearing date May 22nd, 1858, and "added to the Punjab Irregular Force." The epic of the storming of Delhi was then a tale only eight months old, while Lucknow had been retaken finally only two months before the Regiment was raised. The army of the Nana Sahib had been dispersed, but the process of stamping out the smouldering embers of rebellion was not completed until May of 1858. Meanwhile Sir John Lawrence, that great administrator, had been occupied with plans for the reorganization of the Indian Army. "Driven," as he put it, "by the sheer necessity of our position," he had played a dominant part in the suppression of the mutiny by enlisting to that end many thousands of Sikhs and others who, but a few years before, had owed allegiance to the Sikh Raj. But, as he himself realized perhaps more clearly than anybody else, there was grave danger attending the continuance of such a policy. So, bearing in mind the invaluable services rendered by Gurkhas at Delhi and elsewhere during that critical time, it is not surprising that one of the earliest changes to take effect should be the raising of a Gurkha regiment with its home in Hazara, where Abbott had played a lone hand against Chattar Singh at the time of the second Sikh War. Under the orders referred to above the Regiment was to be formed at Abbottabad, and the nucleus was to be provided by transferring to it from other corps all those borne as Gurkhas on their rolls. The units which were called upon to contribute were the 1st, 2nd, 3rd, and 4th Sikh Infantry, the Corps of Guides Infantry, twenty-four regiments of Punjab Infantry, and nine Punjab Police battalions. Of these the majority furnished men only in ones and twos (some of those detailed actually had no Gurkhas on their rolls), but the quotas sent by the

Guides and 2nd Sikhs were of considerable strength, and were organized as the two flank companies of the new formation.

Armament. As regards armament, the intention had been that it should consist of two grooved rifles. These were of course muzzle-loaders, and fired a spherical bullet encircled by a ring of lead, the purpose of which was to engage the grooves on the charge being fired. The bullet was liable to stick occasionally in the bore, and for this reason every man carried a small wooden hammer, with which, when the need arose, he hammered on the ramrod. Only the contingents of the Guides and 2nd Sikhs were in possession of these weapons on arrival, and, forming as they did the flank companies, they retained them. The others had only muskets, so arrangements were made to provide them with short, smooth-bore fusils until such time as rifles could be made available. In the event, they were destined to wait years for them.

Dress. The dress prescribed for the Regiment was green, but in this case, too, difficulties were encountered. It was found that clothing of the correct shade and texture was unprocurable from the clothing agency, and recourse was had, perforce, to local supplies, which proved far from satisfactory.

British Officers. The officers appointed to the Regiment in the original Gazette were Lieutenant C. J. Nicholson of the 31st Native Infantry, as Commandant, and Captain H. F. M. Boisragon, Lieutenant of Police, as Second-in-Command. Lieutenant Nicholson never took up the appointment, so to Captain Boisragon, who was shortly afterwards gazetted a Brevet-Major for his services in the Mutiny, fell the task of raising the Hazara Goorkha Battalion, and his is the honour of having first commanded it. Others to be appointed to the Regiment very soon after its formation were Captain H. Close, 27th Bombay Native Infantry, Lieutenant P. W. Powlett, 58th Native Infantry, as Adjutant, Surgeon H. B. Buckle, and Assistant-Surgeon W. G. W. Clemenger.

Dress of British Officers. The uniform adopted for officers both British and Native (as they were then called) consisted of " a loose tunic of rather light green, a red silk sash, green silk puggree intertwined with a steel chain, shield at back, and pistol in belt, in addition to the sword." The red silk sash and the shield failed to meet with the approval of Brigadier-General Neville Chamberlain, commanding the Punjab Irregular Force, and in accordance with instructions issued by him they were done away with in 1859.

Accoutrements. The accoutrements issued to the Regiment were black, and an application for permission to carry colours was refused; two facts which would appear to indicate a " Rifle " tradition from the very start.

By the end of June, 1858, the transfers from other corps, with very few exceptions, had arrived in Abbottabad, and were housed in dilapidated lines built by the 3rd Sikhs as temporary shelters in 1853. Not for long were they destined to remain in them, for an outbreak of cholera soon rendered their occupation inadvisable, and, as a result, they were to a great extent evacuated, some of the men being sent into camp on Habiba, and a large detachment to Mansehra.

Lines.

The early days of the district—early only in relation to the existence of the 5th Gurkhas—cannot but hold some interest for those who are likely to read this narrative. For those who have done their part in building the reputation of the Regiment, the mere mention of names may serve to call up pleasant memories; while for those who come after, even the very brief reference to the period, which is all that space will permit, may save much searching of records no longer very easily accessible.

Hazara and Abbottabad.

Before our annexation in 1849, Hazara was under Sikh rule. The first Sikh War had been fought in 1845, and one of its results had been the establishment of a British Residency at Lahore. To this were attached British officers in the capacity of assistants, who were employed in making assessments and delimitating boundaries within Sikh territory.

Hazara, at first, remained outside the scope of these officers, being taken from the Sikhs and ceded as an appanage of Kashmir to Raja Gulab Singh in 1846. The inhabitants resented the transfer, and were so successful in making trouble for the ruler of Kashmir that in 1847 he gave willing consent to an exchange of territory. The district thus returned to the Sikh fold, and secured for itself the services of James Abbott, an assistant to the Resident at Lahore, who was sent to make a revenue assessment on behalf of the Sikh Darbar. His first task was the pacification of the country, still buzzing like a disturbed wasps' nest as the result of previous mismanagement and oppression.

At that time every place of importance, and several which would appear to have been of no account at all, boasted a fort, some built by the Sikhs and others by previous occupiers of the valley. Many, of which no trace now remains, must have been standing in a fair state of preservation when the Regiment was raised, and their gradual disappearance since then must have effected a considerable alteration in the aspect of the country. Climb any of the more prominent hills to the east of the cart-road between Dehdar and Mansehra, and the chances are that you will find on top ancient foundations, possibly a few blocks of faced stone, and leading up to them from water in a *nullah* below, the remains of a zigzag path. Even in comparatively recent times the site of the fort built in 1821 by Hari Singh at Nawanshahr, though marked only by a wet ditch and a mass of irises, was known to everybody in the garrison under the name of the " Purana Kila."

Abbott's headquarters were at Haripur, though actually he can have spent but very little time in the place. For his original measures of pacification he had the backing of Sikh troops. Arriving to take up his work in June, 1847, he very quickly brought about a state of tranquillity. Occupying himself first with the Tarkhelis of Gandgarh—the long range of hills flanking the Hazara trunk road on the west between Hasan Abdal and Haripur—Harry Lumsden and John Nicholson co-operating, he next turned his attention to the Dhunds, dwellers in the hilly tract about the south branch of the Haro River west of Murree; and by the end of November was free to bend his energies to administrative work.

Then came the second Sikh War, which, beginning in April, 1848, ostensibly as an insurrection headed by Diwan Mulraj of Multan, quickly developed into a struggle between British and Sikhs for possession of the Punjab. By August the Sikh troops in Hazara, under the leadership of Chattar Singh, one of the most influential of the Sikh Sirdars, definitely threw in their lot with the rebels, notifying the fact by the murder of Canara, an American battery commander in Sikh service at Haripur. At this time two Sikh regiments were encamped on the Pakhli Plain beyond Mansehra, while the remainder, numbering about 2,000 and comprising Artillery and Cavalry as well as Infantry, were quartered in the fort at Haripur. Nothing daunted, Abbott proceeded to hold them in play with his levies. Such was his hold on the affections of the people of Hazara that his own safety was always assured. His energy was boundless, and we find him dashing from one end of the district to the other. His finest effort was to march thirty miles from Nara (ten miles north-west of Haripur) to Salhad, and then finding that he had been wrongly informed, and that the Haripur troops were not trying to effect a junction with those of Pakhli, after only an hour's rest to start off on a forty-mile march in the opposite direction in an attempt to head off Chattar Singh and the Haripur force from Hasan Abdal. Inevitably, given such poor material to work with, he failed in the end to prevent the Pakhli regiments from breaking out southwards, despite his utmost efforts and those of John Nicholson—who came to help him—to block the Dumtaur Pass. The levies merely melted away and the Sikhs walked through.

His most anxious time came with the approach of an Afghan force in January, 1849, for, unable to withstand the blandishments of their co-religionists, several of the most prominent of his followers went over to the enemy. Crossing the Indus at Attock the Afghans advanced towards Sherwan, fifteen miles west of the existing cantonment of Abbottabad, where Abbott had built a small house, and whither he had deemed it prudent to retire on their approach. Fortunately his following was not tempted to the uttermost, for the Sikh need was great, and having reached Bharu Kot, one march only from Sherwan, the Afghan army turned about to go to the help of its allies. The war came to an end in February, 1849, the Punjab was annexed by the British, and Abbott became the first Deputy-Commissioner of Hazara. In 1850 he was given as assistant, Neville Chamberlain, whom we have already met in his later capacity as Brigadier-General commanding the Punjab Irregular Force. In 1852 occurred the bloodless expedition against the Kaghan Saiyads.

Colonel Mackeson was in command, and unfortunately there was a disagreement between him and Abbott regarding the location of posts. There could be only one end to such a dispute when, as in this case, the junior officer refused to give way, and, despite his great aptitude for his work and his previous fine record, Abbott was made to leave the district. He was succeeded as Deputy-Commissioner by Herbert Edwardes. After the annexation the garrison of Hazara had been fixed at two regiments of the Punjab Irregular Force and a mountain train of six guns. These had been cantoned hitherto at Bharu Kot, some miles to the north of Haripur across the Dor River. For reasons of health and climate that place was considered unsuitable, and one of the first acts of the new Deputy-Commissioner was to select a site for a new cantonment. That eventually chosen was the ground upon which the lines and bungalows now stand, and out of compliment to his predecessor he christened the place Abbottabad. Herbert Edwardes held charge of Hazara for less than a year, and was succeeded by Major Becher. With the help of only one regular battalion, a handful of police, and levies raised by himself, the latter safely piloted the district through the storm of the Mutiny and did good work in rounding up the mutineers of the 55th Native Infantry. We find him still in charge in the year of the raising of the Regiment.

Abbottabad, then, had been in existence for barely five years when it became the home of the 5th Gurkhas. It bore small resemblance in those days to the garden which it has since become. The lines were very poor and hardly fit for occupation. Those in which the Regiment was first housed were on the site of the present 1st Battalion lines, while the existing Abbott (1/6th) lines mark the locality occupied by the other battalion of the Frontier Force stationed in Abbottabad. Of trees, now too many, there were then few or none at all. The nakedness of the place is very marked in the photographs taken in 1862. General Villiers Stuart, who was in the habit of noting down interesting information imparted to him throughout his service in the Regiment, writes as follows:—

" It is often forgotten, may be not known, that all the trees of any age in cantonments, and those also on many of the nearer Brigade Circular hills, were planted by a Subadar Major of the 5th Goorkhas, one Parbal Gurung by name."

He also mentions that the pine-trees to the north-west of the lines, on the edge of the big *nullah* which runs down from the Rukh, were intended to provide firewood for married men and their families, those on the range being expected to do the same for the bachelors.

Early Days.

The Regiment being now provided with a background, it is time to return to the record of its growth and general development. On account of an outbreak of cholera, to which reference has been made, sanction was accorded to the building of new lines. Lack of funds demanded that much of the labour should be undertaken by the men themselves, and they were employed in quarrying stone and cutting timber until the end of the year. This work appears to lack certain requisites as a form of training for a newly raised unit of a force liable to be called upon at any moment to take an active part in safeguarding the frontier, and that, perhaps, was the view taken by the Brigadier-General. Be this as it may, he ordered that the Regiment should abandon manual labour, and the lines were accordingly completed under contract.

In October, 1858, the first recruiting party was sent out, not to Nepal, be it noted, but to Kumaon. The recruits enlisted were Gurkhas, Garhwalis, and Kumaonis, each class in approximately equal numbers. Many years were to elapse before the Regiment confined its efforts to the recruiting of Magars and Gurungs of Central Nepal; and allowing that the mingling of races may have augmented the difficulties of administration in quarters, in the field it appears to have answered well enough. December, 1858, must be regarded as a landmark in the life of the 5th Gurkhas, for in that month, though still under strength, it was first reported on as fit for service.

In 1859 an attempt was made to start a Gurkha colony. A small area of land immediately north of cantonments was bought by Government in the hope that a proportion of the men of the Regiment, with their families, instead of returning to Nepal on completion of their service, would take up a part of the colony land and make their homes there. In accordance with ideas held in those days the scheme if it succeeded would simplify recruiting, while establishing a small, dependable Hindu community in the midst of a population hitherto entirely Mohammedan. It is doubtful whether these hopes would have been realized even under more favourable auspices; in actual fact the quality of the land was so poor that nothing would grow on it, and the scheme was accordingly abandoned.

With the following year, 1860, the Regiment may be considered to have left childhood behind it and to have attained full stature as

The Church.   The "Dovecote."   The Mess.   General's Bungalow.

Looking towards Mansehra.
Two Views of Abbottabad, 1864.

a fighting entity of the Punjab Irregular Force. That such, anyhow, was its own opinion is attested by the fact that in January it is heard of as volunteering *en masse* for service with the China Expeditionary Force then being organized to wipe out the stigma attaching to the earlier lack of success of a combined British and French naval enterprise against the Taku Forts.

Expedition against Mahsud Wazirs. That offer was not accepted, but the disappointment occasioned by the refusal was shortly allayed through the receipt of orders, on March 21st, 1860, requiring that the headquarters and 400 bayonets should be held in readiness to proceed on active service. On March 23rd, only two days after the receipt of the warning order, the Regiment marched out of Abbottabad *en route* for Tank.

The object of the expedition, with which the 5th Gurkhas were to gain their first experience of active service, was the punishment of the Mahsuds, who were the terror of that part of the border which lay within several days' march of their strongholds at Kaniguram and Makin. The patience of Government in face of their misdoings had been at last exhausted by their action of a month before, when three thousand of them came down into the plain with the intention of destroying Tank. On that occasion they were unlucky to meet more than their match in the person of Saadat Khan, the Ressaldar commanding the detachment of the 5th Punjab Cavalry which formed the garrison of the Tank outpost. Receiving timely warning of the approach of the Mahsud *lashkar*, by denuding the nearer posts and calling to his assistance the mounted levies of the Nawab of Tank, he succeeded in collecting a body of Cavalry nearly 200 strong. Going to meet the enemy he found that they were still too close to the hills for his purpose, so he first lured them farther into the plain by a ruse which proved as successful in this case as in much earlier days—when practised by the Normans at Senlac and by Joshua at Ai—and then charged them, having first taken the precaution to intercept their retreat. The Mahsuds left three hundred dead on the ground, while the casualties of Saadat Khan's small force numbered only one killed and sixteen wounded.

To fulfil the object of the expedition, a mixed force of Cavalry, Artillery, and Infantry had been organized with a strength of about 5,000, excluding levies, and the command had been given to Brigadier-General Neville Chamberlain. The route chosen was the southerly approach by the Tank Zam, and in the event of the Mahsuds refusing our terms it was intended, after visiting Kaniguram and Makin, to proceed via the Tauda China and Khaisora to Bannu.

After a march lasting twenty-six days the Regiment, 464 strong, joined the force on April 17th at Kot Kirghi-ki-Ziarat. Major Boisragon having been granted furlough, Major O. E. Rothney had been sent from the 4th Sikhs to take command, and thus began for that distinguished officer his connexion with the 5th Gurkhas which was to last throughout fourteen years. Other officers who accompanied the Regiment were Captain Close, who had joined it at Lukki, and Lieutenant H. L. C. Bernard, who had replaced Lieutenant Powlett as Adjutant in January of the previous year.

By April 19th the force had reached Palosin. On the 20th, leaving sufficient troops under the command of Colonel Lumsden to cover the collection of supplies and keep open communication with the plains, General Chamberlain proceeded with the remainder to carry out a reconnaissance in the direction of Kaniguram via the Shahur Tangi. He met with almost negligible opposition, and that only at the defile, and after completing his survey and destroying the strongholds of certain selected offenders he began his return march from Barwani on the 24th. Palosin was reached on the 26th.

During the absence of the main column the camp at Palosin had been attacked, and the Regiment, while undergoing its baptism of fire, had acquitted itself most creditably. The force under Colonel Lumsden consisted of the 3rd Punjab Cavalry, the Guides, 4th Sikhs, 24th Punjab Infantry, the Hazara Goorkha Battalion, and certain details. The camp was sited on level ground on the left bank of the Tank Zam. Two strong piquets were posted, one upstream of it in a tower at a distance of about 800 yards, and the other downstream on a steep-sided knoll. Immediately northwards of the camp the ground rose abruptly, and along the edge of the table-land so formed was a chain of smaller piquets. The interval which had elapsed since the departure of General Chamberlain had passed quietly. Except for a few marauders, with whom shots were exchanged on the 22nd, no enemy had been seen in the vicinity, nor had news come to hand of a hostile concentration. The calm was rudely broken in the early morning of April 23rd. Day had dawned, and the *reveillé* had just sounded when the alarm was given by a volley fired by some of our men on the high ground north of the camp. This was followed by a rush of about three thousand tribesmen, who overwhelmed the piquets and secured the edge of the plateau. From there they opened a tremendous fire on the camp, while a body of swordsmen, five hundred in number, dashed straight for the area occupied by the Guides. Routing some levies they at once became engaged in a hand-to-hand encounter with the men of the Guides, who taken at a disadvantage were forced to give ground.

Colonel Lumsden, the moment the alarm was given, had taken charge of his inlying piquet in person, and posted it on the high ground where it was in a position to enfilade the attackers. Major Rothney, meantime, had formed the Regiment, and with the 4th Sikhs in support fell on the enemy's flank. The Guides by then had succeeded in checking the momentum of the first fierce onslaught, and the counter-attack on the flank had the effect of turning the check into a rout. Hustled beyond the confines of the camp the tribesmen were allowed no time to rally. Led by the Gurkhas a vigorous pursuit was initiated and kept up for three miles over the hills, the enemy being very severely handled. The loss sustained by the small British force in the short-lived but violent affray amounted to 63 killed and 166 wounded. In the Regiment the casualties were 12 men wounded, 2 mortally. The following extract from Colonel Lumsden's despatch bears fine testimony to the conduct of the 5th Gurkhas in their maiden encounter:—

"Whilst this was going on on the right, Major Rothney formed his Goorkhas on the ridge, and supported by the 4th Sikh Infantry advanced on the enemy's flank, bearing down on the mass of Wazirs on the table-land above with undeniable steadiness. . . . The Goorkhas were in front all the way, and although quite a new regiment their skirmishing over difficult ground was the admiration of all who witnessed it."

After the return of the main column to Palosin on April 26th, efforts were made to induce the enemy to accept our terms. They would none of them, however, so there was nothing left for it but to advance on Kaniguram and Makin. The camp at Palosin was broken up on May 2nd and the force moved on to Shingi Kot, where there was a last faint hope that the maliks might be encountered prepared to give a satisfactory answer to the proposals which had been submitted to them. Never a malik came in, so on the 3rd the march was continued, and contrary to expectation it was found unnecessary to fight for the Ahnai Tangi. The enemy, however, put up a stiff fight next day at the Barari Tangi, where at one period matters went none too well with the right attack under Lieutenant-Colonel Green, when the retirement of the 3rd Punjab Native Infantry endangered the guns. The situation was restored by Captain Keyes and the 1st Punjab Infantry, and two hours later the entire position was in our hands. The Regiment's part in the action was the clearing of the ridges beyond the Tangi. Kaniguram was reached on April 5th, the force halting there until the 8th, while further attempts were made to bring the Mahsuds to terms. These were without result, so leaving Kaniguram on the 9th the column encamped at Makin on the 10th, and spent the following day in destroying towers and burning villages, the Mahsud opposition being almost entirely confined to insulting epithets shouted from the surrounding hills. From this point onwards the expedition was a mere promenade. Marching via Razmak, Razani, and the Khaisora the force reached Bannu on May 20th, there to be dispersed.

The Regiment left Bannu on the 23rd and arrived back in Abbottabad on June 11th.

In his despatch covering the period of the expedition the Force Commander paid a tribute to Major Rothney which well bears repetition. He wrote:—

"I would beg to draw special attention to the conduct of Major Rothney, commanding the Hazara Goorkha Battalion, for I consider he displayed that promptitude of decision and correctness of judgment which of all qualifications evince fitness for command, and which, in addition to his other acquirements as a soldier, mark him as an officer of high promise."

ITEMS OF INTEREST, 1860–1861

Furlough. Five days after the Regiment returned to Abbottabad, furlough was opened. Considering the time of year few of the Gurkhas can have reached their homes, and it would be interesting to learn—but records are silent on the subject—where the furlough men went and how they spent their period of well-earned rest.

Change of Command. In December, 1860, Major Rothney was appointed Commandant of the Regiment, Major Boisragon, who was still on furlough, being transferred to the 4th Sikhs, with whom he remained until his retirement from the Service in 1881.

1861. Merely for the pleasure to be derived from the sound of the old names, it is permitted to record that in February, 1861, the non-combatant establishment of the Regiment was reduced by 5 lascars, 2 bildars, and 1 weighman.

In June the number of companies was reduced from ten to eight, and the total establishment of all ranks from 961 to 712.

The first peace-time inspection of the Regiment of which the written result has come down to us was carried out by Lieutenant-Colonel Wilde, C.B., acting on behalf of Brigadier-General Chamberlain in September, 1861. It occupied seven days and embraced "all points connected with drill, duty, and interior economy." On completion of his labours Colonel Wilde wrote:—

"I report for the Brigadier-General's information that I consider, after a long and careful inspection of every part of it, that the Hazara Goorkha Battalion is in an excellent state of discipline, and its efficiency reflects credit on Major Rothney and his officers."

This year further witnessed a most important change in the designation of the Regiment, which was to be known in future as the 5th Goorkha Regiment or Hazara Goorkha Battalion, "and it is to take rank after the 32nd Regiment Native Infantry (Pioneers)."

PALOSIN CAMP
APRIL 23rd 1860

(Based on plan in Nevill's "Campaigns on the North-West Frontier" by permission of John Murray)

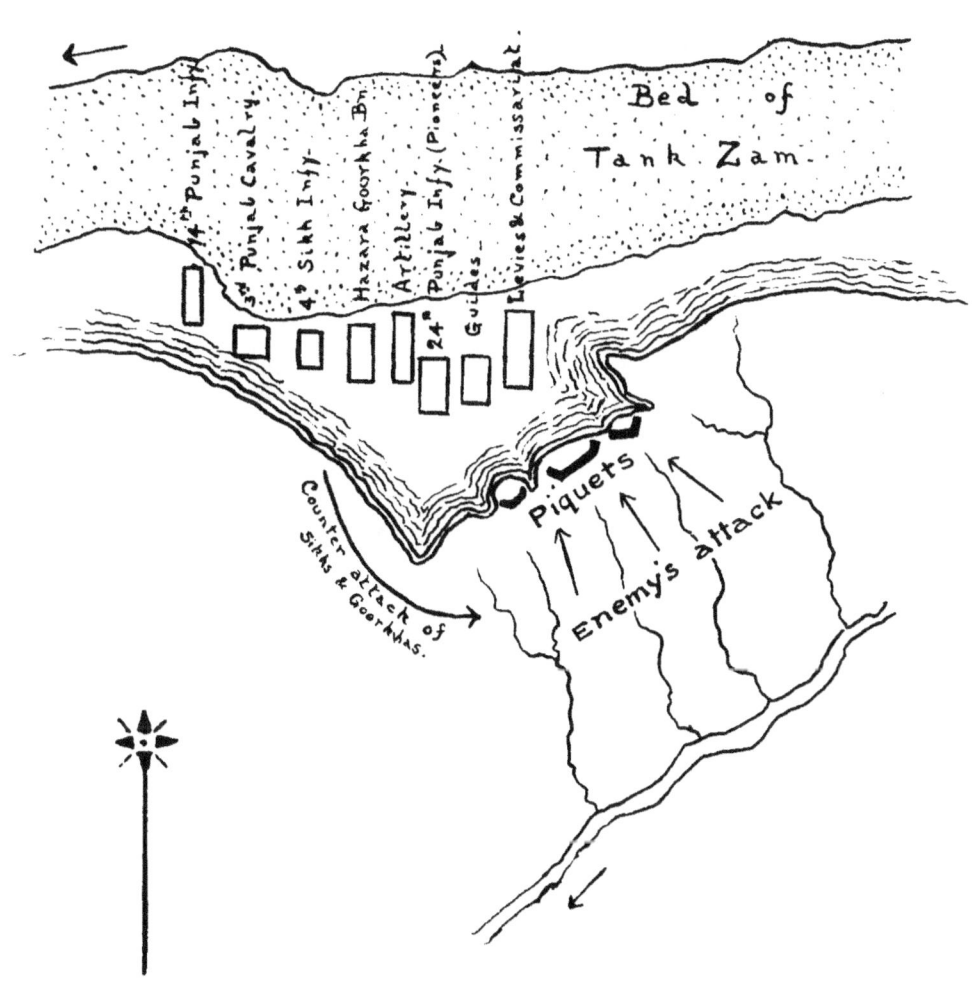

CHAPTER II

1863 TO 1878

Two years of peace in Abbottabad, and then another spell of active service. It had been our experience since the annexation of the Punjab and of the Sikhs during the twenty odd years immediately preceding that event, that trouble on the frontier anywhere from the Black Mountain to the Malakand was invariably traceable to the Hindustani Fanatics. It was so on this occasion.

1863.
The Ambela Campaign.

A detailed study of the history of this colony is of quite absorbing interest, embracing as it does not only their remarkable development in the country of their adoption, but also a system of the most elaborate intrigue which had its roots in far away Bengal. A brief survey only is possible in this place. The founder of the colony was a bigoted Wahabi Musalman named Saiyid Ahmed Shah of Bareilly. At one time he had been the companion-in-arms of a noted Pindari leader, Amir Khan, a Pathan of Buner, and from him he learnt something of the art of war. His most prominent attribute was a fanatical hatred of all non-Musalmans, and his principal occupation the preaching of Jehad. After a period spent at Delhi in acquiring Arabic he started out to make the pilgrimage to Mecca, going via Calcutta and preaching on his way. It was so that he acquired the prestige in Bengal which was later to stand him in good stead by gaining for him money and recruits towards the furtherance of his frontier schemes.

In 1823, having journeyed from Mecca via Kandahar and Kabul, he appeared in Yusafzai with a small following. Such was his eloquence that the Pathans rallied to him in large numbers, and in 1827 we find him setting out to besiege Attock. Despite a serious reverse sustained at the hands of the Sikhs under Ranjit Singh, he managed to re-establish his position, and by 1829 he had subdued Amb and the whole of the Yusafzai tract, and occupied Peshawar. From that point onwards his fortunes declined. The Sikhs harried him relentlessly; he forfeited the regard of many of his co-religionists owing to his attempted reforms, and on a chosen day, by the concerted action of his enemies, a number of those still loyal to him were done to death at the hour of evening prayer. With those who remained to him he fled to Balakot, in Hazara, augmented his following, and again dared the Sikhs to come on. A battle was fought, he himself was killed, and three hundred only of his men made good their escape. These repaired to Sitana on the right bank of the Indus between Khabal and Amb. It was the stronghold of Saiyid Akhbar, the most prominent survivor of the colony, and he assumed the mantle of Saiyid Ahmed Shah. Such was the origin of the Hindustani Fanatics. They never again attained to their former status, but remained to stir up strife and to preach the doctrine of bloodshed for many years to come. The British first sent an expedition against them in 1853, when it is intriguing to note that the armament of the small force under Colonel Mackeson included six wallpieces and six Zamburaks. Further expeditions followed in 1857 and 1858. As a result of the latter they were driven out of Sitana, and an undertaking was exacted from the Gaduns and Utmanzais that they would never again allow them access to their lands.

From this point onwards the course of events has a direct bearing on the campaign in which the Regiment was about to play its part. In 1861 the Gaduns and Utmanzais, having failed to keep out the Hindustani Fanatics, were subjected to a blockade. This had the desired effect. In 1863 these tribes again broke their engagements, and the blockade which was again imposed proved without result. The Hindustanis remained in forbidden territory, attacked the camp of the Guides at Topi, and instigated outrages in Amb and on the Black Mountain. Government therefore decided to act. Orders were issued for the concentration of a comparatively large force, and the command was given to Brigadier-General Neville Chamberlain.

In the case of previous expeditions the Hindustani Fanatics had always made good their escape into the hills. On this occasion it was decided to make a circuit by the Ambela Pass, come down on their principal stronghold at Malka from the north, and either destroy them utterly in their own hills or force them across the Indus into the arms of a second column disposed on the left bank. The line of advance selected could only be used with the consent of the people of Buner. Unfortunately, for reasons of secrecy that consent could not be obtained beforehand, but it was thought that their dislike of the fanatics and their religious differences would cause the Bunerwals to maintain an attitude of friendly neutrality. The force was organized in two columns. Of these the Hazara column was to remain at Darband, where its presence would impress the tribes while it awaited eventualities, and the Peshawar column, under the personal command of General Chamberlain, was charged with the execution of the more active element in the plan outlined above.

The line of the frontier in the area with which we are now concerned runs generally north and south. Of the approaches through which the Hindustani Fanatics could be threatened from the west, the Ambela

Pass lies to the north and the Darhan Pass to the south, the distance separating them being some seven miles in a straight line. It was the latter of the two approaches which had been used on the occasion of the expedition of 1858, and the concentration of the Peshawar column was purposely arranged to foster the belief that the advance would again be by that line. The original point of concentration for the majority of the units composing the column was Swabi, which, from its position well to the south, could give no indication of the route to be taken. On October 18th the Force Commander himself went to the Darhan Pass, and at the same time two mountain train batteries, the 1st Punjab Infantry, and the 5th Gurkhas were collected at that place. Next day the rest of the column moved to Nawa Kala, seven miles south-west of the Darhan.

The stage is now set for the Regiment to play its part. It had already taken its share in the fruitless blockade organized earlier in the year, one company having been stationed at Tarbela from the early part of August, there to remain with a troop of the Guides until the beginning of active operations. Major Rothney having been obliged to take sick leave, Major J. P. W. Campbell of the 1st Sikhs was in command, while other British officers to accompany the Battalion were Captain Close, Lieutenant Codrington, and Lieutenant Oliphant. Lieutenant Sym remained in command of the depot at Abbottabad, and Captain Bernard had charge of the Tarbela detachment. Lieutenants Bird and Taylor and Ensign Serle joined towards the end of the expedition.

The Regiment left Abbottabad on September 15th and marched to Sherwan. There it remained for over three weeks, and it was not until October 10th that it went on to join the Peshawar column of the force, arriving at the Darhan Pass on the 18th.

It is worthy of note that none of the Indian regiments was allowed tentage, either for the men or for the British officers, until December.

Soon after dark on October 19th the small force from the Darhan Pass started for Ambela. Arrived at Parmalao it was joined by 200 Cavalry, the Guides Infantry, the 5th Punjab Infantry, and the 20th Punjab Native Infantry, and came under the command of Lieutenant-Colonel Wilde. Though the distance on the map is a bare eight miles from Parmalao to the Ambela Pass, yet such were the difficulties encountered from the nature of the track and the darkness that it was sunrise of the 20th before the mouth of the pass was attained. Here a halt was called, partly in order to rest the troops and partly to allow of the nearer approach of the main portion of the force, which had left Nawa Kala at 1 a.m.

On restarting the units under Colonel Wilde were employed in securing the high ground flanking the route on either side. By the early afternoon the summit of the pass was reached, and as evening fell the main body began to arrive. It was midnight, however, before the guns came in, while another forty-eight hours were to elapse before the last of the baggage animals struggled to the Kotal. The distance from Nawa Kala to the head of the pass was not more than a dozen miles, and the difficulties of the track alone cannot account for this extraordinary delay. The fact is that the expedition had been decided on in a hurry against the advice both of Sir Hugh Rose, the Commander-in-Chief, and of Neville Chamberlain himself. Each of these distinguished officers, consulted separately, advised the postponement of operations until the following spring. The root cause of the trouble, then, was lack of preparation. In a private letter to his brother Crawford, written from the camp at Darhan on the very day on which the forward move was made, General Chamberlain went so far as to say: " I never before had such trouble or things in so unsatisfactory a state. Carriage, supplies, grain-bags—all deficient."

On the 21st a reconnaissance was pushed down the Chamla Valley, and while the rest of the army is waiting for its baggage there is an opportunity to survey the ground. The Ambela Pass leads direct from Rustam in Yusafzai on the west, to the Chamla Valley on the east. Just on the Chamla side of the pass is comparatively flat open ground where the camp had been made. Standing in the camp, and facing towards the Chamla Valley, the observer has on his left the Guru massif, towering above the Kotal, partly covered with trees. Jutting out from its side at a height of approximately 1,000 feet above the camp and distant from it about one mile is a large outcrop of tumbled rock, which was christened the Eagle's Nest. On the right the hills are lower, their most prominent feature an isolated rocky pinnacle, with its pointed summit on a level with the Eagle's Nest, which was designated the Crag. In front the defile opens out, the ground dropping in terraces to the head of the Chamla Valley. The pass into Buner cuts through the range of hills which rises above the left bank of the Chamla stream.

The reconnoitring party which had left camp on the morning of the 21st was obliged to fight its way back into camp, those trying to bar its progress being identified as Bunerwals. There could no longer be any doubt, therefore, that this section, instead of remaining neutral, had joined the Hindustani Fanatics, and in the light of this knowledge it became necessary to make a fresh appreciation of the situation. The people of Buner were known to be guided in their conduct by the Akhund of Swat, a spiritual leader with a very wide influence among the tribes. The expeditionary force sent to deal with a small coalition of the tribes having their settlements in the immediate vicinity of Mount Mahaban would now be called upon to face a powerful confederation recruited from the whole vast tract of country lying between the Indus and the confines of Kabul. To advance was out of the question; the line of communications cut, the force would starve. To retire was unthinkable, except in the last resort. General Chamberlain therefore decided to strengthen his position at Ambela, and to hold on there in the hope that time and the efforts of the politicals would effect a weakening of the confederation and so give him his opportunity later. The subsequent course of events proved the wisdom of his decision.

During the rest of October and on into November the force had to fight stubbornly to retain its hold on the pass, and the Regiment was engaged almost daily. From the 22nd to the 24th the troops worked hard, strengthening the defences and improving communications. Piquets were posted north and south of the camp, notably at the Eagle's Nest and the Crag, and the defile was blocked front and rear by breastworks. Colonel Wilde was put in charge of the right defences and Colonel Vaughan of those on the left.

On October 25th occurred the first serious collision with the enemy. Major Keyes with the 1st Punjab Infantry was manning the defensive works on the south side of the camp. Early in the morning he found a large number of the enemy in occupation of a ridge situated at a short distance to his front. Deeming them too close for safety he attacked and drove them from the ridge, which he proceeded to occupy. Beyond was a conical hill, and there the tribesmen took their stand. On the situation becoming known in camp, reinforcements were sent out to Major Keyes. When they arrived he distributed the sharpshooters of the 71st Highland Light Infantry and 101st Royal Bengal Fusiliers along the ridge, and withdrew the men of his own regiment to await under cover, with the 5th Gurkhas, the arrival of the Hazara Mountain Battery. By 4 p.m. the battery was in position and opened fire, its first shell uprooting a standard planted on the conical hill. At the same time the 1st Punjab Infantry advanced, supported by the 5th Gurkhas, and, helped by the covering fire of the sharpshooters, drove the enemy from the hill. In his despatch the General described this affair as " a brilliant exploit, managed with great skill."

It is worth noting that the British regiments of the force were armed with Enfield rifles, which were considered to be far more effective than the old " two groove."

On October 26th the Regiment was again in action, this time on the other side of the camp in the neighbourhood of the Eagle's Nest. An attack had been anticipated on the previous day and Colonel Vaughan had accordingly been reinforced with the Hazara Mountain Battery, 30 sharpshooters drawn from the two British regiments, a company of the 71st and the 5th and 6th Punjab Infantry. It is interesting again to note the employment of sharpshooters. They evidently had a

C

definite covering-fire rôle throughout the campaign. The expected attack on the Eagle's Nest came at day-break on the 26th, and was made with the utmost determination. Two enemy standards were actually planted within a few feet of the piquet wall, and Major Brownlow with the 20th Punjab Native Infantry was hard put to it to maintain his position. It was only by the united efforts of the reinforcing troops that the tribesmen were eventually dislodged, and the result was only attained at the cost of a number of casualties. The Regiment was not included among the original reinforcements, but was sent from camp to secure the left flank of the attacking troops. Having helped to preserve it the Regiment next day occupied the Eagle's Nest, returning to its quarters in camp on the 29th.

General Chamberlain, as the result of his appreciation of the altered situation brought about by the hostility of the Bunerwals, had pressed for reinforcements. Of these the first to arrive were the 4th Gurkhas, who marched into camp on the 28th.

October 30th was a day of great activity. The Crag piquet had been lost during the night and had to be retaken. This was successfully accomplished by a combined movement of the 1st Punjab Infantry and the 20th Punjab Native Infantry. While the latter took the position in flank the former scaled the pinnacle in the face of very stubborn opposition. Their detachments were led by Fosbery and Pitcher, whose gallantry earned for each of them the award of the Victoria Cross. Some idea of the degree of resistance offered may be gained from the fact that the tribesmen left 54 dead and 7 wounded in the immediate vicinity of the breastwork, where space was so restricted that the garrison at that time had to be limited to twelve men under a non-commissioned officer. Meantime a strong attack delivered by a large body of Swatis had developed on the front of the camp. They "had established themselves within a few yards of our position, and had attacked the guns of Captain Griffin's battery," when the 5th Gurkhas were called upon to deal with them. It was no new experience for the men, and their response was as ready now as it had been at Palosin, three and a half years before. Forming rapidly, they soon had the Swatis on the run, and the guns were saved. The action cost the Regiment its first casualties of the campaign—one Native officer and five rank and file being killed, and six rank and file wounded. Writing in a despatch forwarded to the Government of India under date October 31st, General Neville Chamberlain referred to this episode as follows:—

"The first result of the combination between the Akhoond and the Moolvie was an attack upon the right piquets of the camp early yesterday morning by the Hindoostanees, and an almost simultaneous attack upon the front of the camp by the Swatees. The front attack was repulsed. Some of the enemy behaved with considerable boldness, and afforded an opportunity for the 5th Goorkha Regiment to make a spirited charge."

For a time relations between the Force Commander and the Regiment were a little strained over the matter of this charge, and the following passage from the old Regimental Record is worth quoting, both as showing how seriously was regarded an error of judgment committed on service, and as giving a clear indication of the confused nature of the fighting on that day. It may be taken that the passage does not reflect in the least degree on either of the officers concerned in the affair.

"Part of the Regiment advanced farther than Brigadier-General Chamberlain intended; but, as the 'advance' (bugle sound) was sounded, and there was much noise and excitement, it was an unfortunate occurrence for which there was no remedy; but Brigadier-General Chamberlain, hearing that Captain Close had sounded the 'advance,' ordered that officer under arrest, and convened a Court of Inquiry, of which Colonel D. Probyn, C.B. and V.C. (Commanding XIth Bengal Cavalry) was President; but it having been proved that Brigadier-General Chamberlain had himself ordered the bugler to sound the 'advance,' Captain Close was released from arrest."

The enemy appeared to pause for breath after their activities of the 30th, contenting themselves with shooting into camp from points of vantage on the surrounding hills. Advantage was taken of the lull to improve communications to the rear, and to start work on a road towards Buner, to be used in case of an advance.

On November 6th Major Harding of the 2nd Sikhs was in command of the detachments of different units detailed to cover the work on the road to the front, and among these was a company of the Regiment under Lieutenant J. S. Oliphant. All went well until the early afternoon, when the order went out that the working parties should return to camp, followed by the covering detachments. The working parties got in safely, but the covering troops were heavily attacked. The broken nature of the country beyond the Crag piquet made communication very difficult. Major Harding was early wounded, and co-ordination became wellnigh impossible. In the end each detachment had to fight its way back to camp independently. Lieutenant Oliphant was so severely wounded that he afterwards died from the effects.

In the confusion of the withdrawal a number of the men greatly distinguished themselves. Three sepoys devoted themselves to trying to save the life of Major Harding after he was wounded. They were completely surrounded by the enemy, and only abandoned their attempt after Major Harding had been killed; actually while borne on the back of a sepoy named Jangbir Thapa. They reached camp with the greatest difficulty. Three others rescued Lieutenant Blair, R.E., who was defending himself against three of the enemy. The Gurkhas killed all three of the assailants, one of whom had grappled with the officer and was found to be wearing a suit of chain armour. The casualties sustained by this company in the withdrawal were seven killed and seven wounded, besides Lieutenant Oliphant.

During the spell of comparative inactivity a great deal of work had been done on the Crag piquet, until it had become capable of holding a garrison of 160. On October 12th Major Brownlow was in charge of the Crag, and that night he was called upon to beat off one vigorous attack after another. On the morning of the 13th he was relieved by Captain Davidson of the 1st Punjab Infantry. Again the piquet was attacked, this time in even greater force.

Captain Davidson was killed, and for the second time the position was lost. Its immediate recapture was of vital importance; any troops who could be got quickly under arms were therefore called upon, and among these was a company of the Regiment. There was no withstanding the *élan* and determination of the counter-attack now launched and before long the Crag was once more in our possession. The honours of the day went deservedly to the 101st Royal Bengal Fusiliers, but the Company of the 5th Gurkhas did its share, and lost two men wounded.

On November 17th the Regiment enjoyed a small success while employed on artillery escort duty in the direction of Khanpur, several of the enemy being killed. They were again engaged on the 18th, but before dealing with their experience it is necessary to touch on the altered dispositions which were then coming into effect. The improvement in communications to the rear, which has been referred to, entailed changing the advanced base from Rustam to Parmalao, and the construction of a road to that place, which running behind the high ground to the south of the pass was defiladed from the Guru Mountain. The work had been completed, and this fact, taken in conjunction with the alignment of the new road to the front, made it possible to abandon the pass as a line of advance. Following on that it had been decided to move the camp farther to the south, and to withdraw the Eagle's Nest and the other piquets on the same side of the defile.

The striking of the old camp and the withdrawal of the piquets were interpreted by the enemy as a general retreat. They swarmed into the pass from every side, and made a vigorous attack on the small piquets to the south which guarded what had now become the left of the position. The defenders were driven out, and the camp was placed in jeopardy. 'As luck would have it, at this juncture the Regiment returned from another spell of escort duty to Khanpur, and their help was at once enlisted to restore the situation.

While the right wing under Major Campbell safeguarded the exposed face, 90 men under Captain Close went to the assistance of the 14th

Native Infantry,[1] who were about to embark on an attempt to retake the piquets which they had been forced to abandon. Captain Close's detachment found that the nature of the hill-side provided cover for the enemy which was impervious to their fire. To fulfil the mission entrusted to them they charged down among the rocks and bushes, drove the tribesmen headlong into the defile, and established themselves on the declivity. There they were exposed to a galling fire from the front and flanks, but they maintained their position until late in the afternoon.

The troops on their right being driven back, it then became imperative to withdraw in order to avoid encirclement. The movement, though carried out successfully, was not unattended with loss, the casualties numbering nine killed and five wounded. They took up a fresh position higher up the slope, and, other troops co-operating, the ground was cleared of the enemy. Shortly afterwards darkness intervened to put an end to the action. The right wing had also been engaged, but not at such close quarters, and finished the day with a loss of only two men wounded. On November 20th the Crag piquet was lost for the third time, and the entire Regiment played a prominent part in its recapture. It had been held by 200 men, half of them provided by the 101st Royal Bengal Fusiliers and half by the 20th Punjab Native Infantry. Beginning their effort at 9 a.m. and continuing until 3 p.m. the tribesmen had assailed the piquet, but in vain. Then, as the result, apparently, of some deplorable misunderstanding, the north side of the Crag was left without defenders, and despite the utmost endeavours of the rest of the garrison the enemy gained possession. From its position in relation to the new camp it had assumed even greater importance than before. General Chamberlain at once ordered up the 71st Highland Light Infantry and the 5th Gurkhas, arranged for artillery covering fire, added the 5th Punjab Infantry to the strength of the attacking column, and himself led the way towards the hill.

Major Campbell was wounded while the Regiment was formed up preparatory to advancing, and Captain Close being on piquet duty elsewhere, it fell to Lieutenant Codrington to command on this occasion. The Highlanders took the direct line, the 5th Gurkhas and 5th Punjab Infantry moved round the exposed flank, and the enemy were routed. The General himself was wounded during the advance, but remained with the attackers until the summit was won. The casualties in the Regiment numbered three killed and nine wounded.

Brigadier-General Neville Chamberlain had not been in the best of health at the start of the campaign; indeed, he was about to proceed on sick leave when his orders reached him. The wound was not the least

---

[1] 14th Sikhs. The two battalions were not destined again to be so closely associated until fifty-two years later, in Gallipoli in 1915.

serious of the seven sustained by him between 1842 and 1863, and he found himself unable longer to exercise command. On November 30th he was relieved by General Garvock. Meanwhile his hope that time would prove his ally appeared likely to be realized. For days on end the enemy remained passive, certain sections had already quitted the field, and the Bunerwals managed to convey a hint that if the British would take the offensive they would stand aside.

General Garvock therefore decided on a general advance, choosing as successive objectives the village of Lalu beyond the conical hill, Ambela Village near the head of the Chamla Valley on the left bank of the stream, and the pass into Buner. Reinforcements had continued to arrive from India, with the result that after leaving a garrison of three thousand for the camp he was still in a position to dispose of a force of nearly five thousand for his offensive. These he divided into two columns, the right under Colonel Turner, the left under Colonel Wilde. The Regiment formed part of the left column, and with it played a very distinguished part.

On the morning of December 15th the advance began. Turner's column moved off in the direction of Lalu, but, its further progress checked by large bodies of the enemy to its left front in occupation of the conical hill which had been the scene of the action of October 25th, it secured the ridges to the south and east of that feature and awaited the arrival of the left column. The Regiment leading, Wilde's force prepared to attack the enemy's formidable position. When it arrived on the alignment of the right column a general assault was launched, both columns advancing with great dash and sending the enemy flying into the valley beyond. The conical hill itself and the ground to the west of it fell to Wilde's men. There they consolidated, what time Turner went forward and destroyed Lalu. On the left the enemy came again, giving the Regiment more than one fine chance of showing its qualities of speed and initiative. Three times the 5th Gurkhas charged, inflicting heavy loss on the enemy and giving him no opportunity to remove his dead and wounded. So swift and unexpected was the Regiment's action on one of these occasions that they captured one of the tribesmen's jealously guarded standards. It was the only flag taken in the entire campaign, and as such, a prize well worth the winning. For sixty-five years it has occupied a place of honour in the Mess in Abbottabad, and it is to be hoped that it will always be cherished there to bear its silent testimony to the fine spirit which has animated the Regiment from its earliest days.

These successes were won with a loss of three killed and nine wounded. That night the two columns bivouacked on the ground won, and on December 16th the advance was continued towards the Buner Pass. The Regiment again led the left column, and the enemy, disheartened by his losses of the previous day, vacated one strong position after another without firing a shot. The village of Ambela was destroyed, and the right column pressed on in an attempt to intercept the enemy hordes making for Buner. On the left of this force were the 23rd Pioneers, commanded by Crawford Chamberlain. While moving across a stretch of broken ground they were charged by a band of Ghazis, about 250 strong, and lost heavily. The Ghazis, on the other hand, were practically wiped out. The pass leading into Buner was reached and occupied, and with darkness the greater part of the force went into bivouac near Ambela Village.

This proved to be the last engagement of the campaign. Next morning the Bunerwals made formal submission, and agreed without reserve to the terms imposed. They undertook as one of the conditions to destroy the village of Malka under the supervision of British officers. This was duly effected.

On December 20th the troops returned to camp, and on the 23rd, the officers delegated to supervise the destruction of Malka having returned on completion of their mission, the Ambela force was broken up.

One last piece of work remained to be done. On January 1st, 1864, the Regiment found itself forming part of a force of 3,000 for the subjugation of the Gadun tribes and the destruction of the settlements of the Hindustani Fanatics south of Kotla. Marching through the Gadun country to the Indus they met with no resistance. Mandi, Sitana, and the Hindustani forts at Khabal were levelled with the ground, and on January 10th the 5th Gurkhas arrived back in Abbottabad. They had been absent for nearly four months, of which three had been spent under fire; they had bested the enemy on every occasion on which they had encountered him; they had greatly enhanced their fighting reputation among their comrades of the Punjab Irregular Force, and had elicited from the Buners the confession that they feared the 5th Gurkhas more than any other regiment. Two British officers had been wounded, of whom one died from wounds, one Native officer had been killed, and of the rank and file 27 had been killed and 40 wounded.

Items of Interest, 1864 to 1868

The happenings of the next few years need not long detain us.

1864. In March, 1864, in accordance with the new system then introduced, the British officer establishment was reorganized as follows:—
Commandant, Major O. E. Rothney;
Second-in-Command and Wing Officer, Captain H. P. Close;
Left Wing Officer, Lieutenant E. Codrington;
Adjutant, Lieutenant J. S. Oliphant;
Quartermaster, Lieutenant J. M. Sym;
First Wing Subaltern, Lieutenant A. Broome;

Lieutenant Oliphant died of wounds, and so never took up his appointment. Lieutenant Sym officiated as Adjutant in his place.

In July sanction was received for the introduction of Kilmarnock Caps to replace the turban hitherto worn. All the oldest photographs show these as worn with a tilt to the left. General Villiers Stuart writes that the present fashion came in with the Afghan War.

1865. It was during the following year that the designation of the Punjab Irregular Force was changed to Punjab Frontier Force. At this time the command of the Force had passed from Neville Chamberlain to Brigadier-General A. T. Wilde.

1868.
Second Black Mountain Expedition.

After four and a half peaceful years spent in Abbottabad, with only a mild outbreak of cholera in 1867 to mar their serenity, the Regiment again saw active service. Agror and the Black Mountain beyond no longer provide occasion for frequent visits from one or other battalion of the Regiment, as they did formerly, so a short account of the long, tree-covered ridge which we see so often when our work takes us onto the nearer hills will not be out of place.

Darband on the Indus makes a good starting-point. Just upstream of Darband the Unar flows in from the north-east, having passed Oghi some fifteen miles back (measured in a straight line). In the angle so formed lies the southern part of the Black Mountain. Its crest-line has a north-easterly trend from the junction of the two rivers to Chittabat, fifteen miles distant as the crow flies. Thence it turns sharply north-west to the Machai Peak for two and a half miles before running due north for a further distance of approximately ten miles, where the two prominent spurs into which the ridge has divided meet the Indus, which at this point flows from east to west. Its average height is about 8,000 feet, though isolated peaks reach nearly to the 10,000 feet level. For the most part it is thickly wooded throughout its length.

The boundary between Independent Territory and British India, in which is included Feudal Tanawal, leaves the Indus about six miles north of the point where it is joined by the Unar, and climbs a spur to the crest of the ridge at Baradar. Thence it follows the crest-line as far as Chittabat, leaving it there to continue generally in a north-easterly direction.

Generally speaking, the western slopes are inhabited by Yusafzai tribes, and the eastern slopes between the crest-line and the British boundary, by Swatis. The Yusafzai tribes, taking them from south to north, are the Hassanzais, the Akazais, and the Chigharzais. The Swatis comprise the inhabitants of Tikari and Daishi, whose lands march with Northern Agror; the Nandiharis, who occupy two fertile valleys running down to the Indus at Thakot and whose nearest British

POSITION ON THE AMBELA PASS
OCT. 20TH – DEC 16TH 1863.
("From plan in "Frontier and Overseas Expeditions from India")

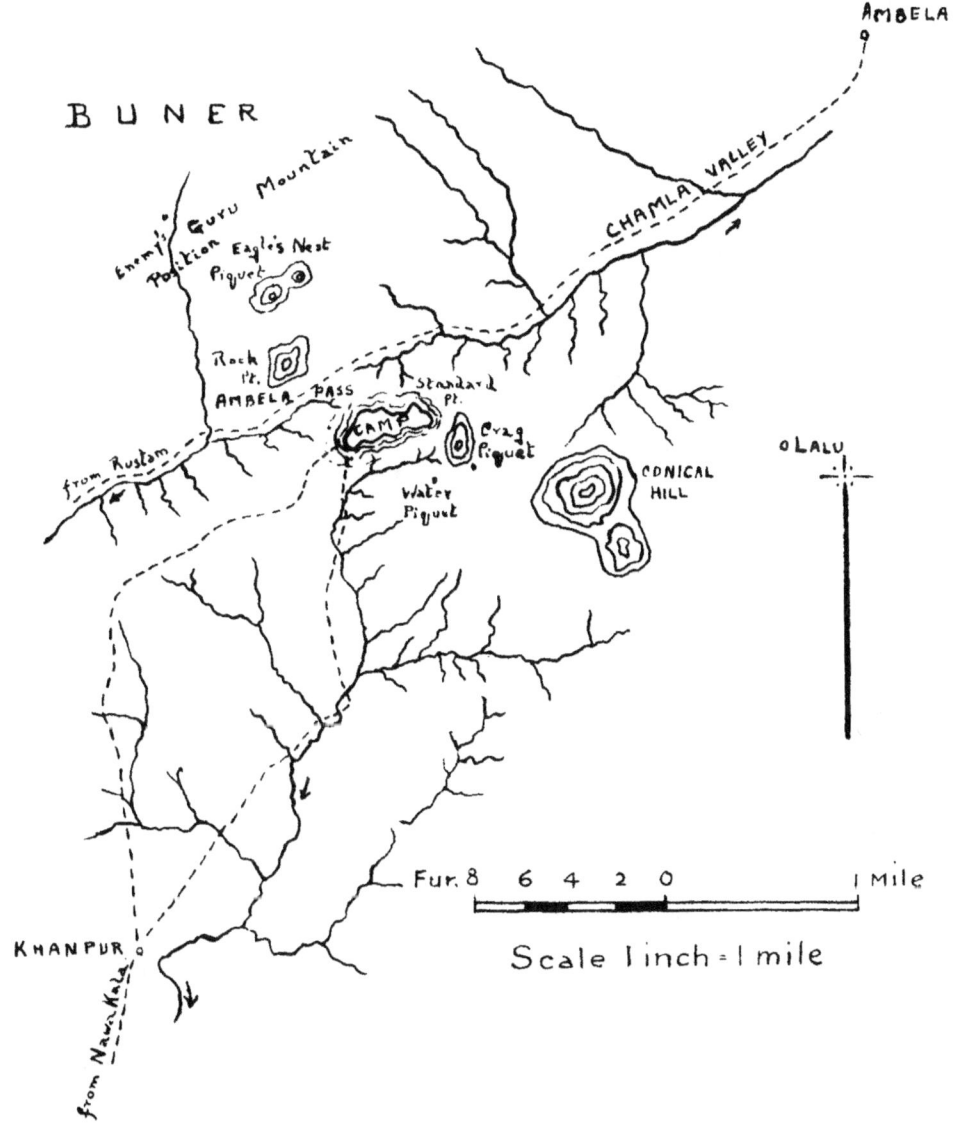

neighbours are the Swatis of the Konsh Valley; and the Allaiwals, who, living to the north of the Musa-Ka-Musalla range, are strictly speaking outside the Black Mountain area. Lastly, mention must be made of the Pariari Saiyads. Their origin is uncertain, but they have found a home for themselves in two small valleys on the eastern face of the mountain, situated between the British border and the country of the Chigharzais.

So much for the country which the Regiment was so soon to enter for the first time. The immediate cause of the second Black Mountain Expedition—the first had been in 1852—was an attack by a combination of Hassanzais, Akazais, Chigharzais, and Pariari Saiyads on the police post recently established at Oghi for the better control of the tribes. The news of this outrage was received in Abbottabad on July 30th, 1868. At 3 p.m. the Regiment was ordered to march immediately to Agror. By 8 p.m. it had left the station fully equipped for service, and Oghi, thirty-nine miles distant by the track of those days, was reached on the evening of the 31st. To appreciate at its proper value the merit of this performance the season of the year has to be taken into account.

In addition to the 5th Gurkhas, Colonel Rothney had under his command the Peshawar Mountain Battery and a number of local levies. Among these latter was a contingent of Tanaolis under the personal command of the Khan of Amb, Muhammad Akram Khan. These rendered good service, but the remaining levies were found to be of little value.

The rôle of the small force under Colonel Rothney was merely the safeguarding of the district until a punitive column could be collected. There was evidence to show that the Khan of Agror, Ata Muhammad Khan, had engineered the attack on the post. He was promptly arrested and sent to Abbottabad. For the rest, it was a case of acting on the defensive and hoping for better things. Conditions at this period are summed up in the old Regimental Record as follows:—

"From August 2nd to 12th the Regiment remained in camp at Ughi Agror without having any opportunity of coming to close quarters with the enemy, who by this time occupied the valley in considerable force (variously estimated at from 4,000 to 7,000 men). The picket and fatigue duty was harassing and incessant; the men had often no time to cook from one day's end to another; the nights were spent under arms at the breastwork round camp, which had been hastily thrown up and was strengthened at night by the men's tents, which were struck and rolled up for the purpose, and by the grain-bags, mule-saddles, etc., from the Regimental Bazar."

The fact that it was Colonel Rothney who held command, and the 5th Gurkhas, with their previous experience of two hard-fought frontier campaigns, who furnished the bulk of the troops engaged, is sufficient proof that a sangared breastwork was not constructed because circumstances prevented its construction. That the work could not be undertaken helps to a realization of the " harassing and incessant " nature of the duties imposed.

The enemy concentration in the valley grew daily in numbers, drawing in representatives of yet more tribes, including some from the far side of the Indus.

A number of villages in British territory were burnt, and British subjects were murdered. On August 7th the tribesmen began to collect at the foot of the Khabbal Hill, only one and a half miles to the northeast of the camp, and their attitude was threatening. Having been reinforced by a squadron of the 16th Bengal Cavalry, on August 12th Colonel Rothney took the offensive. Covered by the fire of the Peshawar Mountain Battery the Infantry advanced against the Khabbal Hill. The enemy made no stand, but began to disperse, firing as they withdrew from the valley. Colonel Rothney himself and two sepoys of the Regiment were wounded. In his "Gazetteer of the Hazara District"—surely one of the best ever compiled, and, as a book to read, worthy of a less unattractive title—Mr. H. D. Watson writes: " A feature of the engagement was a bold dash up the slope over seemingly impossible ground, made without waiting for orders, by Akram Khan and his Tanaoli Sowars."

The small force at Oghi was left in undisturbed occupation of the valley until at the end of September the Regiment was incorporated in the Hazara Field Force as a unit of the 1st Brigade under Brigadier-General R. O. Bright.

As seems to have been customary in those days, the command of the expeditionary force was given to the Brigadier-General commanding the Punjab Frontier Force—on this occasion Brigadier-General A. T. Wilde. More than any incident of the actual campaign, the size and composition of his force gives food for thought. At Darband, Abbottabad, and Oghi he had one horse artillery battery, two field batteries, two mountain batteries, three regiments of Native Cavalry, three battalions of British Infantry, two companies of sappers and miners, a detachment of telegraph sappers, and nine battalions of Native Infantry, besides the " Commissariat." Orders for their concentration had been issued early in August; it was considered inadvisable to weaken the frontier garrisons at the time, so the units of the force were drawn from stations as far south as Cawnpore; yet, with no railways to speak of, this large force had been collected, equipped, and supplied at the three places mentioned before the end of September.

The feat appears the more remarkable when are considered the nature of the tracks on which the force depended for its communications

Kit Worn about 1865.

Kit worn in 1882.

the lack of resources in the country, and the enormous number of animals to be provided for. These last included elephants, which, in parts of India where they are in common use, consume their 800 lb. of green fodder a day. That they did not starve is proved by the well-authenticated exploit of a gunner officer who, chagrined at the aspersions cast upon the mountaineering abilities of his little pets, took them to the very top of the Machai Peak itself! Of the troops previously enumerated a British Infantry battalion, a regiment of Native Cavalry, and a battalion of Native Infantry had been sent to Darband. The remainder concentrated at Oghi, and were organized into two brigades, the second under Colonel Vaughan, with a reserve column to remain at Oghi pending developments under the command of Colonel Rothney. Further, a contingent of an approximate strength of 1,200 had been sent from Kashmir, but it was found unnecessary to use them.

The sight of an array so imposing within easy striking distance of their homesteads was too much for several sections of the tribes, who hastened to make their peace. Others, who included the Chigharzais, Akazais, Pariari Saiyads, and the men of Daishi still gave no sign of penitence, so on October 3rd the advance up the Black Mountain began. The direction taken was almost due north, the 1st Brigade moving on the left and occupying Mana-ka-dana. On the 4th the advance was continued. The objective of the 1st Brigade was the Chittabat Hill, and in expectation of a fight the 2nd Brigade, which had bivouacked about Kilagai in the night, was ordered to support it, leaving the levies on the Barchar spur to protect the right flank. In the attack on Chittabat the 5th Gurkhas acted in support of the 1st Gurkhas. The position was carried with slight loss, and the Regiment bivouacked on the crest of the knoll.

On the 5th an attack was made on the Machai Peak, a position of great natural strength, the capture of which was bound to have considerable moral effect. The Regiment on this occasion supported the 20th Punjab Infantry, comrades of the Ambela Campaign. The approach to the summit was over difficult ground, very steep and rocky, and allowing of manœuvre only on the narrowest of fronts. Thanks to the effective covering fire of the mountain batteries the objective was gained at a cost to the attackers of only eight casualties, one being a man of the 5th Gurkhas, who was killed. The Regiment bivouacked that night just beyond the highest point of the Machai. That, as the highest part of the range, was a suitable position from which to overawe the tribes and formed, too, a favourable starting-point for such punitive measures as might appear still to be necessary. It thus happened that the Regiment was still in occupation of its lofty eyrie when on the night of October 6th-7th the weather changed for the worse. It turned bitterly cold; rain fell and then snow, and the troops, who had neither tents nor baggage, were subjected to a spell of intense discomfort. The capture of the Machai Peak gave cause to those of the tribesmen who had proved recalcitrant to modify their attitude of hostility, and the destruction of some villages of the Pariari Saiyads completed their conversion to a belief in the blessings of peace. Soon all had made their submission, and leaving the Machai on the 10th the Regiment arrived next day at Dilbori, there to form part of a column of observation under Colonel Brownlow, what time a second column marched through Nandihar and Tikari with the object of showing the flag. The Regiment arrived back in Oghi on the 22nd, and on October 25th set out on its return march to Abbottabad.

Aftermath of second Black Mountain Expedition, 1869–71.

The troubled aftermath of this expedition shows clearly the futility of lenient treatment when dealing with these tribes. For less than nine months was there peace in Agror.

In pursuance of the normal routine adopted after the expedition the right wing under Major Close marched out to Oghi for detachment duty on January 30th, 1869, to be relieved in April by the left wing. After a three months' tour they in turn were replaced by a similar detachment of the 3rd Punjab Infantry.

In July, 1869, the tribesmen of the Black Mountain again began to give trouble. Villages in British territory were burnt and British subjects were murdered. Accordingly, on October 1st the Regiment at its full available strength was ordered to Oghi. Shahtut, a village of the Akazais lying within our borders, had been assessed for revenue as one of the results of the late expedition, and was largely concerned in the contemporary unrest. Its destruction was therefore decreed. The Regiment, with the detachment of the 3rd Punjab Infantry, started from Oghi on the 7th, and reached the village early on the morning of the 8th. The inhabitants, knowing what to expect, fled on the approach of the troops, and the village was entered without loss. The houses were burnt, cattle and goats captured to be divided among the men, and all crops found standing were destroyed. This summary action had a good effect for a time, the tribes remaining quiescent throughout the winter, and in January, 1870, the Regiment returned to Abbottabad. In April there was a recrudescence of trouble, the Akazais with a clan of the Hassanzais being the offenders. On the 17th the headquarters left Abbottabad to join the left wing, which had been quartered there since March. Colonel Rothney found himself with insufficient troops to deal with the raiders as they deserved, and had to content himself with destroying the crops round the ruins of Shahtut, the Akazai lands there having been declared forfeit. The restoration of the Khan of Agror shortly afterwards appeared likely to bring tranquillity to the

1870.

valley, and on September 7th the Regiment returned to Abbottabad. Following the burning of three outlying hamlets by the Akazais in June, 1871, the headquarters and 200 rifles again set out for Oghi on the night of June 19th–20th. The prompt retaliatory measures undertaken by the Khan of Agror, which earned him the censure of Government, had their effect, and the party was soon back in cantonments.

Items of Interest, 1868 to 1876

In September, 1868, the establishment was increased by 40 privates, giving a total of 640 sepoys, or 80 per company.

In September, 1869, the Regiment suffered severely from an epidemic of fever, which was raging throughout the district. On the 16th they went into camp on the hills to the west of cantonments, but the exposure in tents appeared rather to aggravate the disease.

During December, 1869, lines were sanctioned for the troops at Oghi, and the Regiment helped to build them.

In September, 1870, a full complement of rifles was received of the pattern short Enfield 1852 with bayonet, the Regiment having been selected as one of the corps of the Native Army to which the issue was sanctioned. On December 20th, 1872, the Regiment marched out of Abbottabad to join a camp of exercise near Hasan Abdal. On February 12th, 1873, the camp of exercise was broken up and Abbottabad was reached on the 16th. In the old Record no mention is made of the weather.

On January 16th, 1874, short Enfield rifles with swords were received to replace the short Enfield rifles with bayonets.

The Regiment was inspected by Brigadier-General Keyes on April 20th, 1874, and again while in camp at Sherwan on November 24th, 1875.

Departure of Colonel Rothney, 1873.

On October 29th, 1873, Colonel O. E. Rothney, C.S.I., was promoted to the rank of Brigadier-General. He had taken over command when the Regiment had been in existence for only two years. He left it seasoned by the rigours of three arduous campaigns and with a reputation second to none in the Punjab Frontier Force. His farewell order marks a stage in the growth of the Regiment, and it is fitting therefore that it should be given a place in this narrative. It was published to the Regiment on November 9th, 1873:—

"It is with much regret that Colonel Rothney takes leave of the Regiment which he has commanded for thirteen years past. Although gratified with the honour done to him in his advancement to a higher command, that consideration cannot for the time dispel the pain and reluctance with which he parts from his old comrades with whom he has been happily associated for many years, and to whom he feels he owes very much. In quitting his present command Colonel Rothney congratulates the Regiment (still comparatively young) on the honourable name which it has gained for itself. The excellent service it has done in three hill campaigns is recorded in despatches; its state of efficiency and discipline has frequently been commended by superior authority; and Colonel Rothney himself fully testifies to the loyal, soldierly, and cheerful spirit which animates all ranks in the Regiment.

"He gratefully acknowledges that this is mainly due to the able and zealous exertions of the officers serving under his command, and he tenders to each and all of them his hearty thanks for the cordial support he has always received from them, and for their soldier-like solicitude for the honour and well-being of the Regiment. He takes leave of them with earnest wishes for their welfare, and he will ever remember with pleasure his long association with them as their brother-officer.

"He desires to thank also the Native officers, non-commissioned officers, and soldiers of the Regiment for their exemplary conduct, soldier-like spirit, and alacrity in the performance of duty while under his command.

"Colonel Rothney wishes the 5th Goorkha Regiment 'Farewell.' He will always watch their fortunes and career with keen interest, and he feels confident they will continue to maintain this good name, and will strive by their discipline and conduct to uphold the honour of the Punjab Frontier Force."

Colonel Rothney was succeeded in the command of the Regiment by Colonel P. F. Gardiner, who joined on May 30th, 1874.

Expedition against the Jowaki Afridis, 1877–78.

In October, 1877, orders were received for the headquarters and 280 bayonets to proceed to Lakha Talao, a village situated just outside Jowaki Afridi territory, about fourteen miles due north of Kushalgarh. The right wing of the Regiment was selected, and the small force left Abbottabad under Colonel Gardiner on October 10th.

The Jowakis, against whom the expedition was directed, are a section of the Adam Khels, and occupy the south-eastern portion of that salient of Afridi country which juts out oddly into British territory across the Peshawar–Kohat road. They had earned punishment by their conduct during the previous July and August. Hearing that Government had under consideration the revision of allowances paid to the tribesmen for keeping open the Peshawar–Kohat road, they jumped to the conclusion that they would lose their share, which amounted to Rs. 2,000 a year. It was unearned increment, as their territory did not touch the road at any point, and they were therefore powerless to safeguard traffic on it, however excellent their intentions. Actually the payment was to have been continued, but was to have been made dependent on their keeping intact that part of the road and telegraph line between Kohat and Kushalgarh which ran close to their inhospitable hills. However, they had too little patience to await the outcome of the revision, and began to raid, plunder, and burn. A quick dash by three small columns had been made into their country in August, but had failed to bring them to terms. It was therefore decided to undertake operations on a larger scale.

Hostilities began on November 9th, 1877. Brigadier-General Keyes, commanding the expedition, divided his force into three columns for the purpose of a combined move on Paia, one of their more important villages lying in the heart of their country. The 5th Gurkhas, with a section of No. 2 Mountain Battery and 280 bayonets of the 5th Punjab Infantry, constituted No. 3 column under the command of Colonel Gardiner. No. 1 column starting from Kohat entered Jowaki territory from the west; No. 2 column starting from Gumbat, about midway between Kohat and Kushalgarh, entered from the south; and No. 3 column from the east. The Regiment with No. 3 column was engaged at Kakhto and had one man wounded. The three columns united at Paia and spent the next few days in burning villages and destroying towers in the vicinity. On October 14th the force moved westwards from Paia to Shindih, which meant for all except Colonel Gardiner's column a return on their tracks. It proved to be a very exceptional year in the matter of the weather. At Shindih the rain came down in torrents, bringing operations to a complete standstill. The men of the Regiment had to subsist as best they might in the open, under conditions of intense discomfort, but bore their sufferings with accustomed cheerfulness.

After weighing alternatives General Keyes decided on Jamu, a short distance northwards, as his next objective; but apprehensive regarding his line of withdrawal after the work of destruction should have been completed he asked for the co-operation of a force from Peshawar, having as its object the weakening of hostile opposition by means of a threat from the north-west. This was agreed to, and December 1st was fixed for the start of the operation.

The Peshawar column was delayed through the interruption of its communications, caused by a sudden rise in the water-level of the Indus, which swept away the bridge of boats at Attock. By December 3rd, however, it was ready and a few days later, having made good the passes leading over the range of hills into the Bori Valley northwards of Jamu, had established itself on the ridge.

The force under General Keyes meanwhile had left Shindih on December 1st in accordance with the original programme; by means of an early start and the rapidity of its movements again divided into three columns, had taken the enemy unawares, and had occupied the Jamu Valley. December 2nd to 4th were spent in the execution of further punitive measures, in surveying the country and in reconnaissance. While the Peshawar column was similarly employed in the

Bori Valley, General Keyes broke fresh ground to the north-east to destroy the village of Ghanba, notorious in that part of the frontier as the resort of all the worst characters for miles around, and considered to be impregnable owing to the difficulties of its approaches.

Still the Jowakis remained obdurate, and objectives for the expedition were becoming scarce. One was found, however, in the Pustawani Valley, an almost inaccessible glen leading out of Jowaki territory in a north-easterly direction. A combined movement of both forces was planned, but again the start was delayed by rain, which rendered the *nullah* tracks impassable. It was December 31st, 1877, before the columns could get under way, but once begun, the enterprise was a complete success. The troops remained in the country until the middle of January, 1878, and then withdrew, leaving only a small mixed force on the northern ridge to watch developments. They had not long to wait; the Jowaki Jirgah hastened to come in, and accepted without reserve the terms imposed. The wing of the Regiment returned to Abbottabad on March 18th, 1878. Their casualties had been few— one Subadar and three men wounded—but they had been called upon to do a great deal of hard work of a harassing nature, had endured considerable hardship, and through it all had well maintained the reputation of the Regiment.

On May 20th an inspection was carried out by Brigadier-General F. S. Roberts, V.C., C.B., who had lately taken over command of the Punjab Frontier Force from General Keyes. It was the Regiment's first official meeting with its future Colonel, the commander under whom it was destined so soon to serve and to gain fresh honour and renown.

In September Colonel Gardiner relinquished command of the Regiment and was succeeded by Major A. Fitzhugh.

CHAPTER III

THE SECOND AFGHAN WAR

NOVEMBER, 1878, TO DECEMBER, 1879

Causes.

FORTUNATELY it is not necessary to enter very minutely into the causes of the second Afghan War in order to appreciate the part played in it by the Regiment. The first Afghan War was fought because, after driving Dost Mohamed into the arms of the Russians through our justifiable refusal to forward his designs for the recovery of Peshawar from the Sikhs, we rashly insisted on deposing him and giving Afghanistan a nominee of our own as ruler in the person of Shah Shuja. We realized, when too late, that we had backed the wrong horse, and that interference in Afghan affairs was not lightly to be undertaken. When, therefore, in 1873 Dost Mohamed's successor, Shere Ali, nervous on the score of his country's integrity through the fall and retention, contrary to Russian promises, of Khiva, asked the Indian Government for material assistance in case of need, the Indian Government, bitten before, was shy of committing itself a second time, and refused.

The refusal of help in Shere Ali's case had much the same effect as in the case of his father before him, though now with more justification. It drove him to favour Russia at the expense of England. At that time no particular anxiety was felt regarding the possibility of Russian aggression. The two countries had lately arrived at some sort of agreement regarding their spheres of influence, and Russia had, further, given an undertaking not to send her agents to Kabul. This mildly complacent attitude, however, could not longer be maintained in the face of the continued southward extension of the Russian frontiers during the next two years. It was felt that we must have a British agent at Herat who could keep the Government in effective touch with the situation across the Afghan frontier, and in 1876 the new Viceroy, Lord Lytton, was authorized to make the promise of aid, previously withheld, in exchange for permission to establish a British agency at Herat or elsewhere. That permission was never given; Shere Ali by now believed that Russian help would be better worth securing.

Then in 1877 came the Russo-Turkish War, when the fixed determination of Great Britain that Russia should not pluck Constantinople among the other fruits of victory seemed, at one time, to make war between England and Russia inevitable. In anticipation Britain called 5,000 Indian troops to Malta. Russia did better; she not only massed troops at the Oxus ferries, but sent a mission under General Stoleitoff to effect an offensive and defensive alliance with Afghanistan. It was only when news was received of the conclusion of the Berlin treaty, bringing peace to Europe, that Stoleitoff's instructions were modified.

The immediate danger of war with Russia passed, but meantime there was the Russian mission, which we could not allow to sway unchecked the counsels of the Afghan ruler. There was, too, the question of our prestige to be considered. Accordingly a British mission with Sir Neville Chamberlain at its head left Peshawar for Kabul on September 21st, 1878, to be turned back by force at Ali Masjid. This insult could only be met by a declaration of war, and preparations were made accordingly. One eleventh-hour chance was given to Shere Ali in case he should experience a change of heart. A full apology for recent happenings was demanded by November 20th: meantime our preparations would go forward, and failing its receipt by the date given, his country would be invaded.

Plan of Operations and Preliminary Movements, October, 1878.
It was eventually decided to form three columns for the invasion of Afghanistan: one at Sukkur for an advance from Quetta on Kandahar, a second at Kohat for an advance by the Kurram Valley to Khost, and a third at Peshawar for an advance to Dakka through the Khyber. The Regiment found itself allotted to the Kurram Field Force under the command of General Roberts, and left Abbottabad for Kohat on October 2nd, 1878. The British officers who accompanied it were Major A. Fitzhugh (Commandant), Major W. H. Unwin, Captain J. Cook, Captain C. F. Powell, Lieutenant C. C. Chenevix Trench, and Surgeon-Major G. Farrell. Lieutenant A. R. Martin joined only a few days later, and Lieutenant C. C. St. E. Lucas on November 23rd, after the Regiment had left Thall.

Kohat was reached on October 15th, and during the sojourn there preparations were made for a lengthy campaign, which included the dispatch to Gorakhpur of a strong recruiting party.

At that time the Kurram Valley was included in Afghanistan, much against the inclinations of its Shiah inhabitants, the Turis, and the fort at Thall constituted our most advanced outpost in that direction. There the final concentration of the Kurram Field Force was to be effected, and for that place the Regiment set out on October 23rd. Having arrived at its destination on November 2nd, in common with the rest of the army detailed for active service, it was faced with a period of waiting. By November 15th the concentration of the Kurram Field Force had been completed, and its composition was then as follows:—

"F" Battery, "A" Brigade R.H.A.;
1 Squadron, 10th Hussars;
"G" Battery, 3rd Brigade R.A.;
2nd Battalion, 8th Foot;
Wing, 72nd Highlanders;
12th Bengal Cavalry;
No. 1 Mountain Battery;
7th Company Bengal Sappers and Miners;
2nd (Punjab Frontier Force) Infantry;
5th (Punjab Frontier Force) Infantry;
5th (Punjab Frontier Force) Gurkhas;
21st Punjab Infantry;
23rd Pioneers;
29th Punjab Infantry;

making a total of 5,335, with 13 guns. The strength of the Regiment at this time was 438 of all ranks.

During the stay of the Force at Thall, General Roberts, having previously referred the question, was able to assure the Turis that they might consider themselves as British subjects from that time forward, and the release conveyed by that assurance from the Sunni tyranny of Afghanistan was undoubtedly an important factor in the success of the operations on this front. One other incident of that period is worth recording as showing that the conditions in the immediate vicinity of Thall have undergone little change in the last fifty years. On November 14th a sepoy of the Regiment was murdered by Waziris while fishing on the right bank of the Kurram.

November 20th came, and Shere Ali still kept silence on the subject of the protest addressed to him, so on the 21st the forward move began. In his "Forty-One Years in India," Lord Roberts tells us of his fears regarding the possible inadequacy of his force for the task before it, and relates that when for the first time they saw the men of the Regiment with their smooth, hairless faces and cheerful looks, even the women were heard to marvel that we should take beardless boys to fight with Afghan warriors.

Beginning of Hostilities, November, 1878.
There were no signs of misgiving, however, when at 3 a.m. on November 21st the Kurram Field Force set out towards the still distant line of the Safed Koh. The track of those days ran for a considerable distance in the bed of the Kurram River, and the necessity to improve it in many places to permit of the passage of guns and animals made progress slow. It left the Kurram at a point some

thirty miles from Thall to cut across in a north-westerly direction the bend made by the river after passing Ahmadzai, so shortening the distance to the Afghan fort of Kurram, which stood on the left bank about eight miles south of the existing cantonment of Parachinar. All went well during the march; the Turis—as also the Jajis of the right bank—proved friendly, and Kurram Fort was reached on November 25th. The Afghans had abandoned the place, leaving a gun behind them, nor could reliable information be obtained regarding their whereabouts and intentions. Reconnoitring forward for fifteen miles, it was ascertained that their army, reported to number 18,000 with 11 guns, had but lately passed through Habib Kila, and was then engaged in preparing a position on the Peiwar Kotal.

Leaving an advanced depot at the Kurram Fort the rest of the Force set out at 5 a.m. on November 28th to gain contact with the enemy, and after marching for nine hours the Regiment formed in order for attack.

Advance to Peiwar Kotal, November, 1878.

The advance was continued for a further six miles without, however, encountering opposition in any form, and having by that time arrived within two miles of the Kotal itself the Force prepared to bivouac. The fire of the Afghan guns soon made it apparent that the spot selected was uncomfortably close to the hostile position. A more suitable place was found about a mile and a half to the rear, and there camp was formed.

During the march the 29th Punjab Infantry under Colonel Gordon had been sent forward to reconnoitre the pass. While the rest of the column was occupied in establishing piquets, and in making all snug for the night, Colonel Gordon's command had attracted unwelcome attention from the enemy. The Regiment was thereupon sent out to cover its withdrawal, and by skilful use of ground accomplished its mission with the loss of one man dangerously wounded. First blood to the Afghans!

The information brought in by the reconnoitring party was to the effect that the approach to the Peiwar Kotal was very difficult, and indicated that a frontal attack would entail very severe loss. This was confirmed next day from the personal observation of the Force Commander. As a result, General Roberts decided to halt where he was until an alternative route could be found, offering a better prospect of success.

As will be seen from the sketch, the Afghan position astride the track leading over the pass ran generally from south-west to north-east, along a high ridge which rose to a height of about 2,000 feet above the level of the valley. It faced generally south-east, and bold spurs descending abruptly from the main feature flanked the track on either side. The southern slopes of the easterly spurs were covered with trees, and beyond the final feature ran a *nullah*, at the head of which was the Spingawai Kotal, situated to the east of the main position. Here it might be that a way would be found to turn the Afghan defences.

While ordering a careful reconnaissance of the Spingawai route General Roberts elaborated measures to deceive the enemy. His efforts in that direction appeared to meet with complete success. It was known that the enemy had posted a detachment at the Spingawai, but as far as could be ascertained no reinforcements were sent in that direction; while, on the other hand, movements of men and guns were observed in the main position which could only have as their object the repulse of a frontal attack.

On the 30th was received the report on the approaches to the Spingawai Kotal. On the information it contained the General arrived at the decision to make a turning movement during darkness by that route in the greatest strength which he could make available, and to leave about 1,000 men under Brigadier-General Cobbe to hold the enemy in front and to guard the camp.

Action at Peiwar Kotal, December, 1878.

The force selected for the turning movement was composed as follows:—

    4 Guns F.A., R.H.A.;
    Wing, 72nd Highlanders;
    No. 1 Mountain Battery;
    2nd Punjab Infantry;
    29th Punjab Infantry;
    5th Gurkhas;
    23rd Pioneers.

The distance to be traversed was considerable, while obstacles to progress were expected, so 10 p.m. on December 1st was fixed as the starting-hour for this force.

With so many possible Afghan sympathizers in his camp, General Roberts had taken the precaution to say nothing of his plans to anybody, with the exception of one or two selected Staff officers. It was not till after dark on December 1st that he assembled commanding officers and communicated his intentions.

In absolute silence the force fell in to begin its march, the policy of deceiving the enemy pursued to the last, for the normal number of lights was left to burn, and not a tent had been struck. At the appointed hour the leading men of the 29th Punjab Infantry, which was in the van, moved eastwards out of camp. In " Forty-One Years in India," Lord Roberts gives an account of the contretemps which might so easily have wrecked his schemes, and which caused him to bring the 5th Gurkhas to the front of the column.

In the East there was just that faint light which comes before full dawn when the enemy became aware of the approach of the force.

"At this moment two shots from the enemy's look-out sentries alarmed the picket on the Kotal. The advance party of 5th Goorkhas immediately formed up from column of fours into a company line, and led by Major Fitzhugh and Captain Cook rushed straight at a barricade which now became apparent about fifty yards to their front. The remainder of the Regiment extended and swarmed round the flanks of the obstacle, which was carried in very brilliant style."[1]

Speedy as their action had been, the clearing of the first barricade took just so much time as allowed the leading company of the 72nd to come up with them. Higher up the slope the flashes of Afghan rifles could be seen against the background of a more formidable defensive work, and now unmindful of fatigue in the excitement of the contest, Gurkhas and Highlanders together charged up the steep hill-side and drove the enemy headlong into the forest. Yet a third breastwork could be discerned through the trees ahead, and again, with hardly a pause, they dashed to the assault, and the Spingawai Kotal was won.

The next phase of the action is best told in the words of the "Historical Record of the 5th Goorkha Regiment," printed in 1886:—

"The enemy fled, and were pursued to the right front by a large proportion of the Regiment. The light was so uncertain, day having hardly broken and the trees being very thick, that it was hard to distinguish friend from foe. Captain Cook found himself confronted by a considerable number of the enemy, who were attempting to save one of their guns. He collected a few men and charged the party of the enemy, who fled, leaving many dead on the field. During this operation Captain Cook saved the life of Major Galbraith, Assistant-Adjutant General, by engaging and throwing down an Afghan soldier who was in the act of shooting at Major Galbraith."

For the act of bravery here recorded, and for his gallant leading in the assault, Captain Cook was recommended for the award of the Victoria Cross, which in due course was bestowed on him.

The casualties of the Regiment in this brilliantly executed assault were two rank and file killed, two Native officers and fifteen rank and file wounded. The pursuit of the enemy through the dense forest had inevitably caused a certain degree of dispersion. A pause was therefore made for purposes of reorganization and the replenishment of ammunition. The battery R.H.A., of which the guns were being carried on elephants, and two of the Infantry regiments were still toiling up the gorge leading to the Kotal, but the vital importance of deriving the utmost possible advantage from the surprise so far

---

[1] Sir F. Roberts's despatch dated December 31st, 1878.

The Capture of the Spingawai Kotal, December 2nd, 1878.

(From the painting by Vereker Hamilton)

achieved was deemed to outweigh considerations of mere strength, so no time was wasted before making a fresh move. The direction of the advance was now west, and for a time all went excellently well. No enemy was seen, and there was nothing to show that he had yet been apprised of the threat to his flank and rear. After proceeding cautiously for two hours the Afghans were encountered strongly entrenched on the far side of a deep depression. When he came to make his dispositions for attack, however, General Roberts found to his consternation that he had with him only the 29th Punjab Infantry. After a time, fearing that his inactivity would incite the enemy to a counter-move, he sent forward the Sikh companies of the 29th, but withdrew them almost at once on realizing that they were too weak numerically for the task. Just then there arrived not only the 72nd and 5th Gurkhas, who had been the victims of loss of touch, but also the horse battery with the 2nd Punjab Infantry and 23rd Pioneers, for whom earlier in the morning it had been considered inadvisable to wait.

The Force Commander now directed the 23rd Pioneers to make an attack across the hollow. They tried, but failed because it was found possible to advance only on the narrowest of fronts, heavily enfiladed from both sides. Happily at this juncture a rapid survey discovered a way farther to the north which not only turned the enemy's barricades immediately opposite, but exposed the rear of the main position to the fire of the attackers.

A further reinforcement now appeared on the scene. The 5th Punjab Infantry had formed the right of the holding attack, launched, as previously planned, in conformity with the progress of the envelopment, and diverted from their proper course by an impassable *nullah* had made for the sound of the firing.

After minor readjustments among the units of his force—made to ensure the greater safety of the wounded—and the strengthening of his hold on the ground so far won, General Roberts went on with the remainder—which included the Regiment—along the newly found route in the direction of the Peiwar Kotal. Concealment of his manœuvre was no longer a consideration; his mountain guns opened fire, and the Afghans, realizing at last that they had been circumvented, retreated hurriedly *en masse*. This gave the troops of the holding attack their opportunity to push right into the position, and they were quick to seize their chance. The 12th Bengal Cavalry took up the pursuit. As to the turning column, darkness overtook them before they could reach the pass, so tired but happy they bivouacked where they then found themselves. At that height the cold was intense, but fortunately wood was plentiful, so the night was spent in comparative comfort. Continuing their advance at daybreak they soon reached the Kotal, and it could then be seen how terror must have lent wings to the Afghans in their flight; guns and baggage waggons and camp equipage all had been left behind, while thousands of rounds of ammunition and much war material of other kinds fell into our hands.

The awards for gallantry gained by the Regiment in the Peiwar Kotal action are duly set out in the appropriate appendix, but passing reference is allowed in this place to the Orders of Merit bestowed on Subadar Ragobir Nagarkoti, who was destined to die fighting in the Deh-i-Mozang Gorge on December 14th, 1879, and on Havildar Parsu Khattri, who was one day to rise to the rank of Subadar Major and to prove himself one of the finest soldiers ever bred in the Regiment.

Reconnaissance of Shutargardan, December, 1878.

The rôle originally assigned to the Kurram Field Force had been twofold. In his book Lord Roberts details his objects as "in the first instance the occupation of the Kurram Valley and the expulsion of all Afghan garrisons south of the Shutargardan Pass, and in the second, as opportunity might offer, the pushing on of reconnaissances into the Khost Valley and, if military considerations would admit, the dislodging the Amir's administration from that tract of country so as to prevent the Kabul Government drawing supplies from it." The first object had been achieved, for the Afghan garrisons, to say nothing of the little matter of an Afghan Field Force, had fled— no one could say whither, but to a point at least many miles on the safe side of the Shutargardan Pass. Still, in view of eventualities the reconnaissance of the pass was itself an undertaking well worth while, and plans were laid accordingly. A halt of two days was made at the Peiwar Kotal Camp, and the time was spent in getting up tentage and supplies and in arranging for the occupation of the position during the winter months. Further, the opportunity was taken to evacuate the sick and wounded to the advanced depot at Kurram Fort. On December 6th, leaving only a small guard for the camp, the Force advanced to Ali Khel. The foot of the pass was reached on the 8th, and next day a thorough reconnaissance was made. From the top of the pass, at a height of 11,000 feet, an uninterrupted view was obtained over the Logar Valley leading down to Kabul, and it appeared that no obstacle intervened to block the advance of a force in that direction should the contingency arise. It did.

On December 10th the Force returned to Ali Khel. From its position between the two passes, at the intersection of a number of important tracks, that place was well adapted to form an advanced post of observation for the Kurram line. The necessary measures,

PAIWAR KOTAL AND SPINGAWAI PASS

(From The Afghan Campaigns 1878-1880 by Sidney H. Shadbolt by permission of Sampson Low, Marston & Co. owners of the copyright)

PAIWAR KOTAL

Zabardast Kala

Koterai

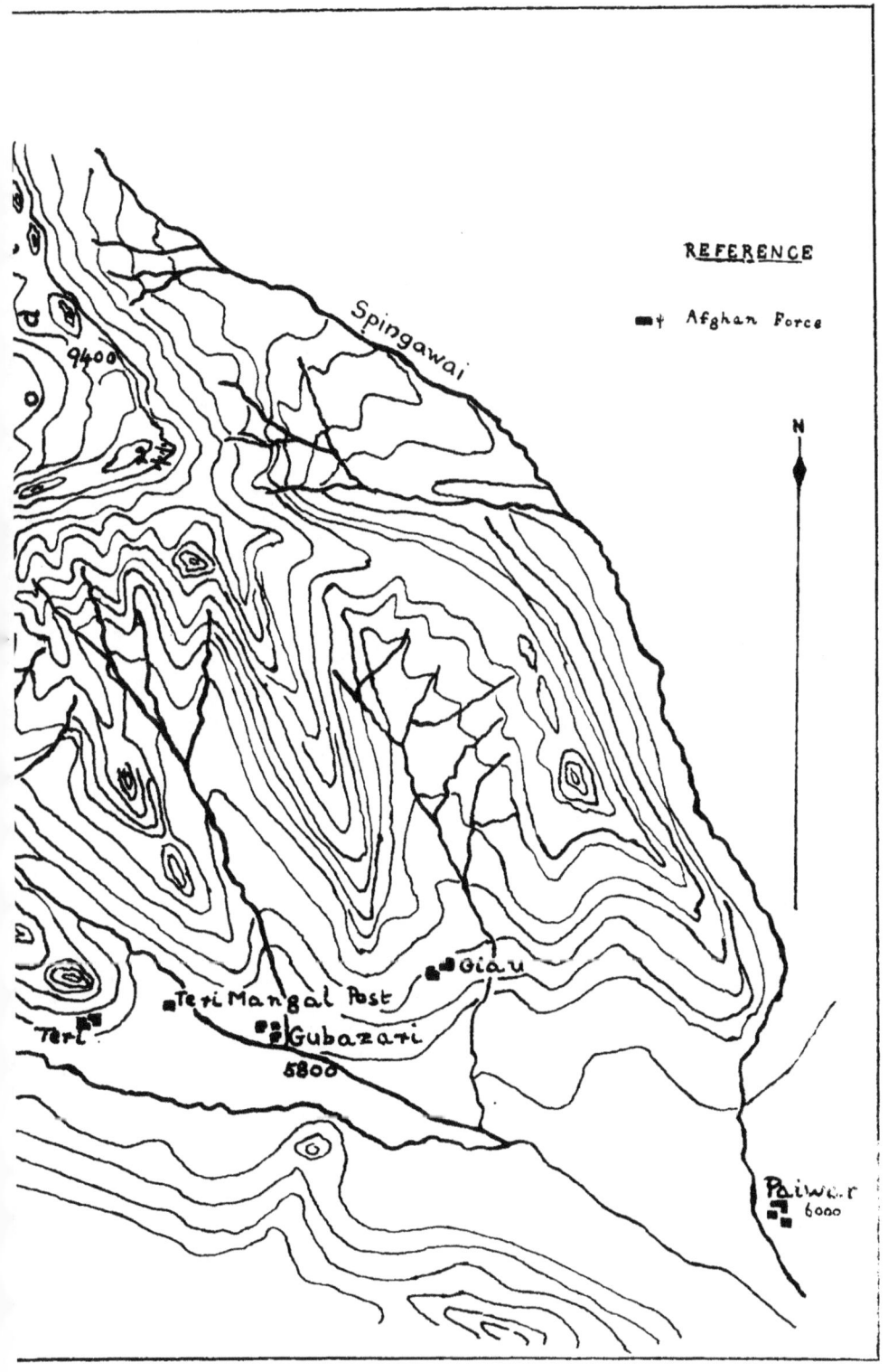

THE 5TH ROYAL GURKHA RIFLES (F.F.)

both political and military, were taken for the establishment of such a post, and on their completion General Roberts was free to return to Kurram Fort, there to prepare for the visit to Khost.

True to his purpose of seeing as much of the country as possible he chose instead of the Peiwar route one farther to the west. The demands in men of Ali Khel and the Peiwar Kotal had reduced the mobile part of the Force to the mountain battery, Wing 72nd Highlanders, 5th Gurkhas, and 23rd Pioneers. This small column left Ali Khel on December 12th, its route lying first west and then south, and halted for the night at Sapari. The road to be traversed next day was reported to be difficult, descending very steeply from the Sapari Pass and then entering a narrow, rocky defile five miles in length, which often barely gave room for a loaded camel to go through. Warning, too, had been given by some friendly maliks that attack might almost certainly be expected during the passage of the defile.

Action at Monghyr Pass, December, 1878.

On December 13th the Regiment fell in at 2 a.m. to provide baggage guards for the transport and with the remainder to furnish a rear-guard to the column. A detachment had been sent on to occupy the Sapari Pass overnight, so it was expected that such trouble as might be in store for the small force would not be encountered until after passing that point. For the Regiment it was to prove otherwise; the transport encountered an ice-slide right across the track soon after leaving camp: animals lost their footing, a long delay occurred, and it was only through the unceasing endeavours of the baggage guards that it was enabled to reach the summit of the pass by noon. From there the 23rd Pioneers, supported by the 72nd and the mountain battery, were sent ahead to secure the exit from the defile. They arrived only just in time, large bodies of tribesmen appearing on the scene just as they were in position. Foiled in their attempt in that direction, while some made friendly overtures others turned their attention to the rear-guard. Almost from the moment of leaving the Sapari Pass the Regiment was continuously engaged. Hearing that the transport was being fired on, and that an officer had been hit, Major Fitzhugh went forward with two companies, leaving the rest of the Regiment under Captain Cook to protect the rear. About a mile and a half down the defile he found Captain Goad of the transport department lying in a doolie very severely wounded. Round him were a sergeant and three privates of the 72nd, who had been hard put to it to hold their ground against numbers of the enemy. After seeing the small party into safety Major Fitzhugh rejoined the rear-guard, which, withdrawing slowly and harassed without intermission, had been most skilfully handled by Captain Cook. The defile was cleared before dark, and that night the Force halted at the village of Keria.

Sir F. Roberts's appreciation of the work done by the Regiment on this day was expressed in his despatch of December 18th, 1878:—

"The conduct and steady behaviour of the 5th Goorkhas on the occasion merit my warmest commendations. For nearly five hours this Regiment maintained a rear-guard fight over most difficult ground with a bold and active enemy thoroughly acquainted with the locality, and so successfully was this duty performed that not a single baggage animal or load was lost. It is therefore my pleasure and my duty to bring the gallant conduct of this fine Regiment once more to the special notice of His Excellency and the Government of India."

After mentioning each British officer by name, and paying a tribute to the Native officers and non-commissioned officers collectively, the despatch continued:—

"But the 5th Goorkhas did not perform their duty without sustaining severe loss. Captain Powell, who was most forward and gallant in the fight, was very severely wounded, and three Goorkha sepoys were killed and eleven wounded, of whom one has since died. The whole Force mourns the loss of these brave men."

Captain Powell soon afterwards died from his wounds.

For his gallantry in this affair of the Monghyr Defile, Sepoy Kishanbir Nagarkoti gained for the first time the award of the Order of Merit, which he was subsequently to win on no less than three other occasions during a fine fighting career. Besides him three men gained the coveted honour in this action, as well as the hospital assistant, Shankar Dass.

From Keria the fort at Kurram was reached without further trouble, and there the Regiment stayed for a great part of the winter.

Kurram Valley, 1879. In January, 1879, General Roberts visited Khost in fulfilment of the second part of the rôle originally allotted to his force. On this occasion he left the Regiment behind, but a detachment of 200 rifles joined him later. He reached Matun on January 6th, took over the fort, and accepted the surrender of the Afghan Governor. There was a collision next day with the tribesmen, and though they were driven off without difficulty, losing 100 men by capture in addition to killed and wounded, and being forced to part with hundreds of sheep and cattle and large stores of grain, it was clear that occupation of the country was out of the question in view of the size of the Force and its many commitments. So after completing a survey of the valley the column returned to the Kurram at the end of January.

On April 1st, 1879, the Regiment marched to Ali Khel, whither it had previously sent a detachment 200 strong to support Brigadier-

General Thelwall, who had been left in charge in that area, and there it stayed for the rest of the summer.

Meantime much had occurred in Afghanistan to change the political situation as it had existed at the time of the outbreak of hostilities. Soon after he heard of the defeat of the Afghan force at the Peiwar Kotal the Amir—Shere Ali—had fled the country, giving out that he went to enlist Russian aid. His son, Yakub Khan, was then allowed to pass from his prison stool to a throne, and with the death of his father in Turkestan in February became Amir indeed. Truly life was not lacking in incident for a member of the Durani Royal House! At that time Sir Donald Stewart held Kandahar, while the Peshawar Valley Field Force under Sir Sam Browne had occupied the Khyber with the Dacca Plain beyond, and pushed forward through Jalalabad to Gandamak. These altered conditions justified the reopening of negotiations, and early in May we find Yakub Khan visiting the camp at Gandamak. By the end of the month a treaty had been concluded whereby in return for a subsidy the Amir agreed to British protection and control of territory which included the Kurram Valley, Peshin, and Sibi, to the residence at Kabul of a British representative with a suitable escort, and to the deputation of British agents to visit the Afghan frontiers in the interests of both parties to the treaty. No specific reference was made to the exclusion of Russian agents, but Yakub Khan bound himself in general terms to conduct his relations with foreign States in accordance with the advice and wishes of the British Government.

Thus it seemed that a satisfactory solution had been found for all points at issue, and politically the way was now clear for the withdrawal of the British forces. Orders were issued for the evacuation of Afghan territory by the Khyber Field Force immediately, and by Sir Donald Stewart's army as soon as climatic conditions should permit. Sir Frederick Roberts's force was to stand fast, pending the settlement of the newly acquired Kurram Valley territory.

Queen's Birthday Parade, May 24th, 1879.

From a regimental point of view the most interesting event of this period was a parade held in honour of the Queen's birthday on May 24th. The available striking-force was located at that time on a plateau four miles east of Ali Khel, and, in his "Forty-One Years in India," Lord Roberts tells of the fine appearance of the troops, and of the consternation of the tribesmen, called in to admire, on the firing of the *feu de joie*. He adds:—

"At this parade I had the great pleasure of decorating Captain Cook with the Victoria Cross, and Subadar Ragobir Nagarkoti, Jemadar Pursoo Khatri, Native Doctor Sankar Dass, and five riflemen of the 5th Gurkhas with the Order of Merit for their gallant conduct in the attack on the Spingawi Kotal, and during the passage of the Mangior Defile. It was a happy circumstance that Major Galbraith, who owed his life to Captain Cook's intrepidity, and Major Fitzhugh, whose life was saved by Jemadar (then Havildar) Pursoo Khatri, should both have been present on the parade."

Major Cavagnari's Mission, July, 1879.

The settlement of the valley entailed attempts, successful on the whole, to establish friendly relations with the tribes on its borders and a thorough reconnaissance of possible routes. In these activities the Regiment took its share, and in July it formed part of the escort to the British mission under Major Cavagnari, who had been chosen as our representative at Kabul. On arrival at the Shutargardan Pass the mission was passed on to an Afghan Sirdar and his following, who thenceforward became responsible for its safe conduct, and the British troops returned to their camp.

Massacre at Kabul, September, 1879.

But little more than a month had passed when black tragedy intervened to set at naught the provisions of the treaty and to put in motion again the machinery of war. On September 3rd, 1879, the British Residency in Kabul was besieged by mutinous elements of the Afghan regular forces, and despite the heroic resistance of the members of the Embassy, and of its escort of the Guides, all within were done to death. Yakub Khan was absolved from the stigma of direct participation in the crime, and his Commander-in-Chief, Daud Shah, was credited with an attempt to save Sir Louis Cavagnari and his following, but these considerations did but enhance the difficulty of exacting retribution. The Amir represented himself as suffering persecution at the hands of his mutinous soldiery, and threw himself on the mercy of the British. At the same time he exerted himself to stir up hatred against them with the object of creating opposition to a renewed advance on Kabul. Captain Conolly, Political Officer at Ali Khel, was the first to hear of the disaster, and immediately telegraphed the news to Simla, whither Sir Frederick Roberts had previously been called for work unconnected with Afghanistan.

Campaign Reopened, September, 1879.

The shock of the tragedy was not allowed to postpone the decision to act, and to act at once. Sir Donald Stewart was to recall as many of his troops as could be made available, for the reoccupation of Kandahar; the Kurram Field Force, made up to the strength of a division and rechristened the Kabul Field Force, was to advance on Kabul under Sir Frederick Roberts; and yet another division under Major-General R. O. Bright was to be assembled to hold the line of the Khyber and the plain beyond as far as Jalalabad. At the same time the Amir was informed of the proposed moves and of the reasons for them. As a preliminary to the advance on Kabul orders were issued to Brigadier-General Massy, who was commanding in the absence of Sir F. Roberts, to seize and hold the Shutargardan Pass. In fulfilment of this object the Regiment left Ali Khel on September 8th, 1879, and camped at Karatiga to await the arrival of the 7th Company Sappers and Miners, and the 23rd Pioneers. Two days later these units reached Karatiga, and at 2.30 a.m. on the 11th the Regiment led the advance from that place towards the Shutargardan. By sunrise the head of the pass had been made good, and there the small force entrenched, pending the development of the situation.

Lack of transport was the main obstacle to rapid concentration, but by making full use of local resources the work of collecting supplies and of moving up units destined to take part in the advance was achieved step by step. Under the new organization of the Force the Regiment was intended to form part of General Baker's 2nd Infantry Brigade with the 72nd Highlanders, 3rd Sikhs, 5th Punjab Infantry, and 23rd Pioneers. Taking part in the move on Kabul there were besides four batteries of Artillery, including the Kohat and Derajat Mountain Batteries, a Cavalry brigade under General Massy and the 1st Infantry Brigade under General Macpherson. Two brigades of Infantry were organized for work on the lines of communication. As the situation developed, many factors combined to stultify the original plan of organization, with the result that it became necessary to employ units quite independently of their original allotment to brigades.

Kushi, the point of entrance into the Logar Valley for a force coming from the Shutargardan, was chosen as the place of forward concentration, and there the Regiment arrived on September 24th. In due course it was joined by the remaining units chosen for the advance, while on September 27th no less a person than Yakub Khan, the Amir himself, came into General Baker's camp. His presence was to prove a source of considerable embarrassment to Sir Frederick Roberts, for he used the freedom which was necessarily allowed him, in view of the relations which were supposed to exist between the British and the Afghan ruler, in order to intrigue with the leaders of his reputedly rebellious subjects, and to strengthen their resistance.

On October 2nd the Regiment with the rest of General Baker's brigade marched ten miles down the Logar Valley to Zargan Shahar, there to join up with the Cavalry brigade, and some Infantry under General Massy who had arrived two days before. On the 3rd, headquarters and the rest of the column left Kushi, and, picking up the Zargan Shahar force *en route*, made their way to Saiadabad.

It has to be borne in mind that transport did not suffice to lift the whole force, small as it was, at one time. Though the entire personnel, exclusive of followers, amounted to only 6,600, the system perforce adopted was to advance one part of the column and on arrival at the camping-ground to send back the animals of the train to bring on the remainder next day. So it came about that when on October 5th Charasia was reached—a group of villages distant about eleven miles from Kabul—General Macpherson. with a mixed detachment of Cavalry, Artillery, and Infantry, 1,200 strong, was still a day's march in rear.

Action at Charasia, Oct. 6th, 1879.

At Charasia, despite the protestations of the Amir, there were signs that a further advance would be strongly opposed. Yakub Khan's own conduct during a meeting with certain of his officials from Kabul gave rise to suspicion, our Cavalry patrols drew hostile fire, and towards evening groups of tribesmen began to collect on the hills north of the bivouac. In face of these indications the Force Commander's first care was to send back his transport animals to bring up General Macpherson's brigade with the least possible delay; his next, to plan the seizure at dawn on the morrow of the high ground commanding his chosen route. So we come to the first important action of the renewed campaign, the Battle of Charasia.

In this neighbourhood the Kabul River and its tributary the Logar flow on parallel courses in a direction just east of due north at an average distance of four miles apart. To the east, some five miles beyond the camp site, the Logar passes through the Sang-i-Nawishta Gorge, and alongside the river lay the track to be followed by the force in its advance to Kabul. In continuation of the heights bounding the defile a series of bold, rocky ridges runs out to the west, and extending as far as the Kabul River forms a defensive position of great natural strength for the purpose of resisting an enterprise against the capital from the south.

The conviction that delay would only make his task the harder had decided the Force Commander to seize the Sang-i-Nawishta Pass, not awaiting the arrival of General Macpherson's detachment. Accordingly, while it was yet dark, very early on October 6th, the Cavalry moved out towards the objective; but daylight revealed hordes of Afghans taking up their positions methodically on the hills, and the patrols were forced to retire, pursued by hostile fire.

Influenced, doubtless, by our movements of the evening before, and by the action of the Cavalry, the enemy appeared to be concentrating his main strength about the Sang-i-Nawishta and the high feature immediately to the west whose summit stood 1,700 feet above the plain. On a spur running down from it towards the Logar were located sixteen of the enemy's guns, twelve being in position on the crest and four more near the foot of the slope.

Farther to the west, and rather nearer to the attackers, was a second and lower ridge, its highest point about 1,800 feet above the level of Charasia, and by delivering his main assault against this feature while holding the enemy elsewhere, General Roberts planned to turn the Afghan position. Small wonder that he should come in time to regard this action as the most critical of his career! His decision to attack was taken in the full knowledge that holding the position in front was a large part of the Afghan regular army reinforced by strong contingents of irregulars, whose numbers increased moment by moment; that the hills to the east and west of the Charasia Plain were vantage-points for hordes of tribesmen only awaiting a favourable opportunity to make a descent on the encampment; that his own force was divided, the rear portion faced with the prospect of fighting its way through stiff opposition to join him; and, finally, that failure would entail annihilation for his devoted troops, and disaster without remedy for British prestige in the East. His commitments were many, and left him with no safety margin to meet the unforeseen; for four companies of the 5th Gurkhas and a squadron of the Cavalry had gone back with the transport, while of the remaining troops some were needed to guard the camp and others to watch the enemy on the flanks.

When morning broke, the troops were disposed in accordance with the original intention of seizing the Sang-i-Nawishta Pass and repairing the road. A measure of redistribution was therefore necessary to give effect to the change of plan necessitated by the altered conditions. The main attack on the western ridge was entrusted to Brigadier-General Baker, whose command was made up of 2 guns No. 2 Mountain Battery, 2 Gatling guns, detachment 12th Bengal Cavalry, 72nd Highlanders, 300 rifles 5th Gurkhas, 200 rifles 5th Punjab Infantry, and No. 7 Company Sappers and Miners. Having assembled his small force, on whose efforts so much depended, in the enclosures about Charasia, he decided to leave there his field hospital and reserve ammunition while he pushed on with the remainder. This entailed a requisition for more troops to guard his impedimenta, and he was sent the remainder of the 5th Punjab Infantry, 450 men of the 23rd Pioneers, and 3 field artillery guns.

Leaving the shelter afforded by the enclosures around Charasia at 11.30 a.m., the attackers were confronted by the rugged ridge, in some parts inaccessible, which formed the right of the Afghan position. Towards Charasia a well-marked spur thrust out from the main feature, flanking the line of advance on the left, and while one company of the 72nd took this as their objective, the rest of the regiment extended away to the right and made for the face of the ridge. They were met by a galling fire from Afghan regulars and the inhabitants of the surrounding villages who were in occupation of this part of the position. The company of the 72nd, which had been directed on the buttress spur, gained a point of vantage on its crest, but were unable to make further progress in face of the odds opposing them. Two companies of the 5th Gurkhas, under Captain Cook, V.C., were therefore sent up to give fresh impetus to the blow aimed at this vital point. Those of the 72nd who were advancing against the face of the hill were likewise brought to a standstill, the check in this case being due as much to the difficulties of the ground as to the resistance offered by the enemy. To meet this situation the front of the 72nd was prolonged to the right by putting in the remaining two companies of the 5th Gurkhas, while 200 rifles of the 5th Punjab Infantry were echeloned in rear of the left flank of the Highlanders. The completion of these fresh dispositions, however, did not bring immediate success. The enemy was very strongly posted, many approaches to him were barred by the extremely difficult nature of the ground, practically all the available reserves had been thrown in, and the action had reached a very critical stage. Success hung in the balance, and the scales could be tipped favourably only by the efforts of the three companies, one of Highlanders, two of Gurkhas, fighting their way forward by the spur on the left.

Lord Roberts speaks of the "intense excitement and anxiety" with which he watched events at this point. The Afghans, by now alive to its importance, were rushing up reinforcements from other parts of the battlefield, and success, if it were to be achieved at all, must be won quickly. Thanks in great measure to the intrepid conduct of Private Macmahon of the 72nd and a few Gurkhas, who, regardless of the hail of bullets, could be seen pushing ahead up the precipitous hill-side, the enemy were driven from the summit in the nick of time. From this point enfilade fire could be brought to bear along the crest of the main ridge, and so came their chance for the remaining companies of the Regiment and of the 72nd and for the 5th Punjab Infantry. The general advance was sounded, and moving with great dash and gallantry, helped not a little by the fire of their comrades on the left, they gained the top of the hill. Sir F. Roberts wrote in his despatch of October 20th, 1879: "The enemy fought well to the last, and charged close up to the 5th Goorkhas, who, however, commanded by Major Fitzhugh, repulsed them with heavy loss. In this affair Lieutenant and Adjutant Martin was very forward."

Driven from the ridge, the Afghans occupied a second position about 600 yards in rear. Reorganizing, the attackers again advanced, with the 72nd on the left, two companies 5th Gurkhas in the centre, and two companies of the 23rd Pioneers on the right. In support were the rest of the Pioneers and the 200 men of the 5th Punjab Infantry. Covered by the fire of the two guns of No. 2 Mountain Battery, they skirmished their way forward, and were presently joined by two companies of the 92nd Highlanders, detached from Major White's force, which had been detailed for the holding attack on the enemy's left. With this fresh impetus, they could no longer be resisted, and on the Afghans' further withdrawal the turning movement may be said to have been completed.

As just noted in passing, Major White of the 92nd Highlanders (afterwards famous as General Sir George White, V.C.) had been commanding on the right of the British line. His action, first in capturing a detached hill south of the entrance to the Sang-i-Nawishta Gorge, and later in sending help to the main attack, had contributed greatly to the success of the operation as a whole.

It was nearing four o'clock in the afternoon when General Baker finally gained possession of the high, rocky ridge which had been his objective. The rapid retreat of that part of the Afghan Army opposing him exposed the right flank of the enemy holding the hill immediately west of the pass; while General Baker changed direction to continue his advance towards the Sang-i-Nawishta, Major White gained possession of the defile, and one company of the 92nd, ascending the hill to the west, captured the twelve mountain guns which the enemy had abandoned in their flight down the reverse slopes.

Resistance was now at an end. One squadron of the 5th Punjab Cavalry, with a detachment of the 9th Lancers, took up the pursuit, only to be checked, however, at the Kabul River. Seeing their dilemma from his position on the hills, General Baker used his mountain guns to shell the enemy rear-guard, and sent the 5th Punjab Infantry and 23rd Pioneers doubling plainwards to their assistance. The enemy was forced to loose his hold on the river crossings and continue his retreat, but darkness coming with the close of day put a stop to further enterprise. Thus ended the first important action of the renewed campaign. The victory had been won at a surprisingly small cost, when are considered the numerical superiority of the Afghans and the strength of their positions. Out of a total of eighteen killed and seventy wounded, the Regiment's casualties were four killed and several wounded. Allowing full credit for the qualities displayed by the 72nd and the remaining units of General Baker's command, it can justifiably be claimed that the dash and determination of the 5th Gurkhas at the most critical stage of the action had contributed materially towards the success achieved.

Events following the Action, and Occupation of Kabul. The all-important defile having been rendered secure, the tired troops bivouacked for the night on the ground won.

General Macpherson's force, left a day's march in rear, arrived at Charasia at nightfall, and next day, October 7th, the right half battalion under Major Sym, which had been sent back with the transport required to bring it in, rejoined headquarters on the heights above the Sang-i-Nawishta Pass. These same heights project northwards towards the Deh Mazang Gorge, through which flows the Kabul River a short distance to the west of Kabul City. Their highest point is the Takht-i-Shah, and their most northerly feature is known as Sher Darwaza. The corresponding doorway on the left bank of the river is formed by the Asmai Heights.

On the morning of October 7th, Sir F. Roberts, with a part of his force, pushed forward to Beni Hissar, two miles south of the Bala Hissar, the great fortress and arsenal of Kabul. There he learnt that an Afghan army, composed in part of the vanquished of the Charasia battle, was encamped on the Asmai Heights, and he decided to disperse it immediately. Starting very early on the 8th, General Massy's Cavalry brigade made a wide detour via the Siah Sang Hill and the deserted cantonment of Sherpur, north of the city, and blocked the Afghan lines of retreat to the north and west. Later in the day General Baker, with a small force, advanced laboriously along the top of the ridge from his position above the Sang-i-Nawishta to the Sher Darwaza feature, only to find that he had too few troops for the accomplishment of his task. He therefore sent for reinforcements, in which were included two companies of the Regiment under Major Sym. They arrived too late for employment that day, and during the night the enemy succeeded in slipping away unperceived. On October 9th Major Sym's two companies were joined by the remainder of the Regiment. The 12th having been selected as a suitable date for the official entry into the Bala Hissar, it fell to the Regiment, with the 67th Foot, to find the garrison of the fortress. On that day, then, leaving only one hundred men with two guns to hold the Sher Darwaza Heights, the 5th Gurkhas took up their new quarters.

Explosion in the Bala Hissar, Oct. 16th, 1879. Three full days only had passed when, on October 16th, there occurred the disastrous explosion which took toll of the garrison to the number of twenty-two killed, among whom were Subadar-Major Bhagiram Gurung, five Havildars, one Naik, and five Sepoys of the Regiment.

"Subadar-Major Bhageeram Goorung had served the British Government with zeal and fidelity for upwards of thirty years, and had served in ten different engagements and expeditions with honour, and he had lately been raised to the rank of Bahadur in recognition of his long and faithful service."[1]

The tragedy was only relieved by the friendly action of the men

---

[1] Extract from Regimental Order No. 491, dated October 18th, by Major Fitzhugh.

of the 72nd, described by Lord Roberts in the following passage taken from his "Forty-One Years in India":—

"There was given on this occasion a very practical exemplification of the good feeling existing between the European soldiers and the Gurkhas. The 72nd and the 5th Gurkhas had been much associated from the commencement of the campaign, and a spirit of camaraderie had sprung up between them, resulting in the Highlanders now coming forward and insisting on making over their greatcoats to the little Gurkhas for the night—a very strong proof of their friendship, for at Kabul in October the nights are bitterly cold."

Well it was that, on hearing of the accident, the Force Commander gave orders for the immediate evacuation of the Bala Hissar, for two and a half hours later came a second and more violent explosion. The Regiment encamped for the night on the Siah Sang, and next day marched into the Sherpur Cantonment, where the entire force was to be accommodated. On the 19th Major Sym's detachment rejoined from the Sher Darwaza, and the work of building barracks was put in hand.

CHAPTER IV

The Second Afghan War—*continued*

October, 1879, to the Conclusion of Hostilities

For the Regiment, after its arrival in Sherpur, there followed a comparatively uneventful spell, lasting some seven weeks. This period was not without its influence on the fortunes of the British in Afghanistan. Yakub Khan, the ex-Amir, who had abdicated voluntarily in October, was sent to India, and the civil administration of the country was undertaken temporarily by the Force Commander, who was given the local rank of Lieutenant-General to enable him to assume command of all troops in Eastern Afghanistan. From Kabul detachments were sent eastwards to join hands with General Bright's division, the line of communication with India via the Logar and Kurram Valleys was abandoned, and a new route opened through the Lataband Pass, which was preferred to the Khurd-Kabul with its tragic memories of the massacre of 1842. Kabul thus became linked with the base in British India by the natural line of communication leading through the Khyber Pass.

Sherpur, Oct.–Dec., 1879.

Meantime, those among the inhabitants of Afghanistan who were not dominated by our occupation of the capital had time to review the situation and to arrive at an appreciation of the numerical weakness of the forces opposed to them. Resenting from the beginning the presence of a foreign army in the country, they were stimulated to action by the preaching of their religious leaders, foremost among whom was the old Mullah, Mir Muhammad, styled Mushk-i-Alam, or "Fragrance of the universe." The action decided on was a combined movement of the tribes living to the north, west, and south of Kabul against Sherpur, with the object of killing and plundering the infidel wherever this might be possible, and of driving the remnant from the country.

At the beginning of December news was received at headquarters that the hostile movement had begun, though the danger was minimized, either deliberately or through ignorance, by those of the Afghan Sirdars on whom the Lieutenant-General was perforce dependent for information. The decision was taken to advance from Kabul in order to deal separately with each confederation of tribesmen before they could join forces for a combined attack.

The most pressing need for the moment appeared to be the defeat of the enemy advancing from the west, who were under the command of Muhammad Jan, and plans were laid accordingly. Two columns were detailed. Of these, one, under Brigadier-General Macpherson, was given the double rôle of preventing a junction between the Kohistani gathering from the north and Muhammad Jan's force, and of forcing back the latter on to a second column, under the command of Brigadier-General Baker, which, moving first south through Charasia and Chihildukhtaran, was then to turn west, and eventually take up a position astride the Ghazni Road not far from Beni Badam.

Operation West of Kabul, Dec. 8th–14th, 1879.

For this operation the Regiment was apportioned to General Macpherson's column, of which the composition was 1 squadron 9th Lancers, 2 squadrons 14th Bengal Lancers, 4 guns F. A. Battery, R.H.A., 4 guns No. 1 Mountain Battery, 67th Foot, 3rd Sikhs, and 5th Gurkhas.

On the morning of December 8th a big parade was held of all the troops lodged in the Sherpur Cantonment, to impress the inhabitants of Kabul before denuding the place of the greater part of its garrison, and in the afternoon the column marched three and a half miles to Kila Aushar on the road to Arghandi, where it was anticipated that contact would be made with the tribes from Maidan and Ghazni under the leadership of Muhammad Jan. A halt at Kila Aushar was ordered for December 9th, to allow General Baker to develop his encircling movement, and the opportunity was taken to reconnoitre to the north and west. The intelligence gathered as a result of reconnaissance led to a modification of the original plan, for the Kohistanis, instead of hurrying southwards to join Muhammad Jan, were discovered to be standing fast in the neighbourhood of Karez Mir, eleven miles north-west of Kabul as the crow flies, while numbers of tribesmen from Ghazni and Maidan were observed moving northwards from Arghandi to their assistance.

Action at Karez Mir, Dec. 10th, 1879.

To meet this situation, General Macpherson was ordered to go north instead of west, and to deal with the Kohistanis before joining issue with the forces of Muhammad Jan. The country being ill-suited to Cavalry, he was directed to leave two squadrons and his horse artillery guns at Kila Aushar, and he was thus left with only one squadron of the 14th Bengal Lancers and four mountain guns while engaged on this service.

The valley in which lies Karez Mir is flanked on the west by a long ridge, which passes within two miles of the village and continues in a direction due south for a further six miles before dropping to the plain. The track from Arghandi, fourteen miles west of Kabul, to Karez Mir is carried across this ridge by the Surkh Kotal, so to prevent further reinforcements reaching the Kohistanis it was first necessary to secure the pass. Marching at 7 a.m. the column found itself, little more than three hours later, in the vicinity of the Surkh Kotal. Disposing the remainder of his force so as to ensure concealment from the direction of Karez Mir, General Macpherson sent the cavalry to reconnoitre towards the village. The prospect from the ridge disclosed a number of Afghan standards dotted about the country to the west, and a considerable body of enemy advancing from the north. The Cavalry, too, had news of importance, for a message was shortly received from them to the effect that about 2,000 Kohistanis held a position on three small under-features near Karez Mir, and that groups of tribesmen were moving rapidly from a westerly direction to join them.

The Brigadier-General acted with the promptitude demanded by the occasion. The Afghans advancing from the north had approached within striking distance in complete ignorance of the presence of a British force on the ridge. An advanced party, consisting of two companies of the 67th and two of the 5th Gurkhas, these last led by Captain Cook, was sent at once to tackle them. Making skilful use of the ground, unperceived the four companies gained a point separated from the enemy by only fifty yards, and thence, breaking cover, they fell on them and sent them flying headlong. After launching his advanced party, the Commander's next care was to provide for the safety of the ridge by leaving there two guns with five companies of the 3rd Sikhs and one of the 67th. Theirs was the important task of protecting the rear of the attackers while withstanding all attempts to reinforce the Kohistanis from the west.

These arrangements in train, General Macpherson, with the remainder of his force, followed in the footsteps of the four companies which had preceded him, and which were even then engaged at no great distance in driving the enemy towards the main position west of the village. For the main attack the six companies of the 5th Gurkhas were disposed on the left, and the five companies of the 67th on the right, while the remaining three companies of the 3rd Sikhs were detached eastwards in support of the Cavalry, to whom had been assigned the rôle of harassing the enemy's left and threatening his retreat. So rapidly did the troops take up their tasks, and such was the *élan* displayed in their advance, that the Afghans immediately opposed to them offered no resistance, but fled incontinently to the main position. Those previously stationed there fought stoutly for a time, but presently their hearts failed them in face of the ardour of the British attack, and they, too, beat a hasty retreat. Their discomfiture was completed by the fire of the two mountain guns, which, moving with extraordinary rapidity, arrived just in time to turn defeat into a rout.

The merit of the original dispositions was seen when the tribesmen to the west of the ridge, hearing the sound of firing, hurried forward with the object of joining in the battle. Finding the pass occupied, and all vantage-points securely held, they returned whence they had come without striking a blow. The casualties sustained by the Regiment in this brilliant little affair numbered only two wounded, one, as ill luck would have it, being the Commanding Officer, Major Fitzhugh. Yet once again Captain Cook, V.C., distinguished himself, the conspicuous gallantry he displayed being brought to notice.

Situation on December 10th (Evening). At the end of the day Sir Frederick Roberts had the satisfaction of knowing that his plan, based on the intention to defeat in detail the separate bodies of the enemy, had been successfully initiated. The confederation of southern tribes had not yet materialized, the Kohistanis from the north had been dispersed, and there remained for the moment only Muhammad Jan and his henchmen in the neighbourhood of Arghandi.

The disposition of his own forces on the evening of December 10th appeared to favour his decision to destroy Muhammad Jan on the morrow. About thirteen miles north-east of Arghandi lay Macpherson, ready to sweep towards Arghandi next day. The other arm of the vice was provided by General Baker's force, which by dint of strenuous marching had arrived within striking distance of the Ghazni Road at a point about eleven miles south-west of Arghandi. The horse artillery guns and two squadrons of Cavalry, which had been left at Kila Aushar, had returned to that place after an abortive attempt during the afternoon to round up the defeated Kohistanis. For the operation of December 11th the strength of this small mounted force was augmented by a squadron from Sherpur, and General Massy was sent to take command. Briefly the plan was that Macpherson should march at 7 a.m., cross the Surkh Kotal, and, with the assistance of Massy's Cavalry, drive the enemy into the arms of Baker's force.

Events of Dec. 11th, 1879. Whether success would have been achieved had there been no misconceptions and no resulting departure from the Lieutenant-General's instructions is matter for conjecture in view of Muhammad Jan's numerical superiority. His strength was estimated at 10,000, a number far exceeding anticipation. Actually the events of December 11th emphasized the truth of Robert Burns' dictum about the " schemes of mice and men." General Macpherson began his march fifty minutes late, the Afghan Sirdars failed to keep the Force Commander in touch with General Baker, and General Massy, striking south too soon, was isolated from General Macpherson's force and became prematurely engaged with the entire *lashkar* of the enemy advancing from Arghandi.

Early in the morning Sir Frederick Roberts rode out from Sherpur with the intention of taking personal control of the combined operation. Warned by the sound of firing that the engagement had begun much in advance of the time planned, he galloped for Kila Kazi. The ground presently allowing him a view, he saw at once that his scheme had miscarried; Massy with his diminutive force was already heavily committed, the enemy appeared to number hardly less than 10,000, and there was as yet no sign of the approach of either Macpherson or Baker. His first care was to secure the line of retreat by ordering up 200 rifles of the 72nd at Sherpur to hold the Deh Mazang Gorge; his next to help in extricating the guns, which were in difficulties. These, owing primarily to mishaps due to the roughness of the ground, had to be abandoned, despite the heroic efforts of the Cavalry to gain time by charging repeatedly in face of overwhelming odds. No whit less worthy of praise was the conduct of this handful of mounted men when, the guns jettisoned, the withdrawal was at last in train. By their skill and daring they held up the enemy advance and enabled the 72nd to reach the pass in time to cover the passage through of the hard-pressed little force. The enemy, the gate to Kabul barred against them, turned aside, and a number of them made for the Takht-i-Shah Hill, overlooking the city from the south-west. The guns were recovered later.

This brief description of the contretemps is necessary because it inaugurated that rapid deterioration in the situation which would otherwise be unintelligible. Our main concern, though, is with the Regiment, and so we return to the doings of General Macpherson's column. Leaving Karez Mir shortly before 8 a.m., the force had crossed the Surkh Kotal and made several miles beyond it on the way to Arghandi, when the sound of guns was heard in the direction of Kila Kazi. Taking in the situation with barely a pause, General Macpherson made his arrangements to meet it. He diverted his transport towards Kabul via the Kafir Jan Defile, and detailed for it an escort consisting of two companies of the 5th Gurkhas under Captain John Cook and four companies of the 3rd Sikhs, with whom, as it happened, was the latter's younger brother. We shall hear of them again. Then with the rest of his force he advanced towards Kila Kazi. They had not gone very far when they encountered a number of tribesmen who had been engaged with General Massy's force, now in full retreat and approaching Deh Mazang. These prepared to dispute a further advance, and the 67th, 3rd Sikhs, and 5th Gurkhas were deployed against them. The threat proved enough for the Afghans, who made for the hills before the attackers could reach them. The next three hours were spent in hunting isolated bands of the enemy from one vantage-point to another; the British troops clearing the enclosures near the village, while the 3rd Sikhs and 5th Gurkhas chased them along the hill paths round about. At 3.30 p.m. the force made a rendezvous at Kila Kazi, where it was intended to stay the night. The Lieutenant-General, however, had other work for them, and ordered them to Deh Mazang. There the main body went into bivouac, but the Regiment was sent on to Sherpur, where it arrived at midnight.

While General Macpherson had been thus engaged in lowering the *moral* of a part of the Afghan *lashkar* elated at their success against General Massy, he had been in danger of losing his baggage. After turning off the Arghandi Road towards Sherpur, the transport entered the Kafir Jan Defile. There it was attacked by overwhelming numbers of tribesmen who had remained concealed till then in the villages of Paghman. At the moment of their onset there were available to meet them only the two companies of the Regiment commanded by Captain Cook. He, as always, proved equal to the occasion. Leading a bayonet charge, he succeeded in holding off his assailants for a period just long enough to allow of the arrival of the companies of the 3rd Sikhs, till then employed in the rear. The vigour displayed in the tactics of the men of both regiments was too much for the Afghan stomach. The convoy was allowed to continue its march unmolested to Sherpur, and not a single item of property fell into enemy hands. Captain Cook himself was knocked down by a stone and stunned; of his men one was killed and two were wounded, while his brother, who had been very forward in the fight, was shot through the chest, the bullet passing close to his heart.

General Baker's column, too, had been engaged on this eventful day. Unable to get in touch with the Lieutenant-General or with General Macpherson, he pushed on towards Arghandi, and late in the day was obliged to fight for a pass near that place which gave access to the Chardeh Plain. The gap secured, he bivouacked there for the night, and arrived at Sherpur on December 12th.

It was the ill fortune of Sir Frederick Roberts to have his plans frustrated on this fateful December 11th by a series of mishaps which he had foreseen and against which he had provided. Instead, now, of his columns scouring the country and mopping up the enemy in detail, they were concentrating for the defence of the capital itself. It will be seen in due course how difficulties were overcome and a successful *dénouement* evolved.

Takht-i-Shah Action, Dec. 12th-14th, 1879.

On arrival at Sherpur the Regiment found preparations already made to resist an attack on the cantonment. Despite its exertions of the past two days, it was allowed but a very brief respite under the shelter of the defences, and daylight of December 12th saw it again on the move to rejoin General Macpherson at Deh Mazang. The reason for the sudden order lay in the necessity to recapture the Takht-i-Shah Hill, now put into a state of defence and held by the Afghans in great strength. It will be seen, on looking at the map, that the Bala Hissar, dominating Kabul City from the south, was situated on comparatively high ground, which rose westwards to the Sher Darwaza Hill. This in turn was but the northernmost feature of a range running north and south, which boasted a high peak, known as the Takht-i-Shah, separated by a dip in the ridge from the aforementioned Sher Darwaza. It is necessary to note, further, that a spur ran out in an easterly direction from the Takht-i-Shah towards the village of Beni Hissar.

Major Fitzhugh being incapacitated by his wound sustained in the fighting at Karez Mir, the command of the Regiment devolved temporarily on Major J. M. Sym. The capture of the peak had been entrusted to General Macpherson. Tied as he was to the Deh Mazang Gap, he could spare only a part of his force for the accomplishment of his task, and this detachment he placed under the command of Colonel Money of the 3rd Sikhs.

From Sherpur the Regiment marched straight to Deh Mazang, and immediately on arrival two companies were detached to Baber's tomb, tucked under the western shoulder of the Sher Darwaza, to act as escort to two guns of No. 1 Mountain Battery which had been detailed to support the attack. The remaining companies then climbed the 1,800 feet to the summit of the Sher Darwaza, and joined Colonel Money, whose force was now composed of detachments of the 67th Foot and 72nd Highlanders, numbering 215 rifles, 150 rifles 3rd Sikhs, and 195 rifles 5th Gurkhas.

With the 5th Gurkhas leading, and the 72nd and 3rd Sikhs supporting them, the attack began. The first objective was a feature across the saddle, from which a well-marked spur led upwards to the Takht-i-Shah. It was very strongly held by the Afghans, and its capture entailed a prolonged and obstinate struggle. When eventually it fell to the pertinacity of our men, it was found to give but little assistance towards the attainment of the ultimate object. The great natural strength of the position had been enhanced during the previous night by the construction of stout breastworks, the approach to it by the connecting spur could be undertaken only on the narrowest of fronts, there was a complete absence of cover, and the numbers of the enemy holding the hill, already large, were being constantly swelled by posses of tribesmen streaming in from the south. Alive to all these difficulties, the Lieutenant-General concluded that to persist in the attempt to storm the peak from one direction only would be a useless sacrifice of life, and he accordingly issued orders to hold on to the ground won, but to defer the final advance on the summit until such time as General Baker's brigade should be available to co-operate.

This was destined to be the closing episode in the career of the gallant John Cook, who fell wounded while in the act of leading his men towards their goal. Other casualties sustained by the Regiment in this action were one sepoy killed and one havildar and five sepoys wounded.

General Baker's brigade having arrived at Sherpur from Arghandi on the evening of December 12th, on the morning of the 13th he was directed to launch an attack on the Takht-i-Shah from the south-east. His command had been strengthened by the addition of the Corps of Guides, the first reinforcements to reach Kabul via the Khyber Pass.

To ensure that his attack should be made in the direction ordered, it was necessary for General Baker to reach Beni Hissar and to deploy from there. His advance guard of the 92nd Highlanders, under Major White, while still some distance north of Beni Hissar, saw hordes of the enemy hurrying out of the village to gain the spur which runs down to it from the Takht-i-Shah. Showing his usual resource and initiative, Major White changed the direction of his advance and raced for the centre of the spur, with the object of interposing between them and their friends on the hill above. Supported by the Guides and covered by the fire of guns, he struck the leading groups of the enemy as he gained the crest. Followed a spirited bout of hand-to-hand fighting, in which the Afghans proved no match for the Highlanders. Hurled from the ridge they made off to try their luck elsewhere, leaving free the men of the 92nd and of the Guides to devote themselves to the capture of the main position.

In the meantime Colonel Money's small force to the north had not been idle. Taking advantage of the diversion caused by General Baker's attack, they continued their interrupted progress. Under the command of Major Sym, detachments of the 72nd, 3rd Sikhs, and 5th Gurkhas fought their way step by step up the steep sides of the Takht-i-Shah, and succeeded in carrying the summit shortly before 11.30 a.m. There a few minutes later they were joined by the 92nd and the Guides, with the result that the enemy abandoned the struggle and retreated towards the south.

It was to prove in the end but a barren victory, though much was yet to happen before circumstances compelled the force commander to postpone offensive action and to await, concentrated at Sherpur, a more favourable opportunity. The Takht-i-Shah had no sooner been won than news was received of the interruption of General Baker's communications, and of a serious threat against Sherpur cantonment from the east. The 92nd and the Guides were consequently recalled by their commander to enable him to clear the Siah Sang hills and intervening villages, and that done, to garrison Sherpur.

Almost simultaneously Colonel Money withdrew the detachments of the 72nd and 3rd Sikhs to Sher Darwaza, and left only the 5th Gurkhas to hold the Takht-i-Shah.

The situation on the evening of December 13th may be summed up thus. General Baker, after much fighting in detachments, had cleared his communications, and had reached Sherpur. The Bala Hissar was held by the 67th Foot, but control of the city had been lost. General Macpherson, under orders, had released his hold of Deh Mazang, and after sending the 72nd to Sherpur, with the rest of his depleted column had joined Colonel Money on the Sher Darwaza Hill.

During the night the enemy attacked the Takht-i-Shah in considerable strength. Their attempt, however, lacked determination, and the Regiment succeeded in beating them off without losing a man. On the morning of December 14th, it appeared at first that the hard knocks dealt them on the previous day had induced the Afghans to desist from further enterprise and disperse to their homes; from the position occupied by the Regiment not one could be seen. Soon, however, it became apparent that they had quitted the southern environs of Kabul only to concentrate for a fresh stroke to be launched from the north-west. In the ensuing action fought by General Baker to drive the enemy off the Asmai Heights and to cut his communications, the Regiment took no part; they must still hold the Takht-i-Shah against a possible attack.

General Baker, assisted by all that could be spared from General Macpherson's force, assaulted and captured the Asmai Heights, but that was the measure of the day's success. To protect his right during the attack, and to threaten the enemy's line of retreat, he had posted detachments on a conical hill which overlooked the Aliabad Kotal from the north-east. Soon after noon the conical hill was attacked by the Afghans in overwhelming strength, and the defenders were forced to retreat. Even before this, General Macpherson had sent a message to the effect that a large body of tribesmen was advancing from the south, and now, in response to inquiries, he informed Sir Frederick Roberts that seething crowds of the enemy were approaching from north, south, and west. Reluctantly the Lieutenant-General was forced to the conclusion that he could no longer maintain his offensive in face of the enormous odds opposed to him, and it was at this point that he decided to concentrate his forces at Sherpur and await there a more favourable opportunity.

Withdrawal from the Takht-i-Shah, Dec. 14th, 1879.

He accordingly issued orders to both Generals to withdraw to the cantonment. General Macpherson initiated the movement at about 2 p.m. with instructions to the 5th Gurkhas to retire to the Sher Darwaza. Major Sym brought his men off the Takht-i-Shah without loss, covered by the fire of the troops on the Sher Darwaza, and

The Bala Hissar, Kabul, 1879.

Kabul, 1880.

after resting there for a short time, passed through the remainder of the force and entered the Deh Mazang Defile. While traversing the pass the Regiment came under very heavy fire from the Asmai Heights, which had been reoccupied by the enemy the moment General Baker began his withdrawal. Subadar Ragobir Nagarkoti and two sepoys were killed, and two sepoys were wounded. The exit from the defile had not yet been gained when Major Sym learnt that the rear of the column was hard pressed by the enemy. He at once turned the Regiment about, and again ran the gauntlet of the Afghan fire from the Asmai Slopes. His prompt action did not fail of its effect; the 5th Gurkhas played a big part in holding up the pursuit, pressure was relieved, and the force reached Sherpur in safety.

General Baker's withdrawal had likewise been followed up closely, and it was while in command of the rear party that Hammond of the Guides gained his Victoria Cross. By evening, however, the entire Kabul Field Force had found shelter within the walls of Sherpur. Not yet, however, was there rest for the men of the 5th Gurkhas. The defences of the place were still incomplete, and they were at once called on to build a breastwork along the crest of the low Bemaru Ridge, which formed the northern boundary of the cantonment.

The following quotation from the "Historical Record of the 5th Goorkha Regiment" helps to a realization of the demands made on the troops during this period of stress:—

"From the morning of the 11th to the night of the 14th few of the men had had any food, and for the last two days they had no water."

The first few days at Sherpur were comparatively uneventful.

Death of Major Cook, V.C., Dec. 19th, 1879.
By the Regiment the news of the death of Major John Cook on December 19th [1] was received with so deep a sense of loss as to overshadow all other happenings. Sir Frederick Roberts paid tribute to his many fine qualities in a divisional order issued by him on this occasion:—

"It is with deep regret the Lieutenant-General announces to the Kabul Field Force the death from a wound received in action on December 12th of Major John Cook, V.C., 5th Goorkhas.

"2. While yet a young officer, Major Cook served at Ambela in 1863, where he distinguished himself, and in the Black Mountain Campaign in 1868. Joining the Kurram Field Force on its formation, Major Cook was present at the capture of the Peiwar Kotal, his conduct on that occasion earning for him the admiration of the whole force and the Victoria Cross; whilst in the action of the Monghyr Pass he again brought himself prominently to notice by his cool and gallant

---

[1] His promotion for services rendered during the campaign was dated November 22nd, 1879, but was not published to the Force until January 16th, 1880.

bearing. In the capture of the heights at Sung-i-Nawishta Major Cook again distinguished himself, and in the attack of the Takht-i-Shah Peak on December 12th he ended a noble career in a manner worthy of even his great name for bravery.

"3. By Major Cook's death Her Majesty has lost the services of an officer who would, had he been spared, have risen to the highest honours of his profession, and Sir F. Roberts feels sure the whole Kabul Field Force will share in the pain his loss has occasioned him."

Again, he wrote in his despatch of January 23rd, 1880: "By Major Cook's death Her Majesty has lost the services of a most distinguished and gallant officer and the Kabul Field Force a comrade whom one and all honoured and admired."

The feeling of the men of the Regiment is crystallized in the words of Parsu Khattri, spoken many years afterwards, when he had risen to the rank of Subadar Major. They are recorded by Major-General H. J. P. Browne. Referring to Major Cook, he said: "He was the bravest man I have ever seen—braver even than Roberts Sahib, Bahadur, whom all the Regiment considered very brave, above all other men."

Sherpur, December 15th, 1879 to May 8th, 1880.

The loss of one so universally respected and admired was but an incentive to answer, as he would have answered, the call to renewed effort in face of apparent defeat. The defences of Sherpur, begun before the British occupation, formed a rectangle, with its greatest length running east and west. The Bemaru Ridge constituted the north face, and though it overlooked the whole of the interior of the cantonment, it was still devoid of a defensible perimeter. Here, then, the Regiment toiled by day at the construction of a stout breastwork, and night after night manned the defences until the danger of an attack was past. In the defence scheme the 5th Gurkhas were allocated to the western half of the ridge, which lay within Major-General Hill's sector. Their task was at least as important as that of any other unit in the force, though, as it happened, the Afghans, when they did eventually work themselves up to fighting pitch, risked everything on an assault against the eastern face.

Sir Frederick Roberts was determined to resume the offensive as soon as possible, and one of his first acts after making the decision to occupy Sherpur was to send for reinforcements from General Bright's division. Brigadier-General Charles Gough's brigade accordingly moved towards Kabul, and reached Lataband on December 23rd. His near approach at last brought matters to a head. From December 17th onwards the enemy, whose strength had swelled to something in the neighbourhood of 60,000 fighting men, had been demonstrating, sometimes from the direction of Asmai, at others from Siah Sang and the villages to the east. They had even, on occasion, approached near enough to the walls to draw the fire of the defenders. Their attack launched in the early morning of the 23rd was of quite a different character. The defences on the east side had not been built to the height of those on the south and west, and here they made their main effort. Showing real determination they reached the abattis, only to be beaten back with great loss. After an interval they tried again, but this time displayed greater caution, so that they suffered less, and were able to hold their ground at the limit of their advance. To drive them thence the 5th Punjab Cavalry, with four guns, were ordered to make their way out by the gap in the Bemaru Ridge, and fall upon their flank. No sooner had this turning movement made itself felt than the Afghan concentration began to disintegrate. Immediately the rest of the Cavalry was loosed against them; those who had already turned from the fight fled the faster, the rest abandoned hope and melted away, and in an incredibly short time not a man of the enemy remained in the field.

Next morning Brigadier-General Charles Gough marched into Sherpur, and never a shot was fired at his Brigade between Lataband and the cantonment.

Events following the Investment of Sherpur, January to July, 1880.

With the dramatic dispersal of the vast confederation of tribesmen before Sherpur, active operations in the Kabul area practically ceased. Despite the snow, which had added considerably to the discomfort of the troops during the period of investment, columns were sent out from Kabul in various directions. The purpose underlying these movements was sometimes the punishment of ringleaders in the late rising, at others the protection of adherents of the British cause against the resentment of their more fanatical brethren, or, on occasion, merely to facilitate the collection of supplies. The Regiment was not called upon to leave Sherpur until May 8th, 1879. During this interval it was employed mainly in improving the defences, the provision of what was known as an esplanade demanding the destruction of several villages and forts, and of numerous walled enclosures. This esplanade was a cleared space extending to a distance of 1,000 yards on all sides of the cantonment and added enormously to its defensive strength.

The efforts made to put beyond dispute our power to hold Kabul were not confined to work at Sherpur. The Bala Hissar was reoccupied and its fortifications repaired, control of the city was re-established, bridges were thrown across the river, communications were improved, and forts were built at the bridge-head, on the Siah Sang Heights, the Bemaru Ridge, Asmai Koh, and Sher Darwaza.

The object with which Afghanistan had been invaded had now,

in great measure, been accomplished. It had been shown that the arm of the Indian Government was long enough and strong enough to avenge the murder of its representative, organized opposition was at an end, and the moment seemed favourable for settling the future of Afghanistan. The policy decided on was first to pacify the tribes, next to select a ruler for Kabul, and finally, having installed one acceptable to the tribesmen, to withdraw from the country.

For the pacification of the tribes the means chosen was the movement of considerable forces through disaffected areas. In accordance with this plan, Sir Donald Stewart, commanding the forces in southern Afghanistan, left Kandahar at the head of a division at the end of March, 1880. His destination was Ghazni, and after fighting a successful action at Ahmad Khel on April 19th, he arrived there on April 21st. Government meanwhile had concluded that it was desirable to place all the forces in Afghanistan under one commander, and Sir Donald Stewart, being senior to Sir F. Roberts, was chosen. He accordingly proceeded to Kabul and took up his new appointment on May 5th. The division from Kandahar went into camp at Hisarak, in the Logar Valley, and there came under the command of Major-General Hills.

A prospective ruler for Kabul was found in the person of Abdur Rahman, a grandson of Dost Muhammad. British gold in the form of a munificent gift of money to the late Amir Sher Ali had been instrumental in driving him out of Afghanistan in 1869, and since then he had lived in Russia, a pensioner of the Russian Government. Negotiations were opened with him in March, and as soon as it became apparent that they were likely to reach a satisfactory conclusion, the autumn of 1880 was fixed for the withdrawal of the British forces from Afghanistan.

While these important considerations of policy are occupying the attention of those in authority, there is leisure to note that the work done by the Regiment since the reopening of the campaign earned recognition in the shape of awards to certain individuals. Captain Cook's promotion to Brevet-Major has already been noted, and in the same Gazette a Brevet-Lieutenant-Colonelcy was conferred on Major Fitzhugh, "in recognition of services during the late campaign of 1878–79." Details of admissions to the Indian Order of Merit are given in the appropriate appendix, but it is fitting that special mention be made in this place of the promotion from 3rd to 2nd Class in the Order of Sepoy Kishenbir Nagarkoti, "for conspicuous gallantry in action at Charasia," and of the same stout-hearted soldier, now a Naik, from 2nd to 1st Class, "for conspicuous gallantry in action at Kabul on December 12th, 1879."

As previously narrated, the Regiment was kept at Sherpur until

May 8th, 1880. On that date they marched as part of a column under Brigadier-General Baker, who had as additional infantry units the 72nd Highlanders, 2nd Gurkhas, and 5th Punjab Infantry, besides Cavalry and Artillery. The force was accompanied by Sir Frederick Roberts, whose command now consisted of the 1st and 2nd Divisions of the Northern Afghanistan Field Force. Lack of opposition resulted in a mere promenade, but at least one ill-disposed person was punished, a Ghilzai chief named Padshah Khan, having his stronghold razed to the ground, and some valuable reconnaissance work was accomplished. The route followed was south to Hisarak in the Logar Valley, thence west by Baraki Rajan and through the Tangi Wardak to Shekhabad, and so north to the neighbourhood of the Kotal-i-Takht. There the force divided, each part taking a different road to Kabul. The 5th Gurkhas stayed for some time in Maidan, visited Rustum Khel up the valley of the Kabul River, and returned to Sherpur on June 15th.

Throughout this time negotiations were proceeding satisfactorily with Sirdar Abdur Rahman Khan, Amir-elect of Kabul. Concurrently details were worked out for the return of the Field Force to India. On July 22nd, 1880, Mr. Lepel Griffin, the Chief Political Officer with the Force, announced to the Sirdars and notables assembled at Kabul both the decision to accept Abdur Rahman as Amir, and the fact of the impending withdrawal of the army. Just a week later there came with the stunning effect of a thunder-clap out of a cloudless sky the news of disaster in southern Afghanistan.

Maiwand and Its Causes, April to July, 1880.
The causes which were so soon to include the Regiment in the epic march from Kabul to Kandahar are to be found in the happenings at and around the southern capital.

The division which had marched to Kabul under the command of Sir Donald Stewart had been replaced at Kandahar by troops of the Bombay Army under Lieutenant-General Primrose. In April, 1880, rumours began to reach that officer of the preaching at Herat of a *jehad* directed against the British, and of the collection there of an army under Sirdar Ayub Khan, brother of the deported Amir, Yakub Khan. In May a Sirdar named Sher Ali Khan—not to be confused with the father of Yakub Khan—was formally installed as ruler of Kandahar, with charge of the civil administration and the support of Afghan regular troops. His misgivings on the score of the loyalty of those of his troops who were quartered in Zamindawar led him, shortly after his installation, to take up his residence at Girishk on the Helmand, seven marches to the west of Kandahar. Before leaving Kandahar he asked that a brigade of British troops should be sent to Girishk to enable him to control the situation in the danger area.

The political function in southern Afghanistan was divorced from the military, and facilities for gaining reliable information were lacking. The full significance of Ayub Khan's activities was not immediately realized, and for this reason, among others, it was not until July 11th that a brigade under Brigadier-General Burrows reached Girishk. On July 14th Sirdar Sher Ali's troops deserted bodily with their guns and crossed the Helmand *en route* to join Ayub Khan. General Burrows went after them, inflicted considerable loss and recovered the guns. That done, he reviewed his position. The last remnant of authority left to Sher Ali dissolved, there was nothing to keep him at Girishk, whereas military considerations dictated a withdrawal to Kushk-i-Nakhud, 46 miles west of Kandahar, where supplies were plentiful and where he was in a position to bar either of the two roads leading from Herat to Kandahar. July 17th, then, found the brigade encamped at Kushk-i-Nakhud. The intelligence service continued defective, and definite news of Ayub's progress and intentions failed to materialize. It was argued, apparently on unsound premises, that he would avoid a collision and, after crossing the Helmand, turn towards Kelat-i-Ghilzai. When, therefore, General Burrows learnt that Afghan regular Cavalry were acting south of the Helmand, and later that a body of hostile Ghazis had occupied Maiwand, eleven miles north-east of Kushk-i-Nakhud on the road from Haidarabad to Kandahar, he resolved to move to Maiwand.

The brigade set out early on July 27th, unavoidably encumbered by a large and vulnerable transport train. At about 10 a.m., when still some four or five miles from Maiwand, General Burrows discovered that the main body of Ayub's army was passing across his front along the road leading through Maiwand to Kandahar. Almost certainly influenced by faulty information regarding the intention of the Afghan commander, he decided to attack. The enemy, far from seeking to avoid a collision, came to meet him. For a time it seemed that the small British force might hold its own despite the odds opposing it. Mainly owing to the efforts of the gunners it was a matter of hours before the Afghans gained any appreciable advantage. Gradually, however, they succeeded in working round the flanks of the brigade, their batteries crept ever closer to the British line till they were firing at a range of only 500 yards, and their Cavalry never ceased to menace the baggage train in rear. At last there was a rush of regular Herati Infantry and of hordes of Ghazis on the British left and rear; the Native regiments, tried beyond endurance, broke and crowded in on the 66th Foot, who formed the right of the line; the Cavalry made a half-hearted attempt to restore the situation, and failed; all was confusion. Without cohesion, with no formed body to protect its rear, its general evading capture only by mounting behind a Native officer of the Cavalry, the brigade quitted the field—a mere rabble. The 45 miles to Kandahar were covered by the afternoon of the following day. Out of a strength of less than 2,500 men, 971 were reported as killed or missing, and the wounded numbered 168. Four guns were abandoned during the retreat, and of other material the loss in rifles and carbines alone exceeded 1,000 in number.

The immediate result of the disaster was to raise the country-side against the British, and by the evening of July 28th, General Primrose found himself with his division invested within the walls of Kandahar.

Such was the situation which had to be faced when, at Kabul, the reins of Government were about to be handed to Abdur Rahman Khan, sworn enemy of his cousin, Ayub Khan.

Preparations for the Kabul-Kandahar March, July-Aug., 1880.

It was decided to proceed with the arrangements for installing Sirdar Abdur Rahman, and even to adhere to the date originally fixed for the withdrawal of the British forces from Afghanistan. Instead, however, of using the Khyber line for the evacuation of the whole of the northern Afghanistan Field Force, a part only would march by that route. The remainder were to be formed into the Kabul-Kandahar Field Force under the command of Sir Frederick Roberts, and it would be their part to restore the situation in southern Afghanistan before leaving the country via Chaman and Quetta.

The Lieutenant-General was given a free hand in the selection of the units which were to accompany him, and each, when chosen, was given the option of declining the honour. Three commanding officers of Native regiments were unable to respond to the call, on the ground that their men had been long enough away from India; Colonel Fitzhugh was not among these, though the 5th Gurkhas were one of the few selected units which had served continuously since the opening of the first campaign in 1878.

The composition of the Force was one Cavalry brigade, three batteries of mountain artillery, and three brigades of Infantry. The Regiment, with the 72nd Highlanders, 2nd Sikh Infantry, and 3rd Sikh Infantry, formed the 2nd Infantry Brigade under the command of Brigadier-General Baker. Two other Gurkha Regiments were among the elect, these being the 2nd and the 4th Gurkhas, who had arrived on the scene with Brigadier-General Charles Gough's reinforcement after the dispersal of the tribal confederation before Sherpur.

It was decided to begin the march on August 8th, since preparations could not be completed before that date. Much work had to be done in a short time. Sick and weakly men were weeded out, equipment was thoroughly overhauled and renewals made on a generous scale, baggage animals unlikely to stand the strain were exchanged for the pick of those available, and a solution was found for the difficult problem of supply.

The transport consisted of ponies, mules, and donkeys. The scale of baggage allowed for Native units was 160 lbs. for British officers, 30 lbs. for Native officers, and 20 lbs. for soldiers, camp equipment being included in these weights in each case. Rations carried for Native regiments consisted of ata, dal, salt, meat on hoof, and rum, but these were to be considered as a reserve only, arrangements being made to subsist on the country whenever supplies were procurable. Actually the Force arrived at Kabul with three days' rations intact out of the five days' taken from Kabul.

"It is important to draw attention to the quality of the troops constituting the *Corps d'armée*, from which Sir Frederick Roberts's Force was drawn, to lay stress on their superior physique, and to recall the fact that officers and men had gone through together the training of a lengthened period of active service. It is not too much to say that in fighting power and intelligence the troops in question could not be surpassed, whilst their equipment was in the very highest order."[1]

From a regimental point of view it is interesting to note that the duty of collecting intelligence during the march devolved on Captain A. Gaselee, who was destined some years later to command the 1st Battalion.

Kabul–Kandahar March, August, 1880.

When we come to the march itself we find that there is not a great deal to tell. It is chiefly of interest for the prudent boldness of its conception and for the success which waited on its completion. But from the time the Force left Kabul until it arrived in Kandahar, no opposition was met with, and one day was so much like another, that a general survey of the episode will serve our purpose better than a detailed description.

The Force moved into camp south of Kabul on August 8th, 1880, the 2nd Brigade halting at Indaki. The next day marked the beginning of the long journey for the relief of Kandahar. The total distance to be covered was 313 miles. The route lay up the Logar River by Hisarak and over the Zamburak Kotal to Saidabad. Thence into the Ghazni Plain by the Sher Dahan Pass, and so by the age-old caravan route through Ghazni and Kalat-i-Ghilzai to Kandahar.

Always a very early start was made, partly to obviate marching during the hottest time of the day, and partly because so much work remained to be done after reaching the camping-ground, that it was essential to complete the march with several hours of daylight in hand. During the earlier stages the starting hour was usually fixed at 4 a.m. As the altitude decreased and the character of the country changed from

---

[1] Extract from lecture by Lieutenant-Colonel E. F. Chapman, delivered at the Royal United Service Institution in 1881, and quoted in "The Second Afghan War, 1878–80, Official Account."

hills to barren plains, the heat grew more intense, so that before reaching Kalat-i-Ghilzai, the column was on the move as early as 2.30 a.m.

Great heat by day, cold during the night—the variation in temperature during the twenty-four hours sometimes covered a range of 80°—sand storms, lack of water, and the choking dust raised by the marching columns, all were amongst the hardships which the troops were called upon to endure.

At the end of the day's march it was necessary to arrange for the supply from local resources of rations and firewood for the men and of grain and fodder for the animals. That done, there still remained the work of distribution to units. Everywhere fuel was scarce. When not otherwise procurable houses were purchased, and the wood resulting from their destruction was issued to British troops. This source, however, could not meet the requirements of the Native regiments, so often it happened that the men, after a hard day's march, had to scour the surrounding country and dig up the roots of southernwood to provide themselves with fuel for the evening meal.

The march discipline of the Force was excellent. Once every hour a halt of ten minutes was made, the eight o'clock halt being extended to twenty minutes to allow the troops to eat a hurried meal. Wherever the ground was suitable the march was carried out in several parallel columns, each covered by its own rear-guard, while the Cavalry protected the front. Marching steadily every day from August 9th to 23rd, the 225 miles from Kabul to Kalat-i-Ghilzai were covered in fifteen days. For the Regiment the march from Barak-i-Barak to Saidabad on August 12th proved unusually arduous. The Zamburak Kotal had to be crossed *en route*, and because there was a probability that the Afghans would dispute its passage, the 2nd Brigade was sent in advance with the Cavalry to secure it. Actually there was no opposition, but the ascent of the pass was found to be difficult. No baggage reached the brigade, the night was unusually cold, and the men were forced to rest in the open with no more clothing than they had worn during the day while marching with the thermometer registering 92° in the shade. A detachment of the 5th Gurkhas, 100 strong, held the summit of the pass during the night, and they, at a height of over 7,000 feet, suffered most. Another trying march was that from Ghazni to Ergatta on August 16th. The distance was twenty miles, the baggage animals were so distressed that it was found advisable to unload them and to allow them to graze for two hours, a severe dust-storm blew throughout the afternoon, progress was very slow, and the rear-guard did not reach camp till 9 p.m. At Ergatta no supplies were procurable.

The Force halted at Kalat-i-Ghilzai on August 24th, and arrangements were made to evacuate the garrison, which was taken on to

Kandahar. On reaching Tirandaz, 53 miles from Kandahar, a message was brought in from that place to the effect that the siege had been raised on the 23rd, and that Ayub Khan had withdrawn to Mazra, a short distance north of the city. The need for extreme haste, then, was over, and Sir Frederick Roberts resolved to accomplish the rest of his journey by more easy stages. He himself succumbed to the extreme heat on the 27th, and was barely fit to ride a horse when Kandahar was reached on August 31st.

The first part of the mission entrusted to the Kabul-Kandahar Field Force had now been accomplished. Three hundred and thirteen miles had been covered in twenty-one days of actual marching. Two days only had been given to rest. The near approach of the men from Kabul had of itself been effective in raising the siege of Kandahar. The second part of the task yet remained to be done, and no time was lost before setting on foot preparations for the defeat of Ayub Khan.[1]

Battle of Kandahar, Sept. 1st, 1880. North-west from the walled town of Kandahar, where the Bombay division had taken refuge, runs from north-east to south-west a long serrated rocky ridge. Before terminating in the plain which bounds Kandahar on the west, it throws off three spurs, which we may name conveniently from their nearest villages the Ahmad Khan Spur, nearest to the town, the Pir Paimal Spur farther west, and beyond that again the Jaliran Spur, running down westwards towards the Argandab River. The Pir Paimal Spur is traversed, not far from its point of junction with the main ridge, by a pass known as the Babawali Kotal, which carries the road to Khakrez. South-west across the valley from the Ahmad Khan Spur rises another rocky ridge above the walls of Old Kandahar, and partially filling in the intervening ground are the low features known as Piquet Hill and Karez Hill. The valley beyond these low hills is thickly treed, with numerous walled enclosures about the villages of Abbasabad, Kaghanak, Gundi Mulla Sahibdad, and Gundigan.

The terrain described was to provide the scene of the impending battle. The action will be described as briefly as possible, since the Regiment was to be called upon to take a less conspicuous share than usual in its successful issue.

Having seen his troops into camp between Karez Hill and Old Kandahar, Sir Frederick Roberts next turned his attention to reconnaissance. By evening he had all the information he required, and he proceeded to make his plan.

---

[1] The following statistics, taken from the "Official Account," give an insight into the difficulties of the march. Of 8,627 transport animals which left Kabul 1,050 died or were reported as missing on the way, and 2,159 were unfit for work on arrival at Kandahar. Ponies fared worse, having only 1,077 effective out of an original total of 2,954. Donkeys did best, arriving with 85 per cent. effective.

A Group of Officers about 1865.

Lt. J. M. Sym. Surgeon J. R. Johnson. Lt. J. S. Oliphant. Lt. A. P. Broome.
Capt. H. P. Close. Major O. E. Rothney, C.S.I. Lt. F. C. Codrington.

A Group of Officers about 1880.

Lt. C. C. Chenevix Trench. Lt. W. R. Yielding.
Lt. C. C. St. E. Lucas. Major J. M. Sym. Lt.-Col. A. Fitzhugh. Capt. E. Molloy. Lt. A. R. Martin.

The Babawali Kotal itself was the key of the enemy's position, but the Ahmad Khan and Pir Paimal Spurs being very strongly held and entrenched, it appeared that a direct assault upon it could only succeed at the price of heavy casualties. The plan, therefore, resolved itself into a demonstration by the 3rd Brigade against the Kotal from the south, and a turning movement via Pir Paimal by the 1st and 2nd Brigades to take the Kotal in rear. To the Bombay troops were given the duties of taking over piquets, escorting guns, and watching the flanks.

On September 1st the attack began at about 9.30 a.m. Covered by Artillery fire the 1st and 2nd Brigades deployed from the neighbourhood of Karez Hill and advanced, the former on the right against Gundi Mulla Sahibdad, the latter on the left towards Gundigan. Both villages, as well as the enclosures between, were strongly held by numbers of Afghan irregulars, who offered a most stubborn resistance. While in the 1st Brigade the 92nd Highlanders and 2nd Gurkhas bore the brunt of the fighting, in the 2nd Brigade the 72nd and 2nd Sikhs had the principal share. The 5th Gurkhas and 3rd Sikhs were in support. Colonel Brownlow, who had commanded the 72nd throughout the period during which they had been so closely associated with the Regiment, was killed near Gundigan while gallantly leading his men. By 10.30 a.m. Gundi Mulla Sahibdad had been captured. Not long afterwards Gundigan fell to the vigorous assault of the 2nd Brigade, and then both brigades, sweeping forward, turned the end of the Pir Paimal Spur, stormed the village, and had the Babawali Kotal at their mercy. With their line of retreat threatened, the enemy withdrew and attempted a last stand on the Jaliran Spur. It was past noon, and the 3rd Brigade, no longer required to threaten the Afghan left, had been ordered forward to support a further advance. With barely a pause the attack surged onwards, and soon the last remnants of Ayub's army were fleeing down the reverse slope and making for the shelter of villages and gardens in the Argandab Valley. The Cavalry took up the pursuit, but owing to the difficulties of the ground failed to come up with the main body of the retreating enemy.

The victory was complete. The whole of Ayub's camp and all his Artillery was captured, and it was estimated that his casualties in killed alone numbered over 1,000 men. The Battle of Kandahar retrieved the disaster of Maiwand, restored British prestige, not only in Afghanistan, but throughout the East, and crowned with a brilliant success the achievement of the Kabul-Kandahar Field Force.

The casualties in the Regiment were 1 sepoy and 2 camp followers killed, and 2 sepoys wounded. With the rest of the brigade the 5th Gurkhas returned to its camping-ground during the afternoon, to remain at Kandahar till arrangements should be completed for the breaking up of the Force.

THE 5TH ROYAL GURKHA RIFLES (F.F.)

Achakzai Expedition, September, 1880.
Two years had elapsed since the Regiment left Abbottabad, and disappointed once already of its hope of speedy return, it asked no better now than to be quit of campaigning for a season. It was not to be, however. Leaving Kandahar with the 2nd Brigade on September 15th, it arrived at Chaman on the 20th. From there, on the 21st, General Baker led his troops into the country of the Achakzais. The brigade at this time consisted of 80 sabres 3rd Bengal Lancers, 2nd Derajat Mountain Battery, 72nd Highlanders, 2nd Sikh Infantry, and 5th Gurkhas.

The Achakzais inhabit a hilly tract some distance to the east of Chaman. They had chosen the period of our embarrassments at Kandahar to seize the Khojak Pass—about ten miles south-east of Chaman—and to destroy the telegraph line. It was to punish them for these unfriendly acts that the present expedition was organized. They had no big villages, but possessed good grazing lands on the Toba Plateau, and to seize their flocks and herds seemed to offer the readiest means of teaching them a lesson.

The force traversed the Boghra Pass, giving access to Achakzai territory from the west, then turned south to cross the western part of the Toba Plateau, collecting thousands of head of sheep and cattle on the way, and finally passed down the Arambi Valley to reach Kila Abdullah on September 24th. There it was met by the remainder of the 3rd Bengal Cavalry, which had been employed in preventing the escape of the tribesmen to Peshin. Its work finished, the brigade marched by the usual stages to Quetta, where it arrived on September 28th.

At Quetta the 5th Gurkhas bade farewell to their comrades of the 72nd. *Farewell to 72nd Highlanders.* Whether in action, in camp, or on the march, the two regiments had seldom been separated since their arrival in the Kurram in 1878; based on feelings of mutual respect, a sincere and lasting friendship had sprung up between them, and it will ever be a bond uniting them that when Sir Frederick Roberts was raised to the peerage he chose as supporters for his coat-of-arms a soldier of the 72nd Highlanders and a soldier of the 5th Gurkhas.

Quetta was to be the scene, too, of another parting, for there, on October 2nd, Lieutenant-General Sir Frederick Roberts said good-bye to the 5th Gurkhas, among other units specially honoured, in the following Field Force order:—

Sir F. Roberts's Farewell Order.

" The Lieutenant-General cannot permit the regiments and battery marginally noted to leave his command without bidding them an especial farewell as having formed part of the original Kabul Field Force.

9th (Queen's Royal) Lancers.
72nd Highlanders.
92nd Highlanders.
3rd Sikh Infantry.
5th Goorkhas.
No. 2 Mountain Battery.

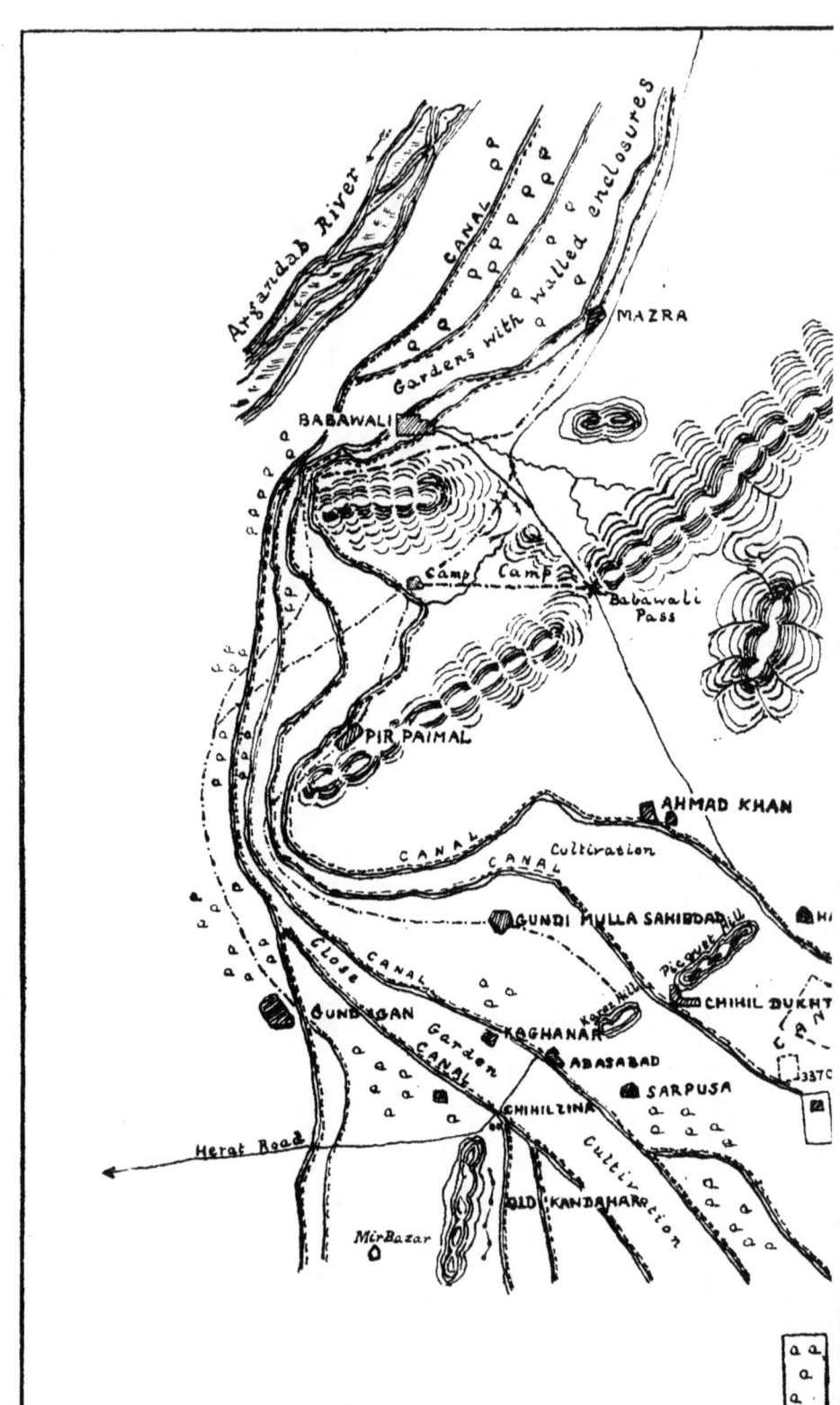

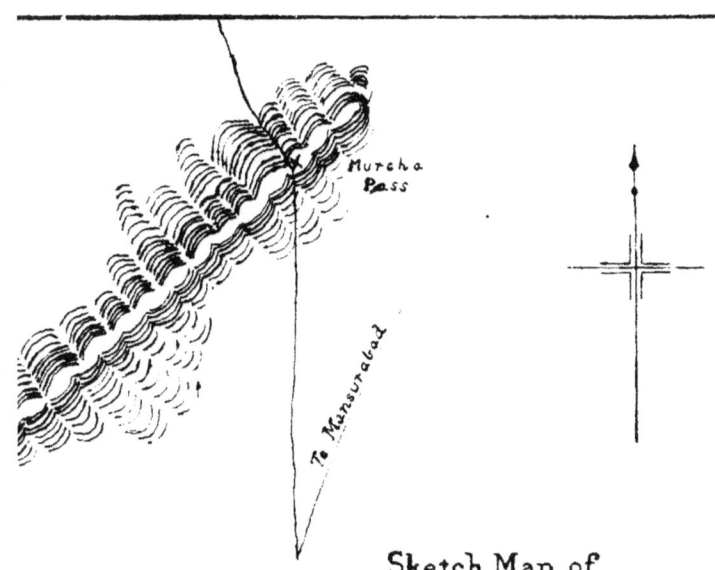

Sketch Map of
KANDAHAR & NEIGHBOURHOOD

From "The Afghan Campaigns of 1878-1880" by Sydney H. Shadbolt
by permission of Samson Low, Marston & Co. owners of the Copyright.

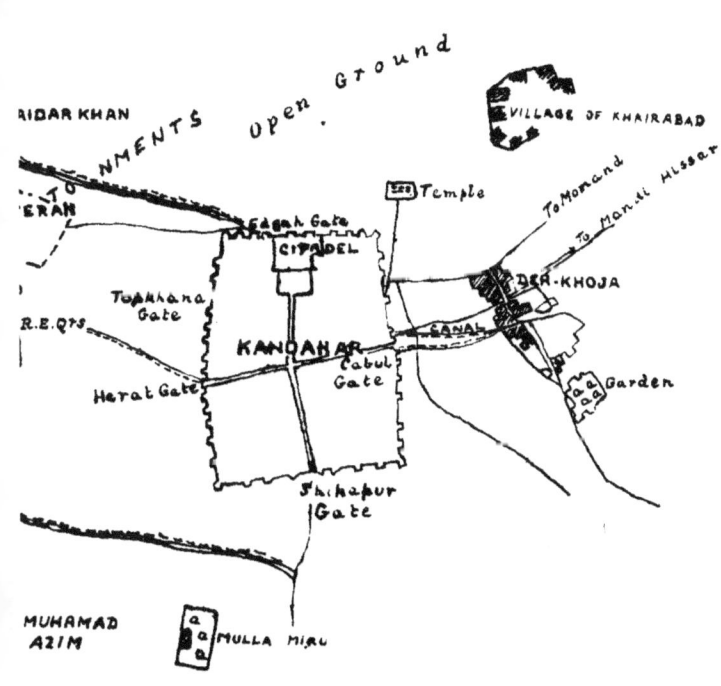

"Sir Frederick Roberts begs to thank these Corps for the excellent service they have rendered during the campaign. No troops could have behaved better either before the enemy or in quarters. Of their gallant conduct in action, the British nation may well be proud, as proud as their Commander is at having been associated with them. The Lieutenant-General desires to acknowledge most cordially the assistance he has received from officers (Native as well as British), non-commissioned officers and men, and to convey to one and all his best wishes for their future welfare."

Marri Expedition, October and November, 1880.
The Regiment had already left Quetta when that order was published, for, halting for only one day, with the 2nd Derajat Mountain Battery it took the road for Sibi on September 30th. Arriving there on October 8th it found itself attached to a force under Brigadier-General MacGregor for the punishment of the Marri tribesmen. Thus one more arduous task fell to the lot of the 5th Gurkhas before they could feel themselves free to seek the rest which surely by now they had well earned.

The composition of General MacGregor's column was as follows:—

3rd Punjab Cavalry;
11/9th R.A.;
2/60th Rifles;
2nd Sikh Infantry;
3rd Sikh Infantry;
4th Gurkhas;
5th Gurkhas.

The Marri country is at the south-western end of the wedge of tribal territory which separates Baluchistan from the Derajat. The inhabitants had brought retribution on themselves by raiding the Harnai line of railway, and by attacking—most successfully from their own point of view, seeing that they carried off treasure to the value of a lakh and a half of rupees—a detachment marching from Spin Tangi to Sibi. They had taken as signs of the end of British dominion in Baluchistan the Maiwand disaster and the investment of Kandahar, and were now to be undeceived. Their territory comprising several rich valleys in which the crops were now standing and more than one village of importance, there were not wanting objectives for the expedition.

The experiences of the Regiment are summed up in the old "Historical Record" as "very trying in consequence of insufficient tent accommodation, bad water, bad roads, and the extreme difficulty of the country."

With the main portion of the column, the 5th Gurkhas left Sibi on October 11th, and marching north along the Harnai branch of the railway, then under construction, reached Babar Kach on the 13th. There the concentration was completed by the arrival of the battery, with one company of the 2/60th and the 4th Gurkhas, who had marched from Harnai.

On the 14th General MacGregor led his force to Mandai (Quat-Mandai), intending to move thence straight on Kahan, the chief settlement of the offending tribesmen, about sixty miles to the south-east. After arrival at Mandai the Commander changed his plan. The Marri clans at this time were allied with those of Luni to the north. This fact decided General MacGregor to thrust in between the allies, and then, having detached the men of Luni from the confederacy, to sweep down into the Marri country from the north.

Leaving a strong detachment at Mandai the column marched thence on October 17th, and on the 18th reached Spin Kach. There it was joined by a small force destined to garrison Thal and Chotiali; and moving now in an easterly direction, it arrived at Thal on October 23rd. At that place the chiefs of Luni made their submission, thus justifying the change of plan.

Up to this point opposition had been negligible, but the marches had proved most arduous. For instance, on the 18th, though the march from Dalujal to Spin Kach was only five miles in length, the rear-guard was actually twenty-four hours on the road. Then again, on the 21st, the column left Kandi at 6 a.m. intending to camp at the Sembar Pass, not more than ten miles away. There it was found that the water supply was brackish and quite inadequate to the needs of the force, so it was necessary to push on. After traversing a further ten miles the advanced guard found water at a well in the Thal Plain, but meantime the transport was in difficulties on the western side of the Sembar Pass, and it was not until 10 a.m. on the 22nd that the rear-guard reached camp. Two hundred and forty baggage animals had to be abandoned on the way; for twenty-eight hours the men had been dependent on the small quantity of cooked food carried in the haversack, and for many hours they had struggled on without water.

Throughout the expedition the marches proved arduous, but the hardships endured were not without result. By adroit manœuvring General MacGregor threatened the tribesmen with complete encirclement, and on the arrival of the force at Mamand on November 2nd, their headmen came in and agreed to the terms imposed.

The route followed from Thal had been east through Chotiali to Bala Dhaka, and thence south-west for five marches, crossing the Kolu Plateau *en route*. From Mamand the column marched to Kahan, arriving there on November 6th. Earnest of complete submission was given by furnishing hostages previously demanded, and by the payment of Rs. 50,000 as a first instalment of the total fine levied. One day's halt was made among ideal surroundings—numbers of fine trees, well-cultivated fields, and plenty of water—and on the 8th the return to British India was begun. The route lay nearly due east by Suji Kach and the Burzen Pass, and the frontier was crossed near Bet Badshah on November 12th. On arrival at Dirigi on the 14th the force was broken up.

The Regiment had left Sibi in excellent health and without one sick man. By the end of the expedition no less than sixty men were *hors de combat*, carried on stretchers or on spare baggage animals, and of these the majority were suffering from dysentery and diarrhœa.

From Dirigi the Regiment marched via Rajanpur and Mithankote to Khanpur, where it arrived on November 24th. Entraining there on the same day, it arrived at Rawalpindi on the 27th. Abbottabad was reached on December 7th, after a long absence of two years and two months.

CHAPTER V

Peace and War, 1881 to 1892

BEFORE going on to chronicle the less eventful years immediately succeeding the second Afghan War, it is allowable to pause for a moment in order to consider the effects of that war on the Regiment. As early as December 18th, 1878, Sir Frederick Roberts had written, " it is therefore my pleasure and my duty to bring the gallant conduct of this fine regiment once more to special notice." Charasia, Karez Mir with the affair at the Kafir Jan Defile, the attack on the Takht-i-Shah and the gallant withdrawal to Sherpur, the Kabul to Kandahar march and the culminating battle, all were yet to come. Each affair in turn served to enhance a reputation already high, and it is a fair claim that by the time the Regiment returned to Abbottabad in December, 1880, it was established in the eyes of fellow-professionals as one of the finest fighting corps in the Service. Not only that, but its fame had even spread beyond the confines of that somewhat restricted circle.

Effects of the Afghan War.

Another effect deserving of notice in this place is the friendship, referred to before, which had been established between the 5th Gurkhas and the 72nd Highlanders. That it was more than skin-deep is evidenced by the action of the men of the 72nd when, after the explosion in the Bala Hissar, despite the intense cold, they freely gave their greatcoats to the men of the 5th Gurkhas. A further proof of comradeship was forthcoming after the return of the Regiment to Abbottabad. The Gurkha ranks, anxious lest separation should bring forgetfulness, on their own initiative subscribed for a shield which bore the following inscription:—

FROM THE

MEN OF THE 5TH GOORKHAS

TO THE

MEN OF THE 72ND (DUKE OF ALBANY'S OWN) HIGHLANDERS

IN REMEMBRANCE OF

THE AFGHAN CAMPAIGN, 1878 TO 1880.

The shield was presented in due course, and in return the men of the 72nd gave the 5th Gurkhas a Drum-Major's staff of ebony with silver mounts and chains, which nowadays occupies a conspicuous position in the officers' mess beneath the "Peiwar Kotal" picture, painted by Vereker Hamilton, brother of Sir Ian Hamilton.

Distinctions Gained. Full details of the distinctions gained during the war by individuals of the Regiment are given in the appendix "Honours and Awards," but some are of sufficient interest to claim a moment's attention in the narrative. Subadar-Major Balbahadur Negi, who had succeeded Subadar-Major Bhagiram Gurung after the latter's death in the Bala Hissar explosion, was appointed an aide-de-camp on the personal staff of the Viceroy in recognition of the services of the Regiment. Every British officer of the Regiment who served received a mention in despatches. Lieutenant-Colonel Alfred Fitzhugh was awarded the C.B. Major J. M. Sym was promoted Brevet-Lieutenant-Colonel, and Captain E. Molloy was promoted Brevet-Major.

In July, 1881, came the announcement that "Her Majesty the Queen, Empress of India, has been graciously pleased to permit the following corps to bear upon their standards, colours, or appointments the words specified below in commemoration of their gallant conduct during the recent campaigns in Afghanistan:—

5th Goorkha Regiment { Peiwar Kotal, Charasia.
Kabul 1879, Kandahar 1880
Afghanistan 1878-80."

Disturbances in Agror, September, 1884. Little occurred to claim attention during the years immediately following the return of the 5th Gurkhas to Abbottabad. In July, 1882, Lieutenant A. A. Barrett was posted permanently to the Regiment, and not very long afterwards he is heard of as doing good work in Agror.

The sequence of events on the Black Mountain Frontier has been followed, in a previous chapter, up to the year 1871. It was not until 1875 that quiet was restored to this part of the border, through the unreserved submission of all the disaffected tribes—the Akazais, the Hassanzais, the Chigharzais, the inhabitants of Tikari and Allai, and the Pariari Saiyads. A period of tranquillity ensued, which ended in 1884 with the eruption in acts of open hostility of the long-standing feud between the Dilbori Khan and the Khan of Agror. The inheritors of the feud were Abdullah Khan of Dilbori and Ali Gauhar Khan of Agror. In April, Abdullah Khan left Dilbori and made his way into the territory of the Pariari Saiyads. There he set himself to foment trouble, and having gained the support of the Saiyads and of sections of the Akazais and Chigharzais as well, in May he raided into the Agror Valley. He was met by the levies of the Khan of Agror, and his following was dispersed after both sides had suffered casualties. The garrison of the Oghi post was increased to 300 rifles, but though raid succeeded raid, the regular troops were given no opportunity of punishing the aggressors. In June, after an unsuccessful attack on the village of Dilbori, Abdullah Khan with his following was driven out of British territory, and the Oghi garrison was again reduced to its normal strength of 100 rifles. For their participation in these outrages a blockade was proclaimed against the Akazais and the Pariari Saiyads with their Chigharzai tenants, while Abdullah Khan himself was outlawed.

Early in September, 1884, a large number of Chigharzai tribesmen moved into Pariari territory. This influx spelt further trouble, and to counter it, advantage was taken of the incidence of the normal relief of the Oghi garrison to double the strength of the post by retaining there the detachment due for relief. The garrison then consisted of 100 rifles 2nd Sikhs and 100 rifles 5th Gurkhas, under the command of Lieutenant Barrett. On September 12th word was brought to that officer of a great gathering of Chigharzais and Akazais, about 1,000 strong, who had planted their standards above the villages of Dilbori and Ghanian on the southern slopes of the well-marked spur which drops eastwards towards the Jal Pass and Kunjgali from the Chitabat Hill. The distance from Oghi Fort was about five miles, and Lieutenant Barrett lost no time in marching against the tribesmen. He took with him 75 rifles 2nd Sikhs, 75 rifles 5th Gurkhas, and 25 police. On this occasion the operation was rather in the nature of a reconnaissance than a serious attempt to disperse the hostile gathering, and after exchanging shots with the Chigharzais and driving them back for some distance, with the approach of darkness the small force returned to Oghi for the night.

At 5 a.m. on September 13th, Lieutenant Barrett again set out for Ghanian, which had been unsuccessfully attacked by the Chigharzais during the night. He had with him the same force as on the previous day, and was accompanied by the Deputy Commissioner, Mr. Clarke. At about 7.30 a.m. he reached the village, and found the enemy, their numbers now estimated at 2,000, strongly posted: some on a ridge above Shahtut Village about a mile to the west, the remainder, as before, less than a mile to the northward, on the southern features of the ridge running down from Chitabat.

Though the odds appeared so great Lieutenant Barrett at once decided to attack. His police he posted in a hamlet about 300 yards north-west of Ghanian to guard his flank from the direction of Shahtut, and leaving a reserve of 30 rifles in the village, with the remaining 120 he crossed the *nullah* intervening between Dilbori and Ghanian, and advanced up the spur which rises from the former village towards the crest of the ridge. At the same time the levies of the Khan of Agror, who had come out to co-operate, were ordered by the Deputy Commissioner to make their way up the ridge from Kunjgali.

As the party from Ghanian disappeared into the *nullah* a number of the enemy started a forward movement down the Mula Kili Spur. They were checked by the fire of the police detachment. Lieutenant Barrett pushed onwards to the crest of the ridge and opened fire. The tribesmen were driven from one position to another, until, unable to withstand the pressure of the combined advance, they at last began to disperse. By 11 a.m., of the entire *lashkar*, 2,000 strong, not a man remained in the field. Their loss was estimated at 6 killed and 20 wounded, while on our side there were no casualties.

Brigadier-General Kennedy, commanding the Punjab Frontier Force, commented on this incident in the following terms:—

"I consider Lieutenant Barrett's spirited conduct of the affair reported testifies highly to his judgment and skill in what must have appeared, until closed with, a serious difficulty, owing to his small detachment being so out-numbered by the enemy."

The Government of the Punjab, when reporting the affair to the Indian Government, wrote as follows:—

"His Honour the Lieutenant-Governor considers that Lieutenant Barrett displayed skill and judgment in his well-conceived and executed attack on a numerically very superior enemy with every advantage of ground and position in their favour, and that the affair was very creditable to the troops engaged."

The Regiment was not again to intervene actively in Black Mountain affairs until one tragic day in the hot weather of 1888. It is therefore unnecessary to delve into the troubled politics of that tract, beyond recording that during the intervening years Chigharzais, Akazais, Saiyads, and Hassanzais all gave cause for complaint at one time or another.

Rawalpindi and Delhi, 1885.
The next events of importance at which the Regiment assisted were the reception of the Amir, Abdur Rahman, at Rawalpindi in 1885, and the big camp of exercise held at Delhi towards the end of the same year. The present Colonel of the Regiment, Major-General Sir J. M. Stewart, has furnished a personal record which covers this period, and it throws such a vivid light on the prevailing conditions that no excuse is needed for quoting in full the passage which deals with this part of his service. He tells first of the incident which decided him to apply for the 5th Gurkhas when he had to make his choice among the regiments of the Punjab Frontier Force.

"Of course, I had heard much of the Gurkha as a fighting soldier, and I knew what a name the 5th Gurkhas had made for themselves in the Afghan War of '78–80. Chenevix-Trench had suggested my applying for the 5th, and said Colonel Fitzhugh would ask for me. Then in the spring of '84 I was on language leave at Rawalpindi. One day on the Mall I saw the very picture of a soldier—a 5th Gurkha perfectly turned out: well-fitted green uniform, forage cap worn at an impossible angle, belts polished like glass, and the man himself excellently set up and moving very smartly. A very cheery Mongolian countenance completed the picture. I had no doubt that here was the regiment for me!

"I joined them in March, '85, just in time to march down to Rawalpindi for the Durbar held in honour of the Amir, Abdur Rahman. The Panjdeh incident occurred during the Durbar. One night after dinner I was offered a horse to gallop in to the Club from our camp in the Khana Plain, to see the list posted up there of regiments detailed for mobilization in the event of war with Russia.

"The 5th were on the list all right, and in brigade with their old friends the Seaforths and 3rd Sikhs. We were hurried back to Abbottabad to prepare, and then Russia climbed down.

"How different the march was in those days!

"The men much the same, but a decided proportion of Garhwalis, Kumaonis, and Khas, who had proved their worth in the Afghan Campaign and had gained many rewards for gallantry. A large percentage of the Regiment had three decorations—the Frontier and the Afghan medals and the Kabul-Kandahar star—a fine sight on a full-dress parade.

"The service uniform was so-called 'khaki' coats—the dye was by no means permanent and the colour very variable—trousers and puttees black; quite smart to look at, but the smell of the dye dreadful! The only smoke was a little clay bowl filled with a rag and a pinch of tobacco, which was passed freely about the ranks. The smell of this, too, was very trying, and it made the men cough immoderately, but they seemed to like it.

"March discipline was indifferent: much straggling, step and dressing disregarded, but the men were cheery and full of conversation. The pace was three miles an hour with difficulty. The Gurkha had got a name as a bad marcher. What a change in a year's time! In October, '85, we left Abbottabad for the Delhi manœuvres and Durbar, which were attended by military representatives of all the European nations. The Regiment did not get back till March, '86, after about six months of camp work. They marched into Abbottabad splendidly: nearly four miles an hour; step, dressing, and handling of arms all of the best—and all due to Colonel Sym, who marched the whole distance at the head of the Regiment, and to the Adjutant, Chenevix-Trench, who worked indefatigably in camp and on the march. Never again could anyone say the Gurkha could not march. And with this improvement in pace on the flat came much greater rapidity on the hill-side."

There is more of equal interest in Sir James Stewart's narrative, but since it deals with a slightly later period we leave it for the moment, to return to it in due course.

At this distance of time the reference to the Panjdeh incident may fail to strike a chord of memory. Early in 1884 Russia had occupied Merv, a position which brought her so close to the indefinite boundary of northern Afghanistan between the Oxus and Hari Rud rivers, that she herself deemed it politic to propose a final delimitation of the doubtful line. Great Britain, consenting, appointed a commission under the leadership of Sir Peter Lumsden, which in co-operation with a Russian commission would demarcate a frontier acceptable to both parties. On one pretext or another, Russia postponed the start of work, and used the time to encroach southwards. The British commission, be it understood, was to act on behalf of Afghanistan. To watch the Russian moves, Afghanistan sent a small force to Panjdeh, at the junction of the Murghab and Kushk rivers. In face of the Russian aggression the attitude of the home Government lacked firmness, with the result that the northern power was emboldened to creep yet nearer to the disputed zone, disregarding its own proposals for a mutual understanding. When a collision appeared likely the British commission, still awaiting the co-operation of its Russian counterpart, moved to Gubran, clear of the direct line of advance on Herat. On April 1st, 1885, a Russian force attacked the Afghans at Panjdeh and drove them towards Herat. The news of the outrage was received with indignant protest both in England and in India. It seemed that an insult so gross and wanton could only be met by a declaration of war, and preparations went forward feverishly. At this critical moment, however, a change of Government occurred at home, and Lord Salisbury's handling of the crisis averted hostilities.

Colonel Fitzhugh's Farewell, September, 1885.

It was on March 20th, 1885, that the Regiment left Abbottabad for Rawalpindi, and on April 14th it returned to mobilize. On October 24th it began its march to Delhi. Between these two events there came a change in command, for Colonel Fitzhugh, having completed his seven years' tenure on September 27th, was succeeded by Colonel Sym.

The Regiment owed much to Colonel Alfred Fitzhugh, C.B., for, taking over command on his transfer from the 4th Sikhs at the beginning of the Afghan War, he had steered it with conspicuous success through a most eventful period. That the Regiment itself contributed to that success is shown in the following extracts from his farewell order. After acknowledging the services of all ranks during the seven years of his command, he continued:—

"During that period many changes have taken place amongst the officers, and Colonel Fitzhugh will not now refer to anyone by name. To do so would be invidious, and the services of the officers and the

Regiment are better recorded in the complimentary orders which have been published by Sir F. Roberts and other Generals than they could be by him.

"Colonel Fitzhugh leaves the Regiment, he trusts, in a very high state of efficiency, thanks to the exertions of all the British officers, and especially the regimental staff, and the co-operation of all ranks.

"Colonel Fitzhugh feels sure that the Regiment will always distinguish itself as heretofore, and that the name of the 5th Gurkhas will remain as celebrated as it is now."

Of the changes amongst British officers, several had occurred quite recently. Lieutenant-Colonel Unwin retired in August, 1884, and shortly afterwards no less than three new officers were appointed: Lieutenant J. O. S. Fayrer in October, 1884, Lieutenant E. de S. Smart in November, 1884, and Lieutenant J. M. Stewart in February, 1885. They were soon to be followed by Lieutenant J. Manners-Smith and Lieutenant Philipps, appointed in 1886.

Delhi, 1886. During the process of mobilizing for war with Russia many defects had come to light, more especially as regards transport and supply. It became one of the main objects, therefore, of the Delhi manœuvres to try out those services. After a march lasting forty-six days the Regiment arrived at Chota Chandu, two stages north of Ambala, on December 8th. There it joined the 2nd Brigade of the 1st Division, Northern Force, and spent some three weeks in brigade and divisional training. Manœuvres on the grand scale began on December 31st, when the Northern Force marched to relieve Delhi besieged by an enemy from the south. On January 7th the opposing sides came into contact at Panipat, a place inured to conflict from three great battles in which there had been no element of make-believe. The war over, the Regiment camped at Delhi on January 14th, and on the 18th took part in a grand review of 35,000 men of all arms. To the discomfort of those present, "heaven's artillery" in the form of a severe thunderstorm refused to be left out of the proceedings, and it brought with it torrents of rain. Nevertheless the Viceroy and the representatives of foreign armies, who were among the spectators, were much impressed by the display.

The return march began on January 22nd, and on March 18th the Regiment arrived in Abbottabad.

Items of Interest, 1881 to 1886

From a regimental point of view the most notable event of 1886 was the raising of the second battalion on October 20th. Marking, as it does, a very definite stage in the life of the 5th Gurkhas, it affords an opportunity to interrupt the narrative in order to set down minor occurrences falling into the period which elapsed between the close of the second Afghan War and the birth of the second battalion.

In 1882 the establishment of the Regiment was fixed at 912—a decrease of 25 men.

In 1883 Subadar-Major Balbahadur Negi was admitted to the Order of British India with the title of "Bahadur."

In 1885 free passages by rail were granted to men proceeding on furlough.

In July, 1886, Brigade Surgeon George Farell, who had been with the Regiment throughout the Afghan War, was appointed Principal Medical Officer to the field force in Upper Burma. He had been connected with the Punjab Frontier Force for twenty-seven years, and in recognition of his distinguished services had been made a Companion of the Bath in the recent birthday honours list. He was succeeded by Surgeon J. A. Nelis.

In July, 1886, the Punjab Frontier Force was transferred from the control of the Lieutenant-Governor of the Punjab to that of the Commander-in-Chief.

Raising of the 2nd Battalion, October, 1886.

The provision of second battalions for the 1st, 2nd, 4th, and 5th Gurkhas about this time was due to Sir Frederick Roberts, then Commander-in-Chief. As the result partly of his experience in command of the Madras Army, he initiated the policy of disbanding certain units of the Indian Army which recruited from among the non-martial races, and of replacing them by newly raised Gurkha battalions. To that end he made special arrangements with the Government of Nepal.

The nucleus of the 2nd Battalion 5th Gurkhas was to be furnished by volunteer transfers from the 1st Battalion of the Regiment and from the three Gurkha regiments serving in Assam. Major E. Molloy was transferred to raise and command the 2nd Battalion, and Captain C. C. Chenevix-Trench went across as senior Wing Commander. Four Native officers, 27 non-commissioned officers, and 119 sepoys were transferred from the 1st to the 2nd Battalion, the majority in November, 1886, and the rest in March, 1887.

The present Colonel of the Regiment (1928) has placed it on record that, from the very beginning, Colonel Sym, abetted by Colonel Molloy, insisted that the relations between the two battalions should conform to the motto, "One Regiment of two battalions," and that spirit still lives.

There is no need to say more about the 2nd Battalion in this place, for its story is fully told elsewhere in this book. For the present the doings of the 1st Battalion claim our attention.

Rebuilding Lines, 1887.

The year 1887 was devoted by the 1st Battalion to rebuilding the lines. Working parties were constantly employed in pulling down the old barracks, while others were detailed daily with the Battalion mules to bring stone from the quarry across the valley. It was now that the lines—later to be known as the Martin Lines, after Sir Alfred Martin—assumed their present shape. A number of buildings have been added since, and the idea of avenues of chenar trees, now such a pleasing feature, originated at a much later date. Brigadier-General Villiers-Stuart's information is to the effect that the lay-out of the previous lines ran at right angles to those which replaced them. The pre-1887 barracks seem to have been far from desirable residences. To save expense the site of each was half dug out of the slope and half built up. From this cause the quarters were very damp. Fungus grew freely on the inside walls, and even attached itself, on occasion, to clothing and accoutrements.

The Battalion bazar, previously sited on the present recruits' parade ground, was moved at this time to the position it now occupies.

Major Battye's Death, June, 1888.

In 1888 occurred the tragic affair on the Agror Frontier, which resulted in the death of Major L. R. Battye and four men of the Battalion, and of Captain H. B. Urmston of the 6th Punjab Infantry.

Major Battye, accompanied by Captain Urmston, had left Abbottabad on June 16th to visit the Oghi detachment. Early on the 18th they took with them 58 rifles from the post and 17 police, and set out to explore the eastern slopes of the Black Mountain, with special regard to the water supply. The way chosen was up the Barehar Spur, and after climbing for some hours a halt was made for breakfast. From the halting-place the route lay northwards along the crest of the main ridge, which also formed the boundary line between Agror and independent territory. While the main body took a line below the crest on the British side of the border-line, it seems that Major Battye himself, with the advance guard, moved along the divide. Not far from the point at which they struck the crest-line they passed through the little hamlet of Chappra, inhabited at this time of the year by Gujar tenants of the Akazais. These strongly resented the passage of the troops; shouts were raised, a few shots were fired, and a shower of stones came hurtling between the tree-trunks. Major Battye, wishing above all things to avoid bloodshed, continued his advance, and anxious to spare his assailants, would not even allow the men to open their ammunition. Favoured by the ground the Gujars pressed on behind the small column, and unceasingly harassed its rear. Matters became so critical that Subadar Kishanbir Nagarkoti—he of the Monghyr Pass, Charasia, and the Takht-i-Shah—at last urged Major Battye to allow him to open fire. Still swayed by the desire to avoid bloodshed, that officer refused, and tried instead to persuade the enemy that he came in peace. They, by now, were beyond persuasion; meeting with no retaliation they became ever more daring, and every moment their numbers swelled as fresh partisans ran up to the sound of firing.

Convinced, in the end, that he must either fight or leave the ridge, Major Battye chose the second alternative, and covered by a small rear-guard under Havildar Garba Sing Thapa, began to descend towards the village of Atir.

The withdrawal had not long been in progress when a message came in from the rear-guard saying that Havildar Garbu Sing had been wounded. Accompanied by Captain Urmston and Subadar Kishanbir Nagarkoti, Major Battye retraced his steps. Unfortunately the main body knew nothing of what was happening behind, and communication being difficult owing to the thickly wooded nature of the country, it was soon beyond sight and hearing down the hill-side. The further retirement of the small rear-guard was held up for some time while a stretcher was brought for the wounded Havildar. When at length it did get under way, it was only a matter of minutes before the enemy realized that it was completely isolated from the rest of the detachment. Gaining confidence from their immensely superior numbers the assailants pressed on.

To cover the withdrawal of the stretcher party there were now left only the two British officers, of whom Captain Urmston was unarmed, the Subadar, a naik, three sepoys, and a bugler. Helped by the trees the tribesmen were right in among the forlorn little party. One, leaping from cover, dealt Captain Urmston a blow with a hatchet. Another, with a sword, wounded Major Battye severely in the shoulder. He turned, to find himself confronted by an infuriated opponent armed with sword and shield. He was defending himself as best he could in his weakened state when Subadar Kishanbir came up and ran his assailant through the body. With two wounded officers to succour, their retreat cut off, and their own small numbers reduced by casualties, the plight of Subadar Kishanbir's handful was indeed desperate. They went on a short way, when Major Battye sank to the ground, exhausted from loss of blood. It appears that he never completely recovered consciousness. Concerned only to defend his officers to the last, the Subadar showed superb courage. Urging his three remaining men to fight on, he set them a fine example by his gallant and undaunted bearing. Using his pistol, with his own hand he killed several of the enemy, and, aided by his soldiers—soon reduced to two—succeeded for a time in keeping the enemy back. The end came when Major Battye was hit through the neck, and almost immediately afterwards Captain Urmston, too, was killed.

With nothing left to fight for, Subadar Kishanbir's next care was for the recovery of the bodies. The task was manifestly beyond the powers of himself and his two men, surrounded as they were by a pack of tribesmen thirsting for their blood. By some miracle they succeeded in getting clear away, and speeding down the hill they caught the main body at the village of Atir. The Subadar then led the detachment back to the scene of his last stand, and bore the bodies of both officers to Oghi.

The post was reached in safety, although, before evening fell, both the Khan Khel Hassanzais and the Pariari Saiyads had collected to the sound of firing. Of the enemy, six were killed.

Major Battye's death was announced to the Battalion in the following Battalion order dated June 20th:—

"It is with much sorrow that the commanding officer has to announce to the Regiment the death of their second-in-command, Major L. R. Battye, who was killed on the Black Mountain on the 18th instant, in a gallant endeavour, with the aid of a few men, to carry away Havildar Garbu Sing Thapa, who had been wounded, and Colonel Sym is fully assured that this sorrow is equally shared by all ranks in the Regiment. Major Battye had served in the 5th Goorkhas for nineteen years, and during this time his noble and consistent character, his entire unselfishness and love for his fellow-men, coupled with an absolute devotion to his duty, had gained him the admiration and affection of all with whom he came in contact, and furnished a bright example of a true soldier's life. By Major Battye's death the Regiment has lost a friend and comrade whom they will long mourn.

"The undermentioned Native officer and men gallantly stood with Major Battye till he was killed:—

Subadar Kishanbir Nagarkoti.
No. 1476 Naik Dhansing Saru, "A" Company.
„ 2684 Sepoy Indarbir Thapa, "D" Company.
„ 2685 Sepoy Motiram Thapa, "C" Company.
„ 2687 Sepoy Chandarbir Thapa, "H" Company.
Bugler Kalu Nagarkoti, "H" Company.

"The commanding officer deeply regrets that, with Major Battye, Naik Dhansing Saru, Sepoy Chandarbir Thapa, and Bugler Kalu Nagarkoti also fell, but the loyalty, courage, and devotion of all were such that it is fit their names should be recorded in the history of the Regiment, the honour of which they have done so much to uphold." [1]

All three survivors of the rear-guard gained awards for gallantry. Indarbir Thapa and Motiram Thapa were admitted to the Third Class of the Order of Merit.

The problem of a suitable award for Subadar Kishanbir Nagarkoti was more difficult. As sepoy he had been admitted successively to the Third and Second Classes of the Order of Merit. In the rank of Naik he had been admitted to the First Class of the Order, and at first sight it seemed that it was not in the power of Government to confer on him any higher distinction. The difficulty was overcome by admitting him to the pay of the First Class of the Order in the rank of Subadar

---

[1] In the contemporary account, written by Colonel E. Molloy, from which many of the facts are taken, it states that Havildar Garbu Sing Thapa died of his wound soon after the withdrawal began.

—hitherto, in accordance with precedent, he had drawn Order of Merit pay in the rank of Naik—and by making a special award of a gold bar, to be worn on the ribbon of the Order.

The murderous attack on Major Battye's party led directly to the third Black Mountain Expedition. The Battalion found itself among the units selected to take part. Orders issued on September 7th for the assembly of the expeditionary force stipulated that battalions would proceed at a minimum strength of 600. It happened that through the good offices of the Commander-in-Chief, Sir Frederick Roberts, to the 1/5th Gurkhas had fallen the honour of providing the Viceroy's guard, and in April two complete companies had been sent to Simla under the command of Lieutenant J. M. Stewart. It now became essential to arrange for the return of these two companies, but at first Simla showed some reluctance in releasing them. Fortunately Sir Frederick again intervened, and they returned just in time to take part in the expedition.

Third Black Mountain Expedition, Sept.–Nov., 1888.

Even so the Battalion was still under strength owing to the large number of recruits and furlough absentees. Recourse was therefore had to the 2nd Battalion, who provided 100 rifles under the command of Lieutenant A. H. G. Kimball.

Among British officers of the Battalion were several who have not yet been mentioned. Lieutenant G. H. Boisragon and Lieutenant C. H. Davies had been appointed in 1887, and Lieutenant F. F. Badcock in June, 1888. In August, Captain G. Hawkes and Lieutenant F. W. Evatt had come across from the 2nd Battalion, the former taking Major Battye's place as second-in-command.

Before going on to the story of the expedition it is interesting to note that this was the first campaign in which the Battalion used the Martini-Henry rifle. The new weapons had arrived to replace the old Sniders during July.

Since 1868 the people of the Black Mountain had multiplied their offences, until now there was a long score due for settlement. Those concerned were the Hassanzais, the Akazais, the Saiyads and Chigharzais of Pariari, and the inhabitants of Tikari. Against all, fines, greater or less in amount, were outstanding. Of late, too, the Hindustani Fanatics, under their aged chief, Abdullah Khan, had taken a hand in affairs and so earned punishment. Later, though they did not appear in the original indictment, the Allaiwals, too, were included in the scope of the operations.

The command of the expeditionary force was given to Major-General J. W. McQueen, C.B., A.D.C., who had at his disposal two brigades and a reserve column. Each brigade was subdivided into two columns, the First Brigade, commanded by Brigadier-General G. N. Channer,

V.C., providing the 1st and 2nd Columns, and the Second Brigade, under Brigadier-General W. Galbraith, providing the 3rd and 4th Columns. The command of the 1st Column was given to Colonel J. M. Sym, who had under him:—

>No. 4 Hazara Mountain Battery (4 guns).
>1st Battalion Northumberland Fusiliers.
>3rd Sikhs.
>1st Battalion 5th Gurkhas.
>Half No. 3 Company Sappers and Miners.
>Two Gatlings.

It is unnecessary to enter into the composition of the rest of the force, but we may note as interesting the inclusion in the 3rd Column of 300 of the Khyber Rifles under Major Muhammad Aslam Khan, and in the Reserve Column of two battalions of Kashmir Infantry under General Indar Singh. The Seaforth Highlanders were represented by their 2nd Battalion.

The plan of campaign was as follows. To subdue the Hassanzais and Akazais by an advance of the 1st, 2nd, and 3rd Columns up the eastern spurs of the Black Mountain, while the 4th Column threatened them on the west by moving up the Indus from Darband. For the 4th Column was reserved the additional task of dealing with the Hindustani Fanatics, whose stronghold lay across the river near Palosin. The Reserve Column to remain for a time about Oghi and in occupation of the Chattar Plain. Then, after some modification of the original organization, to detach part of the force northwards for the subjugation of the Pariari Saiyads and Tikariwals.

All went according to plan. Active operations began on October 4th.

First Phase, Oct. 4th to 20th, 1888. On that day the 4th Column advanced from Darband up the left bank of the Indus, and encountered strong opposition beyond Towara. Included in the ranks of the enemy were numbers of Hindustanis from across the river. The tribesmen lost heavily, and were eventually driven off in the direction of Kunhar. Kotkai was reached that evening.

Meantime, on the eastern side of the Black Mountain the 1st Column had climbed to Mana-ka-Dana, the 2nd Column to a point above Barchar, and the 3rd Column to Sambalbat. Next day they reached the crest.

The next two weeks were spent by all four columns in improving communications and in destroying villages and crops. From their bivouacs on top of the ridge the three columns sent parties in all directions to scour the surrounding country, and, dominated as they were, the tribesmen offered but little resistance. The 4th Column, after spending some days in reconnaissance from Kotkai and Towara, advanced through Kunhar to Ghazikot. Thence on the 18th it crossed the river and entirely destroyed the Hindustani settlement at Maidan.

These punitive measures soon began to take effect. On October 19th the Akazai jirgah came in, and signs were not wanting that the Hassanzais, too, were preparing to submit. The time had come, therefore, to change the centre of activity to the more northerly tract, but before turning our attention that way it will be as well to see how the Battalion had fared during the first phase of the operations.

The Battalion in the First Phase.

The 1st Column, to which the Battalion belonged, concentrated at Bagrian at the end of September. From September 29th to October 3rd, working parties were employed daily in making a road from camp to the Jal Pass, and thence along the ridge towards Mana-ka-Dana.

When, on October 4th, the general advance began, the 1st Column set out for Mana-ka-Dana, about 3,500 feet above the starting-point, three companies of the 5th Fusiliers formed the advance guard, and two companies of the 1/5th furnished the rear-guard, the remainder of the Battalion, with the exception of 50 rifles detailed as escort for the Hazara Mountain Battery, being at the tail of the main body. The movement was covered by the guns of the 8/1st South Irish Division R.A. from a position on the Atir Spur. Their fire proved effective, for of the small party of the enemy which gathered to oppose the advance they killed three and drove off the rest. The Northumberland Fusiliers accounted for a few more after reaching the crest.

It was found that the northern spurs running down from Mana-ka-Dana, which in 1868 had been covered with thick forest, were at this time bare, having been completely denuded of trees. Some difficulty was experienced in finding water, but a supply was eventually discovered to the south-west of the highest point and about 600 yards distant from it.

The night was spent in discomfort. It rained hard, and as no provision had been made for tents, but little could be done to ameliorate conditions which, at that elevation, proved most trying. The enemy took advantage of the thick weather to attack the supply area, which lay within the perimeter of the Northumberland Fusiliers. They were driven off, but only after causing considerable damage. In a rush of swordsmen they wounded five followers, and then got away with sheep, goats, and a number of mules.

Next day, the 5th, leaving two companies of the Northumberland Fusiliers and two of the 3rd Sikhs at Mana-ka-Dana, the column moved to Chittabat, on the crest of the ridge. There was little opposition, but the track along the north side of the ridge was found to be very difficult. All day the sappers worked on it, fired at occasionally by parties of enemy hidden in the trees, and it was dark before the baggage arrived at the bivouac. For water the troops had to depend on what they could collect from two small buffalo wallows filled from the rain of the preceding night.

On the 6th two companies of the Battalion were left to guard the camp, while the rest of the Battalion went to Mana-ka-Dana as escort to the baggage animals of the column, sent down to Bagrian to replenish supplies. At the same time detachments of the Northumberland Fusiliers and 3rd Sikhs moved in the direction of the Doda Hill in search of water. This was found in a *nullah* running down in a north-easterly direction between Chittabat and Doda, but in order to secure the supply it was first necessary to clear the last-named feature, which had been occupied by the enemy in considerable strength. In the attack which followed, the tribesmen lost heavily, their village of Landa was burnt, and their standing crops were cut and sent, with considerable quantities of stored forage, to the bivouac at Chittabat.

From the 6th to the 29th the Battalion took a hand in most of the punitive operations carried out from Chittabat for the coercion of the still recalcitrant tribesmen. During the first part of this period constant storms, accompanied by rain and sleet, made the climate very trying. The men, however, soon hutted themselves with branches of pine-trees, and despite the weather there was but little sickness. For some few nights the enemy caused much annoyance by sniping the bivouac, and the 3rd Sikhs, who were more exposed than the other units, sustained several casualties.

As to the more active side of the campaign, apart from road-making and convoy work, the Battalion assisted in overrunning the country of the Akazais and Hassanzais from end to end. It was present at the destruction of the villages of Biran, Darai, and Saidra. The last-named is a Pariari village, and there was found the pole of a dandy which had been lost on the occasion of the attack on Major Battye's party—sure indication of the participation of the Saiyads in that outrage.

Second Phase.
The second phase of the expedition comprised the punishment of the Pariari Saiyads and Tikariwals and that visit to Allai which had no place in the original plans. To execute his designs General McQueen decided to employ two columns. Those selected were the original 1st Column, strengthened by the addition of the 34th Pioneers and one company Seaforth Highlanders, and a newly constituted 5th Column, composed of units taken from the original 2nd, 3rd, and Reserve Columns. To set free the 1st Column for its appointed task it was arranged that the 2nd Column should relieve it at Chittabat, while the 3rd Column, disposed to the south of it, held certain features of tactical importance and connected up with the 4th Column, distributed along the Indus.

The relief was carried out on October 20th. On that day, while the rest of the 1st Column moved to Mana-ka-Dana, detachments of the Regiment and of the 3rd Sikhs escorted a survey party to the Machai Peak. They encountered no enemy, and later in the day rejoined the column at Mana-ka-Dana.

The striking-force was now to work over country which had been left untouched by the expedition of 1868. On October 21st both columns advanced and bivouacked in the vicinity of Chirmang. This move was sufficient of itself to bring in the Tikari maliks and induce prompt payment of fines. A halt was made at Chirmang to allow time to the Saiyads for an eleventh-hour repentance and to enable General McQueen to reconnoitre the country. At the end of two days the head-men of Pariari had made no gesture of submission, and accordingly, on the 24th, a mixed force, 1,000 strong, drawn from both columns, advanced through the Pariari glen, in which lay their principal settlements, and destroyed the villages of Garhi and Kopra. These were chosen as being the least accessible, and the work done, the force returned to Chirmang, leaving the Pariari Saiyads with matter to ponder. To drive the lesson home it was decided to pay a visit to Thakot on the Indus, a place which had hitherto been left severely alone as being too difficult of approach.

Visit to Thakot, Oct. 25th, 1888. As a preliminary to the Thakot visit, both columns went forward on the 25th and 26th, the 5th Column halting at Dabrai and the 1st Column at Maidan. A wing of the Battalion, under Captain A. A. Barrett, was left at Chirmang. On the 27th certain movements were undertaken with a view to concentrating a flying column at Serai, beyond Dabrai. The headquarters of the Battalion remained at Maidan, where it was joined by the wing under Captain Barrett on the 29th.

The flying column, taking with it only one blanket per man, greatcoats, and one day's rations, began its march to Thakot early on the 28th. The village was reached without fighting, and the whole force promenaded through to the strains of "You're owre lang in coming, lads," played by the pipes of the Seaforth Highlanders. It was left to the local inhabitants to draw the inference that the lads might have come before, and could always come again.

Although the Thakot villagers themselves were submissive, it was found necessary to punish the inhabitants of Lora, opposite Thakot on the left bank of the Nandihar stream. They, as well as the men of Daut across the Indus, shot into the camp during the afternoon. After destroying Lora and shelling Daut, the flying column returned to Serai on the 30th.

During its stay in Maidan the Battalion was employed in making a road towards Allai. October 30th had been appointed to Arsala Khan, chief of the Allaiwals, as the last day on which his submission would be accepted. He failed to take advantage of the period of grace allowed to him, and orders were therefore issued for an advance on the 31st. In preparation for the advance Colonel Sym, accompanied by a detachment of 200 rifles of the Battalion, carried out a reconnaissance towards the Ghorapher Pass. For the invasion of Allai the composition of the two columns had been modified, and it is not without interest that picked marksmen from the Royal Sussex Regiment, the Suffolk Regiment, and the 24th Punjab Infantry were attached to the 1st Column—a reversion to the methods of the Ambela Campaign.

In the Allai Country, November, 1888.

On October 31st the force halted at the Mazrai Pass and a reconnaissance was made of the Ghorapher Pass leading into Allai. During the next day's march it became apparent that the Allaiwals intended to make a show of resistance at the gateway of their country. After ascending gradually for a few miles, the 1st Column, which was leading, found itself at the foot of a precipitous rise. Above were great masses of granite boulders, giving shelter to groups of the enemy, who presently became visible. Soon there broke out the sound of the playing of pipes and beating of drums, and not long after, shots were fired from the thick forest on the left of the line of advance. The attack was led by the Northumberland Fusiliers and Khyber Rifles, with the 1/5th Gurkhas in support. Covered by the fire of the guns the leading troops approached the crest; the sound of pipes and drums was stilled, and the defenders sought safety in flight.

Brigadier-General Channer then moved forward along the crest to Kage Oba, taking with him the Northumberland Fusiliers, 1/5th Gurkhas, and the Khyber Rifles. A good site was found for the bivouac, with a plentiful supply of water, but such were the difficulties of the ascent to the pass that no baggage could be got up to the troops. At an elevation of 9,000 feet, without food, blankets or greatcoats, the men suffered much from exposure. Fortunately the enemy showed no signs of activity, so that it was soon found safe to light fires.

November 2nd was spent in improving the road to the rear and in helping the transport forward. Even so, the last of the baggage animals did not reach Kage Oba until after dark, and some idea of the difficulties of the steep ascent is to be gained from the fact, officially recorded, that fourteen mules fell from the path and were killed. On the same day a reconnaissance was made towards Pokal, the stronghold of Arsala Khan. Towards evening, news was brought that the Khan himself had fled the country, but that his eldest son, with a considerable following, was preparing to resist a further advance. The detachment of the Battalion detailed to escort the baggage had one man wounded.

On November 3rd, 200 rifles of the Battalion formed part of a small mixed force under Brigadier-General Channer, which set out from Kage

Oba with the object of destroying Pokal. The distance to be traversed was seven miles, and the march entailed a descent of 4,300 feet. For the first two miles the path followed approximately the contour of the hill, and then ran down a narrow spur thickly covered with pine-trees and undergrowth. In places the ground on either side was so precipitous that the skirmishers were obliged to keep to the ridge. This gave an opportunity to the enemy, concealed in the undergrowth, to fire on the column at very close range. Quick to seize their advantage, they caused several casualties, the Battalion losing one man severely wounded. The tables were turned on them, however, when Pokal was reached, for they were caught by our fire while retreating across the open and suffered heavily. The village and its tower were entirely destroyed, the mosque alone being spared, and at 1 p.m. the force began its withdrawal. The Allaiwals followed up closely till within one mile of Kage Oba, but again they were made to pay for their temerity. Brigadier-General Channer, in his despatch, estimated their losses at from 80 to 100 killed. The Battalion digest of services is more conservative, and gives 60 killed and wounded.

Visit to Pokal, Nov. 3rd, 1888.

The destruction of Pokal marked the end of active operations. Leaving Kage Oba on November 3rd, the 1st and 5th Columns reached Maidan on the 4th. A representative jirga of the Pariari Saiyads came in there the same evening, and on the 7th the fine imposed on them was paid in full. It now only remained to withdraw the field force to British territory. The crest of the Black Mountain had already been evacuated; by the 10th the troops from Maidan had been concentrated in Agror, and by the 13th the Indus Valley column had closed on Darband.

Final orders for the dispersal of the force were received on November 11th, and on November 18th the Battalion found itself back in Abottabad.

Dispersal of Expeditionary Force, November, 1888.

One interesting feature of the '88 expedition is the number of residents in British territory who joined the enemy. They came from Hazara, from Rawalpindi, and from as far afield as the Jhelum district. That they were not backward in the fight is proved by the fact that many of these "foreigners" were recognized among the enemy casualties. Few of them can have had anything in common with the tribes against whom the expedition was directed; they stood, apparently, to gain nothing and to lose everything, and the inference is that they were actuated by religious zeal.

It will have become apparent by now that the old Battalion was seldom left for long to enjoy the blessings of peace, but the end of the Black Mountain Expedition of 1888

1889.

did actually mark the beginning of a short respite from the rigours of active service.

During the period of calm which followed, the most interesting event with which the Regiment was connected was Lieutenant Francis Younghusband's exploration of the passes leading through the great divide between Chinese Turkestan and India, from the Karakoram Pass in the east to the Pamirs in the west. The most important objective given to him was the Shimshal Pass, whence the bandits of Hunza had recently issued to raid a caravan passing between Leh and Yarkand, and he was to return down the Hunza Valley through Gilgit to Kashmir. As escort he was given Havildar Surbir Thapa, a naik, and four sepoys of the Regiment. Strangely enough there is no mention of the part played by these men in the records of either battalion, but a full account of the adventurous journey is to be found in Sir Francis Younghusband's "Wonders of the Himalaya," published in 1924. Unfortunately there is room here only for certain incidents which illustrate the impression produced by our men on a young officer of a regiment of British Cavalry, who had previously travelled from Peking to India and had met many types of hillmen and of hardy nomads.

Lieutenant Younghusband's Journey of 1889.

Leaving Abbottabad early in July, 1889, the party marched to Leh by the Sind Valley and the Zoji La. Necessary preparations undertaken at Leh were completed by August 8th, and on that day they set out for the Karakoram Pass (19,000 feet), which was crossed on August 19th. Shahidula, whence the Hunza raiders had carried off a number of Kirghiz, was reached on the 23rd. From there the route lay to the Yarkand River, a tributary of which gave access to an outlying range christened Aghil by Lieutenant Younghusband on his previous journey in search of the Mustagh Pass. From the pass leading through into the Oprang Valley a wonderful view was obtained of the great Karakoram peaks from the north. There lay the main work of exploration, and the greater part of September and half October were passed in a search for possible routes leading from the Oprang, across the great divide, to India. After braving many dangers, the party reached the Shimshal Pass on October 15th. Descending the Hunza Valley but a short way, they retraced their steps and descended to the Yarkand River, preparatory to reconnoitring the passes giving access to Hunza from the Taghdumbash Pamir. *En route* they fell in with the Russian explorer, Captain Grombtchevsky. On November 8th they again crossed into Hunza, this time by the Mintaka Pass, and from there made their way to India.

Now for the part played by the six men of the 5th Gurkhas. Sir Francis Younghusband tells of his visit to Abbottabad to pick up his escort.

"On the parade ground the next morning I found the six Gurkhas drawn up, dressed in their new rough mountain kit. . . . So each, as I finally approved him, gave a broad grin of satisfaction, and was a source of envy to the whole assembled Regiment. . . . As they bundled themselves into their *ekkas* and perched themselves up by the drivers they grinned more broadly than ever, and trotted off amid the wild cheers of their comrades. It was a great send-off. And they deserved it, for they were the sturdiest and stoutest little men in the Regiment."

Not far beyond Domel the cart-road ended and the men were put on ponies. "They are splendid little men on foot, but ponies they knew nothing about, and for some days now they spent their time in tumbling off. But Gurkhas take everything with a grin, and they seemed to get more enjoyment out of falling off than of stopping on."

At Shahidula a Durbar was held, the men wearing their full-dress uniform, and there the leader asked for information about Darwaza, the Hunza Fort guarding the northern exit of the Shimshal Pass. A Khirgiz told him that "the outpost was a fort with a wall on each side of it at the top of a ravine, and that the first man to appear would certainly be shot. This sounded unpleasant, but I turned to the Gurkha corporal and said in chaff that in that case I would send him first." The naik did not forget. On arrival at Darwaza some seven weeks later, Younghusband went forward with three men, leaving the Gurkhas to cover his retreat in case of a hostile reception. "I descended into the ravine, crossed the frozen stream at the bottom, and was proceeding towards the fort when I was joined by the Gurkha corporal, who had run breathlessly after me, saying that at Shahidula I had promised that he should be allowed to go first." After hairbreadth escapes from avalanches while searching for the Saltow Pass, the party reached Suget Jangel in the Oprang Valley. "From there on September 23rd I set out with some of the Gurkhas to explore a great glacier region to the westward. Again heavy snow fell, and we had a cheerless time on the rough moraine, amidst the crevasses and *séracs* of the glacier, with only occasional glimpses of the great peaks of the main range. However, nothing damped the spirits of the Gurkhas. These conditions only seemed to brighten them up, and a joke about looking for some soft stones to lie on kept them in roars of laughter every evening. It had originated in some officer in the Afghan War. But the Gurkhas never tired of it, and the havildar would repeat it with the same success every evening."

When the Russian party was encountered, Captain Grombtchevsky expressed a desire to see our Gurkhas on parade. "I was delighted at the chance of showing them off. So I had up the havildar and told him that in an hour's time he must turn out for inspection by the Russian officer, and go through the manual and firing exercises. I said that the reputation of the whole Indian Army was in his hands, as these were the first Indian troops the Russian had seen. He said, ' Very good, Sahib, we will show the Russian what the Indian Army is like.' And presently they turned out very smart and clean. They were in the finest condition, after all the hard work they had had, and had a splendid soldier-like look about them. And they went through their exercises with the finest precision. The Russian was delighted, and quite taken aback. He said he had not realized that these were regular soldiers. He had imagined that Indian soldiers were irregular. And he asked me to congratulate them.

"When I went to tell the havildar he said, ' I know what the Russian officer has been saying: he has been saying how small we are; but you tell him we are the smallest men in the whole Regiment, and all the rest are taller than he is.' "

In his book Sir Francis Younghusband pays a tribute to the endearing qualities possessed by our men, when he tells of his parting with them. " A few days later I parted with my Gurkhas. Tears were in their eyes as we said good-bye. Before they left the Regiment—so they now informed me—they had been told by their head Native officer that if anything happened to me not one of them was to return alive to bring disgrace upon the Regiment. They had been prepared for any sacrifice, but I had looked after them so well they had had no hardships at all, they said, and they wished to thank me. Rough, sturdy little men they were, but a fund of tender sentiment lay beneath their rough exterior—and, in high moments like our parting, a true gracefulness as well."

Changes among British Officers.

The year 1889 saw changes among the British officer personnel which are not without interest. Colonel Sym went on leave to England in April, and Colonel V. E. Hastings was appointed temporary Commandant in his place. Lieutenant the Honourable C. G. Bruce was posted to the Battalion in May, and joined early in June. In October, Lieutenant J. Manners-Smith left for the political department, where we shall hear of him again before very long, though not in the rôle of a suave and polished diplomat. During Colonel Sym's absence on leave the welcome news arrived that he had been made a Companion of the Bath.

The Lighter Side of Manœuvres, 1889–1890.

Towards the end of the year the Abbottabad Brigade marched down to Rawalpindi to join a camp of exercise, which provided occupation until the end of January, 1890. The occasion is only of importance because it gave rise to a few of those pleasing incidents which, in a close community such as an officers' mess, will raise a smile so long as the memory of them endures. The incident of the bleached bone, the incident of the ban on Mr. B———'s stories, the episode of the metamorphosis of the Colonel's horse, all happened during this camp of exercise.

Mr. Kipling's centurion Parnesius, in conversation with Dan and Una, spoke of " little jokes and sayings that every family has." Regiments have them, too, and as often as not they have no meaning for anyone from outside. On the occasion of a brigade parade there lay on the ground a small, insignificant bone, bleached white by the Punjab sun. The 2nd Battalion were there, commanded temporarily by Colonel Gaselee. The order came to him, " You will dress your Battalion on that bone!" Unable to believe his ears he paused before complying, and narrowly escaped arrest.

The hero of the second incident is still going strong, and does not want his identity disclosed. An attitude so retiring is understandable in one who says of himself at that period of his career, " Ah, me! I was a pale young curate then!" All the officers of both battalions were present in the officers' mess. As happens in such gatherings, weighty matters had been under discussion, when it was seen that the youngest subaltern was about to overcome his natural reticence and speak. The temporary C.O. of the 1st Battalion made haste to ensure his continued silence. He cut in with, " Now then, no more of your stories, Mr. B——."

This same C.O. owned a horse, in colour khaki, with white face, pink nose, and white eyes like a water buffalo. Solicitous for the comfort of the animal, he had procured for its protection on manœuvres a fine new suit of horse-clothing. This, being made of Cawnpore blankets sewn together, was warm and comforting for the quadruped, but the durzi who sewed had introduced a colour scheme of his own. He had bound the edges with tape of that harsh pink touched with mauve so dear to the native heart. The sais—no admirer of beauty unadorned—had extended the scheme to the headstall, and had caused the eye fringe to be dyed in the same shade. There came a night of heavy rain, followed at early dawn by a sound of lamentation in the horse lines. Wondering what had happened, a few of the younger officers went to see.

" To-day," said the saises, " is appointed for the General's parade, and behold, protectors of the poor, the horse of the Colonel Sahib Bahadur." They beheld! The dye had run from his trappings and had spread itself generously over the animal's person. From quarters to withers he was speckled and ringstraked in shades of vermilion and mauve, and his china-white eyes stared stonily from a crimson countenance.

For the young officers it was indeed an alarming spectacle. Though innocent for the nonce, their reputations were such that their most solemn denials would avail them nothing in face of the accusation which would inevitably be brought against them. Their only remedy, to find a means of restoring the horse to its original sub-fuse colouring. First they tried scrubbing, but the dye, so ready to run before, now proved capable of withstanding their utmost efforts. Parade time was approaching, so in desperation they called in the mess barber and ordered him to shave the brute. He did his best with a "cut-throat" razor, but the brute proved unwilling, with the result that his last state was much worse than his first. Fortunately for the young officers the parade was taken by Brigadier-General G. N. Channer, V.C., who had been bidden to luncheon afterwards in the mess. He had noticed —as who would not?—the 100 per cent. disability of the C.O.'s charger, and rightly divined that it was responsible for the trace of thunder in the atmosphere. In his cheery way he set himself to dispel the gloom, and succeeded so well that all ended happily. The lighter side of manœuvres, and of active service, too, would provide material for many a volume well worth reading, but for us it is time to return to more serious matters.

Black Mountain Promenade, October, 1890.

February 8th, 1890, marked the return of the Battalion from Rawalpindi, and when it next left Abbottabad its face was set again towards the Black Mountain.

As one result of the expedition of 1888 the tribes had acknowledged the right of the British to march troops along the crest of the mountain at will. To keep open the right of way Sir John McQueen was ordered to take a small force to the Black Mountain in October, and to obviate causes of friction, jirgahs of all the tribes affected were invited to Abbottabad in September. They refused either to send jirgahs or to stand by their agreement regarding the right of way.

On October 17th, Sir John McQueen marched out of Abbottabad with the Derajat Mountain Battery, 500 rifles of the 4th Sikhs, and 350 rifles from each battalion of the 5th Gurkhas. His instructions were to avoid fighting, while ensuring that tangible evidence should be forthcoming regarding the feeling of the tribes.

Oghi was reached on October 19th, and there the small force found itself storm-bound throughout the two following days. Weather conditions improving, on the 22nd reconnoitring parties were sent up the Barchar and Sambalbat Spurs. On both, enemy parties were in position not far from the crest of the main ridge. Holding that the tribesmen had not yet committed themselves, Sir John, with the greater part of his force, ascended the Barchar Spur on the 23rd, and bivouacked at a point some distance beyond the village. During the night the enemy worked down the spur and fired into the bivouac. Here was the evidence required, and if confirmation were needed, it was furnished next morning, when numbers of tribesmen were seen on the mountain-side above preparing quite obviously to resist a further advance. Orders were then given for a withdrawal to Oghi, and at the same time a letter was sent which made it quite plain to the enemy that for them the evil day was but postponed.

The force was not molested during its descent to the plain. It left Oghi on October 26th, and arrived back in Abbottabad on the 28th.

The day of reckoning came for the Black Mountain tribesmen when the Hazara Field Force was ordered to concentrate at Darband and Oghi by March 1st, 1891. In the expedition which followed, the Regiment was represented by the 2nd Battalion, and an account of its doings during this, its first experience of active service as a battalion, will be found recorded in a later chapter. The main interest of the campaign lies in the strategical plan, for though a small force was sent to Oghi as a precautionary measure, the usual lines of advance up the eastern spurs were abandoned, and the thrust was delivered by two columns operating from Darband.

Black Mountain Expedition of 1891.

To the 1st Battalion was assigned the rôle of remaining in a state of readiness at Abbottabad while holding Oghi with a detachment. The immediate result was that the Battalion lost about half its number of British officers, for all who could, sought active participation in the expedition. Lieutenant Boisragon was attached to the Guides, Lieutenant Fayrer to the 4th Sikhs, Lieutenant Badcock became a brigade transport officer, and Lieutenant Bruce was appointed orderly officer to Sir William Lockhart. In little more than a month they were clamouring to get back; it was a year of small wars, and on April 6th the 1st Battalion was ordered to Miranzai.

The Battalion had passed close to the scene of the projected expedition on its way to the Kurram in the autumn of 1878. Then, however, its objectives lay far afield, and there had been no reason to regard with particular interest the long ridge of the Samana which flanked its line of march on the north, nor yet the succession of valleys and hills interposing between the Samana and the Safed Koh. Now it was to fight in that region, and it is well, therefore, to take a brief survey of the theatre of operations.

Second Miranzai Expedition of 1891.

Travelling towards the Kurram Valley from Kohat, the route lies for a number of miles on the left bank of the Kohat Toi. Fifteen miles west of Kohat, that stream is joined by the Khanki River, and in the angle between them the Samana Ridge has its beginnings, to continue westwards for some twenty miles, at a height of 2,000 to 3,000 feet above the Miranzai Plain. North of the Samana three streams run parallel from west to east: the Khanki, the Mastura, and the Bara. The watersheds between them comprise long parallel ridges, moulded in much the same pattern as the Samana itself, and bounding the horizon on the north stretches the white panorama of the Safed Koh.

Of the inhabitants of this part of the frontier, the several divisions of the Orakzais occupy the Samana, the Khanki Valley, and the greater part of the Mastura Valley beyond; while northward of them the Bara, Bazar, and Khyber Valleys, Maidan and the Kajuri Plain are inhabited by Afridi clans. During January and February of this year (1891) certain Samil sections of the Orakzais had been compelled to make restitution for previous misdemeanours and to tender complete submission by a force under the command of Sir William Lockhart. Under the terms of the agreement entered into at the close of the campaign, they consented to the establishment of British posts and the construction of roads on the Samana Ridge. To give effect to this clause of the agreement, when the punitive column withdrew from Orakzai territory, working parties were left on the Samana, and the 29th Bengal Infantry was detailed for their protection.

Not unnaturally the occupation of the Samana by British troops was regarded by the Orakzais as a whole, and even by a number of sympathizers among the Afridis, as a threat to their independence. They taunted with cowardice those sections which had lately accepted terms, and so worked on their feelings that on April 4th they engineered surprise attacks on the widely separated escorts and drove them from the ridge.

No time was lost in initiating retaliatory measures. Sir William Lockhart was then commanding the reserve brigade of the Hazara Field Force at Darband, on the Indus. Selected to command the troops detailed for the second Miranzai Expedition, he received his orders and left Darband with his staff on April 6th—only two days after the outbreak. On April 7th his brigade began its march to Kohat, accompanied by all its transport.

To return now to the 1/5th Gurkhas in Abbottabad. We have seen that orders reached them on April 6th, but immediate compliance was rendered extremely difficult owing to scarcity of transport. Two days of intense effort, however, saw the problem solved, and on April 8th the Battalion left Abbottabad. Marching by double stages they reached Hasan Abdal on the 9th, and moving thence by train as far as Kushalgarh they arrived in Kohat on April 11th.

Hangu, at the foot of an outlying feature of the main Samana ridge, had been selected as the point of concentration of the expeditionary force. By April 16th the concentration had been completed, and the force had been organized into three columns. Of these the 1st Column was placed under the command of Colonel Sym, the command of the Battalion devolving accordingly on Captain A. R. Martin. At the time of leaving Abbottabad the only other British officers available had been Lieutenants Smart and Philipps and Surgeon Major Nelis, but by the time active operations began Lieutenants Fayrer, Boisragon, and Badcock had rejoined from the Hazara Field Force, Lieutenant Stewart from Burma, and Captain Barrett from the adjutancy of the Calcutta Volunteers. The strength of the Battalion was just over 600.

In the operations which followed we are mainly concerned with the activities of Colonel Sym's column, composed of No. 3 Mountain Battery R.A., 1st Battalion King's Royal Rifles, half No. 5 Company Bengal Sappers and Miners, 1st Punjab Infantry, 27th Bengal Infantry, and 1st Battalion 5th Gurkhas.

Capture of Samana, April 17th–20th, 1891.
On April 17th the advance began, the 1st Column moving direct on Lakka, on the crest of the Samana, and the other two columns skirting the base of the ridge as far as Darband. The 1st Column, led by the 1/5th Gurkhas, reached Lakka unopposed, and from there Sir William Lockhart directed the 2nd Column on to the Darband Kotal, and the 3rd Column on to Sangar. The route of the 1st Column now lay along the crest of the ridge. On reaching the Darband Kotal it was found that the 2nd Column had arrived, and strengthened by the addition of the 27th Bengal Infantry, it was sent on down to Gwada, a village due north of Sangar on the right bank of the Khanki.

The 1st Column then continued its advance, and on reaching Tsalai found itself opposed by small parties of the enemy strongly posted among rocks. The King's Royal Rifles, who were now leading, took the position in their stride, but with the loss of their Colonel, wounded, and of several of their men. From Tsalai it did not take long to reach Sangar, where the 3rd Column was encountered, and there they bivouacked for the night.

Mastan is the name given to that part of the Samana interposing between Sartop and Gulistan. It may be described as a narrow, undulating plateau, opening out in places to a breadth of several hundred yards, rocky for the most part, and covered here and there with coarse grass and scrub, which holds an infrequent black partridge and an occasional hare. It fell to a combined movement of the 1st and 3rd Columns carried out on April 18th. There was a sharp skirmish when Sartop was reached, resulting in casualties on both sides, but, the Battalion having but a small part to play, its details need not concern us. At the end of the day the 3rd Column was left to hold Mastan, and the 1st Column returned to Sangar.

Owing to difficulty in supplying the 2nd Column down in the valley at Gwada, it was moved up to Sangar on the 19th. On that day the 1st Column remained halted, but the 3rd Column found itself opposed to large bodies of tribesmen who had collected with the object of recapturing the ridge. When evening fell the column was disposed along the plateau, facing north, its right on Sartop and its left on the cliffs of Saragarhi. Owing to the wide distribution of his command, Colonel Brownlow found himself without an adequate striking-force. On April 20th, therefore, he demanded reinforcements, and there were sent up to him from Sangar the Peshawar Mountain Battery, the 2nd Punjab Infantry, and four companies each from the King's Royal Rifle Corps and 1/5th Gurkhas.

These reinforcements reached Colonel Brownlow at a point east of Saragarhi at about 1.30 p.m. He at once made dispositions for an attack on Saragarhi, to be carried out by the 1/5th Gurkhas with the King's Royal Rifle Corps in support, and arranged for a simultaneous assault on the neighbouring village of Ghuztang.

The instructions given to Captain Martin were to attack the village of Saragarhi and clear it of the enemy. Then to capture and clear the hills beyond, and to hold on to his position during the time required for the destruction of the towers in Saragarhi.

Now Captain Martin was a past master of the art of mountain warfare, with a particular penchant for the *arme blanche*. Making a rapid study of the ground he directed his leading companies to advance by a covered way. Supported by the fire of the mountain battery they succeeded in getting close to the enemy before their movement was detected. Then, while the skirmishing companies dashed forward with fixed bayonets, the remainder opened a devastating fire at short range on the tribesmen thus taken by surprise. The piquets surrounding the village were taken at the charge, the half-battalion swept through, and the enemy fled in all directions, leaving their dead and wounded on the ground and throwing away their rifles as they ran. The momentum of their spirited advance carried the men of the 1/5th Gurkhas beyond the village and straight through to the hills on the far side. These they held while Saragarhi and Ghuztang were destroyed with their towers, and then, the work completed, they returned to Sangar.

The whole affair had lasted but half an hour. The losses in the Battalion were only two men seriously wounded, while the enemy casualties numbered about 60 killed and 240 wounded. This phenomenal success was due to the element of surprise introduced into the original plan of attack, the *élan* displayed by the men, and the terror inspired in the enemy by the threat of the bayonet. Short as the action was, and few as were our casualties, April 20th is deservedly kept as a regimental holiday.

Before returning to join the rest of the 1st Column at Sangar the Battalion received the warm thanks of Colonel Brownlow, commanding the 3rd Column. Besides Captain Martin, those who took part in the action were Captain Barrett, Lieutenants Philipps, Boisragon, and Currie (attached from the 2nd Sikhs), and Surgeon Major Nelis.

For Colonel Sym's column the next few days proved uneventful. The 2nd and 3rd Columns were employed in operations beyond Gulistan in the vicinity of the Chagru Kotal, and a number of villages on the northern slopes of the ridge were destroyed. These measures were not without effect, for the Afridis, some of whom had opposed the 2nd Column on April 23rd, sent in a jirgah on the 24th, and terms were also made with one or two sections of the Orakzais.

Visit to Sheikhan, April 29th– May 3rd, 1891.

Sir William Lockhart had intended, after dealing with the Samana villages, to visit the head of the Khanki Valley. Hearing, however, that the Alisherzai and Mamuzai sections of the Orakzais were inclined to tender their submission, he decided to improve the occasion by first showing the flag in their country of Sheikhan. The settlements in this tract are to be found clustered for the most part in the Lagardara and Daradar Valleys, of which the former runs parallel to the Khanki, joining the Kohat Toi at Ustarzai, and the latter runs from north to south past the head of the Lagardara valley, and joins the Khanki directly below the point where Fort Lockhart now stands. Access from the Lagardara into the Daradar Valley is by the Kharai Pass.

The 1st Column was destined for this operation, but before orders were actually issued, on April 27th two companies of the Battalion, under Lieutenant Boisragon, marched from Sangar to relieve the 1/4th Gurkhas in the posts on the lines of communication at Hangu and Chikarkot. The distance from Sangar to Chikarkot by the only route suitable for transport was twenty-six miles, and the country was now sweltering through the early days of the hot weather. Bearing these circumstance in mind it becomes apparent that the march was a severe test of endurance for the company taken by Lieutenant Boisragon to Chikarkot. The post was reached at 9.30 p.m. The detachments had no sooner entered on their new duties than it became necessary to recall them, for on April 28th the 1st Column, and with it the 1/5th Gurkhas, concentrated at Hangu, ready for the projected visit to Sheikhan. Starting in the heat of the day, Lieutenant Boisragon with the one company retraced his steps for fifteen miles to Hangu, arriving there at 8 p.m. Though they had covered forty-two miles in thirty-six hours under far from favourable conditions, they were quite ready to leave Hangu with the column next morning.

Little interest attaches to the Sheikhan visit, apart from that which lies in the sight of new country. On April 29th the column, accompanied by Sir William Lockhart, reached Mir Ashgar. From there it ascended the Lagardara Valley, halting on successive days at Dran and the Kharai Pass, and destroying *en route* the towers of Lagardara and Dran. During the night spent on the pass it rained in torrents, and it was without regret that the column began the descent into the Daradar Valley on May 2nd, and marched to Star Kili. Leaving there the greater part of his force, Colonel Sym with an escort moved up to the Nakatu Pass at the head of the valley, destroyed a tower in Takhtak Village on the far side, as an answer to threats uttered by the inhabitants, and returned before dark to Star Kili. The force, having completed its mission, marched to Gwada on May 3rd, and from there made its way back to Sangar.

The conclusion of the operation marked the end of active participation by the Battalion in the campaign. Soon after Sir William Lockhart's return to the Samana all important sections of the Orakzais either accepted terms or made overtures for peace. It remained only to complete the punishment of the Mishti clan by destroying the towers of Khandi Mishti in the presence of the assembled jirgahs, and to prove to the tribes living at the head of the Khanki Valley that none was beyond the reach of retaliation, by a march to the Alisherzai Kotal, which connects the head waters of the Khanki with the Kharmana Valley. To carry out his project Sir William Lockhart employed the 2nd Column, which left Gulistan on May 10th and returned, its object successfully accomplished, on the 15th. During its absence the Battalion was attached to the 3rd Column holding Mastan, and it rejoined Colonel Sym's force at Sangar on May 16th.

End of Miranzai Expedition, June, 1891.
The second Miranzai Expedition may be written down as one of the most successful small wars ever fought on the frontier. For the Field Force no further work could be found, and orders were issued for its gradual dispersal. The Battalion left the Samana on June 7th, and arrived back in Abbottabad on the 14th.

For his part in the expedition the services of Colonel Sym were brought to special notice. Sir William Lockhart wrote in his despatch:—

"Colonel J. M. Sym, C.B., 5th Gurkha Regiment, commanded the 1st Column and maintained his reputation as a good soldier in the field. His ability and war experience have always made me feel that any work entrusted to him would be thoroughly and satisfactorily carried out."

Captain Martin and Lieutenant Bruce, the latter in his capacity of orderly officer to the G.O.C., were also mentioned in despatches.

Hunza-Nagir Expedition, 1891–1892.
From the sun-baked rocks of the Samana and the heat of the Miranzai Plain, the scene changes to the snows and glaciers of the stupendous mountain masses in the most northerly corner of Kashmir. By way of introduction to the story of a detachment of the

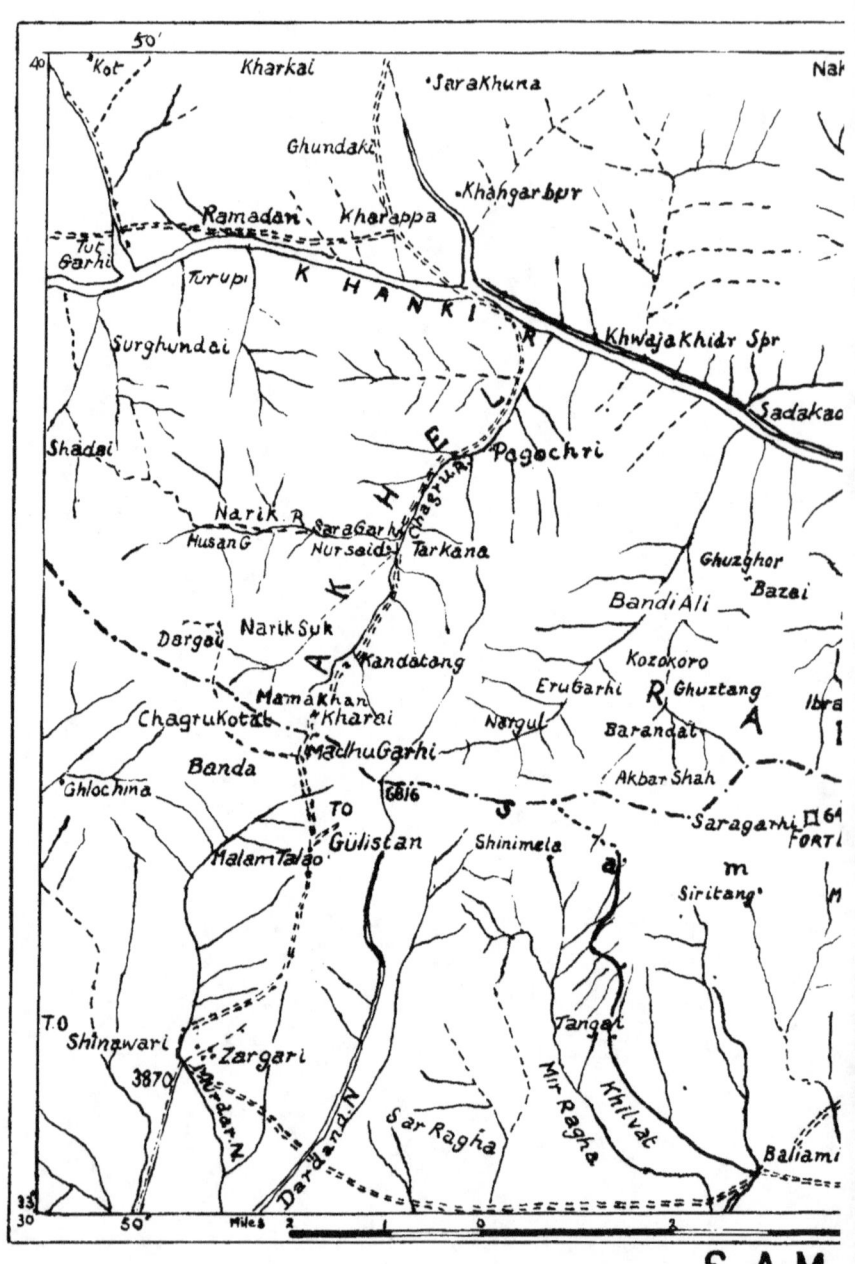

SAM

(Taken from Vol II. Frontier and
Note. Crest of Samana Ridge i

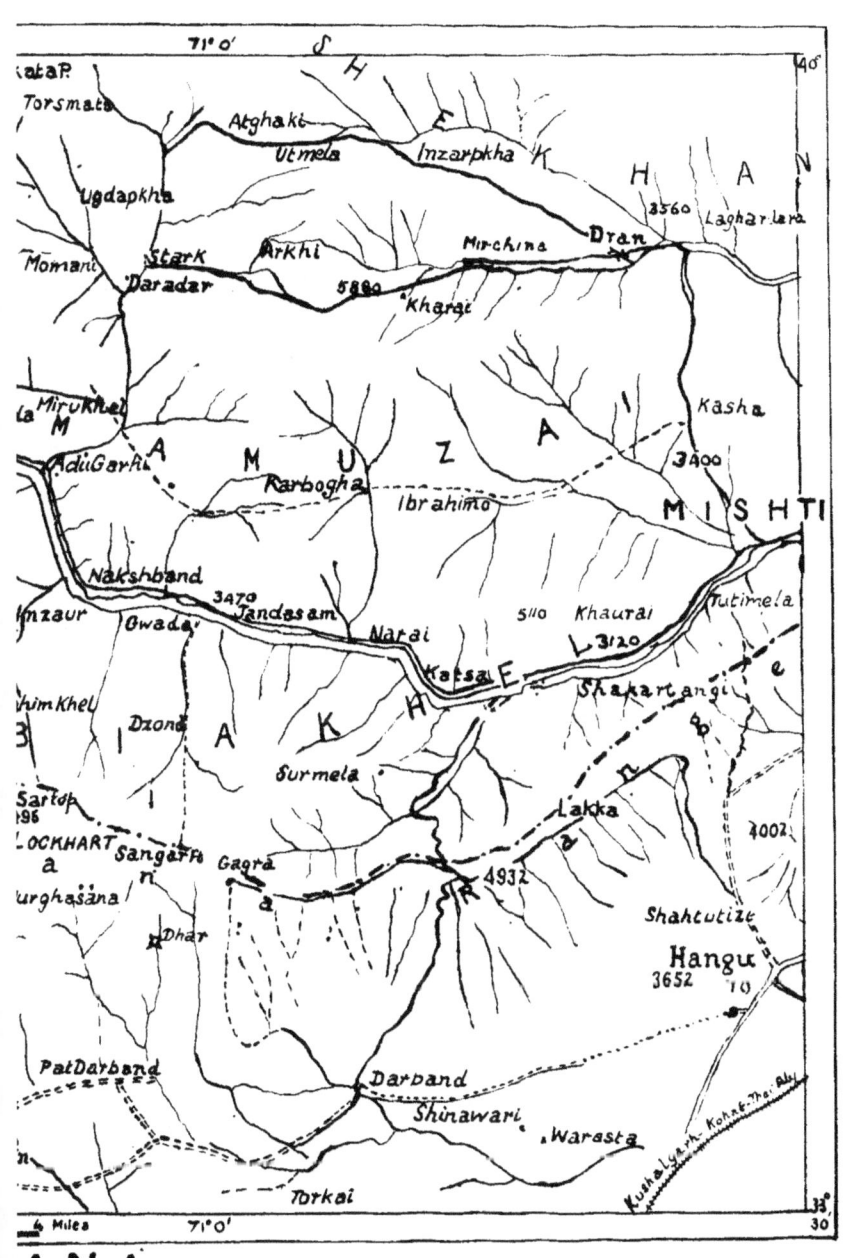

ANA.
(Overseas Expeditions from India)
indicated by chain-dotted line.

Battalion in the Hunza-Nagir Expedition, an experience which befell Lieutenant J. M. Stewart in the autumn of 1891 is well worth telling. It is given in his own words. "Manners-Smith and I were both in Gilgit on special duty. Colonel Sym allowed me to go provided I returned to take up the adjutancy when he handed over the command to Colonel Gaselee. I returned in October and met our detachment crossing the Burzil on their way up. The weather was terrible, and it was then that Barrett lost some of his toes from frostbite, and Badcock also was considerably affected by the cold.

"I had rather an interesting experience just before. The Russians had come down on to the Pamirs, and a small party had crossed the Hindu Kush, and even compelled Frank Younghusband, then our agent in Yarkand and Kashgar, to withdraw from the Taghdumbash Pamir. I was sent up by Algie Durand with a few Pathans of the 20th P.I. and my two Gurkha orderlies to safeguard him, as he had no armed men with him. My orders were to insist on the withdrawal of the Russians and, if necessary, to fire on them. What an international incident that might have provoked! But they disappeared before I arrived, and so I lost possible celebrity."

The incident here recorded, besides placing us geographically, puts us into direct connection with the events about to be described, for the importance to us of the passes from Hunza to the Pamirs, and the favour shown by the Kanjutis to the Russians at British expense in the matter of access to them, were among the causes leading to the expedition.

Kanjut Country and People.
A study of the map of northern Kashmir will show the Hunza (Kanjut) River rising at the western end of the Karakoram Range, and flowing generally south to join the Gilgit River a short distance below Gilgit post. At Nagir it makes a sharp bend to the west, and flows for some twenty miles in that direction to Chalt before again turning south towards Gilgit. Between its head waters and Chalt the country on its right bank is Hunza territory, while that on the left bank belongs to Nagir. Access to this out-of-the-way corner from Kashmir is over the Tragbal and Burzil Passes, down into the Indus Valley at Bunji—unbearably hot in summer—and then up the Gilgit River to its junction with the Hunza River.

For many years the people of Hunza and Nagir, though often at odds with each other, had combined on occasion to give trouble to the Kashmir Durbar, which, up to recent years, had proved quite incapable of dealing with them. They acknowledged no master, though conceding to China a certain right of interference in their affairs, were not above listening to the blandishments of Captain Grombtchevsky and his Cossacks, raided freely into British territory for slaves, and, especially in the case of the Hunza Tham, had a sense of their own importance amounting to the ludicrous. This last was largely fostered by the ease and impunity with which they gathered in the wealth of the caravans plying between Leh and Yarkand. The military ineptitude of Kashmir had led to the re-establishment, in 1889, of the Gilgit Agency, and at the same time special service officers had been deputed to organize and train the Dogras and Gurkhas of the Kashmir Imperial Service troops. By 1891 the military situation had improved to an extent which justified the employment in the field of the Imperial Service troops backed only by a small number of regulars. A pretext for their employment was to be found in the continued misbehaviour of the Thams (rulers) of Hunza and Nagir, which culminated in May, 1891, in an abortive enterprise against the Kashmir outposts of Chalt and Chaprot.

In September, therefore, the Thams were informed that the time had come to make roads through their country, and that if they chose to resist they must take the consequences. In anticipation of resistance a section of the Hazara Mountain Battery and a detachment, 200 strong, of the 1/5th Gurkhas were ordered to Gilgit from Abbottabad.

Captain Barrett was detailed to command the detachment of the Battalion, and with him were Lieutenants Boisragon and Badcock. Lieutenant Gorton, R.A., was in command of the section of the mountain battery. They left Abbottabad on October 4th, and on the 14th reached the foot of the ascent to the Tragbal Pass.

Crossing of Burzil Pass, Oct. 26th, 1891. The crossing of the passes so late in the season was a risky undertaking. Both the Tragbal (11,800 feet) and the Burzil (13,500 feet) boast long, exposed stretches liable to be swept by devastating blizzards which, at their worst, give no hope of survival for man or beast caught in the icy blast. It was therefore necessary to take precautions. The small force was divided into three parties: the first under Captain Kemball, of the 2nd Battalion, who was going to Bunji on special duty; the second under Lieutenant Gorton; and the third under Captain Barrett himself, assisted by Lieutenant Boisragon.

The first two parties succeeded in crossing both passes without serious mishap, though there were a few casualties from frostbite. The third party was less fortunate. When it arrived at the Kashmir end of the Burzil Pass on October 25th, the weather was threatening. Arrangements were made with the Tahsildar of Gurais for the provision of ponies to go in front and tread a path through the deep snow. These, however, did not materialize, and the passage had to be made without their help. The detachment reached the long, exposed down which is the pass, to find that a blizzard was blowing strongly. Somewhere beneath the thick mantle of snow ran the road lately constructed by Spedding and Company: the trouble was to find it. From the first, difficulty was experienced with the baggage mules, which wandered constantly into the deep drifts on either side, and could only be set on their way again by dint of the most strenuous exertions. Early, too, many of the drivers began to fail, and the escort had a hard task to keep them moving. It was noon when the head of the column reached the summit of the pass, and the descent to Chilam Chiki began. Progress, beset with difficulties before, now became increasingly arduous. As the afternoon wore on, the cold became intense; it began to freeze hard and the wind was bitter. The track became a slide of ice; every animal in the train fell down not once nor twice but scores of times, and for the escort the labour seemed endless of unloading, heaving the unfortunate animals to their feet, and loading up again. Evening came, night followed, and through the darkness the slow advance must continue, for to halt there meant death from exposure. It was 1.30 a.m. when the head of the column reached camp, and the rear-guard, after a night of ceaseless effort, arrived some hours after sunrise. The blizzard had taken a heavy toll of the detachment. Captain Barrett himself was among those who suffered most severely. He was on the sick list for five months, and lost several of his toes. Of fighting men twenty-nine were frostbitten, four being incapacitated for further service, and eight of the regimental followers were also affected. Among the mule drivers there were no less than fifty-three cases of frostbite, and of this number several died from the effects.

Composition of Force. The passes once negotiated, no further marching difficulties were encountered. On November 6th, Lieutenant Badcock, who had been left behind at Baramulla to bring on a Gatling gun, caught up the detachment at Astor. Gilgit, the headquarters of the Agency, was reached on or about November 15th, and there, to his own chagrin and the regret of all ranks, Captain Barrett had to remain with the remainder of the sick until they could be evacuated. From Gilgit the detachment, now commanded by Lieutenant Boisragon, moved in two parties to Chalt. Of these the first arrived on November 21st and the second on the 29th, by which latter date the whole field force was assembled there, ready to advance. The composition of the Hunza-Nagir Field Force was unusual. Besides the troops from Abbottabad the only regulars were about half a dozen Bengal Sappers and less than 30 rifles of the agency escort which had been provided by the 20th Punjab Infantry. The Raghu Pertab and Bodyguard Regiments of Kashmir Infantry and the Puniali Levy made up the remainder, and brought the fighting strength of the force to a total of about 1,130 rifles. In addition, 200 of Spedding's Pathans, working on the road, had been armed and enrolled to form an engineering corps. Lieutenant-Colonel Algie Durand was in command, Captain Twigg was D.A.A.G., Captain Colin

Mackenzie was D.A.Q.M.G., Captain Fenton Aylmer was commanding R.E., Captain Stewart and Lieutenant Manners-Smith were Political Officers, and Surgeon-Captain Roberts was Principal Medical Officer.

The day on which concentration was completed (November 29th) saw the despatch of Colonel Durand's ultimatum to the Thams. Their answer, received on the 30th, breathed defiance, and the decision was taken to deal a first blow against the pseudo-sanctity of Kanjut territory by capturing the fort of Nilt.

Advance from Chalt, Dec. 1st, 1891.

Chalt, the point of concentration, is situated on the right bank of the Hunza River, whereas Nilt is about nine miles upstream on the left bank. The crossing was effected on December 1st after the seizure, unopposed, of a kotal in the ridge which abuts on the right-angled bend made by the river at this point. On December 2nd the *reveillé* sounded at 5 a.m., and by daybreak the head of the column was approaching the saddle. It was a fine day, and in the light of early morning the fort of Nilt, away to the east, was presently visible from the top of the kotal. It stood among terraced fields on the very edge of a high cliff overlooking the river-bed. Behind it the deeply cut ravine of Nilt ran down from the Rakaposhi Glacier to join the river, and beyond was a background of mighty hills, their lower slopes precipitous and bare, but crowned towards their crests by growths of pine. The route to be followed by the attacking force, after descending steeply from the kotal, lay across a flat interposed between the hills and the river. Broad to start with, the flat narrowed gradually as Nilt was approached, until, at a point about 300 yards from the fort, where a subsidiary spur encroached from the main feature, it was only some sixty yards wide. This spur shut out all view of the fort from the flat ground to the west of it. Upstream of Nilt, on the right bank of the river, was Maiun; standing at the junction of another big ravine with the Hunza River, and facing Maiun, on the same side as Nilt, was the fortress of Thol.

Storming of Nilt, Dec. 2nd, 1891.

The little force, with its numbers of baggage coolies and mules, wound its way over the kotal and on to the flat beyond. There a halt was called to allow the rear to close up, and when the troops again advanced they formed on to a broad front in line of columns. Two deep *nullahs* traversed the plain from right to left, and at both the path had been cut away, converting them into formidable obstacles. It was after one o'clock when the men of the 1/5th Gurkhas, who were leading, drew level with the projecting spur and sighted the fort in front of them. They at once came under the well-aimed fire of the defenders, but advancing by section rushes they succeeded in reaching a position from which they could shoot at the loopholes of the fort at close range. On their right the Puniali levies, with the backing of the

The Nilt Position.
(From a Photograph presented by F. H. Bridges.)

handful of men belonging to the 20th Punjab Infantry, were led by Captain Colin Mackenzie and Lieutenant Manners-Smith to the top of the projecting spur. From that vantage-point they commanded the interior of the fort, but they could help but little towards further progress, for the defenders manning the loopholes were out of sight, and the rest wisely remained under cover of the bullet-proof buildings. The guns, unable to follow the Punialis owing to the precipitous character of the spur, opened fire from a bluff overlooking the river on the left, but their shells proved useless against those stout walls.

For the moment it seemed that an impasse had been reached. In front was the fort, its walls 14 feet high and 8 feet thick, built of stone cemented with mud and strongly reinforced with stout baulks of timber. It stood four-square with flanking towers at the angles and midway along each face. There was but one entrance to it—a gateway at the south-west corner—but this, again, was screened by a second wall, 8 feet high and loopholed for musketry. Further protection was afforded by a steep-sided ravine, running along outside the curtain wall, which had been filled with branches to form a dense abatis. Another abatis had been constructed to block the space between the south-west corner and the projecting spur. On the left a high cliff fell sheer to the river-bed; behind was the perpendicular descent to the Nilt Ravine, and on the right rose the hills.

A situation so desperate demanded desperate measures to meet it. Lieutenant Boisragon, with the men of the 1/5th Gurkhas, was ordered to take the fort by assault after Captain Aylmer, accompanying him with his sappers, had blown in the gate. Colonel Durand had only just issued his orders when he was seriously wounded, and the command of the force devolved on Captain Bradshaw.

The moment they learnt what was required of them the Gurkhas rushed forward to assault the western wall of the fort, but were soon checked at the abatis. A party of half a dozen, with whom were Lieutenant Boisragon and Captain Aylmer, hacked a way through with their *khukris*, and then, finding shelter as best they could from the fire of the defenders, delivered at almost point-blank range, worked their way round to the small gate leading through the outer wall. This they quickly battered down, to find themselves faced by the main entrance, strongly constructed of timber, heavily barricaded with stones, provided with loopholes through which the enemy was shooting busily on to the ground in front, and recessed back from its flanking towers, from which a cross-fire was brought to bear on the same point. Miraculously the members of the small party were spared to carry out the remainder of their task. While Lieutenant Boisragon and his half-dozen Gurkhas neutralized as far as possible the fire from the gate and the flanking towers, Captain Aylmer ran in with Sapper Hazara Singh, placed his slabs of gun-cotton, tamped them with stones and lit the fuse. While engaged in this act of heroism he was wounded in the leg—the range so close that his clothes and skin were seared by the flash of the powder, but with the help of his devoted henchman he succeeded in crawling to a safe distance, under the shelter of the inner wall, to await the explosion. To the disappointment of those who waited there, tensely expectant, nothing happened, for the fuse proved faulty. Captain Aylmer, a second time braving certain death, crawled back and again ignited the charge. Again he was wounded, his hand crushed to pulp under the weight of a great stone dropped from the wall above. This time his heroism was rewarded; there followed a deafening report, stones and fragments of wood filled the air, and under cover of the cloud of dust the men of the 1/5th Gurkhas carried the breach.

Up to this moment only the two officers with their diminutive following had succeeded in reaching the gate. They were now joined by Lieutenant Badcock and a few more men, who found their way through the abatis just as this critical stage in the assault was reached. Of the rest, while the majority of the 1/5th detachment still strove to penetrate the obstacle, the guns and the covering party, unaware that the gate had been breached, maintained a heavy fire on the defences, while Captain Colin Mackenzie, Captain Twigg, and Lieutenant Manners-Smith, with a few of the 20th Punjab Infantry, gained the ditch on the south side.

For the party at the breach a fierce hand-to-hand conflict ensued in the narrow alley-way leading from the gate to the interior of the fort. Sepoy Kharak Sing Thapa and Sepoy Bahadur Rana were killed almost at once, and several others were wounded. Captain Aylmer, despite his wounds, killed several of the enemy before, faint with pain, he was carried back to the shelter of the ditch outside. With their numbers so depleted, it became only too evident that the devoted handful would be unable to carry the fort; indeed, nothing but their grim determination enabled them to retain their hold on the position already won. Leaving Lieutenant Badcock to contest the gateway, Lieutenant Boisragon went to collect reinforcements. A most hazardous undertaking it proved, for he must again run the gauntlet of fire from the gateway towers, must brave the bullets and shells of his friends still shooting briskly at the fort, and must wander from group to group beyond the abatis, a target for the Kanjut marksmen still manning the loopholes only a few yards away. That he returned unscathed from his errand is one of the incredible facts of that incredible afternoon. During his absence Lieutenant Badcock had been hard put to it to maintain his position. Picking up a rifle he shot down some of the enemy who pressed on him and his party in the narrow alley, then, heading a counter-charge, he drove the assailants back into the maze of the interior. During this spirited encounter he was severely wounded in the arm, but his dash and courage had their reward, for Lieutenant Boisragon arrived with reinforcements to find the gateway still held.

The detachment of the 1/5th Gurkhas now surged into the network of passages inside the stronghold, to be followed soon by the men of the Kashmir regiments. On the part of the enemy a general withdrawal began to the formidable defences sited on the far side of the Nilt Nullah. A few of the more daring spirits remained to contest final possession of the stronghold, some to be captured, others to be driven from one place of hiding to the next, until, ere evening fell, the place was clear.

Colonel Durand's original intention had been to push on a part of his force with the object of gaining a footing on the right bank of the Nilt Ravine. The enemy had foreseen this possibility, and had guarded against it by cutting away all paths leading down the precipitous left bank to the *nullah* bed below. A further advance was therefore postponed, and Captain Bradshaw contented himself with sending up the guns to pound a strong sangar situated on the far side to guard the crossing. Then, leaving a strong detachment to hold the fort, he collected the rest of the force to camp in the terraced fields about half a mile distant from the post.

Small as were the forces engaged, the capture of Nilt deservedly ranks high among the achievements of the Regiment. Out of a total of 3 killed and 32 wounded in the entire force, the detachment of the 5th Gurkhas lost 2 killed, 2 died of wounds, and 20 wounded. The wounded included Lieutenant Badcock and Jemadar Jangia Thapa. No less than nine men of the Regiment gained the Indian Order of Merit "for conspicuous gallantry displayed at the storming of Nilt." For his part in the affair Lieutenant Badcock received the Distinguished Service Order, while on Lieutenant Boisragon was conferred the most coveted distinction of all—the Victoria Cross. Of those outside the Regiment, Captain Aylmer also gained the award "for Valour," and it will be conceded that the distinction can seldom have been better earned.

The anxious period which followed the storming of Nilt may be described in the words of Colonel Durand's despatch.

Checked before Thol-Maiun Position, Dec. 3rd–9th, 1891.

"The force was halted for the night at Nilt. In front of it was the great ravine rising from the river-bed to the glaciers some thousands of feet above. The far bank was lined with sangars which commanded every possible track up it. Its height varies from 600 feet, where it joins the river bank, to 1,200 feet, and it is absolutely precipitous. To the left of the force ran the Hunza River, on the opposite bank of which was the strongly fortified place of Maiun, standing on the high cliff of the river and full of men. Half a mile up the river on the left bank was a strongly fortified *ziarat*, from which to the junction of the great ravine ran one continuous line of sangars.

"During the night all the sangars were strongly reinforced, and those exposed to shell fire were provided with such heavy roofs as to defy the seven-pounders.

"On the morning of December 3rd an advance was attempted, but was abandoned after a loss of one man killed and seven wounded, including Lieutenant Gorton, R.A.

"Every sangar on the opposite hill was held in great force. The path leading down from the fort was precipitous, impassable for mules, and swept from end to end by a searching fire, while the path by which the enemy had fled the day before, and which ran up a cliff on to the cultivated land above the river, had been broken away and encumbered with abatis. It was, moreover, barred by a large sangar holding about a hundred men, which during the night had been so strengthened as to be bomb-proof.

"In this difficult position the force remained for seventeen days stationary, whilst endeavours were made to find a means of attacking Maiun on the opposite bank of the river."

In the end it was not by Maiun that the advance was made. Among those who were employed night after night in searching for possible lines of attack was a Dogra sepoy of the Kashmir Bodyguard Regiment. His name was Nagdu.

Attack on Thol Cliffs, Dec. 20th, 1891.

After much patient study of the ground he concluded that a way existed, possible for cragsmen, though extremely hazardous, up the face of the cliffs immediately facing the blockhouse constructed on the crest of the projecting spur above the fort of Nilt. His first attempt, when he set out by night with a dozen men to capture a sangar, was a failure, owing to the vigilance of the enemy, but, nothing daunted, he tried another line, and succeeded in reaching a point close to four enemy sangars which overlooked a scar on the face of the hill made by the rolling down of showers of rocks. When he reported his discovery, Captain Colin Mackenzie, who commanded in the temporary absence of Captain Bradshaw, decided to attempt the storming of the sangars by this difficult approach. It was at best a desperate venture, but no better solution could be found and the need was great. Encouraged by the long delay, the Kanjut tribesmen were planning a raid on the lines of communication, and it was known that the dwellers in the Yasin Valley had composed for the moment their perennial differences, and were preparing to combine against us.

The plan of attack was simple. On the night chosen, before moonrise at 10 p.m., Lieutenant Manners-Smith, accompanied by Lieutenant Taylor, was to lead out 100 men of the Bodyguard Regiment, and, under, cover of darkness, to reach a point in the Nilt Ravine immediately below the four sangars overlooking the declivity explored by Nagdu. With the coming of daylight this party was to climb the cliff and assault the enemy breastworks, what time a detachment of picked shots covered their movement from a position on the projecting spur above Nilt Fort.

At 7 p.m. on December 19th Manners-Smith paraded his men, and started for the selected hiding-place in the ravine. Nerves were on the stretch, and there was momentary consternation among those left behind when, an hour later, shouts and the sounds of tom-toms were heard from the direction of Maiun. The relief was great when these soon resolved themselves into the noise of an ordinary merrymaking, evidence that the first important move was undetected, and ground for hope that the defenders of the sangars would be less vigilant than heretofore.

Well before daylight on the 20th the covering detachment left camp to take up positions on the projecting spur. It consisted of 50 rifles of the 5th Gurkhas, 25 of the 20th Punjab Infantry, and 60 taken from the Kashmir regiments, and was divided into four parties, each to concentrate its fire on one sangar. In addition there were the two seven-pounder guns.

Dawn comes late at this time of year in the valleys enclosed by these stupendous hills. It was 8 a.m. before there was light enough to see clearly, and at that time fire was opened on the four sangars across the ravine. Soon after the climbers left their shelter and embarked on the ascent. So steep was the cliff that they remained hidden from the occupants of the breastworks above them and from the defenders on either side. The sangars which formed their objective were situated at a height of more than 1,200 feet above the bed of the ravine. Watched anxiously by their comrades across the *nullah*, they surmounted laboriously one difficulty after another, until with only 400 feet still to be negotiated the advance party of fifty Gurkhas with Manners-Smith faltered, cast right and left, and finally came to a standstill. The cliff above them rose sheer, and there was no way up even for the most skilled of cragsmen. Descending to the *nullah*, at 10 a.m. they made a fresh attempt by a different route. This time no impassable obstacle barred their path, and the leading men reached a point only sixty yards distant from the nearest sangar. Only then was the movement of the storming party discovered by the enemy. They were seen first by the occupants of Maiun Fort, who gave the alarm by beating tom-toms, and whose message, shouted from breastwork to breastwork, presently reached the defenders of the four sangars which formed the extreme left of the hostile position. These, spurred to greater energy by the danger confronting them, showed courage and resource, and some of them, braving the intense fire of the covering party, left the shelter of their sangars to release the piles of rocks kept ready against just such an emergency. It was fortunate that those taking part in the assault had already quitted the points most exposed to these stone avalanches, but, even so, a few were wounded.

Displaying great coolness and judgment, Lieutenant Manners-Smith worked forward gradually towards the objective. Seizing every chance that offered, with the foremost of his men he presently reached the comparatively flat ground on which the sangars were sited. Of these the first was rapidly surrounded, shots were fired through the opening in its rear, and with no further preliminary a rush was made for the interior. Among the first to enter was Lieutenant Manners-Smith's orderly, Harkia Thapa by name, whose conspicuous gallantry earned for him the award of the Indian Order of Merit. Of the defenders a number was killed before they could effect their escape, and of those who fled, several were accounted for by the fire of the covering detachment and of the parties stationed in the fort of Nilt. With the arrival of more men from below, the remaining three sangars were cleared, and then no time was lost in dealing with the neighbouring breastworks on the mountain-side. The effect of this brilliant coup was completely to turn the enemy's left flank and to threaten his retreat. Realization of this came almost at once. Long lines of fugitives could be seen streaming up the valley from the strong places of the *Ziarat*, Maiun, and Thol.

No sooner was the success of the assaulting party assured than orders were given for pursuit. Detachments were sent to deal with Thol and Maiun, and leaving a minimum garrison for the fort at Nilt, the rest of the force, led by the men of the 5th Gurkhas, pushed rapidly up the valley and reached Pisan, seven miles distant from Nilt.

End of Enemy Resistance.
The action of December 20th brought about the final collapse of enemy resistance. The big lower sangar immediately opposite Nilt Fort was surrendered by its occupants, numbering nearly one hundred, without resistance, and a strong position just west of Pisan was abandoned precipitately on the approach of our troops.

To Lieutenant Manners-Smith was made the coveted award of the Victoria Cross. On his skill as a climber, on his great personal courage, and, even more, on his determined spirit which refused to entertain the idea of failure, had depended the success of the enterprise, and seldom, indeed, has the distinction been better earned. Considering the scale of the operations the enemy losses were heavy. More than 100 dead were counted on the Nagir side of the river alone, and 118 prisoners were taken. The casualties on our side were almost negligible.

On December 21st a small force, in which were included one hundred men of the Battalion, made a forced march of twenty-seven miles to Nagir, receiving, *en route*, the submission of the Tham of Nagir. His ally of Hunza had fled, pursued by a band of his own warriors, and on the 22nd, Baltit, the Hunza capital, was occupied by a detachment of

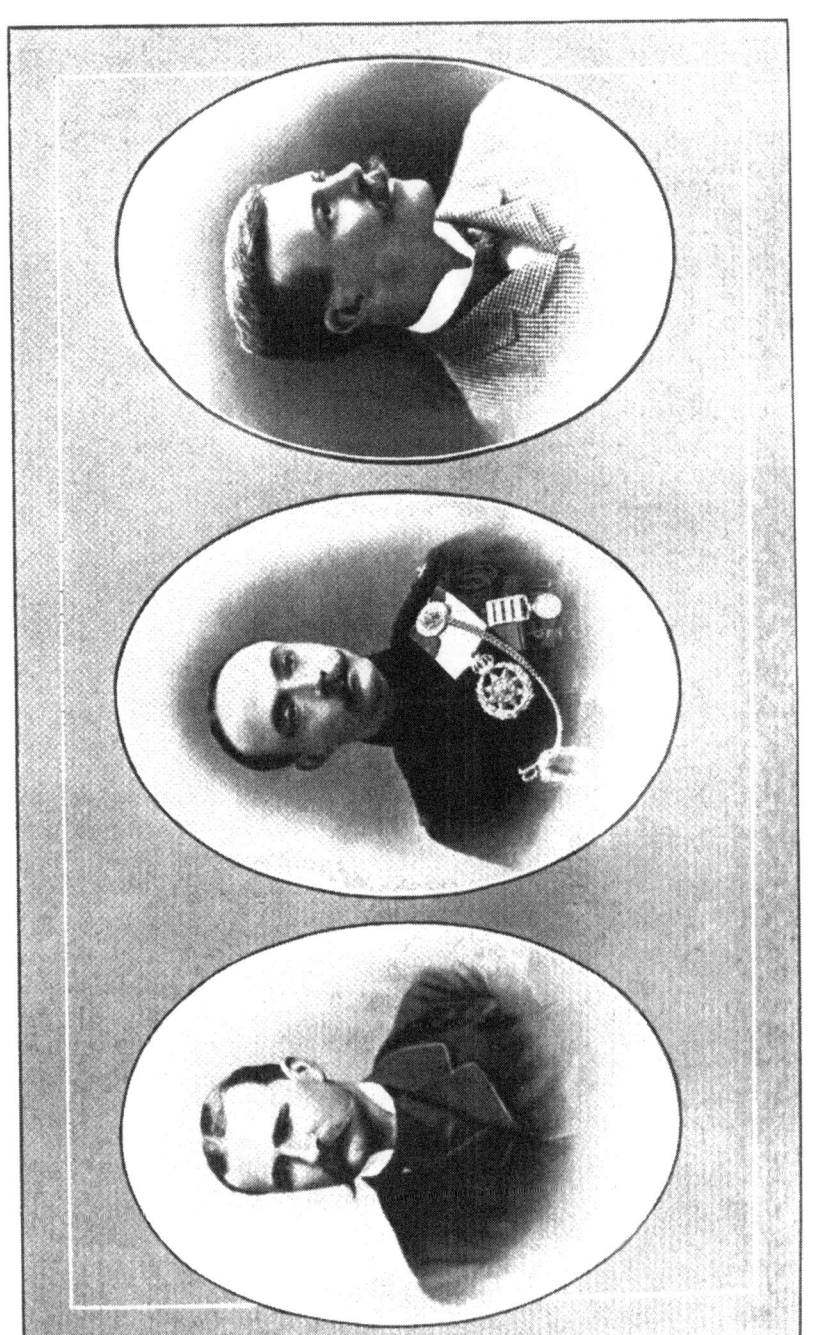

J. Cock.   G. H. Boisragon.   J. Manners-Smith.

Three who gained the Victoria Cross.

THE 5TH ROYAL GURKHA RIFLES (F.F.)

the 5th Gurkhas. The succeeding days were occupied in making temporary arrangements for the administration of the country, and these completed, the 5th Gurkha detachment returned to Gilgit on January 12th, 1892. Then the field force was broken up.

Return to Abbottabad, October, 1892.
The detachment remained at Gilgit until the end of August. During June Captain Barrett and Lieutenant Badcock were sent to England on sick leave, and Captain Kemball, who had been on special duty at Bunji, assumed command. From Gilgit a move was made to Astor, and then, on relief by the 15th Sikhs, in two parties the detachment set out for Abbottabad on September 10th and 11th. When Baramulla was reached on the 25th a case of cholera occurred, and it became necessary to halt there for five days. Fortunately the epidemic did not spread, and October 10th saw the arrival of the party in Abbottabad. Well might Colonel Gaselee say, in the order published by him after his inspection of the detachment on its return, "the reputation of the Regiment has been fully maintained."

ITEMS OF INTEREST, 1887–1892

With effect from June 21st, 1887, Subadar-Major Bhagatbir Thapa was admitted to the 2nd Class of the Order of British India.

New accoutrements, known as the Mackenzie equipment, were received and issued to the Battalion in December 1887.

In December, 1887, the Government of India sanctioned the elimination of the words "Hazara Goorkha Battalion" from the designation of the Regiment.

In June, 1888, in order to provide the 2nd Battalion with its complement of mule transport, the transport establishment of the Battalion was fixed at 130 animals—previously there had been over 200—with 3 Jemadars, 5 Duffadars, and 48 syces.

In 1889 the entertainment was sanctioned of 15 recruit boys.

In September, 1891, recruit boys were done away with.

During 1892, Second-Lieutenant S. D. Ketchen, from the Seaforth Highlanders, was appointed to the Battalion on probation, and Second-Lieutenant C. R. Johnson was transferred from the 44th Gurkha Rifles.

In 1892, Subadar Kishanbir Nagarkoti went on pension on reaching the age of forty-four years. In recognition of his exceptional services he was granted a special pension of Rs. 20 a month for life in addition to the ordinary pension of Rs. 30 a month.

Change of Command, October, 1892.
While the detachment of the Battalion was engaged in winning fresh laurels for the Regiment across the Kashmir passes, for those who remained in Abbottabad the passage of time was marked by a few events of considerable importance. In October, 1892, Lieutenant-Colonel A. Gaselee, C.B., who had officiated for Colonel Sym since the

latter's departure on one year's furlough, was appointed to succeed him in the command of the Battalion.

Of extra-regimental activities in this period, chief interest centres round Mr. Martin Conway's visit of exploration to the Karakoram Mountains. Lieutenant the Honourable C. G. Bruce, an athlete *hors concours* who had already established a considerable reputation as a climber, was detailed to accompany the party, and with him went four riflemen of the Battalion. They were Parbir Thapa, Harkbir Thapa, Amar Sing Thapa, and Karbir Burathoki, and "the most ready and valuable assistance which they rendered throughout" won for them high praise from the leader of the expedition. Subsidized by the Royal Society and the Royal Geographical Society, Mr. Conway came from England with other members of his party intending to make a thorough survey of the passes of the Karakoram, of the great glaciers of that region and of their tributaries, and to collect biological, botanical, and geological data. Setting out in April, 1892, they explored the hitherto unknown Hispar Glacier and the pass of the same name, were the first to traverse the Nushik La, and the first, too, to make known the secrets of the Upper Baltoro. Their most conspicuous mountaineering feat was the ascent of a minor peak which they christened Pioneer Peak, and it gives some idea of the scale of the mountains in that locality when it is known that the height of this lesser summit was 22,600 feet. The fine painting of the giant Mount Godwin-Austen, which hangs on the north wall of the present anteroom, is a permanent reminder of the expedition.

Lieutenant Bruce with Karakoram Exploration Party, April, 1892.

This same month of April witnessed yet another Black Mountain imbroglio. It will be remembered that during the previous year the 2nd Battalion had taken part in an expedition against the tribes. On its conclusion the Isazai clans had agreed to the perpetual exclusion of the outlawed Hashim Ali, but now came the news that the Hassanzais and the Mada Khel had agreed to the settlement of his family in their lands. They were warned of the consequences of their action, and, as a precautionary measure, the two battalions of the Regiment with the 1st Kohat Mountain Battery were ordered to Agror. Leaving Abbottabad on April 27th the force reached Oghi on the 29th. As the result of a few cases of cholera, camp was changed more than once, but the end of May found the three units settled on a spur above the village of Bagrian. There they remained until the end of September, suffering a good deal from malarial fever towards the end of that time.

Occupation of Agror, April, 1892.

The hot weather had passed, and still Hashim Ali with his family was harboured by the Hassanzai and Mada Khel clans of the Isazai. Orders were accordingly issued for the assembly of a field force at

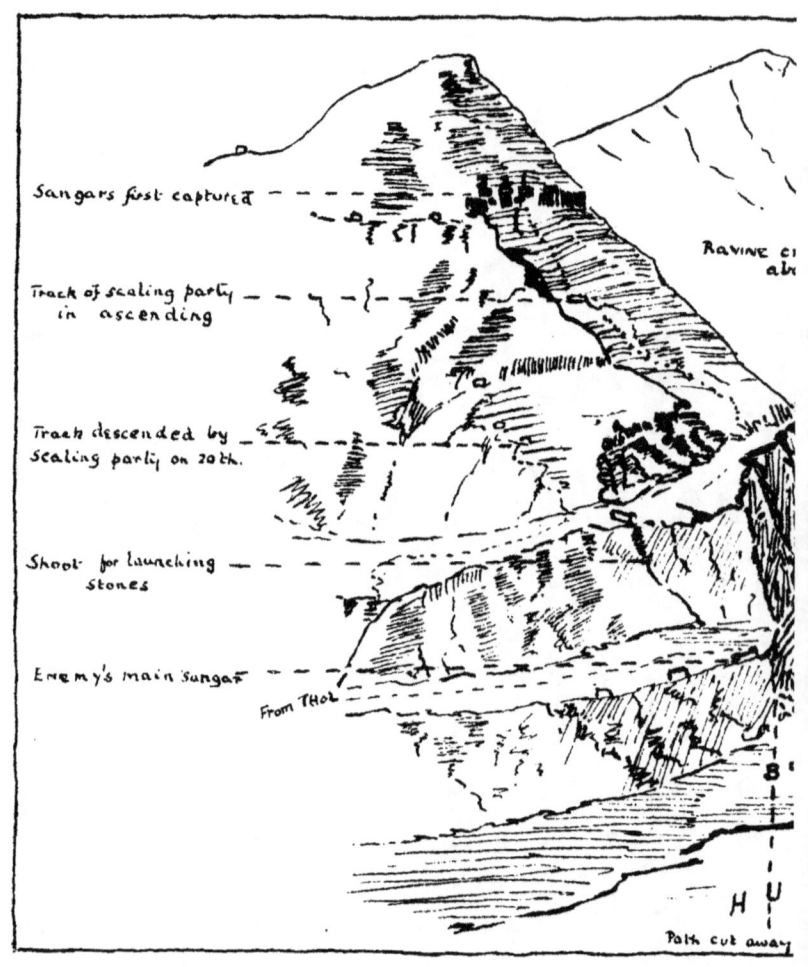

VIEW OF NILT RAVI[NE]
LOOKING S[OUTH]
(Taken from Vol. I. Frontier and O[verseas...])

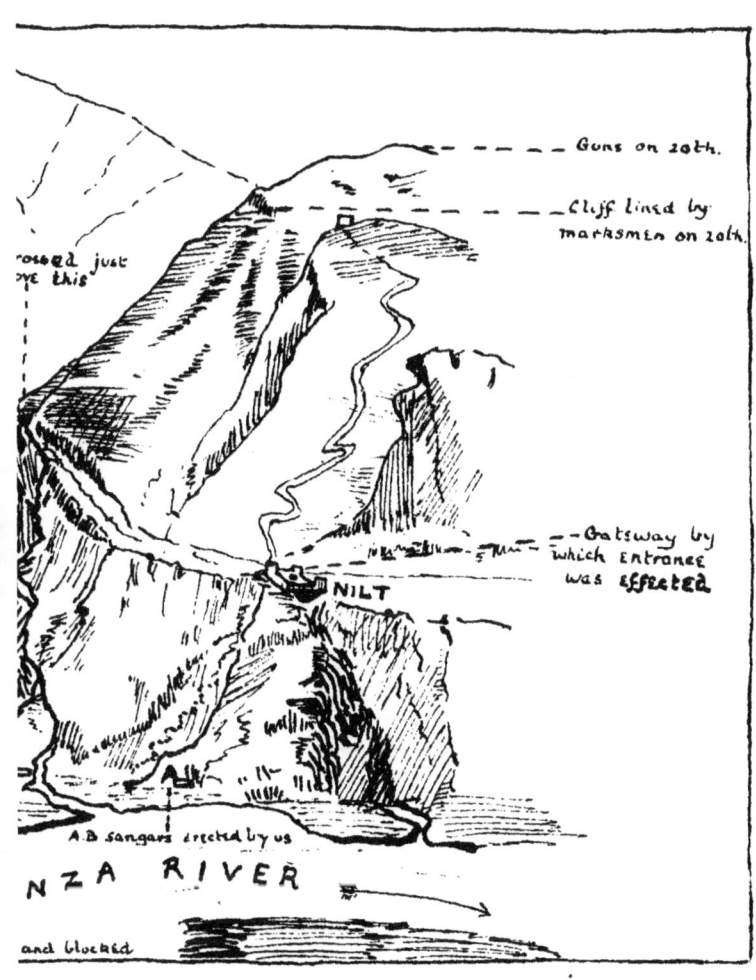

INE FROM MAIUN

OUTH.

Overseas Expeditions from India.)

Darband, with the object of expelling the outlaw and of punishing the tribesmen who had failed to abide by their engagements.

Isazai Expedition, Sept.-Oct., 1892.

The Battalion marched from Agror on September 29th and joined Sir William Lockhart at Darband on October 1st. The subsequent operations lack interest, for the enemy offered no resistance and tamely submitted to the destruction of their villages. It is worth noting, however, that a Maxim gun, manned by a detachment of the Yorkshire Light Infantry, was used on this occasion for the first time in India. Having accomplished its object the force withdrew, and on October 20th the Battalion reached Abbottabad. For ten days previous to this date it had been necessary to camp outside cantonment limits as the result of an outbreak of cholera at Darband.

It will be noticed that hitherto in this narrative, when referring to

Change of Designation.

private soldiers of the Regiment the term " sepoy " has been used. As early as February, 1891, a G.G.O. had been published which changed the designation of the Regiment to the 5th Gurkha (Rifle) Regiment, and further decreed that the term " rifleman " should be substituted for " sepoy." For some reason the old records continued to use " sepoy " after the publication of the order, but from 1893 onwards the new appellation begins to occur. The change was of considerable importance, and undoubtedly helped to foster *esprit de corps*.

CHAPTER VI

A Record of Changing Conditions

Transition. The narrative has now reached a period which may be taken as marking the transition from the old order to the new. Sir James Stewart has something to say about this in in the record from which we have previously borrowed. "In peace time life was certainly less interesting. For the officers, games were limited—no football, no golf, no polo; tennis irregular, two courts at the top of the station occasionally used; the mess a small one, only eight officers and nearly all of them married. We shared a very genial mess with a frontier battalion and a frontier battery, but even so, in the hot weather, dining members were few.

"Shooting was better. Kharki Jheel gave excellent duck and snipe, chikor and pheasant were plentiful. Kashmir was not overrun (the road in had not been made), and fine heads could be got fairly easily in the Kaj Nag. Everything was much cheaper—food for man and beast, servants, rents, etc.—but the pay was less.

"For the men the tale is somewhat the same—they had few amusements. Rugby football had been tried, but without success. Perhaps they went more into the district and got more sport, but the attractions of the bazaar were more pronounced. The start of 'soccer' was strange: few could kick the ball at all, but about 1890 we had a good many young officers between the two battalions who knew the game, and progress was rapid. About the same time, too, the increase in the number of officers made polo possible. So both officers and men obtained healthier amusements.

"With only eight officers the Wing system was the only possible one. A very junior officer often found himself in command of a wing, and sometimes even of the Regiment. Much less was expected, much less was obtained."

The conditions here described were not to be changed in a day, but with the passing of the years they did undergo modifications. It is not necessary in this place to say anything about the work of the Battalion, since the story of gradual development tells itself as the narrative proceeds. As regards the pastimes of officers and men, however, a few words will not be out of place, even though, to deal at all adequately with the subject, it is necessary to anticipate events.

Shooting.

Shooting in the old days was a great standby, and occupied much spare time. For the men, it may be, there has been no great change. Starlings are still plentiful in the valley, and still, of a holiday morning, the fields and roadsides are thronged with Gurkha sportsmen who stalk warily, with muzzle-loading fowling piece poised, to get several birds in a line, or kneel to take careful aim into the brown of the flock feeding on the ground. The little Gurkha ladies, meantime, tramp sturdily the edges of the streams, and pause, here and there, to gather watercress.

But for those dependent for their sport on birds other than starlings there has been a marked falling off in the opportunities offered. Colonel F. W. Evatt, in a letter, speaks of the days of plenty. "'Jimmie' Stewart refers to an incident when two hundred quail were bagged within 200 yards of the Mansehra road, just beyond the rifle range. This is no tall story; I myself carried one of the guns, and Lethbridge the second. The only variation in the account is that the bag was 199 birds; more could not be added as the cartridges had given out!" Then Major-General H. P. Browne has memories of good bags got within walking distance of the mess. "I remember Ketchen getting fifty couple of snipe in the Stony Jheel (Unwin's Pool) and the Mirpur Jheel in one day, working alone with a dog. I also remember fifty couple of chickor being shot in the *nullah* behind Dehri waterworks, the recruits being employed to drive. Big bags of duck were made at Karki on the road to Oghi, and at Tora Pind near Torbela." Such delights may be enjoyed no more. Quail no longer use this route in their migrations; except for a few weeks very late in the season the two valley jheels are practically bare of duck and snipe, and all the slopes of Sirban and Habiba, in a normal year, hardly hold six coveys of chikor between them.

In the matter of big game the outlook is less gloomy, and excellent heads are added to the regimental collection from time to time. Browne's curly $55\frac{1}{2}$-inch markhor still holds the mess record for length, but Erskine has lately brought a grand head from Gilgit which runs it very close, while the average of other trophies from Kashmir is steadily improving.

Fishing.

If game birds have shown a growing tendency to disappear from their previous haunts, fish, more faithful or less affected by the depredations of local inhabitants, still frequent the waters of the district. Probably there is less time now for the pursuit of the gentle art than in the earlier days of the Regiment, and to the modern exponent it seems that previous generations of mahseer can never have been so capricious as their successors of the present day. But the fish are there, and sometimes they are caught. The keen spirits of the Regiment still journey to

Torbela—now approachable by a motor road; still tempt the lower reaches of the Siran with fly and spoon; and with mulberry, melon seed, locust, and frog, each in its season, still ruffle the limpid waters of the Cheblat from Wah to its junction with the Haru. The men are no whit behindhand; no stream within walking distance of a camp will remain unvisited; damming and diverting rivers, netting, tickling, and stunning with a *khukri*, as well as more orthodox methods, all are still in vogue; while it remains one of nature's mysteries that a rain-filled hollow which but yesterday was sun-baked mud, to-day will yield store of fishlings to the Gurkha's lure on the end of a piece of string. It is matter for regret that the " Trout Club " is no more; the efforts of A. H. G. Kemball, ably seconded by C. R. Johnson and A. B. Hay-Webb, to restock the Kalapani stream, had begun to bear fruit when the Great War interrupted their labours. Otters and two-legged poachers, allowed a free rein, soon ruined the hatcheries, and nowadays the Kalapani holds no trout. Mercifully it has been ordained that this should not be the end of trout culture in the district. Under the ægis of the Forest Department other streams have now been stocked, notably the upper reaches of the Siran. A motor road leads from Abbottabad through Shinkiari up the left bank of the river, new bungalows have been built, and other steps taken to make plain the path of the fisherman, so that, before a decade has passed, Hazara maybe will vie with Kashmir as a paradise for the ardent angler.

Football. More than other changes which the years have wrought, the cult of association football has given pleasure to the men. If we except Nigel Woodyatt, of the 3rd Gurkhas, the chief credit is due to F. G. Lucas, of the 2/5th. For many years players were few, and any piece of moderately flat ground served their needs. Gradually the game spread to regiments other than the 3rd and 5th Gurkhas, the presentation of a cup by the 3rd Gurkhas for competition among all units of the brigade provided an incentive for the attainment of a higher standard, and football became established as *the* game of the Gurkha soldier. In the Regiment it was for long the 2nd Battalion which excelled, and it was their then commanding officer, Colonel J. M. Stewart, who first thought of extending the playing areas by levelling the ground beyond the Battalion bazaar on the south side of the Murree road. The work was begun in 1907, and six years of uninterrupted labour resulted in two almost perfect grounds. On the bazaar side a double row of chenar trees affords a grateful shade, and from them a bank of turf slopes down to the green grass of the field of play. The far side, too, is lined with chenar trees, and beyond the ground again drops glacis-wise and green to the lower level of the golf-links. The example set by the 2nd Battalion was later followed by others, and with the acquisition by the cantonment of all the land as far as the Link road came a further opportunity to increase the area reserved for football. South of the Murree road the newly bought land being taken up for a second polo ground, the 1st Battalion secured a lien across the way, and by dint of much labour and some expenditure of money there made four good grounds. With a fifth, provided by the levelling and turfing of the recruits' parade-ground, it is possible to ensure a game for nearly four hundred men on a holiday afternoon. The result is that nowadays nearly everybody plays, and there are competitions to suit all degrees of skill. The cup presented by the 3rd Gurkhas has already been mentioned; it is generally known as the Gurkha Brigade Cup. His Highness the Maharaja of Nepal presented a trophy shortly after the close of the Great War, which is at present competed for on the league system by those who have survived to the semi-finals of the Gurkha brigade tournament. In all districts there is an annual competition for units of the Indian Army, and for these the two battalions of the Regiment enter regularly wherever they may happen to be quartered. There is the Punjab Frontier Force football cup, played for in Kohat, which more often than not is held by one or other battalion of the 5th Gurkhas, although the 1st Sikhs are still serious rivals as they have been for many years past. The 5th Fusiliers cup, presented some years before the Great War by the 1st Battalion of that regiment then stationed at Rawalpindi, is open to company teams of the four battalions of the 5th and 6th Gurkhas. Finally, in the 1/5th, platoon teams, consisting of seven men a side, compete during the hot weather for a challenge shield presented in 1924 by Lieutenant-Colonel H. E. Weekes. From this brief account it will be seen that football plays a large part in the lives of the men.

The Hill Race.

Another interest was provided in the early 'nineties with the introduction of the annual *khud* race. None who ever witnessed the event is likely to forget the experience. Unsurpassed among athletic contests as a spectacle, it had important consequences, for it not only established the reputation of the Gurkha as practically invincible on the hill-side, but also had the effect of speeding up hill-work generally. Once the competition became fairly established, entries were numerous, and from some ten battalions there would collect between thirty and forty competitors, all as fit as a special diet and a long course of training could make them. The men ran barefooted, dressed in singlets and shorts. The race was run over a steep and rocky hill-side, so precipitous in many of the downhill portions that the ordinary plainsman would need to use his hands. Not so the trained Gurkha, who would drop full speed from one rock to another eight feet below, land on one leg and bring the other forward to continue unchecked his headlong career. A fairly typical course would work out something like this. First a rise of about 900 feet, very abrupt, rocky, and bare. The runners, heads well down, hands put out occasionally to steady themselves, would take this at a seemingly unhurried jog-trot, ascending well over 100 feet to the minute. Next would come a long slant to the top of a ridge, and for half a mile or so the competitors, beginning to string out, would straighten up and stride out boldly despite the uneven surface. Then a steep descent of 500 feet or so, providing the spectators with their first real thrill as they watched the leaders fairly hurl themselves at the declivity, bounding from foothold to foothold, arms high in air, and seeming barely to touch the ground. Again a testing spell against the collar, and the big field would be well spread out, the rearmost, perhaps, just beginning to breast the rise as those in front settled to another longish run over comparatively flat ground. Finally, the great run-in, maybe 1,000 feet of sheer *khud*; sharp-edged rocks, great rounded boulders, or tussocks of rough grass, nothing served to check the tremendous pace of the leaders, with their perfect sense of balance and their muscles all attuned to answer to the culminating demand for speed.

More than any other, C. G. Bruce was responsible for the institution of the race, and for those who remember those days his notes will be full of interest.

" The Hill Race was first introduced as a protest against the attitude which considered that Gurkhas could not compete on equal terms with Punjabis, Sikhs, etc. 1890 was the first year, at the Punjab Frontier Force sports. The race was run to the south of the parade ground on a course which lasted about ten minutes. There were about 133 starters of all classes. The first thirty-three places were won by the 1st and 2nd Battalions of the 5th Gurkhas, the first Punjabi coming in 34th.

" There were three annual local races afterwards, and in 1894 the 5th Gurkha Challenge Cup was given. The first race was run on a short course of fourteen minutes, also south of the parade-ground, and was won by Deoram Thapa, with Harkbir Thapa second (both of the 1/5th), and the celebrated Budhiparsad (1/3rd Gurkhas) third. This man won the race for the next seven years. The rules of the race gave the winning regiment the option of holding it at their own station, or of naming the course, and in consequence it was held for many years at Almora, and finally at Lansdowne. Then by mutual consent it was run at Bakloh, when the winner proved to be Dharmjit Pun, of the 1/5th; nor did Budhiparsad win again, although he competed some eleven times, his greatest opponents being the winner of the first year, Deoram Thapa, and Harkbir Thapa, who also competed eleven times, always placed, but never winning.

" Dharmjit Pun won the cup on four occasions until beaten finally by Tulbir Gurung, of the 1/6th. In the meantime there had been other winners—namely, Santbir Thapa of the 1/3rd, and Maniraj Gharti of the 2/6th. The latter, who was the victor in the 1907 race at Abbottabad, was thought to have injured himself, and was not entered a second time until 1914, when he again won, beating on that occasion the redoubtable Tulbir Gurung, who had proved invincible during the intervening years. Thus it happened that the trophy was in the possession of the 2/6th Gurkhas when the Great War put a stop to further contests.

"The race was run over various types of hill, and the length of the course was from twenty-three to thirty-three minutes—the actual longest course run, on the slopes of Sirban. During the twenty years in which runners entered a great deal was learnt, naturally, of the best methods of training them, and the times made in later years were, generally speaking, in advance of the earlier times.

"Of the many competitors of the first class who entered, it is probable that Budhiparsad was the finest of all, although there were several candidates who, failing to win either from mishap or from some other cause, yet showed signs of being nearly as good, notably Ragobir Thapa, 1/5th. Many other competitors won open races against all classes brought against them, notably an open race at Landi Kotal in March, 1898, which was won by the 2/5th detachment of the Gurkha Scouts against all-comers, men coming in specially to compete from the open country, from Tirah, and from Afghanistan.

"One of the most exciting of all such events was when General Lockhart's relief column was in Wana in 1894, and a great race was got up by the Political Officer against the local Mahsuds and Wazirs. Running to order, Harkbir, clad only in running shorts, carried off the field at a terrific pace, the Mahsuds and Wazirs after him. Ragobir and Karbir Burathoki, meanwhile, ran cannily. The little ruse was successful, the race being won easily by Ragobir, with Karbir second and Harkbir third, and the field well in the background.

"During the tour of duty of the 1/5th in Chitral in 1903-04, the annual race against the Kafirs and Chitralis was won by Jaman Sing Thapa. In that year the Battalion was also successful in the race for the Gurkha cup, run off at Abbottabad, for Dharmjit Pun and Balbahadur Thapa, who happened to be serving in the depôt, came in first and second.

"During the time that Lord Kitchener was Commander-in-Chief a challenge issued from the Headquarters Staff at Simla. The challengers contended that the Gurkha could not compete with the Pathan uphill. Gurkha partisans, represented by H. J. P. Browne, then holding an appointment at Simla, accepted the challenge. I was charged with the selection and training of the Gurkha runners, and confined my choice to men of the two battalions 5th Gurkhas only. Pathans were selected both from Frontier Militia and from regular regiments of the Indian Army. During the race competitors were required to climb some 3,000 feet, no single stretch of downhill occurring in the entire course. The result of the match was a runaway victory for the Gurkhas, all four of whom finished well in front of the first Pathan to arrive at the winning-post.

"One of the most notable of all the running performances ever done by the Regiment was in 1899. Havildar Harkbir Thapa was with me in England for six months, and after two months' travelling in Switzerland we went to Skye and wandered in the Chuchullin Hills. As the result of an argument between McLeod and some of his ghillies, and possibly egged on a little by Professor Collie of our party, a small bet was made that Harkbir would not run from Sligachan Inn to the top of Mount Glamaig and back in an hour and a quarter, the ghillies saying that their dogs could not do this. The distance is two miles open moorland to the foot, and a rise of 2,817 feet to the summit. Harkbir accomplished it by himself—no pacemaker, no preparation—in thirty-seven minutes to the summit, and eighteen minutes back to the inn without fatigue. Apparently this record remains to the present day; many athletes in the North have tried to beat it, but so far none has come near to equalling it.

"I might add that in the athletic records of the Regiment by far the best flat runner ever turned out was one Manglu Damai, who in his time proved himself good enough to take on all-comers of whatever class. He was, in his way, a freak, who flourished about 1886."

As mentioned before, an interruption occurred to the series of contests in the form of the Great War, and the race has not since been revived. There is a general feeling that excellent as were the results of the competition, post-war conditions hardly allow of individuals being trained up to the pitch of fitness necessary for so exacting a test. While those interested agree that the trophy should be run for with the object of providing a standard of speed, the majority consider that the competition should take some other form. It seems probable that it will shortly be revived in the form of a relay race.

Both before and after the institution of the *khud* race the Regiment was very forward in the field of mountain exploration. *Mountain Exploration.* To the Guides must be given pride of place when it comes to assessing the extent of ground covered. They worked on rather different lines, however, their men being employed more often than not on secret service duties, and for intimate exploration of the Himalayas the 5th Gurkhas yield the palm to none. Again recourse will be had to the notes of Brigadier-General the Honourable C. G. Bruce, who himself took part in the majority of expeditions with which the Regiment is concerned, and whose knowledge of the Himalayas is unrivalled.

"The first party sent out accompanied Sir Francis Younghusband in his first descent into Hunza in 1886, and consisted of two non-commissioned officers and four men. Later on Harkbir was orderly to Sir James Stewart when he crossed over the Khora Bort Pass and traversed the Pamirs in the direction of Margelan, to extract Sir Francis Younghusband, who had been detained by the Russians.

"Then came Sir Martin Conway's expedition to the Karakoram, the two most notable features being the discovery of the great Hispar Glacier and the climbing of Pioneer Peak (about 23,000 feet), the highest actual summit reached up to that date. In this both Harkbir Thapa and myself took part.

"This was followed by the tragic attempt on Nanga Parbat, when Mr. Mummery and his two Gurkha orderlies, Ragobir Thapa and Guman Sing Gurung, lost their lives. There were two attempts actually to climb Nanga Parbat by the north-west face—the first undertaken by Mr. Mummery, Dr. Collie, and Ragobir, the second by Ragobir and Mummery alone. These were the two most difficult actual climbs yet made in the Himalayas, being, from a technical point of view, equal to the most difficult fancy climbs in the Alps, and performed at a very much greater elevation. Indeed, the whole of that expedition was most strenuous. For instance, the abortive attempt, in which I took part, to cross the north-western ridge of Nanga Parbat kept us out on the mountain for two days and two nights. Mummery and the two Gurkhas were killed when endeavouring to make a pass between Nanga Parbat itself and the Gonala Peak to the north of it, intending to descend eventually into the Buldar-Rakiot Valley. They were swept away by a great avalanche which fell from high up on the side of Nanga Parbat.

"Later, Subadar Karbir Burathoki and I accompanied Mumm and Dr. Longstaff in an exploratory visit to the peaks of Upper Garhwal. The chief incident was the ascent of Mount Trissul (23,400 feet), which remained till last year (1928) the highest *summit* yet reached, though not the highest point on the earth's surface attained.

"Then followed numerous expeditions in out-of-the-way parts of Suru and on the Zaskar borders, in Kashmir, in Kulu, and in Lahoul. Among other climbs one well worth noting here was that in which the late Subadar-Major and Honorary Captain Kulbahadur Gurung accompanied Dr. Neave and Captain Corrie, R.E., in the first ascent of Mount Kolahoi in Kashmir. Then, again, two orderlies were detailed from the Regiment to proceed with the Filippo de Filippi Expedition in their survey of the heads of the Zemu and Ziachen Glaciers. On the declaration of war in 1914 these two orderlies were given the unenviable task of escorting back to Kashmir certain Italian officers who were members of the expedition, as it was not known at that time on which side Italy might come in.

"Apart from Himalayan exploration, on three occasions the Regiment has had representatives in the Alps. The first occasion was when Parbir Thapa accompanied me on a winter campaign in 1891. The next when Sir Martin Conway took with him Amar Sing Thapa and Karbir Burathoki on his journey from end to end of the Alps in 1894. During the last quarter of the journey these two were Sir Martin's sole companions. And, lastly, the often mentioned Harkbir Thapa led Dr. Collie and myself for two months in 1899.

"This by no means completes the tale of mountaineering achievements of men of the Regiment, for on various occasions they have found themselves on the tops of minor peaks in different parts, including the Kashmir border and Kaghan. In this last-named region some fifteen summits have been scaled, most notably Mali-ka-Sar, the highest point in the range, which was climbed from the ridge facing the Kashmir border by Captain Battye and four of the men in 1912. This is the pyramid-shaped peak seen from Abbottabad, of which the height is 17,345 feet."

Like the *khud* race, mountaineering is in abeyance. Officers of the Regiment still tramp over the nearer hills, still climb the more accessible of the Kaghan Mountains, and with aching muscles and laboured breathing still struggle over rocks and shale in Kashmir in pursuit of ibex and markhor; wherever the officer goes, a few of the men go, too. But of mountaineering as a pursuit in itself, there is none now with the knowledge and experience of a C. G. Bruce, and the revival of Himalayan exploration awaits, for the present, the coming of a mountaineer.

Other pastimes mentioned by Sir James Stewart in the passage quoted at the beginning of this chapter are polo, tennis, and golf. If we add racquets, squash racquets, and cricket, and say something of the development of each, we shall have material for a comparison of the older conditions with those obtaining later.

Polo.

Polo, when it did come in with the late 'eighties or early 'nineties, was taken up keenly by a number of officers. Ponies were small, they could be bought cheaply, and their keep formed but a comparatively small item in the monthly budget, so that even the poor subaltern, serving eleven years for his captaincy, could play without straining too severely his resources. The game may have been slower in those early days, but was no less a test of nerve and horsemanship than in the later period of big ponies and enhanced prices. A tournament, instituted in 1908 in connection with the celebration of the jubilee of the Regiment, became the precursor of an annual tournament, in which a number of outside teams compete, while the Regiment is generally represented. Only once has the tournament been won by a regimental team, when, in 1912, the cup was carried off by the 2nd Battalion, represented by Harington, Duncan, Heyland, and Wellesley. At one period the 2nd Battalion were regular in their attendance at the P.F.F. and Indian Infantry tournaments. They came near to winning the latter in January, 1910, when, after beating the Guides Infantry by 6–5 in the semi-final, scoring five of their goals in the last chukker, they were beaten by one goal by the 2nd Gurkhas in the final. Nowadays there are two polo grounds in Abbottabad, the second having been made after the Great War on the site of old *makhai* fields south of the Murree road. With enhanced facilities in the matter of grounds, polo is becoming increasingly difficult for the infantryman of small means. While it is true that the polo fund, started in 1908 under the auspices of (then) Colonel J. M. Stewart, does help to meet the initial high cost of ponies, their keep is so expensive that the number of players grows fewer year by year.

Tennis.
As regards tennis, the "two courts at the top of the station" long ago disappeared, and the venue was changed to the present club. There are to be found six good gravel courts, and, as is to be expected, in view of the universal popularity of the game, they are generally all in use. The Regiment usually boasts more than one player of merit, and of recent years the 5th and 6th Gurkha group has figured prominently in the Army Championships at Queen's Club. In 1925 the doubles championship was won by Alexander of the 5th and Emmott of the 6th, while other players of the group who would always have to be reckoned with are Broadway and Bernard.

Golf.
Golf is another game of which the lure attracts an ever-increasing number of players, and Abbottabad does its best to keep pace with the times. The old circular nine-hole course has been transformed into a good, sporting course of fourteen holes, and it is possible to play an entire round without once being forced to play one's second from the middle of a game of football. The greens are good and are improving, and not a hole but has some golfing interest and possibilities of very serious trouble for him who tops his tee shot, or errs by too great a margin from the appointed way.

Racquets.
Racquets, alas! is dead in Abbottabad. The court built by the Regiment and sold to the club was in great demand up to the war, and many fine players had taken their exercise in its somewhat dark interior. Of them all, Sheppard of the sappers was pre-eminent, and it is evidence of his extraordinary fitness that no game was so hard but it left him with breath for a laugh. In the Regiment, F. F. Badcock was outstanding in his time, and he continued to play, and to play well, even after he

lost an arm in Tirah. After him came Skipwith and Harington, who scored a number of successes in the North of India championships, the latter especially putting up a wonderful performance in 1909, when, in the absence of Sheppard and Wilson-Johnston, he won every event in the tournament. There was a short-lived revival of racquets after the war, but the expense proved too great for the majority of players, and there came a time when no one entered the court for weeks together. With the death of the cheery old Pathan marker, Makhmud, who was reputed to have exchanged a favourite wife for a fighting quail, it was realized that the glory had departed, and in 1923 the court was sold to a missionary society. Squash has taken the place of racquets, and claims many more devotees than ever did the faster game. There are two courts in the club, the gunners have another in their mess, and one has now been provided for the Artillery School at Kakul.

Cricket.

Cricket in Abbottabad has its lean and fat years, but few seasons pass without the playing of an occasional match. There have always been cricketers in the Regiment—some like J. M. Stewart and C. E. B. Champain of county form, while others, like Turner and Alexander, might have played for a county had the opportunity come their way. The 2/5th football grounds make an ideal setting for cricket, with their green grass, the fine sloping bank of turf for spectators, and the chenar trees. Unfortunately the demands of football seldom allow of their use for cricket, and matches against Rawalpindi and other of the nearer stations must more often be played on the edge of the old polo ground.

Apart from the vicissitudes attending the sports and pastimes of officers and men, a few changes of a more general character may be mentioned before we revert to the story of the first Battalion.

The Mess.

The mess will form a convenient starting-point. Although the cantonment came into existence several years before the Regiment was raised, there is no record of the construction of any building as an officers' mess prior to that event. The original mess-house may be seen in one of the early photographs of Abbottabad reproduced in Chapter I. From the beginning it was the property of the officers of the Regiment, though the other officers stationed in Abbottabad also found a home there. From the original cottage-like building it expanded into a good-sized mess, of which the officers of the 5th Gurkhas had every reason to be proud. Gradually it became filled with trophies of war and of the chase. Old weapons and captured standards found a place on its walls, and year by year the collection of heads improved. The Buner standard, the 72nd Drum-Major's staff, the chain-mail and drums and flags from Nilt, as well as the trophies of the Great War, all serve as a reminder of the prowess of men of the Regiment, while the horns of markhor and ibex, ovis poli and ammon, burhel and oorial, thar and barasingha, buffalo and bison, not to mention a goodly assortment from Africa, speak of hard lying and considerable self-sacrifice on the part of a number of venturesome spirits. As time went on the units in the station increased in number, while of each the complement of British officers was augmented. The old house could no longer accommodate them all, and about 1902 the gunners left for a mess of their own at the top of the station. The 6th Gurkhas, who had arrived in Abbottabad as the 42nd from Assam, continued to share the mess with the two battalions of the 5th until after the raising of their 2nd Battalion. In 1906 they repaired to a temporary mess in an existing bungalow, pending the completion some years later of the fine house they now occupy. Shortly after the conclusion of the Great War the 5th Gurkha Mess ceased to be the property of the officers of the Regiment, being taken over by Government on payment of Rs. 30,000. Many of those who have left the Regiment would find difficulty in recognizing their old abode, for the opportunity was taken when a new roof had to be provided, about 1909, to make extensive alterations. The old anteroom was converted into a spacious entrance hall, a cardroom was added in the angle between this hall and the billiard-room, a new anteroom was built on the east side of the dining-room by removing the covered-in verandah and throwing out the old wall flush with its exterior, and a conservatory was added on the south side of the building. The work was in charge of C. R. Johnson, who did wonders with the limited amount of money available. Great interest is nowadays shown in the garden, where a number of new borders have been dug. Always beautiful in the spring, if only by reason of its roses, it can usually show a wealth of bloom throughout nine months of the year. Tulips, hyacinths, daffodils, anemones, ranunculus, crocus, and other bulbs begin to flower in March, and carry on well into April. They are overlapped by the early summer annuals—antirrhinum, stocks, wallflowers, pansies, and suchlike, by herbaceous things and roses. By the time these show signs of flagging, monsoon flowering plants are ready to take their place, the last of all to be overcome by frost being the cannas, which outstay even chrysanthemums, dahlias, zinnias, and balsams, and show scarlet, orange, carmine, and salmon-pink almost to the end of December.

Water Supply. To later arrivals in Abbottabad it is always matter for wonder how in former times the garrison managed for water. Even twenty-six years ago, when there were four battalions and three batteries, there was but the one supply from the *nullah* above Dheri Village. Then came the pipe-line from Kakul; but even so, with no increase in the garrison, there soon began occasional scares of a shortage of water, and during the summer, gardens often fared badly. To these two supplies has now been added a third, the Kalapani having been tapped in the neighbourhood of the old trout hatcheries, but no sooner had it been opened than a warning was issued impressing on householders the necessity for using it sparingly.

Houses.

Another puzzle to a later generation is house accommodation. In the past twenty-five years at least seven new bungalows have been built in cantonments, and yet the surplus which can find no home is enough to support three hotels, which before were non-existent. Incidentally, it is significant of a change in outlook that not a single house is owned by a British officer; all, without exception, have passed into the hands of Indians.

Other Changes.

Other changes comprise the establishment of the motor-car in popular favour, the extension of roads, and the coming of the railway. On returning from leave one no longer scrambles sleepily from the train at Hasan Abdal to be jolted over forty odd miles of road in a shabby old *tonga*. Instead, one leaves the main line at Taxila—formerly Serai Kala—reaches Havelian after about two-and-a-half hours' train journey on the branch line, and then is carried up the hill in an American motor-car. The toot of the motor-horn has ousted the blast of the *tonga*-driver's bugle, and where before one halted to mend a trace or patch the harness with a piece of string, one now sits in the dust to watch the chauffeur change a punctured tyre. Nevertheless, despite modern invention and the march of science, Abbottabad remains surprisingly the same. There is the same feeling of being apart from and rather better than the rest of the world, the same atmosphere of camaraderie combined with a friendly rivalry, and the same determination to let no one pass us in the race. There are more tin roofs in the villages, but irises still bloom in the graveyards, the dog-rose still flourishes on the Brigade Circular, and in autumn the bracken still turns a golden brown below the cliffs of Sirban.

CHAPTER VII

KAGAN, WAZIRISTAN, AND TIRAH, 1893 TO 1898

Move to Kagan, 1893.
When the narrative was interrupted to show how time had wrought changes, and how the old order differed from the new, the 1st Battalion had just arrived back in Abbottabad from the Isazai Expedition. The theatre in which it was next required to interest itself was Kagan, the long valley which forms, as it were, an arm thrust out from Hazara towards Chilas. The Shinakis and other independent tribes had been giving trouble, and from November, 1892, and on into the early months of the following year, the Kashmir troops from Gilgit had been actively engaged against them. During that time the 23rd Pioneers were at work on the Kagan–Chilas road. With the end of the cold weather and the consequent opening of the Babusar Pass, Kagan became accessible from Chilas, and the trouble appearing likely to spread to the Kohistanis, there was a possibility that they and the tribes already embroiled might either attack Chilas itself or cross into Kagan with the object of harassing the convoys and working parties on the road.

As a result of this situation, on April 22nd, 1893, the 1/5th Gurkhas and No. 1 (Kohat) Mountain Battery were directed to prepare to move at once to Kagan on orders being received. The threat of hostile action by the tribes did not materialize at this stage, but the Battalion remained in a state of readiness. In August there was a recrudescence of trouble, and a wing of the 1/5th, comprising 6 British officers, 7 Gurkha officers, and 350 rank and file, together with 2 guns of the Kohat Mountain Battery, was sent to deal with it. Colonel Gaselee, who a short time before had been made an A.D.C. to the Queen, had gone to England in April, and in his absence Captain A. A. Barrett commanded. One new officer accompanied the Battalion in the person of Lieutenant H. J. P. Browne, who had joined on April 14th.

The wing left Abbottabad on August 29th and reached Besal, towards the head of the valley, on September 7th, having covered the distance of 123 miles in ten successive days of marching. Detachments of a strength of 2 N.C.O.'s and 12 rifles were dropped at Kagan, Naran, and Battakundi, and Captain J. M. Stewart with 100 rifles was posted between Battakundi and Burawai.

The 23rd Pioneers and two companies of the Bengal Sappers and Miners were already at Besal when the wing arrived there. The presence of this comparatively strong force proved effective in keeping the peace in this out-of-the-way corner of the frontier, and at no time between September 7th and November 8th did the Kohistanis give cause for interference with their activities. It is true that letters, despatched apparently by the tribesmen and threatening dire trouble for the invaders, were constantly received in camp, but these were later traced to one of the Saiyads of the valley for whose benefit the temporary occupation had been arranged.

Convoy escort work and roadmaking occupied much of the time. Major-General H. J. P. Browne tells of a good piece of work by one of the post commanders.

A sapper officer, visiting his post, had examined a big *nullah* nearby with a view to bridging it. The post commander no sooner heard of the officer's intention than he set to work with the men of his detachment. In the most scientific manner he felled several enormous paludar trees (*Abies Webbiana*) and fixed them across the gap. When a short time afterwards the officer returned with his sappers to begin his task, he was amazed to find the bridge already completed. It was still standing in 1914.

The height of the camp at Besal was 11,500 feet, and as winter approached, the cold became intense. In October the Pioneers crossed the Babusar into Chilas, and a detachment of 30 men from the Battalion, under a Gurkha officer, was posted at the foot of the pass eight miles beyond Besal. By the end of the month it had become apparent that no further trouble was to be expected. Captain Stewart's command accordingly left the valley accompanied by the mountain guns, and on November 8th the rest of the wing marched from Besal and reached Abbottabad on the 17th.

Visit of General Brackenbury, 1894.
Apart from the Kagan visit the year was uneventful. In March, 1894, Colonel Gaselee returned from leave, and in the following month a visit was paid to Abbottabad by the military member of the Viceroy's Council, Lieutenant-General H. Brackenbury, C.B. At a parade of the garrison he presented the insignia of the Order of British India to Subadar Parsu Khattri Bahadur, and part of the address which he made on that occasion may well be quoted here:—

" The 5th Goorkhas have gained a reputation not only in India, but throughout Her Majesty's dominions, for the finest qualities which soldiers can possess—devotion to duty and undaunted gallantry in the field. In travelling round the frontier I have had the opportunity of seeing most of the regiments of the Punjab Frontier Force which has worthily attained so high a character for its distinguished services, and

I felt that I could not be content until I had come to Abbottabad to see those fine regiments which are stationed here and of which I had always heard such high praise. And now I have seen you on parade I know that all that I have heard must be true."

Making every allowance for the obligation to say what will please at a function of the kind, there is enough here of genuine commendation bestowed by a member of the Government who was also a soldier to make his hearers proud of their Regiment and of their connection with the Punjab Frontier Force.

With the Waziristan Field Force, Dec., 1894 to March, 1895.

The closing days of 1894 saw the Battalion setting out for the scene of the Regiment's first encounter with the Queen's enemies. In April, 1860, it had received its baptism of fire at the camp at Palosin, and now, after a lapse of nearly 35 years, it was to wander once more among the strong places of the Mahsuds—Jandola, Ahnai, Marobi, Makin, Shahur, Kundiwam, and Wana— names which were to become familiar, too, to a later generation. In November, 1893, Sir Mortimer Durand, conferring with the Amir at Kabul, had arrived at an agreement regarding the demarcation of a boundary line between Afghanistan and the independent tribes across the British border. The work of delimitation was actually begun in the autumn of 1894, and the beginning of November found the boundary commissioners with a strong escort encamped at Wana in Southern Waziristan. Before dawn on November 3rd the camp was rushed by some 1,500 Mahsuds, followers of that notorious firebrand, the Mulla Powindah. The brunt of the attack was borne by the 1/1st Gurkhas, who behaved with great gallantry; the assailants were driven outside the perimeter, and, pursued by the Cavalry, lost heavily. On the British side the casualties numbered 45 killed and 75 wounded.

An offence so grave could not be overlooked. Terms were offered: compliance with them to be regarded as tantamount to reparation for wrongs done, their rejection to be visited with stringent reprisals. Meantime preparations would go forward for an invasion of the heart of the Mahsud country. Thus it came about that on November 30th the Battalion marched from Abbottabad to Hasan Abdal, whence it took train to Darya Khan, to reach Dera Ismail Khan on December 4th. Being much under strength, owing in part to a fever epidemic which followed in the train of the monsoon, 4 Gurkha officers and 170 other ranks were attached from the 2nd Battalion. The British officers who took part in the expedition were Colonel Gaselee, Captains Fayrer and Crawford, Lieutenants Davies, Bruce, Johnson, Ketchen, and Browne, and Surgeon Lieutenant-Colonel Bookey in medical charge.

From Dera Ismail Khan the Battalion set out on December 7th, and following the Tank Zam route, reached Jandola on the 11th. There it was incorporated in the 2nd Brigade Waziristan Field Force, under the command of Brigadier-General W. P. Symons, C.B. For the execution of those measures of reprisals which would be demanded by non-compliance with the terms offered, Sir William Lockhart's force consisted of three brigades. Of these the troops of the original delimitation escort formed the 1st, and would advance from Wana to Kaniguram. The 2nd Brigade was earmarked for a move from Jandola to Makin, and the 3rd was held in readiness to march to Razmak from its place of concentration at Mirian, near the junction of the Khaisora with the Tochi River.

During the period of negotiations it was apparent that many influential *maliks* were for peace, but in the end the turbulent Mulla was too strong for them. By December 12th, the date marking the end of the period of grace, no settlement had been effected, and on the 16th orders were received for the brigades to advance on their objectives.

The Battalion, with the 2nd Brigade, reached Makin on the 21st. The Mulla Powindah's village of Marobi was destroyed *en route*, a few shots were fired into camp at night, and isolated attempts were made by a few bold spirits to harass the baggage of the column. Otherwise the march was without incident, and of organized opposition there was none. On the same date the 1st Brigade reached Kaniguram after experiencing considerable hardship owing to the condition of the road, and the 3rd Brigade arrived at Razmak.

1895.

Next, measures were devised for the punishment of those sections of the Mahsuds who had taken part in the attack on the camp at Wana. For this purpose the force was divided into six small columns, each destined to overrun some enemy retreat in the neighbourhood of the great Pir Ghal Mountain. The 1/5th Gurkhas, with two companies of the 2nd Punjab Infantry and a half-company of sappers and miners, was given the task of sweeping out the Potwala Ravine. This column, like the others, began operations on Christmas Day, destroyed settlements and towers, collected considerable store of forage, and rounded up many head of cattle. After bivouacking out for two nights it returned to camp at Makin, having met with no opposition. There it remained until January 5th, 1895. Its stay was marked by heavy foraging and escort duties, so that often it was with difficulty that time could be found to cook. The weather, too, was very cold, but despite the fact that in many units pneumonia took a heavy toll, in the Battalion the men stood the exposure well and there were very few cases of sickness. In view of subsequent developments in the Tirah Campaign it is interesting to find it recorded that " on one or two occasions whilst at Makin the value of having trained scouts was proved. They were able to beat the Waziris on their own ground when sneaking about to fire on convoys, etc."

Signs were not wanting that the punishment inflicted on the offending sections was beginning to prove effective. Before the end of December, news was received that the Mulla had fled to Birmal, and a move had been made in the direction of compliance with the terms originally imposed. It was decided, therefore, to concentrate the Field Force at Jandola preparatory to initiating a series of movements in another part of the country. The 2nd Brigade left Makin in company with Sir William Lockhart on January 5th, and reached Jandola on the 8th. The remaining two brigades had already taken their departure, the 1st moving via the Shaktu and the 3rd via the Shinkai Algad. By January 9th concentration had been completed at Jandola. From there the 3rd Brigade was sent back to Mirian and the 1st Brigade was ordered to take the Gumal route to Wana. The 2nd Brigade left Jandola on January 13th, and moving up the Shahur reached Kundiwam in the Khaisara Valley on the 19th. The Battalion was detached *en route* with the 14th Sikhs and a section of sappers and miners to carry out a small punitive expedition against the Machi Khels. The task was completed successfully in two days, and the 17th saw the 1/5th Gurkhas back with the rest of the brigade two marches short of Kundiwam.

The 2nd Brigade was destined to remain at Kundiwam until the final withdrawal of the troops from Waziristan, but on January 22nd the Battalion, now a unit of divisional troops, severed its connection with Brigadier-General Symons' command and marched with Sir William Lockhart to Wana. During the spell of comparative leisure enjoyed at that place was held the historic race mentioned in the last chapter when our representatives triumphed over all comers.

While still at Kundiwam, Sir William Lockhart had interviewed the leading *maliks* of the offending sections and had propounded the conditions on which their submission would be accepted. While waiting for his interview to bear fruit he pushed forward the business of boundary delimitation which had been interrupted by the attack on the camp at Wana. While a strong escort from Wana accompanied Mr. King, who was entrusted with the delimitation of the boundary from Wana to Khwaja Khidr, the divisional troops, including the 1/5th Gurkhas, were detailed as part of the escort to the party which was to carry out a similar task from Khwaja Khidr to Charkhel and Laram. This entailed, in the first place, a march to Bannu. With the 2nd Battalion Border Regiment, 20th Punjab Infantry, No. 2 Company Sappers and Miners, and the Maxim gun detachment of the Devonshire Regiment, the Battalion left Wana on February 5th and, moving via Tank and Pezu, reached Bannu on the 17th. Next day they marched to Mirzail, ten miles west of Bannu on the Tochi River, and halted there for a week. At Mirzail a junction was effected with the 3rd Brigade, which had left Jandola, it will be remembered, about a month before, and on February 25th the whole force began its journey up the Tochi. Six days of continuous marching brought it to Sheranni, some nine miles west of Datta Khel on the Upper Tochi, and there a meeting took place with the Afghan boundary commissioners in accordance with arrangements previously made.

When two days out of Mirzail the Battalion sustained its only casualty of the campaign, a rifleman being mortally wounded by a prowling Wazir when on duty with a camel-grazing guard.

The Battalion's share in the expedition ended with the arrival at Sheranni. The Mahsuds had already given proofs of a change of heart, the last of the hostages demanded from them were surrendered on March 4th, and Sir William Lockhart felt justified in submitting proposals for the withdrawal of the bulk of the troops to India. Enough remained to ensure the protection of those engaged in completing the demarcation of the boundary. On March 8th Sir William himself left Sheranni for Bannu and took with him the 2nd Battalion Border Regiment, the 1/5th Gurkhas, and the Maxim gun detachment of the Devonshire Regiment.

To those acquainted with the frontier, the campaign is chiefly of interest from the contrast it presents to the most recent expeditions against the Mahsuds. The immunity enjoyed by comparatively small columns, and the ease with which they traversed every part of the country, are very striking. Whether the Mahsud of the present day is really a better fighter than his elders of a generation ago is open to question. It is more probable that the numerous successes scored by him against untrained troops in the earlier part of the campaign of 1919–20 are responsible for his greater enterprise and boldness in our latest encounters with him. The moral is obvious.

On arrival in Bannu on March 16th the Battalion found itself cast for a spell of garrison duty. At this time a small British force, under Captain Townshend, was beleaguered in the fort at Chitral, and while Colonel Kelly was engaged in his wonderful march from Gilgit, preparations went forward for the mobilization of a relief force which was to bring succour from the south via the Malakand Pass. It was confidently expected that the 1/5th Gurkhas would form part of the relief force, and every endeavour was made to re-equip the Battalion and make it fit for a new campaign. The disappointment was the greater, therefore, when its recent return from Waziristan was given as a reason for sending the 13th Bengal Infantry in its place.

On April 4th the return march to Abbottabad was begun. The route followed was by road to Peshawar via Kohat, thence by rail to Hasan Abdal, and so by the usual familiar stages to Abbottabad, which was reached on April 15th.

The honours accruing to the Battalion from the Waziristan Campaign were a mention in despatches for Colonel Gaselee, and a mention and brevet of Lieutenant-Colonel for Major Martin, who had done good work as Assistant-Adjutant-General on the Headquarters Staff.

At Abbottabad, 1895-96.

There followed a quiet time in Abbottabad until the unaccountable frenzy which shook the entire frontier in 1897 once more drew the Battalion from the paths of peace. In 1895 occurred the death of two riflemen, in company with M1. Mummery, on the north-west face of Nanga Parbat. They were Ragobir Thapa and Guman Sing Gurung. In February, 1896, a short absence from Abbottabad was caused by the attendance of the 1/5th at a small concentration of troops at Rawalpindi. They were brigaded with the 1st Battalion Gordon Highlanders and the 3rd Rifle Brigade. Otherwise the chief interest of this period attaches to changes among officers. At the end of April, 1896, Colonel Gaselee left to take up the appointment of officiating Colonel on the Staff at Cawnpore. He was succeeded by Lieutenant-Colonel A. R. Martin, whose permanent appointment as Commandant was to date from June 29th, 1897. Lieutenant W. D. Villiers-Stuart joined, on transfer from the 20th Punjab Infantry, on September 29th, 1896. In the same year Subadar Parsu Khattri Bahadur, I.O.M., became Subadar-Major and was shortly afterwards admitted to the 1st Class of the Order of British India with the title of Sirdar Bahadur. But a little later, in April, 1897, Subadar Jangia Thapa was admitted to the 2nd Class of the Order. This officer had for a time been one of Sir Frederick Roberts's orderlies during the Afghan War and earned the nickname of "Bullets," because it was commonly accepted in the Regiment as a fact that he had once been hit on the forehead by a bullet which had been completely flattened without, however, causing him the least discomfort.

Chamkanni Blockade, Feb.-Aug., 1897.

The year 1897 was to prove the most stormy ever experienced on the North-west Frontier since British influence along the borderland had supplanted that of the Sikhs. It was not, however, the general uprising of the tribes from the Indus to the Tochi which was responsible in the first instance for the transference of the headquarters and right wing of the Battalion from Abbottabad to the Kurram River: the train had been laid for that explosion, but the match had not been applied. For reasons which need not be specified, a blockade had been ordered of the Chamkannis, a tribe located at the head of the Kharmana Nullah which joins the Kurram at Sadda, and it was for the enforcement of the blockade that the 1/5th Gurkhas were called on.

The headquarters and right wing marched out on February 3rd

with a strength of 6 British officers, 7 Gurkha officers, and 360 other ranks. Lieutenant-Colonel A. R. Martin was in command, and with him were Captain Kemball, Lieutenants Bruce, Ketchen, and Villiers-Stuart, and Surgeon Lieutenant-Colonel Bookey. Twice before, the journey to Kohat and beyond had been a prelude to active service, and it was to be so again. On arrival at Sadda, some 35 miles beyond Thal on the left bank of the Kurram River, a standing camp was formed and the necessary arrangements were made to render the blockade effective. The stay there lasted until May 10th, when a move was made 15 miles farther to the west to a spot on the Kirman Nullah not far from Ahmadzai. On August 8th camp was again shifted, this time to Parachinar; but even before that, warning had been given of the coming storm, so it will be as well, at this point, to say something about the rising as a whole.

Frontier Unrest, 1897.

It happened that after the Mahsud campaign of 1894–95, to all seeming an unwonted calm settled on the frontier. Beneath the surface smouldered the fires of religious fanaticism which circumstances, barely noticed at the time, were presently to fan into flame. To an extent far greater than was realized, the tribesmen resented the boundary delimitation begun in 1894, fearing the loss of their independence. The Mullas, religious leaders of the tribes and opposed to any settled form of government, took advantage of this feeling of resentment, fostered it by enlarging on added grievances of their own imagining, and preached *jehad* as the only remedy. The most active among them were the Hadda Mulla, Najm-ud-Din, in Mohmand territory; Sadullah, known as the "Mad Fakir," who incited the people of the Swat Valley; and the Aka Khel Mulla, Saiyid Akbar, who preached to the Afridis. The Mulla Powindah failed to obtain a hearing among the Mahsuds and Wazirs. The task of these turbulent priests was made the easier firstly by the fact of the recent victory of the orthodox Turks over the infidel Greeks, and secondly by events in Afghanistan, where the Amir had lately assumed the title of "Zia-ul-Millat wa ud-Din" (Light of Union and Faith), and had also produced a book, "Takwin-ud-Din," which treated of *jehad*.

The peace of the borderland was first broken at Maizar, on June 10th, by the treacherous attack of the Madda Khels on the escort of the Political Officer, who had gone there from Datta Khel to settle various local questions. This was followed, on July 26th, by a wholly unlooked-for outbreak at the Malakand and Chakdara. Well on towards evening the officers from these posts were playing polo at Khar: at nightfall they were with difficulty holding their own against thousands of Swatis, whose religious feelings were inflamed to the pitch of frenzy by the fulminations of the "Mad Fakir." Nearly two months later, on August 7th, a *lashkar* of four or five thousand Mohmands crossed into British territory, burnt and looted the village of Shankargarh, and threatened Shabkadr Fort. Finally, on August 23rd, began the Afridi attacks on the Khyber forts, which fell one by one until two days later all had passed into enemy hands. Allied with the Afridis were the Orakzais who, immediately following the Khyber débâcle, became extremely active on the Samana and, aided by the Chamkannis, menaced the security of the Kurram posts.

Each outbreak entailed a separate expedition, the most important being that undertaken by Sir William Lockhart with a large force against the Afridis and Orakzais. Our present concern is with this last, for not only did the headquarters and wing of the Battalion stationed in the Kurram take an active part in the operations of the Tirah Expeditionary Force, but the 1/5th Gurkhas as a whole provided more than one-third of the original total strength of the famous Gurkha scouts.

Gurkha Scouts. The idea was not new of employing Gurkhas to carry out special tasks in hill warfare against a trans-border enemy. We have seen how men of the Regiment were used at Makin in the campaign of 1894–95 to counter the marauding tendencies of the Mahsuds, and even before that their peculiar aptitude for such work had been given scope on the Black Mountain. The Tirah Expedition, however, was the first occasion on which an organized body of Gurkha scouts formed part of the original order of battle. The men were chosen from the 1/5th, 2/5th, and 1/3rd Gurkhas, " specially trained to work on the steepest hill-sides, and selected for their wiry physique, fleetness of foot, and skill as marksmen." [1]

The 1/5th contingent consisted of Lieutenant the Honourable C. G. Bruce, 1 Gurkha officer, and 55 rank and file. The total strength of the scouts was about 120 rifles; they were commanded by Captain F. G. Lucas of the 2/5th and were given a third British officer in the person of Lieutenant A. B. Tillard of the 1/3rd Gurkhas.

Plan of Campaign in Tirah. The outstanding events of the campaign are familiar to those who have served on the frontier. It was the Afridi boast that none had ever entered their country without their full and free consent, and in order to upset that proud claim an invasion was planned from the south. Crossing the Samana Range by the Chagru Kotal the force would enter the Khanki Valley inhabited by the Orakzais. From there the Sampagha Pass would give access to the Mastura Valley, whence Maidan and Bagh, at the head of the Bara River in Afridi Tirah, could be reached by way of the Arhanga Pass.

During the time needed for preparation the enemy were extremely active on the Samana and in the Kurram Valley. To deal with them,

[1] "The Campaign in Tirah, 1897–98," by Colonel H. D. Hutchinson (Macmillan & Co.).

flying columns were formed from the troops available, but General Yeatman-Biggs, operating from Hangu, failed to save the small Samana post of Saragarhi, where on September 12th a havildar and 20 men of the 36th Sikhs were all killed, fighting to the last, and he effected the relief of Gulistan only just in time on September 15th. Colonel Richardson, with the Kurram Valley brigade, reached Sadda on September 5th, his arrival serving to frustrate the intentions of a big Orakzai *lashkar* which threatened to overwhelm the post. At that time the wing of the Battalion at Parachinar formed part of a small movable column under the command of Major Vansittart. Their numbers were very inadequate for the task of safeguarding the valley, and the coming of reinforcements extracted them from an awkward dilemma.

Samana and Kurram, September, 1897.

On September 16th the wing moved out of Parachinar, and after a trying march, joined Colonel Richardson in the camp overlooking Sadda. "At 10.30 p.m. the Sadda camp was attacked from the direction of the Kharmana Defile. The advanced piquet of the 5th Punjab Infantry was driven in by a sudden rush of the enemy, assisted by villagers living three miles east of Sadda. The retirement was admirably covered by the steady company volleys of the 5th Gurkhas under Lieutenants Ketchen and Browne, and the section volleys of the 5th Punjab Infantry. The portion of the camp attacked was the east face, held partly by the wing of the 5th Gurkhas under Major Vansittart, ... and partly by a wing of the 5th Punjab Infantry. The plan of the attack had evidently been carefully thought out, the face held by the Gurkhas being kept engaged by several hundred of the enemy, whilst the main attack was made on the south-east corner, held by the 5th Punjab Infantry. ... All the troops actively engaged were in position in the shortest possible time, and the first two steady and precise volleys of the gallant Gurkhas disabused the enemy's mind as to the possibility of effecting an entrance in that quarter. ... The discipline of all ranks was excellent, and although the casualties among the horses and transport were heavy, the order that prevailed throughout the attack of three hours spoke highly for the arrangements of the column and for the quiet energy of all the British and Native officers when exposed to a fire to which there was no opportunity of response. The enemy was estimated at 2,000 strong; their casualties were unknown, but from a visit to Badhura Village it was apparent that large numbers were wounded, the dead having already been buried."[1]

Attack on Sadda, Sept. 16th, 1897.

After helping to repel the attacks just described, the wing remained at Sadda for only a week, and returned to Parachinar on September 23rd.

[1] "The Risings on the North-west Frontier, 1897–98" (Pioneer Press, 1898).

There Colonel Martin rejoined on return from furlough, but he was shortly afterwards given a staff appointment, and only came back to the Battalion on the conclusion of the campaign.

Invasion of Tirah, October, 1897.

Meantime preparations went steadily forward for the invasion of Tirah, and it becomes necessary to follow for a time the fortunes of the main column in order to get an idea of the work done by the scouts. The force was organized in two divisions. The 1st Division was commanded by Brigadier-General W. P. Symons, C.B., and consisted of the 1st Brigade under Brigadier-General R. C. Hart, V.C., C.B., and the 2nd Brigade under Brigadier-General A. Gaselee, C.B., A.D.C. The 2nd Division was commanded by Major-General A. G. Yeatman-Biggs, C.B., and consisted of the 3rd Brigade under Colonel F. J. Kempster, D.S.O., A.D.C., and the 4th Brigade under Brigadier-General R. Westmacott, C.B., D.S.O. The Gurkha scouts were Army troops. With the Headquarters Staff was Captain F. F. Badcock, D.S.O., who held the appointment of Field Intelligence Officer, while Captain I. Phillips was D.A.A. and Q.M.G. on the staff of the Lines of Communication.

Dargai, October 18th and 20th, 1897.

By the middle of October concentration was nearing completion, and Sir William Lockhart wrote in his despatch of December 9th:

"I consequently issued orders for the march of the Main Column on the 20th and following days from Shinawari to Khorappa. . . . Meanwhile the road from the Chagru Kotal towards Khorappa was being improved by military and hired labour. . . . It was reported, however, that the troops and labourers thus employed were being so molested by the enemy's sharpshooters, who occupied the heights to the west of the Chagru Defile, especially by those living in a small village called Dargai, about 1,800 yards to the left of the road shortly after it crosses the crest of the pass, that the improvement of the road could not be continued until the heights had been cleared. . . .

"I therefore determined to attack and destroy the village of Dargai, while by a simultaneous flanking movement I seized the heights overlooking the valley to the west. . . ."

In this way there came to be fought the first of the two actions for the possession of the Dargai Heights. The troops left Shinauri very early on the morning of the 18th. While General Westmacott moved straight on the Chagru Kotal with the object of creating a diversion by means of a frontal attack, General Kempster embarked on a long turning movement which would bring him in on the right and rear of the enemy's position and enable him to strike a decisive blow from the west. Attached to General Kempster's command for the day were the scouts of the 5th Gurkhas, who were given the important task of leading the advance. While for General Westmacott all was plain sailing, for the turning column the way was beset with difficulties owing to the rocky and precipitous nature of the ground to be traversed. A few miles out of camp all mules, including those of the mountain battery, had to be returned, since it was impossible for them to go farther. In these circumstances the work of the scouts was invaluable, relieving, as it did, the troops in rear of many of the burdensome duties involved in their own protection. Even so, it was long after they were expected when General Kempster's troops arrived within striking-distance of Dargai, though their steady advance from a direction threatening the enemy's line of retreat made much easier the task of the column carrying out the frontal attack. Soon after noon the Orakzai defenders quitted the shelter of their *sangars* and fled towards the Khanki Valley. Dargai was then destroyed, and at 3 p.m. the two columns joined hands. There remained the return to camp, since lacking arrangements for the supply of rations and water, it was considered impossible to remain in possession of the ground won. Attracted by the sound of firing, large numbers of tribesmen had collected from the direction of the Sampagha Pass. "The return to Shinawari via Chagru Kotal in the face of such overwhelming numbers, with darkness growing rapidly, was a most difficult and dangerous operation; but so well conceived were General Kempster's dispositions, so admirable the manner in which the troops, both British and Native, carried them out, and so great the assistance afforded by the mountain Artillery both from Chagru Kotal and the Samana Suk, that the enemy did not dare to press an attack home, and after Chagru Kotal the return to Shinawari was practically unmolested."[1]

The second attack on the Dargai Heights was carried out on October 20th. In this action the scouts of the Regiment were given only a minor part to play, but those of the 1/3rd Gurkhas under Lieutenant Tillard were prominent in helping the advance of the 1/2nd Gurkhas across the bullet-swept stretch of open ground, which was later the scene of the well-known exploit of the 1st Battalion Gordon Highlanders. Partly, perhaps, because the plan of attack made no provision for a turning movement, casualties were heavy, but by 3 p.m. the position had been won and the troops went into bivouac in the vicinity of the Chagru Kotal.

Khorappa, in the Khanki Valley, was reached on the 21st. It was necessary to halt there for a week while arrangements were made for the next forward move, and during that time the enemy never ceased from troubling. Not a night passed but the camp was heavily sniped, and as ill-luck would have it, Captain Badcock was one of the victims.

[1] "The Risings on the North-west Frontier, 1897-98" (Pioneer Press, 1898).

A large-bore bullet passed through his left elbow while he was sitting at dinner, and it was found necessary to amputate his arm near the shoulder. In spite of this handicap, when peace came again he was still a formidable opponent at lawn tennis, and at racquets could hold his own against the best players to be found in Northern India.

Capture of Sampagha Pass, Oct. 29th, 1897.

Sir William Lockhart's next objective was the Sampagha Pass, leading into the Mastura Valley. To the attack launched against it on October 29th the Orakzais offered but a feeble resistance, while the help afforded to them by their Afridi allies was almost negligible. The scouts of the 5th Gurkhas, however, found an opportunity to distinguish themselves. Attached to General Gaselee's brigade they took their share in the capture of the main approach to the pass, and then, two companies of the Queen's supporting them, they worked their way up a spur on the east of the kotal where numbers of the enemy were trying to interpose between the Yorkshire Regiment and the 3rd Sikhs. While engaged in the task of heading back this body of tribesmen, Havildar Kaman Sing Burathoki did brilliant service. His attention was caught by the movements of a gang of Pathans prowling among the rocks of the steep hill-side, and he at once set himself to spoil their plans. He manoeuvred his section with such skill that he took the tribesmen completely by surprise. Opening fire at very short range before they were aware of his presence he killed a number of them, whereupon the rest fled precipitately, leaving their dead on the ground.

Capture of Arhanga Pass, Oct. 31st, 1897.

At the capture of the Arhanga Pass two days later the scouts of the Regiment were again attached to General Gaselee's brigade, which was given the task of dealing the decisive blow on the enemy's left, while the 2nd Division, led by the scouts of the 3rd Gurkhas, attacked frontally. "The Battalions of Gaselee's Brigade (with whom for the day were the 5th Gurkha Scouts, some eighty in number, under Captain Lucas and Lieutenant Bruce) climbed steadily up the ravines on his (the enemy's) left, and at ten minutes to ten exactly their leading files reached the crest of the hill. The ascent was a very steep one, though well sheltered the greater part of the way from direct fire, and there was admirable rivalry for the honour of being the first to top the summit. As nearly as possible the Yorkshire Regiment and the 5th Gurkha Scouts arrived at the same time, but the Queen's, the 3rd Sikhs, and the 4th Gurkhas were all close up, and the performance of the whole brigade was excellent."[1]

Over the Arhanga Pass the force moved into Maidan about the head waters of the Bara River. During the prolonged stay made there

[1] "The Campaign in Tirah, 1897–98," by Colonel H. D. Hutchinson (Macmillan & Co.).

for the replenishment of reserve supplies the scouts were constantly engaged with small parties of the enemy both by day and night, and were often called upon to stalk hostile snipers during the hours of darkness. On the night of November 15th–16th, Lance-Naik Karbir Burathoki brought off a most brilliant coup when he surprised a numerous band of marauders and killed six of them, losing only one of his own men during the encounter.

Maidan and Bagh, November, 1897.

Throughout the time spent in Maidan the Zakka Khels proved the most irreconcilable of all the Afridi clans, and it was partly to mete out punishment to them that a force was detached to visit Saran Sar on November 9th. With this operation, and with the disaster which befell a company of the Northamptons during the withdrawal, the scouts had no concern, but when the movement was repeated two days later to show that sound tactics would always prevail over tribal cunning, Sir William Lockhart was careful to choose General Gaselee's brigade for the demonstration, and to send with them the Gurkha scouts.

"General Gaselee, long well known as the Colonel of the 5th Gurkhas, and an officer of vast experience in frontier fighting, directed the movements with great judgment, and though the Afridis again followed up the retirement, they never got a look in at all. . . . It was an entirely successful and satisfactory day, and in a Brigade Order, General Gaselee conveyed Sir William Lockhart's appreciation of the day's work by the troops."[1]

The enemy scored another success on November 16th, when they overwhelmed a party of the Dorsets during the withdrawal of General Kempster's brigade from the Waran Valley, but again the scouts had no part in the misfortune.

They are next heard of on November 18th, when a beginning was made with the transfer of the camp from Maidan to Bagh. The force engaged consisted of the 2nd Brigade with the divisional troops of the 1st Division. No serious opposition was encountered until after arrival at Bagh. No sooner did the tribesmen realize, however, that the troops had come to stay, than they gathered in great numbers and disputed possession of every vantage-point. Here the scouts were in their element. Throughout eleven long hours they were actively engaged with the enemy, and by skilful use of ground, forced them to abandon position after position.

"The Gurkha scouts of the 5th Gurkhas did excellent service on November 18th, killing several of the enemy, and many more were seen being carried away wounded."[2]

[1] "The Campaign in Tirah, 1897–98," by Colonel H. D. Hutchinson (Macmillan & Co.).
[2] "The Risings on the North-west Frontier, 1897–98" (Pioneer Press, 1898.)

THE 5TH ROYAL GURKHA RIFLES (F.F.)

Again in General Westmacott's reconnaissance to Dwatoi, carried out between November 22nd and 24th, the scouts earned great distinction, and Havildar Kaman Sing Burathoki, Rifleman Maniram Pun, and Lance-Naik Goria Rana; all of the 1/5th, were awarded the Order of Merit for conspicuous gallantry displayed on this occasion.

Events in Kurram Valley, Oct.–Nov., 1897.

While the Gurkha scouts had been occupied in Tirah, the Chamkannis and certain Orakzai sections across the watershed in the Kurram basin, had persisted in their defiant attitude. Sir William Lockhart decided to deal with them before proceeding to his next move in the main theatre—the overrunning of the Bazar and Bara Valleys. This decision was to bring together for a spell the scouts and the Kurram wing of the Battalion. It will be convenient, therefore, at this point to go back a little, and to follow the fortunes of the wing subsequent to its return to Parachinar after the attack on the camp at Sadda.

For more than a month nothing occurred to demand the active intervention of the wing of the 1/5th Gurkhas. On November 3rd, however, they were called to Sadda by Colonel W. Hill, commanding the Kurram movable column, in connection with the assembly of a strong *lashkar* in the Kharmana Defile.

On November 7th the movable column[1] entered the Kharmana Defile with the object of carrying out a reconnaissance in force. During the advance over a distance of some seven miles but little opposition was encountered. Piquets were posted to protect the route, and at 1 p.m., the purpose of the reconnaissance accomplished, the force began to withdraw. By that time the enemy had mustered in strength, and the men of the 1/5th Gurkhas who furnished the rear-guard were soon hotly engaged. About a mile had been covered in the direction of camp when a long delay was occasioned by a piquet of the Kapurthala Infantry, which failed to acknowledge the signal to withdraw. Encouraged by the check, the tribesmen directed a strong attack on the rear-guard. No strangers to these tactics, the 5th Gurkhas were ready for them. With a loss to themselves of one killed and three wounded they beat off the attack and handled their assailants so severely that they made no further attempt to molest the column. On receipt of a report that the piquet had come in the march was resumed, and the column reached Sadda before evening fell. During the night the officer commanding the Kapurthala Infantry made the

---

[1] Maxim-Gun Detachment Royal Scots Fusiliers.
100 Lances Central India Horse (mounted).
100 Lances Central India Horse (dismounted).
100 Rifles 12th Bengal Infantry.
260 Rifles 1/5th Gurkhas.
400 Rifles Kurram Militia.
100 Rifles Kapurthala Infantry.

discovery that his piquet had not rejoined as reported. Those missing consisted of a Subadar and 35 men, and subsequent investigation showed that in attempting to rejoin the rear-guard they had taken a wrong line, had been trapped in a *nullah* where a jungle fire was burning, had been found there by a party of the enemy and had been killed to a man after the withdrawal of the column to camp.

There happened nothing else of moment on the Kurram side until, on November 29th, Colonel Hill once more took his column up the Kharmana to meet the force from Bagh which was to co-operate with it in punishing the Chamkannis.

That force left Bagh under the command of Brigadier-General Gaselee on November 26th. The route lay westwards up a tributary of the Bara River, known as the Kahu Darra, then over the Durbi Khel Pass, and down a small affluent of the Kharmana to Dargai, the principal settlement of the Massuzai. The advance was led by the Gurkha scouts, stiff opposition was encountered, and there were several casualties. Owing to the difficulties of the way and the dangerous character of the heights flanking the route, only short marches could be accomplished, and it was not until the 30th that a junction was effected at Lwara Mela with the Kurram movable column.

Actions at Thabai, December 1st and 2nd, 1897.

No time was wasted, for on the very next day, December 1st, the united forces set about the punishment of the tribes which still refused to comply with the terms offered them. While General Gaselee himself penetrated the Lozaka Defile with a compact little column to receive the submission of the Gar Massuzais, Colonel Hill, with the troops detailed below, moved on Thabai, the principal stronghold of the Chamkannis.

Left Column (Lieut.-Col. C. Gordon).
2 Maxim Guns, Royal Scots Fusiliers.
150 Sabres 6th Bengal Cavalry (dismounted).
300 Rifles 12th Bengal Infantry.
150 Rifles 1/5th Gurkhas.
100 Rifles Kapurthala Infantry.

Right Column (Lieut.-Col. G. Money).
Gurkha Scouts.
150 Sabres Central India Horse.
Kohat Mountain Battery.
¼ Company Bombay S. and M.
2/4th Gurkhas.

Thabai itself was about six miles north of the camp at Lwara Mela, and the approaches to it were by two parallel defiles. Of these the more easterly took off from the camp and gave access to the village from the south, while the other ran up from a point about two miles west of Lwara Mela and led round to the western side of the settlement.

The right column, accompanied by Colonel Hill, used the eastern approach, and led by the Gurkha scouts, arrived unopposed at a kotal overlooking Thabai from the south at 10 a.m. From there the mountain guns opened fire on the enemy, who could be seen in their positions about the village. The left column, which had a more difficult route to traverse, had arrived meanwhile at some outlying hamlets about one mile to the west of Thabai. Enemy snipers posted on the surrounding heights here found an opportunity to harass the advanced guard, but their fire was soon silenced by the Maxim guns of the Royal Scots Fusiliers, which came into action on a scrub-covered knoll situated conveniently in the defile.

"The Engineer party with a strong escort then proceeded to burn and destroy the hamlets. Signalling communication was now established with No. 1 Column, and orders were sent by Colonel Hill, who was with that column, to proceed right up the defile to Thabai and join hands with him, he being then within one mile of and overlooking Thabai. Colonel Gordon at once issued orders for the 1/5th Gurkhas to proceed, followed by the Maxim guns, the 6th Bengal Cavalry, the Kapurthala Infantry, and the 12th Bengal Infantry. The defile was very narrow, in some places not more than 50 yards across, with precipitous cliffs on either hand rising to 800 or 1,000 feet above the bed of the river. On debouching from the defile at Thabai the head of the column turned to the south to join Colonel Money, whereupon the enemy, following their invariable plan, appeared on the high ground over the ravine and commenced a heavy fire. The 1/5th Gurkhas and the 6th Bengal Cavalry at once extended to cover the withdrawal of the remainder of the force through the ravine, and while this was being done Lieutenant Richmond Battye of the 6th Bengal Cavalry was killed. A little later the two companies of the 1/5th Gurkhas and the 6th Bengal Cavalry, after debouching from the defile, came under a trying fire from the enemy's sharpshooters on the opposite hill. The enemy had excellent cover among trees, with the additional advantage of being posted above the Gurkhas and the Cavalry, who were on the edges of rice terraces which formed the side of the slope up which they had to retire to join Colonel Money's column. It was during this period and among these troops that most of the casualties of the day occurred." [1]

In the Battalion two riflemen were killed, and Lieutenant Villiers-Stuart and two riflemen were wounded. The removal of the casualties up a steep slope under a heavy fire proved very difficult, and it was for the courage he displayed on this occasion in getting Lieutenant Villiers-Stuart to a place of safety that Subadar-Major Parsu Khattri was promoted from the 3rd to the 2nd Class of the Indian Order of Merit. Others who distinguished themselves at the same time were Havildar Bir Sing Gurung and Rifleman Birkhdhoj Khattri. For Lieutenant Villiers-Stuart his wound was a great misfortune. Good at games and a keen rider, the after-effects of a badly shattered knee were to debar him from his favourite pursuits throughout the rest of his service. But he never allowed his disability to affect his physical

[1] "The Risings on the North-west Frontier, 1897–98" (Pioneer Press, Allahabad, 1898).

efficiency as a soldier, and it is still remembered of him that a few years before the Great War he marched his double company the 32 miles to Mansehra and back at an average speed of four miles an hour, and himself walked with them every step of the way.

The rest of the story of the first day's fighting at Thabai is soon told. The two columns joined hands a little to the south of Thabai, and the work of covering the further withdrawal to camp was taken up by the Gurkha scouts. There was a great race between them and a strong party of the enemy for the possession of a line of hills which commanded the route to be followed in the retirement, the Gurkhas, by a great effort, winning on the post. Foiled at this point the enemy appeared to lose heart, and camp was reached with little more fighting at 7.30 p.m.

December 2nd, the anniversary of Peiwar Kotal and Nilt, was once more to prove a great day in the annals of the Regiment. Colonel Hill again moved against Thabai, taking with him the force detailed below:—

Advanced Guard.	*Main Body.*	*Rear-Guard.*
5th Gurkha Scouts.	½ Batt. The Queen's Regt.	2/4th Gurkhas.
200 Rifles 5th Gurkhas.	Kohat Mountain Battery.	
	½ Battalion 3rd Sikhs.	

The route followed was that taken by the right column on the previous day. On approaching the kotal overlooking Thabai the advanced guard encountered strong opposition from about 300 tribesmen, who fought with great determination behind a series of strongly made *sangars* situated on the hills to the west. It fell to Captain Lucas and his scouts to deal with them, supported by the wing of the Battalion under Major Vansittart. The action of the scouts is thus described by Colonel C. E. Calwell in his book entitled, " Small Wars: Their Principles and Practice."

" There were 80 of these scouts engaged—on this particular occasion they were moving rather ahead of one flank of the column operating against Thabai. When the enemy was observed in some force on high ground they first had to scramble up some precipitous slopes. Then on approaching the crest they found in front of them three successive spurs, each one *sangared* and held by large bodies of tribesmen. Captain Lucas waited until he saw the leading company of the 5th Gurkhas coming up in support; then telling off one half of his command on one flank to sweep the first lot of *sangars* with independent fire, he himself led the other half from the other flank to charge this nearest position. To the wild delight of the Gurkhas the Chamkannis, on seeing the little party rushing forward, stood up, fired a desultory volley and got their knives out. It looked as if there was to be a scrimmage such as the scouts had been thirsting for. But the enemy could not

Subadar-Major Parsu Khattri, I.O.M., Sardar Bahadur.
1859 to 1900.

stand the combination of approaching bayonets and of a withering fire which the happy dispositions adopted for attack brought about. They wavered a moment and then fled, leaving behind them several dead to the credit of the firing half of the scout company. The two other spurs were cleared in the same way, and finally when the hillmen streamed away over the crest and across terraced fields below, the Gurkhas shot them down from above with deadly effect. Twenty or thirty of the enemy were killed, and not a single scout was even wounded."

The companies of the 1/5th Gurkhas in support were not quite so fortunate; Major Vansittart himself was wounded and two riflemen were killed. The taking of the main Chamkanni position paved the way to the complete and final destruction of their stronghold. Then came the time for withdrawal, which all accounts describe as " unmolested." The incident which accounted for this immunity is described below in the words of Brigadier-General the Honourable C. G. Bruce, who, of course, was present with the Gurkha scouts.

" The scouts' action in the morning of turning the Chamkanni position through steep cliffs, and the rushing by Captain Lucas of a number of *sangars*, was completed by the most successful ruse, employed by Lieutenant Browne on retirement. The troops consisted at this point of the scouts and half a battalion of the 1/5th Gurkhas. To retire from the Chamkanni position a descent of 1,500 feet was necessary, followed by an ascent of nearly 1,000 feet. As the evening approached, the Chamkannis were gathering as usual in confident anticipation of an hour's care-free sport. The scouts cleared off the position early, leaving the final retirement to Lieutenant Browne. With great skill he placed his men along the ridge, leaving an open and ascending glacis to his front, but ensuring on his own side good cover immediately available. When the rest of the force began to withdraw he slackened his fire, giving the impression of a dwindling number of rifles holding the position, but did not retire his men, only keeping them tight under cover. When the firing had completely ceased, the Chamkannis broke cover and rushed for the ridge, only to be met with rapid fire from Lieutenant Browne's men, the result being that they suffered very considerable and unexpected casualties and were so demoralized that it became possible to carry out the withdrawal immediately without further molestation, though at a great and suitable pace."

A spectator of the day's work was Lord Methuen, who expressed great admiration of the qualities of speed and resource displayed by the men of the Regiment.

Next day (December 3rd) the Kurram movable column returned towards Sadda, and with it went the wing of the 1/5th Gurkhas. The tribes in the Kurram Valley had had their fill of fighting, and on

December 23rd the wing moved back to Parachinar. There it remained until its return to Abbottabad on February 22nd, 1898. On the same day the Gurkha scouts began the return march to Bagh, which was reached via Khanki Bazar and the Chingakh Pass on December 6th.

Before undertaking the punishment of the Chamkannis, Sir William Lockhart had issued orders for the evacuation of the Tirah and for the concentration of his forces near Bara Fort a few miles south-west of Peshawar. It was his intention to continue punitive operations from there in the Bara and Bazar Valleys, and to arrange for the reoccupation of the Khyber. The 2nd Division was to reach its destination by a march down the Bara River, while the 1st Division, following at first the course of the Mastura River, reached the point of concentration by way of the Sapri Pass. The Gurkha scouts accompanied the 2nd Division, and gave a very good account of themselves during a period which embraced some of the hardest rear-guard fighting ever experienced on the frontier. Early on the second day out they were prominent in the capture of a hill commanding the entrance to the Rajgal Valley, and in the fighting which came afterwards in the valley itself they were well to the fore.

March down Bara Valley, December 7th–14th, 1897.

Owing to interruptions caused by the difficult passage of the Dwatoi Defile and the visit to the Rajgal Valley to punish the Kuki Khels, the march towards Bara Fort can hardly be considered to have begun in earnest until the 10th. Each day the tribesmen pressed hard on the rear-guard; there was heavy sniping at night, and as the men fell in of a morning a few would fall victims to the bullets of the ever-active tribesmen. The river was crossed and re-crossed, the weather turned cold and cheerless, and for three days rain fell almost incessantly causing intense discomfort. The rearmost troops seldom succeeded in reaching the camp at nightfall; instead they had to remain out in the open, guarding the transport which had been left behind, without baggage, sometimes without food, and once even without water. The Gurkha scouts had their full share of all these hardships, but thanks to their previous training and their fine physical condition their efficiency was not impaired.

Barkai, near Bara Fort, was reached on December 14th. The troops of the 1st Division had already arrived there, and in addition Sir William Lockhart had at his disposal Brigadier-General Hammond's Peshawar column for the execution of his future plans. These provided for the further punishment of the Zakka Khels by the destruction of their settlements in the Bazar Valley and the reoccupation of the Khyber.

The first-named task was entrusted to the 1st Division, while the re-establishment of the Khyber posts was reserved in the main for

Brigadier-General Hammond's column. Meanwhile the 2nd Division, which had endured so much in its march down the Bara, was to be given a rest. Not so the Gurkha scouts, who were apportioned to General Gaselee's column for the invasion of the Bazar Valley by the Chora route, a move which was to be carried out simultaneously with that of a second column under General Symons marching parallel on a more northerly track through Alachi.

Operations in Bazar Valley, December 25th–28th, 1897.

Despite their openly expressed defiance, the Zakka Khels made no great show of resistance. December 24th found the scouts encamped with the column at Lala China. On Christmas Day they marched to Chora, and on the 26th reached China, the principal settlement of the valley. On the way the rear-guard was engaged with small parties of the enemy, and sustained several casualties. The next day was devoted to the destruction of China, and on the 28th hard blows were exchanged as the force made its way back to Chora. That marked the end of fighting for the Gurkha scouts. They remained in the Khyber for some weeks, and during that time negotiations were carried on with those sections of the tribes which had not yet made their submission. These seemed likely to bring peace, when, on January 29th, 1898, troops of the 2nd Division experienced a serious reverse at Spin Kamar, a pass leading into the Bara Valley from the Kajuri Plain. There was a possibility that the tribes, encouraged by their success, would again harden their hearts and refuse to make terms. Should that happen, a spring campaign would become necessary, and Sir William Lockhart accordingly arranged to increase the efficiency of his forces by increasing the number of Gurkha scouts.

Their strength was raised to a total of 8 British officers, 7 Gurkha officers, and 660 rank and file, they were armed with the Lee-Metford rifle, and to enable them to become familiar with the new weapon they were sent to Peshawar for a short course of training before rejoining the 1st Division in the Khyber. Under the new organization the contingent from the 1st Battalion consisted of Lieutenant the Honourable C. G. Bruce, Lieutenant H. J. P. Browne, 3 Gurkha officers, and 220 rank and file. The 2nd Battalion quota was even larger, numbering 240 rifles under Captain F. G. Lucas, Lieutenant M. H. P. Barlow, and Lieutenant M. R. W. Nightingale. The total was completed by detachments from the 1/1st and 2/3rd Gurkhas. It was while the reorganized scouts were awaiting developments at Landi Kotal that they won a great victory in a hill race run against local Pathans.

Strength of Scouts increased.

It soon became evident that the Spin Kamar affair had not had the effect anticipated. Gradually the various sections of the tribes complied with the terms imposed, until finally even the Zakka Khels came in and made their submission. With the resulting dispersal of the Field Force the existence of the Gurkha scouts as an organized body came to an end, and in April, 1898, the several contingents returned to their peace stations.

End of the Campaign, April, 1898.

To do full justice to the work of the original scouts would need far more space than is available here. The following notes contributed by General Bruce will help towards a better idea of their achievements.

"I might point out that we were employed with every brigade in succession, that we covered the advance of most troops, seizing the heights in the dark, and were usually left to find our own way home. When a mistake had been made, as on the Saran Sar, we were sent out to repeat the performance. On occasions chasing home at night was often a difficulty owing to the fact that our covering parties, usually furnished and placed a mile or two behind us, frequently considered us as their covering parties and went off home in peace and comfort. Getting back on these occasions required considerable activity. Work at night, other than seizing points before dawn, consisted in stalking small sniping parties, and was very exciting if not always very successful. Karbir, however, brought off a very brilliant coup in stalking a party of Afridis and accounting for some six of them.

"In those days when volley firing was in vogue, the enemy frequently dodged the word of command most successfully. Many of our little local successes were gained by utilizing these words of command; men were specially posted to take advantage of the carelessness of the enemy after a volley had been fired."

General Bruce tells two stories which are in lighter vein.

"One of the most nervous incidents during the retirement down the Bara Valley was after an order had been issued that there was to be no further looting of villages. The scouts marched passed Sir William Lockhart with every haversack stuffed with chickens. Luckily the Gurkha face can look more innocent than anything on earth!

"After the burning of the China Bazaar in the Zakka Khel country, the scouts, increased to the strength of almost a battalion, were collected at Landi Kotal. There we were visited by Mr. Lionel James, the well-known war correspondent. He lunched with us and mentioned that he was to call on his uncle, Colonel W——, a dour and terrible veteran whom he had not seen for fifteen years. He called him Uncle Opey, and at first seemed to have misgivings about the coming interview. He went on lunching with us and then was led like a lamb to the slaughter. 'Uncle Opey,' said the long-lost nephew, 'Uncle Opey, old dear, I am damned drunk!' We fled—it was no business of ours."

The distinctions gained by the Gurkha scouts were many. In the Regiment, apart from the awards made to the rank and file, Captain

Lucas and Lieutenant Bruce were both mentioned several times in despatches, both earned brevet promotion to the rank of Major, and the former was given the Distinguished Service Order.

Sir William Lockhart wrote in his despatch:—

"During the present expedition the scouts drawn from the 3rd and 5th Gurkhas have proved especially valuable. Being trained mountaineers and accustomed to guerrilla warfare, they were able to climb the most precipitous hills, lie in ambush at night, and surpass the tribesmen in their own tactics."

CHAPTER VIII

1898 TO 1914

BETWEEN the years 1860 and 1898 the Regiment has perhaps a longer list of campaigns to its credit than any other Infantry unit of the Indian Army. Now comes a time in the history of the 1st Battalion when for sixteen years it applied itself to maintaining its efficiency without once having its work put to the final test of war. It was often asserted by those to whom the lot had fallen in a groundless fair, that Gurkha battalions remaining always in one station were handicapped in the race with other units which moved from place to place and saw more of the world. For the 5th Gurkhas, at any rate, no such handicap existed. They enjoyed a climate which allowed of training at fairly high pressure all through the year; available at their doors were hills suited to the practice of every phase of mountain warfare, and plains appropriately accidented by their Creator for the obvious purpose of staging realistic battles against a well-armed and highly organized enemy. Every winter they attended some concentration of troops, rubbed shoulders with cavalrymen, sappers, and gunners, and compared notes with British Infantry battalions and with all classes of the Indian Army. One or more of their officers were present at most of the campaigns fought between 1898 and 1914, and returned to impart the knowledge gained by new experiences. Both battalions were represented in China, where J. M. Stewart, E. B. C. Boddam, M. R. W. Nightingale, and F. H. Bridges saw service in the Boxer Rising; in course of time officers joined who had been through the war in South Africa; D. M. Govan served with Mounted Infantry in Somaliland; C. M. Crawford, in the position of a military attaché, was a witness of some of the fiercest fighting of the Russo-Japanese War, and it became his custom afterwards to come into the mess and convey his impressions in short, nervous sentences punctuated with the exclamation, "What is war? Blood! Blood!"

Among those who accompanied the Tibetan Mission were J. M. Stewart and G. P. Sanders, while in the Abor Expedition and others undertaken at the same time against tribes of the North-east Frontier, A. M. Graham and A. B. Hay-Webb played a distinguished part.

Enough has been said to show that life in Abbottabad during peacetime did not entail stagnation on a hill-top; just how the time was spent and what the profit of the work will appear as the narrative proceeds, and it will help towards gaining a truer conception of the life of the Battalion if we deal first with certain events which were common to every normal year.

The training year began with the hot weather. During the earlier part of the period now under review detachments were many and British officers were few. Inevitably the training of each sub-unit could not be made continuous, and we find that a particular company would spend a month or more cutting wood in the neighbourhood of Phulkot and then go into camp for its annual training under a specially selected officer. Even after the introduction of the double-company system in 1901 it was necessary for a year or two to continue this method. For example, on the Samana in 1901 all four double companies went through a special course of training under Major C. G. Bruce, and in August 1902 the same officer took two double companies into the hills above Kalapani for a like purpose. With the increase in the number of British officers which came with Lord Kitchener's reforms it was found possible for a double company commander to carry out the training of his own unit, and beginning with the year 1903 this was the procedure invariably adopted. It became the custom to form summer camps whither, as a rule, two double companies would migrate accompanied by the recruits. The most pleasant of all such camps were those in the Kagan Valley, Paya and Shagram on the left bank of the Kunhar above Kawai, and Naddi on the right bank with Musaka-Musalla for a background. In such surroundings, with no other distractions than those provided by hill, forest, and stream, with a minimum of men absent from any parade and in a perfect climate, it is not surprising that the time spent in summer camp was found to give good value.

Training.

With the coming of the cold weather there were generally camps of exercise or manœuvres in some part of the plains country to the south of Abbottabad. Occasionally these were postponed until after Christmas, with disastrous consequences, but more often they were held in November and December.

Inspections came towards the end of the training year, and the reports were invariably favourable. The following extracts are not without interest. Inspecting in 1899, Major-General C. C. Egerton wrote, " An excellent spirit pervades all ranks." Major-General Sir A. R. Martin remarked in 1908, " A thoroughly efficient Battalion in all respects. Special attention is directed to developing the rifle efficiency." In 1910 Lieutenant-General Sir Jocelyn Woodhouse noted " a fine Battalion and fit in all respects. Maxim gun mules and section above the

Inspections.

average." Lieutenant-General Sir James Willcocks said in 1911, " A first-class fighting Battalion very well trained."

Detachments.
Mention was made above of detachments. Of these some fell regularly to the Battalion in its turn, others were merely incidental. Of this latter class were the Simla detachment provided in 1898, the guard over the camp of Boer prisoners at Kakul furnished in 1902, and the Murree detachment sent in 1905. Of the former kind were the Phulkot woodcutting party; the detachment for duty at the School of Musketry, Changla Gali; the guard for the Artillery Practice Camp at Hatti, and the " puttee party " which went to Sopor and other places in Kashmir to buy puttees and blankets for the half-mounting store.

The employment of a number of men on cutting wood needs a word of explanation. Less lucky than the 2nd Gurkhas, who have their own forest reserve, the men of the Abbottabad garrison have always been obliged to spend an unduly large proportion of their hard-earned pay in providing themselves with firewood. To relieve them in part of the burden, from 1893 onwards trees were procured *in situ* by negotiation with the Forest Department, and these were then felled and split by Battalion labour and floated down the Daur River to Dumtaur. In this way firewood could be obtained much more cheaply than by purchase in the open market. Usually two companies at a time would be employed on this work; the men revelled in the return to surroundings which were not unlike those of their own homes, and the hard manual labour kept them fit.

Autumn Fever.
In the words of the " Gazetteer of the Hazara District," " The chief malady from which the district suffers is malarial fever. This is worst in the damp plains of Pakhli and Haripur, but when the summer rains are abnormally heavy and the maize crop exceptionally high, as was the case in 1906, it is very prevalent everywhere." In the days of which we are now writing it was a factor which had always to be reckoned with, and each succeeding Commanding Officer gave the subject prominence when writing up the year's doings in the digest of services. At that time the fields of maize, with their drainage ditches containing stagnant water, came right up to the 2/5th lines and the brigade parade-ground, and it was not until, years later, the cantonment was extended in that direction to include all ground as far as the Link Road that the evil was abated.

1898.
The years immediately succeeding the return from the Kurram were uneventful. In 1898 three new officers joined —H. A. Holdich, F. H. Bridges, and C. E. Bateman-Champain. The Battalion again had the honour of providing the Simla detachment, and its absence, combined with the

despatch of an unusually large furlough party, left few men available for training. Those who remained were put through a special course of musketry fired in the hills at unknown ranges. The details of the practices were worked out by Captain Fayrer, who succeeded in arousing great interest in the experiment. It is significant of the progressive spirit underlying the system of training that the need for experiment should have been realized while volley firing was still in vogue and while the authorities still approved a normal musketry course which comprised only deliberate shooting at an iron target bearing a large black bullseye standing out from a snow-white ground.

1899.

The first manœuvres attended by the Battalion after the conclusion of the Tirah Campaign took place in the country round Attock in February and March of 1899. They are notable on two counts; the first that, despite the time of year, the exercises were not brought to a premature end by bad weather; the second that the tactics of the South African War were anticipated by the use of Mounted Infantry. Major-General H. J. P. Browne relates that " as many men as possible of the Battalion were hastily mounted on transport mules to gallop forward and seize an important position. The route was strewn with thrown Gurkhas, but sufficient arrived to deny the position to the enemy."

Since June, 1898, Colonel Martin had been officiating as Deputy-Adjutant-General at Army Headquarters. In June, 1899, he was confirmed in the appointment, and the command of the Battalion therefore passed to Lieutenant-Colonel A. A. Barrett, who had been second-in-command of the 2/5th. Of these two distinguished officers the former was destined to rise to the command of a division and the latter, after finishing his time in command of an army, to attain the rank of Field-Marshal. The Regiment takes an equal pride in the careers of both.

In this year, when the weather was at its hottest and all were longing for the alleviation which the rains would bring, orders arrived for the despatch of a strong detachment to escort arms and ammunition to Chilas. Two Gurkha officers and 100 rank and file were detailed for the duty under the command of Lieutenant Villiers-Stuart, and on July 18th they began their march. At first the heat was very great; then came the rains, which brought a drop in temperature, but added enormously to the difficulties of the road; and finally, as the Babusar Pass was approached, the cold became intense. From these causes the march proved extremely trying, but the detachment returned to Abbottabad on August 15th with its mission successfully accomplished, and Colonel Barrett recorded of it that " it was carried out in a most creditable manner by Lieutenant Stuart and those serving under him."

In December the sad news was received of the death at Chilas on the 15th of the month of Captain C. H. Davies, who was on special duty at the time with the Kashmir Imperial Service troops. He had been twelve years in the Regiment, and during that time had endeared himself to all ranks, who sincerely deplored his loss.

1900.

The year 1900 is memorable for the introduction of the double-company system in the Indian Army. Instead of the two wings of a battalion there were now four double companies for purposes of administration. The four officers next in seniority to the Commanding Officer were appointed double company commanders; the remainder were known as double company officers, but after filling the posts of Adjutant and Quartermaster there was seldom more than one available for other work. Each company was under the direct command of a Subadar who had a Jemadar to assist him. It is not necessary to go further into the system, but it may be noted that it was very well suited to the needs of the Indian Army, and possessed the advantage that it gave to Gurkha officers more obvious and more definite responsibilities than they were later to enjoy under the platoon organization.

In February, Subadar-Major Parsu Khattri, Sirdar Bahadur, retired on pension. A most loyal and devoted servant of Government, he possessed qualities of head and heart which cause him to be spoken of even now in the Regiment with affection and respect. It was fitting that Colonel Barrett should write of him for permanent record in the digest of services, " The officer commanding cannot allow this distinguished Native officer to retire on pension without placing on record his appreciation of the very valuable services he has rendered to Government." He was succeeded by Jangia Thapa, another well-known character who has already been mentioned in these pages. This officer had the unusual experience, for a Gurkha, of visiting Australia, being selected towards the end of the year to accompany the contingent which was to represent India at the inauguration of the Australian Commonwealth on January 1st, 1901.

In May the Battalion was re-armed with Lee-Metford rifles. Prior to the issue of the new weapons a party composed of selected N.C.O.'s and drill men under the Adjutant, Captain Browne, was sent for instruction to the 2nd Battalion of the Queen's Regiment. Major-General Browne tells of a camaraderie which culminated in a great dinner given by the N.C.O.'s of the Queen's to the N.C.O.'s of the 5th Gurkhas. He notes, in passing, that the proceedings would not have been approved by the more zealous members of the Army Temperance Association. Our men presented their hosts with *khukris* as a token of their appreciation of the splendid hospitality extended to them. In August the Lee-Metford rifles were withdrawn for reissue to the China

Order of Merit Men, 1899.

Standing.—Birkhilurg Khattri, Thabai, 1897. Bhagathir Thapa, Nilt, 1891. Motiram Thapa, Black Mountain, 1888. Parsu Khattri, Peiwar Kotal, 1878, and Thabai, 1897. Kanan Sing Burathoki, Nilt, 1891, and Tirah, 1897. Harkia Thapa, Nilt, 1891. Karbir Burathoki, Nilt, 1891, and Tirah, 1897.

Kneeling.—Motiram Pun, Tirah, 1897. Goria Rana, Tirah, 1897. Naudia Thapa, Nilt, 1891. Goria Gharti, Tirah, 1897.

Expeditionary Force then mobilizing for service against the Boxers under the command of Sir Alfred Gaselee.

On September 16th, on receipt of a warning order, preparations began for a move to the Samana. Four days later the Battalion marched to Sultanpur, and running three normal stages into one, reached Hasan Abdal on the 21st, after a march of thirty-two miles. On arrival at Kohat on the 25th they were retained there for garrison duty until November 4th, when they once more set out along the well-remembered road which runs through Hangu and Patdarband to Fort Lockhart. On November 7th the Samana posts were taken over from the 1st Punjab Infantry. This gave a distribution on the Samana itself of 517 at Fort Lockhart, 127 at Gulistan, and 70 at Shinauri. In addition a small guard remained at Hangu.

1901.

The time spent on the Samana passed peacefully; the tribesmen had not yet forgotten the punishment administered four years earlier, and there was never any threat of trouble. Companies underwent their annual period of training, and again a special course of musketry was fired. For the rest, the men were constantly employed in hard manual labour, and it is possible that no other battalion has ever done quite so much to improve the place during less than a year's stay on the long ridge which overlooks the plain of Miranzai. To the 1/5th Gurkhas must be given the credit for the construction of the whole of the west hornwork and of two complete sets of barracks in the south hornwork, the roofing alone being undertaken by the Military Works Department. They were also responsible for the levelling of a camping-ground to the north of the existing parade-ground, and for the building of the cookhouses which are just outside the fort walls to the south and west. Finally, as was to be expected under a Commanding Officer whose knowledge of plant life was only equalled by the pleasure he took in seeing things grow, a great deal of tree-planting was done. The varieties chosen were willows, walnuts, and apricots, and despite the dry and rocky nature of the soil many are to be seen to this day, some to the north-west of the pond which lies between the fort and the Civil lines, and others along the ridge to the west in the direction of the parade-ground.

It is meet that the records of a Regiment which was to bear the title of Royal should contain a reference to the death of Queen Victoria which, in January of this year, plunged the Empire into mourning. Her lively interest in the welfare of India and of those who served her there were well known, and the following message sent by her after the action at Peiwar Kotal is but typical of many others which served to strengthen her hold on the loyalty and affection of her soldiers.

"I received the news of the decisive victory of General Roberts, and the splendid behaviour of my brave soldiers, with pride and satisfaction, though I must ever deplore the unavoidable loss of life. Pray inquire after the wounded in my name. May we continue to receive good news."

The sojourn of the Battalion in the Samana posts came to an end in August. On the 27th it marched down the hill, reaching Kushalgarh on September 1st. Going on from there by train to Hasan Abdal it proceeded stage by stage along the Hazara Trunk Road, to arrive back in Abbottabad on September 5th. It had proved a very hot march, undertaken at the beginning of the most unhealthy season of the year, but so fit had the men become as the result of their strenuous work in a good climate that they suffered no ill-effects, and withstood much better than usual the baneful influence of the Hazara autumn.

The return of the Battalion to Abbottabad was followed by a period of great activity. Two companies were struck off to undergo a special training under Major Vansittart and Captain Browne; scouting, as in previous years, was in the capable hands of Major Bruce, who took charge of a large class of 82 men; and musketry, already dealt with, had to begin all over again owing to the receipt in October of new Lee-Enfield rifles to replace the Mark IV Martinis issued in August, 1900. While shooting was in progress an unfortunate accident occurred which led to the suspension of firing pending investigation of possible defects in the weapons. The cause of the accident satisfactorily explained, shooting was resumed.

Turning for a moment to events outside the narrow confines of Abbottabad, chief interest attaches to the Waziristan blockade. The only officer of the Battalion to see service on this occasion was Lieutenant Villiers-Stuart, attached with Major Lucas of the 2nd Battalion to the 17th Bengal Infantry. That unit had never before served on the frontier, and through no fault of its own at first found difficulty in adapting itself to unfamiliar conditions. It is not surprising, therefore, that there should have been occasional moments of anxiety for the two officers of the 5th Gurkhas, but their previous reputations and their considerable experience of mountain warfare stood them in good stead, and there is reason to believe that their efforts were appreciated.

Before the end of the year the 42nd Gurkha Rifles, later to be known as the 6th Gurkha Rifles, came from Assam to make their home in Abbottabad. Their arrival entailed the departure of the Frontier Force battalion hitherto quartered in the station, and it might be supposed that the removal of this link with the outside world and the consequent absence of contact with any element other than Gurkha would result in a certain loss of efficiency through the want of a suitable object for emulation. Nothing of the kind happened. The new-comers as soon as they got into their stride proved serious rivals, stimulating always to fresh endeavour. Side by side with this rivalry there grew a comradeship which, born and fostered in the pleasant peace-time atmosphere of Abbottabad, was to grow to full stature through association in Egypt, Gallipoli, and Mesopotamia. In all that really matters the 5th and 6th Gurkhas are as one regiment.

Just a year had passed since Captain Davies's death, when news came of the loss of another good officer. On December 8th Captain Ketchen, then serving with the Kurram Militia, met with a fatal accident while out shooting with his orderly on the Safed Koh.

1902.

In 1902 a new experience came to the Abbottabad garrison with the establishment of a camp at Kakul for the accommodation of Boer prisoners of war. They numbered several hundred, and the duty of guarding them was shared between the units of the garrison and two companies of the Rifle Brigade from Rawalpindi. They proved to be harmless souls, none too clean in their persons but often clever with their hands, and much of their time was spent in turning out articles which they sold as souvenirs to the residents of Abbottabad. Peace having been restored in South Africa, the camp was broken up in November, but sad to relate a number had succumbed to the climate, and their bones rest in the little cemetery on the edge of the big *nullah* bordering the Kakul cantonment on the east.

In August the Battalion suffered yet another bereavement in the death of Captain M. H. P. Barlow. He held the appointment of Station Staff Officer, Kohat, and during the hot weather contracted typhoid fever. To the regret of all who knew him he succumbed to its effects at Fort Lockhart on the 12th August.

About this time there were many changes among the British officer personnel of the Battalion, and it will be convenient to depart from strict chronology in order to record them all in one place. D. M. Govan joined on transfer from the 2nd Battalion on December 1st, 1901, and Major Kemball came back as second-in-command in June, 1902. Those who joined on first appointment were A. M. Graham in September, 1902, E. C. de R. Martin in April, 1903, and the Honourable A. C. Murray in September, 1903. In May, 1902, the Battalion said good-bye to Major Vansittart, appointed to the command of the 8th Gurkhas, and just a year later Ivor Philipps retired from the Army, claimed by important interests at home.

1903.

In 1903 the Battalion again left Abbottabad for a spell of service elsewhere, but before going on to speak of the good days spent in Chitral we must give our attention to two events which happened in the earlier part of the year.

The first of these was the introduction of the Maxim gun and the formation of a machine-gun section. Two guns arrived from the arsenal at the end of 1902, but their mechanism and handling were wrapped in mystery, and to elucidate them with the help of the data then available was a task requiring both patience and industry. The first machine-gun officer of the Battalion was H. M. Battye; after spending several months in preliminary spade-work, in August he took his newly formed section to Thandiani and there continued their training on more advanced lines. The good work begun by him was later pushed on by W. D. Villiers-Stuart. Himself of a mechanical turn of mind, with an eye for detail, and possessed of great administrative capacity, he succeeded in producing a very high standard of efficiency, and it was not long before the machine-gunners themselves began to take such an immense pride in their work that there was justification for their claim to be looked upon as a kind of miniature *corps d'élite*.

The second event referred to above was the loss of the "colony" land granted to the Regiment in 1859. It will be remembered that a plot of ground had been allotted with the object of forming a Gurkha colony, but that the scheme had failed because no one could be found to settle there. Poor as the soil was, it had been found possible to grow on it maize and several varieties of vegetables, so in 1861 Major Rothney, while still awaiting permanent settlers, had put the ground under cultivation and had initiated the custom of dividing the resulting profits among the married men of the Battalion. Now after forty-four years of uninterrupted possession the colony land was reappropriated by Government for the erection of barracks to be occupied by a newly raised battery of mountain Artillery. In representing the regimental side of the case Colonel Barrett pointed out that the custom of dividing profits had continued uninterruptedly since 1861, that the principle of providing land for cultivation was apparently admitted by the grant to the 2nd Battalion of a similar plot in 1887, and that the loss of the profits would entail real hardship for married men. He asked that by way of compensation, Government would provide a sum of money which would be used to form the nucleus of a family relief fund on the lines of that maintained by the 2nd Gurkhas. Correspondence on the subject was continued over a long period, but the application for compensation was finally rejected, and it became harder than ever for the married Gurkha to turn out smart and clean while at the same time providing his family with the bare necessities of life.

Chitral, September, 1903, to October, 1904.
On September 15th, 1903, the Battalion, strengthened by a double company of the 2nd Battalion under Major F. G. Lucas, D.S.O., marched out of Abbottabad bound for Chitral. With Lieutenant A. E. Johnson attached from the 2/1st Gurkhas and Lieutenant F. E. Wilson, I.M.S., in medical charge, the number of British officers was brought

1. Major-General Sir John Munro Sym, K.C.B. 2. General Sir Alfred Gaselee, G.C.B., G.C.I.E.
3. Lieut.-General Sir Alfred Robert Martin, K.C.B. 4. Major-General Sir Arthur Arnold Barrett, K.C.B.
5. THE K.C.B. CUP,
presented by Four Ex-Commandants of the Regiment in 1911.

up to twelve. Captain F. F. Badcock, D.S.O., remained at Abbottabad in command of the depot.

The Chitral Campaign had been fought in 1895, and one of its results had been the permanent occupation of the country by a small British force. The garrison consisted at this time of a battalion of Infantry and one section of a mountain battery stationed at Kila Drosh, one hundred and thirty miles beyond our administrative border, with a detachment at Chitral itself, twenty-four miles farther northwards. For many years it was the custom to send Gurkha battalions in turn to garrison the post, reliefs taking place annually in the autumn.

Reaching Nowshera on September 23rd the Battalion halted there to take over warm clothing together with a large convoy of supplies, ordnance stores, and treasure. From Nowshera it went on with the escorting troops, and crossing the Lowarai Pass without difficulty, arrived at Drosh on October 11th. It is interesting to note that on this march the men wore for the first time the newly introduced felt hat with a broad brim. Between Hasan Abdal and Dargai the weather was very hot, but thanks to the protection afforded by this type of head-dress the Gurkha ranks felt little discomfort and remained in the best of health.

During the time spent in Chitral, Major Lucas's double company of the 2nd Battalion retained its identity, with the result that the Infantry of the garrison consisted of five double companies. Of these, during the winter months, one double company was quartered at Chitral and the remaining four at Drosh. Up to Christmas wood-cutting was the chief occupation, and it left but little time for anything else; but with the coming of the new year systematic training became possible, and helped by favourable conditions, progress was very rapid. But favourable conditions alone fail to account for the enormous strides made in Chitral; there was at work some other powerful influence which cannot be defined. It must have happened to most officers that they have gone on parade expecting nothing out of the ordinary, to find that instructions, however expressed, are understood at once; that the men can do nothing wrong, working indeed as though collectively inspired; and that perfection is attained with no expenditure of effort on the part of the man in charge. So it was with the training carried out for the most part in various camps in the hills around Drosh. The results obtained were excellent and set up a new standard to be worked for in future years.

For the first time the system was tried of detailing one double company to furnish all duties for a week at a time. This ensured for the remainder uninterrupted periods of three weeks' duration with a full complement of men, and so great were the advantages conferred by this method that it has been the usual practice ever since when it has been found possible to adopt it. During the hot weather Drosh itself becomes very unhealthy, and previous occupants had suffered much from the peculiar type of fever which is rampant there at that season. From the middle of May to the middle of September, therefore, the garrison was reduced to only one double company. With the exception of the double company in Chitral the rest of the Battalion was accommodated in camp, one double company at the " Retreat " Camp situated four miles up the Drosh Nullah at a height of 7,000 feet, the remaining two at Madaglasht, a delightful spot at a considerable distance from Drosh up the Shishi Khol Valley. The Drosh garrison was relieved every ten days from the Retreat Camp, and by ringing the changes on Drosh, Chitral, Retreat, and Madaglasht it was possible to ensure that no double company had more than two periods of ten days at Drosh, while all had six weeks in the splendid climate of Madaglasht. Here, at a height of 10,000 feet, were open grassland, fine stretches of forest, and hills which were good to work over, and in these ideal surroundings companies underwent their annual course of training. Twice a month double companies marched over the Lohigot Pass (14,000 feet) to visit the R.A. camp in the Gulan Gol. The distance was twenty-two miles and men carried their own food and bivouacked in the open. For recreation there was shooting, which was excellent of its kind. Markhor and oorial in particular were found to be plentiful, and many were the good heads brought in; while for the sportsman in less ambitious mood, chikor were there in their hundreds. Driven by an army of beaters they would fairly hurtle downwards from the high ground above, and the reward was only to him who swung an incredible way ahead and never checked.

In connection with the markhor shot in Chitral it is interesting to note that the horns are straighter than those of the heads brought from Kashmir, while the " spread " is less, and it is the experience of those in the Regiment who have done the most shooting that the farther east you go the greater is the spread and the more pronounced is the spiral twist. The two extremes are to be seen in the straight-horned markhor of the Safed Koh and Suleiman Ranges and the outward sweeping spirals of the species to be found in Astor.

The men, as was to be expected, were perfectly contented in their surroundings; in their spare time they could wander at will over the hills armed with the company fowling-pieces, nor ever return empty-handed, and the many streams of that country-side were for them a source of endless delight. Khud-running was another pastime which received encouragement, and it has already been recorded that they challenged the Chitralis and beat them on their own ground. This was no light achievement, seeing that some of the best runners were at the depot, and that these were successful in the same season in winning the 5th Gurkha challenge trophy.

Reverting for a moment to the subject of training, it is not without interest that the 1/5th Gurkhas anticipated by many years the general practice of the Army by awarding badges for proficiency in various branches of work. These badges could be earned by passing regimental tests in such subjects as drill, machine-gun, Mounted Infantry, range-finding, and scouting, and to this incentive to do good work is due in great measure the rapid progress made during the training season of 1904.

The only other outstanding event was the appointment as Colonel of the Regiment of Field-Marshal Earl Roberts, V.C., K.G., K.P., G.C.B., O.M., G.C.S.I., G.C.I.E. In the foreword to this book Sir Ian Hamilton speaks of him as " the finest commander of troops in action and under fire the British Army has known since the days of Marlborough." Small wonder that the Regiment was proud of the honour done to it, and glad to renew its connection with one whose gifts of leadership had inspired its doings in good times and bad alike throughout the stirring period of the second Afghan War.

The pleasant sojourn in the valley of the Kunhar drew towards its end; by the middle of September the Battalion was again concentrated at Drosh, and route-marching became the order of the day in preparation for the long trek back to Abbottabad. On October 11th the relieving garrison, consisting of the 1/1st Gurkhas, marched in, and on the 17th the 1/5th Gurkhas bade a regretful farewell to Chitral and set their faces towards India. On November 11th they arrived back in Abbottabad. Before the end of the year Subadar-Major Jangia Thapa, Sirdar Bahadur, retired on pension, and was succeeded by Bishnu Thapa, whose medals, presented by his widow and displayed nowadays in the anteroom of the officers' mess, attest the distinguished part played by him during his long and honourable career.

1905 to 1914. After the return of the 1/5th Gurkhas from Chitral until, ten years later, they moved out to take part in the Great War, there were no long periods of absence from Abbottabad. During all that time there happened nothing of outstanding importance, but the yearly round was made up of a number of minor incidents which had their influence on the Battalion's development, and which for that reason are worth recording. Such incidents are concerned with changes in equipment, movements and training, postings and appointments of officers, and certain minor happenings which do not lend themselves to classification. In dealing with the record of these ten years it will be convenient to treat of each of these subjects in turn.

Of the many changes in equipment and clothing which took place about this time, some were initiated by Army Headquarters, others were the result of unremitting efforts towards improvement on the part of the Battalion itself. From higher authority came the bandolier pattern of equipment and the short Lee-Enfield rifles received in July, 1905. The adoption of aluminium water-bottles in December, 1901, the introduction of the broad-brimmed field-service hat in September, 1903, the wearing of rucksacks begun early in 1905, the substitution of brown bayonet scabbards and *khukri* frogs for black in 1906, and the invention of the waterproof cape in the same year were all due to Battalion efforts. That all these innovations have stood the test of time is a tribute to the sound judgment of those responsible, and if further proof is wanted of the practical nature of these changes it is to be found in the action of other units, which soon followed the example set by the Battalion. The wearing of shorts was the result of the experience of the Gurkha scouts in Tirah, but official approval was not easily obtained, with the result that several years elapsed before their universal adoption as an article of dress. It is interesting to find that as early as 1907 the Mills-Burrows equipment was sent to the Battalion for trial. As then designed it was found to be unsuited to its purpose, and a report was sent in pointing out defects and suggesting modifications.

Changes in Equipment.

Under the head of "movements" a record can be made conveniently of training-camps and manœuvres as well as of other occasions when the Battalion left Abbottabad in fulfilment of some object not directly concerned with training. An analysis of the years 1905 to 1913 shows that the man in the ranks spent some eighty days in every year in camp, that nineteen training-camps were arranged for companies, and that on sixteen occasions the whole Battalion marched out of the station for Battalion training or to take part in manœuvres or, as happened twice in 1908, to join a brigade held in reserve while operations were in progress on the frontier. In addition to these, recruits' camps were formed annually in the hills during the hot weather, while from time to time demands were made on the Battalion for detachments to do duty at such places as Murree, Changla Gali, Attock, and the Artillery Practice Camp at Hatti. Obviously it would be tedious and unprofitable to give the details of all these moves, and only those will be touched on which have features of special interest.

Movements and Training.

During the cold weather of 1905–06 His Royal Highness the Prince of Wales visited India, accompanied by the Princess. His itinerary, of course, included Rawalpindi, where it was arranged that he should see the final stages of manœuvres during the early part of December. With the rest of the Abbottabad brigade the 1/5th Gurkhas took part in the exercises leading up to the final clash between the two armies. As the climax approached, the Battalion found itself near a brigade of guns in action. All appeared to be going well, the guns getting their ranges and firing scientifically, when a senior staff-officer galloped up, very red in the face from heat and fury. Not completely *au fait* with modern methods of fire direction he yet made it plain that what he wanted was noise. Dashing along the line of guns he yelled, " Fire salvos, damn you! Fire salvos!" And the gunners, with their customary adaptability, " made it so."

The Battalion went through its first Kitchener test in 1906. Lord Kitchener, then Commander-in-Chief in India, aimed at increasing the efficiency of the army in India by introducing the element of competition into the annual inspection of battalions. Under the rules framed by him all battalions carried out the same series of exercises, marks were allotted on a common basis, and the winning unit held the Chief's challenge cup for a year.

The exercises began with a fifteen-mile march under service conditions, followed immediately by an attack on a position, the defending enemy being represented by service targets, and ball ammunition being used as a test of shooting efficiency. The inspecting officer was, as a rule, the Brigade Commander—in this case Major-General J. B. Woon, C.B.—and the entire business, comprising, as it did, almost every phase of normal warfare, occupied several very strenuous days and nights. Excellent as the idea was in principle, it suffered from the grave practical disadvantage that conditions could not be made the same for all units throughout India, and after two years' trial the competition was abandoned. The last test carried out by General Woon in 1907 provided the occasion for F. F. Badcock's famous appreciation of the situation, brief but masterly. During a rear-guard action, with the 1/5th retiring southwards along the grass *rukh*, he found himself in position with his double company waiting to cover the retirement of the lines in front. Suddenly two battalions of the enemy charged him in rear from the cover of the Brigade Circular trees, where, but for an unfair ruse, they could never have arrived. One glance behind, and then he sized up the situation and issued instructions all in one breath: "*Dushman! Salaharu! Bhag!*"[1] Himself he led the way.

In 1908 occurred the Bazar Valley and Mohmand Expeditions. It was not the fortune of the 1st Battalion to take an active part in either, and on February 10th it left Abbottabad and moved to Peshawar, where it was retained as part of Major-General Watkis's 3rd Brigade, distributed between Peshawar and Nowshera. Two brigades proved ample for the task of subjugating the Zakka Khels, and so quickly

[1] " The enemy! the swine! run for it! "

was the result achieved that *Punch* produced a cartoon on the subject entitled, " Willcocks's Week-end War." During the expedition the 2/5th worthily maintained the reputation of the Regiment. Both battalions returned to Abbottabad on March 14th, and it was characteristic of Colonel Kemball that, wishing to leave the 2nd Battalion a clear field to enjoy the welcome provided on arrival, he led the 1/5th into the Salhad Nullah and so by a back way into the station.

The Mohmand Expedition proved to be a much more serious affair than that against the Zakka Khels which preceded it, and from May 4th until June 6th the Abbottabad brigade was concentrated on the railway between Serai Kala and the Margalla Pass, ready to move if required. Both battalions found themselves encamped at the pass, beneath the shadow of Nicholson's monument. There was a scare of cholera, the weather was very hot, water was none too plentiful, and flies swarmed everywhere. A popular pastime was fly-catching by hand with the help of a match dipped in treacle, and those who were there probably remember a great match between the two Commanding Officers, time-limit half an hour. It was the hottest period of a very hot day, and as the wretched insects found it cooler underneath the mess table than anywhere else, both distinguished officers were presently grovelling on the floor, sweating profusely. Colonel Kemball, with his angling tricks, proved a formidable opponent, but Colonel Stewart showed a dogged perseverance which refused to acknowledge defeat, and the result, it is believed, was a tie. A very pleasant memory is the violin-playing of Bird, the Sapper. He would come out from Rawalpindi after his work was done, play most beautifully all through the evening and far into the night, and make the return journey by jumping onto a goods train as it slowed before entering the tunnel.

The Rajoia manœuvres, which were held from October 25th to 29th, 1908, are memorable because they provided the first occasion for an extensive use of the telephone. Everywhere signallers were to be met squatting on the ground chanting, " I wa-a-ant the Adjutant Sahib," that being the approved opening to conversation by telephone in those days. Some time was to elapse before a thorough knowledge was acquired of the working of the instrument, and it is on record that in 1909, during manœuvres, a brigade signalling officer held up the Bombay mail for two and a half hours between Burham and Hasan Abdal by tapping in on the wrong line.

The inter-divisional manœuvres of 1909 ended in torrents of rain, and on their conclusion both battalions of the Regiment and the 1/6th Gurkhas went into standing camp at Rawalpindi for two months. It was a valuable experience for men and officers, who had many opportunities of meeting other branches of the Service both at work and

1/5th Guard, Boer Prisoners' Camp, Abbottabad, 1902.

Recruits Bridge-building, Abbottabad, 1906.

play. The standard of football was improved by frequent encounters with the teams of British regiments, especially the X Hussars, who lived near by, and a most pleasing feature of the sojourn in Rawalpindi was the *entente* established with the 5th Fusiliers.

As regards training apart from manœuvres, a few occurrences are worth special notice. That the Battalion was ahead of its time in the ideas held on musketry instruction is evidenced by the nature of the special course fired in 1906. At that time the annual musketry course was confined almost entirely to deliberate shooting at ranges up to 1,000 yards, and a man might repeat each practice an unlimited number of times until he made a score good enough to count for purposes of classification. Colonel Kemball considered that something more than that was required to make a good battle shot, and the special course was framed with the idea of making the men shoot with accuracy and at the same time quickly. Snapshooting (not rapid firing) was taught by making men throw up and fire without aim at a large target at close ranges.

After the experience of 1897 it was only natural that instruction in scouting should occupy an important place in training programmes. In the frontier fighting of 1908 scouts were not employed as an organized body; but the lesson of Tirah had not been forgotten, for towards the end of that year a divisional camp was formed at Kalabagh in charge of Major Bruce. His task was to teach the art of scouting to selected men from every battalion in the division, and in spite of differences in language and physique the results he obtained were excellent.

Finally, in this connection reference must be made to the first reservists' training carried out by Major Bruce at Gorakhpur in 1909. It says much for his reassuring influence and for the spirit animating the men that no feeling of discouragement followed the occurrence of two unfortunate accidents which resulted in loss of life. The first was the explosion of a number of bombs which were to be used to represent Artillery fire during a field day. The man carrying the bombs was killed and several of the party were severely injured. Lieutenant Molloy, who was in charge, though himself badly shaken by the explosion, did very good work in attending to the wounded.

On the occasion of the second accident a detachment taking part in a field day was crossing a railway bridge when it was surprised by a train which came unexpectedly round a bend. For those who had actually begun to cross there was no escape, with the inevitable result that some were killed and others badly hurt. Both accidents formed the subject of official inquiry, and in both cases it was found that no blame attached to those responsible for the training. More important still, the reservists bore their misfortune with admirable fortitude, and after performing certain ceremonies designed to avert further calamity, continued their work with a good will and energy deserving very high praise.

Three changes of command occurred during the period under review.

British Officers. In February, 1905, Colonel A. A. Barrett was promoted Colonel on the Staff, Belgaum, and was succeeded by Lieutenant-Colonel A. H. G. Kemball.

The latter, though offered a brigade on the conclusion of his period of command in 1910, preferred to seek peace and the delights of fishing in British Columbia. His place was taken by Lieutenant-Colonel G. H. Boisragon, V.C.

In 1906 the Indian Staff College opened its doors, and for the first course, held at Deolali, the Battalion had a representative in the person of Captain H. J. P. Browne. His example was followed by Captain H. A. Holdich, who, having qualified for Camberley, was given a nomination to the Quetta seat of learning, and joined early in 1908.

Other changes comprised the joining of several new officers, whose names will be found in the appropriate appendix; the appointment on transfer from the 2nd Battalion of Major F. W. Evatt as second-in-command in 1906; the retirement of Major J. O. S. Fayrer and Major F. W. Evatt in 1909, and of Captain the Honourable Arthur Murray in 1911; the transfer to command the 1/6th Gurkhas of Major the Honourable C. G. Bruce in 1913 and the appointment as second-in-command of Major E. B. C. Boddam in the same year.

In the cold weather of 1911–12 the North-east Frontier of India provided the *mise-en-scène* for a punitive expedition against the Abors. A. B. Hay-Webb accompanied the force in the appointment of boat transport officer. His unflagging energy and great organizing capacity were not to be defeated by the vagaries of the river, nor by the dilatory methods of waterside villagers, and to his efforts was largely due the success of the supply system on the lower reaches of the Dihang. He soon became known as "The Pirate," because, his business being the provision of boats, he always found means to procure them. His reward was a mention in despatches.

At the same time a mission was undertaken into the country of the Hill Miris away to the west. There Captain A. M. Graham found himself in military charge. The inhabitants resented the intrusion of the small force of military police, and one day, as dawn was breaking, made a rush on the jungle-surrounded camp. Roused by a cry from the quarter-guard sentry Captain Graham hurried out to find the hillmen in the act of penetrating at one corner of the camp. Without hesitation he dashed in among them and shot a dozen of the assailants with his own hand. The remainder thereupon fled. His great personal courage earned for him the award of the King's Police Medal.

Miscellaneous Incidents.

Heretofore no mention has been made of that branch of regimental activity which is concerned with music. Fortunate, as a rule, in its bandmasters, and happy in having several officers with a trained knowledge of music, the Regiment seldom had cause to complain of its band. In this connection there came a time, however, when trouble arose over the regimental march past, " Hieland Laddie." It was an excellent tune, but had been adopted by so many British units that wherever the Regiment went it found itself under the necessity of asking permission to play its own march past. In 1905, therefore, a change was made, and for " Hieland Laddie " was substituted "Moreen," an old Irish air brought to light by W. D. Villiers-Stuart.

The same year saw a considerable advance in the provision of amenities in the lines. It had been Colonel Barrett's constant aim to increase the comfort of the men and of their families. When he left he gave a sum of money to be used in building a bath-house, and the way having been shown, the canteen fund was called on to provide a second.

In 1908 the Regiment celebrated its Jubilee. For nearly a week Abbottabad was *en fête*; there were dinners and dances, polo and football tournaments, a cricket match in which the Regiment defeated the World, a gymkhana, sports, a khud race, and a grand torchlight tattoo. A big party of N.C.O.'s from the Seaforths was made welcome, and we had the pleasure of entertaining a number of their officers, while every unit of the Frontier Force sent its representatives. The opinion was unanimous, when the time came to clear away the debris, that the celebrations had been worthy of the occasion.

In January, 1911, the Crown Prince of Germany came to Abbottabad. An account of his visit is given in the next chapter, which deals with the doings of the 2nd Battalion before the Great War, but as a matter of general interest it may be stated here that in the mess he made a good impression. His English was excellent, he spoke well and vivaciously, and he appeared genuinely interested in shooting and other sports.

From the heir to the throne of Germany we turn to our own Royal House. In May, 1910, the world mourned the death of King Edward; the year 1911 was one of pageantry and splendour designed to mark the accession of King George. To attend the coronation of His Majesty in London the Battalion sent Subadar Amrit Mal. In December was staged the great *durbar* at Delhi, when the Emperor of India and his consort moved before their subjects in splendour never before equalled even in the Imperial City. On this occasion the Battalion was represented by several distinguished Gurkha officers who had served their time and gone on pension, as well as by a few who were still on the active list. They included pensioned Subadar-Major and Honorary Captain Bishnu Thapa, Sirdar Bahadur; Subadar-Major Harkbir Thapa, I.O.M.; pensioned Subadar Motiram Thapa, I.O.M.; pensioned Subadar Birkhdhoj Khattri, I.O.M.; Subadar Goria Rana, I.O.M.; pensioned Subadar Karbir Burathoki, I.O.M.; and Jemadar Maniram Pun, I.O.M.

No account of those pleasant times could be considered complete without a reference to Lord Roberts's cup. The Colonel of the Regiment soon after his appointment presented a magnificent silver rose-bowl for the encouragement of rifle-shooting in the two battalions. A day would be chosen in the late spring when Abbottabad was at its best, and in the early morning the company teams selected to compete would repair to the ranges. Between the two ranges on the young green grass beneath the pines, breakfast would be spread for the officers, and at no great distance the wood-smoke could be seen rising from the fires where tea was prepared for the men. The days that linger in the memory were fine, the air crystal-clear; the spring sunshine was tempered by a gentle breeze, and the long shadows of the pines lay across the firing-points. The shooting was taken seriously enough, since it was no small honour for a company to have its name engraved on the cup; but because no other work was done on that day the spirit of holiday was abroad. The test imposed was a strenuous fire and movement practice, entailing much hard running and quick shooting, and great was the excitement as each company in turn finished firing and enthusiastic partisans awaited the announcement of the score. To the generosity of Lord Roberts it was largely due that the Regiment developed a zest for practical shooting at a time when conditions, in general, were inclined to be too artificial.

And now, for a time, we break off the story of the 1/5th Gurkhas, to follow the fortunes of the 2nd Battalion from its raising until the outbreak of the Great War.

Colonel E. Molloy, C.B.
Raised 2nd Battalion, 1886.

CHAPTER IX

THE 2ND BATTALION, 1886 TO 1914.

Origin and Constitution, 1886.
THE early history of the 2nd Battalion 5th Royal Gurkha Rifles (Frontier Force) is the history of the 5th Gurkhas during the first thirty-eight years of the Regiment's existence. The traditions of the old corps are its inheritance; the deeds of the men who fought at Palosin, at Ambela, in Afghanistan and on the Black Mountain are inalienably its inspiration.

In 1885 Sir Frederick Roberts became Commander-in-Chief in India. In his "Forty-One Years in India," referring to his efforts to render the Army in India as perfect a fighting machine as it was possible to make it, he writes: "The first step to be taken towards this end was it seemed to me, to substitute men of the more warlike and hardy races for the Hindustani sepoys of Bengal, the Tamils and Telagus of Madras, and the so-called Mahrattas of Bombay. . . . No comparison can be made between the martial value of a regiment recruited amongst the Gurkhas of Nepal or the warlike races of Northern India, and of one recruited from the effeminate peoples of the south."

Sir Frederick lost no time, but at once took steps to effect those changes which he considered necessary. One result of his efforts was the issue by the Government of India of a special circular dated October 1st, 1886, which decreed the raising of a second battalion of the 5th Goorkha Regiment or Hazara Goorkha Battalion. To the history of that newly-constituted representative of the old traditions we now turn.

In its organization the new battalion was "to be of the same established strength as the 1st Battalion, and in all respects similarly equipped." It was to be formed by volunteer transfers from the 5th Goorkha Regiment and from the three Assam Regiments (42nd, 43rd and 44th Goorkha Light Infantry), the numbers volunteering to be limited to one hundred per regiment of all ranks. In the end 150 men were transferred from the old Regiment, that number including 4 Gurkha officers and 27 non-commissioned officers, but of the rest for whom provision had been made, twelve only were forthcoming from the 42nd and from the other two battalions none at all. The reason for the failure of the Assam regiments to provide men is to be found in their impending departure to take part in the Burmese War. To complete the establishment of the new battalion, there was no alternative other than direct recruitment from Nepal. Thanks to the strenuous efforts made by Captain Chenevix-Trench and Captain Eden Vansittart 400 recruits were obtained in 1887 and 319 in the following year. They were of a fine stamp, and the rapidity with which they mastered their work was truly remarkable, for no later than 1889, when the average length of service of the men of the 2/5th can hardly have reached two years, we find them reported on as " fit for any active service."

In October, 1886, the old Regiment was commanded by Colonel Sym, whose second-in-command was Major E. Molloy. It fell to the latter to raise and command the new unit, and the story goes that both commandants sat together over the long roll of the 5th Goorkha Regiment and applied their united experience and knowledge of the men to the selection of a suitable nucleus for the 2nd Battalion. This incident is typical of their attitude towards the existence henceforward of two battalions, for they insisted from the beginning that no differences should be allowed to mar the happiness of their relations and that each must work on the same principles, since the reputation of the Regiment must be the equal responsibility of both. The date on which Major Molloy assumed command was November 10th, 1886. The following is a complete list of the officers appointed to the 2nd Battalion on its formation :—

        Commandant ... Major E. Molloy.
        Wing Commanders Major A. Gaselee.
                             Major Lorne Campbell.
        Wing Officers ... Captain C. Chenevix-Trench.
                             Lieutenant Eden Vansittart.
                             Lieutenant A. H. G. Kemball.
                             Lieutenant A. S. Rooke.
                             Lieutenant C. M. Crawford.
                             Lieutenant W. Hudson.

Lines.

For quarters, arrangements were made by Sir John McQueen, commanding the Punjab Frontier Force, to house the nucleus of the Battalion in the mountain artillery lines rendered vacant by the absence of the battery in Burma. Meantime, the Military Works Department began the construction of the existing 2/5th lines, later to be named after General Sir Alfred Gaselee. Their position at the north-east corner of the cantonment, close to the cultivated ground of the valley, caused them to be very unhealthy during the autumn months, but that defect was afterwards remedied by extending the cantonment for a considerable distance to the north and east. The improvements effected by successive commanding officers have been many, and include the planting of trees, the making of drains, the levelling of ground for parades and games and the building of bath-houses and institutes. The oldest and finest of the chenar trees were there before the lines were built, but Colonel Molloy, and later Colonel Hawkes, were responsible for the planting of many more; the oak trees by the office came from England in the time of Colonel E. W. F. Martin; the line of eucalyptus trees below the followers' quarters, the well-grown camphor bushes beside the Murree Road, the lines of chenar trees bordering the football grounds, as well as the levelling of the grounds themselves, were the work of Colonel Stewart; the layout of the new quarter-guard and the building of the tea-shop were planned by Colonel Champain; finally, the levelling of the recruits' football ground was done by Lieutenant-Colonel H. T. Molloy.

The rifle range was completed by the end of November, 1888, and was taken into use at once for the firing of the Battalion's first annual course of musketry. The rifle used was the Martini-Henry, which had replaced the old Snider only during the previous July, and, if we may judge by the earliest inspection reports, the results were satisfactory. Very early in the career of the 2/5th Sir John McQueen wrote of their work: "Their steadiness and smartness on parade, and the intelligent way in which they handled their rifles, calling for special mention."

Black Mountain, 1888. The Black Mountain expedition of 1888, though it came too soon to give the Battalion as a whole a chance to win its spurs, yet provided experience of active service for a number of men. As related in a previous chapter, a detachment of 100 rifles under Captain Kemball accompanied the 1st Battalion throughout the campaign, while a similar detachment under Captain Chesney went to Darband on the Indus for duty at the advanced base which had been established there. As ill-luck would have it, a severe outbreak of cholera occurred at Darband. In the narrow confines of the camp it soon spread to Captain Chesney's party, and several cases ended fatally. Later in the campaign the detachment was ordered to Oghi, where it remained until active operations ceased and all other troops had been withdrawn from Agror.

Progress during early years, 1888-1890. With 80 per cent. of its strength consisting of recruits, of whom a large proportion only joined in 1888, it is natural that the Battalion should have spent the first few years of its existence in Abbottabad. Strenuous years they must have been, too, for those charged with the creation of a fighting entity from a small nucleus of trained men and more than 700 recruits, but their hard work had its reward in 1889, for in that year the 2/5th was pronounced fit for service. The report, marking as it does an important stage in the development of the unit, may be quoted in full :—

"The 2/5th Goorkha Regiment is in a thoroughly efficient state and fit for any active service. The men have been well selected, and are a fine body of young soldiers. They are well set up, carefully trained and steady under arms. The state of discipline in the corps is most creditable to the officers, and the musketry condition is satisfactory. All establishments are complete and efficient, and there is a fine soldierly and willing spirit amongst all ranks."

These excellent results did not escape the watchful attention of the Commander-in-Chief, who wrote in the same year : "I am much pleased by the progress made by this young battalion, which reflects great credit on Colonel E. Molloy and the officers under him."

In December, 1889, "this young battalion" first marched out of Abbottabad to take its part in training with other troops. The occasion was the camp of exercise at Rawalpindi, to which a reference was made in Chapter V. The lighter side only is touched on there, but the manœuvres were not without their instructional value, and the men returned to Abbottabad in January, 1890, the richer for their experience and with their outlook appreciably widened.

In October, 1890, 350 rifles under the command of Major Hawkes, accompanied Sir John McQueen to the Black Mountain. It will be remembered that the object of this visit was to test the feeling of the tribes, and that these gave evidence of their repudiation of the agreement made in 1888 by firing into the bivouac and by preparing to oppose the further advance of the small force encamped above Barchar. Thereupon Sir John withdrew to British India, and preparations were begun for yet another Black Mountain expedition. In that expedition the 2/5th were to gain their first experience of active service as a battalion, but some months were to elapse before the opening of hostilities, and meantime there was no departure from the ordinary routine of training. In November and December there were manœuvres near Attock. The weather especially at Camp Akora in December, was atrocious, and the exercises as a whole were described at the time as the "wettest on record." Colonel E. Molloy being appointed to the command of the 1st Brigade, the command of the Battalion devolved on Major Hawkes. From the neighbourhood of Akora the return march to Abbottabad was made across the Yusafzai Plain via Torder and Swabi, and the Indus was crossed by the bridge of boats at Pihur.

Black Mountain Promenade, October, 1890.

Attock Manœuvres, November-December, 1890.

With the coming of the new year, preparations began for the punishment of the Hassanzais and Akazais, the tribes mainly concerned in the hostile demonstration of the previous October. The command of the expedition was given to Major-General W. K. Ellis, C.B., who had at his disposal two columns for operations on the Indus side of the mountain, and a third and much smaller column to watch events from Oghi. An additional brigade was kept in reserve at Rawalpindi.

Black Mountain Expedition, 1891.

The plan of campaign entailed an advance from Darband along the Indus by the left, or river, column, and a simultaneous movement across the lower slopes of the mountain by the right, or Tilli, column. This variation of the method followed in previous campaigns was dictated by the situation near the Indus of all the principal settlements of the two offending tribes.

Arrangements were made to complete concentration at Darband and Oghi by March 1st, but owing to bad weather the force was not finally assembled ready to move until the 11th. The arrival of the 2/5th at Darband furnishes an incident which, for the qualities it displays of endurance under suffering, of eagerness to be in the fight and of unquenchable zeal for the good name of the Regiment, may well serve as an example to the young soldier for all time. For some days past Subadar Dalbir Ale had been ailing, but had insisted on doing his work as though nothing had been the matter with him. On reaching Darband he collapsed before the Battalion had been dismissed. Surgeon-Major Duncan found him lying on the ground unconscious, and there he died almost at once. Medical examination showed that the cause of death was the bursting of an internal abscess; for him the march must have been a long drawn-out agony, but no word of complaint had passed his lips, and it is fitting that the memory of his great spirit should be perpetuated.

At Darband the 2nd Battalion joined the Tilli column, which was under the command of Brigadier-General A. D. Hammond, V.C. The remaining units were the 9th Mountain Battery, 1st Royal Welch Fusiliers, Wing 32nd Pioneers and Khyber Rifles.

The advance of both columns began on March 12th. The route of the Tilli column lay up the long spur which ascends from the point of junction of the Unhar River with the Indus, and it proved so steep and difficult when the frontier line was reached that the transport was left behind. On this march the Battalion formed part of the advanced guard under the command of Colonel Molloy. That night was spent in the open near the crest of the ridge in the neighbourhood of Pailam, and fortunately but little rain fell, though the weather was threatening. Tilli, the immediate objective of the right column, was reached next day (13th), and there a prolonged halt was made. The original intention had been to employ General Hammond's force in over-running the Khan Khel country about the upper waters of the Shal Nullah and the

Akazai lands beyond, and to supply it by a track to be constructed through Tilli towards Ril and Kangar. Owing to the great difficulties presented by the rocky and precipitous nature of the hills to be traversed that plan was found to be impracticable, and the task of supplying the troops even at Tilli was subject to so many interruptions that the column was eventually withdrawn to the Indus Valley. If, for the Battalion, the stay at Tilli brought no fighting, it yet provided plenty of work and entailed a fair measure of hardship. Weather conditions were vile and rations none too plentiful, but spirits never flagged; there were camp fires and sing-songs of an evening, and to all their tasks the men brought that cheerfulness and goodwill which is the special characteristic of the Gurkha soldier.

The left column, meantime, had been fully occupied on both sides of the river in the valley below. The Hassanzais and Akazais were not in fighting mood, and left to themselves would have made immediate submission, but the Hindustani fanatics were once more on the warpath, and there was skirmishing with small gatherings of the enemy at Nadria, Ghazikot and Kanar. The 21st March saw the column encamped on the right bank of the Indus in the Palosi Plain, with a detachment guarding the bridge of boats at Kotkai and with outposts established at a few points of tactical importance.

Before this, the decision had been taken to bring the Tilli column to Palosi, but first it had a mission to accomplish. North-east of Tilli just south of the upper Shal lay Seri, the stronghold of Hashim Ali, chief of the Hassanzai and almost sole cause of contemporary unrest. The leader himself was known to be absent from home, soliciting help from the Mian Gul of Swat, but to destroy his village would teach a much-needed lesson to the tribes and would have its influence in bringing about their early submission.

On March 21st, therefore, a flying column organized from the troops at Tilli, set out for Seri. The advanced guard consisted of a wing of the Battalion and the Khyber Rifles, with Colonel Molloy in command. The going proved very difficult, and the weather, threatening at the start, grew rapidly worse. Ril was occupied, and by nightfall the advanced guard had reached Abu, a place of tall cliffs. There they were caught in a heavy snowstorm, and having no baggage, they sought shelter in some wretched cattle sheds. Colonel Muhammad Aslam Khan, commanding the Khyber Rifles, nearly lost his life through the collapse of the particular hovel in which he had taken refuge, and, to the veteran fighter's disgust, he was so badly hurt that it became necessary to send him back next day. Seri was reached on the 22nd, its defences were demolished, and then, its work accomplished, the flying column returned to Tilli.

On March 24th General Hammond moved down to join the river

Part of the Nucleus of the 2nd Battalion, with E. Vansittart, Adjutant.

2/5th on the Range: Old Style "Volley Firing."

column at Palosi, but of the Battalion one wing only accompanied him, the rest being distributed in detachments to hold Tilli, Ril and Makranai.

It will be seen from the map that upstream of Palosi the Indus forms a big loop round the foot of the great spur which interposes between the Shal Nullah and the main stream at this part of its course. Palosi is on the right bank at the lower end of the loop, and opposite to it on the left bank the Shal Nullah joins the Indus at Bakrai. The upstream end of the loop is marked by the village of Darbanai. When General Hammond's force reached Palosi on the 24th, the river column had already thrown a flying bridge across the river at Bakrai, and thanks to a good piece of work by Colonel Gaselee, then commanding the 4th Sikhs, had established a strong piquet at Diliarai, situated on the crest of the great spur mentioned above. To ensure complete control of this part of the river and of the country on either side, it only remained to gain possession of Darbanai. With that object in view, General Hammond set out on March 25th, taking with him Number 9 Mountain Battery (less one section), the Royal Welch Fusiliers, two companies 11th Bengal Infantry, wing 2/5th Gurkhas and the Khyber Rifles. The route chosen lay up the Shal Nullah and then over the main ridge to the village which occupied a commanding position on the far side, 1,500 feet above river level. The going was very rough, and for the mountain battery especially progress was slow. By 1 p.m. the infantry had gained the saddle joining the Darbanai spur to the Diliarai heights, but the guns were still some distance behind. On their arrival the advance began, with the Khyber Rifles on the right, the 2/5th Gurkhas on the left and the Royal Welch Fusiliers supported by the 11th Bengal Infantry in the centre. At once it became apparent that the tribesmen were present in considerable strength and were prepared to make a show of resistance. They opened fire from the main ridge and from the direction of the village itself, and the fact that they lost some forty of their number is proof that they were prepared to do more than merely shoot and run away. Soon, however, they began to lose heart in face of the steady advance of the British troops, and before the village was reached resistance was at an end. The column went into bivouac for the night at Darbanai and prepared to make a stay of several days.

On March 27th the Battalion sustained its first casualty in a more serious encounter with the enemy. Upstream of Darbanai and situated towards the extremity of the next spur jutting out river-wards from the main feature, lies the village of Surmal. There had collected a body of 500 Chigharzais, who, heedless of warnings, refused to disperse and assumed an attitude of defiance. In the action which followed the Khyber Rifles again took the high ground to the east, the Battalion made a flanking movement inside them, and the Welch Fusiliers moved straight on Surmal. The 11th Bengal Infantry were in support. The 2/5th Gurkhas found themselves faced with a stiff climb over most precipitous ground, but by a great effort they succeeded in arriving at their objective at the same time as the Welch Fusiliers. Up till then the enemy had held on sturdily to their position, sheltered as they were under the brow of the hill. Now, however, a heavy fire directed on them by both regiments caused them to retire in confusion after suffering heavy losses. One company of the Battalion had gone wide in the track of the Khyber Rifles, and had surprised and dispersed another large party of tribesmen in the hills above the villages. Their lack of success both at Surmal and on the heights was a severe blow to the Chigharzais, and ended effectually their opposition to the movements of the expeditionary force. Their casualties were estimated at 120—a very large proportion of the total number engaged. On the British side one man of the 2/5th was killed, and in other units a few were wounded.

The story of the rest of the campaign is soon told. For some time prior to General Hammond's action of the 27th reports had come in of a hostile gathering in the neighbourhood of Baio. Every day added to the size of the concentration, and, as a precautionary measure, the Reserve Brigade was moved to Darband from Rawalpindi. The coalition comprised contingents from a number of the trans-Indus tribes, and their presence was a source of embarrassment to General Ellis, whose original instructions failed to cover the problem which had arisen. Reassuring messages were sent, and at the beginning of April the *lashkar* began to disperse. On April 7th the Reserve Brigade was withdrawn from the field force to follow its commander, Sir William Lockhart, to Miranzai. By this time the Hassanzais were ready to submit; a thorough reconnaissance had been made of their trans-Indus territory, and, on that side of the river, there was nothing left to do. The Akazais, however, still held out, and Hashim Ali had not yet been surrendered. Arrangements were made therefore for the transfer of all troops to the left bank, and for a change of base from Darband to Oghi.

End of the Campaign, June, 1891.

Under the new scheme the 2nd Brigade (General Hammond) remained at Darbanai and the 1st Brigade (General Williamson) at Seri, with numerous detachments at points of tactical importance. As the result of punitive measures undertaken during April, the Akazais at last agreed to the terms imposed. Both they and the Hassanzais, however, insisted on their inability to surrender the person of Hashim Ali, who had fled the country. His perpetual banishment was therefore substituted for the surrender of his person in the terms of settlement, and in June the field force was broken up. Leaving only a brigade under General Hammond in occupation, to ensure compliance with the terms imposed, the remaining troops returned to India, and the 2/5th Gurkhas to Abbottabad.

For the part it played in this, the last of the Black Mountain expeditions, the Battalion received a special mention in the despatch of the Commander-in-Chief.

Following the withdrawal of the Hazara Field Force certain changes were made in the arrangements hitherto in force for the administration of this part of the frontier. They included the payment of allowances to a number of the tribal chiefs and the raising of a body of Border Military Police, recruited from the independent clans across the boundary line. The function of the Military Police was, generally, to maintain peace in the Black Mountain area and particularly to ensure the continued exclusion of Hashim Ali. To back them, a strong detachment from the Abbottabad garrison was posted at Oghi. These changes had taken effect by November, 1891, when the remaining brigade too was withdrawn.

Further trouble with trans-Indus Tribes, 1892.

Notwithstanding all precautions, Hashim Ali very soon caused further trouble. At the end of March, 1892, he visited Baio to arrange for himself a sanctuary with the trans-Indus Hassanzais and the Mada Khel. His return seemed likely to cause a fresh outbreak, and in April a column consisting of the Kohat Mountain Battery and the two battalions of the Regiment under the command of Colonel Molloy, was hurried out to Oghi to reinforce the 2nd Battalion detachment under Major Hawkes, already stationed there. It was not intended to use force if that could in any way be avoided, and resort was had to other means of unravelling the tangled skein. In this way there came to be entrusted to Colonel Molloy a very delicate and somewhat hazardous mission. The one way to bring peace to the Black Mountain seemed to be the apprehension of Hashim Ali. The maliks were known to be exasperated with him and his machinations, and by negotiation with them it was arranged that the ex-chief of the Hassanzais should be brought to Pabbal Gali, there to meet a representative of the Government. Colonel Molloy was selected for his tact, experience and knowledge of frontier politics. One morning he rode out alone from Oghi and met Hashim Ali on the hillside. Contrary to his expectation, and to the undertaking given by the maliks, he found himself confronted by a number of armed men, the personal following of Hashim, who assumed a threatening attitude. Their mere presence, let alone their blustering demeanour, meant ruin to Colonel Molloy's slender hope of success, but concealing his conviction of failure, he used all his powers of persuasion in an attempt to induce Hashim Ali to accompany him to Oghi. Inevitably his effort was abortive, and he rode back to the post, as he had left it, alone.

No greater success attended the efforts made to effect the expulsion of Hashim Ali from the lands of the Isazai across the river, and consequently troops were assembled at Darband at the beginning of October to secure by force what could not be accomplished by peaceful persuasion. As narrated at the end of Chapter V, the expedition met with no opposition. Both battalions of the Regiment took part in the operations, which began with the destruction of Baio on October 6th, and virtually ended with the demolition of the defences of Garhi and Nawekili on the 8th. Three days later the troops returned to Darband and the column was broken up. Colonel Molloy, admittedly an authority on inter-tribal relations in this region, had been averse to the despatch of the expedition from the beginning, and had previously sent in a detailed report on the situation in which he stated his views. Nevertheless, it can at least be claimed for the Isazai Field Force that its activities had the effect of securing the banishment of Hashim Ali and so bringing peace to the Black Mountain.

Isazai Expedition, 1892.

Later in the month of October the Battalion returned to Abbottabad, destined to remain there undisturbed for several quiet years. It was soon after that event that Colonel Molloy's health began to give cause for anxiety, and in April, 1893, under medical advice, he sought rest in England. In his farewell order reproduced below, he expressed his sense of obligation to those who had served under him; what the Battalion owes to him is at least equally deserving of remembrance.

1893.

"On leaving the battalion which he has had the honour of raising, Lieutenant-Colonel E. Molloy desires to place on record the thanks which he feels are due to all those who have so loyally and so ably assisted him during the time of his command. To the officers, both British and Goorkha, but especially to the former, his thanks are due for their zealous co-operation which has enabled the Battalion to attain a standard of efficiency of which he considers all ranks may feel justly proud. He trusts that the system to which more than anything else this is attributable, of allowing all those entrusted with authority scope to exercise it effectually, will always be pursued, for not only has its success, both in the field and quarters, been established beyond doubt, but also because it tends more than anything else to foster and maintain that spirit of *esprit-de-corps* which is the very life of the Regiment, and which will enable it, should occasion arise, to encounter and overcome whatever may be the undertaking before it.

Farewell Order of Colonel E. Molloy.

"It is with deep regret Lieutenant-Colonel E. Molloy bids everyone farewell, but he leaves the Battalion in good hands, and he is confident its efficiency will be more than maintained. He relinquishes the command with every wish for its welfare, prosperity and fame."

Lieutenant-Colonel George Hawkes succeeded Colonel E. Molloy in the command of the 2/5th Gurkhas on November 10th, 1893. The years of peace spent in Abbottabad brought to the 2nd Battalion much the same experiences as to the 1st. It is a record of steady progress in work and of the maintenance of the happiest relations between officers and men, but a detailed account would result in a mere repetition of what has already been set down, so only events which are of particular interest will receive attention here.

Snowfall.

Except as an uncomfortable incident of campaigning, any mention of snow has been omitted from the 1st Battalion record. In a normal Abbottabad winter, however, it is a factor to be reckoned with, and the heavy falls which occurred during January and February, 1893, are not lightly to be passed over. For thirty years Hazara had experienced nothing to equal them, and they played havoc with the ordinary routine of the station. When the Jab Nullah flows muddily between banks of cotton wool and the maize stumps in the fields are covered by a dazzling white blanket, while ragged-edged clouds hang low on the nearer hills, training is in abeyance and games cannot be played. The eucalyptus trees lose their symmetry as their branches snap noisily under the weight of snow, and even the tougher *chirs, biars, kangars* and *chenars* are hard put to it to survive intact the burden put upon them. Then there is nothing to be done but fall in the companies in any kit and take them for long tramps over the hills. By long-established custom the bonds of discipline are relaxed, the sight of a hare will scatter a whole battalion as the men go leaping and yelling in pursuit; snowball fights will break out on the smallest provocation, and with the exception of the Colonel Sahib, whose person is sacred, no British or Gurkha officer can rely on his commission to protect him from the missiles of both contending parties. They are good days, thoroughly enjoyed by everybody, but it is as well, perhaps, that their number is limited.

1894, 1895.

The years 1894 and 1895 hold little of permanent interest. In April of the former year, when Sir Henry Brackenbury visited Abbottabad and made that stirring speech from which an extract is quoted in Chapter VII, he presented the insignia of the Order of British India to Subadar-Major Bhimal Sahi, the first Gurkha officer of the 2nd Battalion to be so honoured. In 1896 two companies of a strength of 4 Gurkha officers, 8 Havildars and 162 rank and file, were attached to the 1st Battalion for the expedition against the Mahsuds. They took part in the operations at Makin, Kundiwam, Wana and Sheranni, and returned to Abbottabad in April, 1896. Major-General H. J. P. Browne mentions that on the march from Wana to the Tochi the Battalion passed through Pezu where many articles of mess property were found in the dak bungalow, by the old *abdar*, Gurditta. They had disappeared more than fifteen years before when the Regiment was on its way back to India at the end of the Afghan War, but how they got to Pezu, which is many miles north of the route followed in 1880, is a mystery which has never been cleared up.

Chitral, 1896-1897. Early in 1896 the 2/5th were ordered to proceed to Chitral. Leaving Abbottabad on April 21st, they arrived at Kila Drosh on May 14th. Barely a year had passed since the Chitral campaign had been brought to a successful conclusion, and conditions were not the same as those ruling when the 1st Battalion was stationed there some years later. The garrison was larger, headquarters and most of the troops remained at Chitral itself instead of at Drosh and, in comparison with the complete freedom enjoyed later on, movement was restricted. The delightful climate of the upland valleys could not be exploited by the formation of summer camps, and from May to September the heat at river level proved very trying. During the winter heavy falls of snow interfered with training. Officers and men, however, enjoyed the change, and a very happy year was spent in this, the northernmost outpost of the Indian borderland. The Battalion was confronted with a very heavy task in the early spring of 1897 when the time for its relief drew near. It was sent south to clear the Lowarai Pass to allow of the passage of the relieving troops. In many places there were drifts over thirty feet in depth, under the vast accumulation of snow it was often difficult to ascertain the alignment of the road and working parties must always be on their guard against avalanches which were a constant menace. Undeterred by these adverse conditions the men, in the highest spirits, worked strenuously and well, and deservedly gained high praise for their achievement in clearing the pass before the arrival of the relieving column in April. In May, 1897, the Battalion returned to Abbottabad.

When later in the year the whole frontier was ablaze, the 2/5th were debarred from taking an active part in suppressing the risings owing to the absence on furlough of double the usual quota. From their ranks, however, came nearly half the total number of the famous Gurkha Scouts, and it was they who provided the commander of that splendid body of men in the person of Captain F. G. Lucas. When Sir William Lockhart decided on increasing their numbers to the strength of a full battalion, Lieutenants Nightingale, Barlow and Warburton left Abbottabad in February, 1898, with a second contingent of 220 picked men to join the original scouts at Landi Kotal. The excellent work done by Captain Lucas earned for him a brevet majority and the award of the Distinguished Service Order, while among the rank and file there were many who gained distinction. The original scouts fought at Dargai, the Sampagha and Arhanga Passes, Maidan, Saran Sar, the Bara Valley and China; their story has been told in an earlier chapter.

After two years spent in Abbottabad the Battalion again set out for a tour of duty elsewhere. This time their destination was the Samana, where from March, 1899, until March, 1900, they furnished the garrison of the posts, with headquarters at Fort Lockhart. In May Colonel Hawkes went to England, and Brevet Lieutenant-Colonel E. W. F. Martin came from the 1st Gurkhas to officiate for him until confirmed in the appointment of Commandant in May, 1901. The Samana has already been described and enough has been said earlier in this narrative to give an idea of the kind of existence led by a unit quartered there. In the case of the sojourn of the 2nd Battalion it has to be remembered, however, that the tragedy of Saragarhi had been enacted less than two years previously, and it was necessary to observe precautions which later could be dispensed with. Compensation was found for this drawback in the excellence of the climate which resulted in continuity of training of a maximum number of men. The effects of this were apparent when Major-General Waterfield carried out an inspection soon after the return of the Battalion to Abbottabad. His report ran " A smart, well-turned-out battalion who seem to maintain the traditions of their corps."

Samana, 1899-1900.

While on the subject of inspections it is convenient to give extracts here from reports covering the period which preceded the outbreak of the Great War. In 1893 Sir George White saw the men on parade soon after he succeeded Lord Roberts as Commander-in-Chief. He expressed his extreme satisfaction with their steadiness and added: " they are just as good and smart when no one is looking at them."

Inspections, 1893-1908.

In 1904 Sir Edmund Barrow wrote: " An excellent Regiment in every respect with immense *esprit-de-corps* and with the advantage of a very good lot of British officers. The men are smart in handling arms and in their general bearing. They are very good on the hillside. There is no tendency to over-centralize."

In 1908 the Lieutenant-General commanding the Northern Army noted: " Quite up to the best of the Gurkha Battalions."

Many other distinguished officers carried out inspections at various times, including Sir William Lockhart, Sir Power Palmer, Sir Corrie Bird, Sir Charles Egerton and Lord Kitchener, and without exception their reports were favourable.

From the time of its return from the Samana early in 1900 until its next spell of active service with the Zakka Khel expedition in 1908, the 2nd Battalion record resolves itself for the most part into a chronicle of minor happenings relating to the doings of officers, changes in equipment and other details of administration and interior economy, excursions from Abbottabad on manœuvres, reliefs on detachments, and progress in shooting and games. There are certain events of that period, however, to which greater importance attaches, and these first claim our attention.

Abolition of Punjab Frontier Force, 1903. On March 22nd, 1903, the Punjab Frontier Force ceased " to exist as a separate body after fifty-four years of honourable and distinguished service." Henceforward it was to survive only as a name incorporated in the titles of those units whose deeds had brought it fame. At the time of its dissolution the force was commanded by that very distinguished soldier, Major-General Sir Charles Egerton, K.C.B., D.S.O., A.D.C., who concluded his farewell order with the words : " The Major-General Commanding earnestly hopes that the camaraderie and *esprit-de-corps* which have been so strong a characteristic of the Punjab Frontier Force, may always endure and not be permitted to die out." After twenty-five years it is possible to see the complete realization of that hope, and for those regiments who, like the 5th Gurkhas, have the privilege of writing themselves " Frontier Force," their original connexion with that *corps d'elite* must always be an inspiration and an incentive to go forward in the spirit of its great traditions.

Abbottabad, of course, ceased to be the headquarters of the Punjab Frontier Force, the garrison was organized as a war brigade with its own brigade commander and staff, and, administered at first by the Peshawar Division, in 1904 was transferred to the Rawalpindi Division.

Appointment of Lord Roberts as Colonel of 5th Gurkhas, 1904. On June 3rd, 1904, took effect the appointment as Colonel of the Regiment of Field-Marshal the Right Honourable Frederick Slade Earl Roberts, V.C., K.G., K.P., G.C.B., O.M., G.C.S.I., G.C.I.E. The 2nd Battalion, equally with the 1st, was proud of the renewal of its connection with the great leader, and the 5th Gurkhas soon had reason to be grateful for his lively interest in its welfare.

Visits of Lord Kitchener, 1903 and 1906. Lord Kitchener twice visited Abbottabad during his term of office as Commander-in-Chief in India, first in October, 1903, and again on September 10th, 1906. On the second occasion he did the Regiment the honour of accepting an invitation to dinner. There was a feeling of nervousness among the young officers when the evening began, for they had been warned to keep their eyes on their plates lest Lord K. should resent their stares, and, as he was reputed to have done elsewhere, walk abruptly out. The Chief's geniality and genuine interest in his surroundings soon ended the constraint. With the exception of Lord Kitchener himself, who stood by and encouraged the proceedings, every senior officer in turn was " chaired " round the Mess to the accompaniment of a cheerful noise beaten out on the Nilt kettle-drums, and few who saw it will forget the picture of Sir Beauchamp Duff extended on the floor, his arms entwining the leg of a sofa, while all the subalterns of both battalions hauled respectfully but firmly on his legs in their determination to do him similar honour.

Officers, 1900-1908.
The doings of British officers during this period are not without interest. In 1900 occurred the polyglot expedition to China, and in the contingent sent from India the Battalion was represented by Captain J. M. Stewart who was given the appointment of D.A.Q.M.G., 2nd Brigade; Captain E. B. C. Boddam, in command of the 3rd Coolie Corps; Lieutenant M. R. W. Nightingale, as Assistant Brigade Commissariat and Transport Officer of the 2nd Brigade; and Lieutenant F. H. Bridges, who was attached to the Hong-Kong Regiment. In 1901 Captain Stewart was given a brevet majority for the good work done by him in China, and Captain Boddam went to the Staff College at Camberley. In 1904 Captain Stewart left to command the 1/9th Gurkhas at Dehra Dun.

In February, 1905, while the Battalion was on manœuvres at Khanpur, the sad news arrived of the death of Colonel E. Molloy, first Commandant of the 2/5th Gurkhas. He was at Lugano on a short visit when he contracted pneumonia, the effects of which proved fatal. His knowledge of the men, and his ready sympathy had endeared him to all the Gurkha ranks, and his loss was deeply felt by those who had served under him.

In September, 1906, the Battalion suffered another bereavement in the death of Colonel E. W. F. Martin, who was at that time officiating in the command of the Brigade. His were just those qualities to gain for him the affection as well as the respect of his subordinates, and it was with very genuine sorrow that the Regiment assembled to do honour to his memory at the little cemetery among the pines.

To succeed Colonel Martin, Lieutenant-Colonel J. M. Stewart returned from the 1/9th Gurkhas. Those who joined during this period were H. T. Molloy, in 1903; G. P. Sanders and T. Luck, in 1904; J. D. Crowdy, in 1905; H. R. C. Lane, W. V. Brett and R. C. Duncan, in 1906; F. Skipwith and A. A. Heyland, in 1907.

Among Gurkha officers mention must be made of the promotion to Subadar-Major of that distinguished soldier, Amar Sing Thapa in 1905, and of the transfer of Bidan Sing Adhikari in 1906 to occupy a similar position with the 1/9th Gurkhas.

Details of administration and interior economy which seem worthy of permanent record include the following :—Two maxim guns were received in July, 1902, and 24 men were selected and put under training to form the gun detachments. Felt hats for wear in field service order were introduced in September, 1903. Aluminium cooking pots were bought from Battalion funds and brought into use in 1904. Short M.L.E. rifles were issued in July, 1904. The miniature range east of the old quarter-guard was built in 1905, and two bath-houses were erected in the same year with money given by the mother of Bugler Chuni Damai, to perpetuate the memory of her son, who had lately died. She handed over a sum of Rs.896, and the buildings serve also as a perpetual reminder of her devotion.

Administrative Changes, 1902-1907.

For some part of every year the Battalion was absent from Abbottabad, the occasion being provided by training camps or manœuvres, and once by a tour of garrison duty in relief of a unit quartered elsewhere. These excursions gave an opportunity of comparing the results of training carried out in Abbottabad with corresponding results achieved in other places, and they successfully countered the tendency to develop an outlook too parochial. In January and February, 1902, the 2/5th took part in the Yusufzai manœuvres, and twice had the experience of ferrying across the Indus with their baggage and transport animals complete. In October of the same year they marched down the cart-road prepared to relieve the 2nd Sikhs in Kohat, that regiment being then under orders for Somaliland. On arrival at Hasan Abdal something occurred to modify the original plans, and they halted there for two months. Eventually, however, they did reach Kohat, and they formed part of the garrison of that station from the end of December until their return to Abbottabad at the end of February, 1903. In December, 1903, manœuvres took place in the vicinity of Rawalpindi, and from that time onwards the Battalion took part in all those concentrations of troops mentioned in connection with the 1st Battalion in an earlier chapter of this narrative. With the rest of the Indian Army it completed in the Kitchener tests of 1905 and 1906, and the success it achieved under the severe conditions imposed gained for it a word of praise from the inspecting officer, General Woon. In the autumn of 1905 the 2/5th again had a glimpse of Chitral. Starting with the escorting column on September 14th, they went as far as Kila Drosh, and returned on December 8th, very hard and fit as a result of nearly two months of continuous marching.

Movements, 1902-1907.

The occasions were many when a part only of the Battalion left Abbottabad for one purpose or another. In 1903, for instance, Major Lucas with 4 Gurkha officers and 121 rank and file was attached to the

1st Battalion to complete their numbers during their stay in Chitral; detachments were frequently required for duty at Murree, Changla Gali and elsewhere, and seldom a year passed but the companies and the recruits went into summer camp. As early as 1894 a hot weather camp had been formed at Thandiani, but it was not until some years later that a similar procedure became a regular feature of the year's training. The locality usually chosen was Huli-ka-Dhana, beyond Thandiani, where the climate was excellent, the water supply plentiful and the ground available for training of sufficient extent to meet requirements. Other places were tried, such as the Bhogarmang Valley and Kagan, but the former was found unsuitable and the latter, though ideal on every other count, proved inconveniently distant.

Shooting and Games.
The only shooting competition in which the Battalion was wont to take part at this period was the annual match against the 1st Battalion for the cup presented by Lord Roberts. This was won by the 2nd Battalion in 1905 and again in 1907. The same year marked the beginning of a sequence of football victories, for, beating the 2/10th Gurkhas in the finals, the Battalion team was successful in winning the Gurkha Brigade cup. Trained originally by Major Lucas, the team was generally of more than average strength. Its two outstanding players were Hari Thapa, a back, whose long, raking kick often turned defence into attack, and Harkia Thapa, a very skilful centre-forward. Among British officers, "Boy" Warburton, until his tragically sudden death, was a veritable tower of strength.

It may be that it is only their remoteness—enhanced, perhaps, by the intervening upheaval of the Great War—which lends to those days a glamour seemingly absent from the serious business of soldiering in these present times. Would it occur to anyone now to take the arrangements made by Army Headquarters and convert them into material for a mere light-hearted jest? Such things were done then, and here is a story sent by Colonel F. W. Evatt to prove it.

"There was the great jest of the Japanese attaché which attracted the attention of the Commander-in-Chief. The attaché was timed to arrive on a Monday, but the station staff officer got a wire postponing his visit. The guest had been told off to the care of Chesney, who knew French, the reputed common tongue in which communication was to be kept up. It occurred to some bright spirit—possibly F. H. Bridges—that it would be a pity to disappoint Chesney, ignorant as yet of the change of plans, so he selected a Mongolian, coached him in his part, dressed him in European clothes and drove him to Chesney's bungalow. All went according to plan, and while the host entertained his guest with French conversation and photographs of local interest, the disguised rifleman kept the ball rolling for quite a time with 'Oui, Oui.'

Eventually the conspirators entered and broke it to Chesney that 'Yamagachi' was Tilbir Thapa of his own double company." Moreover the rifleman was exactly like a Japanese.

Despite his mental brilliance, Major Chesney was inclined to be absent-minded, and once during field firing at Morkalan had been known to wander, whistling cheerfully and playing an inaudible tune on his buttons, into a line of bullet-swept targets which he had himself put in position.

Zakka Khel Expedition, February, 1908.
Early in 1908 the 2/5th again saw active service when they took part in the expedition against the Zakka Khels of the Bazar Valley, a locality previously visited by the Gurkha Scouts under Major Lucas in December, 1897. Justification for the expedition was to be found in the repeated raids made into British territory by members of the tribe. These culminated on January 28th, 1908, in a daring enterprise against Peshawar city, when a policeman was killed, others were wounded and property of an estimated value of one *lakh* of rupees was carried off to the hills. Thereupon preparations went forward secretly for the mobilization of two brigades and a reserve brigade, to be placed under the command of Major-General Sir James Willcocks, K.C.M.G., C.B., D.S.O., for the punishment of the Zakka Khels.

On February 2nd, 1908, the Battalion was warned to be ready to move at a moment's notice to take part in the Nowshera manœuvres. On February 4th this warning was followed by a definite order to mobilize for service on the frontier, and later on the same day came detailed instructions for entrainment at Hasan Abdal at 2 p.m. on the 6th. This was short notice indeed, and preparations went forward far into the night. By the morning of February 5th all was in readiness, and at 10 a.m. began the long march of forty-two miles to the railway at Hasan Abdal. Arriving there at 1.30 p.m. on the 6th, it was found that haste had been in vain; there was no knowing when entrainment would take place, and meantime the Battalion would pitch camp and await with what patience it could muster the receipt of further orders.

Some days were spent at Hasan Abdal while the Home and Indian Governments corresponded by telegram regarding the exact scope of the expedition. There were daily trips to Rawalpindi to gather the latest crop of rumours and to buy articles of campaigning kit. A strong draft arrived from the 2/6th Gurkhas, and at last on February 11th the Battalion entrained for Peshawar, where it arrived some hours after darkness had set in. The British officers present were Colonel Stewart, Major Lucas, Major Badcock, Captain Johnson, Captain Champain, Captain Skipwith, Lieutenants Sanders, Molloy, Lane and Duncan, 2/Lieutenant Heyland, and of the 2/6th Gurkhas, Lieutenants Beeman, Sparrow and Hackett.

Topography. The Bazar Valley, the goal of the expeditionary force, is the valley of the Bazar stream which flows through it from west to east to join the Khyber stream four miles south-east of Lala China. Some twenty miles long, it is separated from the Khyber Valley on the north by the Alachi Hills, and from the Bara Valley on the south by the Sur Ghar range. On the west it rises gradually towards the lofty, snow-capped range of the Safed Koh. Through the northern barrier of hills towards the west end of the valley the Thabai and Tsatsobi passes lead into Afghanistan, while farther to the east the Bazar, Bori, Alachi and Chora passes give access to the Khyber. The easiest approach is from Lala China, in the Khyber, over the Chora pass to Chora village. Thence westward to Walai, for a distance of six or seven miles, the valley is narrow, but at Walai it opens out into the China plain, the village of China itself lying about three miles farther to the west, half encircled by a long spur running out from the main watershed to the north.

Plan of Campaign. General Willcocks's plan of campaign was to move the bulk of his force to Walai by the Chora Pass, and to send a flying column under Colonel Roos-Keppel to carry out an encircling movement from Landi Kotal over the Bazar Pass to China. The flying column was to consist of a half battalion, 2/5th Gurkhas (300 rifles) and the Khyber Rifles (800 rifles), while the main column comprised two brigades, the first commanded by Brigadier-General Anderson, and the second by Major-General Barrett. The reserve brigade, which included the 1st Battalion of the Regiment, was distributed between Nowshera and Peshawar.

Advance from Peshawar. Under these arrangements, when the Battalion arrived in Peshawar it found itself under the unwelcome necessity of dividing, and at noon on February 12th the right half, under Major Lucas, took train for Jamrud preparatory to joining the Khyber Rifles at Landi Kotal. On the 13th, a fine, bright day typical of the cold weather of northern India, the well-worn road leading westwards from Peshawar was once again the stage for scenes so often enacted there before, as the two brigades of the main column streamed along it towards the Khyber to the music of the regimental bands and the skirl of the pipes, while seemingly endless trains of camels and mules raised clouds of dust in their rear. Nominally the 2/5th Gurkhas formed part of the 1st Brigade, made up, besides, of the 1st Bn. Royal Warwickshire Regiment, 53rd Sikhs and 59th Scinde Rifles, but on this, as on many future occasions, they were attached to the 2nd Brigade, composed of the 1st Bn. Seaforth Highlanders, 28th Punjabis, 45th Sikhs and 54th Sikhs. That night was spent in camp at Jamrud, and next day the force marched to Lala China, just short of Ali Masjid in the Khyber.

On February 15th active operations began. For the entry into the Bazar Valley General Willcocks had arranged that, simultaneously with the advance of the flying column from Landi Kotal, the 2nd Brigade, equipped as lightly as possible, should move ahead by the Chora Pass and, securing the main tactical features of the Zakka Khel portion of the route, should make for the neighbourhood of Walai. The half-battalion of the 2/5th was again attached to the 2nd Brigade, and extricating itself with some difficulty from the broken ground on which it had bivouacked, set off at daybreak with three days' rations in the haversack and only 7 lbs. of bedding for the men. From Lala China to Chora, with its white fort set imposingly on the left bank of the Bazar stream, is a distance of seven miles, and on this part of the route, traversing as it does the country of the friendly Malik Din Khel, no opposition was encountered. About a mile west of Chora the track enters Zakka Khel country, and here it is entirely commanded by the lofty ridge known as Tsapara, rising above the left bank of the stream.

Occupation of Tsapara Hill, February 15th, 1908.
The advanced guard reached this point at midday, and at once came under the fire of a body of the enemy posted on the slopes of the ridge. The advance of the column was checked, and during the short pause which ensued a message came to Colonel Stewart instructing him to clear the Tsapara feature and to hold it during the night with the object of securing communication with Chora.

The half-battalion advanced rapidly up parallel spurs and, driving the enemy before them, were soon in possession of the crest. The only casualties were amongst the mules of the machine gun section and first line transport, which had been sent to shelter in a deep *nullah* near the foot of the slope. They came under heavy fire from enemy snipers retiring from the ridge, and two of them were hit. Companies were distributed along the crest and, under the protection of covering parties, at once set to work to build sangars for occupation during the night. To secure the left flank a piquet of the 4th Double Company was posted on the east end of the ridge. During the hours of darkness a bold attack was made on it by a party of Zakka Khels. The first indication was a heavy burst of firing from the direction of some high ground situated at no great distance, and soon the sentries, who happened to be two tough old soldiers, passed the word that the enemy were close at hand. From man to man the whisper passed " Ayo! Ayo! " and in a moment everyone was on the alert, ready to repel a rush. Near at hand all was still, but peering intently into the darkness, the occupants of the sangar could just discern moving figures only thirty yards away—evidently a party which had crept up under cover of the supporting fire from the high ground. Now these, too, opened a heavy fire, and the flashes from their rifles serving to give the direction the men of the piquet replied. For some time the interchange of shots continued, and then again silence reigned. Throughout the night periods of quiet alternated with bursts of heavy fire; at one time the enemy, growing bolder, threw large stones over the sangar wall, and never for a moment could vigilance be relaxed. With the coming of daylight the tribesmen at last withdrew, and then it was found that the fire of the piquet had accounted for three of their number. On our side there were no casualties, but three more mules were shot.

To complete the story of February 15th it is only necessary to say that the remainder of the 2nd Brigade had bivouacked near Walai, and that the 1st Brigade, with the baggage columns, had halted for the night at Chora.

Advance to Walai, February 16th, 1908.
On February 16th the 28th Punjabis arrived to take over the Tsapara piquets, and the half-battalion 2/5th Gurkhas, sending down its mules to proceed by road, set out on a long, stiff climb over the hills to Walai. While this movement was in progress, considerable numbers of the enemy were seen in front, who appeared to be hotly engaged with some of our own troops endeavouring to make their way up the hill from the valley below. Grasping the situation, Colonel Stewart decided to lend a hand, and with his half-battalion began a turning movement which would bring it out on the hills overlooking the enemy who were opposing the advance from the valley. All went well until it arrived at its objective, when the moment it appeared on the crest of the ridge, it came under heavy machine-gun fire directed on it by the guns of the battalion it was trying to assist. Every effort was made to obtain recognition, but without success. Even the very gallant action of a signaller named Maidhar Gharti, who set up his heliograph under a storm of bullets and flashed it repeatedly on the machine guns, failed to stop their fire. Eventually the half-battalion was obliged to seek shelter behind the ridge and continue its advance to Walai. On reaching Walai it fell in with Major Lucas and the right half-battalion, which had left Landi Kotal at 4 a.m. on the 15th to arrive at China by way of the Bazar Pass on the evening of the same day after a very hard march. Having spent the night at China, where the enemy snipers had been busy, on the morning of the 6th they had come on to Walai to join the 2nd Brigade.

Walai had been selected by Sir James Willcocks as the site of a standing camp for his force. From this it is not to be supposed that the view from the surrounding hills showed orderly rows of white canvas in the plain below, for there were no tents. It was merely the place from which the force would issue daily to harry the Zakka Khels, and to which it would return when the day's work was done. In this part of the Bazar Valley there are two main branches of the

Bazar stream, which run nearly parallel about two miles apart and unite at a point 1,500 yards south-east of Walai. The camp was situated on either side of the northern branch. It was overlooked on the west and south by the Khar Ghundai feature, known also as Seaforths' Hill, situated between the two branches, and by a spur running down from Sara Paial, named 45th Sikhs Hill, which rose above the right bank of the southern branch. On the north and east the camp was commanded by the Zir Ghundai feature, and by a range of low hills which curved round towards the junction of the streams. All these features were strongly picketed, and an inner line of defence was provided by a breastwork built round the camping ground.

The night of February 16th/17th, like most nights spent at Walai, was disturbed, for the Zakka Khels were inveterate snipers. On the 17th the 1st Brigade moved in from Chora, and the Battalion being sent across the *nullah* to join them and to take over a part of the perimeter in the north-west corner of camp, set to work to dig for itself what are expressively known as "funk holes." Men of other regiments in the brigade stood round and smiled at this display of energy, for they had found Chora quiet enough, but a night spent without cover taught them wisdom, and they were quick to follow this prudent example.

China destroyed, February 18th, 1908.
China, a few miles west of Walai, a place of many towers, springs of good water, of fruit trees and fertile fields, is the only settlement of real importance in the valley, and against it the initial efforts of the expedition were directed. On the 18th the Battalion formed part of a mixed force under General Barrett for the capture and destruction of China. Leaving camp before daylight the 2/5th and Seaforths made a slight detour to bring them on to the low ridge half encircling China from the north, while the rest of the force moved straight on the objective. The attack delivered by the 2/5th and Seaforths, as the hills were approached, met with some opposition, and 2/Lieutenant MacFadyen of the latter regiment was mortally wounded. Advancing with great rapidity the Battalion soon reached the crest of the ridge, the enemy withdrawing towards Tsatsobi and Thabai, and dispositions were made at once to hold the position throughout the day. Meanwhile, the rest of the force had reached China from the east, and the work of blowing up towers, collecting firewood and fodder and destroying the fruit trees and the water supply was begun. The retirement to Walai began about 4 p.m., and, in accordance with their usual practice, the enemy collected magically from nowhere and attempted to follow up. The pace of the Battalion and the excellence of its covering arrangements were effective in keeping them at a distance, but on the

Beginning of Week-End War, 1908 : 2/5th Digging in on reaching Walai.

End of Week-End War : Zakka Tribesmen bringing in Rifles.

other flank they succeeded in getting close to No. 3 Mountain Battery in fairly open country, and the gunners with their escort and the 54th Sikhs were for a time hotly engaged. The 54th Sikhs, however, proved equal to the occasion, the enemy were driven off, and the further withdrawal proceeded according to plan. Before 6 p.m. the whole force had reached the shelter of the camp piquets, and the enemy, who had lost heavily, would seem to have had their fill of fighting, for during the night not a shot was fired.

It is unnecessary to describe in detail the subsequent operations carried out from Walai, since they differed little in their general character from those of the first day. Each entailed an advance encountering slight opposition, a pause and protective arrangements while some work of destruction was performed, and a withdrawal followed up with considerable determination until the vicinity of camp was reached. It was customary to employ the two brigades alternately, but the Battalion was unaffected by this arrangement, for it invariably accompanied that brigade for which active employment had been found. On the 19th China was again visited, this time by General Anderson's Brigade, and the Battalion was given the task of safeguarding the left flank, where the 54th Sikhs had come to close quarters with the enemy on the previous day. On this occasion, although the tribesmen did their best to harass the retirement, they met with no success.

Reconnaissance to Tsatsobi, February 20th. On the 20th only four companies were available for active operations, the remainder being on piquet. The half-battalion accompanied a column detailed for the destruction of Sarmando and Kwar, and for a reconnaissance in the direction of the Tsatsobi Pass. There was much long-range fire from the hills, but no casualties on our side, and the column returned to camp, its mission successfully accomplished.

Attack on Halwai Position, February 21st, 1908. The operations of the 21st were on a larger scale, both brigades being employed for their execution. For some days past the enemy had been gathering in considerable numbers at Halwai, six miles west of Walai, and General Willcocks seized the opportunity to attack them and destroy the village. The 2nd Brigade moved south of China, leaving the 28th Punjabis *en route* in occupation of the China Hill to cover the subsequent withdrawal of the force, and sending the Seaforths to hold a position on the hills south-east of Walai. The Battalion, with the 1st Brigade, moved north of China, and crossing the Sarwakai Pass, advanced southwards across the plain to attack frontally the Halwai position. Moving with great speed, the 2/5th soon gained possession of the hills and inflicted a number of casualties on the retiring enemy. The towers of Halwai were destroyed, the stacks of timber burnt, and then the withdrawal began. Both brigades now took the line south of China, and for a time all went well. Parties of the enemy, however, had managed to approach unobserved the position of the 28th Punjabis on the China Ridge, and when that battalion began its withdrawal it found itself under heavy fire, delivered from the crest at close range, and suffered a number of casualties. Emboldened by this success the tribesmen pressed hard the further withdrawal of the Seaforths in the plain to the south, and it was while directing the retirement at this stage that their commanding officer, Major the Honourable D. Forbes-Sempill, was killed.

Events from February 23rd to 28th, 1908.
The Battalion paid another visit to China on the 23rd, and next day was employed on convoy duty towards Chora. A large *jirga* of Afridis having arrived in camp, who offered to negotiate with the Zakka Khels, hostilities were suspended for two days. The opportunity was taken to organize a khud race, open to representatives of all Indian units in the force. With Pathans of every class available in the ranks of the Khyber Rifles, the three Frontier Force regiments and the 28th Punjabis, competition was likely to be keen, and the Battalion was none too sanguine of success. However, it entered three runners and hoped for the best. The course selected was from the bed of the *nullah* to the crest of the Khar Ghundai and back again, and as only one flag was used to mark the turning point at the top of the hill, there was ample scope for competitors to choose their own line. When the race started it was seen that while the Gurkhas made straight ahead for the steepest part, which in actual distance provided the shortest way to the summit, the remaining runners kept rather to the left in order to have the advantage of the more gentle declivity of a convenient spur. For a time it seemed that the Gurkhas had chosen wrongly, so slow appeared their rate of progress up the precipitous face of the hill. Nevertheless, two out of the three were the first to round the flag, and when it came to the downhill run, there was no hope for anyone else. Ratanbir Pun arrived first at the winning post, and Chandra Sing Gurung second. Dilaram Thapa, who had hurt his foot, was fifth, being beaten by two Pathans of the 28th Punjabis.

It was about this time that Sir James Willcocks had an amusing encounter with one of our men. Meeting the rifleman one morning, taking a letter towards the field post-office, he was about to pass him by, when the little man saluted smartly and approached.

"Are you the biggest General Sahib here?" he asked.

"I am," answered Sir James.

"Will you post this letter for me?" came the odd request.

"But why not take it to the field post-office?" suggested the General.

"It is a very important letter to my wife in Abbottabad; I do not trust the field post-office; it does not use stamps. But if the big General Sahib will send my letter with his own, it will without doubt arrive."

Sir James good naturedly took the letter and, as he afterwards told Colonel Stewart, sent it to post with his own mail.

On February 27th the Battalion took over all the camp piquets, preparatory to the final withdrawal from the valley. As ill-luck would have it, the weather turned very cold; there was heavy rain during the daytime and snow fell at night. Bedding had been stacked ready for immediate despatch, and the men therefore had nothing but their greatcoats. Although negotiations for a settlement were actually in progress, firing at night was heavier than on any previous occasion, so that from every point of view, the time spent on piquet duty from the 27th to the 29th proved the most uncomfortable period of the expedition.

Withdrawal from Bazar Valley, February 29th, 1908.

The Afridi *jirga* which had gone to Halwai on the 25th to settle terms with the Zakka Khels, returned on the 28th, its mission successfully accomplished. On the same day orders were issued for the evacuation of Walai. On the 29th the camp was broken up, and the withdrawal began. The 2/5th left their piquet positions, and acted as rearguard to the force as far as Chora, where they spent the night. On the 30th they again took up the duties of rearguard until Lala China was reached, when they closed and proceeded independently to Jamrud. Testimony from the enemy's side to the success of the expedition is to be found in the following extract from the "Political Report of the Bazar Valley Expedition, 1908."

" The Afridis, who are no mean judges of hill fighting, express themselves amazed at the handling and conduct of the troops as unlike anything they have seen or heard of, and the fact that they have obtained no loot in mules, rifles, stores or ammunition, on which they confidently counted to compensate them for their own losses, has given them a strong distaste for expeditions conducted on these novel lines."

The Battalion had borne itself in accordance with its traditions, and had worthily upheld the reputation of the Regiment. A most pleasing feature of the expedition had been the opportunity it afforded of renewed association with the old 72nd Highlanders, of whom Sir James Willcocks wrote in his despatch: "The Seaforths have throughout the operations proved themselves a very fine battalion." At the same time he wrote of Lieutenant-Colonel J. M. Stewart: "An excellent Battalion Commander who was frequently assigned difficult duties which he invariably carried out satisfactorily." Others of the Battalion who were mentioned were Major F. G. Lucas, D.S.O., and

Subadar-Major Amar Sing Thapa. Lieutenant-Colonel Stewart was promoted to a brevet colonelcy and was honoured by being appointed A.D.C. to the King. Subadar-Major Amar Sing Thapa was admitted to the second class of the Order of British India.

Return to Abbottabad, March, 1908.
On March 2nd the 2/5th reached Peshawar, and there foregathered with the 1st Battalion. From Peshawar the whole Regiment returned by the usual stages to Abbottabad, where they arrived on March 14th. In Nowshera, where the Regiment spent a night, the Battalion Pipers were much to the fore. They had a critical audience in the Seaforth Highlanders, who were stationed there, but managed to survive the ordeal with credit. There was a great guest night on that occasion, when the Officers of the Seaforths entertained the Officers of the 5th Gurkhas. Dim recollections remain of a climbing race up the great bamboo poles of the Mess tent, when G. P. Sanders just managed to defeat one of the Seaforths who was known as Cupid, but ruptured a small blood vessel in his thigh as the result of his too rapid descent.

1908 to 1914.
Of the remaining years before the Great War, nearly everything worth telling has been said in an earlier chapter. The jubilee of the Regiment was celebrated in April, 1908, and the Battalion team again won the Gurkha Brigade Cup, beating the 1/3rd Gurkhas in the finals. In the great Khud race Ratanbir Pun was second.

In May the Battalion went to Margalla, as part of the reserve brigade for the Mohmand Expedition, and returned to Abbottabad in June. January 1st, 1909, marked the fiftieth anniversary of the transfer of the Government of India from the East India Company to the Crown. To commemorate the event a proclamation parade was held, and the announcement was made of certain benefits which were to accrue to the Indian ranks of the Army. These included an increase in pay and a free issue of firewood.

In 1908 Subadar-Major Amar Sing Thapa went to England in the train of the Prime Minister of Nepal, and in 1911 Jemadar Ram Sing Thapa was selected to attend the coronation of His Majesty King George V. During this period there were a number of outstanding successes in the field of sport. The Gurkha Brigade Football Cup was again won in 1910, and the Punjab Frontier Force Cup was carried off by the Battalion in two successive years, 1909 and 1910. The 5th Fusilier Cup was played for for the first time in 1912, and was won by the 2nd Double Company, another double company of the Battalion, the 3rd, also reaching the final. In 1909 W. G. Harington, who, originally a gunner, had joined the Battalion the previous year, won every event in the Northern India Racquets Championships. In 1910 a polo team of the Battalion reached the final of the Native Infantry

Tournament. In 1909 "D" Company won the Lord Roberts Cup with a record score.

On January 14th, 1911, the Crown Prince of Germany visited Abbottabad. In the morning he witnessed a tactical exercise framed somewhat on the lines of those associated at that time with his own country, for the entire garrison, consisting of four battalions and four batteries, carried out a massed attack on the hill above the range, and with blank ammunition made such an uproar as can seldom have been equalled on a field day. Later the Regiment entertained him at luncheon, and the admission had to be made that in the Mess he made a very good impression. He said that His Majesty King George had told him that he must visit the 5th Gurkhas while in India. After luncheon he sent two telegrams, one to the King, saying that he had acted on his suggestion, and another to Lord Roberts, Colonel of the Regiment.

A few days later came a letter from the Crown Prince, enclosing a telegram from His Majesty. It ran:—"Thank you for your kind thought of me. Glad you lunched with 5th Gurkhas. Hope you are enjoying yourself."

For some years the Regiment was proud of its possession of a signed photograph presented by the Prince, but this ceased to have an existence soon after the outbreak of the Great War.

In October, 1911, Colonel Stewart was given an important staff appointment in Burma, and was succeeded by Lieutenant-Colonel F. G. Lucas, D.S.O. Of the many improvements inaugurated by the former it is satisfactory to be able to record that the levelling of the football grounds was finished little more than a year later. Once known irreverently as "Jimmy's Folly," the levelled area now provided a stretch of turf not to be surpassed for its purpose in the whole of India, and the day will come when the chenar trees, having got their girth and growth, will make of it one of the pleasantest places in the station.

Of those years before the Great War it can truly be said that there was an attractiveness about them not so easily associated with the less settled period which followed it. Rifle green has made way for khaki on all occasions; the three arms—cavalry, infantry and guns—have been supplemented by aeroplanes, tanks and gas; that which was simple has become complicated. The time has come to follow those great events which wrought the change, and breaking off the story of the 2nd Battalion, we turn our attention to the 1st Battalion, about to take its part in the Great War.

PART II.

THE FIRST BATTALION IN THE GREAT WAR

British Officers of the Regiment, taken in Abbottabad shortly after the Outbreak of the Great War, 1914.

Top Row.—Capt. O. E. Todd. Capt. W. G. Harington. Capt. M. F. Reaney, I.M.S. Lt. K. C. S. Erskine. Lt. Beatson, I.M.S. 2/Lt. F. E. Le Marchand. Capt. R. C. Duncan. Lt. A. A. Heyland. Capt. G. Turner.

Middle Row.—Capt. G. P. Sanders. Lt.-Col. E. B. C. Boddam. Lt.-Col. G. H. Boisragon, V.C. Lt.-Col. F. G. Lucas, D.S.O. Major C. R. Johnson. Major M. K. W. Nightingale. Capt. J. D. Crowly.

Bottom Row.—Lt. R. L. Beddy. 2/Lieut. H. A. Wollesley. Lt. C. A. Gouldsbury. 2/Lieut. R. M. Bruce. Lt. H. J. Cummins. Capt. D. M. Givan.

CHAPTER I

EVENTS FROM AUGUST 4TH, 1914, TO MAY 30TH, 1915.

Mobilization,
5-8-14 to
17-8-14

THE news of the outbreak of war between Great Britain and Germany was received in Abbottabad on August 5th, 1914. The momentous intelligence was accompanied by an order to the 1/5th Gurkhas, among other units in the station, to mobilize for active service. For several reasons there was no prospect of attaining a state of complete readiness for service immediately upon receipt of the order. The season of the year was against the possibility of any such undertaking; the rains had set in, a large proportion of the rank and file of the Battalion was on furlough in Nepal, a number of the British officers was on leave in England, and, finally, in order to complete the field service strength of the unit it was necessary to call up the reservists.

This, of course, did not prevent everything possible being done to ensure the completion of mobilization as rapidly as circumstances would permit. In view of the large number of men affected, and the inaccessibility of their homes in many cases, the response to the notices of recall may be taken as a fine tribute to the nature of our relations with the men who serve with us. By November 1st—that is, a full month before the normal end of their period of furlough—135 men, out of 153 to whom notices had been sent, had rejoined at headquarters, and similarly, of 100 reservists, only 12 had failed to respond.

Meantime, those Indian mountain batteries in the station which had been warned for service, being handicapped to a far less extent than the Gurkha units by the considerations set out above, had completed their preparations and gone, the 27th Mountain Battery to East Africa, and the 23rd and 30th Mountain Batteries to Mesopotamia.

Of the Gurkha battalions in Abbottabad, the 1/5th and 1/6th Gurkhas only had been warned for service, and this warning being confined to a simple order to mobilize, the question of their probable destination could only be a matter for surmise. On October 11th, 1914, however, their doubts were in part dispelled by the receipt of instructions to hold themselves in readiness to embark for foreign service. The 1/6th Gurkhas were the first to move. They left Abbottabad on

October 28th to form part of the 29th Indian Infantry Brigade, under Brigadier-General H. V. Cox, C.B., and in due time sailed from Karachi, with Egypt as their immediate destination. After their departure the 1/5th Gurkhas were not left for long to take their ease in their peace station. Being warned on November 1st, 1914, to be ready to move at very short notice, at 10 a.m. on November 3rd they received definite orders to entrain at Havelian at 6 p.m. on the same day.

Accordingly at 2 p.m. the Battalion set out, feeling that the great adventure had really begun. Only to glimpse the sea was for men who had never been within a thousand miles of it an adventure; to sail on it, to see fresh countries the other side, and there to fight against a civilized enemy comprised a succession of unexpected happenings outside the day-dreams of the most imaginative Gurkha. To speed the Battalion on its way and to wish it luck there had come the 2/5th Gurkhas, the 2/6th Gurkhas, nearly all residents in cantonments, and a strong contingent from the Bazar. Their expressions of good will, so heartily conveyed and so obviously sincere, were very greatly appreciated. The sister battalion, though left behind for the moment, was soon to be called upon to take an active part in the war, and in Mesopotamia, throughout three long years, it found no lack of scope for the exercise of its qualities. Before long, indeed, there was no unit which had its home in Abbottabad, but found itself participating in one or other theatre of operations.

The marching-out strength of the 1/5th Gurkhas was 12 British officers, 17 Gurkha officers, 808 other ranks, besides followers. The British officers who accompanied the Battalion were:—

Lieutenant-Colonel G. H. Boisragon, V.C. (Commanding);
Lieutenant-Colonel E. B. C. Boddam;

Major M. R. W. Nightingale; Major D. M. Govan;
Captain H. M. Battye; Captain G. Turner;
Captain W. K. Brown; Lieutenant D. I. B. Lloyd;
Lieutenant R. L. Beddy; Lieutenant K. C. S. Erskine;
Lieutenant H. J. Cummins; Captain M. F. Reaney, I.M.S.

The Gurkha officers with the Battalion were:—

Subadar-Major Harkabir Thapa, I.O.M.; Jemadar Gopal Gurung;
Subadar Dhanraj Gurung; Subadar Dhanjit Gharti;
Subadar Juthia Gurung; Subadar Amrit Mal;
Subadar Tilbikram Thapa; Subadar Karbir Thapa;
Jemadar Rabi Gharti; Subadar Partiman Rana;
Jemadar Gajarsing Thapa; Jemadar Dhansing Gurung;
Jemadar Biraj Gurung (i); Jemadar Harishankar Gurung;
Jemadar Pemnarain Thapa; Jemadar Gobinde Pun;
 Jemadar Biraj Gurung (ii).

The first halt on the journey proved to be Lahore, where the 1/5th arrived at 4 p.m. on November 4th. On arrival, instructions were received to detrain and proceed to a standing camp at Lahore Cantonments. By this time it had become known that the Battalion was to form part of the 28th Indian Infantry Brigade, commanded by Brigadier-General Sir G. J. Younghusband, K.C.B., and consisting of the 51st Sikhs (F.F.), the 53rd Sikhs (F.F.), the 56th Rifles (F.F.) and the 1/5th Gurkha Rifles (F.F.)

Some days went by, and for lack of a better reason it was surmised that the halt was occasioned by the decision to concentrate the Brigade in Lahore, but this conjecture proved to be wrong. At 1 p.m. on November 15th the Battalion entrained for Karachi.

During this journey came the news of the death of Field-Marshal Earl Roberts, Colonel of the 5th Gurkhas. Caring nothing for his own comfort, and banishing all recollection of the slights put upon him by his countrymen because he had tried to warn them against this very danger which was now upon them, he had striven only to devote all his great qualities, his prescience, and his influence to his country's service. In the pursuit of this aim he had gone to France to help and encourage the Indian troops. Amongst them his was still a name to conjure with, and we may be certain that he succeeded in his endeavour. The effort, however, proved too much for his strength, already overtaxed by his ceaseless exertions, and he died of exposure without seeing England again.

Here, if ever, Milton's lines apply:—

> "Nothing is here for tears, nothing to wail
> Or knock the breast, no weakness, no contempt,
> Dispraise or blame, nothing but well and fair,
> And what may quiet us in a death so noble."

Major-General Sir John Munro Sym, K.C.B., who had relinquished the command of the 1/5th Gurkhas in 1893, became Colonel of the Regiment in his place.

Arriving at Karachi docks on the morning of November 17th, the Battalion embarked on the s.s. *Barpeta*. She proved to be a comfortable, well-found ship of some 8,000 tons, belonging to the B.I.S.N. Company, and while on board all ranks received every consideration from her captain and officers. Special mention must here be made of the gifts sent on board through the agency of "The Ladies' Patriotic League of Karachi." These consisted of tea, dried fruits, chillies, and cigarettes for the men, and of books for the officers. Needless to say they were very greatly appreciated, as, too, were the parcels sent later on by the "Ladies of Lahore," and "the Comforts Committee

Voyage to Egypt, 17-11-14 to 4-12-14.

of Abbottabad," containing bundles of winter and summer clothing, cigarettes, writing-paper, and other luxuries. These derived an added value from the fact that they were received at a time when such things were very hard to come by.

Though the loading of the *Barpeta* was completed on November 17th, it was necessary to delay her departure until other members of the convoy should be ready. Leaving the wharf on the 18th, she anchored in the harbour, only, however, to move out on the 19th and take up a fresh anchorage outside. Finally, on the early morning of the 20th, she weighed anchor and steamed westwards escorted by the R.I.M.S. *Dufferin*. On the morning of the 22nd was encountered a large convoy of twenty steamers which had sailed from Bombay, escorted by the French Cruiser *Dupleix*. From this point the whole convoy proceeded together in a "line-ahead" formation of six parallel columns. Thanks to the fine weather, there was very little sickness, and it was found possible to keep the men fit by means of running drill and physical training. The needs of ponies and mules in this respect were met by the provision of a cinder track laid on the deck, on which they were exercised twice a week. On November 26th Aden was passed, and on December 3rd the convoy anchored off Suez to await orders. On arrival, it was found that the *Barpeta* was only one of forty-four ships collected there, all of them bringing men, horses, or guns to help win the war, and hailing from New Zealand, Australia, and India.

On the evening of December 4th orders were received to disembark for service in Egypt. The *Barpeta* accordingly went alongside, and the work of unloading began. Working until midnight, and resuming in the early morning, the ship was completely cleared and the baggage loaded on to the train in record time. The rapidity with which they worked, and their silence, won for the men golden opinions from the captain of the *Barpeta*.

Ismailia.
From Suez the Battalion proceeded in two trains to Ismailia. Headquarters and the left half Battalion left Suez at 8.30 a.m. on December 5th, to be followed by the right half Battalion at 2.30 p.m., and by 6 p.m. that evening all had reached their destination.

The situation on the Canal at this time may be summarized as follows: The Turks, German-led, were known to be making preparations for an attack on the Canal, and it was confidently expected that this would develop against some portion of the line between Port Said and Suez at no very distant date. On our side provision had therefore been made to deal with any force which could reasonably hope to cross the desert from the direction of Beersheba. Ismailia itself, situated about midway from the two extremities of the Canal, was selected as the headquarters of the "Canal Defence Force," commanded by

Major-General Wilson, C.B. This force consisted of six Indian Infantry brigades, which were distributed on the Canal from south to north as follows:—

From Suez to southern end of Great Bitter Lake	1 Brigade
From southern end of Great Bitter Lake to Serapeum	1 Brigade
From Serapeum to El Ferdan	1 Brigade
At Kantara	1 Brigade
At Ismailia	The Reserve

The force at Ismailia was composed as follows:—

1 Indian Infantry Brigade;
1 Brigade Imperial Service Troops;
1 Cavalry Brigade, Imperial Service Troops;
2 Indian Mountain Batteries;
1 Section Royal Flying Corps;
Egyptian Troop Details.

The defence of Ismailia consisted, in the first place, of a fortified post on the eastern bank of the Canal, covering the ferry. The normal garrison of this post was one battalion, but it was constructed to accommodate two battalions in case of an enemy attack or other emergency. Secondly, there was El Ferdan, a post similar to the main work, but considerably smaller and situated on the eastern bank of the Canal, seven miles north of Ismailia. Its normal garrison was a double company, which, in time of emergency, could be increased to half a battalion. Thirdly, there was an intermediate defence work known as the "Bench Mark," two and a half miles north of Ismailia, and capable of accommodating half a battalion. Its situation was some two and a half miles to the north of Ismailia.

The camping-ground selected for the Battalion at Ismailia was found to be a strip of desert sand, three-quarters of a mile west of the ferry. The water supply from pipes was good and plentiful, and arrangements had been completed for the incineration of refuse. During the time that the Battalion remained in camp at Ismailia, the health of all ranks was very good. Cases of fever and dysentery were rare, and almost the only serious cause of complaint, from a medical point of view, arose from the number of lice in the clothing and bedding of the men. This particular trouble was put an end to by the provision of steam disinfectors in February, 1915. During the months of December, January, and February the climate was, generally, all that could be wished for. From time to time, though, a strong wind would blow, and on such occasions the driven sand made life a burden. December and part of January were spent in training, and the work done calls for no special comment. The men's amusements were not neglected, and a football tournament was organized for Gurkha units serving in Egypt. Four battalions took part, and the 1/5th, by beating the 1/7th Gurkha Rifles in the finals, succeeded in carrying off the trophy, a bronze sphinx, which is now to be seen in the mess at Abbottabad.

On January 13th three new officers joined the Battalion, viz.: Second-Lieutenant N. C. Cosby, Second-Lieutenant I. G. Knowles, and Second-Lieutenant Johnson. The last-named was shortly afterwards transferred to the 40th Pathans, while that regiment was on its way to France.

Early in January information was received to the effect that seven Turkish divisions, together with a motley throng of Bedouin irregulars, of an estimated strength of from ten to fifteen thousand, had collected in Southern Syria, under the command of Djemal Pasha, who had as his Chief of Staff a German officer, Colonel Kress von Kressenstein. This, together with other indications, showed beyond question that the threat against the Canal would materialize, and it was anticipated that an attack would be made towards the end of the month. Consequently the activities of all troops on the Canal were directed to the strengthening of the string of fortifications on the eastern bank, and to the construction of a series of entrenchments on the western bank, which ran without interruption—except where the presence of lakes rendered them unnecessary—the entire length of the waterway, from Suez to Port Said. Further, the country round Kantara was inundated, war vessels were stationed on the Timsah and Bitter Lakes, and both naval and military patrols were organized to keep watch on the Canal fairway and the desert to the east.

El Ferdan. Arising out of these activities, from January 1st, 1915, onwards the Battalion was required to furnish one double company and the machine-gun section as garrison for El Ferdan Post. The defences here consisted of a line of trenches dug on the circumference of an arc, the chord of which, some 400 yards in length, rested on the Canal bank. The trenches themselves were sited on the slopes on the high mounds which had been left during the excavation of the Canal. The outlook from the post, to the south, east, and north, was over a sandy plain, dotted here and there with low bushes. To facilitate supply, a small pier was erected, and communications were improved by the construction of a ferry which connected the post with the opposite bank. Water was brought daily by launch and stored in tanks on the Canal bank. The defences were completed by the erection of barbed wire entanglements and by the provision of flares, while further to guard against eventualities a mine was laid in an angle of the post.

1. Early Days in 1915: Eel Fishing on the Banks of the Suez Canal.
2. More Fishing on the Canal.
3. 1/5th Machine Gun mounted against Submarines on the s.s. " Annaberg " en route to Gallipoli.

On January 21st, 1915, an advanced party of the enemy, estimated at 700 Infantry and 200 Cavalry, was definitely located by our aeroplanes within forty miles of the Canal. As a precautionary measure, all ships passing through the Canal were protected by means of sandbags, and defensive positions were occupied according to plan. In the area with which the Battalion was concerned, the East Lancashire Territorial Artillery, consisting of six batteries sent from Cairo, took post on the western bank with the 20th Battery a thousand yards north of El Ferdan. The left-half Battalion, under Lieutenant-Colonel E. B. C. Boddam, left Ismailia to form the garrison of Bench Mark Post, while the Right Wing and Battalion Headquarters, under Lieutenant-Colonel G. H. Boisragon, V.C., performed a similar service in the case of El Ferdan.

Turkish Attempt on Canal, 21-1-15 to 12-2-15.

Meanwhile, the Turks were continuing their advance, and on January 25th three separate enemy columns were located. The southern column, estimated at a strength of 3,000, was at Bir Mabeiuk, and was reported to be heading for the Suez section of the defences. The central or main column, of an estimated strength of 30,000, was marching on Ismailia, and its advance guard had occupied Moia Harab and Wadi-um-Muksheib. The northern column, about 6,000 strong, was reported in close proximity to El Kantara, which post it attacked half-heartedly on the evening of January 25th. It was anticipated that El Ferdan, too, would be attacked that night, but in this case expectations were not fulfilled.

25-1-15.

On January 26th, H.M. ships *Swiftsure*, *Ocean*, *Minerva*, and *Clio* entered the Canal, and the last-named, under the command of Captain Mackenzie, R.N., was detailed to assist in the defence of the El Ferdan section. On the same date the New Zealand Infantry Brigade and a number of Australian units were brought up from Cairo to take part in the operations. From the 26th onwards the proximity of the enemy necessitated constant readiness in case of attack. The Battalion worked hard in improving existing defences, and kept unbroken watch on the approaches to the Canal. By day the Bikanir Camel Corps did excellent and willing service in patrolling the country in the vicinity of the posts. By night the duty of observation devolved on the personnel of the armed launches which had been fitted out for the purpose. On January 27th occurred an incident worth passing mention. At 10 a.m. a Cavalry reconnoitring party of considerable strength, which had been sent out from Ismailia, was proceeding in a northerly direction about two miles east of El Ferdan. Suddenly a dozen or more shells were seen to burst, apparently right among the men and horses of the party. Anticipating an attack the garrison of the post immediately stood to, but no enemy appeared, and no further shelling occurred. Later it became known that H.M.S. *Clio*, having received no warning of any intended movement of our own troops east of the Canal, had mistaken the patrol for an enemy party, and acted accordingly. Fortunately, despite the excellence of the shooting, no serious damage was done.

On January 29th the passage of ships through the Canal was resumed after a hold-up of traffic which had lasted for several days. The resulting procession formed a spectacle not easily forgotten. Passenger steamers almost beyond counting, fifteen transports filled with Australian troops, a submarine and numerous other craft steamed by within 100 yards of the positions occupied by the Battalion. It was a curious experience that of exchanging shouted conversations with the passing ships at one moment, and returning the next to observe the movements of the enemy on the distant hills.

It was during these days of waiting that on two occasions the footmarks of an enemy patrol, which had been engaged on a midnight prowl in the vicinity of the post, were observed by our men with the coming of daylight. To discourage further enterprise in this direction, on the night of January 30th–31st a party, under Subadar-Major Harkabir Thapa, was told off to lie up for them. At about midnight five men were seen moving cautiously over the sand, and fire was opened. At least one man was hit, who was brought in later, and daylight further revealed numerous packets of dynamite which had been thrown away by the Turks in their flight. On January 29th, 30th, and 31st, there occurred minor skirmishes at Kantara, at Kubra, which is east of Suez, and in the neighbourhood of Ismailia. East of El Ferdan, too, constant enemy movement was observed, and on

1-2-15.
February 1st the Turks could be seen distinctly in the act of constructing gun emplacements and trenches within six miles of the post. H.M.S. *Clio* accordingly moved to a position five hundred yards south of the defences, and from there opened fire with her 4·7-inch guns. It is to be presumed that some damage was done, but no definite information on this point was forthcoming. About this time the practice was introduced of reinforcing the permanent garrison of El Ferdan by detachments, about a hundred strong, of Australian and New Zealand troops in frequent reliefs.

The happiest of relations were at once established between the Colonials and our men, each race quite obviously highly approving the qualities displayed by the other, though by what strange means they arrived at mutual comprehension will always be one of the mysteries attending any war which brings together the Gurkha and the English-speaking soldier.

Early on February 2nd a reconnoitring patrol of the 56th Rifles fell in with an enemy force of all arms about four miles east of the

Ismailia Ferry. Fire was opened and continued for some little time, but since, owing to the disparity in numbers, no decisive result could be looked for, our party eventually broke off the action and withdrew after suffering slight loss. In the early afternoon of the same day news was received by telephone that an enemy force of 3,000 was marching on El Ferdan. No sooner had the defences been manned than with the utmost suddenness there arose a most violent sand-storm, which rendered the trenches wellnigh untenable.

Parapets crumbled; eyes were blinded and faces cut by the whirling sand. Ears, mouth, and nostrils were filled with it, making breathing difficult and hearing almost impossible. It permeated the working parts of rifles so that bolts jammed and there was no possibility of opening fire. Finally it blotted out the sun, and darkness almost Egyptian prevailed. Bayonets were fixed, and tensely expectant, the men awaited the attack. Followed anti-climax, for when at 5 p.m. the storm ceased, not a sign of the enemy was visible. At 2 a.m. on February 3rd, however, an attack did actually materialize. It was carried out by a force of only 400, and proved a fiasco. Losing direction in the darkness the attackers missed the El Ferdan defences, and moving some two hundred yards to the south, found themselves on the bank of the Canal itself. Having arrived there they began to shoot vigorously at the *gare* immediately opposite, but a few rounds fired into their flank from the southern trenches of El Ferdan were sufficient to show them that they had blundered, and standing not upon the order of their going, they went whence they had come, never to reappear. At 8.30 a.m. a Turkish battery opened fire at a range of 6,000 yards on the *gare*, the railway station, and on H.M.S. *Clio*. The cruiser was twice hit, but no damage was done. The enemy battery and the cruiser kept up an interchange of shots throughout the day. A number of shells fell close to the post, but none burst within the actual defences, and no casualties occurred.

Meantime the enemy's main attack had been directed against that part of our line intervening between Serapeum and Tussun. Beginning at 3 a.m. on the 3rd the Turks continued their efforts throughout that day, and during part of February 4th. Covered by their guns the 23rd Turkish Division moved straight on the Ferry Post, which was held by the 51st Sikhs and the 56th Rifles. None succeeded in reaching their objective, while their losses were very heavy. Mention must be made of the work of the warships, both French and British, stationed on Lake Timsah, which did great execution against the Turkish batteries. The total enemy losses in this attack were estimated at over 3,000, viz.: 1,000 killed and drowned, 650 prisoners, and 1,500 wounded. Our casualties were 115 killed and wounded. There was no general counter-attack on our part, and on the night of February

6th–7th the enemy began an unmolested retirement to Beersheba, taking with them the whole of their Artillery and train. During the attack the depot camp of the Battalion under Lieutenant Lloyd came in for some heavy shelling. The followers collected there behaved with the greatest coolness, and it is on record that the sweepers were more concerned to make proper provision for the conservation intact of the incinerator bars than themselves to seek safety under cover.

The left wing of the Battalion which, it will be remembered, was located at the Bench Mark Post was given no opportunity of taking part in these operations, while at El Ferdan the part played by the right wing was confined to the minor happenings already chronicled. At this time the nights were bitterly cold, and on February 4th rain fell in torrents, causing a good deal of discomfort. A few deserters came in to surrender, amongst whom was a certain Syrian Christian. This man had been employed as batman to a Turkish Artillery officer, and in order to escape the more quickly had stolen his master's horse, fully equipped with sword, note-books, great-coat, etc. Our acquisition of these articles is worth passing mention as forming the first instalment of enemy property to fall into the hands of the Battalion in the course of the Great War.

On February 5th a double company of the 1/5th, accompanied by the machine-gun section and a detachment of a hundred New Zealanders, marched from El Ferdan, a distance of four miles, to the position lately occupied by the enemy. There they found their battery emplacements, and numerous trenches and dugouts for the Infantry, all carefully camouflaged with bushes in order to avoid detection by our aircraft. Several burst shells were seen actually inside the trenches, testifying to the accuracy of our gunfire, while there were other unmistakable signs of casualties inflicted on men and animals. On the evidence, too, of the equipment which had been abandoned it would appear certain that numbers of the Infantry had been in a great hurry to quit the front-line trenches.

Ismailia after Turkish Attack, 12-2-15 to 9-3-15.

After February 5th, excitement engendered by the Turkish attempt on the Canal began to abate, but it was considered necessary for some days to continue the maintenance of a state of immediate readiness in case of attack, and it was not until February 12th that permission was given for the removal of boots and accoutrements at night. Meanwhile, with the assistance of Territorial Sappers the defences were further strengthened by means of barbed wire, flares, mines, and bomb-proof shelters. On February 12th the Canal was reopened for traffic after sunset, and all night long a procession of ships passed by, their searchlights maintaining a continuous blaze of light on the camp and Canal banks. About this time, too, steam-dredgers and pile-drivers made their reappearance, and there was a resumption of the normal activities of the Canal, clear evidence of the fact that, for the time being at least, the Turkish menace was considered to be at an end.

On February 14th the Battalion was relieved at El Ferdan and the Bench Mark Post by the 51st Sikhs, and returned to its former camp behind the Ismailia Ferry. On February 15th arrived the first draft from India, consisting of fifty other ranks, and on the same day short leave was opened for officers.

Move to Suez Section, 10-3-15.
After a few weeks spent uneventfully at Ismailia, orders were received to entrain for an unknown destination. It was only after entrainment that information was furnished to the effect that the Battalion would proceed to the Suez section of the Canal, there to relieve the 30th Brigade (General Mellis's), which was under orders for Mesopotamia. The defences to be taken over consisted of three posts, known as Kubri, Baluchistan, and Shatt. All were situated on the eastern bank of the Canal, were strongly fortified, and were of a size to accommodate considerable garrisons. A few yards only in rear of each post ran the Canal, while to north, east, and south the outlook was over a limitless stretch of desert. The relief took place on March 12th, Kubri being occupied by headquarters under Lieutenant-Colonel Boisragon, V.C., Baluchistan by some 300 rifles under Major Nightingale, and Shatt by a similar number under Lieutenant-Colonel Boddam. It was known that an enemy force occupied Nekl, eighty miles distant, and though the Turks were reported to be showing little activity, the greatest vigilance was necessary to ensure the interception of hostile raiding-parties, which might attempt to approach the Canal in order to drop mines in the fairway, or by any other means, to interfere with the traffic. That being the case, continuous observation and ceaseless patrolling were once more the order of the day.

22-3-15.
Despite the enemy's reported inertia, however, on March 22nd a Turkish column, consisting of the 3rd Battalion 30th Regiment, with Artillery, machine-guns, and Cavalry, succeeded in eluding the vigilance of our spies and aeroplanes, and at 5.30 a.m. made its appearance at a point no more than two miles distant from El Kubri. The advance guard of the column, four hundred strong, under German officers, fell in with a patrol of nine men of the 56th Rifles. The latter put up a sturdy fight, losing two killed and three wounded, and inflicting on the enemy losses amounting to twelve killed and fifteen wounded. The sound of firing roused the neighbouring posts, and as soon as there was sufficient light one of our batteries posted on the western bank of the Canal opened fire on the Turkish advance guard, which was then in retreat, and inflicted

casualties. The 56th Rifles and the Hyderabad Imperial Service Lancers were sent four miles into the desert in the direction of the enemy retirement, and remained in observation throughout the day. Further, an aeroplane reconnaissance was organized from Ismailia, which eventually succeeded in locating the enemy's camp, hidden amongst the sand-dunes some nine miles to the east of Kubri. Thereupon the decision was arrived at to attack the Turks next day.

Attack on Turks East of Kubri.   During the night of March 22nd–23rd, the 51st and 53rd Sikhs were brought up from Suez, and at 6 a.m. a column, composed as under, marched eastwards from Kubri into the desert.

Commander.
Lieutenant-Colonel G. H. Boisragon, V.C.

Advance Guard.
Major Nightingale.
1 troop Hyderabad I.S. Lancers, C.D.G.H. Companies, 1/5th G.R. Captain Brown, Captain Turner, Lieutenant Lloyd, Lieutenant Beddy.

Main Body.
1 squadron Hyderabad I.S. Lancers (less 1 troop), 5th Battery R.F.A. (T.), 51st Sikhs (Lieutenant-Colonel Beadon), 53rd Sikhs (Lieutenant-Colonel Davis), detachment Bikanir Camel Corps.

For some hours the column continued to march without stopping, and the loose sand provided very heavy going. At 9.45 a.m., however, came the welcome news that our aeroplanes had located the enemy two miles to the northward, and the column having changed front to face in that direction, a halt was called. The distance traversed so far was about nine miles. The strength of the hostile force was estimated at 200 Cavalry, a field battery, and 800 Infantry, and no time was lost in issuing orders for an attack. The Cavalry which during the march had protected the left flank of the column, was now transferred to the right or eastern flank of the attack, with instructions to co-operate as opportunity should offer. Of the Infantry, the 1/5th Gurkhas and 51st Sikhs provided firing-line, supports, and local reserves, the former on the right, while the 53rd Sikhs were held in reserve with column headquarters, the 5th Battery R.F.A., and the detachment of the Bikanir Camel Corps.

That there might no longer be any doubt in the matter, the enemy shortly after 9.45 a.m. announced the fact that he had become aware of our presence by sending over some shells from his field battery, of which one or two fell among a group of Cavalry, which had formed part of the advance guard, causing it to retire somewhat hastily. At 10 a.m., dispositions for the attack having been completed, the advance was begun in Artillery formation. The ground to be traversed was entirely devoid of cover, and sloped gently upwards for something over a thousand yards, the undefined crest-line, with the ground beyond, forming the position occupied by the enemy. Very shortly after starting the advance guard came under comparatively heavy fire from hostile guns, machine-guns, and rifles. Thanks in great measure, however, to the assistance given by our own battery, casualties were few, and the advance continued without interruption. Before the crest-line could be reached it became apparent that the enemy had no intention of making a prolonged stay, and soon afterwards he was in full retreat. Nothing was to be done but to go in pursuit of him, and a stern and wearisome chase it proved.

The retirement was most skilfully conducted by the hostile Commander, Colonel von Trommer, and our Cavalry, possibly through lack of experience, failed to take advantage of its opportunities. The burden of the pursuit thus fell on the Infantry, whose task was not made easier by the fact that the country to be traversed consisted of a weary waste of sand-dunes, crossing and re-crossing, meeting and separating in all directions like the waves of a troubled sea. Advancing steadily, the men would climb steeply thirty feet to the summit, only to drop down thirty feet on the other side, to start again and continue the process interminably, while the wind blew incessantly and drifted the loosely packed sand. At noon orders were received to stop the pursuit, and at 2 p.m. the return march was begun. The Canal was reached at 8 a.m., the men being very exhausted as the result of their twenty-six-mile march across the sand.

The total casualties sustained by the column were five killed and fifteen wounded, the 1/5th losses amounting to only three wounded. As a result of the operation a considerable quantity of ammunition, both for guns and rifles, fell into our hands. This had been abandoned by the enemy in his camp, but he succeeded in removing all his Artillery and transport. The official estimate of the Turkish losses was fifty killed, but it is possible that they were not so heavy. Five wounded Turks were captured by the Battalion, and it was curious to note that they received the kindest of treatment from the men. It is safe to surmise that an Arab or Mahsud similarly situated would have fared very differently.

No further military operations of importance took place on the Suez section of the Canal, though it was still necessary to guard against the activities of small enemy parties. On March 28th an unusually violent sandstorm caused great discomfort, and it happened that on this day a detachment of 200 rifles under Captain W. K. Brown was required to march to Bir Mabeiuk, fifteen miles east of Shatt, there to prepare a landing-ground for an aeroplane which had been detailed to carry out a reconnaissance to Nekl. Worse conditions for a march can hardly be imagined, and it is not difficult to realize that the small force experienced a very trying time before reaching its destination.

From this time onwards the hot weather season may be said to have set in; the country was infested with locusts, and flies were innumerable. Despite these conditions, however, the general health of the men did not suffer, and cases of dysentery were few, while as an off-set to the trials set out above the bathing and fishing to be had in the Canal were a source of never-ending delight.

Suez, 15-4-15 to 14-5-15.

On April 15th, on relief by the 53rd Sikhs, the Battalion moved into Suez for a rest. The camping-ground at that place was entirely devoid of shade, and much exposed to wind and dust. Garrison duties, too, were found to be very heavy, so that no great advantage can be said to have accrued from the change.

Outpost Duty at Shaloufa. 15-5-15 to 26-5-15.

In these circumstances none was found to mourn when orders were received to relieve the 51st Sikhs in their posts to the north of the sector previously occupied by the Battalion. The relief was effected on May 15th, headquarters proceeding to Shaloufa and a detachment to Gurkha post. Duties were very similar to those previously undertaken in the defensive sector farther south, and may be summed up as ceaseless patrolling and constant readiness in case of attack. The heat increased day by day, and, efforts to obtain ready-built wooden huts having failed, the Battalion was instructed to hut itself. Consequently all men who could be spared from the defences were busily employed in making bricks, quarrying stones, and other similar tasks, and doubtless there would have resulted a regular garden city in the desert had not destiny decided that it was time for the 1/5th Gurkhas to do a turn on another stage. On the night of May 26th the telephone conveyed an order to move to Suez next day on relief by the 51st Sikhs, and to prepare for immediate embarkation *en route* to the Dardanelles. Having concentrated at Suez by the evening of the 27th the Battalion entrained on the 29th, and reached Port Said on the same day. That night was spent on the wharf, and on the 30th the Battalion embarked on the transport *Annaberg*, which up to the outbreak of war had plied for cargo in the service of a German firm. So ended the first period of service of the 1/5th Gurkhas in Egypt.

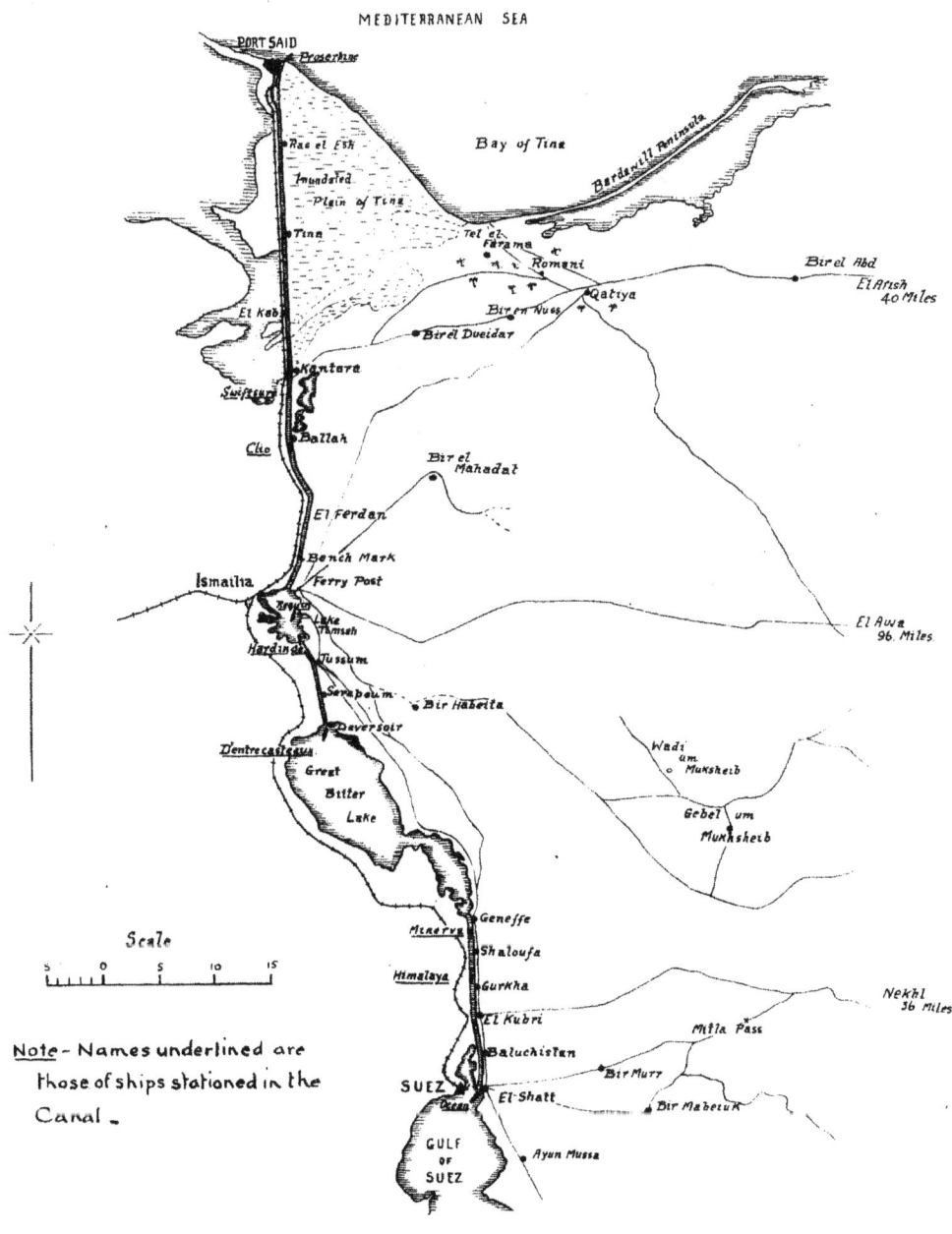

CHAPTER II

THE BATTLE OF JUNE 4TH,
AND SUBSEQUENT EVENTS TO JUNE 27TH, 1915

Summary of Gallipoli Campaign before Arrival.

THE sequence of events prior to the arrival of the Battalion on the Gallipoli Peninsula may be briefly summarized as follows:—

Early in the year it had occurred to one or more among His Majesty's Ministers who shared in the responsibility of directing the war, that great results were to be hoped for from a subsidiary offensive conducted in the first instance against Turkey and beginning with the forcing of the Dardanelles and the capture of Constantinople. Whether the expedition was justified or not will always form matter for discussion, and opponents of the enterprise will doubtless continue to quote Lord French's dictum to the effect that "the detailment of troops and war material to the Dardanelles was undoubtedly the chief cause" of the failure of the French and British offensive in 1915 in Champagne and Artois.

On the other hand, affairs on the Western Front appeared temporarily to have reached a condition of "stale-mate," and so rich were the prizes to be gained as a result of a successful offensive in the subsidiary theatre—direct and uninterrupted communication with Russia, the Balkan States actively for us or harmlessly neutral, the downfall of Turkey, the almost complete encirclement and consequently stricter blockade of the Central Powers—and so nearly, in the event, was success achieved, only to be snatched away by sheer ill-fortune, that not to have made the attempt rather would appear to need justification. Be that as it may, the attempt was decided on, and a fleet having been collected at Lemnos, from mid-February onwards a series of attacks was made on the land forts guarding the Dardanelles, with the object of opening a passage to the Sea of Marmora. At first the efforts of the Navy appeared likely to meet with success, but as the ships penetrated farther into the Straits, sweeping arrangements were found inadequate to cope with the Turkish stratagem of floating down mines with the current, and after suffering heavy loss in capital ships it became necessary to desist. In the meantime an expeditionary force had been dispatched to Lemnos under the command of General Sir Ian Hamilton. It had not originally been intended to use this force to open a road to Constantinople by way of the Gallipoli Peninsula, but by March 22nd, the conclusion having been reached that the Navy alone could not force the passage to the Dardanelles, it was decided to begin arrangements for a landing.

The first step was to effect a redistribution of men and stores in the transports conveying the force, and for this purpose the ships were ordered to Egypt. Consequently it was not until the latter part of April that the necessary arrangements could be considered sufficiently complete to allow of the attempt being made. The Turks, meanwhile, warned by the bombardment of the forts and by the presence in Egypt of our expeditionary force, had taken steps to render invasion either by the Peninsula or by the Asiatic shore of the Straits a matter of extreme difficulty. A force of from 35,000 to 45,000 men had been made available to oppose a landing, the Straits were swept by guns in concealed positions, strong works had been constructed to cover all probable landing-places, and arrangements had been made to facilitate the transfer of troops from one shore to the other in case of necessity.

In face of such odds it would appear incredible that a landing could be effected, but on April 25th the " Battle of the Landing " was fought; and thanks to the co-operation of the Navy, to the gallantry of the British and French troops engaged, and to uncertainty in the minds of the enemy regarding the actual points at which landing would be attempted, lodgments were effected at Anzac, near Ari Burnu, and at several places on both sides of the Cape Helles in the south of the Peninsula. The French division, under General d'Amade, which had secured a footing at Kum Kale on the Asiatic shore, was withdrawn on the 26th.

As was to be expected in an achievement which has no parallel in history, casualties were very heavy, and Sir Ian Hamilton, who had long been pressing for a brigade of Gurkhas, or, failing that, for an Indian Brigade from Egypt, was allowed to draw on General Sir J. Maxwell's force for Major-General Cox's 29th Brigade, which consisted of the 14th Sikhs, 69th and 89th Punjabis, and the 1/6th Gurkhas. The brigade landed on the Peninsula on the night of April 30th–May 1st, and played its part in the first and second battles of Krithia, and in subsequent operations. Later it was thought advisable to send the two Punjabi battalions to France, and orders were issued for their replacement in the brigade by the 1/5th and 2/10th Gurkhas.

We left the Battalion on board the *Annaberg* in Port Said harbour.

En route to Dardanelles, 30-5-15 to 3-6-15.

Before embarkation a depot had been formed at Suez, and there were collected all men surplus to field-service strength, officers' chargers, and surplus kit. The British Officers who accompanied the Battalion to take part in the second episode of its great adventure were Lieutenant-Colonel Boisragon (commanding),

Lieutenant-Colonel Boddam; Majors Nightingale, Govan, and Battye; Captains Brown and Turner; Lieutenants Lloyd (Quartermaster), Beddy, and Erskine (Adjutant); Second-Lieutenants Cosby and Knowles; and Captain Reaney, I.M.S. (Medical Officer).

At 9.50 a.m. the *Annaberg* left Port Said, lustily cheered by the 2/10th Gurkhas, who had just arrived on the wharf preparatory to following in our wake. There was more noise, too, of a heartening nature at the harbour exit, where a French battleship passed and deputed its band to play " Tipperary " and other martial airs, but mostly "Tipperary." Ideal summer weather was experienced throughout the voyage, and on June 1st and 2nd, while passing among the islands of the Grecian Archipelago, anyone whose thoughts were that way attuned had ample material for rhapsody. It was doubly hard then that, with every prospect pleasing, attention should have to be given to considerations of enemy submarines. Their probable presence, however, constituted a very real danger; it was necessary to keep a sharp look-out and, as a further precaution, the Battalion machine-guns were mounted in the stern, ready to deal with a periscope should it appear.

Lemnos was reached early on June 2nd, its great harbour crowded with shipping—French and British men-of-war, and a whole fleet of transports, headed by the stately *Mauretania*. At 2 p.m. began the transhipment of baggage to two Fleet sweepers, and at 7 p.m., distributed in these, with never a light showing, the Battalion sailed for Gallipoli. The anchorage at Cape Helles was reached without mishap, and immediately arrangements were put in hand for getting ashore. The spot appointed was " V " Beach, the scene of so many gallant exploits on the preceding April 25th, and to reach it a further redistribution, this time into trawlers, became necessary. That accomplished, each trawler in turn ran alongside the jetty built out from the *River Clyde*, of famous memory, and there discharged its freight.

Disembarkation at " V " Beach, 3-6-15. Disembarkation having been completed by 3 a.m. on June 3rd, the Battalion was conducted northwards by road to within a short distance of Gully Ravine. There a suitable place having been found, dugouts were constructed in the face of the cliff, and in them was spent the greater part of that day. Some diversion was created by enemy shells, which burst at frequent intervals on the cliff above, and sprayed their bullets harmlessly into the sea a few yards distant. In the course of the day visits were paid by General Cox, and the Battalion found itself posted to the 87th Brigade of the already famous 29th Division. The other units constituting the brigade were the Dublin Fusiliers, Munster Fusiliers, South Wales Borderers, and Border Regiment.

At the time of the arrival of the 1/5th Gurkhas, as the result of the scheme adopted for the landing of the expeditionary force, it was divided into two portions. The northern portion comprised the Australian and New Zealand Army Corps, under the command of General Sir W. R. Birdwood, which, having effected a landing near Ari Burnu, was holding a line from Fishermen's Huts, as its northern extremity, southwards astride the lower end of the spurs leading up to the high ridge of Sari Bair, to a point on the coast about 1,200 yards south of Ari Burnu. That part of the expeditionary force operating in what may be termed the "southern area," comprised the 29th Division, including the reinforcements from Egypt to which previous reference has been made, the Naval Division under General Paris, and a French division, composed largely of Senegalese troops, commanded by General d'Amade. In that order, with the Indian troops on the extreme left of the 29th Division, they had established themselves on a line running from a point three miles north-east of Tekke Burnu to one mile north of Eski Hissarlik Point, and thence southwards to the coast. In both cases the Turkish front-line trenches were situated, generally, at a very short distance—in some cases only a few yards—from our own.

General Situation and Terrain.

A very brief description of the terrain is necessary for a proper understanding of operations conducted on the Peninsula. With the exception of a few localities, very limited in extent, where the beaches used in the landing gave a few yards of foreshore, from the southernmost of the two promontories bounding Suvla Bay, past Tekke Burnu and Cape Helles to Eski Hissarlik, and thence for some distance north-eastwards, the cliffs rose almost sheer from the sea, seldom less than 40 to 50 feet in height, and often attaining an altitude greatly in excess of these figures. The northern area was dominated by the Sari Bair Ridge, which culminated in the high peak of Koja Chemen Tepe (1,000 feet), 5,000 yards north-east of Ari Burnu. The southern area was dominated by Achi Baba (715 feet), situated 2,500 yards east of Krithia Village. From these two heights descended numerous spurs. Those from Sari Bair, on nearing the sea, formed, with the intervening dry water-courses and ravines, a tumble of broken ground, covered for the most part with low scrub and coarse grass which extended to the shore; but in the case of the southern area a considerable stretch of terraced fields intervened between the foot of the spurs and the top of the cliffs.

Before ever landing troops on the Peninsula the conclusion had been reached that the possession of Achi Baba would give command of the Narrows, and thus make a way for the Fleet to open water and Constantinople. Previous efforts had been made to accomplish this end, notably in the

Battle of June 4th.

Lancashire Landing ("W" Beach) from Cape Helles End.

"V" Beach and Sedd-ul-Bahr from Cape Helles.

fighting which immediately followed the landing on April 25th and the attacks sustained throughout three days from May 6th to May 8th. These attempts had failed in their ultimate object, partly through lack of adequate Artillery support of the kind required, and partly through want of a sufficient number of troops in reserve. A further attempt had been planned for June 4th, and in this the Battalion found itself billed to take a part. Leaving its place of rest at Gully Beach on the evening of June 3rd it moved northwards and occupied the support trenches immediately in rear of the 1/6th Gurkhas and 14th Sikhs, to whom had been entrusted the extreme left of the line in the southern area.

At 8 a.m. on June 4th the battle began with a bombardment of the hostile positions, the guns of the Navy participating. The while a blinding dust-storm raged, the Artillery continued the work of destruction until 10.30 a.m., when a halt was called for the space of half an hour. Recommencing at 11 a.m. the bombardment was maintained for a further period of twenty minutes. At the end of that time all troops manning the front-line trenches fixed bayonets and lifted them high above the parapets. This action led the Turks to expect an immediate assault and, acting on this misconception, they rushed men into their trenches, until then lightly held. Our guns, thus made a present of their targets, began again to shell in earnest, and only desisted on the stroke of midday, when our assaulting troops, accompanied by bomb-throwers, left their trenches and made for the enemy across the open.

For some time it appeared that this attack at least was not to be doomed to failure. On the extreme right the French were successful in carrying the trenches to their front and the Haricot Redoubt beyond, which had long been a thorn in their flesh. To the left of them the Naval Division captured and held a Turkish work of great strength, and not to be outdone by the sailors their next-door neighbours, the Manchester Brigade, with whom were associated the Lancashire Fusiliers, made a charge which resulted in the storming of two lines of enemy trenches and yet retained sufficient momentum to carry the attackers on until they had made good the lower slopes of Achi Baba. From the position attained, the ground rose beyond them clear to the summit, and had a reserve been available for use at this juncture, in all human probability the key of the Narrows would have been won this day. Nor had matters gone less well farther northwards.

Next to the Manchesters the 88th Brigade of the 29th Division, after a hard-fought struggle with the bayonet, succeeded in capturing the enemy's front-line trenches, while on the extreme left of the attacking line the 14th Sikhs forced their way through the maze of stout wire entanglements guarding the Turkish defences, which had remained intact despite the efforts of our Artillery, and compelled the enemy to retire. This achievement cost them in killed and wounded, 450 men out of a total of 600 engaged, including the loss of 23 British and Indian officers.

This initial success achieved all along the line proved the high-water mark of our gains in the battle. Soon came the ebb. The French, struggling desperately, by means of a tornado of shells and bombs were forced out of the Haricot Redoubt. The Naval Division, its right flank in the air as the result of the French retirement, could no longer retain its position, and returned to the original line. The Manchester Brigade, despite the fact that its right flank was now in turn exposed, continued to hold tenaciously to the ground won, its Commander declaring that his men were prepared to do so indefinitely. Eventually, however, a fresh attack by the French, timed in the first instance for 3 p.m. and then postponed for an hour, having finally failed to materialize, it became necessary to withdraw the brigade, and by 6.30 p.m. it had retired under orders to the original Turkish front-line trenches.

The results of the battle may be summarized as a gain of 200 to 400 yards over a front of three miles, the infliction of severe losses on the enemy, and the capture of 400 prisoners. Against these material advantages must be set the fact that our flanks had made no appreciable advance, while our casualties totalled approximately 7,000, a full three-quarters of them sustained on the top of what at one time appeared to be a victory cheaply won.

So much for the action as a whole. To understand the part played in it by the 1/5th Gurkhas it is necessary to look back for a moment to the events of the morning. The 1/6th Gurkhas were holding Gurkha Bluff, and in the noontide offensive their outstanding achievement had been the action of a single double company, which under Captain Birdwood had worked its way round by the cliffs to the north of the bluff and gained a footing in a Turkish communication trench, which formed the enemy main artery of communication in that part of the line. There they had contrived to maintain themselves for some twenty minutes, but being strongly attacked by superior numbers of the enemy armed with a copious supply of bombs, to which they had not the wherewithal to reply, they had then been forced to retire, Captain Birdwood himself being mortally wounded and some 20 of his men killed. The 1/5th Gurkhas meanwhile remained in the trenches occupied by them overnight, expecting at any moment to be called upon in their rôle of local reserve to support the left of the attack in the advance on Krithia. That advance was destined never to take place, but, instead, a most hazardous enterprise was reserved for the Battalion, and one which was to prove a very severe test of its qualities in this its first experience of warfare as waged on the Peninsula.

At 3 p.m. orders were received to the effect that the Battalion was to hold itself in readiness to cross the bluff, gain the beach beyond, and thence turning inland, storm the cliffs preparatory to seizing an important communication trench, afterwards known as J11A, which ran back in a north-easterly direction from the right of the enemy's line. The operation, though now planned on a larger scale, was almost identical with that undertaken by Captain Birdwood's double company of the 1/6th Gurkhas earlier in the day. It in no way detracts from the merit of the morning's performance to state that very different conditions now prevailed. Then it had been a comparatively simple matter to gain the objective; the trouble began after a lodgment had been effected. By the time the 1/5th Gurkhas were called upon to act, however, the Turks had become fully alive to the danger threatening their right flank. In their trenches and redoubts in this area they had massed, as was subsequently estimated, about 8,000 men and 40 machine-guns; the approach to the spurs, by which alone access was to be had to the communication trench, was open to the fire of a hostile battery at a range of 300 yards; and from prepared positions sited on the summit of the cliffs the enemy could bring to bear on troops attacking up the spurs a heavy cross-fire from machine-guns and rifles.

Lacking inside information it is not possible to hazard a guess as to the connection of the attack about to be described with the progress of events generally. At 3 p.m., when preliminary orders reached the Battalion, there was still hope that the renewal of the offensive on the part of the French—to which, of course, the Naval Division was to conform—would restore the ground originally gained and render safe the somewhat precarious situation of the Manchester Brigade. Under these circumstances it is not difficult to understand that a threat against the enemy's communications would render easier the task of the French and the Naval Division by putting him under the necessity of diverting troops to deal with it, thus weakening his power of resistance in the area farther south. By 5 p.m., however, at which time the turning movement by the Battalion was actually initiated, the hope of a renewed offensive had been dashed through failure of the French to respond, and it may be that it was still thought advisable to proceed with the operation in the expectation that it would assist the withdrawal of the Manchester Brigade. At 5 p.m., then, the 1/5th collected in the ravine at the southern end of Gurkha Bluff, from which could be seen the ground over which the attack was to be made. The general features were pointed out by Lieutenant-Colonel Bruce commanding the 1/6th Gurkhas, who as the result of a full month spent on the Peninsula, had become thoroughly familiar with his surroundings.

From the crest of the bluff the ground sloped steeply to the narrow strip of beach beyond, and from the beach the cliffs stood up to a height of 200 feet and more, their surface scattered with scrub and coarse grass. The cliffs were not perpendicular, and from their crests ran down in sharp, narrow spurs to the water's edge, the soil being a composition of rough limestone detritus, which crumbled to the tread. Three spurs were selected, and dispositions made for the attack as follows:—

The 3rd Double Company (Major Battye and Lieutenant Cosby) was detailed to the farthest spur, and would form the left of the attack; the 1st Double Company (Captain Turner), following the leaders, was to take the centre spur; and the 4th Double Company (Major Govan and Captain Brown) was reserved for that nearest to the starting-point. The reserve consisted of the 2nd Double Company (Major Nightingale and Second-Lieutenant Knowles). In the order given each company in turn broke cover, crossed the open ground, and rushed down the slope to the beach. Once there it was found necessary to proceed in single file until both wings and the centre of the attack arrived at the foot of the spurs which would lead them to the objective. The movement did not long escape the notice of the hostile battery referred to above, which opened a heavy fire of accurately burst shrapnel on the attacking troops. A number of casualties occurred, among them, as ill-fortune would have it, being both the commanding officer and the second-in-command. Colonel Boisragon was shot through the knee-cap, and owing to his position it was not found advisable to move him during daylight. He remained under the shelter of a rock, and from there kept in touch with events until the retirement of the Battalion after nightfall. Colonel Boddam was hit through the thigh, but managed to crawl back some distance to a permanent shelter, where he was found later and taken to hospital on a stretcher.

The 1st, 3rd, and 4th Double Companies, meanwhile, had turned inland and begun the ascent of the spurs. As they climbed, the conformation of the ground above them gave protection from the hail of shrapnel which till then had continued to harass the advance. It was, however, only to exchange a lesser for a greater evil, for they now became exposed to a heavy cross-fire from both rifles and machine-guns, brought to bear on them from concealed positions at the top of the cliffs. The situation which had now arisen was such that only by means not available to the Battalion would it have been possible successfully to cope with it. The knife-edge character of the spurs rendered impossible the formation of an adequate fire front; the available covering-fire, owing to the conformation of the cliffs and the facilities for concealment possessed by the enemy, was unsuccessful in producing any appreciable reduction in the volume and intensity of the hostile fire; and the

Looking North along the Coast from Cape Tekke.

Gully Beach (looking South).

possibilities of a concerted rush in order to gain the objective was ruled out by the distance to be traversed over difficult ground in face of an enemy who could bring to bear the full power of his weapons against troops disposed in depth on very narrow frontages. At the same time full credit must be given to the 1/6th Gurkhas for their efforts to assist the advance by means of a well-sustained fire from their position on Gurkha Bluff; nor must mention be omitted of a certain torpedo-boat destroyer which, from its position out at sea, used its guns to the best effect possible under the very difficult conditions prevailing.

To complete the story of the part played by the Battalion in this battle of June 4th it will be convenient from this point to follow the fortunes of each double company in turn. It is not possible at this stage, however, to describe in detail the ebb and flow of progress on each spur. An outline only of the achievement in each case can be given, and it must be left to the imagination of the reader to supply the atmosphere of " confused noise and garments rolled in blood "—the atmosphere, in fact, inseparable from any " battle of the warrior," whether the period be that treated of in the Old Testament or the early summer of 1915.

The 4th Double Company on the right made good progress up to a point and, having arrived within a comparatively short distance of the crest, attempted to carry it with a rush, to be swept back by a shower of bombs and the concentrated fire of machine-guns. Undeterred by this initial failure the leading lines charged afresh, only, however, for the assault to be broken as a result of the hopeless odds to which it was opposed. Again and again the attempt was renewed, always to meet the same fate. On one of these occasions Captain Brown, placing himself at the head of his men, drew his sword—he was probably the only officer on the Peninsula who wore one—and waving it high in the air, dashed upwards in the direction of the crest. He was shot dead, together with Jemadar Harishankar Gurung and a number of those who followed him.

The story of the happenings on the centre spur could be told in almost the same words. Near the top of the cliffs, No. 1 Double Company found its way barred by a concealed trench. No effort was spared to capture it, but without result. Captain Turner was shot through the head, and died instantaneously, and a number of his men, too, were either killed or wounded. Lieutenant Beddy, who up to this time had been covering the advance of the companies with machine-guns from a concealed position near the 6th Gurkha trenches, saw Captain Turner fall, and leaving his place of comparative safety ran out across the open in the hope of arriving in time to lend a hand. By some miracle he succeeded in traversing the greater part of the intervening distance, but he was then hit in the side, and died the same night. On the left the 3rd Double Company was called upon to undergo a very similar experience. Finding himself unable to make headway against the heavy fire from front and flanks, Major Battye gave orders to dig in and wait for a more favourable opportunity for a further advance. Very shortly afterwards, however, Major Battye himself was shot through the head, and Subadar Amrit Mal was wounded. One last effort was made to obtain the objective by pushing in No. 2 Double Company on the centre spur. The official language of the order which announced the award to Major Nightingale of the D.S.O. for the part played by him, will serve to describe this phase of the action. The wording runs:—

". . . for distinguished gallantry in leading an attack up a difficult spur after he had been wounded. He reached the crest, and was again wounded, but coming back a few yards he rallied his men and again led them on. He was wounded a third time, but still endeavoured to advance till he fainted."

In the course of these successive assaults Subadar-Major Harkabir Thapa was wounded in the foot and Subadar Juthe Gurung in the leg. The latter, gallantly refusing assistance, bandaged his own wound and was on the point of rejoining his company when a second bullet shot him dead.

It was now well on towards evening; of 11 British officers, 4 had been killed and 3 wounded, and it had become apparent that without adequate Artillery support and a plentiful supply of bombs, renewed assaults could only result in a useless waste of life without yielding any compensating advantage. Further, owing to the lack of necessary leadership, following on the heavy casualties among British and Gurkha officers, and in consideration of the fact that the element of surprise would be wanting, nothing was to be gained from a renewal of the attack after dark. With the utmost reluctance, therefore, orders were issued for a withdrawal to the position occupied in the morning. The remainder of the Battalion reached the place appointed without mishap, but the orders failed to reach No. 3 Double Company, now commanded by Second-Lieutenant Cosby, which consequently remained in occupation of its advanced position until 2 a.m. on June 5th. At that hour Second-Lieutenant Cosby, arguing from the non-receipt of orders that the remaining companies were no longer in possession of the spurs on his right, concluded that to stay longer was to court disaster. Leaving a few men to cover the retirement he effected a successful withdrawal, and managed, too, to take with him all his wounded. His decision had been taken only just in time, for not only was the double company called upon to repel a strong attack delivered by the enemy immediately opposing it, but it had also to deal with small parties of Turks, who were in occupation of the ground vacated by the remainder of the

Battalion. As was to be expected, it went hard with the men of the covering party. Naik Dhan Sing Gurung, who was in command, was captured. In no way cast down, however, he watched his opportunity, and, wresting himself free from his captors, sprang over the cliff. Reaching the beach in safety he fell into the hands of another body of Turks. These, optimists that they were, proceeded to march off with him in the direction of their lines, but breaking loose again he sought safety, this time by plunging into the sea. Weighed down as he was with equipment and boots, he swam out under a hot fire, and then, turning parallel to the coast, went on until he finally succeeded in landing within the confines of the allied position.

The casualties sustained by the Battalion in the course of the day were as follows:—

	Killed.	Wounded.	Total.
British Officers	4	8	7
Gurkha Officers	2	8	5
Other Ranks	27	90	117
Grand Total	33	96	129

British Officers Who Fell.

Hedley Battye came of a family which had given many of its members to the service of their country. The death on active service of his father—also of the 5th Gurkhas—and of his uncles are part of the history of the Indian Army. Brought up in an intensely religious atmosphere, his outlook was governed by his early training. High principled and very genuine, what was given him to do he did with his might, and so won for himself in large measure the esteem and affection of the Regiment.

Gerry Turner had been educated at Fettes, and, like his brothers, won early distinction as a player of games. Had he remained at home he would have made a name for himself as a Rugby footballer and cricketer. Strong in body and mentally sturdy he brought to his problems a habit of clear thinking which was of the greatest service to him professionally. He had many friends, of whom the most intimate was little Beddy, and it was during the time that either one or both of them played for the Battalion team that the Gurkha Brigade and P.F.F. football cups were won by the 1/5th Gurkhas for the first time in their football history. As Adjutant for some years before the war, he knew and was known by all, and there was not one among those who served with him who did not feel deeply the loss occasioned by his death.

The manner of Wynyard Brown's death was typical of him. Generous and impetuous, it was his wont to dash boldly at the task which lay before him. He was an exceptionally fine rider, quick to establish a feeling of confidence between himself and his mount, and had won prizes for jumping in very good company. Increased responsibilities—for he had married a year or two before the war—gave the necessary ballast to his impulsive nature, and had he lived he might have gone far in his profession.

R. L. Beddy was small of stature, but with a great heart. Active and energetic, he never knew when he was beaten, and to see him at football go straight and hard, caring not in the least what stood between him and his objective, was a lesson in courage for the onlooker. He and Turner were as David and Jonathan, and it was his desperate anxiety on his friend's account when he saw him fall that led to his own death.

It is instructive to note in passing that the total number of bombs issued to the Battalion to enable it to gain its objective and to hold it against counter-attack was twenty-five. The Turkish supply, on the other hand, was practically unlimited. Another urgent need was an adequate supply of Artillery ammunition. The reserve for all guns on the Peninsula at the end of this battle stood at the absurdly low figure of 800 rounds. These two facts are given as throwing some light on the difficulties attending an offensive, but it is fair to add that in neither case is the shortage to be attributed to any fault on the part of the men on the spot. Home resources were still only partially organized, and the things were not to be had.

Graves of Officers. Of the officers killed in this action, Captain Turner and Lieutenant Beddy were buried side by side near the edge of Gurkha Ravine, quite close to the graves of Captain Birdwood and Captain Whytehead, of the 6th Gurkhas, and in due course wooden crosses were put up to mark the spot. The bodies of Major Battye and Captain Brown were not recovered.

Disposal of Wounded. The wounded were tended at No. 108 Indian Field Ambulance, which was in charge of Major W. R. Battye, I.M.S., a brother of H. M. Battye of the 5th Gurkhas, and on the morning of June 5th were evacuated in lighters to hospital ships and transports. The less serious cases were accommodated at Mudros, while others were distributed among the hospitals at Malta and Alexandria. A few men found themselves on ships bound for England, and these, on arrival, were treated at the Hardinge Hospital at Brockenhurst.

On the morning of June 5th, the missing 3rd Double Company having joined up at daylight, the Battalion found itself together once again in the ravine near Gurkha Bluff. Major Govan assumed command, and in accordance with orders a move was made with a view to completing the newly constructed Indian Brigade in a position in rear of the left of the line. Besides Major Govan, Lieutenants Lloyd and Erskine, Second-Lieutenants Cosby and Knowles, and Captain Reaney, I.M.S., still remained to fight another day.

5-6-15 to 27-6-15.

Full of incident as were the days to those taking an active part in events, a day-by-day record of periods intervening between one general action and the next would yield neither pleasure nor profit. For the purpose of this narrative it is sufficient to state that from June 6th to June 14th, and again from June 23rd to June 27th, the Battalion occupied the right sector of front-line trenches allotted to the Indian Brigade on the extreme left of the Allied line in the southern area, the interval from June 15th to June 22nd being passed in reserve. June 28th saw the beginning of another big battle.

It would be doing less than justice to the men, however, to pass without comment the fact that, dragged off shipboard in the darkness and pushed straight into a fight attended with every unfamiliar circumstance, with most of their British officers *hors de combat*, and a hundred and more of their comrades out of the running, they were still fit to take their place in the front-line trenches only the day after the conclusion of the battle. A training system based on decentralization of authority undoubtedly helped towards this result.

While neglecting wearisome detail, a slight description of the life in front-line trenches and in reserve is necessary to a proper understanding of the prevailing conditions.

The trenches, generally, were situated at distances varying from 50 to 200 yards from those of the enemy. The intervening no-man's-land was a litter of rotting corpses, mostly Turkish, and of other debris of the battlefield. The stench was overpowering, flies bred and throve in noisome hordes to an extent which would have caused Pharaoh hastily to relax his grip on the children of Israel, and lice added their quota to the burden of existence. By day the enemy's Artillery more often than not gave considerable trouble, especially the "Asiatic Algies," as they were christened, fired from the direction of Kum Kale; by night, musketry fire from one side or the other rattled almost incessantly, and both by day and night snipers were active, causing a certain number of unavoidable casualties. Constant spade work was necessary, both for the repair and improvement of existing trenches, and for the excavation of new works. This, in addition to ordinary trench routine duties, provided exercise and employment for all ranks by day; and that the hours of darkness might not be devoid of incident, parties of men were dispatched into no-man's-land, sometimes to glean information regarding the doings of the enemy over the way, more often for the purpose of collecting the rifles of the dead, for which there was a crying need. In this difficult and dangerous task Rifleman Ranbir Gurung of "A" Company, and Lance-Naik Ujirsing Gurung of "D" Company, particularly distinguished themselves. During its two tours of front-line trench duty at this period the Battalion's casualties totalled forty-one.

The reserve position may be imagined as situated about 800 yards in rear of the firing-line—still somewhat noisy, but not exposed to direct hits from the enemy's guns and rifles, and possessing the inestimable advantage that it afforded an opportunity of bathing and washing clothes. Properly to appreciate this boon requires a ten days' exposure to the uninterrupted attentions of flies, lice, and fleas. Duties in reserve comprised the furnishing of certain piquets for the protection of the ground in the vicinity, and the detailing of platoons to form local and brigade reserves. In addition men were constantly employed in making roads, carrying rations, and digging trenches.

Contemporary Events on Other Parts of the Line.

Two events of importance took place in the Helles Sector during the period under review. On June 10th the Border Regiment and the South Wales Borderers carried a portion of the hostile trenches, and despite vigorous counter-attacks, which entailed hard fighting throughout the night, they succeeded in holding all the ground won. On June 21st the French gained a brilliant victory. Assisted by a heavy bombardment of the Turkish line, in which British guns and howitzers and the warships of both nations participated, an attack was launched against the formidable works situated on the line of the Kereves Dere. The 2nd French Division on the left captured all first- and second-line trenches opposite its front, including the long-coveted Haricot Redoubt. The 1st Division on the right twice stormed all its objectives and was twice driven back. General Gouraud then issued an order which it is impossible to refrain from quoting.

" From Colonel Viont's report it is evident that the preparation for the attack at 2.15 p.m. was not sufficient.

" It is indispensable that the Turkish first line of trenches in front of you should be taken, otherwise the gains of the 2nd Division may be rendered useless. You have five hours of daylight; take your time, let me know your orders and time fixed for preparation, and arrange for Infantry assault to be simultaneous after preparation."

Result: an attack brilliantly executed, 600 yards of trenches captured, all gains held despite furious counter-attacks, and a total for the day of 7,000 casualties inflicted on the enemy. The French losses in killed and wounded were about 2,500.

Before passing on to the Battle of June 28th it should be placed on record that Sir Ian Hamilton inspected the sector held by the Indian Brigade on June 14th, and subsequently issued the following message:—

"The G.O.C., M.E.F., wishes all ranks to know that the good work done by the Gurkha regiments under his command has been specially brought to the notice of the C.-in-C. in India. He has been asked to telegraph to the Maharaja of Nepal to this effect."

CHAPTER III

BATTLE OF JUNE 28TH,
AND SUBSEQUENT EVENTS TO AUGUST 5TH, 1915

Battle of June 28th.
SHORTLY after the June 4th battle, news reached the Commander-in-Chief of the projected dispatch to Gallipoli of new divisions, fresh batteries of Artillery, and, most important of all, an adequate supply of ammunition for both guns and howitzers. Plans were duly laid for their effective employment, but it was not expected that they would be available for a big attack much before the end of July or the beginning of August, and in the meantime it was not to be thought of that the force on the Peninsula should sit still with folded hands awaiting " the day." After the French success of June 21st, in which it will be remembered that the British guns did their share, there was just sufficient shell left to the batteries for one more battle on a grand scale. It was so that there came to be fought the Battle of June 28th.

The plan was to push forward the left of the line in the Helles Sector, pivoting on a point S.W. of Krithia about one mile from the sea, and, at the limit of the ground won, to form a new front facing generally eastwards. The execution of this plan involved the capture of five lines of enemy trenches west of Saghir Dere, and of two lines east of that feature. The trenches west of the ravine had been labelled by the Staff J9, J10, J11, J12, J13, those to the east being known as H12, and so on to H16.

The 29th Division was now commanded by General de Lisle, who had taken over from General Hunter Weston on June 4th, on the promotion of the latter to the command of the VIII Corps. All that it was possible to accomplish by hard work and hard thinking had been done to make the present venture a success. The orders issued were comprehensive but clear, the question of the Artillery preparation had received very careful consideration, an understanding had been arrived at with the French regarding assistance to be given by their guns, and arrangements had been made with the Navy to ensure the co-operation of certain units of the Fleet. Finally—and this had a most important bearing on events—a push was to be made in the Anzac Sector in the hope of diverting reinforcements which might otherwise be available to help the Turks opposing the main attack farther south.

The 87th and 86th Brigades of the 29th Division were given the task of capturing the trenches which interposed between the Saghir Dere and the sea, while the 156th Brigade was detailed to carry out the attack on the opposite side of the *nullah*. At the southern end of J9 and J10, situated just within the loop formed by their junction, was a strong Turkish advanced post, well sited and very heavily wired, known as the Boomerang Redoubt. The cracking of this particularly hard nut was entrusted to the Border Regiment. Lastly, the Indian Brigade was required to extend the gains of the 87th and 86th Brigades.

The battle began at 9 a.m. with a bombardment of the objectives by our heavy artillery. During this stage very material assistance was rendered by the French. At 10.20 a.m. the field guns and howitzers, backed up by H.M. ships *Talbot, Scorpion,* and *Wolverine,* began to take a hand, primarily with the object of destroying the enemy's wire. In this, it may be said at once, they were most successful. The Boomerang Redoubt referred to above, because it was expected to offer a particularly stout resistance, was further subjected to the attentions of certain trench mortars borrowed from the French for the purpose, with the result that when at 10.45 a.m. the Border Regiment broke from cover and dashed to the assault, they reached their objective with comparative ease.

As the time approached for the general assault of the Infantry, the Artillery bombardment increased in intensity. The entire landscape was blotted out by a thick curtain of yellow dust, which swirled and eddied with the wind until a stronger gust would part it to reveal for a moment the white smoke-puffs of the bursting shrapnel or the clouds of darker vapour rising from the impact of high-explosive shell. At 11 a.m. range and fuse were lengthened, and synchronizing with this the 87th Brigade on the left and 156th Brigade on the right quitted their trenches and advanced resolutely on their objectives. West of Saghir Dere the 87th Brigade carried three lines of trenches—J9, J10, and J11—and, despite the heavy shrapnel-fire to which they found themselves exposed while crossing the open ground, their casualties were surprisingly light.

East of the ravine the Royal Scots succeeded in making good two lines of trenches, but farther to the right the remainder of the 156th Brigade met with strong opposition and failed to make progress. This set-back was in no way attributable to want of courage or determination on the part of the troops engaged, but was simply due to the fact that, the supply of Artillery ammunition being strictly limited, it had been considered advisable to concentrate on the trenches nearer the sea as being more important, with the result that farther inland the wire remained uncut and the opposing troops unshaken.

Returning to the area west of the ravine the 86th Brigade at 11.30

a.m. advanced through the victorious 87th Brigade, crossed the long stretch of open ground beyond J11, cleared J11A, and effected lodgements in J12 and J13. The entire length of these two trenches did not come into our possession only because towards their south-eastern extremities they were commanded by the rising ground on the far side of the Saghir Dere. The retention by the Turks of that part of them which lay nearest to their communications caused much hard fighting and many casualties to the Indian Brigade throughout this and the following few days. Despite the partial check sustained by the 156th Brigade, the object of the attack had now been realized almost in full. Following the successful advance of the 86th Brigade the Lancashire Fusiliers by inclining half right had linked up with the Royal Scots east of the ravine, with the result that a continuous line, facing generally eastwards, had been established along the limit of the area of operations.

Action of Indian Brigade. Now to describe the part played in the action by the Indian Brigade, and more especially the doings of the 1/5th. During the progress of the main attack the 2/10th Gurkhas, the 1/6th Gurkhas, and the 1/5th Gurkhas, in that order, made their way northwards under the cliffs, following at first much the same route as had been taken by the Battalion on June 4th.

It is necessary to realize that, except on the right of the attack, the newly won trenches had been very badly damaged by our Artillery bombardment, in many places to an extent which suggested that no trench had ever existed. The first duty, then, of the Indian Brigade was to take over from the 86th Brigade J11A and those portions of J12 and J13 which had come into our hands. The 2/10th Gurkhas were the first to turn inland, and having reached the crest, established themselves in a length of J11A lying to the south of its junction with J12. Here they set to work to repair the damage done by our guns, and suffered a number of casualties in the process. They were eventually relieved by the Munster Fusiliers and Inniskilling Fusiliers.

When it came to the turn of the 1/6th Gurkhas they, too, turned right handed, and took over the part of J11A which lay between the points at which it was joined by J12 and J13. In addition they occupied as much of J13 as was in our possession. They will be heard of again in the account of the ding-dong struggle which ensued for the possession of J13. The 1/5th pressing on beyond the 1/6th reached a point outside the limit of the advance of the 86th Brigade. Once there it became apparent that a certain spur running downwards to the sea at some distance northwards of the junction of J13 with J11A would form an excellent *point d'appui* for the extreme left of the new line. Until that should be secured this flank, resting as it did at the junction mentioned, with no means of communication to the shore, must remain distinctly in the air, and there was no saying how long a respite might be granted before the Turks should realize the fact and act accordingly.

The task to be undertaken by the Battalion, then, was from the junction, to dig a trench in prolongation of J11A, as far as the friendly spur, and thence to follow the line of it left-handed to the shore. There was a considerable measure of danger attending the work, those engaged on it being subjected to a heavy fire from the enemy section of J13 and also from the higher ground on the opposite side of the *nullah*. By this time, as the result of much practice the men had become expert sappers, so that notwithstanding casualties the trench was soon completed, to be duly handed over to the 1st and 2nd Double Companies " for keeps " throughout the hard fighting which was to follow.

During the course of the afternoon it became apparent that the Turks were in no mood tamely to submit to the loss of ground occasioned by our success in the morning's assault. They probably realized that, given space in which to maintain and manœuvre a few more brigades, the Allies would be in a position to render extremely precarious their hold on the high ground commanding the Narrows and the Asiatic shore, the loss of which would open up to the Fleet a road to the Sea of Marmora and thence to Constantinople itself. This retaliatory spirit showed itself in the form of counter-attacks launched from the *nullah* running past the eastern extremities of J12 and J13, the weight of which threatened more than once to overwhelm the left of the line.

The fighting which resulted from the Turkish counter-offensive against the left of our line was of a nature so confused that the framing of any concerted plan was impossible. It was left to Commanders on the spot to meet the needs of the moment with such means as lay immediately to hand, and to give any clear and connected account of events from the evening of June 28th to July 5th is, therefore, a matter of considerable difficulty. Survivors can tell of what happened in their immediate vicinity, but their knowledge of events being limited as a rule by their environment—in other words, by a seething mass of men engaged in a life-and-death struggle in the bottom of a trench rising many feet above the level of their heads—they are in no position to connect their own actions with the equally strenuous efforts of detachments to the right or left of them.

It will help to a better understanding of the bare facts about to be chronicled if it is borne in mind that the positions of units holding these trenches were always fluctuating; that reliefs for which arrangements had been made could not always be carried out in their entirety, with the result that there was often a sprinkling of British troops among the Gurkha units engaged and vice versa; and finally, that though the enemy's main efforts were directed into the channel provided by J13 there was in addition much movement across the open.

Fighting in J13, June 28th to July 5th, 1915.

With these considerations to help towards the filling in of the picture it is now possible to resume the account of events on the extreme left of the Allied line. Throughout the afternoon the 1/5th continued to dig, with the object, as has been said, of securing a *point d'appui* for the exposed flank. Towards evening, however, the 2nd and 3rd Double Companies were pulled out of the line to rest and feed. There had barely been time to snatch a mouthful when at about 6 p.m. orders were received to clear the Turks out of that portion of J13 which they still held, and to secure it against a further irruption of the enemy. Major Govan put himself at the head of the 4th Double Company and led it into the trench, to be followed by the 3rd Double Company under Second-Lieutenant Cosby. With considerable difficulty they made their way past men of the 1/6th Gurkhas and a party of British soldiers—to which the Royal Fusiliers and Inniskillings had each contributed their quota—until the head of the slender column gained contact with the enemy, who was found to be starting on a bombing attack of his own down the trench in the direction of J11A. As before, the Battalion's supply of bombs was hopelessly inadequate to the needs of the occasion, while that of the Turks appeared, as usual, to be inexhaustible. Nevertheless Major Govan, with the help of the mere handful of men whom the restricted space would allow to act, succeeded in holding the hostile attack for a time.

Meantime Second-Lieutenant Cosby, anxious to ascertain the state of affairs in front, left his double company for the moment and began to struggle through the congestion which intervened between him and the head of the column. While still on the way he heard " turmoil and shouting " to his right, so looked over the parapet, to find that the trench was being charged by a detachment of British troops from the direction of J12. By the exercise of the full lung-power at his command he managed to make them understand that their efforts, though well intentioned, were directed against their own side, whereupon they dropped quietly into J13, thus adding considerably to the congestion. Second-Lieutenant Cosby then continued his journey, and having found Major Govan was immediately sent back to collect more bombs. A few minutes later there was a sound behind him of increased enemy activity, and in the confusion which followed there occurred a rush of British troops across the open ground south of the trench in the direction of J11A. They had carried with them a few of our own men, and deeming that under these circumstances his own presence at the front would prove an asset even more valuable than a fresh supply of bombs, he retraced his steps with the intention of rallying the men and administering a check to the enterprise of the Turks. With room to move about progress was more rapid than had previously been the case. As always, given a leader the men proved ready to do all that was required of them. With his following, despite the fact that he was now suffering from a wound in the arm, Second-Lieutenant Cosby succeeded in clearing J13 up to the point where it was joined by a Turkish communication trench running in from the north. Near this spot was found the body of Major Govan, who had apparently been killed instantaneously while gallantly striving to cope with the increased violence of the enemy's attack.

The most that could be hoped for, until a fresh stock of bombs should arrive, was to hold the Turks to the positions then occupied by them. To this end Second-Lieutenant Cosby decided on the construction of a barricade at the limit of the ground won. Material was to hand in plenty in the form of sandbags from the Turkish communication trench; the problem was how to cover the working party in the absence of bombs and handicapped by the fact that the trench was so deep as to deprive the men of the use of their rifles. Eventually the difficulty was overcome by scrambling up the sides, and, pressed close to the parapet and the tops of traverses, assuming a position, precarious it is true, but possessing the advantage that it enabled fire to be brought to bear on the bays beyond the barricade. Work now proceeded apace, the barricade was duly completed, and on top of it a machine-gun was mounted which was to prove effective in holding the enemy off for an hour or two to come.

On Major Govan's death Lieutenant-Colonel Bruce assumed the direction of affairs as far as both 1/5th and 1/6th Gurkhas were concerned, establishing his headquarters not far from the junction of J13 with J11A, and using companies from both battalions to execute his designs as circumstances demanded.

D. M. Govan, known in the Regiment as "Dod," was a fine soldier. Always fit and hard, he never spared himself, and under his calm, unruffled leadership the Battalion had maintained a stout heart despite the shock administered in its first action on June 4th. Essentially an outdoor man, he was a good rider, and could hold his own with a shotgun in any company. His was the spirit to rise to an emergency, and the more on that account was his loss to be deplored.

At about 8 p.m. Lieutenant-Colonel Bruce withdrew the 3rd and 4th Double Companies of the 1/5th for a short spell of rest, relieving them by two double companies of the 1/6th under Captain Abbott and Lieutenant Poynder. About half an hour after the relief had been effected, the Turks renewed their attempts to bomb their way down the trench. As long as on our side bombs were available, no great difficulty was experienced in pressing them back. As soon as the supply failed, however, the machine-gun and barricade proved inadequate of themselves, in the face of a determined effort, to repel the attackers, who, owing to the existence of traverses, could not be kept beyond bombing distance, and were consequently in a position to render untenable the bays on our side of the barricade. In these circumstances, and because the remaining two double companies were still hard at work digging on the new alignment, Colonel Bruce decided again to call up the lately relieved 3rd and 4th Double Companies, and to use them in diverting the pressure from Captain Abbott and his men. Nothing was to be gained by employing them in J13 itself, so, on arrival, they were placed in position behind a low breastwork which had been constructed a short distance to the east of J11A. With this as their base of operations, they were required, upon matters becoming critical in J13, to detach parties to make a rush across the open, fire their rifles in the faces of the Turks, and return—what was left of them—to the starting-point. It was a desperate business, but more than once during the night, led always by Second-Lieutenant Cosby, the rush was made, the rifles were fired, and the 1/6th Gurkhas, hard pressed, found temporary relief. Second-Lieutenant Cosby was again wounded, this time in the head, but managed to carry on until the morning.

Within the trench success and failure were alike dependent on the bomb supply. At a comparatively early hour the enemy had carried the barricade erected by the 1/5th. That obstacle removed the replenishment of our stock of bombs entailed a Turkish retreat; the supply exhausted, the enemy surged forward again, the odds then overwhelmingly in his favour. At one time an attempt was made to dig southwards and connect up with the 86th Brigade in J12, but beyond the fact that the men strung out to work were of assistance in repelling a Turkish counter-attack directed against that trench, the numbers available being unequal to the task, they could accomplish little, and were subsequently recalled. At about midnight the enemy succeeded in forcing the men of the 6th Gurkhas almost to the end of J13. A fresh stock of bombs materialized just in time. Armed with these Captain Abbott and his party stormed their way back through the trench, and had driven the Turks almost to their original position when the leader fell, seriously wounded. Still fighting sturdily with the means at their disposal, his men were losing ground, when Lieutenant Poynder initiated a bayonet charge. Though failing in its purpose of clearing the trench, it had the effect of checking the hostile advance, and paved the way to the measure of success which resulted from the night-long struggle, for dawn saw a new barricade erected on the spot occupied by the original work and our own men in possession.

J13 was to prove a fruitful source of trouble for both the 5th and 6th Gurkhas for some time to come, and because it will not be possible to go so fully into the incidents of future encounters, a somewhat lengthy description is given in this instance, principally with a view to providing material for a correct picture of the ups and downs of the fighting as it continued through the following nights and days. It will be convenient at this point to abandon the narration of events in their exact sequence, and to complete the account of the happenings in J13.

Possibly for reasons not unconnected with the repulse of the strong Turkish counter-attack, of which mention will be made later, June 29th and the night of June 29th–30th passed in comparative quiet. On the night of June 30th–July 1st, however, there was a recrudescence of enemy activity in J13. On this occasion, again, lack of bombs left no alternative but to fall back slowly in face of the limitless supply commanded by the Turks. Man after man sacrificed himself unhesitatingly by taking his place at a traverse and attempting to hold the attack with rifle fire. The expedient was tried, too, of keeping up a continuous fire with a maxim-gun mounted on the top of a traverse, but still the hostile progress was not stayed. The curse of the situation was those traverses. They gave absolute protection to the Turks against the fire of our rifles and machine-guns, but none to our men against the enemy bombs. Eventually, however, on our side, too, some of these missiles were collected, with the result that the enemy was driven back to the point from which he started. Lieutenant Poynder was largely responsible for our success in this action, but was wounded before the achievement was complete.

Further Fighting in J 13, June, 1915.

On July 1st the enemy renewed his attempt with consequences which appeared likely at one time to prove serious. There was a moment when our men found themselves forced right out of J13, with the possibility of being driven farther. The attack, however, had been checked just sufficiently to allow of the collection of a fresh store of bombs. A volunteer party was rapidly organized, consisting of bombers of both the 5th and 6th Gurkhas. These drove back the Turks and held them at a point about half-way along J13. This allowed of a second detachment being pushed into the trench, which, equipped with the necessary tools, proceeded to erect a barricade at the junction of J13 with J11A, to cut away the traverses beyond, and to lay a barbed-wire entanglement for some distance along the trench in the direction of the enemy. At the end of twenty minutes the covering party returned, having run short of bombs. The enemy was not far behind, but, the work completed, it was a matter of a few seconds only to clear the trench, and the first Turk to appear fell with a bullet through the head fired from one of the loopholes in the parapet. The entire episode reflected great credit on all concerned, and special mention must be made of the good work done by Lieutenant Erskine, who was not only largely responsible for the success of this particular achievement, but had previously distinguished himself on two occasions by leading attacks from a flank against J13, besides at this time bearing the responsibility attaching to the command of the battalion, with all which it entailed.

As a result of the measures taken on July 1st, the Turks were in no position to give further trouble in J13. On our side one more attempt was made to bring the trench within our own system of defence. On July 3rd a bombing party of the 14th Sikhs, assisted by a few men from the 5th and 6th Gurkhas, was detailed for the task. The enemy was forced to abandon his first barricade, but his second defied all the efforts of the attackers to carry it by storm, and the party was obliged to return without accomplishing its object.

The abortive attempt of July 3rd marks the end of the fighting in J13, at least as far as the Indian Brigade is concerned. Before leaving the subject altogether, however, it is as well to draw attention to a mistake which has crept into Sir Ian Hamilton's "Gallipoli Diary," where he deals with the events of this period. On page 361 occurs a statement to the effect that the Gurkhas lost their trench on the night of July 1st–2nd, and that the Inniskilling Fusiliers retook it for them with a loss of all their officers except two. This was not the case, the actual facts being as recorded above.[1]

Turkish Counter-attacks. The sequence of events was interrupted at the point reached with the coming of daylight on June 29th. The time has now come to resume the story from that point and to give some account of the more important incidents which occurred on the remainder of the front held by the 5th and 6th Gurkhas. In their newly won position both battalions alike were called upon to submit to day-long shelling by the hostile guns. On first experience of them the H.E. projectiles especially proved very trying. The noise of their explosion was tremendous, and though the effect was very local, they caused much damage to the trenches and were responsible for a steady increase in the casualty roll. Considerable difficulty was also experienced in the matter of supply. Everything, including water, had to be brought from Gurkha Beach, a distance of over a mile; and since at many places the route was exposed to enemy fire at short range, it was necessary to make the trip under cover of darkness. The men suffered considerably in consequence, the lack of sufficient water being especially felt, but they acquitted themselves full soldiery, nevertheless, and fought and dug as circumstances demanded.

The morning and afternoon of June 29th were spent in completing the defensive works begun on the previous day. At 5.30 p.m., however, the comparative calm was broken by a heavy bombardment of our trenches, which, for the space of an hour, were subjected to a storm

---

[1] A scrutiny of material not previously available shows that the reference in the "Gallipoli Diary" is to a trench further to the south. The statement is accurate, but the 5th and 6th Gurkhas were not concerned.

Panorama of the Suvla Position, fro[m]

Panorama of "V" Beach, taken from

m the Turkish Position on Koja Chemen Tepe.

the end of the Pier built out to the "River Clyde."

of both shrapnel and H.E. shell, and to an uninterrupted fire from enemy rifles and machine-guns. At 6.30 p.m. the hostile batteries lengthened their range, and it became apparent that the Turkish Infantry was about to issue from its trenches. On our side, supports were therefore moved up close to the firing-line and preparations made to meet the threatened attack. A few moments only of waiting and it materialized, to be crushed by the fire brought to bear on the attackers from our trenches, from our shore batteries, and from the guns of H.M.S. *Scorpion*, which had taken up a position in support of the left of the line to meet just such a contingency. As ill luck would have it, Lieutenant Lloyd, who had taken over command on Major Govan's death, was wounded in the arm while waiting for the attack to develop and had to betake himself to hospital. This left Lieutenant Erskine as the senior British officer, with Second-Lieutenant Knowles to assist him, besides Captain Reaney, I.M.S., as Medical Officer. To the very great regret of all, the last-named officer was killed on July 1st by a shell which exploded in the Hospital. He had been indefatigable in his care of the wounded, both during the battle of June 4th and also in the course of the present fighting. Over and over again he visited the firing line, impelled thereto by his high sense of duty, and his skill and devotion were equal to every demand.

Up to this time there existed a feeling among the men that in their encounters with the Turk, through no fault of their own, they had had by no means the best of it, and all were anxiously awaiting the occasion to do as they had been done by. The opportunity was not long in coming, and that the removal of all grounds for discontent might be the more complete, they were presented by the Turks with two chances of getting even.

Towards evening on July 2nd, after a day which had passed uneventfully except for the usual morning shelling, the Turks began the heaviest bombardment of our trenches yet experienced. As the enemy fire increased in intensity, the noise of the detonations became absolutely deafening, until men were stunned and bewildered by the sheer volume of sound. It came as a relief, therefore, when the range was lengthened in preparation for the Infantry assault. The Turkish trenches at this point were about 150 yards from our own, and, in the failing light, the serried ranks of the enemy could be seen in the act of breaking from cover. Simultaneously both 5th and 6th Gurkhas opened a murderous fire on their front, while the Artillery caught them in flank. No troops in the world could have stood in the face of such a storm, and the attack just melted away. Not yet convinced of the futility of their efforts, they renewed the Artillery bombardment, and again attempted to assault. Once more as they left their trenches they were met by a tremendous volume of rifle fire and by the accurately burst shrapnel of

R

our Artillery. For a moment they wavered, falling in heaps where they stood, and then the survivors, a small remnant only, shattered and demoralized, of two fresh Turkish battalions fled in disorder to the ravine. Their dead in front of our trenches alone numbered 600, and it was estimated that their total casualties amounted to 2,000.

The part played by the 5th and 6th Gurkhas in repelling this attack received recognition in the form of the following message:—

"The Lieutenant-General commanding the 8th Army Corps congratulates the 5th and 6th Gurkha Rifles on their gallant and successful action in repelling the strong Turkish attack on the night of July 2nd–3rd, and on having inflicted such heavy casualties on the enemy."

The slaughter amongst the Turks just recounted, however, pales by comparison with that dealt out to them on July 5th. Before the first glimmer of dawn every available enemy gun, those on the Asiatic shore participating, started throwing their projectiles indiscriminately all over the Helles area. The Asiatic batteries alone fired 1,900 shell, some 700 of these falling on Lancashire Landing, and in all the total number of rounds expended must have exceeded 5,000. The firing, however, was wild in the extreme, so much so, indeed, as to appear to be unaimed. In the attack which followed an entire Turkish division took part, picked troops from Adrianople.

At 3.50 a.m. they were seen to debouch from the ravine opposite the positions held by the 5th and 6th Gurkhas. Taught by their previous experience the men were not slow to seize their opportunity. Supports were rushed up, and a withering fire was opened on the densely packed mass which showed as a darker shadow against the dimly lighted background. Almost at once the guns, too, began to take their part in the work of destruction, and, posted as they were to a flank, did vast execution by means of enfilade fire magnificently directed. Further, to add to the utter hopelessness of their task, the attackers were raked from the other side by the quickfirers belonging to one of the two destroyers which had already proved of great assistance in repelling hostile counter-attacks. For an hour the Turks continued their despairing efforts but then came a lull.

Incredible as it may seem this was not to prove the end, and that they could be persuaded to try again, faced as they were with certain destruction, and warned, as they must have been by the litter of dead and dying which strewed the ground between the opposing trenches, is evidence no less of the heights of courage to which human nature may rise than of the fighting qualities of the Turkish soldier. Persuaded they were, however, and at the end of half an hour fresh masses were seen to emerge from the ravine. Line after line they came to attempt the impossible, only for line after line to be swept away by the tornado of fire which assailed them. But always were found men to replace those who fell. As though determined on self-immolation, ever larger and more densely packed became the columns which now swarmed into the open. They were mown down in heaps; annihilated. Except for the grisly reminder left upon the ground, whole companies, even whole battalions, were obliterated as though they had never been.

Extraordinary scenes occurred in our own trenches, now so congested by the presence of the supports that many men were unable to find standing room at the parapet. Some of these overcame the difficulty by climbing on to the parados, and shooting from there over the heads of their comrades in front. Others were seen to hand their rifles to their more fortunately placed friends, whose own weapons had become too hot to hold. Throughout four long hours the Turks continued to pile up their dead, but then came the end. Of that division which, before daylight, had advanced to the attack there was left none to try again. Lying out on the no-man's-land between their trenches and ours were some two thousand corpses, and this number by no means completes the tale of dead alone, for the unseen scores which filled the big ravine and every little *nullah* in this part of the line could not be included in the count.

Contemporary Events. It is convenient to regard the fighting which occurred between June 28th and July 5th as one continuous battle, the first stage marked by our initial success of the 28th, and the second by the various attempts of the enemy to regain the ground they had lost. Taking this view it is as well to touch briefly on those incidents in other parts of the line which had a direct bearing on the operation as a whole.

The most important of these was the demonstration made from Anzac on June 28th, for the purpose of diverting enemy reinforcements. This took the form of an attack on the low ridge covering Gaba Tepe, and was entirely successful in its object. About the time that the Anzac push began to make itself felt, large Turkish columns, evidently on their way to Krithia, turned back to meet the new menace, and, as luck would have it, came under the fire of our destroyers, and lost heavily. Had these reinforcements reached their original destination, matters might have gone very badly for us in the Helles area. As a sequel to this the Turks made a strong counter-attack on the night of June 29th–30th against the positions occupied by the New Zealand Mounted Rifles and Australian Light Horse, and were most bloodily repulsed.

The only other occurrence of any moment was the dashing advance of the French on the morning of June 30th, when they succeeded in adding another strong Turkish redoubt, the Quadrilateral, to their gains of June 21st.

Rest at Imbros.

The repulse of the big Turkish attack on July 5th marked the end of serious fighting for the 1/5th Gurkhas in the Helles area. The entire Indian Brigade was badly in need of a rest for purposes of reorganization and refitment.

Including the Staff, only eight British officers remained in the brigade, and every unit was very much under strength. On July 6th the Battalion was relieved by the Inniskilling Fusiliers and moved back to Gurkha Beach, whence, on the 9th, it proceeded to Imbros.

The casualties sustained by the Battalion in the fighting which occurred between June 28th and July 5th are given in the following table:—

	British Officers.	Gurkha Officers.	Other Ranks.	Total.
Killed	2	1	27	30
Wounded	2	2	65	69
Total	4	3	92	99

The losses cannot be regarded as heavy, when against them is put the very serious damage done to the enemy during this period.

Nearly a month was spent at Imbros, the time being fully occupied in making good the deficiencies in personnel and material caused by the continuous fighting of the preceding four weeks. A double company of the 2/5th Gurkhas arrived, and in order to ensure its retention as a complete unit under its own officers, the 2nd Double Company of the 1/5th, having lost the most heavily in killed and wounded, and being without any British or Gurkha officers, was distributed among the remaining three double companies. This arrangement resulted in the 2/5th detachment becoming the 2nd Double Company of the Battalion for the time. Details of its experiences will be found in Part III.

The 1/5th had every reason to be grateful for this reinforcement, the value of which only appreciated with the opportunity, not long in coming, to show the stuff of which it was made. The strength of British officers was further augmented by the return from hospital of Lieutenant Lloyd and Second-Lieutenant Cosby, and the attachment for duty of officers from other regiments, viz. Captain G. Tomes, 53rd Sikhs, and Lieutenants Greene and Birkbeck, 92nd Punjabis, while, on July 15th, Lieutenant-Colonel Firth of the 2/10th Gurkhas was appointed to take temporary command. Additions to the strength from all sources brought the battalion total up to the respectable figure of 825, excluding 11 British and 19 Gurkha officers.

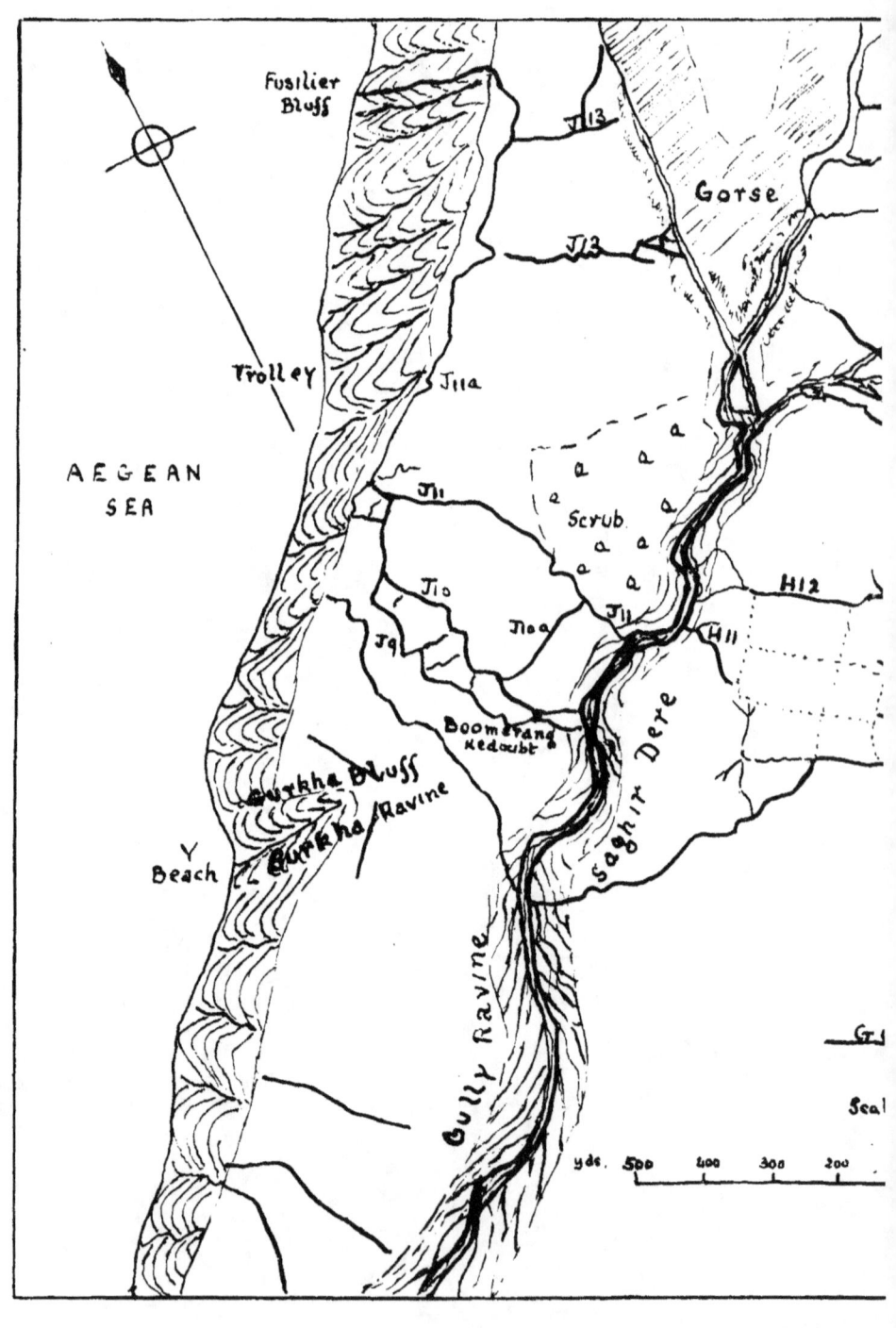

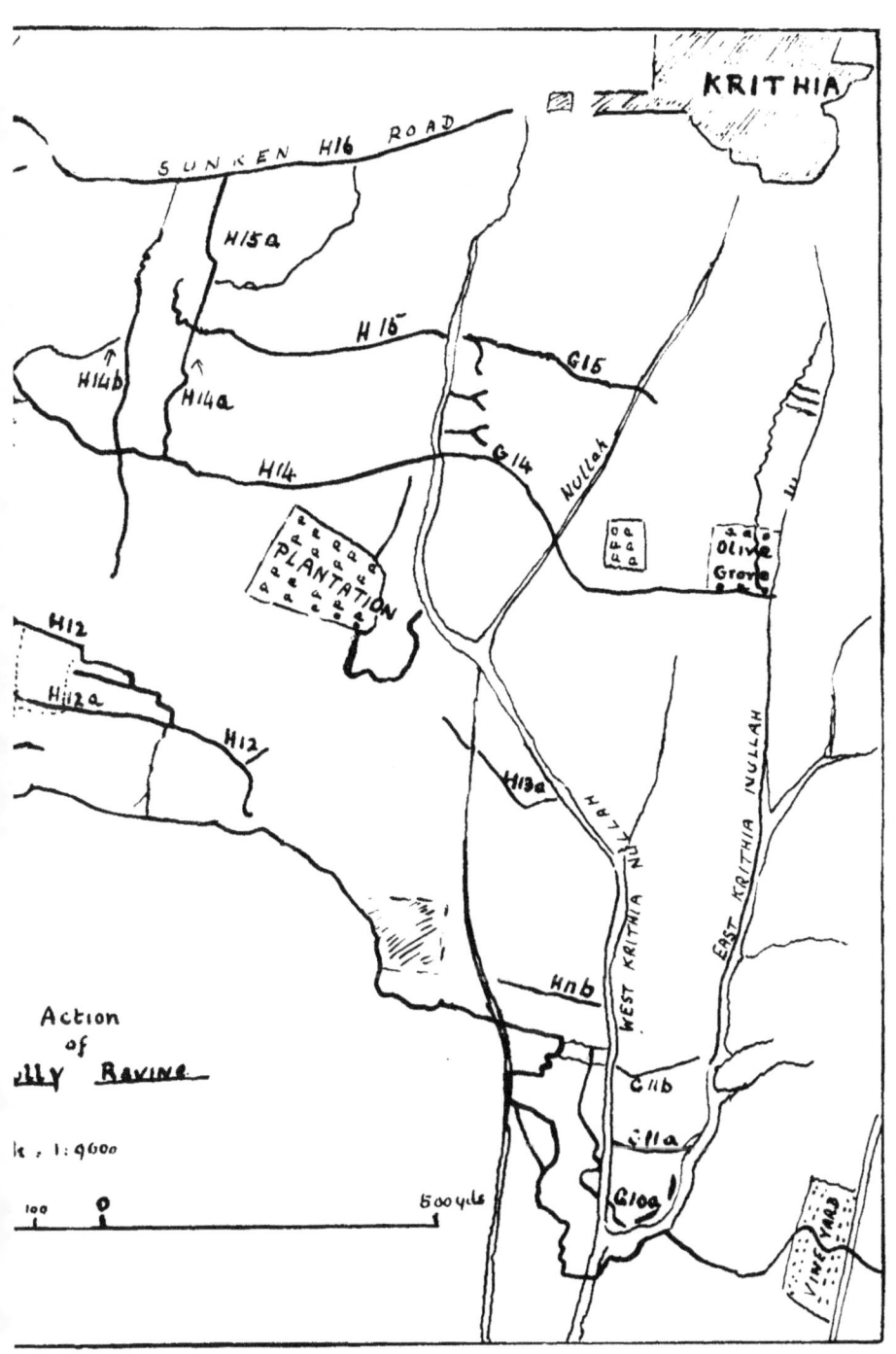

Action of
Gully Ravine

k . 1:9600

On July 15th the Battalion was paraded with the remainder of the brigade for an inspection by the Commander-in-Chief, Sir Ian Hamilton, who complimented all ranks on the good work they had done. Still more to the point, he was much struck by their cheerful demeanour, a sure indication that the *moral* of the men had not suffered as the result of their trying adventures.

On the same day occurred an incident which, though it bore no fruit, is worth recording as showing that Gurkhas had done nothing to mar the reputation gained by them in former years. During the fighting of mid-July in the Helles area, two territorial battalions had been surrounded by the Turks, and it had become a matter of the utmost urgency to gain touch with them. It was decided as the most likely method of achieving this purpose to send a party of Gurkha Scouts through the Turkish lines, and the 5th and 6th Gurkhas were called upon to furnish men to carry out this extremely hazardous task. They were duly selected and placed under the command of Havildar Kulbahadur Gurung of the 1/5th, but just before they sailed information was received that they would not, after all, be required, the Territorials having themselves found a way out of the *impasse*.

By the end of July it became apparent that fresh schemes were maturing for the confounding of the Turks. On the 29th the Indian Brigade severed its connection with the 29th Division, and became an independent formation at the disposal of G.H.Q. Previous to this the troops of the new division had been seen to be busy practising landing operations; training in night-work was carried out, maps of the country round Kum Kale were issued—this, in view of the real destination of the troops, was done to deceive—and finally actual orders were given for a move at short notice. On August 2nd Colonel Firth, with other commanding officers, left for an unknown destination, and on the night of August 5th–6th, the Battalion embarked on the Egyptian mail-boat, to find itself at 2 a.m. on the 6th off the coast of Anzac. This, then, was to be the scene of the next struggle.

CHAPTER IV

BATTLE OF AUGUST 6TH–10TH, AND SUBSEQUENT EVENTS TO AUGUST 20TH, 1915

Plan of Attack, August, 1915. REFERENCE was made, at the beginning of the last chapter, to plans for a renewed offensive on a grand scale on the arrival from England of fresh divisions and an ample supply of ammunition for the Artillery. These had been accumulating during the past weeks at Imbros, Mudros, and Mitylene, until, by the beginning of August, the concentration—if concentration it could be called under the circumstances—was complete. The new formations proved to be the 10th, 11th, and 13th Divisions, composed entirely of units of the New Army, and all as yet untried. Of these the 13th Division and the 33rd Brigade of the 11th Division had been sent straight to the Helles area to gain experience as soon as they arrived. For lack of space on the mainland, the remainder of the 11th and the whole of the 10th Division remained in the Islands until the time came for them to take part in the operations.

The object of the projected attack was to establish a position across the Peninsula north-westwards from Maidos which would give access to the Narrows, and to provide for it a protected line of supply from Suvla Bay. The means adopted to attain this object were:—

(1) A holding attack vigorously executed by the troops in the Helles area to pin the Turks to their ground and prevent them from detaching reinforcements northwards.

(2) A main attack, driven home by the troops at Anzac reinforced by the Indian Brigade and the 13th Division, to drive the enemy from Sari Bair and the high ground adjoining that feature, and obtain command of the Narrows.

(3) A turning movement by the X Corps (10th and 11th Divisions), which was to be landed at Suvla Bay and in its vicinity as soon as the main and holding attacks had been fairly launched, designed to threaten the enemy's right flank and loosen his hold of Sari Bair. That accomplished the IX Corps was to co-operate in the main attack by means of a strong thrust on Sari Bair from the north and north-west.

The plan was bold and simple in conception, deserving of success — with the element of luck working ever so slightly in our favour it would have succeeded. The preliminary arrangements for its execution,

1. Officers' Dug-outs, Anzac. 2. Anzac, looking South along Coast.
3. Anzac Front: Quinn's Post to Lone Pine.

however, were complicated in the extreme, entailing as they did, to take two items only, the previous landing and maintenance on the mainland, unobserved by the Turk, of some 30,000 men with their complement of guns, animals, and stores; and the concentration, in accordance with a strict time-table, of large bodies of troops separated, in some cases, by 120 miles of sea. Despite these difficulties and many others the task was successfully accomplished, and on August 6th the great offensive was launched.

Though our principal concern is with the main attack, to confine ourselves to its progress would result in no accurate appreciation of the achievement born of the tense struggle of the next few days in this area. For a proper understanding of events it is essential to trace the broad outlines of the operations conducted to the north and south of Anzac, and to fix in our minds the important tactical features of the country over which the advance was to take place. The topography of Helles being already known, the consideration of these tactical features can be limited to an examination, firstly of the objectives of the attack from Anzac, and secondly of the ground which was to prove the undoing of the IX Corps.

The objectives of the main attack lay along the great ridge of Sari Bair, which ran generally in a north-easterly direction from a point near the southernmost limit of the Anzac position. The first abrupt rise culminated in a feature known as Lone Pine, some 400 feet high, of which the seaward slopes only were in our possession. Thence rising always to the north-east, it is a two-mile journey by map—a much greater distance on the ground—past Baby 700 and Battleship Hill to Chunuk Bair (750 feet). The culminating peak of the range, known as Koja Chemen Tepe (1,000 feet) lies one mile to the north-east of Chunuk, and between the two is Hill Q, the prize for which the Battalion was to fight, but which it was not destined to win. Chunuk Bair throws off to the westward a spur named the Rhododendron Spur, north and south of which the ravines of Chailak Dere and Sazli Beit Dere run downwards to the sea. At its western extremity Rhododendron Spur rises again suddenly to form the steep, scarped underfeature of Table Top. Beyond the Chailak Dere, the Aghyl Dere takes its course, the two *nullahs* separated by the high ground known as Bauchop's Hill. Northwards again of the Aghyl Dere are the Damakjelik Bair and the Kaiajik Aghala, low-lying hills which provided the *mise-en-scène* for the fighting of part of the 13th Division. The last feature to be remarked in this part of the battlefield is the Abdel Rahman Bair, a bold spur, thrust out northwards as a buttress from Koja Chemen Tepe itself.

Description of Terrain.

The setting for the attack of the IX Corps from the direction of Suvla Bay was of a nature very different. The bay itself, bounded to the north and south by the promontories of Suvla Point and Nibrunesi Point, is shallow, and the ground for some distance inland of it low-lying and nearly flat, a description more especially applicable to the Salt Lake, bone-dry at this season of the year. Running parallel to the coast north-eastwards from Suvla Point is the ridge of Kiritch Tepe Sirt, scrub-covered and rising to a height of 650 feet, which formed the northern limit of this area of operations. The southern boundary was formed by the valley of Biyuk Anafarta, which runs westwards from the village of that name down towards the sea. Between the head of this valley and Kiritch Tepe Sirt, which it joins, is a range of hills some four miles in length and lying at a mean distance from the Suvla coast of three to four miles. Its average height is probably about 700 feet, and from near its centre, in close proximity to Anafarta Sagir, there juts out into the plain in the direction of the Salt Lake a long spur, at the extremity of which are situated the important tactical features of Scimitar Hill or Hill 70 and Ismail Oglu Tepe. Again to the west of these, and about midway between them and the Salt Lake, are Yilghin Burnu and Chocolate Hill.

It will be realized from this description that the terrain of itself presented a formidable obstacle, but there was in our favour an element of surprise that had been introduced into the scheme of attack, and actually the Turkish force immediately available to oppose the Suvla landing, was estimated as only one regiment, one squadron, some Gendarmerie and 12 guns. The distribution of the remaining enemy forces was 36,000 available to oppose the holding attack near Krithia, 27,000 to meet the thrust from Anzac, and 37,000 in reserve in the battle area. In addition, 45,000 were near Keshan, and could arrive in three days, and 10,000 were available on the Asiatic shore. Obviously, then, to reap the benefit conferred by the surprise landing near Suvla, it was all important to lose no time in pushing home the attack in that region. In the event, failure to do so deprived us of a victory otherwise well deserved. An adequate idea of the part played by the Battalion in this battle can only be conveyed by first sketching in broadest outline the principal events in each theatre of operations.

Disposition of Enemy Forces.

The holding attack in the Helles Sector was launched on the afternoon of August 6th. The fighting was of a nature most desperate, the 29th Division and the Lancashire regiments engaged there greatly distinguished themselves, and though little material gain can be recorded as the result of a battle lasting almost without interruption throughout seven days, the main object of the attack was achieved, for not only were all Turkish forces in that area pinned to their ground, but the necessity was even imposed on the enemy of calling for reinforcements on the sectors to the north.

The Helles Attack.

The Anzac Attack. The objectives of the central attack from Anzac were the Chunuk Bair Ridge, Hill Q, and Koja Chemen Tepe. Its success depended on the co-operation of the divisions to be landed at Suvla on the night of August 6th–7th. The Anzac lines being completely invested, special arrangements were necessary to allow of the attack being launched. As a preliminary, the 1st Australian Brigade, on the evening of August 6th, made a most gallant assault on the Turkish trenches on Lone Pine, captured them despite desperate enemy resistance, and held on to their gains in face of repeated counter-attacks throughout the fighting of the following days. Next, four columns were organized, which, for purposes of convenience, may be designated the Right Covering Column, the Right Attacking Column, the Left Attacking Column, and the Left Covering Column. The Right Attacking Column, consisting of the New Zealand Infantry Brigade, was entrusted with the task of capturing Chunuk Bair, moving to its objective via the Sazli Beit and Chailak Deres. To help it on its way, the Right Covering Column—New Zealanders—was to open up the defiles by the seizure of Old No. 3 Post, Table Top, and Bauchop's Hill. The Left Attacking Column, with the fortunes of which we are mainly concerned, consisted of the 4th Australian Brigade and Cox's Indian Brigade, with our old friends the 21st (Kohat) Mountain Battery (F.F.) to provide Artillery support.

Advancing by the Aghyl Dere, it was to drive the Turks from their positions on Koja Chemen Tepe and Hill Q, relying, for the accomplishment of its task, on the co-operation of the Suvla Bay divisions. To guard its flank, and all unknowingly to form a link with the Suvla attack, the Left Covering Column—Welsh troops—was to effect the capture of Damakjelik Bair. The 29th Brigade of the 10th Division and the 38th Brigade of the 13th Division were to be in reserve. Further, to divert the enemy's attention from the main objectives of the attack, Australian mounted troops, consisting of the 1st and 3rd Light Horse Brigades, at dawn on the 7th were to rush from their trenches at Quinn's Post and on Walker's Ridge against the slope of Chunuk Bair running down south-westerly towards the sea.

The operations of the covering columns began at about 9.30 p.m. on the night of August 6th. Despite the obstacles presented by the nature of the country and the darkness, they had gained all their objectives by dawn, and the attacking columns had entered on their tasks. In the case of the right column of assault, progress was at first good, and Rhododendron Spur fell an easy prize. This may be attributed in part to the heroism of the Australian mounted troops, who had attacked at dawn in accordance with their programme and had sacrificed themselves in their endeavour to carry out the task imposed on them. Then, however, came a check, the fact being that the operation entrusted to the left column of assault proved wellnigh impossible of accomplishment.

A long night march carried out by two brigades over a route unreconnoitred and of extreme difficulty, resulted inevitably in loss of touch. Delay was unavoidable in face of the necessity for redistributing troops to different objectives, great heat as the day wore on, and absence of water. The day ended with communication barely established and everyone exhausted from the combination of hard work and thirst endured under a burning sun. On the 8th the New Zealanders, reinforced during the preceding night by the 7th Gloucesters and 8th Welsh Pioneers, established themselves on the crest of Chunuk Bair. The Australians on the left lost very heavily, and eventually failed in their very gallant attempt against Abdel Rahman Bair, while between them the Indian Brigade, supported now by the 39th Brigade, could do no more than gain a little ground in the neighbourhood of the Farm in the course of their enterprise against Hill Q. Then came the fateful August 9th, when with any assistance from the direction of Suvla, success must inevitably have been achieved.

Pivoting on the New Zealanders' position on Chunuk Bair, an attack was organized on Hill Q, supported by the guns of the fleet, and intended to be further strengthened by a force of five battalions under General Baldwin. The 6th Gurkhas, with some of the 6th South Lancashires, advanced with great dash and actually gained a position astride the ridge between Hill Q and Chunuk Bair, whence they looked down on the Dardanelles and the Asiatic shore beyond. But the expected reinforcement failed to materialize. The five battalions under General Baldwin had gone astray in the darkness; through some most grievous error the naval bombardment recommenced, punishing heavily the devoted handful on the ridge, a strong Turkish counter-attack was initiated, and, fighting desperately, our men were forced far down the seaward slope. This proved to be the beginning of the end, for next day, August 10th, two tired battalions of the 13th Division, which had taken over from the New Zealanders during the preceding night, were overwhelmed by a very strong Turkish counter-attack and driven from the crest of Chunuk. Wave after wave the enemy surged down the slopes of Sari Bair.

At first there was no withstanding the fierce onslaught; General Baldwin was killed, and much of the ground, so hardly won, abandoned. The situation was saved by the fire of our Artillery and of the machine-guns of the New Zealand and Indian Brigades. After fierce hand-to-hand fighting in the thick scrub, a line was eventually re-established along the lower spurs of the great ridge, and this, growing stronger day by day, formed a barrier which the Turks never succeeded in breaking through.

To tell the story of the Suvla attack is to touch on one of the great tragedies of the war. Admirable preliminary Staff work resulted in a landing which was attended with almost every circumstance of surprise. Three landing-places were used, one known as "A" Beach, near the centre of the Bay, and the remaining two, known as "C" and "B" Beaches, south-east of Nibrunesi Point. By dawn on August 7th the 10th Division was ashore, and such opposition as the Turks could offer had been overcome. The 11th Division soon followed, though in this case there was some confusion, and the hour of 2 p.m. saw some 25,000 of our men established on a line running east of the Salt Lake from Karakol Dagh in the north to Yilghin Burnu in the south. It was at this point that the well-laid plan began to "gang agley." Rapidity of execution was vital to its success, but instead there came delay, which in the end brought failure. Lack of leadership and of the offensive spirit—this latter sapped by the pangs of thirst and physical exhaustion due to the great heat—may be taken as the main causes contributing to the *débâcle*.

The Suvla Attack.

Throughout the night of August 7th–8th, and again on the 8th, isolated attempts were made to advance, but there was no cohesion and, with some notable exceptions, no *élan* in the attack. The Turkish snipers, working in thick scrub, were handled with consummate skill, and since on our side even the smallest units failed to maintain touch, they produced results in holding up the advance which were out of all proportion to their numbers. By August 9th, despite the personal efforts of the Commander-in-Chief, the golden opportunity had been allowed to slip away. The Turks grew hourly stronger, and as time passed the operations tended to assimilate ever more closely to the conditions of position warfare. On August 10th nothing remained but to abandon temporarily the hope of a grand success, and to consolidate our lines on the limit of the ground won.

As already stated, the 1/5th Gurkhas formed part of the left column of assault in the central attack. The task before it was no easy one, but it is needless at this point to dwell on the difficulties with which the force was called upon to cope, since the principal amongst these have been referred to elsewhere. The night march which was to bring the column within striking distance of its objectives was timed to begin at 10.30 p.m. on August 7th, but some of the troops having failed to reach the rendezvous at the appointed time, a start was not made till 11.30 p.m. The 4th Australian Brigade led, followed by Column Headquarters, 1/5th G.R., 2/10th G.R., 1/6th G.R., New Zealand R.E., 21st (Kohat) M.B., and 14th Sikhs, in the order given. To the 1/6th was assigned the rôle of supporting the Australians in their attempt on Koja Chemen Tepe, while to the 14th Sikhs was given the

The 1/5th Gurkhas in the Attack, Aug. 6th and 7th.

task of acting as a reserve to the 1/5th and 2/10th in their attack on Hill Q, which they were to approach via the southern fork of the Aghyl Dere.

Trouble arose at the very commencement of the enterprise. Missing the prepared exit the leading troops made their way over a deep trench through a narrow gap in the wire, and, hoping to retrieve the misfortune of a late start, set a pace which proved much too fast for those in rear. Inevitably big gaps occurred in the column, with the result, in the case of the 1/5th, that while three double companies took the correct route, the 3rd Double Company, marching in rear of the Battalion, turned southwards too soon, and made an isolated attempt against Hill Q, which, though gallant in the extreme and almost successful in attaining the objective, in the end averted disaster only through good luck, combined with the unrivalled ability of the men to move rapidly in the hills.

The story of the doings of the 3rd Double Company will be told later.

The remaining three double companies just before dawn, having reached the point where the Aghyl Dere bifurcates, prepared to deploy for the attack. The 1st Double Company took the left of the line, the 2nd Double Company, composed of men of the 2/5th, was in the centre, and the 4th Double Company, with the machine-guns, on the right. Somewhere to the left of the Battalion, but not in touch with it, was the Australian Brigade, and away to the right, their whereabouts, however, unknown, were the 3rd Double Company of the Battalion and the 2/10th Gurkhas. As the morning wore on the 1/6th Gurkhas, who had been called upon to reinforce the Australians, finding themselves unable to progress in that direction, swung right-handed until they, too, found themselves thrusting upwards from the slopes of Sari Bair. From this it will appear that the movement lacked cohesion as regards the larger units taking part in it, while even in the smaller units intercommunication became a matter of the utmost difficulty, so rugged and broken was the terrain and so dense the scrub which covered the hill-sides.

The direction taken by the three double companies of the Battalion, now deployed, was from the point of bifurcation mentioned above, towards the summit of Hill Q. Progress at first was rapid, but the thick cover was infested with enemy snipers, with the result, when even sections became disintegrated, that impetus was lost. The nature of the fighting may be gauged from the numbers found missing at the end of the day. Small groups and individual men still struggled forward, not knowing where danger lay, but only that it was imminent, and that the blow might fall from front, flanks, or rear. Often it must have happened that a man fell to a sniper's bullet, and that his comrades, only a yard or two away, knew nothing of it. The heat grew ever more intense as the day wore on, and the men, already exhausted by their exertions of the preceding night, suffered much from thirst. At last, with the summit of Hill Q still distant some hundreds of yards, orders were issued to close and establish a line between the two forks of the Aghyl Dere, about half a mile in advance of the morning's position of deployment. Throughout the afternoon and evening men continued to straggle in, for with companies and sections all abroad delay in the receipt of orders was unavoidable, and by nightfall the Battalion, less the 3rd Double Company, was in occupation of the position indicated.

At dawn on August 8th—the day which saw the New Zealanders established on the crest of Sari Bair—the attack was

August 8th. renewed. The leading lines attained a point within 300 yards of the summit of Hill Q, only to be met with machine-gun fire of such intensity that further advance must have spelt annihilation. Once more it became necessary to issue orders for a retirement, and by midday the attackers had returned to their trenches, taking with them thirty-five Turkish prisoners. There they were joined by the missing 3rd Double Company, and it will be convenient at this point to give an account of its doings during the preceding thirty-six hours.

At dawn on August 7th Lieutenant Cosby, commanding the double

The 3rd Double Company in the Attack. company, made the discovery that, owing to the enforced neglect of rules which govern the conduct of night marches, touch with the remainder of the Battalion had been completely lost. With improving visibility, figures wearing slouch hats could be discerned on the slopes of Sari Bair away to the right. Under the mistaken impression that these figures indicated the position of the Battalion the Double Company Commander made in their direction, only to find, on arrival at communicating distance, that they were New Zealanders. A parley ensued, in which Colonel Sutton, who just then put in an appearance with two companies of the 2/10th Gurkhas, also took part. Nothing having occurred to modify the original intention, which as far as the Gurkhas were concerned entailed the capture of Hill Q, it was decided to organize an attack, and attempt to push on to that point. At the time of reaching this decision the New Zealanders had established themselves along a false crest north-westwards of the culminating point of Chunuk Bair, and distant some 600 yards from the summit of Hill Q. Preliminary dispositions were made under the cover afforded by the false crest, which resulted in the New Zealanders attacking on the right, and the Gurkhas, led by " F " Company of the 1/5th and supported by the two companies 2/10th, on the left. As soon as the first wave topped the rise, it came under intense machine-gun and rifle fire directed on it from a redoubt situated near the summit of Hill Q. Once over the crest the ground, thickly covered in scrub, sloped downwards for some hundreds of yards to a cornfield, whence it rose again to the Hill Q Redoubt, about 100 yards away. Traversing the downward slope at top speed the leading lines of "F" Company reached the shelter of a low stone wall conveniently situated in the middle of the cornfield. At this point there was also a small stone hut, and this having been occupied as a look-out post, a halt was called to permit of a survey of the position. It proved to be none too promising. The New Zealanders, subjected to a raking enfilade fire from Chunuk, had been forced to retire, and of the two double companies of the 2/10th, not a sign was visible. Of "E" and "F" Companies of the 1/5th there were some 30 men at the stone wall, while the remainder were in the cover of the scrub which edged the cornfield. The field itself had now become the object of very particular attention from the Turkish machine-guns, a fact, however, which in no way deterred the men, who, using the shelter of the bushes to form small groups, continued to dash across it to join their comrades at the wall. It had become necessary to arrive speedily at a decision regarding further action. To attempt, unsupported, the capture of the redoubt would be tantamount to suicide. To retire would prove almost as costly, and, in view of the proximity of the objective and the efforts already made, was an alternative to be adopted only as a last resort. Under the circumstances it remained only to hold on in the hope that help would arrive; should it fail to materialize, a retirement at dusk was still possible, and would be attended with less risk.

Acting on this decision signals were made to those in the bushes to remain where they were, and at the same time steps were taken to improve the position at the wall. This was nowhere more than two feet in height, and since the Turks maintained on it a continuous fire with rifles and machine-guns, all movement entailed in digging had to be undertaken beneath such inadequate shelter as it afforded. Lying face downwards the men scraped away with their entrenching tools until a sufficient depth had been reached to allow of the use of picks and shovels. Work then went forward rapidly, and it was not very long before complete immunity had been secured against enemy fire from the redoubt. Then followed a period of waiting. For ten long hours the men lay here, exposed to a fierce sun and suffering much from thirst. There were a few casualties, as was inevitable in view of the volume of fire brought to bear on a confined space, but on the whole they were fortunate in this one matter. During the morning some distraction was caused by the fire of our own naval guns directed against the summit of Hill Q. Some of the shells dropped unpleasantly close, a condition of affairs which was soon remedied by the waving of black and yellow flags provided before the night march began to show the progress of our advance.

The incident leads to speculation regarding the high hopes of success which must have been entertained by our gunners, when so early in the attack they were asked to lift their fire for fear of hitting their own Infantry. As the long day wore on, hopes of support began to wane, and were finally abandoned. On the approach of dusk, preparations were made for a retirement, and it was then seen that the Turks had become alive to the situation and were creeping through the dense scrub southwards of the cornfield for the purpose of getting astride the line of retreat. Hopelessly outnumbered, there was nothing for it but to rely on speed of foot, and this realized, the movement conformed to the accepted tenets of hill warfare. Hampered though they were with their wounded, they easily outdistanced their pursuers, and though the enemy machine-guns reopened, in the failing light they did no damage. The difficulties of the party were not yet at an end, however. Lieutenant Cosby was entirely ignorant of the whereabouts of the remainder of the Battalion, while of the New Zealanders and the half-battalion 2/10th G.R., not a trace was to be found. It appeared to him probable, too—so far in advance of the rest of our forces had been his position—that other bodies of Turks might have interposed between his double company and the sea. Slackening speed as the danger in rear became less imminent he made a hurried reconnaissance, and struck the head of a ravine which, as evidenced by the corpses and other debris of the battlefield bestrewing its length, had served as a line of approach in the morning's advance. Down this ravine the double company made its way, presently to fall in with a small party of its own men who, having become mixed up with the 2/10th Gurkhas, had retired under orders from Colonel Sutton. The night of August 7th–8th was spent in the ravine, and next day, men having been sent out early to search for it, a junction was effected with the remainder of the Battalion.

August 8th, then, found the whole Battalion occupying a defensive position in the Aghyl Dere foothills, about half a mile due west of the summit of Hill Q. Our losses had been considerable.

Casualties. Of British officers, Lieutenants Birkbeck, Hunter, and Fletcher had been killed, and Captain Harington and Lieutenant Erskine wounded. Of Gurkha officers, Jemadar Pemnarain Thapa had been killed, Subadar Karbir Thapa and Jemadar Amarsing Thapa were missing, and of the remainder three had been wounded. The losses amongst the other ranks comprised 44 killed, 15 missing, and 195 wounded, the total casualties of the Battalion in the two days' fighting thus amounting to 265.

August 9th. August 9th passed in comparative quiet as far as the 1/5th were concerned. Several Turkish counter-attacks were successfully repulsed and a number of enemy snipers accounted for, but no part was taken in the important happenings on the hills to the south. This may seem strange in view of the achievement of the 1/6th Gurkhas on this day, but it has to be borne in mind that the attack of the Indian Brigade against Hill Q was never intended to be launched from the direction of Chunuk. The 1/6th had arrived at their position of August 9th through swinging right-handed when unable to progress in the direction taken by the Australian Brigade. The remainder of the Indian Brigade was not similarly affected.

August 10th.

On August 10th the 1/5th became embroiled in the general Turkish counter-attack which succeeded in regaining the crest of Chunuk. The Battalion had received a reinforcement of 100 men of the Australian Brigade, who behaved with great gallantry, and helped materially to stem the tide of attack. When eventually the Turkish remnant retreated, broken and demoralized, our line was still intact, and the men were ready to meet any call which might be made upon them. Heavy casualties had been inflicted on the enemy, one machine-gun especially finding a magnificent target. Though its backsight was knocked off by a bullet, and its barrel casing pierced in many places, the No. 1 continued to fire, pouring a continuous stream of bullets into the flank of a packed mass of Turks and causing them to retire in disorder. An attempt was then made to take advantage of the situation by organizing one last attack in the hope of gaining the summit of Hill Q. A gallant response was made, but no support was forthcoming, and a strong wire entanglement proved an efficient bar to further advance. Evening found the Battalion in occupation of the original position; to north and south matters had come to a standstill, and at this point may be said to have ended the Battle of August 6th–10th.

Events after the Battle.

It was on this day, the 10th, that Captain Tomes, who, it will be remembered, had joined from the 53rd Sikhs in Imbros, was sent across to take command of the 1/6th, but he was killed almost immediately while effecting the relief of men in the front-line trenches. Fortunately for the Battalion other officers now began to arrive to replace those who had been killed or wounded. On August 11th came Lieutenant Cummins and Captain Bailey, the latter the well-known explorer who, inured to hardship as he was, must have found the heat, flies, and stench of the Peninsula a poor exchange for the snows and solitudes of Tibet. On this date Lieutenant Lloyd left to command the 1/6th G.R. in place of Lieutenant Tomes. He was killed on the 14th while accompanying General Cox in an inspection of the piquet line. On the night of August 11th–12th five officers reported their arrival, Captains Molloy and Hay-Webb, Lieutenant Nepean, and Second-Lieutenants Roberts and Phillips.

The next few days were spent in consolidating the position and in improving communications with the units on the right and left. The enemy was seen to be engaged in the same task, and the attempts of each side to interfere with the progress of the other gave rise to considerable unpleasantness which culminated in a fierce duel, carried on with machine-guns and rifles, on the night of August 12th–13th.

On August 13th the 1/5th Gurkhas were relieved by a New Army battalion of the Hampshire Regiment, and with the rest of the Indian Brigade moved to a new position on the slopes of the Damakjelik Bair, where they began at once to dig themselves in. This position ran westwards from a point on the northern slopes of Damakjelik Bair nearly due south of Kabak Kuyu, and then bent north-westwards to Kazlar Chair. It was occupied from right to left by the 14th Sikhs, 1/6th Gurkhas, and 2/10th Gurkhas, with the 1/5th in reserve. On the left it connected with the IX Corps, and on the right with the New Zealanders, who occupied the northern and eastern slopes of the Damakjelik Bair.

From August 13th to 20th the Battalion remained in reserve, but was nevertheless kept busy digging trenches and clearing brushwood in front of the line. More often than not the work had to be done under fire, with the result that every day brought its small toll of casualties. There was the usual plague of flies, and while the days were intensely hot, the nights brought with them a cold breeze. Sweating by day and shivering by night the men suffered considerably from fever and dysentery, and so it came about that of the total strength of 573 a number was in hospital.

On August 15th Lieutenant-Colonel Firth, D.S.O., was placed on the sick list, the command of the Battalion devolving on Captain Molloy. On the 16th Second-Lieutenant Knowles rejoined, and on the 17th Lieutenant Greene and Second-Lieutenant Roberts were posted to the 1/6th G.R.

August 20th was to mark the end of the brief respite from active operations, for on the 21st began the last big battle of the campaign.

CHAPTER V

BATTLE OF AUGUST 21ST, 1915,
AND SUBSEQUENT EVENTS TO THE EVACUATION

Object of the Attack. AFTER the battle described in the last chapter it was decided, in view of enemy superiority both in numbers and position, that to strike a decisive blow against the Turks was no longer possible under existing conditions, and that any such attempt must be delayed until the arrival of reinforcements, amounting to 150,000 men, and the replenishment of stocks of ammunition and other material. At the same time the opinion was held that to leave the Turks in undisputed possession of the ground then occupied by them would be to jeopardize such gains as had resulted from the battle. A review of the position showed that the capture of Hill 70 (Scimitar Hill) and Ismail Oglu Tepe would not only free the Suvla area from the constant threat of bombardment by the enemy's Artillery, but would close to him the Anafarta Valley for the passage of his reinforcements, and also provide a convenient starting-point for future operations at such time as the arrival of fresh troops should render feasible their inception.

Plan of Attack. To General de Lisle was entrusted the execution of the plan. For the attack on the two essential objectives the 29th Division was brought up from the southern area, while the force was further strengthened by the addition of the 2nd Mounted Division of Yeomanry. The area of active operations was limited to the north by Hill 70, and to the south by Hill 60 (Kaiajik Aghala). That part of the line which lay northwards of Sulajik was to be held passively by the 53rd and 54th Divisions.

For the actual assault three columns were formed. Of the 29th Division—now commanded by General Marshall—the 87th Brigade was to move against Hill 70 and the 86th against Ismail Oglu Tepe. The 88th, which had lost the most heavily in the previous fighting, was to form the divisional reserve. South of the 29th Division the 11th Division of the IX Corps was to capture the trenches to its immediate front in the vicinity of Hetman Chair, and that accomplished, to advance to the assistance of the 29th Division and attack Ismail Oglu Tepe from the south. The third column, commanded by General Cox and consisting of Australian, New Zealand, British, and Indian troops, was to secure the wells at Kabak Kuyu and Susak Kuyu, seize the important tactical feature of Hill 60, and establish itself on a line in continuation of that attained by the 11th Division. The 10th Division, as corps reserve, would be in the vicinity of the mound known as Hill 10, and the Yeomanry Division, acting in a similar capacity, was to take up a position in the first instance behind Lala Baba. The assault was timed for 3 p.m., and was to be preceded by an Artillery bombardment of half an hour's duration.

A just appreciation of the achievement of the troops engaged in this battle must depend on a realization of the following considerations: The advantage of surprise was no longer with us; the enemy, having been given ample time in which to strengthen his positions, had made full use of his opportunities; and finally, the afternoon brought with it a strange white mist, quite unprecedented in our experience of the Peninsula. This last rendered practically futile our Artillery bombardment and obscured our objectives, but allowed to the enemy a clear view of our men silhouetted against the western sky.

Attack of 29th Division.
The 29th Division advanced to the attack with an *élan* wholly in keeping with its previous record. Under a murderous fire, the 87th Brigade surged far up the slopes of Hill 70, and the leading lines even reached the trenches at the top. On their right the 86th Brigade, though partially disorganized by the blazing scrub to its front, was almost successful in reaching its objective. In the case of both brigades, however, intense Artillery fire from north and south-east, and a continuous stream of machine-gun bullets from the crests, proved an impenetrable bar to final achievement. Again and again the assault was renewed, but no help being forthcoming from the 11th Division to the south, they were forced, in the end, to dig themselves in a short distance below the Turkish trenches.

Attack of Yeomanry Division.
Meantime, as soon as it appeared probable that the 29th Division might require assistance the 2nd Mounted Division of Yeomanry was ordered to take up a position behind Yilghin Burnu. On its way from Lala Baba it came under a heavy fire of shrapnel, but the behaviour of the men under these trying circumstances was magnificent, and their formations were maintained in a manner which would have done them credit under the conditions of peace manœuvres. From the position at Yilghin Burnu the division was sent into the attack at about 5.30 p.m. Called upon, as they were, to overcome not only the enemy resistance, but also the blazing scrub of the hill-side, progress was necessarily slow. They reached the leading lines of the 29th Division, and one battalion succeeded in capturing an underfeature between Hill 70 and Ismail Oglu Tepe, which it took for the latter objective. There, however, their success ended. The losses in the attack of the two

divisions amounted to nearly 5,000; in view of the failure of the 11th Division it appeared useless to renew the assault, and during the night orders were issued for a retirement to the original line.

It will be remembered that the objectives of the attack of the 11th Division were firstly the enemy trenches north and south of Hetman Chair, and secondly Ismail Oglu Tepe from the south. Advancing at 3 p.m. the 34th Brigade secured the northern sector, but nothing further was accomplished. The 32nd Brigade, which should have operated against Hetman Chair and the communication trench connecting that place with the Ismail Oglu Tepe position, lost direction, and the 33rd Brigade, sent up with the express purpose of correcting this error, fell into precisely the same trap. With these two mistakes the offensive in this part of the line came to a standstill.

Attack of the 11th Division.

The operations of General Cox's force provided the only real success of the day. The scheme of attack in this area comprised three phases.

Attack on Kaiajik Aghala and the Wells.

The capture of the Turkish trenches north-east of the Kaiajik Dere and of Hill 60 itself constituted the first phase. The operation, timed to begin at 3 p.m., was entrusted to General Russell, who had at his disposal the New Zealand Mounted Rifles, some 500 men of the 4th Australian Brigade, one British battalion of the 29th Brigade, and a company of New Zealand Sappers. The remainder of the 4th Australian Brigade was detailed to cover the advance.

The second phase comprised the capture of the well at Kabak Kuyu, and was timed for 3.10 p.m. Under cover of the rifle and machine-gun fire of the South Wales Borderers the assault was to be carried out by the 5th Connaught Rangers, the movement being directed by Lieutenant-Colonel Agnew, the Commander of the 29th Brigade.

The third phase was the advance of the Indian Brigade under Lieutenant-Colonel Palin, in conjunction with the attack of the 11th Division on its left. The first objective given to it was a line running from Susak Kuyu through Green Patch Farm to Kabak Kuyu, and then, in the event of the assault on the latter place proving successful, the left of the line was to push on some 600 yards to a spot known as Dervish Ali Kuyu, whence a position was to be established to link up southwards with General Russell's force on Hill 60.

General Russell's attack was only partially successful. A lodgment was effected on the south-western slopes of Kaiajik Aghala, but Hill 60 was not won. Communication trenches were dug to connect with the Australian position on the north-eastern slopes of Damakjelik Bair, and the new gain in ground was consolidated, with the result that

Operations of General Russell's Force.

the Turkish bombing attacks, initiated during the night, were frustrated. On the morning of the 22nd the attack was renewed by the 18th Australian Battalion, which had just arrived. An advance was effected of 150 yards, but enfilade fire then drove them back to the original line. Under cover of this attack, however, the New Zealand Mounted Rifles pushed forward some eighty yards, and were successful in holding on to their gains. This assault brought to an end our enterprises against Hill 60 for the time being. It was destined finally to fall a prize to General Russell's force on August 29th.

Attack on Kabak Kuyu. Soon after the initiation of the operations just described, the 5th Connaught Rangers advanced against Kabak Kuyu. This battalion was composed of young men, full of keenness, and hitherto unblooded. They moved with the utmost dash and disregard of the enemy's fire, seized the well, and the enemy posts in its vicinity, and then reformed to continue their advance in the direction of Hill 60.

Advance of Indian Brigade. For the advance on its objectives the Indian Brigade was disposed with the 2/10th Gurkhas on the left and the 1/5th Gurkhas on the right, forming firing line and supports, while the 1/6th Gurkhas moved at a distance of 800 yards behind as reserve. To the 14th Sikhs was given the rôle of covering the advance from the trenches previously occupied by the Canterbury Battalion of the New Zealand Mounted Rifles. Leaving their positions of assembly at 3.30 p.m., the two leading battalions came under heavy fire, and after an advance of 500 yards were definitely checked for a time. Receiving fresh impetus, however, from the support companies, they again moved forward. On the left the 2/10th Gurkhas gained possession of Susak Kuyu, and on the right the 1/5th made good the ground in the vicinity of Green Patch Farm. True, this line was still some hundreds of yards short of the final objective of the brigade, but with the 11th Division failing to progress on their side, and with General Russell's force checked on the lower slopes of the Kaiajik Aghala, no useful purpose was to be served by pushing on. The night was spent in consolidating the ground won, and by morning the not unsatisfactory result had been achieved of ensuring uninterrupted connection throughout the new line and also with the troops on the right and left. The results of the attacks of the Indian Brigade may be summarized as the capture of several important wells, and a gain in ground of 800 to 1,000 yards.

1/5th Gurkhas in the Attack. It remains to give a few details regarding the doings of the 1/5th Gurkhas in this attack. Leaving their position under the cover afforded by Damakjelik Bair at about 2.30 p.m., they formed up behind the forward piquets of the 1/6th Gurkhas, ready to advance as soon as the Connaught Rangers, from the trenches of the South Wales Borderers on the right, should begin their attack on the advanced Turkish trenches at Kabak Kuyu. Here they underwent the very trying ordeal of enduring passively hostile shrapnel fire, which took its toll from among the waiting ranks.

It was no light task which was laid on the Battalion. In front of the 1/6th piquet line the ground, devoid of cover, fell glacis-wise to the level stretch beyond which were situated the Turkish trenches dug for the protection of the wells, and their strong points on the face of Hill 60 itself. The area over which the advance was to be made was further exposed to the enemy artillery on the slopes of Chunuk Bair.

In Captain Molloy's dispositions for the attack the 3rd and 4th Double Companies furnished firing-lines and supports, and the remaining two double companies were retained by him as his local reserve. When the Connaught Rangers launched their spirited attack, the Turks opened on them with rifles and machine-guns not only from Kabak Kuyu, but also from Hill 60 and the vicinity of Green Patch Farm. Through the fire directed on the Rangers from the right of the Turkish line, the 1/5th were called upon to advance.

Difficulties were encountered from the outset. Issuing through gaps in the wire which covered the 1/6th piquet line they had first to effect a very rapid deployment, and then to change direction to face their objective—this, too, under a hail of shrapnel bullets and the enfilade fire of rifles and machine-guns. Nothing daunted, Captain Hay-Webb led off with the 4th Double Company, taking the declivity at a run in the hope of gaining a modicum of cover on the level ground below. While traversing the slope he was mortally wounded and died shortly afterwards in the dressing-station. Captain Bailey followed closely with the 3rd Double Company, and, adopting similar tactics, had succeeded in gaining the level ground when he was hit through both legs. With that the advance came to a temporary standstill some three hundred yards from the objective.

Battalion headquarters, meanwhile, was moving forward by a covered way, and presently arrived at a position favourable for observation. Seeing the lack of movement, Captain Molloy instructed his Adjutant, Captain Cummins, to go across to the leading companies, and to get them on again in short rushes. Eagerly Captain Cummins went to perform his hazardous task. Gallantly he placed himself in front of the foremost line, and, shouting to the men to follow him, he led them in a series of short bounds towards the enemy trenches. His brave effort was of no immediate avail; he himself was killed, and with him fell many of those who followed. His body was recovered by the 1/6th Gurkhas that night, far in advance of the line on which the companies had checked. Round him lay a number of those whom he had led, and it was seen that all had been shot in the head.

It now became apparent that away to the right the attack of the Connaught Rangers had been completely successful. This made it the more necessary that the Battalion should draw level with them, and in the hope of achieving this object, Captain Molloy returned down the covered way to the original forming-up line, where the first Double Company, under Captain Nepean, awaited a call on its services. After receiving his orders, Captain Nepean moved off with his company, Captain Molloy accompanying him to show him the way. The route taken was the defiladed approach which had previously been used to good purpose. By its means the double company was enabled to reach the line of Green Patch Farm, and to gain touch with the Connaught Rangers. With their co-operation the Turks were driven back and a line was established north and south of Green Patch Farm, and thence along the lower slopes of Hill 60 to Kabak Kuyu. Thus a very real success was achieved, but, almost as soon as won, it came very near to frustration owing to a premature order for withdrawal to the Connaught Rangers. Fortunately, Captain Nepean was able to get into touch with Colonel Jourdain, who, on matters being explained, averted the impending *débâcle* by postponing the move of his battalion until reinforcements should arrive.

Having seen the 1st Double Company established, Captain Molloy, grasping the importance of holding the new line, at great personal risk went back to find the remainder of the Battalion, with a view to organizing and consolidating the position of Green Patch Farm. The good work done by this officer received no recognition at the time, but it is gratifying to be able to record that, partly through the intervention of Colonel Jourdain, commanding the Connaught Rangers in 1920, long after the Gallipoli honours lists were closed, his services were proved to have been so exceptional that a special award was made to him of the Distinguished Service Order.

With the arrival of the remaining three companies work went forward apace. The machine-guns were sited to cover the consolidation, firing line and support trenches were completed, and patrols, under Lieutenant Cosby, were sent out to gain touch with the troops on either flank. The Connaught Rangers having been withdrawn at dusk, a detachment of 100 men of the 14th Sikhs was sent up to fill the gap between the right of the 1/5th and the Australian left. Similarly, to the north, the right flank of the 2/10th having been driven back by heavy fire from Hill 60, the 1/6th Gurkhas were used to straighten the line. By the morning of the 22nd a continuous system of trenches had been dug along the entire length of the front occupied by General Cox's force; northwards it connected with the right of the 11th Division, and southwards with the Anzac defences. This, however, is somewhat to anticipate events. Returning to the evening of the 21st, the Turks were not yet done with. At about 10 p.m. Lieutenant Cosby came upon a number of the enemy who appeared to be intent on sniping our working parties from the shelter of the scrub. With the help of his men he succeeded in cutting them off, and 15 of the party were made prisoners. Unfortunately, a few snipers had already taken up their positions, and of these one shot at and wounded Lieutenant Knowles before he could be captured. It was his last shot on earth. Next morning the British officers of the Battalion were still further reduced in number, Lieutenant Nepean being wounded while supervising the work of consolidation. Of our officers who had been posted to the 1/6th Gurkhas, Lieutenant Greene was killed during the advance of that battalion to fill the gap which existed on our left.

The battle of August 21st proved to be the last of any magnitude to be undertaken during our occupation of the Peninsula. It only escaped complete failure by the success achieved on the right of the area of attack, which not only resulted in the acquisition of a good supply of water, but also safeguarded our communications between Anzac and Suvla.

The casualties sustained by the Battalion are given in the following table:—

	Killed.	Wounded.	Total.
British Officers	2	3	5
Gurkha Officers	—	3	3
Other Ranks	13	40	53
Grand Total	..	..	61

Lloyd was a Welshman of the best type, apt to be temperamental, but always lovable, and he was one of the most popular officers of his time in the Regiment. His great friend was Gerry Turner, and it would be difficult to find a better pair. He wrote from Gallipoli a few days after the 1/5th had lost most of their officers, and there was no doubt that he had a premonition that his own end was near.

Hay-Webb was one of the quiet, unassuming kind, but with a really good brain. He was shy and reserved in manner, but all who knew him liked him, for he was one of the straightest men imaginable. He was attached to the 2/2nd Gurkhas in France, and while there he proved himself to be resourceful and courageous beyond the ordinary.

Cummins was one whose many excellent qualities were not displayed on the surface. The better one knew him the more one liked him, and

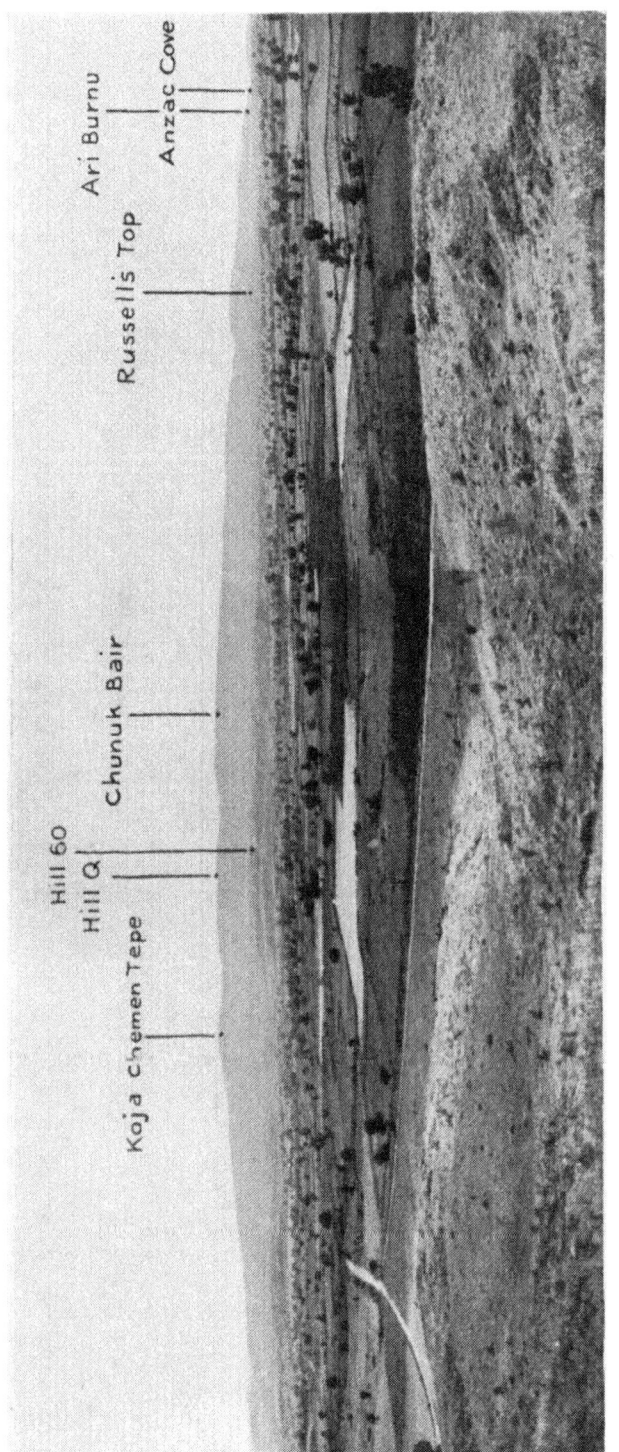

Panorama looking South-East from Chocolate Hill.

the greater the respect one had for him. Very thorough, devoted to the interests of the Regiment, and very brave, his death caused a gap not easily filled.

The day after the battle, Second-Lieutenant Toogood, having joined from England, the Battalion consisted of 5 British officers, 9 Gurkha officers, and 500 other ranks, of which number, however, only 360 were available for duty in the firing-line.

Capture of Hill 60, 27-8-15 to 29-8-15.

No event of outstanding importance occurred until the capture of Hill 60 on August 27th. The enterprise was again entrusted to General Cox, who had at his disposal detachments from the 4th and 5th Australian Brigades, a brigade of the New Zealand Mounted Rifles, and the 5th Connaught Rangers. Quitting their trenches at 5 p.m., the attackers were greeted with an overwhelming fire from enemy field guns, rifles, and machine-guns, momentary relief being afforded only when, the Turks bringing heavy shell to their aid, a number of these fell into their own trenches. On the right, the Australians could make no progress. In the centre the New Zealanders effected a lodgment on Hill 60 itself, to which they held throughout the fluctuations of the fighting on their right and left during the next twenty-four hours, and despite all the Turks could do against them by means of bombs, bayonets, and intense fire from all available weapons.

On the left, the Connaught Rangers assembled for the attack in the trenches of the 1/5th Gurkhas, and it is not without interest that their commanding officer, Colonel Jourdain, later acknowledged in the kindest terms the help he received at this juncture from Captain Molloy and all ranks of the Battalion. Their assault was once more carried out with great dash and gallantry, and they gained all their objectives. Receiving no support, however, during the early hours of the night, outnumbered and outbombed, they were forced to retire.

August 28th saw the New Zealanders alone holding on to their gains. On the 29th, at 1 p.m., the attack was renewed, and the 10th Light Horse, overrunning communication and fire trenches, ousted the Turks from their positions, and gave us final command of Hill 60 and the ground beyond.

Trench Warfare, 30-8-15 to 19-12-15.

After the capture of Hill 60 the entire line settled down to the routine of trench warfare, with its long spells of drudgery, punctuated by moments of intense excitement. There was as yet no whisper of evacuation. The Commander-in-Chief, more firmly convinced than ever that by way of the Dardanelles was a rapid decision to be arrived at, had pressed for reinforcements to enable him to renew the offensive. Up to a point the authorities at home appeared to be in agreement with him, and so it was that hope still flourished and nerved all ranks to endure. Sick and feeble commanders had been replaced, the *moral* of the new divisions improved daily, while that of the veterans was all it had ever been. The *moral* of the Turks, on the other hand, began to show signs of deterioration; so it is a fair contention, bearing in mind these more favourable factors and seeing how very near had we already been to victory, that a renewal of our effort under the conditions contemplated would have opened a way to Constantinople, and thereby brought much closer the end of the World War. It was not to be, however. The Salonika heresy, together with the initiation of a premature offensive on the Western Front, were to lead to the diversion of the Gallipoli reinforcements and the consequent abandonment of the enterprise.

As far as the Battalion was concerned, periods of duty in the front line alternated with spells of rest. On August 30th Captain Molloy was wounded, and until Major Tillard from the 4th Gurkhas (of whom we last heard as an officer of Gurkha Scouts in Tirah in 1897) assumed command on September 8th, owing to the scarcity of senior officers, Major Allanson commanded both the 1/5th and 1/6th Gurkha Rifles. On the day on which Captain Molloy was wounded, Captain Kirkwood joined the Battalion from the 14th Sikhs. The first period of duty in the front-line trenches terminated for the left-half battalion on September 5th, the right half being relieved on the 11th. The time spent in rest generally passed quietly, though even here there was seldom complete immunity from enemy shell fire.

In the front line, on the other hand, there was constant activity, especially during the hours of darkness. Working parties were ceaselessly employed in repairing damage resulting from both shrapnel and high-explosive shells; there was mining and countermining, and the construction of saps to bring us into closer contact with the enemy trench system; there were patrols to be organized and snipers to be posted that no opportunity might be allowed to slide of inflicting loss on the Turks; there was the improvement of the defences to be undertaken by the strengthening of our wire and the digging of supervision trenches—every concomitant, in short, of a war of attrition as learnt by our experiences in France. Finally, a fresh terror was added to life by the introduction of the bombing catapult. Every day brought its toll of casualties, and sickness, too, was responsible for some reduction in strength. As an example, between August 22nd and 28th, one Gurkha officer was wounded, and of other ranks five were killed, forty-one wounded, and fifteen evacuated sick. Fortunately, on September 15th a draft arrived consisting of Second-Lieutenants Cook and Winn, Jemadars Seria Gharti and Balbir Rana, and 100 other ranks. On the same day Captain Harington rejoined from hospital, and on the 18th the return of all men extra-regimentally employed increased the

"What might have been": The Narrows from Koja Chemen Tepe.

Men of the 15th at Damakjelik Bair.

strength of the Battalion to 6 British officers, 9 Gurkha officers, and 535 other ranks.

Extracts from War Diary. A few extracts from the War Diary will probably serve to give a correct impression of the conditions under which the Battalion worked at this time. They are taken from the period covering its second tour of duty in the front line, i.e., from September 20th to October 4th.

"21-9-15.—Night passed quietly. Considerable sniping at our working parties.

"22-9-15.—Night passed quietly. Two casualties in British officers, Second-Lieutenant Roberts and Second-Lieutenant Cook being wounded.

"24-9-15.—Intermittent bursts of firing heard from the direction of Susak Kuyu, continuing all night. 15.30 to 16.15, Turks shelled the firing line with high explosives, only three or four falling in front of sector held by us, remainder going to the left. No damage. Intermittent shrapnel shelling from 16.30 to 18.00 by Turks. Traverses damaged.

"27-9-15.—Patrols went out at 22.00, 01.00, and 04.00, but reported everything quiet. Fire started all along the line, the result of cheering in trenches on the left of our line; stopped at 19.45. During this time nine 6″ H.E. shells were dropped close to our Headquarters, only one of which exploded. No damage done. Also few shrapnel fired at our firing line. At 23.00 aeroplane heard overhead going west, and at 00.05 heard returning E. It seemed to drop three bombs, which appeared to fall near Anzac. 14.00 to 16.00 desultory shelling of our trenches by the Turks.

"29-9-15.—Night passed quietly. Casualties three wounded and none sick."

It must be admitted that certain qualities of imagination are necessary if the incidents described in the above somewhat laconic terms are to be properly visualized. As an example, the last entry quoted—that for September 29th—covers the following episode, which is given in the words of the recommendation of Lance-Naik Harkbahadur Thapa for the award of the Indian Distinguished Service Medal:—

"On September 29th, 1915, he, as a rifleman, formed one of a party of scouts sent to reconnoitre the enemy position. The party lost their way in the dark and were heavily fired on by both sides; one scout was killed, and the Havildar in charge, wounded. Harkbahadur Thapa, though himself also wounded, took command of the survivors, and showing great presence of mind and initiative, succeeded in extricating the party and bringing it back without further loss."

To take another War Diary entry of this period, that for October 3rd. It runs, "The night passed quietly," and this it must be conceded is inadequate to the occasion, for on that day was carried through a rather brilliant minor exploit. The construction of a sap being necessary well in advance of the line held and only forty yards from the Turkish trenches, Lieutenant Cosby called for volunteers. He met with a ready response; under heavy fire, at point-blank range, the work was most efficiently done, and for his part in it Havildar Dalbir Chand was recommended for the award of the Indian Order of Merit.

Despite these omissions, however, the War Diary entries given above, and selected at random, will, if properly considered, give a very fair idea of the " daily round " at that time.

The Battalion's third tour of duty in the front line lasted from October 20th to November 4th. Casualties were rather fewer than had previously been the case, and there occurred nothing which merits special mention here.

The Blizzard. During its fourth tour of duty, however—November 18th to December 1st—occurred the blizzard. It may be that this was responsible for accelerating the decision to evacuate ; in any case it can be stated with absolute conviction that a recurrence of the phenomenon would have left the army unfit for further operations. Even as it was, the force suffered a reduction in numbers equivalent to one-tenth of its total strength, and in some formations the proportion of casualties were very much greater. The 29th Division, for example, lost a full two-thirds of its men through frostbite and exposure. In the 1/5th, too, there were a number of cases of frostbite, but, compared with most other units, the Battalion suffered little from the storm. This was due, not to the fact that the conditions were less severe, but to the remarkable stamina of the men. In the case of the Gurkha, though his brain may become numb when exposed to intense cold his body puts up a stout resistance, and nine times out of ten he survives where others, less hardy, succumb.

When November 26th broke—cold, dull, and gusty—there was nothing to indicate the cataclysm which impended. As the day wore on, however, the wind increased in violence, the cold became more intense, and rain turned to sleet. These conditions were sufficiently wretched, but worse was to follow. Before nightfall there came a thunderstorm, which rent the clouds and brought down a cascade of water on the heads of our men as they crouched in the trenches. These filled rapidly, and in many places it became necessary to quit them, the men improvising such cover as they could on the parados. The Turks on higher ground, less affected than ourselves by the downpour, mistook the movement for an impending attack, and opened a heavy fire on the entire line. Under the circumstances no reply was possible, with the result that our losses were considerable. Before long, however, the enemy's own plight became so bad that he was obliged to desist, and then was created

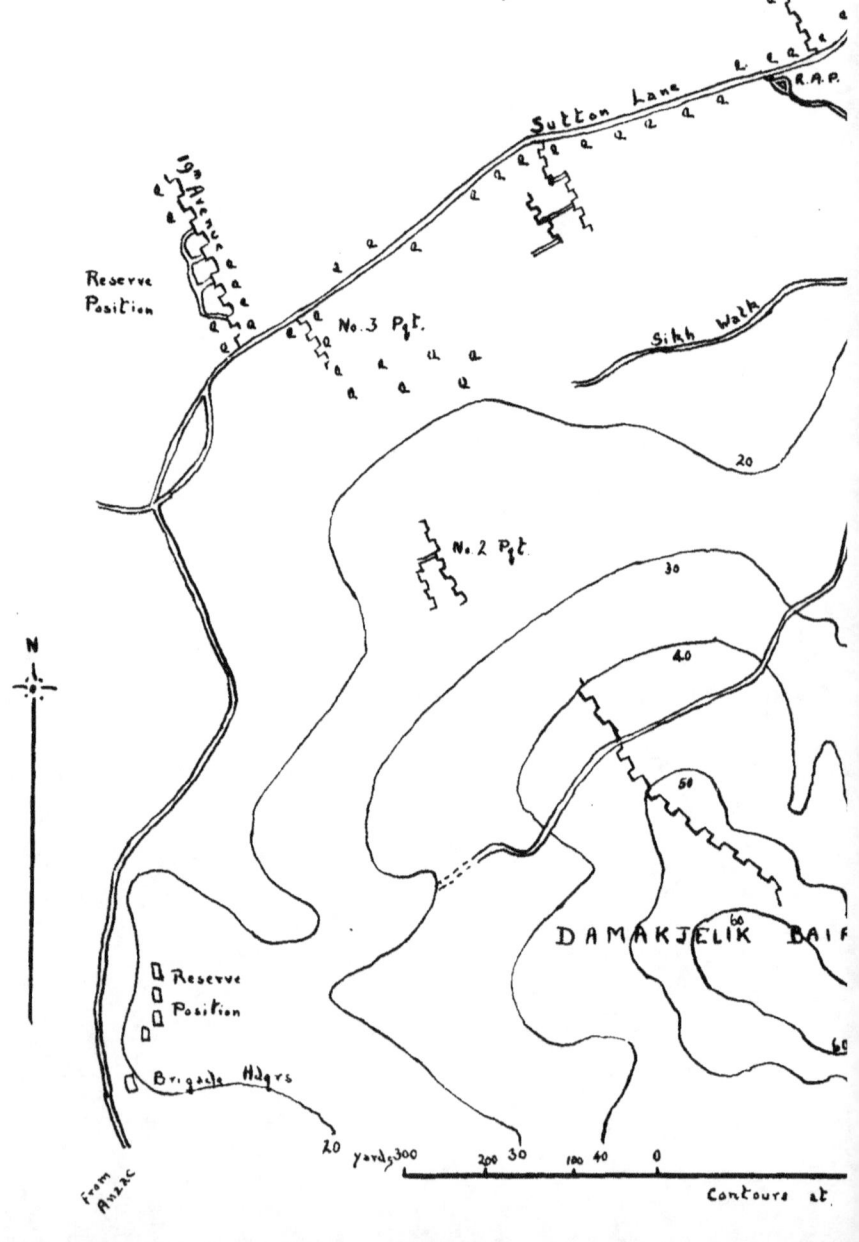

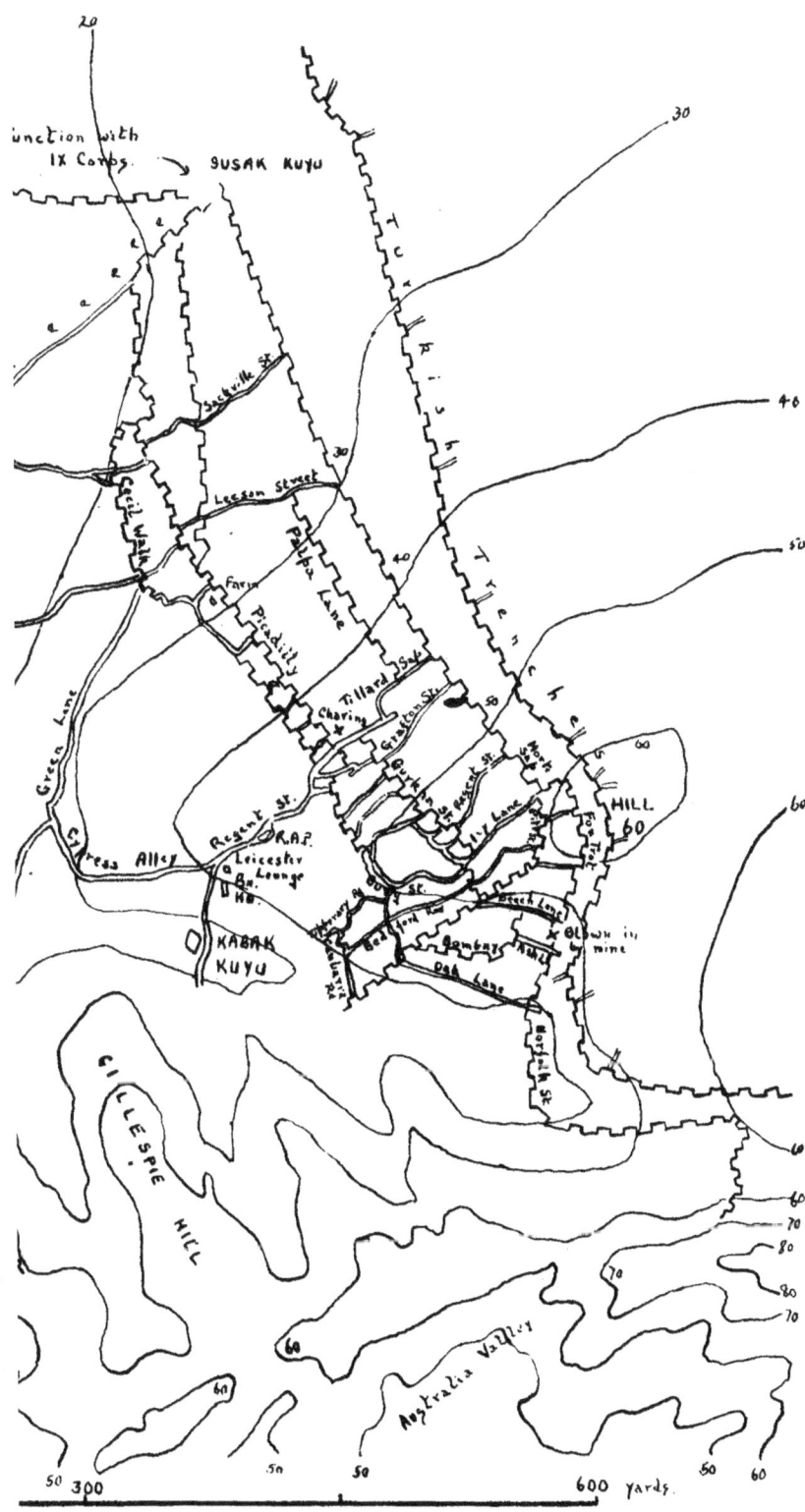

a situation surely without parallel in the records of warfare, where two vast opposing forces, each apparently at the mercy of the other, abandoned for a time their attitude of mutual antagonism and strove only to combat the greater menace of nature in an uproar. It is established beyond shadow of questioning that many were drowned before they could leave their trenches. To quote from John Masefield's "Gallipoli":—

"In one trench when the flood rose a pony, a mule, a pig, and two dead Turks were washed over a barricade together."

All through that night and the following day, except that water no longer poured into the trenches, conditions grew worse. The culmination of misery arrived with the 28th, when the wind blew a full gale, intensely cold, the snow swirled and eddied, water froze in the trenches, parapet and parados collapsed, and frostbite took its heaviest toll. Then came a change for the better, but the storm had already worked untold havoc. At Suvla, Anzac, and Helles, 200 men had died, and not less than 10,000 had been totally incapacitated for further service.

From December 2nd to the 9th the time was passed in reserve.

Last Moments. On December 10th the Battalion again moved up to the front line for what was to prove its last tour of duty. Throughout the nine days which were to elapse before the final evacuation there was considerable activity on the part of both sides. The Turks were particularly busy with their ·75's, while their high-explosive shells were found to be much more effective than had previously been the case. In addition there was much throwing of bombs; machine-guns were seldom idle, and the frequent explosion of Camoflet mines further contributed to the uncertainty of existence. How closely the end was approaching was, perhaps, only realized in full on December 13th, when orders were received for the embarkation of 1,202 of all ranks of the brigade on the following night. Of this number the Battalion provided 112, consisting of 75 Gurkha ranks and 37 followers. Considered as a trial trip for the infinitely greater undertaking yet to come, the success of this preliminary withdrawal gave reason to hope that disaster would be averted. On December 16th arrangements were communicated for the evacuation of the remainder of the brigade on the night of December 19th–20th. To effect a successful withdrawal in the face of an active enemy is rightly regarded as one of the most difficult operations of war. When are considered the immense and added hazards attending this particular undertaking, and, these notwithstanding, the completeness of the eventual achievement, ample justification will be found for the claim of the Commander-in-Chief, that here was a deed without parallel in history.

Though a study of the complete orders for the evacuation would doubtless be profitable, here it will suffice to summarize briefly the action decided on. The clearing of the Anzac and Suvla area was to be effected on two successive nights, the majority of the troops being reserved for the second night. In the Indian Brigade the proportion was 200 to 700. In the case of the final withdrawal three parties were formed. For each party a Commander was appointed; times were given for quitting the trenches, arriving at the beach, and embarking, and the route to be taken was specified. Great stress was laid on the necessity that everything should appear normal, e.g., the usual number of periscopes was to appear above the parapet, and ammunition was to be placed in convenient places to allow those left to maintain the normal volume of fire delivered from the established frontage. Finally arrangements were made which should obviate noise, and everything possible was done to prevent the enemy gaining advantage from the necessity under which we were placed of leaving behind stores and ammunition.

The fateful 19th of December arrived, and brought with it for the 1/5th a grim reminder that all was not yet finished. Morning stand-to was just over when at 8.10 a.m. a Turkish mine exploded just outside Essex barricade. It was one of the most powerful seen in this area: hurled skywards a vast column of earth and stones, damaged the parapets for a considerable distance on either side, and completely obliterated the section of trench in its immediate neighbourhood. Fortunately a party from the sector most affected had just left to clean the communication trenches, and of those remaining, all had a providential escape. Some twenty were buried beneath the debris of the explosion and had to be dug out. Though suffering somewhat severely from shock they were otherwise uninjured. One man was actually not discovered for forty-five minutes, and his comrades had constantly walked over him unknowingly. When extricated at the end of that time he was found to be only shaken by his experience, and on regaining at last the power of speech his first request was for a cigarette. The behaviour of those nearest to the scene was beyond all praise. Immediately following the explosion the Turks opened a furious bombardment with their 75's and prepared to attack. With great coolness and presence of mind Subadar Partiman Rana and Havildar Budh Sing Gurung—the latter had been almost in the centre of the affected area—collected their men and filled the gap. At the same time rapid fire was opened along the remainder of the front, the men in the bombing post at Ash Lane doing especially good work, with the result that the enemy threat failed to develop. The bombardment lasted forty-five minutes, to be succeeded by another of thirty-five minutes' duration; but despite the fact that the fire was well aimed and the shells accurately fused, not a Turk succeeded in breaking through.

Slowly the day passed, to be followed by the early darkness of a

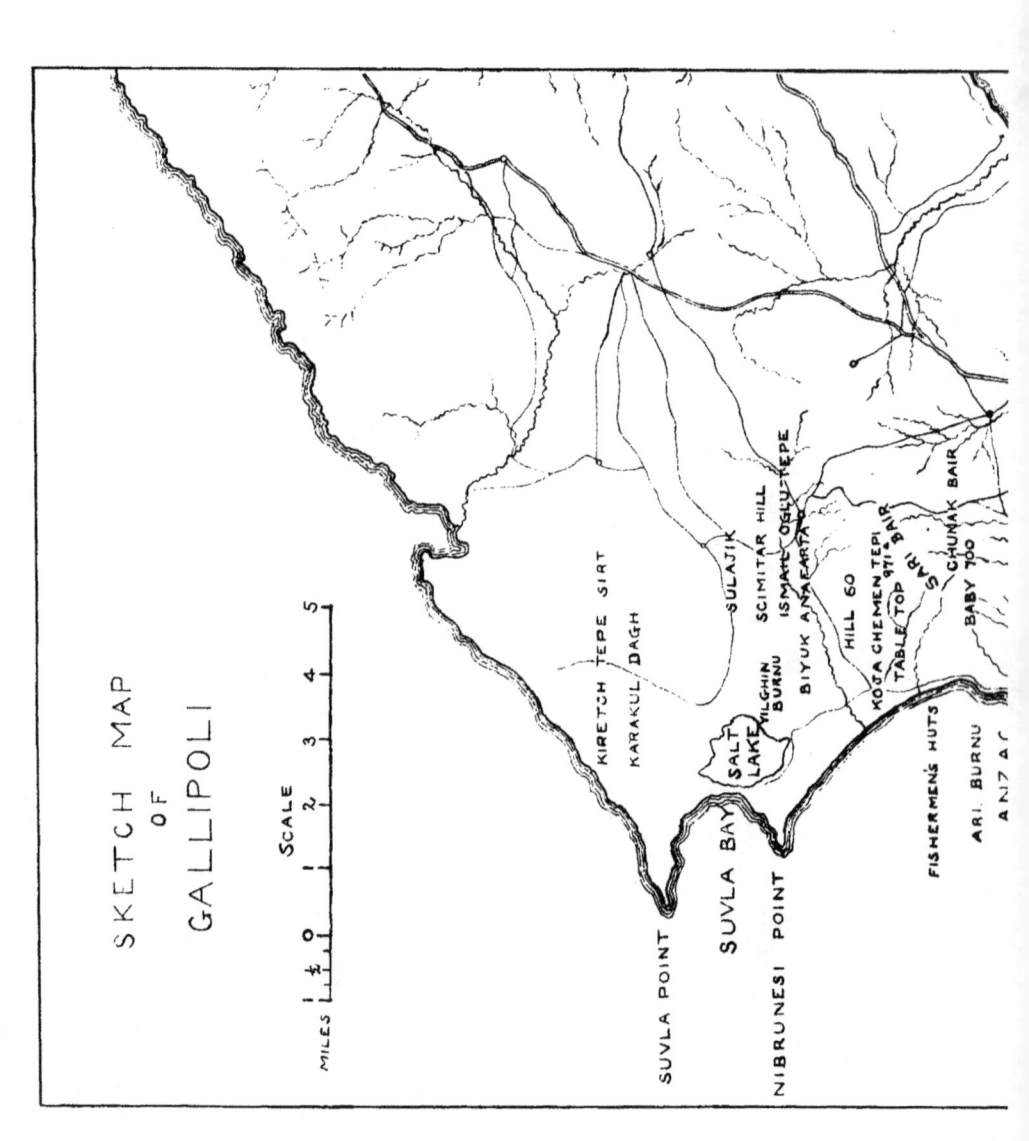

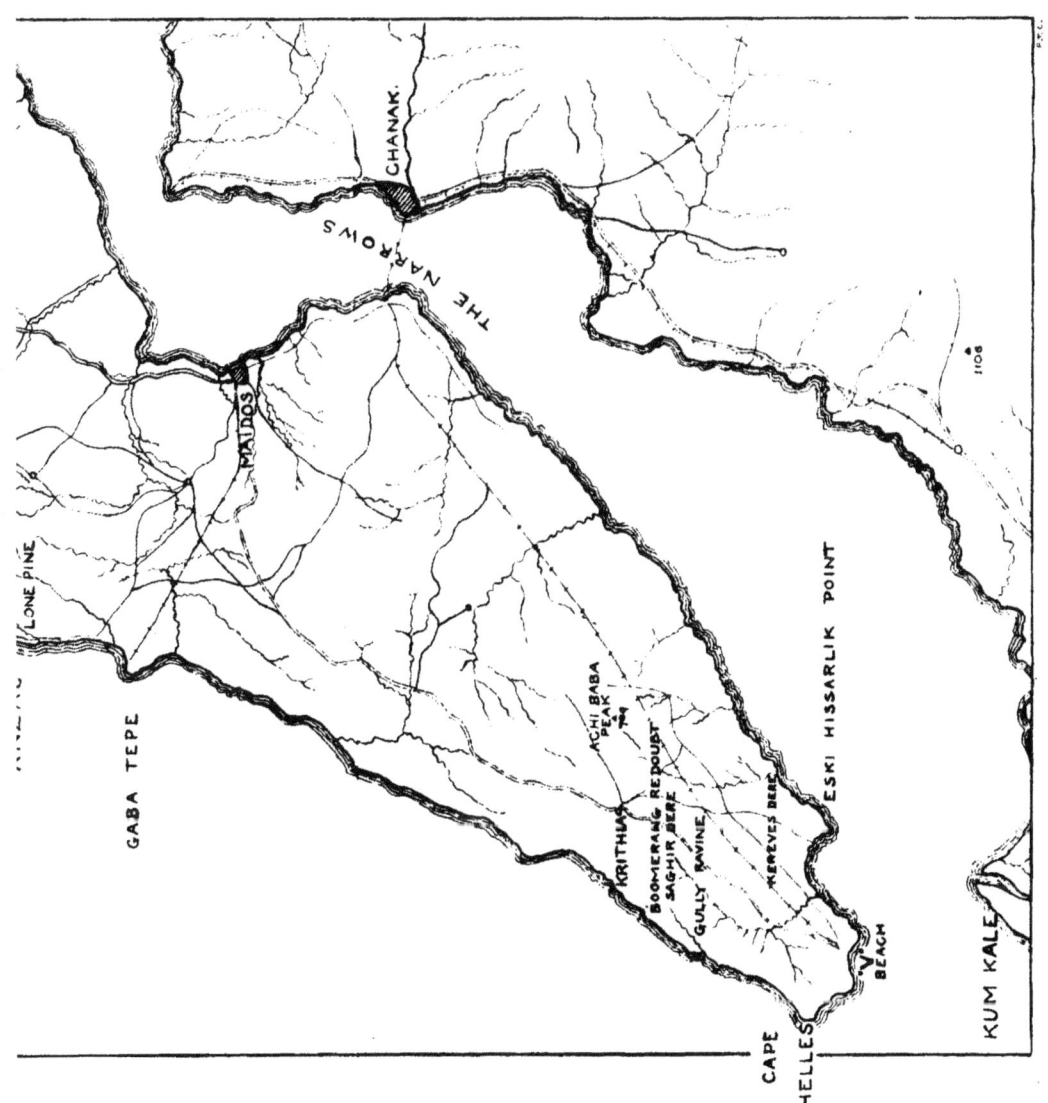

winter's evening. The men of the first party gradually left the trenches, and swiftly and silently made their way to North Beach, Anzac, where they packed themselves on board the lighter and were taken away. A similar procedure was followed in the case of the second party, and by midnight, of the Indian Brigade only eighty of the 1/5th and fifty of the 1/6th were left. An hour and a half must elapse before they were free to go. The tension was great, for should the Turks gain an inkling of the true state of affairs they were doomed men. Still, they fired their rifles and carried on in accordance with orders. At last, however, the word was given, and they, too, went their way, to embark from the piers just south of Asmak Dere. To the 1/5th was given the post of honour, one British officer and twenty-five Gurkha ranks remaining to cover the withdrawal. All went well, and long before daylight on the 20th the troops from Anzac and Suvla were aboard their ships and on their way to Mudros.

"Far called our navies melt away;
On dune and headland sinks the fire."

So ended the Dardanelles Campaign—a very glorious episode. That it should so end could not be other than a bitter disappointment, and the sympathy of all soldiers, of whatever school, must go out to the Commander-in-Chief, who had so nearly achieved victory, only to have it snatched from him through circumstances which neither he nor any other might foresee. For the Battalion there was consolation in the thought that it had maintained its reputation through difficulties and dangers greater than had to be faced by the men of Palosin and Peiwar Kotal, of Charasia and Nilt, and it could await with quiet confidence the next adventure which fate should bring.

CHAPTER VI

INDIA. ARRIVAL IN MESOPOTAMIA

The Evacuation Reviewed.
CALM after storm, and while the distance widens between the men of the 1/5th Gurkhas and the scene of their recent struggles, an opportunity is given to see how the closing episode of the campaign was regarded by those in a position to gauge its difficulties and its inherent dangers. On December 21st, 1915, a Special Order of the Day was published. It is given in full.

"The Commander-in-Chief desires to express to all ranks in the Dardanelles Army his unreserved appreciation for the way in which the recent operations, ending in the evacuation of the Anzac and Suvla positions, have been carried to an issue successful beyond his hopes. The arrangements made for withdrawal and for keeping the enemy in ignorance of the operation which was taking place could not have been improved.

"The General Officer commanding Dardanelles Army, and the General Officers commanding the Australian and New Zealand and 9th Army Corps, may pride themselves on an achievement without parallel in the annals of war. The Army and Corps staffs, Divisional and subordinate Commanders and their staffs, and the Naval and Military beach staffs proved themselves more than equal to the most difficult task which could have been thrown upon them. Regimental officers, non-commissioned officers, and men carried out without a hitch the most trying operation which soldiers can be called upon to undertake—a withdrawal in the face of the enemy—in a manner reflecting the highest credit on the discipline and soldierly qualities of the troops.

"It is no exaggeration to call this achievement one without parallel. To disengage and withdraw from a bold and active enemy is the most difficult of all military operations; and in this case the withdrawal was effected by surprise with the opposing forces at close grips, in many cases within a few yards of each other. Such an operation, when succeeded by a re-embarkation from an open beach, is one for which military history contains no precedent.

"During the past months the troops of Great Britain, Ireland, Australia and New Zealand, Newfoundland, and India, fighting side by side, have invariably proved their superiority over the enemy, have contained the best fighting troops of the Ottoman Army in their front, and have prevented the Germans from employing their Turkish allies against us elsewhere.

"No soldier relishes undertaking a withdrawal from before the enemy. It is hard to leave behind the graves of good comrades, and to relinquish positions so hardly won and so gallantly maintained as those we have left. But all ranks in the Dardanelles Army will realize that in this matter they were but carrying out the orders of His Majesty's Government so that they might in due course be more usefully employed in fighting elsewhere for their King, their Country, and the Empire.

"There is only one consideration—what is best for the furtherance of the common cause. In that spirit the withdrawal was carried out, and in that spirit the Australian and New Zealand and 9th Army Corps have proved, and will continue to prove themselves, second to none as soldiers of the Empire."

With that graciousness which we have grown to expect from the Royal House which we have the honour to serve, His Majesty the King sent a telegram:—

"It gives me the greatest satisfaction to hear of the successful evacuation of Anzac and Suvla without loss of troops or guns. Please convey to General Birdwood and those under his command my congratulations upon the able manner in which they have carried out so difficult an operation."

The congratulations of the Government were conveyed in a telegram from the Secretary of State for War, in which he expressed on their behalf "high appreciation of the excellence of the arrangements for the withdrawal from Anzac and Suvla, and their warm admiration for the conduct of the troops in carrying out the most difficult operation of war."

It remained, then, to go and fight elsewhere.

20-12-15 to 13-2-16. Egypt again.
On December 20th the Battalion arrived at Mudros and picked up the advance party which had left the Peninsula on the 14th. Sailing thence for Egypt in the *Knight Templar* they arrived at Alexandria on December 24th, disembarked on the 25th, and at once entrained for Suez, which was reached at 4.20 p.m. that day.

At this time the strength of the Battalion stood at 489, made up of 9 British officers, 18 Gurkha officers, and 462 Gurkha other ranks. Followers numbered 89. Between December 30th, 1915, and January 3rd, 1916, three drafts arrived from India, which brought up the strength to 14 British officers, 23 Gurkha officers, and 853

T

Gurkha other ranks. The new arrivals amongst British officers were Captain O. E. Todd, who had been in command of the depot at Abbottabad, Captain W. L. Hogg, and Second-Lieutenants Thomson, Trotter, and Bayldon.

There followed a difficult time for everybody. It needed conscious effort to combat the reaction following the previous stress, and many harassing problems of organization presented themselves for solution. Government acted generously in making good losses of personal kit and public equipment, though unavoidable delay occurred in the process of refitting. Then, too, many little presents were received from various sources which helped to mitigate discomfort. On January 22nd, 1916, the Battalion left Suez for post duty at El Kubri East; and there, on the 30th, they said good-bye to Major Tillard, and welcomed in his place Major Villiers-Stuart, who had at last succeeded in getting back to his own Regiment after months of hard fighting in the Ypres salient in command of the 9th Battalion of the Rifle Brigade. At El Kubri some training was undertaken, and the Sisyphus task was imposed of digging trenches in the sand, which, blown by the wind, promptly filled them in again. However, these apparently rather purposeless activities came to an end when orders were received to embark for India, and on February 13th the Battalion went on board the s.s. *Arankola*, which was lying at Port Tewfik.

It is well known to all who have had the pleasure of serving him that the Commander who won the affection and admiration, given in unstinted measure, of the Australian and New Zealand Army Corps, forgets nobody whom he has any excuse to remember, and, true to his reputation, Sir William Birdwood sent a letter to the Battalion, which arrived soon after embarkation.

" I am writing a line to thank you all so much for all the help you gave me at Anzac, and I can assure you that I am really sorry to think that you are no longer in my command. Will you please let the Regiment know how much I look forward to having the good fortune of serving with them again some day."

The receipt of such a letter at this juncture was heartening, and went far towards dispelling the feeling of disappointment engendered by recent happenings.

*India,
February,* 1916,
to March, 1917.

The *Arankola* reached Karachi on February 24th, and there the Battalion took train for Peshawar, which was found to be its immediate destination. Eighteen months of war appeared to have effected but little change in the general outlook in India, and it seemed to occur to few that some slight demonstration of enthusiasm over the return of a battalion which had been considerably knocked about in Gallipoli would not have been out of place. Not all, however, were indifferent. When the train reached Rawalpindi, Sir Gerald Kitson, commanding the Rawalpindi Division, was on the platform. He had come to the station on purpose to see how it had fared with one of his old battalions in its adventures overseas, and he was not unmoved by the changes which time had wrought. Soon after the arrival of the Battalion in Peshawar on February 27th, an arrival which entailed detrainment in the dark, it was further cheered by a message of welcome from His Excellency, the Commander-in-Chief, who telegraphed to the commanding officer:—

"My heartiest welcome to you and all ranks under your command on your return from field service where all have so gallantly and devotedly maintained the best traditions of the Indian Army."

The main reason for the return of the Battalion to India was to enable it to reorganize and refit, and, indeed, the need was great. To facilitate the work the depot was transferred from Abbottabad to Peshawar, and with it came records, stores, and equipment, and a contingent of recruits numbering close on one thousand. Our allies of Nepal had made a noble response to our urgent call for men, but it was a great strain on their resources, and so it came about that recruits were of all ages and of varying standards of physique. Though the impossibility was realized of retaining, under existing conditions, only those who satisfied previous requirements, some weeding out was essential, and during April and May nearly three hundred recruits were discharged as unlikely to become efficient soldiers. Even so, a photograph of the Battalion taken just before it left Peshawar in May, 1916, shows 1,561 of all ranks on parade. Other urgent work comprised the settlement of accounts, adjustment of promotion rolls, applications for family pensions and wound pensions, dispatch to their homes of men discharged, the resubmission of recommendations for honours and awards, and other items too numerous to find mention here. The way of reorganization was beset with many stumbling-blocks, not least among them the scarcity of British officers who had been given an opportunity either to become acquainted with their men or to learn the administrative methods obtaining in the Indian Army. For this the magnitude of the war, with its unprecedented demands on personnel, was alone responsible; the spirit of the Battalion had undergone no change, and eventually the difficulties were overcome and the desired result attained.

An interruption occurred on March 16th, when little more than two weeks after arrival the Battalion marched to Dag, on the road to Cherat, to take part in hill manœuvres. On its return to Peshawar ten days later the work was resumed.

On April 26th Lieutenant-Colonel M. R. W. Nightingale, D.S.O., rejoined, having recovered from wounds sustained on the fateful June 4th, and took over command from Major Villiers-Stuart, whose talents were to be used in a wider field. Leaving Peshawar on May 12th he went to Abbottabad to organize a short course in mountain warfare for Territorial officers and N.C.O.'s, and on May 26th he was appointed Supervising Officer of the Nepalese Contingent at Kakul.

Lieutenant-Colonel Nightingale, D.S.O., takes over Command, April, 1916

It will not be out of place to quote here a telegram from the New Zealanders of Anzac sent to the Secretary of State for War, and forwarded to the Battalion through Army Headquarters at this time:—

" On this anniversary of our great adventure may we New Zealanders tender our tribute to the immortal and glorious valour of the Indian troops with whom we had the honour of serving."

Perhaps too little has been said in the preceding chapters regarding the relations established with these splendid fighters. After August 5th contact was frequent, and the Gurkhas of the Brigade, no less than their British officers, formed a very high opinion of their qualities.

Fortunately for the Battalion it was not to be called upon to spend a hot weather in Peshawar, and May 24th found it marching into Abbottabad after an absence of eighteen months. The work of reorganization was not yet by any means complete, and was continued throughout the summer, while the requirements of training were met by the formation of summer camps, companies being accommodated at Huli-Ka-Danna and Nimbal, and the recruits, to the number of six hundred, at Banda Qazi.

The Battalion Returns to Abbottabad, May, 1916.

It was in the cold weather of 1916–17 that Government initiated the policy of increasing the number of Gurkha battalions in the Indian Army. To the first new battalion to be formed—known originally as the 1st Reserve Battalion of Gurkha Rifles, but afterwards to become the 4/3rd Gurkha Rifles—the 1/5th Gurkhas were required to contribute their quota of men, and accordingly in September two hundred Gurkha officers and Gurkha other ranks left for Rawalpindi, the spot selected to serve as the nursery of the infant unit. Eventually all Gurkha regiments were provided with a third battalion, with the exception of the 4th Gurkhas, who, however, were probably intended to lend their name to one of the two new battalions to which the 3rd Gurkhas stood *in loco parentis*. The recruiting resources of Nepal were further strained by the raising of four battalions of the 11th Gurkha Rifles. On their disbandment, a fate which they shared in common with all the new battalions after the war, the 4/3rd Gurkhas presented to the 1/5th, as one of its progenitors, an unusually handsome cup, which may now be seen in the mess.

With October the period of comparative rest came to an end, for on the 8th of the month the Battalion moved to Nowshera to take a hand in the Mohmand Blockade. A general idea of what was happening on that part of the frontier is to be gained from an extract taken from General Sir Charles Monro's despatch of July 23rd, 1917:—

Mohmand Blockade, October, 1916.

"During the last half of 1916 the attitude of some of the Mohmands became distinctly hostile, and a number of raids were made across the border into the Peshawar area. To prevent these raids, and as a punishment, a blockade was instituted along the Mohmand border and a chain of blockhouses, connected by a wire fence, was constructed and manned."

On arrival at Nowshera the 1/5th Gurkhas formed part of the 3rd Brigade under the command of Major-General Nigel Woodyatt, C.B., to which had been allotted the rôle of an advance into the Mohmand country should this prove advisable. In the event, the necessity for a forward move by the brigade did not arise, for Shabkadr being threatened by a large gathering of tribesmen on November 14th, on the 15th Lieutenant-General Sir Frederick Campbell, using the 1st and 2nd Brigades, attacked and dispersed the *lashkar*. So far-reaching was his action in its effect that the tribesmen, having returned to their homes, attempted no further concentration, and the 3rd Brigade remained in the vicinity of Nowshera until February 9th, 1917. On that day it relieved the 2nd Brigade in the blockade line, the Battalion taking over from the 95th Infantry three company sectors lying between Michni and Shabkadr, with battalion headquarters and the reserve at Subhan Khwar.

Under the normal system in force for the maintenance of the blockade a month would have been spent in the line. Actually the 1/5th Gurkhas had barely settled down to their spell of watch and ward when, on February 11th, orders came in to mobilize for a second period of service overseas.

On February 12th Lieutenant-Colonel E. B. C. Boddam, still very lame from his wound, rejoined and assumed command. He was not destined to stay long, however, in command of a Battalion of his own Regiment, for to his own regret and that of all ranks his injury prevented him, as yet, from taking part in an arduous campaign, and he was shortly afterwards transferred as Commandant of the 3rd Battalion of the 6th Gurkhas.

On February 14th, on relief by the 72nd Punjabis, the Battalion marched to Nowshera, where it made a short stay of three days before entraining for Abbottabad. Barely three weeks were allowed for mobilization, and on March 12th a new adventure was inaugurated with the march to Havelian and entrainment there for Karachi. Those taking part were 13 British officers, 17 Gurkha officers, 981 Gurkha other ranks, and 77 followers. The names of the British officers are of interest, if only to show the changes imposed by two years of war. They were Lieutenant-Colonel M. R. W. Nightingale (commanding); Major W. Evans, 1st Gurkhas; Major F. L. S. Brett, 7th Gurkhas; Captain K. C. S. Erskine, M.C. (Adjutant); Captain N. R. C. Cosby, M.C.; Lieutenant H. D. H. Y. Nepean, Lieutenant J. D. H. Cook, Second-Lieutenant C. S. Baker, Second-Lieutenant W. B. O. Fox, Second-Lieutenant J. W. W. Tregale, Second-Lieutenant K. J. Mackintosh, and Second-Lieutenant A. P. Q. Thomson. Lieutenant U. J. Bourke, I.M.S., was Medical Officer. Of them all only Lieutenant-Colonel Nightingale and Captain Erskine had been of the number which left Abbottabad for Egypt in November, 1914, and both had been seriously wounded in Gallipoli.

Embarkation at Karachi, March 15th, 1917.
The Battalion reached Karachi early on March 15th, and later in the day embarked on the transport *Elephanta*. She formed one of a convoy of eight vessels which sailed next day under the escort of H.M.S. *Pyramus*. The Gulf of Oman was reached on the 19th, and the safety of the convoy being assured during its passage up the Gulf, the *Pyramus* left the units composing it to make their own way to Basra. The *Elephanta*, however, was detained to receive Lieutenant-General Sir George Kirkpatrick, Chief of the Staff in India, who had voyaged thus far in the escorting ship. A rough sea necessitated putting in to the island of Kishm on the northern side of the Gulf, and there Sir George Kirkpatrick came on board. Steaming thence as soon as the transfer had been effected, the *Elephanta* arrived off the well-known bar, fourteen miles from the mouth of the Shatt-el-Arab, early on the 21st. The tide serving, she was able to cross at once, and reached Basra at 3.30 p.m. For lack of a vacant berth she remained at the anchorage until the morning of the 22nd, when she moved four miles upstream to Magil, where the Battalion disembarked.

Arrival in Mesopotamia. March 22nd, 1917.
With the Battalion safely landed in Mesopotamia the question naturally arises, " What brought it there ? " To find an answer it is necessary to recall the sequence of events prior to its arrival, and in doing so the temptation to touch, however lightly, on the thorny topic of side-shows will be firmly resisted.

Review of Events in Mesopotamia up to Arrival of Battalion.
When on October 16th, 1914, the 16th Indian Infantry Brigade of the Poona Division left India, war with Turkey had not been declared, and its objective—not, however, made known until after it had sailed—was no more than the island of Abadan, where it

would be in a position to protect the pipe line and refineries of the Anglo-Persian Oil Company, suppliers of oil to the Royal Navy, and where, it was hoped, its presence would counter anti-British propaganda intended to produce disturbances in the oil area. War with Turkey was declared on November 5th, 1914, and on the 6th, Brigadier-General W. S. Delamain, commanding the 16th Brigade, took Fao. With Turkey in the field the protection of the oil supply entailed stronger action and greater force, so the remainder of the 6th (Poona) Division, held in readiness against this contingency, was sent from India. It was commanded by Lieutenant-General Sir A. A. Barrett, one of the Regiment's most distinguished officers, and while he held the reins the rôle of Force "D" was confined to the fulfilment of the object originally governing its dispatch, and there were no untoward incidents. Basra was occupied on November 21st, and, as vital to its security, Qurna was taken, and the surrender accepted of the Commander of the 38th Turkish Division on December 9th. Followed the Turkish attempt to recapture Basra, which was defeated at the Battle of Shaiba on April 12th, 13th, and 14th, 1915. Ere this, the decision had been taken to increase the strength of Expeditionary Force "D" to that of an army corps, and to enlarge the scope of its operations to include control of the whole of the Basra Vilayet. One result of this decision was the return to India of Sir Arthur Barrett and the assumption of the command of the army-corps-to-be by General Sir John Nixon.

The effective control of the Basra Vilayet entailed an extension of the radius of activity to Amara at least on the Tigris, and to Nasiriya on the Euphrates. Amara, the town itself, was captured by Major-General C. V. Townshend almost single-handed on June 3rd, and the formidable resistance offered by the Turks at Nasiriya was finally overcome by Major-General G. F. Gorringe with the 12th Division on July 25th.

After much discussion, from the existing records of which it would appear that the authorities in India were strongly in favour of a policy involving offensive action, while the India Office sought to curb their enthusiasm, a further advance up the Tigris was undertaken, with Baghdad as the objective. On September 28th, 1915, General Townshend with the 6th Division defeated the Turks at the Battle of Es-Sinn or Kut, and he reached the high-water mark of his success in the early stages of the Battle of Ctesiphon between November 22nd and 24th. Then came the turn of the tide. The Turks were reinforced; General Townshend had not troops enough to meet them, nor transport sufficient to maintain himself so far from his base, and on November 25th he began his retreat.

December 3rd was the fateful day on which the 6th Division

entered Kut-al-Amara, and by December 7th four Turkish divisions, in addition to Cavalry, had closed in on the place, cutting off retreat. This sudden and unlooked-for blow to our prestige demanded urgent action; two brigades with certain additional troops were sent from India, the 3rd and 7th Divisions arrived from France, and, certain necessary adjustments completed, were organized as the Tigris Corps under the command of Lieutenant-General Sir Fenton Aylmer for the relief of Kut. Misinformed concerning the resources of the beleaguered garrison, General Aylmer was forced to act prematurely; in rapid succession were fought the Battle of Shaikh Saad from January 6th to the 9th, 1916, the Battle of the Wadi on January 13th, and the Battle of Hanna on January 21st; but despite the determination of the Commander and the heroism of the troops, the Turks still barred the way to Kut. There ensued a pause in the operations. General Sir Percy Lake had succeeded General Sir John Nixon in chief command, the corps had suffered severely at the last-named battle, and the belated discovery was made that food supplies in Kut would last well into April. For its quality of tragic failure with success in sight the Battle of Dujaila, fought on March 8th, bears comparison with the early August fighting in Gallipoli. Only the necessary permission to the 37th Brigade when they asked for it, or orders to Column "B" to push on into the empty redoubt; only one of these alternatives was lacking, or victory was assured.

General Townshend cut off at Kut-al-Amara, December, 1915.

After the battle General Gorringe succeeded General Aylmer in command of the Tigris Corps, and there followed a further period of consolidation and hard manual labour imposed by the threat of floods. In the end it was the flood peril which turned the scale in favour of the Turks. The corps again took the offensive on April 5th, when the Hanna position being found without defenders, the 13th Division, new arrivals at the Tigris front, pushed on and captured the Fallahiya trenches after dark. Under the handicap of storm and flood the next lines at Sannaiyat proved too strong, despite determined attacks against them from April 6th to 9th, and accordingly attention was turned to the right bank. No greater success, however, attended the enterprise against Bait Isa on April 17th. A last despairing effort was made on April 22nd, the Sannaiyat position again forming the objective, but was frustrated through the agency of mud and water. Kut fell on April 29th.

Kut Falls, April 29th, 1916.

The very day which witnessed the closing episode in the tragedy of Kut-al-Amara saw the Second Battalion of the Regiment set out on their desert march to Nasiriya. They had arrived at Basra from India on March 13th during the breathing-spell which followed after Dujaila, and their transfer to Nasiriya was occasioned by fears for the safety of that place, to which the approach down the Shatt-el-Hai was opened for the Turks through the fall of Kut, situated as it is at the point where the affluent leaves the Tigris.

While there had been a prospect of saving Kut the rôle of Force "D" had been governed by the urgency of that problem. The necessity for wiping out the stigma attaching to the surrender governed in great measure its future action, though the wisdom of advancing to Baghdad still remained in dispute. General Lake never for a moment relaxed his efforts to create a sound organization, and to his unremitting toil were largely due the victories gained by his successor.

General Maude takes over Chief Command, August, 1916.

In July, 1916, the War Office took over the direction of affairs in Mesopotamia, and on August 28th Lieutenant-General F. S. Maude succeeded General Lake in chief command. Among many other changes perhaps the most notable was the appointment of Major-General A. S. Cobbe to the command of the Tigris Corps. All through the hot weather and on into the winter the work of reorganization went forward until in early December all was in readiness for further operations. The mistake was not made of looking too far ahead, for it was decided, as a first step, to try only for a footing on the Hai on the Tigris line, and, should a favourable opportunity occur on the Euphrates, to occupy Samawa.

The Offensive after the Fall of Kut, December, 1916.

The offensive was initiated on December 14th, 1916. The force had now been organized into two corps. Of these, speaking very roughly, the I Corps under General Cobbe faced west on the left bank of the Tigris, which here flows generally from west to east, while the III Corps was on the right bank facing north. Before the I Corps lay the still immensely strong Turkish position of Sannaiyat, and part of its rôle was to pin the enemy there during active operations undertaken by the remainder of the force farther upstream. On December 14th, 1916, a footing was secured on the Hai. Thence, working gradually westwards, the Khudhaira Bend was added to our gains by January 19th, 1917. The next objective became the Turkish salient immediately opposite Kut, the capture of which by February 4th resulted in the withdrawal of all enemy forces to the left bank. Attention was then turned to the Sannaiyat position. After an unsuccessful attempt to capture it on February 17th, it fell to a combined movement on February 22nd, when the I Corps attacked it in front, and the III Corps operated against the Shumran Bend, upstream of Kut.

It is no exaggeration to say that the fate of Baghdad was decided at Sannaiyat. Turkish rear-guards did wonders during the pursuit, and there was, further, the delay of the Diyala crossing, in connection with which March 8th will always be remembered for the heroism displayed by the Loyal North Lancashire; but, short of extensive inundation, which was not attempted, no effort of the enemy could now stop the advance, and Baghdad was entered on March 11th. General Maude's successes had resulted in an extension of the political project, which was now to include the security of the Baghdad Vilayet. So far no mention has been made of the Russians under Baratoff, who were in touch with the Turkish XIII Corps in Persian territory, but a reference to them becomes necessary because the desire to co-operate with them affected decisions taken at this stage. The fulfilment of these two objects—the security, that is, of the Baghdad Vilayet and co-operation with the Russians—necessitated action in several directions, and when the 1/5th Gurkhas arrived in Basra on March 22nd, 1917, the situation was as follows.

Baghdad Taken, March, 1917.

The 7th Infantry Brigade Group was at Faluja, on the Euphrates. The 21st Brigade was at Mushaida, on the right bank of the Tigris, having been left there after the successful action fought in the vicinity on March 14th by the I Corps, of which the remainder had since returned to Baghdad. The 40th Brigade Group was at Daudiya, guarding the bunds on the left bank of the Tigris upstream of Baghdad.

Situation, March 22nd, 1917.

Keary's column, consisting of the 3rd Division less one brigade, with Cavalry, was about to enter Shahraban on its way to join hands with the Russians, who were approaching from Karind.

Nasiriya was still held by the 15th Division, to which belonged General Lucas's 42nd Brigade, of which the 2nd Battalion formed part.

Of the operations following the capture of Baghdad it is the occupation of Faluja which is the main concern of this narrative, since it was the prelude to those major actions on the Euphrates in which the 1/5th Gurkhas was to play its part.

CHAPTER VII

MESOPOTAMIA. THE BATTLE OF RAMADI

The Battalion sets off for Baghdad, March 29th, 1917.

As always happened during the war, no matter how completely equipped a unit might be on leaving India, on arrival in a new theatre of operations it would inevitably lack certain essentials required to meet local conditions; and so it was with the 1/5th Gurkhas on arrival in Mesopotamia. The week spent at Magil was fully occupied in making adjustments imposed by the Mesopotamia scale. Complete readiness was achieved by March 29th, and on that date the Battalion embarked on a riversteamer known as the P.S. 60, and on two barges which, in accordance with river transport usage, were attached one on the port and one on the starboard side. Destined for Baghdad, where great events were in train, the hopes of immediate employment rose high; and that nothing might be lacking to stimulate enthusiasm, while embarkation was still in progress the 2nd Battalion arrived from Nasiriya, bringing with them the welcome news that the two battalions would serve together in the 42nd Brigade commanded by that distinguished 5th Gurkha officer, Brigadier-General Lucas, D.S.O.

The love of travel is the common heritage of man, but on the Tigris the point of satiety is soon reached. Long before, the scenery of Mesopotamia had been summed up by an English soldier in a masterpiece of word-painting which may not be quoted here. The battlefields of a year before were passed in turn, and there was little left to tell of the tragedy each had staged. The monotony of the journey was broken on April 5th, when the P.S. 60 dropped her rudder. She was thus reduced to steering by means of her paddles, and this so retarded her progress that on the 6th the Battalion was enabled to carry out a route-march to Ctesiphon, and to meet her, shorn of the barge in which had been accommodated the mules, no farther upstream than Bostan on the return journey. The men on board again, the advanced base at Baghdad was reached later in the morning, and thence a move was made back to Hinaidi, which had been chosen as the temporary abiding place of the 42nd Brigade composed of the 1/4th Dorsets, the two battalions of the Regiment, and the 2/6th Gurkhas.

It was at Hinaidi on April 9th, while large working-parties were realigning the camp, that Lieutenant H. D. H. Y. Nepean performed the gallant action which earned for him the bronze medal of the Royal Humane Society. A number of men were bathing and washing at the edge of the river, which here runs deep and swift close in to the bank. One, Udbir Gurung, lost his footing and was carried into the stream. He was soon in difficulties, and by the time the alarm was given to Lieutenant Nepean, who was standing fully dressed near by, he had disappeared beneath the surface. Clothed as he was, Nepean jumped in, swam out, and dived for the drowning man. At his first attempt he failed to find him, but, continuing his efforts at grave risk to himself, he eventually succeeded in locating him, and brought him to land.

The rest of April was spent at Hinaidi, and nothing occurred to disturb the routine of training except that on April 13th a warning order was received requiring the Battalion to be ready to move to Baquba, on the Diyala at very short notice. The reason for the order is perhaps to be found in the situation fifty miles north of Baghdad, where, between the Adhaim and the Diyala, General Marshall was operating against the Turkish XIII Corps. After a successful action near Shaila on April 11th he had driven them eastwards onto their entrenched position at Arab-bu-Abin, twenty miles north of Baquba, but an attack carried out against that position on the 13th had failed to dislodge the Turks. On the 15th, however, the latter withdrew of their own accord, and on that day news reached Hinaidi that the prospective move to Baquba had been cancelled.

The Battalion's first taste of active service under Mesopotamian conditions came in the form of a punitive expedition against the Karud Arabs, the area of operations lying on the left bank of the Euphrates some distance to the south-east of Faluja. Instigated, apparently, by the Turks, this section had proved troublesome ever since our occupation of Faluja in March and of Mufraz in early April, until, in the latter month, their misdeeds culminated in the murder of Lieutenant-Colonel Magniac of the 27th Punjabis.

Lucas Column Operations Commence, May 2nd.

The order for the move of Lucas column, the force of all arms under Brigadier-General F. G. Lucas constituted for the purpose of exacting reparations, was issued on May 2nd. Besides the 42nd Brigade (less the 2/5th Gurkhas, who were otherwise employed), the column comprised two squadrons 14th Hussars, 215th Battery R.F.A., 14th L.A.M. Battery, one section Malerkotla Sappers and Miners, and the 130th Machine Gun Company. The plan was to make for Mufraz, the Euphrates terminus of the Decauville railway connecting that river with Baghdad, and thence to move northwards in the direction of the Radwaniya Canal, what time a similar force known as Haldane's column operated southwards from Faluja against the same objective.

The three battalions of the 42nd Brigade left Hinaidi at 2.30 a.m. on May 3rd, and picked up the other units of the column at the Iron Bridge, three miles west of Baghdad. At 9 a.m. a halt was called at no great distance from Tel Raml, but at 4 p.m. the column moved off again to continue marching for another three hours before settling down for the night beside a small stream of which the name has not been preserved. An early start on May 4th resulted in the force reaching Mufraz at 2 p.m., after a hot and dusty march of seventeen miles. The serious business of the expedition began next day, May 5th. With the 1/5th Gurkhas leading, and "B" Company forming the advanced guard, a move was made to Imam Hamza, five miles north of Mufraz, as a prelude to further operations.

There the column formed on a broad front and headed for a hostile village known as Khan Maqdam, which lay four miles farther northwards. During this advance the 2/6th Gurkhas, who were on the left flank, destroyed a Karud village which lay in their path, and sustained one casualty, the result of the explosion of ammunition in a burning house. Meanwhile "C" Company of the Battalion, which was on the right of the line of march, succeeded in rounding up about fifty head of cattle. Otherwise the advance was without incident, and on reaching Khan Maqdam the column halted for the night. Next day, May 6th, the forward movement was continued with the object of driving the enemy, whom it was hoped to find in the neighbourhood of the Radwaniya Canal, onto Haldane's column coming from the north. The 14th Hussars were given the task of closing the way of escape eastwards into the desert, the opposite flank being already blocked by the river. Touch with Haldane's column was established at about 7.30 a.m., and it has to be admitted that the Arabs had succeeded in escaping the trap, for apart from the Artillery and machine-guns, which found a long-range target, and the 14th Hussars, who encountered and engaged with fire a party of about one hundred strong, no unit of the force found an excuse to fire a round. After joining hands the energies of both columns were directed to the destruction of the property of the recalcitrant tribe, with the result, at the end of the day, that to the credit side of the expedition could be placed the death of the principal sheikh and of six other Arabs, the total destruction of two villages with some 500 acres of crops, and the capture of 400 head of cattle and 20,000 rounds of ammunition—this last being mainly of French manufacture. Besides the 2/6th casualty already mentioned, one man of the 14th Hussars was also wounded.

The Advance on Khan Maqdam, May 5th.

Early on May 7th Haldane's column returned to Faluja and Lucas column to Mufraz. The latter halted at Mufraz on the 8th, as there was a possibility that its services might be required in the direction of Hilla, thirty-five miles to the south. That possibility, however, did not materialize, so on the 9th a start was made for Hinaidi and Baghdad, and covering thirty-two miles in two days the 42nd Brigade reached its old camp on May 10th. From the Battalion point of view the expedition was useful in that it afforded proof that the men had quickly become acclimatized. Though the War Diary dealing with this period bristles with the entry, " dusty and very hot," they showed themselves well able to withstand the adverse conditions.

Back to Hinaidi, May 10th.

Less than a week had passed when on May 16th Lucas column was again called upon. Its mission on this occasion was the punishment of an Arab tribe inhabiting the country about Samaikcheh—which lies west of the Tigris about forty miles north of Baghdad—the need for retribution arising from the murder by that tribe of Lieutenant Stables and twenty men of the 47th Sikhs while employed as escort to a survey party.

Lucas Column, Further Operations.

The operations differed little in character from those previously undertaken against the Karud Arabs, but the marches were generally longer, the days were even hotter, and the water available, though plentiful enough at halting-places, was far from palatable. The column concentrated and set out on its northward march on the evening of May 16th, and next day received a most useful, not to say essential, addition to its strength in the 7th Cavalry Brigade, for under prevailing conditions it was impossible for burdened Infantry without the help of mounted troops to retain contact with an unburdened and elusive enemy bent only on melting away. On the 18th the force reached Khor Tarmiya, a small lake about six miles south of Samaikcheh, and from this point certain movements were undertaken to give effect to the plan of operations. Briefly, this was to ring an area of country with the object of rounding up as many as possible of the enemy, and then, closing inwards, to capture livestock and destroy property. To the 8th Brigade from Samaikcheh was given the task of stopping the northern boundary of the area to be enclosed, while one of the remaining sides was effectively guarded by the Tigris. It fell to the 42nd Brigade to block the southern side, and to the Cavalry Brigade to close the way of escape to the west.

After a halt of a few hours at Khor Tarmiya, Lucas column, which now included the Cavalry, moved westwards at 11 p.m. The Infantry having taken up the positions allotted to it, the Cavalry turned north, and, before complete encirclement had been effected, gained contact with a number of the enemy. The results of the expedition may be summarized as a loss to the enemy of sixty killed, the capture of 2,500 head of cattle, and the destruction of much valuable property. Following on two days' halt at the lake-side camp, of which the second was occasioned by a dust-storm which fairly prevented movement, the return march was begun, and the Battalion reached Hinaidi on May 24th. Colonel Nightingale's war diary entry, summarizing conditions in the month of May, is illuminating. It reads: "General health of the Battalion during May was good. Maximum temp. varied from 96° to 104° N.W. winds and dust-storms frequent."

Summer, 1917. The vigorous measures initiated by General Maude had by this time secured Baghdad against the danger of flooding and had cleared the *vilayet* of Turkish forces. The increasing heat forbade further operations, and the army in Mesopotamia prepared to endure as well as possible the burden of the summer. The 42nd Brigade remained at Hinaidi until June 3rd, when it moved to Karada, one and a half miles nearer to Baghdad.

Despite the steadily rising temperature, much hard work was done. A rifle range was made by the Battalion, large working-parties were employed in connection with the Hinaidi–Baquba railway, then under construction, and a complete system of trenches for occupation by a brigade was dug in order that trench warfare might be practised. The steady rise of the mercury in the thermometer was of chief interest during this period. While the daily minimum as recorded inside large double-fly tents remained fairly constant at something between 70° F. and 80° F., the maximum had reached the 110° F. mark by the end of June, and 126° F. on one particular day about the middle of July. Fortunately the health of the men seemed little impaired, and such cases of sickness as did occur were mainly to be attributed to sandfly fever. For the greater part of this period of awaiting the resumption of the offensive, Lieutenant-Colonel Nightingale was acting as Brigade Commander. He returned to the Battalion, however, on August 17th, and it was then that Major Brett, who had been officiating for him, left to command for a month or so the 1/2nd Gurkhas at Baquba.

Events prior to Ramadi. On September 4th the Battalion was re-armed with high-velocity rifles, and the newly constructed range was much in request in order to ensure for each man an opportunity to acquaint himself with the idiosyncrasies of his particular weapon. That acquaintance was made only just in time, for great events were toward, and on the 14th warning was given for a move at short notice to a destination which was not made known. Baggage was limited to operation scale, which meant twenty pounds for officers and ten pounds for other ranks, and no tentage was to be taken. These orders entailed dumping the surplus at Hinaidi Rest Camp, and on the 15th all was in readiness. Though kept in ignorance of the fact, the Battalion had now been drawn into the current of events which was to bear it to Ramadi, but before passing on to the battle it is advisable to glance at the general situation as it existed at this time.

When at the end of the previous cold weather active operations had been suspended owing to the heat, the three bodies of Turks opposing the British in Mesopotamia had been driven back—one along the line of the Diyala to a position on the Jebel Hamrin range, one up the Tigris to a distance of nearly twenty miles north of Samarra, and one along the Euphrates to Ramadi. During the summer it was found that our occupation of Faluja did not adequately safeguard the country between the Tigris and Euphrates against the danger of inundation, and accordingly on July 8th the 7th Brigade Group reached out from Faluja and secured Dhibban, whence it dominated the junction of the Sakhlawiya Canal with the main river.

The First Attempt on Ramadi.

Having gone so far there seemed good reason to try for Ramadi, at that time but lightly held by the Turks. The attack was launched on July 11th, and was making progress when an interruption occurred in the form of a furious dust-storm. That blew itself out, but only to be followed by an abnormal rise in temperature, in face of which it would have been madness to call for further exertion on the part of the troops engaged. A withdrawal was effected during the night to Mushaid, and after waiting there in the faint hope that the Turk would release his hold, only to discover that such was not his intention, on July 14th the much-enduring force moved back to Dhibban.

Our abandoned attempt on Ramadi was regarded by the Arabs as a set-back, and it may be that the desire to restore our prestige was one reason why the opening gambit of the renewed offensive took the form of a move against that place.

Movement on any large scale was for the time being precluded by the intense heat, and it was not till the middle of September that it became sufficiently cool to render the operation practicable. The interval passed without incident, and the War Diary records nothing but a series of high temperatures. On September 15th Major F. L. S. Brett rejoined from temporary command of the 1/2nd Gurkhas.

Preparations for the Second Attempt on Ramadi, September, 1917.

Madhij was chosen as the place of concentration for the operations against the Ramadi position, and the necessary movement orders came through on September 14th. Two days were allowed for preparation and for the disposal of surplus baggage, and on the 16th at 4.45 a.m., 15th Divisional Headquarters and the 42nd Brigade left Baghdad. Halts were made at

Khan Nuktah (17th), Faluja (18th), and Tel Sina Dhibban (19th). The last was our most advanced post on the Euphrates front. On the 20th the 1/5th with a section of field guns formed advanced guard to the column, which reached Madhij without opposition. A distant Turkish patrol was all that was seen of the enemy.

At Madhij the 1/5th took up an outpost position extending from the Euphrates in a semicircle for one and a half miles, with three companies in the line and "C" Company in reserve. They were relieved by the 1/4th Dorsets on the morning of the 21st. The same day there were signs of Arab activity, and a piquet of the 97th Infantry on the left bank of the river was rushed, sustaining several casualties and losing a Lewis gun. On the 23rd the 1/5th moved into a new camp closer to Madhij, and here the same night Major Erskine had the misfortune to be shot through the wrist by a sentry while inspecting the outpost line, the right sector of which was held by "A" and "D" Companies.

On September 25th the 12th Brigade, which had been one march behind, arrived, and completed the concentration of the 15th Division for the attack on Ramadi. The following extract from Sir Stanley Maude's despatches of October 15th, 1917, shows the enemy dispositions and outlines General Brooking's plan:—

"The enemy held an advanced position four miles east of Ramadi on Mushaid Ridge, which runs north and south, and rises some sixty feet above the plain. To the north of the ridge lies the Euphrates River, and to the south the salt Habbaniyeh Lake. The Turkish main position was semicircular in outline, and was sited about one mile to the east and to the south of Ramadi. The eastern front ran along, but behind, the Euphrates Valley Canal, and the southern front across bare sandy downs extending from the Euphrates Valley Canal to the Aziziyeh Canal, which leaves the Euphrates one mile west of Ramadi and flows south. The plan of operations was to turn the southern flank of the Mushaid Ridge, secure a crossing over the Euphrates Valley Canal, and attack Ramadi from the south with the bulk of the column, while the Cavalry operating west of the Aziziyeh Canal threw themselves across the enemy's communications with Hit by blocking the Aleppo Road. Steps were taken to induce the enemy to expect the main attack against his left on the Euphrates, and with this intent the river was bridged at Madhij, and a road was constructed thence up the left bank, while supplies were also collected there."

Description of Terrain. The main action was fought between the Habbaniyeh Escape, which was a large canal two miles beyond the Mushaid Ridge, and the Aziziyeh Canal 1,500 yards farther west. The latter was crossed by a masonry bridge near its junction with the river. It was made passable for

Cavalry after a little work at a point almost due west of the roadway across the Escape. Between the two canals the country held six main features marking roughly the limits of the three stages of the battle. To the right and just west of the roadway across the Escape was Escape Hill, a knoll thirty feet high, which later became the headquarters of the 42nd Brigade. In line with this knoll, and about 1,000 yards to the west of it, was another rise somewhat more prominent, and this eventually formed 12th Brigade headquarters. A mile and a half farther north was a low-lying ridge called "Middle Hill," the west end of which was known as "Double Hill." About 1,700 yards north of this lay Ramadi Ridge on the right and Sheikh Farajah on the left, the village of Ramadi being in a grove of date-palms on the bank of the Euphrates 1,000 yards to the north of the saddle which connected the Ramadi Ridge and Sheikh Farajah.

To the west of the Aziziyeh Canal was a plain encircled on the south and west by a ring of low hills. The highest of these was two miles west of Ramadi, 300 yards from the river, and was called "Cavalry Hill." It was at this point that the Cavalry Brigade took up a position from which it successfully cut the enemy off from Hit, thirty miles to the north.

The Battle of Ramadi, Sept. 28th, 1917. The 42nd Brigade marched from Madhij at 6.30 p.m. on September 27th, and reached the position of assembly at nine o'clock. It then moved forward a mile and a half across the plain in bright moonlight, and arrived unopposed at the position of deployment. No further advance was contemplated for the moment, and a line was taken up along First Knoll and Lower Knoll, and entrenched. Heavy firing was heard in the front line, caused by an enterprising attack by the 2/6th Gurkhas, who had moved across the Escape, surprised a strong Arab post, and secured the roadway by which the column was to have crossed and attacked the next day. Early the following morning the 2/6th occupied Escape Hill, where they were shortly afterwards relieved by the 32nd Pioneers, who had come up during the night to prepare and improve the road.

At 5.30 on the morning of the 28th the 1/4th Dorsets and the 2/6th Gurkhas attacked and captured the Mushaid Ridge. They were heavily shelled during the advance, but sustained few casualties. As they reached their objective the enemy retired, evidently fearing that he was being outflanked. At 8 a.m. the 1/5th received orders to cross the Escape and seize Middle Hill, while the 2/5th were to occupy Double Hill. The 1/5th reached Escape Hill at nine o'clock and began their attack at 9.30. "C" and "D" Companies, less two platoons forming escort to the guns, were forward, and "A" and "B" Companies were held in battalion reserve. The Turkish guns at once opened

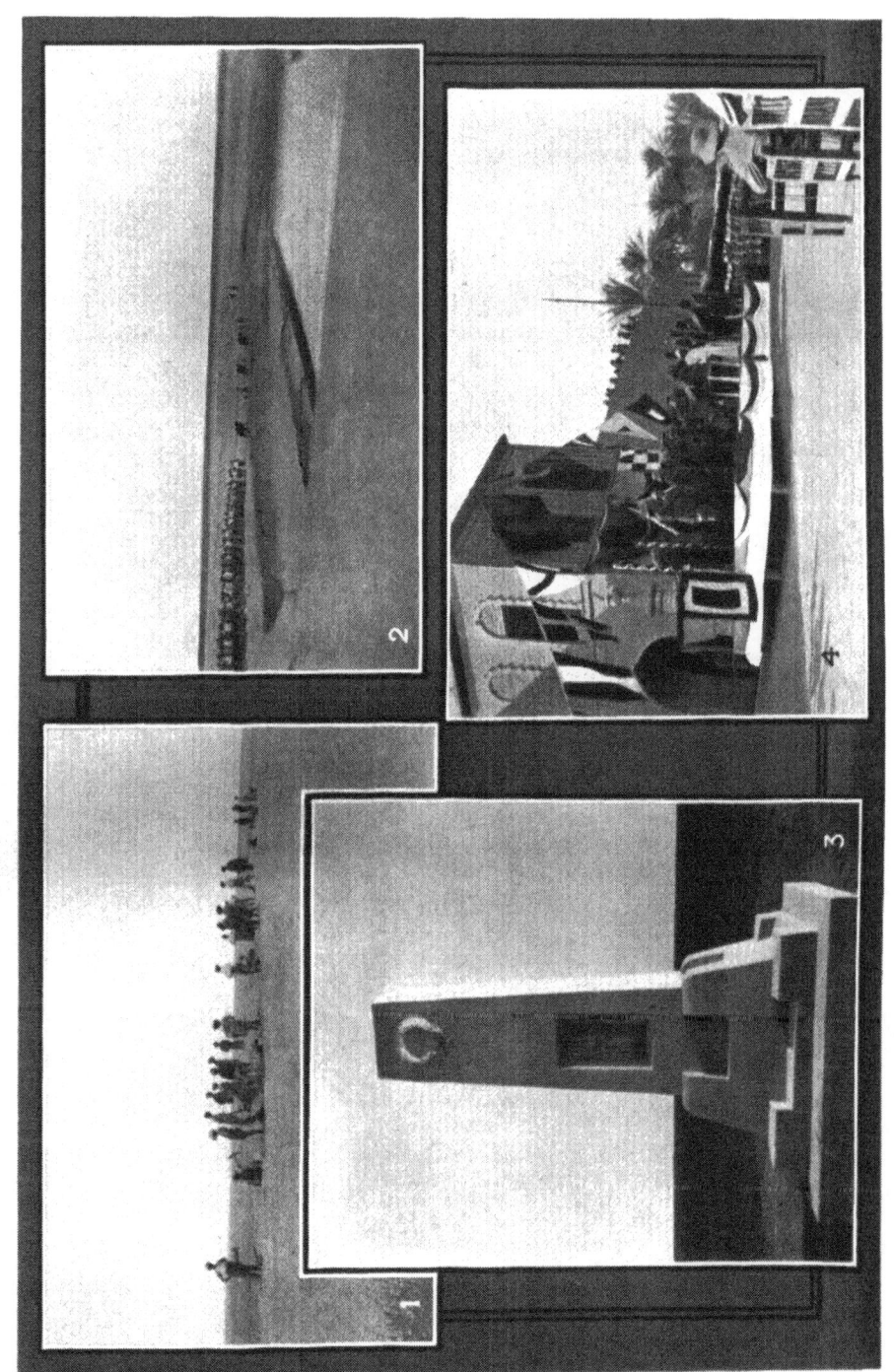

1. Digging Madhij Position, November, 1917.
2. Route March : 15th crossing Dam at Habbaniyeh Escape.
3. Ramadi Memorial on Ramadi Ridge.
4. Proclamation of Armistice by General Brooking at Ramadi.

heavy fire, which increased in intensity as the objective was approached; but fortunately the shells were bursting high, and the objective was made good with slight loss at about ten o'clock. Lieutenant Mackintosh was wounded in the face during this advance, one man was killed, and eight wounded.

During the consolidation of Middle Hill the men took the opportunity of refilling their water-bottles. This was rendered possible by the excellent arrangements for the supply of water by Ford vans by means of which the 15th Division became possessed of a mobility which contributed greatly to the success of the operation, since it made them independent of the river. These vans travelled as much as seventy-five miles between the river and the troops, and were able on occasion to supply water direct to the firing-line.

The 1/5th remained stationary till 12.40 p.m., when it became necessary to exert further pressure on the enemy and pin him to his ground while the Cavalry worked round his rear. Orders were received to attack and occupy the Ramadi Ridge. The 2/5th, who had made good Double Hill were directed from there on the same objective. The Cavalry had taken up a position on the river bank about five miles downstream from Ramadi, and the 50th Brigade had passed across the rear of the 42nd with the object of crossing the Aziziyeh Canal and cutting the enemy's line of retreat. The 12th Brigade was assembled near the Habbaniyeh Lake, ready to operate on the left of the 42nd.

Between Middle Hill and Ramadi Ridge the ground falls thirty feet in the first one thousand two hundred yards, and rises sixty feet in the last five hundred. It was devoid of cover. The ridge is not clearly defined except in the evening light, so that it was not easy to determine when the actual summit was reached. From the ridge the ground slopes gradually down to the river two thousand yards away, while eight hundred yards down this slope were the enemy trenches, with numerous machine-gun emplacements scattered along the Escape at closer ranges.

At 1.10 p.m. the advance began under cover of a heavy bombardment. "A" and "B" Companies formed the firing-line, and "C" and "D" were in reserve some two hundred and fifty yards behind. There was little response from the Turkish guns, but premature bursts from our own caused a few casualties.

The 1st Battalion in the Attack.

At 1.80 the lines deployed and began the ascent of the ridge. Shortly afterwards the descent of the forward slope began, and the leading troops came under a withering fire from guns, machine-guns, and rifles. Being silhouetted against the sky our men formed a conspicuous mark to the enemy well concealed on the ridge, and were forced to halt and lie down. We lost heavily without being able to make any effective reply. Captain Nepean in " B " Company was wounded in the foot, but remained in command till the evening. Subadar Dudbahadur Pun, Jemadar Mansdhan Pun, and twenty-one other ranks were killed, and forty-eight were wounded—all in " B " Company. " A " Company lost thirty-five rank and file killed and wounded. " C " and " D " Companies came up on the right and left respectively, and the former had their Commander, Captain Cook, killed, while Lieutenant Fox and Jemadar Shamsher Gurung were wounded. Their losses in other ranks killed and wounded were thirty. In " C " Company Lieutenant Paterson, Jemadar Kulbir Rana, and forty others were wounded. Battalion headquarters, which had remained in the plain some three hundred yards in rear, also came under fire, and Lieutenant Baker, Jemadar Balwant Rana, and six men were hit.

By about 2 p.m. the enemy fire, which had somewhat died down, developed greater intensity, making further advance impossible. A line was dug just forward of the crest to give cover from rifle fire, and evacuation of the wounded was taken in hand. Captain Bowman, R.A.M.C., and Naik Ansaram Pun worked with the utmost devotion for the five hours remaining before the sun set. The Battalion dressing-station was on Middle Hill in charge of Sub-Assistant-Surgeon Dasram, who worked admirably. As no assistance was forthcoming from the advanced dressing-station on Escape Hill, some 450 brigade casualties had to be evacuated a distance of over two and a half miles from the ridge to Escape Hill entirely under Battalion arrangements.

At 2.15 p.m. two companies of the Dorsets came up on the left of the line, but when they attempted to advance farther, were met by fire of such intensity that they were compelled to fall back in line with the troops holding the ridge. The 2/5th extended the line still farther to the left, losing their commanding officer, Major Harington, in the oblique movement across the enemy's front which was forced on them by the configuration of the ground. At 4 p.m. the 2/6th Gurkhas came up on the right from brigade reserve, and a third company of the Dorsets pushed forward on the left. Still there was no sign of the enemy withdrawing, and he maintained a desultory fire till evening.

As darkness fell it became necessary to decide whether the position
The Withdrawal to Middle Hill. on the ridge should be maintained. There was a possibility of Turkish counter-attacks developing against either or both flanks by covered approaches. Our men had had a long day's fighting and were in need of a respite. Lieutenant-Colonel Nightingale, who was in command of the forward troops, decided, after consulting unit commanders, to advise a withdrawal, as the Cavalry had now turned the enemy's right flank and

it was considered that the Turks could be held to their ground equally well from Middle Hill. Brigade headquarters were two and a half miles behind, and communication was difficult. There was no visual signalling, a wire had not yet been laid, and several orderlies sent with messages failed to return. However, at 7.45 p.m. written orders were received from the brigade agreeing to the withdrawal. The wounded were sent back, and half the troops in the front line retired to a fresh position four hundred yards south of the ridge, while those remaining increased their fire to conceal the movement. At 8 p.m. these also withdrew and took up a position on Middle Hill in good order and without loss. Actually before the withdrawal the enemy was allowing our men to come forward and collect rifles and casualties, so it is probable that he had had his fill of fighting for the day.

On Middle Hill a reinforcement was received of two companies of the 43rd Erinpura Infantry, and a message timed 6.25 p.m. came through from divisional headquarters at Lake Knoll. General Brooking wired:—

"*To all ranks my grateful thanks. You have done splendidly.*"

The Turks Surrender, September 29th. The night passed quietly, but on the morning of the 29th heavy firing was heard: it was from the Turks, attempting to break through the Cavalry blocking their retreat. In the early morning light, patrols were sent out to ascertain the situation as regards the enemy on the ridge. One of these commanded by Captain Cosby came under accurate machine-gun fire, and had to fall back on Middle Hill. Later in the day preparations were being made again to advance to the ridge in co-operation with the 12th Brigade, who were now well round the Turkish right flank, when a line of figures waving white flags made a sudden appearance on the skyline. At 11.40 the following message was received from divisional headquarters:—

"*Cease all firing. Flag of truce with Colonel Costello going out to meet Ahmed Bey.*"

The advance was continued onto Ramadi Ridge and along the west bank of the Escape as far as "Jackson's House." Some Arabs who were found looting were summarily shot, and salvage operations were taken in hand.

The Battle of Ramadi had ended none too soon. Just after the enemy surrender a violent sandstorm arose. Had this come earlier it would probably have influenced the course of the operations, and would certainly have facilitated the escape of the Turks, as visibility was reduced to a few yards. As it was a regrettable incident was narrowly averted during the advance on Ramadi, when two bodies of our troops each mistook the other for the enemy.

The Fruits of Victory.

Ramadi had cost the 15th Division just under one thousand casualties. In return we had captured or destroyed a whole Turkish division numbering about four thousand. Fifteen guns, twenty machine-guns, several thousand rifles, and a very large quantity of miscellaneous war material fell into our hands. The blow was undoubtedly a surprise to the enemy, and its effects were far reaching. The bad impression created by our ineffectual advance in the heat in July was entirely effaced, and our prestige with the disaffected tribes was restored. The late Edmund Candler ("The Long Road to Baghdad") says: "In the Baghdad Villayet Ramadi was recognized as the drop curtain for the Turk. He was nevermore to appear on the boards except as a prisoner."

List of Casualties.

The losses in the 1/5th Gurkhas were: Killed—Captain J. D. H. Cook, Subadar Dudbahadur Pun, Jemadar Mansdhan Rana, Jemadar Dharamsing Pun, and twenty-four other ranks. Wounded—Captain H. D. H. Y. Nepean, Lieutenants G. S. V. Paterson, G. S. Baker, W. B. O. Fox, K. J. Mackintosh, Jemadars Shamsher Gurung, Kulbir Rana, Balwant Rana, and one hundred and forty other ranks. Four men were reported missing.

Immediate awards were made by the Army Commander as follows:—

Nine Distinguished Service Orders, one Military Cross, two Indian Orders of Merit (Second Class), and seven Indian Distinguished Service Medals.

Congratulatory messages to the 42nd Brigade were received from the Brigade Commander, from Sir Stanley Maude, and from the Army Commander, the latter of whom subsequently telegraphed:—

"*1/5th Gurkhas seem to have done particularly well. Convey to them my warmest appreciation of their fine fighting qualities.*"

The Battle of Ramadi gave rise to an extraordinary coincidence which is undoubtedly worthy of record.

"On June 28th, 1915, Havildar Sasidhar Thapa was wounded in trench J13, in Gallipoli. His kit, together with his haversack containing a small black notebook, in which was written the company nominal roll, was left in the trench when he was himself evacuated. Shortly afterwards the trench was occupied by the enemy, after our men had been bombed out. On September 30th, 1917, over two years later, after the Battle of Ramadi, a private of the Dorsets, looking through a Turkish dump, picked up this same notebook and casually handed it to the first person who happened to be within reach. This was no other than Subadar Sasidhar Thapa, its original owner. The book was in exactly the same condition as it had been when lost in Gallipoli."

CHAPTER VIII

THE BATTLE OF KHAN BAGHDADI AND THE END OF THE WAR.

1917—*continued*.
SINCE the Euphrates front had now been cleared of the enemy within striking distance, the left flank of the forces in Mesopotamia was deemed to be secure against the counterstroke down the river, which General Falkenhayn was believed to be contemplating for the recapture of Baghdad. For the moment there was no further work for the 15th Division. Its surplus mechanical transport was withdrawn for employment in the operations about to take place on the Tigris north of Baghdad, and it was able to settle down quietly for the winter. The three brigades were disposed in depth from Ramadi to Faluja, the 42nd being stationed in and around the former.

The 1/5th Gurkhas remained in Ramadi, taking its share of outpost and other duties till October 5th. It then moved with brigade headquarters and the 2/5th to Madhij. This was an unpleasant spot and infested with flies, but the coming of the cooler weather made it bearable. On October 18th a draft of 2 Gurkha officers and 170 other ranks arrived, and in November the following British officers joined: Lieutenants W. A. M. Ferguson, W. R. Ransford, C. H. M. Wingfield, F. E. C. Hughes, P. E. Cayley, and L. A. Foster. Some of these were visitors only, being posted, after a brief stay, to other units. In the same month Lieutenants Nepean and Baker rejoined on discharge from hospital.

On November 17th both battalions of the 5th Gurkhas with two sections of the 130th Machine Gun Company, all under the command of Lieutenant-Colonel M. R. W. Nightingale, moved to Ramadi, where they made a road and constructed defences on the left bank of the river just below the town. After an absence of three weeks they returned to Madhij, having seen nothing of the Turks. On December 18th Colonel Nightingale was given command of the 54th Infantry Brigade at Baghdad and Major F. L. S. Brett took over the Battalion. Before the year ended another draft, 9 Gurkha officers and 177 other ranks, arrived. The majority came from the depot in India, but some were men who had been discharged from hospital.

1918.
The first month of the New Year was spent in training and reorganization. Major F. Skipwith rejoined from Staff employ on January 18th and assumed command. On February 1st the Battalion's establishment of Lewis guns was increased from eight to sixteen. Shortly afterwards the

42nd Brigade moved forward to Ramadi and relieved the 12th on outpost duty. In Ramadi rumour was rife regarding fresh operations impending on the Euphrates front. It was known that the Turks had been reinforced and were concentrating at Hit, while their patrols had pushed forward downstream as far as Uqbah and Nafata. The 15th Division therefore received orders to capture Hit as soon as the necessary arrangements could be made.

Events prior to Occupation of Hit.

To clear up the situation and ascertain the enemy dispositions, Brigadier-General F. G. Lucas moved out of Ramadi on February 18th in command of a small column which included two companies from each battalion of the Regiment. He reached Khan Abu Rayat at midday and received information that a small Turkish detachment was watching the road at Uqbah seven miles farther north. It was decided to attempt the surprise and capture of this party, and the march was resumed at 10 o'clock the same night. At midnight the column reached the position of deployment some 1,500 yards from the supposed enemy post. Here the two 2/5th Companies were ordered to make a detour to cut off the enemy's line of retreat, while one of the 1/5th Companies was to make a frontal attack at 5 a.m. on the 19th. The plan was duly carried out, but failed to bear fruit; the only sign of the enemy was a Cavalry patrol on the far horizon. The disappointed column fell back on Khan Abu Rayat at 11 a.m.

Next day information (which subsequently turned out to be inaccurate) was received that the Turks were about to evacuate Hit. Orders were issued to the troops at Khan Abu Rayat to occupy Uqbah, while the remainder of the division moved forward in close support. On the 21st and 22nd reconnaissances were carried out from Uqbah, and on the latter date British patrols proceeded as far as the enemy wire without being fired on. The enemy was evidently not to be persuaded to disclose his dispositions, and the only sign of him was an aeroplane which bombed and machine-gunned one of our reconnoitring parties without inflicting casualties. The 42nd Brigade therefore withdrew again to Khan Abu Rayat on February 25th. The 59th Brigade went to Uqbah and the 12th to a post six miles upstream from Ramadi. Owing to difficulties of maintenance most of the divisional Artillery was kept at Ramadi and Faluja, while at Khan Abu Rayat the 1/5th were employed in finding piquets and working parties. A post was built and garrisoned by "C" and "D" Companies under Captain Erskine.

Hit Occupied, March 9th, 1918.

On March 8th intelligence, this time authentic, was received that the enemy was withdrawing, and at 5.30 p.m. the 42nd Brigade, less the two companies in the post at Khan Abu Rayat, moved forward to Uqbah.

On the 9th the 50th Brigade occupied Hit and moved forward the next day to Sahaliya, ten miles farther north. "C" and "D" Companies rejoined the 1/5th on the morning of the 11th.

The Turks had retired from Hit and Sahaliya without a shot having been fired, and had withdrawn as far as Khan Baghdadi, abandoning the greater part of their supplies. Their retirement was wholly unexpected, as their defences were formidable; probably it was due to the lesson they had learned at Ramadi and their dread of falling victims to the tactics which had proved their undoing there.

Orders were now received to drive the enemy as far as possible from Hit. Roads were constructed and a large dump of stores and supplies was secretly formed at Sahaliya. Reconnaissances were reduced to a minimum with a view to giving the Turkish troops a false sense of security. Additional mobile troops, including a Cavalry brigade with light armoured motors, were ordered to Hit, but these moved by night and concealed themselves by day. These and other measures taken to conceal our intentions were apparently successful, and it is believed that the opposing Commander was convinced that no further operations on our part were contemplated for the moment.

Khan Baghdadi Plan of Attack.

The plan for the attack on the Khan Baghdadi position resembled that employed so successfully at Ramadi. A strong movement was to be made against the enemy's left, while the Cavalry and armoured cars swung round his right flank. For the purpose of the operation three brigade groups were formed composed of the three Infantry brigades of the 15th Division, each with attached troops. Thus the 42nd Brigade became "Lucas Group" and the 50th "Andrews Group." Part of the 12th Brigade, which was to be carried in Ford vans, was called "Hogg Group," and the remainder formed divisional reserve. The frontal attack was to be carried out by Andrews Group; Lucas Group was to be in support ready to move later round the Turkish right; Hogg Group would carry out the pursuit.

By March 24th the 15th Division was concentrated at Sahaliya and Hit. Andrews Group moved out of Sahaliya early on the night of the 25th–26th, its first objective being the enemy forward position situated about three miles from his main defences and believed to be lightly occupied. Lucas Group followed three miles behind.

The Battle.

About 3 a.m. on the 26th Andrews Group struck the enemy position and, contrary to expectation, found it very strongly held. An attempt to break through proved unsuccessful, and the original plan had to be somewhat modified. It was decided that Andrews Group should move west and attack the enemy right flank, while Lucas Group carried out a simultaneous frontal attack. The movement was to begin at

10.30 a.m. to give time for the Artillery to close up and admit of the men having a meal.

The movements of Andrews Group must have alarmed the Turks, for at 10 a.m. they fell back on their main position. The original plan was therefore again resorted to, and when our advance recommenced at 10.30 a.m. Andrews Group was on the left and Lucas Group on the right. The ground though undulating was not difficult, and by 3 p.m. a position had been reached from which the Turkish trenches could be seen 2,500 yards away. Here there was a halt to admit of the Cavalry completing their encircling movement. This lasted till 4 p.m., when the order to advance came through. A further delay, the reason for which has not been made clear, occurred, but the final phase of the battle began at 5.30 p.m. By a few minutes past six o'clock, under excellent supporting fire from the guns, Andrews Group were climbing the abrupt rise to the enemy position, and the Turkish surrender had begun.

So much for the general progress of the battle. To follow the movements of the 1/5th in detail necessitates slight retrogression.

The Battalion in the Battle of Khan Baghdadi, March 25th.

Lucas Group moved out of Sahaliya at 11 p.m. on March 25th and covered the first seven miles without incident. At 3 a.m. on the 26th they heard the heavy firing caused by the attempt of Andrews Group to take the enemy advanced position, and a halt was called to await developments. A further move forward was made at 5 a.m., but soon after 6 o'clock the news came through of the check to Andrews Group, and the orders for the attack at 10.30 were received. Dispositions were made accordingly. The Dorsets and 2/6th Gurkhas were to form the forward line, the 2/5th would be in support, and the 1/5th in brigade reserve. The Battalion was in the shelter of a large *nullah*, and ample time being available, the opportunity was taken to cook and eat a hot meal.

Intelligence was received of the enemy withdrawal and of the reversion to the original plan of attacking the Turkish main position, and at 10.30 the advance was continued, the group being disposed as already described.

The 1/5th divided into two portions, the right half moving forward and the left remaining with group headquarters. Captain Nepean led " A " and " B " Companies forward with their left on the Khan Baghdadi—Hit road, but the country was broken and touch was difficult to maintain. Eventually, owing chiefly to error in the identification of the correct branch of the road, these two companies found themselves isolated from the remainder of the group and too far forward. They were therefore withdrawn and rejoined the Battalion.

In the final advance the dispositions were slightly modified, the 1/5th changing places with the 2/5th in reserve and support respectively. The 1/5th advanced with "C" and "D" Companies forward and "A" and "B" in support. Its objectives had, however, not been clearly defined, and there was consequently considerable delay. Eventually two knolls were pointed out to the leading companies, one at the eastern extremity of the position and the other some 1,000 yards to the north of it. This information was sent to the supporting companies by runner, but did not reach them. Connection between the two halves of the Battalion was lost, and was not re-established till the action was over. It was fortunate that the consequences of this error were not more serious. Had the Turks been more enterprising they might have taken advantage of it and inflicted considerable loss. Luck was, however, with us, and the advance was successfully carried out. It is necessary to follow the movements of the two portions of the Battalion separately.

The two forward companies, "C" and "D," being unaware that their message had failed to reach its destination, pressed on to the first objective. Even before they reached it, however, it could be seen that the enemy had thrown in his hand and was surrendering to the leading troops. These continued through the position and came to a deep *nullah*, where they captured 25 Turks and some machine-guns. No. 15 Platoon was detached to capture an enemy battery 600 yards distant, and the remainder continued to advance till they reached the second objective. Here they were joined again by No. 15 Platoon, who had left a small guard over the captured guns. This was later relieved by troops from the 50th Brigade, who had apparently received orders to take over all trophies, and they subsequently claimed the credit for the capture of the guns. At 6 a.m. orders were received to fall back on Khan Baghdadi, where the Battalion became reunited. The ground vacated was taken over by the Dorsets, and Hogg Group moved off in their vans to follow up the enemy.

"A" and "B" Companies, having failed to receive the message, moved out of the Wadi Brooking, but could see no sign of the rest of the Battalion. They got as far as the *nullah* in which the machine-guns had been captured by the leading companies, and there reformed and reorganized. Patrols were sent out to try to gain touch with "C" and "D" Companies, but failed to locate them. At this moment Captain Erskine came up from group headquarters, where as second-in-command he had remained, and asked for information as to the whereabouts of battalion headquarters. On being informed of the situation he stated that the Battalion was to return to Khan Baghdadi, and accordingly decided to take "A" and "B" Companies back to that place.

The total casualties in the Battalion in the action were only five wounded, two of these being in the second-line transport.

On March 27th the news of the complete surrender of the Turks was confirmed by General Brooking, who passed the Battalion on his way to the north. The same evening the 1/5th marched to Jubbah, three miles upstream, and joined the rest of the 42nd Brigade, who had arrived a few hours earlier.

The End of Turkish Resistance.
The victory at Khan Baghdadi marked the end of enemy resistance in the Euphrates area. Ana was captured on March 28th, and a large quantity of material fell into our hands. The total of prisoners taken was over 5,000. Salvage work was at once taken in hand, and on this the Battalion was employed till April 13th, when it returned to Ramadi.

Leave to India Opened.
Towards the end of April, Captain Erskine left for India to attend a course at the Staff School, Saugor. On May 14th the Battalion was reorganized in consequence of the the departure of "A" Company, which was transferred *en bloc* to the 1/11th Gurkhas. Leave to India was opened, about 15 per cent. of officers and other ranks being permitted to go at one time. The summer passed quietly in training and garrison duty, companies being sent in turn to Uqbah and Khan abu Rayat.

Summer, 1918.
In August the influenza epidemic swept over Mesopotamia; about two hundred men were attacked, though fortunately there was only one death. Early in September the Battalion had the misfortune to lose Lieutenant Plunkett, commanding "C" Company, who was drowned when bathing. The following officers joined at various times in the summer and autumn. Lieutenant W. R. Watt, M.C., Lieutenant C. E. Simpson; Lieutenant W. R. Thompson, Lieutenant R. Maynard, Lieutenant Pryor, and Lieutenant Whitby.

The Armistice.
The Turks capitulated on October 31st, following General Allenby's brilliant campaign in Palestine and the successful operations of the I and III Corps in Mesopotamia on the Tigris and Kifri-Kirkuk lines. On November 12th the news of the conclusion of the armistice with Germany came through and was celebrated by a three days' holiday.

After the Armistice.
At the end of November orders were received that the 1/5th Gurkhas were to join the I Corps on the Tigris and form part of the Army of Occupation in Mesopotamia. Peiwar Kotal Day was celebrated in the usual manner by the Regiment on December 2nd, and two days later the 1/5th took its departure from the 15th Division, with which it had been so long associated. The march to Dhibban, the railhead on the Euphrates, was most uncomfortable, as rain came down in torrents. Arriving thoroughly soaked the men had to be packed fifty-two into trucks

1. Shergat (Tigris): Ancient Asshur.
2. Entraining at Dhibban en route for India.
3. "Gott Strafe England": A German Drawing on a Wall of the Wrecked Wireless Station at Baghdad.
4. The Residency, Baghdad: Used as G.H.Q.

intended to hold only forty. Abu Rajash was reached early on December 6th, whence after a brief rest, the Battalion marched fourteen miles to Jift, where they joined the 55th Brigade (18th Division) commanded by Brigadier-General Morris, C.B.

On leaving the 15th Division the Battalion received the following farewell order from General Brooking:—

"On the departure from the 15th Indian Division of the 1st Battalion 5th Gurkhas Rifles, F.F., the Divisional Commander feels sure that all ranks of the Division will join him in expressing their great regret at losing the comrades who have for twenty months shared with them so loyally the vicissitudes of active service in Mesopotamia.

"The 1/5th Gurkhas joined the 15th Division in March, 1917, having already gained a great reputation in Gallipoli. This reputation, by steadiness in action and by good comradeship under all circumstances, they have worthily upheld.

"Now, at the victorious conclusion of this great war, the Divisional Commander wishes them farewell and the best of luck in whatever the future may bring."

1919.

Early in January the 1/5th Gurkhas, less "B" Company, which was dropped half-way at Ain Dibs and Bilali, moved up the Tigris to Shergat, forty miles from railhead. On the 17th orders were received which seemed to presage an early return to India. The 1/5th on relief by the second Battalion were to return to Dhibban, and the previous instructions, by which the former were allotted to the Army of Occupation in Mesopotamia, were cancelled. On February 11th a small advanced party under Lieutenant-Colonel Skipwith left for Karachi, and temporary command of the Battalion devolved on Captain Watt until he was relieved shortly afterwards by Captain King-Salter of the 6th Gurkhas. It was laid down that only four regular officers were to accompany the Battalion to India, and that those surplus were to be posted to units remaining in Mesopotamia. Lieutenants Baker, Mackintosh, and Cayley were transferred to the 2/5th, and the four who went to India were Lieutenant-Colonel Skipwith, Captains King-Salter, Nepean, and Watt.

The Battalion Leaves for India, March 2nd.

On March 2nd the Battalion entrained for Baghdad, where they embarked immediately on arrival for Nahr Umar, the new port about eighteen miles above Basra. Headquarters and three companies reached Nahr Umar on the 10th, and "B" Company, for whom there was not accommodation on the same boat, arrived two days later. A week was spent here while all surplus stores and equipment were handed in to the ordnance department. Just before embarkation Captain King-Salter was given a Staff appointment, and Captain Nepean took the Battalion back to India.

On March 16th, "A" "B" and "D" Companies embarked on the *Barpeta*—the same ship by which the Battalion had travelled to Egypt in November, 1914. "C" Company sailed the following day on the *Bankura*. After an uneventful voyage the two vessels reached Karachi on the 22nd and 23rd respectively, and the troops disembarked at once. They were accorded a reception by the Welcome Committee, and moved into the rest camp where they spent two days.

Entraining on March 24th the 1/5th Gurkhas reached Abbottabad three days later. The garrison and civil station turned out to welcome them after their long absence, and the proceedings terminated with the presentation by Brigadier-General Badcock, commanding the Brigade, of the ribbon of the 1914–15 Star to those entitled to wear it. The following was the strength of the Battalion as it marched into the cantonment:—

Arrival at Abbottabad, March 27th, 1919.

British Officers	11
Gurkha Officers	18
Other Ranks	1,030
Followers	56

So ended for the 1/5th Gurkhas the Great War of 1914–18. It is not claimed for the Battalion that it did greater deeds than any other unit of the Indian Army. But this account of its services will hardly have fulfilled its purpose if it does not show that, whether suffering the pangs of thirst in the scrub on Sari Bair, or numbed by the deadly chill of the blizzard on the slopes of Hill 60; whether exhausted by the blinding heat of the Mesopotamian plains, or exposed to wholly unfamiliar dangers on any of a dozen different battlefields, the men were always ready and willing to answer every call that was made upon them. The measure of their effort is the measure of their sacrifice.

Since leaving India in November, until their return at the end of the Great War, they had suffered in casualties:—

	British Officers.	Gurkha Officers.	Other Ranks.
Killed or died of wounds	15	12	221
Wounded	17	12	748
Missing	—	—	4
Died of disease	1	—	40

a total of all ranks of 1,070.

PART III.

THE SECOND BATTALION IN THE GREAT WAR

The War Memorial of the 5th and 6th Gurkhas at Abbottabad, consisting of the Entrance Porch and Wall of the Gurkha Cemetery, erected 1920.

Replica of the Figure of a Gurkha on the Gorakhpur War Memorial. Now in the Officers' Mess, Abbottabad.

The Memorial Tablet in St. Luke's Church, Abbottabad.

THE GREAT WAR MEMORIALS.

CHAPTER I

OUTBREAK OF THE WAR—BRITISH OFFICERS IN FRANCE—EVENTS OF SUMMER, 1915—DRAFTS FOR THE FRONT—"C" COMPANY IN GALLIPOLI

1914. WRITING after the lapse of years it is not easy to record with any degree of accuracy the advent of the Great War to India. The stage was set very far afield; rumour, and what little could be gleaned from a censor-ridden Press, took the place of actual sights and sounds; and all that remains now is a rather hazy recollection of impressions connected with the upheaval of which few then realized the magnitude. A remote corner such as Abbottabad was ill-served with reliable news. The first visible sign of what was afoot was the rush in every sort of vehicle of officers from curtailed summer leave in Kashmir to join their corps—an exodus to be remembered by any who participated. Then came the flood of rumours from sources never ascertained. The bazaar gave birth to the tale of the annihilation of the German Fleet prior to declaration of war, likewise to the equally fantastic story of the annihilation of the B.E.F. in France. Even the Russians at the Scottish railway junction—still plentifully besprinkled with Siberian snow—were faithfully vouched for by someone who corresponded with someone whose cook had an engine-driver for cousin. Later, information became more authentic: the unostentatious departure of brigades from India grew from rumour to fact, faces faded from Club bars, letters remained unanswered, and the lists of ponies for disposal swelled. India was beginning to take part in the war.

The 2/5th Gurkhas were destined to play the part of understudies and to wait some considerable time before changes amongst the principals were to give them a chance in the lead. August, 1914, found them still in the familiar lines in Abbottabad, and all that marked the outbreak was the early recall of furlough men on the 11th of the month. At the same time all the reservists on the books were called to the Colours, and it is creditable that there was hardly an absentee in either category. Some of the officers were fortunate enough to make their entry into the drama straight away. Many will recall tales of controversy between high departments of State regarding the services of those lucky ones whom chance had taken on furlough *ex* India that hot weather, and an unverified impression of the Secretary for War stalking grimly from the portals of the India Office vowing never to darken its doors again. Apparently the War Office won the first round, for Major Champain and Captain Molloy both managed to obtain places in the New Army—that immortal " First Hundred Thousand "—the former being posted to the 9th Battalion the Rifle Brigade, and the latter to the 8th K.R.R. Later, doubtless on account of the crippling officer casualties sustained by the Indian Army Corps in France, the claims of the India Office appear to have received their due, and Captain Molloy went to the 2/2nd Gurkhas near Neuve Chapelle in November, 1914. Major Champain had to wait a little longer, but eventually joined the 1/1st Gurkhas at Festubert in February of the following year.

The following officers were borne on the books of the Battalion when war broke out:—

Lieutenant-Colonel F. G. Lucas, D.S.O. (commanding).
Major C. R. Johnson (second-in-command).
Major H. A. Holdich.
Major C. E. Bateman-Champain (furlough).
Captain F. H. Bridges (Imperial Service Troops).
Captain F. Skipwith.
Captain J. D. Crowdy.
Captain G. P. Sanders (furlough).
Captain H. T. Molloy (furlough).
Captain W. G. Harington.
Captain H. R. C. Lane (with Assam Military Police).
Captain R. C. Duncan (Adjutant).
Captain A. M. Graham (with Assam Military Police).
Lieutenant A. A. Heyland (Quartermaster).
Lieutenant A. Neville Rolfe.
Lieutenant C. A. Gouldsbury.
Lieutenant H. A. Wellesley.
Second-Lieutenant F. E. Le Marchand.
Lieutenant-Colonel M. A. Kerr, I.M.S. (Medical Officer).
Subadar-Major Amarsing Thapa.
Subadar Sankhbir Thapa.
Subadar Lalsing Gurung.
Subadar Mansram Pun.
Subadar Tularam Thapa.
Subadar Madansing Gurung.

Subadar Ramsing Thapa.
Subadar Bilbikram Rana.
Jemadar Naresor Thapa.
Jemadar Hastabir Thapa.
Jemadar Pahalsing Rana.
Jemadar Dalsing Thapa.
Jemadar Balbir Rana.
Jemadar Arjun Thapa.
Jemadar Purnabir Rana.
Jemadar Tikaram Rana.

Of the British officers, seven are still serving at the time of writing (1928), though not all in the 2/5th; but of the Gurkha officers not one remains, the last survivor, Arjun Thapa, having retired as Subadar-Major in 1926.

Death of Lord Roberts. The autumn of 1914 is marked in the annals of the Battalion by the passing of a great soldier whose name was enshrined in the hearts of the older generation of Indian soldiers with an affection seldom, if ever, equalled. On November 14th Field-Marshal Earl Roberts died in France while on a visit to the Indian Army Corps. At the time of his death he was Colonel of the 5th Gurkhas, with whom he had been closely associated since the second Afghan War. There were some serving in those days to whom the slight figure covered with decorations was familiar, and in the minds of those now taking the salt of the *Sirkar* the name lives with those of other almost legendary heroes who did so much for British India.

Captain Graham Killed in Action, December 20th. In the last days of the old year the Battalion sustained its first casualty, the precursor of many to come. Captain Graham had left India in October for France, and in December he was posted to the 2/2nd Gurkhas, then in the line about Rue d'Epinette. He was to survive in the holocaust of officers of the Indian Corps but a very short time, and all ranks were grieved to learn that he had been killed in action at Givenchy on the 20th of the same month. The "History of the 2nd K.E.O. Gurkhas" gives the following account of his death:—

"Our front was held as follows: Captain Graham of No. 3 Company on the right, with Captain Molloy as Company Commander; Major Watt, with Captain Bethell and No. 4 Company, holding the centre; Major Rooke with No. 2 on the left, linking up with the 6th Jats; Major Boileau with No. 1 in reserve. Our two machine-guns were disposed, one on Major Rooke's right, the other with Captain Graham's company, both being under Captain Molloy. At 2.30 a.m. the whole place was shaken by the explosion of a huge German mine under the 'Orchard' parapet, with which our own mine under their western parapet went up in the centre and right trenches, the walls and parapets in many places falling in. This was instantly followed by a deluge of concentrated shrapnel, high-explosive, and machine-gun fire for a few minutes, ending with a rush of the enemy into the 'Orchard' and trenches south of it."

After describing the forcing back of No. 4 Company by the weight of the German attack, the account goes on to say:—

"On our right No. 3 Company and the machine-gun found a good target at first as the Germans issued from their west saphead; but folds in the ground favoured their rush into the 'Orchard' and on to Captain Graham's front. Heavy fighting took place here and on the Seaforths' left front. Captain Graham was killed. The machine-gun, with the exception of some spare parts, was captured, and we had no bombs with which to reply to the Germans, whose attack was chiefly made with those missiles. . . . Captain Molloy, now in command of No. 3, was forced back to the south portion of trench 'C' . . . in trench 'C' Molloy and his men managed to hold on successfully, though separated from the Battalion. . . . Captain Molloy's company held their line steadily until the morning of November 22nd, when the Royal Sussex arrived to relieve them and they were able to rejoin the Battalion. It is certain that but for their dogged hold on their bit of the line by No. 3 Company on our extreme right the Seaforths would have fared far worse, and perhaps have been unable to regain their left trenches, which they had lost in the earlier stages of the fighting."

In the same battle of Givenchy, Lieutenant Neville Rolfe was wounded. He had left India at the same time as Captain Graham, being posted to the 2/8th Gurkhas.

The end of 1914 saw Abbottabad practically denuded of its pre-war garrison. Gradually the various units took their departure: the 1/5th and 1/6th lines were vacated as their occupants received their orders for active service, and the mountain batteries, too, were among the chosen. It is not difficult to understand the chagrin of the 2/5th at finding themselves thus left, as it were, on the shelf. The belief was then generally prevalent that a decision in such a titanic struggle could not be long delayed, and hopes of participation grew less sanguine as the months passed away.

Some new officers joined just before the year ended. These were: Second-Lieutenants R. M. Bruce and A. U. M. Spottiswoode. Major W. B. Ross, M.B., I.M.S., was posted as Medical Officer.

Events at Oghi, 1915. The year 1915 opened with a diversion which might have proved quite welcome as a break in the routine of normal times, but seemed trivial compared with the issues then involved. In January the Civil Authorities made an urgent requisition for military aid at Oghi, a small post in the Black Mountain area normally garrisoned only by a detachment of Frontier Constabulary.

The reason for the summons for troops is referred to briefly in the Commander-in-Chief's despatch of March 9th, 1916.

"In January, 1915, unrest among the Chagarzais on the British border at the Black Mountain necessitated the temporary reinforcement of the Oghi post by regular troops. Quiet prevailed until August, when emissaries from Buner endeavoured to stir up the Black Mountain tribes in the cause of *Jehad*. As a precautionary measure a small column consisting mainly of a detachment of the troops whose services had been lent to the Government of India by the Nepal Durbar, was ordered to Oghi and the neighbouring posts, where they remained throughout September.

"Conditions became normal again in October."

On receipt of the call for troops the right-half Battalion, under Major Johnson, accompanied by a sub-section of Mountain Artillery, left Abbottabad at 1.50 p.m. on January 25th. They covered the 36 miles to Oghi in 14 hours, arriving at 4.0 a.m. on the 26th—quite a creditable march considering that most of it was performed by night. The rest of the column, comprising the 2/6th Gurkhas and the remainder of the 2/5th, left about 3 p.m. on the 25th, arriving at 8.30 the next morning. The trouble, or rather the threat of it, soon subsided, and the troops, with the exception of three hundred rifles under Captain Harington, who remained to augment the constabulary garrison, left again for Abbottabad on January 28th. As noted in Chapter II the autumn again saw the Battalion paying a brief visit to Oghi.

On April 2nd the first draft was sent on service. It was commanded by Lieutenant A. A. Heyland and comprised Subadar Ramsing Thapa, 6 N.C.O.'s, and 28 riflemen. Their destination was France, where they joined the 1/1st Gurkhas on May 4th. Very soon afterwards they were engaged in the heavy fighting which took place round Festubert, and in this action, on the 22nd of the same month, Lieutenant Heyland was killed "while endeavouring to alter the configuration of a captured trench in which his men were being mown down."[1] His loss was keenly felt throughout the Battalion. A young officer of exceptional charm and capacity, he was a great favourite with all ranks, who were now coming to the unpleasant realization of the fact that war always claims the best.

The First Draft.

In June, as the grim toll exacted from the units of the Indian Army in the war theatres swelled, further drafts had to be found. The depot system then prevailing was unable to meet the demand, and sacrifices had to be made by battalions still remaining in India. Sacrifice is not a misnomer,

[1] "With the Indians in France," p. 291.

for where all, as individuals, longed to see service, the necessity of parting with integral portions of such a closely knit entity as a battalion was obviously productive of heartburning amongst those who remained behind.

"C" Company to Gallipoli, June 30th.

The 2/5th were very fortunate in that they were able to serve the Regiment, for their next and largest draft, comprising "C" Company as a complete unit, was sent to the 1st Battalion, who had been fighting in Gallipoli since the beginning of the month and had paid a very heavy price for the privilege. A further reinforcement to the Peninsula was necessary on August 13th, but on this occasion the numbers were smaller. "C" Company was commanded by Captain W. G. Harington, who had with him two British officers (Second-Lieutenant A. Hunter and Second-Lieutenant A. S. Fletcher, both of the Indian Army Reserve of Officers), four Gurkha Officers (Subadar Mansaram Pun, Subadar Dalsing Thapa, Jemadar Budhibal Rana, and Jemadar Tejbir Thapa), and 196 other ranks with 12 followers. They moved down the familiar road to Havelian on June 30th, and reached Karachi on July 2nd, after a very hot journey over the Sind Desert, which is no health resort at that season before the rains break. Immediately on arrival they embarked on the hired transport *Malda*, which carried also details for other Gurkha battalions serving in Gallipoli, and drafts for the Indian Cavalry regiments still in France. The voyage was uneventful, except that the monsoon on its eastward journey assisted Neptune in exacting more than his usual tribute from voyagers wholly unversed in his ways.

On July 11th a call was made at Aden, where the Gurkhas made new friends amongst Australian troops bound for the same destination as themselves. The inclination to fraternize was mutual, and Subadar Mansaram was the honoured recipient of a souvenir in the form of a badge representing an emu, the official insignia of the Australian corps. This he used to display with considerable pride on his headgear, until the chaff of his fellows—usually taking the form of salutes with very exaggerated respect—grew so persistent that he was well advised to conceal it. At Suez on July 16th all Gurkha drafts disembarked and were railed to Ismailia, where the base depot was situated close to the waters of Lake Timsah. Four days were spent here at rest, bathing and seeing the sights, amongst which were aeroplanes, common enough later, but rather amazing on first view. On the 19th "C" Company entrained for Alexandria and embarked on the *Anglo-Egyptian* the next day. They were joined on board by Lieutenant D. I. B. Lloyd and Lieutenant N. Cosby with some men of the 1st Battalion who had been wounded on the Peninsula in the action of June 28th and were being sent back on discharge from hospital.

Mudros Harbour in the island of Lemnos was reached on July 24th.

Here, in truth, were things strange and wonderful to unsophisticated eyes, calculated to arouse the shade even of Ulysses to marvel at the transformation of these blue waters of his voyaging.

So large a collection of shipping and one so heterogeneous could hardly have been matched at that time in any other harbour of the world. The rich prize offered in the city of Constantine had caused every allied nation to bring its standard to the array: Saint George's Cross of Red with the ill-fated Saint Andrew's Blue of the Russian Empire, and the Tricolour of the Republic of France. Battleships swung ponderously to titanic cables, a trickle of steam testifying to their readiness for instant action; destroyers, grim and vicious, lay leashed in line behind them. Here and there a periscope revealed the departure or return of a submarine from very unlawful occasions in the Straits; and in and out among them all scurried the immaculate little naval pinnaces, their business known only to themselves—maybe merely the conveyance of English ale to wash down the Navy's dinners. Transports of every shape and size were overshadowed by the huge bulk of the *Mauretania*, in whose spacious decks a whole brigade had been carried to join the army in the Dardanelles; while the curiously familiar appearance of certain lesser craft called up a fleeting memory of Channel crossings, prelude or postscript to a well-spent leave. Does anyone know what a Nepalese hillman really thought of it all?

"C" Company had but a brief time to spend in contemplation of these new sights; they were practically at their destination. On the night of July 29th–30th they transhipped to a small steamer for the short voyage to Imbros, the small island some fourteen miles from the Gallipoli Peninsula where Force Headquarters were situated. Here they joined the 1st Battalion, who had been resting after their recent heavy fighting at Helles. To follow them farther involves the risk of some repetition, since the narrative of their share in future events of the campaign is naturally one with that of the 1st Battalion which has already been recorded in Part II. A general description of the actions which followed is therefore superfluous, and the following account will be confined as far as possible to such details as are of particular interest to the 2nd Battalion. To preserve the continuity of the narrative some slight redundancy is unavoidable.

In an inspection held shortly after its arrival at Imbros, Brigadier-General H. V. Cox expressed his pleasure at the appearance of Captain Harington's command, which now became No. 2 Double Company in the 1/5th Gurkhas, though for the purposes of the ensuing narrative it will be more convenient to continue to refer to it as "C" Company. The succeeding days were spent in training for the conditions of warfare likely to be experienced in the near future, particularly the practice of night operations.

On the evening of August 6th the Battalion left Imbros. Operations were apparently imminent as each man carried 200 rounds of ammunition, two days' emergency rations, and cooked food for one day, while one waterproof sheet only was allowed to every two men. The short voyage provided further new experiences for "C" Company, as to an ever-swelling symphony of battle music they passed into the operation zone. There was a continuous roar of rifle fire accompanied by the thunder of heavy Artillery with the bursting of their huge shells. Overhead the air crackled with bullets which failed to find their mark in the trenches on the coast and passed over amongst the ships lying off-shore, whose searchlights were constantly busy seeking to reveal what mysteries lay hidden in the darkness.

"C" Company Lands at Anzac, August 6th. At Anzac the landing began at 10 p.m., and by 2 a.m. the whole Battalion was ashore, one rifleman being unfortunately drowned in the transhipment by lighter. At first cover was taken amongst the piles of baggage, stores, and supplies of all kinds lying on the beach, but later a move was made to Reserve Gully. Here the rest of the day (August 6th) was spent in an area about 30 yards square, where partial shelter was afforded by the steep side of the ravine. There was no sleep or rest for anyone. It had been considered very important to avoid disclosing to the enemy the fact that fresh troops had landed on this part of the Peninsula; but Turkish aeroplanes were active, and one which passed over soon after daybreak must have observed the situation, for the area came shortly afterwards under fire from guns of every calibre. This continued throughout the greater part of the day. Closely packed as they were in the gully, the troops could scarcely hope to avoid casualties, but "C" Company was fortunate in sustaining none. During the day General Birdwood, commanding at Anzac, had made a point of seeing personally every British and Gurkha officer, and preparations were made for an early advance. These included careful arrangements for the filling of water-bottles, but owing to the sinking of one of the ships bringing water from Egypt the supply proved inadequate, with the result that many men were obliged to fill up from a brackish source which had been originally set apart for consumption by baggage animals only. The effects of this contretemps were later very apparent.

Operations of August 6th to 10th. The severe operations which were now to take place, beginning on August 6th, have been recorded in detail earlier in this history, and the chronicle of "C" Company must be restricted to its particular movements and actions in the battle. The advance, in the circumstances already described in the account of the 1st Battalion, resulted in an almost inevitable lengthening of the column, and it was at this stage,

At Battalion Headquarters, Damakjelik Bair: Inspection before taking over Trenches.

2/5th Men in a Fire Trench beyond Damakjelik Bair.

after the Battalion had passed through the Australian Brigade in the northern area of the Aghyl Dere, that Captain Harington, whose company was third in the column, ascertained that touch had been lost. Almost immediately the Battalion came under heavy fire from the front, so "C" Company was formed into two lines in single rank and charged up the hill. The Turks were not in very great strength here and fell back, maintaining very heavy fire as they retired. In the charge Second-Lieutenant Hunter was killed and the company suffered some fifteen casualties; but its effort was not wasted, since, in conjunction with a second attack launched by No. 4 Double Company under Captain Erskine on the northern slopes of the Dere, it enabled the 2/10th Gurkhas to advance up the Dere itself.

When it became sufficiently light to see clearly, "C" Company found itself rather awkwardly situated, with the Turks in occupation of a position which ran from a point 200 yards from its left flank close across its front to within 50 yards of its right flank. Fortunately, however, they appear to have been taken by surprise and their *moral* shaken, for they withdrew before very long, leaving behind a considerable quantity of arms, ammunition, and equipment. Captain Harington's plan was now to work along the ridge to his right and establish touch with No. 3 Double Company, and it was while reconnoitring this line of advance that he was wounded, though he was able to issue orders for the company to move to its right by sections. During the execution of this manœuvre Second-Lieutenant Fletcher was killed, and the company was thus left without a single effective British officer. Captain Harington, however, refused to be evacuated and remained in the *nullah* until noon, when it became possible to remove him to hospital. Subadar Mansaram distinguished himself by very good work this day. Going forward alone to reconnoitre, and thereafter leading the company to the front, he succeeded in capturing the ridge. Havildar Chintram Bura also showed conspicuous bravery in the attack, leading his section with considerable skill. Great enterprise and a very fine example to his comrades were shown by Rifleman Kale Gurung. Finding himself unable to use his rifle in the thick scrub, he hit on the device of cutting loopholes in selected places with his *khukri*, and by encouraging others to do the same he was instrumental in establishing fire superiority over the Turks in the immediate vicinity. Though wounded he refused to quit his work until a second wound, sustained later in the day, left him no option in the matter, and he was taken to the rear.

From August 7th to 9th further assaults were launched against the enemy's main position, but "C" Company was not called on to advance. On the 10th the Turks counter-attacked with great violence without achieving any noticeable result as far as this front was concerned.

All their assaults were brought to a standstill, and some prisoners were even captured. During this period Naik Narbahadur Gurung showed conspicuous initiative, and his name was submitted for distinction in the various actions by three British officers, two of them of battalions other than his own. The good work of Rifleman Bhanbir Rana was also noticed. On one occasion he was in support in rear of the firing line with his section when a Turkish attack was made. The sudden and unexpected onslaught temporarily broke the line, whereupon Rifleman Bhanbir, without waiting for orders, followed by his section, made a quick dash for the gap. He succeeded in filling this and so restored a very critical situation.

Captain H. T. Molloy joined the Battalion on the night of August 11th, fresh from his experiences in France. He was posted to "C" Company, but left the next day to take over command of the Battalion from Colonel Firth, whose health would no longer allow him to continue the arduous task which he had assumed some time previously on transfer from the 2/10th Gurkhas. He was sent to hospital, and Lieutenant G. F. Knowles relieved Captain Molloy in command of "C" Company.

On the night of August 13th the Battalion was relieved in the front line by the 10th (Service) Battalion of the Hampshire Regiment, and marched to a position on the southern slopes of the Damakjelik Bair, where it was held in brigade reserve. It remained here until the 20th, obtaining such rest as was possible in face of the constant calls made upon it for trench digging in the advanced positions, for scrub clearing, and for the performance of many other necessary fatigues. On the 21st the 29th Brigade was again sent up to the front line to take part in an attack on Kaiajak Aghala and Hill 60, to be carried out in conjunction with the Australians and other British troops.

Operations of August 21st.
For this operation the Battalion formed up in rear of the piquets of the 1/6th Gurkhas, during which process they came under shrapnel fire and had a few casualties. Their subsequent advance took them across an open slope swept by enemy fire from the ridges and hills to their right front and on the flanks. No effective reply to this was possible in the circumstances, but some loss was inflicted on the enemy, as small bodies of Turks encountered near our front-line trenches were either killed or captured. These were found to be armed with ·22 bore rifles, with which they were able to perform some effective sniping, since the report was practically inaudible at even comparatively short range. "C" Company was on the right of the advance and reached a forward position on the slopes of Hill 60 at about six o'clock in the evening.

There, digging in, they consolidated the line won and were able, despite exposure to very heavy fire, to maintain their ground till darkness relieved to some extent their immediate anxieties.

In this attack Havildar Chintram Bura again distinguished himself by the manner in which he led his section. Keeping it well together he was the first to attain the objective. Thereafter he showed untiring energy in reorganizing his small command, which, by the steadiness of their fire, succeeded in warding off every counter-attack. His judgment in choice of ground undoubtedly saved casualties. Lieutenant Knowles was wounded by a Turk who lay hidden in the scrub some ten yards from the line where our men were digging. Retribution was swift to follow, as men in the vicinity made a rapid dash forward and killed the sniper with their *khukris*.

During the night, which was dark as pitch, considerable tumult in the Turkish lines proved the prelude to a strong counter-attack by the enemy. This came from the crest of Hill 60, and the line of which "C" Company formed part moved forward to meet it. The Turks were met in the open and forced back with considerable loss, including about thirty captured. In the advance Captain Molloy leaping into a trench found it full of the enemy, and his impetuous rush carried him right on top of one of the occupants. Owing to the blackness of the night surprise was mutual, but a rapid appreciation of the situation convinced Captain Molloy that a tight grasp of his opponent was advisable. They remained locked in an affectionate embrace till the opportune arrival of other members of the company, who disarmed the Turk after carefully depriving him of the bomb with which he had doubtless hoped to disintegrate his aggressor had he been given slightly longer notice of his advent.

Assaults on the enemy position on the summit of Hill 60 continued successively for the next ten days. "C" Company did not participate in these, but assisted with covering fire, working hard during the intervals of darkness on consolidation of the line they had occupied. On September 6th they moved to another position on the same line, and here they remained till the 11th, when they were relieved by the 1/4th Gurkhas newly arrived on the Peninsula from France.

Casualties. Losses in the company during August had been heavy. One Gurkha officer had been wounded, and the total of killed and wounded amongst the other ranks was fifty. British officer casualties amounted to five. Second-Lieutenants Hunter and Fletcher had been killed, and Captain Harington and Lieutenant Knowles wounded as already recorded. The fifth, Captain Molloy, received a severe wound on August 30th which made him an absentee from the Battalion for a considerable period. Captain Harington was able to take over the company again on September 15th when he rejoined from India, bringing with him a small draft of eight N.C.O.'s and eighteen riflemen.

As far as the 1/5th Gurkhas were concerned, the remaining period of their stay in Gallipoli consisted of trench warfare. Night raiding and bombing sorties intervened in the monotony of digging trenches, and there were occasional outbreaks of heavy bombardment by the Turkish Artillery. Just prior to the evacuation our forward trenches were in some places no more than fifteen yards from those of the Turks on Hill 60, and this proximity entailed incessant bombing and mining operations, the latter involving the exploding of Camouflet mines at very close quarters. Frequent damage to parapets necessitated repair under hazardous conditions, generally within range of aimed rifle fire. The strain on all ranks was severe, and at one time "C" Company held the front-line trenches for ten successive days without relief. Late in November came the blizzard which had such devastating effects on the devoted troops maintaining their precarious hold on the Peninsula. The men suffered severely from frostbite, and those in the forward positions were unable to obtain proper food or rest for three days on end. Their behaviour was beyond praise during this arduous experience; no complaints were heard, nor did a single man report sick till relief had been completed.

Trench Warfare.

The story of the evacuation and the successful manner in which it was achieved has received its recognition in documents of more general interest. The only point of particular import in these pages is that "C" Company had the honour to be the last to leave Anzac. Under Captain Harington, with whom was Lieutenant Gladstone, it was detailed to cover the withdrawal of the rest of the Battalion who were the last to quit this part of the Peninsula. On December 18th it took over an extended front with the knowledge that it could expect little or nothing in the way of reserves or supports in its rear. On the following day it had to sustain a very hard bombardment by enemy 6-in. howitzers and 75-mm. guns, which was preceded by the explosion of an exceptionally powerful Turkish mine. This did considerable damage to the trenches, and "C" Company lost Jemadar Budhibal Rana, who was so severely crushed that he died shortly afterwards. Subadar Mansaram Pun was wounded. The repair of the broken works entailed much labour of a difficult and hazardous nature, to assist in which it was found possible to send up twenty men of "A" Company in relief of those of "C" who had been badly bruised and shaken.

The Evacuation, December 18th and 19th.

That December 19th was a day of considerable tension is easily understood when it is realized that in the final stages of the evacuation the Turks held their general line of forward trenches as close as from 150 to 300 yards from ours. Indeed, at one point the separation was a matter of merely 100 yards. At 4 p.m. the first party of the Battalion embarked, and the second moved off four hours later, leaving "C" Company to its own resources, except for a few bombers belonging to a British battalion who had been left in a post close at hand. The men obtained what sleep they could in the earlier part of the evening and at midnight, having had but little food during the day, disposed of their emergency rations prior to moving off. At 1.15 on the morning of the 20th, Lieutenant Gladstone took the first party from the trenches to the beach. Captain Harington followed fifteen minutes later with most of the remainder. Finally, at 1.40 the last sections fell in ready to take their departure. The trenches were filled with barbed wire and a few valedictory rounds sped in the direction of the enemy lines. With boots blanket-wrapped to deaden any sound which might reveal their departure the rear party faded from contact with the Turks.

Embarkation was completed without a hitch at a pier near the Asmak Dere, whence the passage to Mudros was made by lighter. There "C" Company joined the remainder of the Battalion on the *Knight Templar*, and sailed at once for Alexandria, which was reached on Christmas Eve. They remained in Egypt till March 14th, when they were transferred to Mesopotamia to join hands once more with their own Battalion.

This had been the first complete unit of the 2/5th Gurkhas to fight overseas, and it was the only one to see service in a European theatre. It was their very good fortune to leave their dead side by side with those of their brothers in the Regiment, and to have some share in the honour gleaned by the 1st Battalion from those few sore-stricken acres of Anzac.

CHAPTER II

1915—Epidemic of Malaria—Mohmand Unrest—1916 and Orders for Overseas—Departure from India and Arrival in Mesopotamia—Operations on Euphrates Front.

1915.

While its representatives were giving a good account of themselves in the main war theatre the rest of 1915 passed uneventfully enough for the Battalion still in Abbottabad. It was now generally realized that the war was not to be of brief duration, and hopes of active participation somehow, somewhere, grew stronger. The ever-present query was how and where; and many guesses, the outcome of the never-ending crop of rumours, were to be hazarded before the question received an answer. The frontier was uneasy—an initial portent of a great restlessness that was not to settle down for many months after the conclusion of the World War, and only after much good blood had been spilt on grim hills and passes. In July tribal gatherings were heard of in Buner, but there was not much disturbance till the middle of August, when that notorious "hot-gospeller," the Haji Sahib of Turangzai, became active in the vicinity of the Ambela Pass. His following comprised several thousand, and he was given a certain amount of support from the Hindustani fanatic colony, who live just over the Indus where the—to them alien—King's writ does not run. The old Mullah had many debts to write paid to, and he was now believed to be contemplating an invasion of British territory at a time when the Raj was somewhat preoccupied elsewhere. However, his time had not yet come, for he and his four thousand odd stalwarts were dispersed at Rustam by a force under Brigadier-General N. Woodyatt and driven back with some loss into the hills from which they had come.

Epidemic of Malaria.

The 2/5th had bad luck in not being able to take part in even this minor operation. In the early autumn one of the periodic epidemics of malaria, which are now happily—owing to adequate drainage and other preventive measures—much less frequent, was experienced in Abbottabad. In fact throughout the Punjab the season was one of the most sickly experienced for years. By the end of July the virus had spread through the Battalion with a vigour unprecedented, at one time three-quarters of the N.C.O.'s alone being non-effective with fever. The hospital was swamped with cases, and every ward was overflowing so that even the verandas became closely packed with beds. In the 2/5th fifty-two deaths were the toll exacted by this single outbreak; and it is not surprising that the unit was declared temporarily unfit for service. The Nepalese battalions at Kakul were in the same bad way. Out of four stationed there, only one could produce sufficient effective men to move to Oghi in August on the occasion already referred to in Chapter I. The Battalion also sent such numbers as were fit to march on this small side-show, which again proved barren of excitement, as the column was only called on to sit still in a perimeter camp outside the old fort for a week or two. December 1st saw everyone back in Abbottabad again. After a few days another temporary ebullience started a fresh hare on the frontier, and orders were received to move to Peshawar to join the 3rd Infantry Brigade. The Battalion moved out of Abbottabad on December 12th, and on the 17th the brigade marched to Nagoman, eight miles from Peshawar on the Mohmand border. By the time it got there, however, the unrest on this part of the frontier had subsided.

Casualties During 1915. During 1915 casualties had been sustained on various fronts. Twenty-two of the rank and file had been killed and eighty-seven wounded, mostly in Gallipoli. The following officers had received wounds in action:—

Lieutenant-Colonel H. A. Holdich, in Mesopotamia on November 22nd.
Major C. E. Bateman-Champain, at Neuve Chapelle on March 13th.
Captain H. T. Molloy, in the Dardanelles on August 30th.
Captain W. G. Harington, in the Dardanelles on August 7th.
Lieutenant A. Neville Rolfe, in France on March 10th (for the second time).

Awards for gallantry had been made to:—
Major H. A. Holdich, promoted to Brevet rank on October 29th, for distinguished service in the field.
Captain H. T. Molloy, D.S.O., for gallantry in action in Gallipoli.

The latter award, though earned on the Peninsula in 1915, was not announced till 1920, in the *Gazette* of June 8th.

Lieutenant-Colonel C. R. Johnson and Captain G. P. Sanders were detailed to assist in the training of the Nepalese contingent, then located in Kakul for the hot weather and Hassan Abdal for the winter. Captain R. C. Duncan was appointed Staff Officer to the Mardan Mobile Column during the operations against the Mohmands from August 26th to November 20th, after which he rejoined and resumed the Adjutancy from Lieutenant Wellesley, who had been officiating in his absence. In April Lieutenant C. A. Gouldsbury was appointed Quartermaster.

Three officers joined on first appointment during the year, and a certain number from the Indian Army Reserve of Officers were attached for duty. The former were Second-Lieutenants H. N. Loch, G. A. Maconchy, and J. C. Coates; and the latter were Second-Lieutenants R. N. Broad, J. E. Roberts, H. E. Winn, N. C. Inglis, H. S. Phillips, R. C. Bayldon, L. J. Hicks, J. C. March, E. A. Saunders, J. B. Fisher, and H. B. Corfield.

1916.
Orders to Mobilize.

The New Year was to bring better fortune than had hitherto been experienced. On January 22nd the long-hoped-for mobilization orders were received: this time it was for service overseas and not for any frontier side-show. A certain amount of rejoicing was pardonable in the circumstances. There was a month of delay waiting for definite orders, but in those days there could be really only one destination for troops from India. On February 23rd the Battalion entrained for Karachi, and by March 3rd the right wing and headquarters had completed embarkation on the *Ekma*, sailing for Mesopotamia the same evening. The remainder, under Captain Sanders, who had succeeded in obtaining a relief in the Nepalese contingent, sailed the following day on the *Arankola*.

Below are the names of the officers who left India with the Battalion for Mesopotamia:—

Lieutenant-Colonel F. G. Lucas, D.S.O. (commanding).
Captain G. P. Sanders (second-in-command).
Captain R. C. Duncan (Adjutant).
Lieutenant C. A. Gouldsbury (Quartermaster).
Lieutenant H. A. Wellesley.
Lieutenant R. M. Bruce.
Second-Lieutenant G. A. Maconchy.
Second-Lieutenant J. C. March.
Second-Lieutenant F. B. Fisher.
Captain R. W. C. Hingston, I.M.S. (Medical Officer).
Subadar-Major Amarsing Thapa.
Subadar Lalsing Gurung.
Subadar Madansing Gurung.
Subadar Hastabir Thapa.
Subadar Pahalsing Rana.
Subadar Naresor Thapa.
Subadar Arjun Thapa.
Jemadar Purnabir Rana.
Jemadar Tikaram Thapa.
Jemadar Kumbhasing Gurung.
Jemadar Giria Thapa.
Jemadar Bhawanand Thapa.

Jemadar Narpati Bura.
Jemadar Maidhar Gharti.
Jemadar Chandrasing Gurung.
Jemadar Goria Gurung.
Jemadar Sahabir Gurung.
Jemadar Pirthibir Bura.

History has recorded practically nothing of the thoughts and impressions of those who now saw the sea for the first time. For the most part the Gurkha, in his philosophical way, took the new sights and experiences rather for granted, but conversations occasionally overheard testified that amusing speculations were indulged in by the more inquiring spirits. The most common query was regarding the manner in which the ship found the way; the track behind was plain to all, but what of the unmarked waste before? The means of propulsion also gave rise to much discussion, and were eventually accepted as beyond the grasp of even the most mechanically minded. These topics exhausted, the barren sea, with an uneventful voyage, grew wearisome, and relief was manifest when by some occult means the ship found its way up the Shatt-el-Arab to Basra, where the whole Battalion disembarked on March 13th. At Magil, where it went into camp, it was joined by drafts, the survivors of France and Gallipoli, who had come via Suez under the command of Captain W. G. Harington, who had with him Captain A. C. Gladstone and Second-Lieutenant R. Bayldon. On the 16th it moved to Makina Masus, where it joined the 42nd Infantry Brigade. This place was then practically a desert, and it was interesting to see it two years later as a large and well-found cantonment.

2/5th Join 42nd Brigade, March 16th.

The other units of the brigade were the 4th Battalion the Dorsetshire Regiment and the 2/6th Gurkhas, the latter old friends from Abbottabad. The introduction to the Dorsets was somewhat unconventional. Apparently there had been an epidemic of " relapsing fever," and the medical authorities had decreed that all clothing was to be passed through the mysterious process which, to quote a war author, at least affords " an awfu' fricht " to the bacteria and larger organisms which may be present. Bereft of their raiment the men of Dorset on the day of the Battalion's arrival were taking the air in the state of their early forefather before the Fall. The climate and locality were not inappropriate.

Although the operations in Mesopotamia were at this time passing through a very critical stage, it did not fall to the 2/5th to take any active part. In November of the previous year Townshend had carried his force beyond Kut to Ctesiphon, only to meet there superior enemy numbers which forced him back to the former place, to endure a siege which began on December 3rd. Hurriedly organized attempts to relieve him during the spring of 1916 had failed to achieve their object, in spite of severe sacrifice and endurance of British and Indian troops. Losses so heavy as practically to decimate the troops engaged were sustained at Sheikh Saad, Hannah, The Wadi, and Falahiyah. Exhaustion and adverse conditions brought the advance to a standstill almost in sight of the goal, and on April 29th Kut and its defenders passed into Turkish hands. There followed a long period of reorganization for the next phase, which opened with Maude's successful advance in December, 1916, and the recapture of Kut-el-Amara.

Basra, 1916. The neighbourhood of Basra was little affected by these operations, and the 42nd Brigade passed an uneventful hot weather. The only people who saw anything of the fighting on the Tigris were a party of one Gurkha officer and fifty other ranks, under Lieutenant Wellesley, who were sent as guard to the Army Commander. These rejoined the Battalion later on at Nasiriya. March was occupied with daily working parties on the Zobeir railway bunds, and the men had their first experience of the sand shovelling of which they were to have their fill before the campaign was over. A change in command gave Colonel Lucas the brigade, and Major Sanders took over the Battalion. Captain Duncan became a Company Commander in his place, passing on the Adjutancy to Lieutenant Maconchy.

Move to Nasiriya. In April it became expedient to investigate the possibility of moving troops from Basra to Nasiriya, and the route across the desert was reconnoitred by Captain Duncan, accompanied by Captain Hackett of the 2/6th Gurkhas. The 42nd Brigade began the march on April 29th. It was a most arduous business: no road existed and the troops plodded over the waste of loose sand in scorching heat with but a scanty supply of water, and that brackish and most unpalatable. Three-quarters of the normal ration only could be issued, and there were no fresh vegetables to be had. Still, few fell out, and the troops came through the ordeal well. Opposition had been expected, as reports received in Basra indicated every likelihood of an encounter with Arabs under Ibn Raschid, a local sheikh; but it was found later that this worthy had thought better of trying conclusions, contenting himself with hovering ten miles off on the flanks. Nasiriya was reached on May 10th without a shot having been fired, and no Arabs were even seen except on the outskirts of the town. The necessity of this transfer to Nasiriya was not very obvious at the time, but the recently published official history makes it clear that it was due to the Turkish investment of Kut, which opened to the enemy a possible route down the Hai. It was only after our subsequent advance towards Baghdad that this line was found to be much less practicable than was first supposed.

THE 5TH ROYAL GURKHA RIFLES (F.F.)

42nd Brigade joins 15th Division, May 10th.

In Nasiriya the 42nd Brigade took its place in the 15th Division under Major-General H. T. Brooking. Camp was made on the left bank of the Euphrates, but two days after arrival the river rose, flooding this ground. A hurried move had then to be made to the right bank. The crossing held its thrills as hardly any transport was available, involving the manhandling of baggage tents, etc., from one side to the other.

During May steps were taken to strengthen the defences of Nasiriya, and extensive works were put in hand to obviate the seasonal flooding from the Euphrates, which is liable to inundate the surrounding country for miles if not restrained. The troops shovelled sand nobly, and the work continued into June, when the Mesopotamian summer began to show what it could do. The thermometer climbed to 118° in the shade, exhausting all but the inevitable oriental bacteria, which it fostered. Cholera appeared, but was taken in hand and claimed only two victims from the 2/5th.

On July 8th, Colonel Johnson, who had come from the depot in India and taken over command in the middle of June, received orders to move down the river to destroy the village of Abdul Hussein, the sheikh of which had proved recalcitrant when asked to call and pay his respects to the G.O.C. At 2.40 a.m. on the 9th the Battalion embarked on river-steamers, which, failing to attain the dignity of names, were known as Numbers 3 and 4, and escorted by the monitor *Greenfly*,[1] reached the village at dawn. The place was deserted, and the column had to be content with blowing up three towers and laying the houses waste. Creating a desert and calling it peace is a pursuit not entirely unacceptable to the Gurkha, so one may presume it was a satisfied Battalion which arrived back at Nasiriya at half-past eleven the same morning.

Work on the defences continued into August, and there was little relief from the growing heat. A grilling afternoon saw the shade temperature touch 121°, interesting as a record, but trying for a hillman to endure. Despite it, health on the whole was good, but no precautions could entirely avert the crop of sores so prevalent east of Suez—known by various names, but all of the same nature, equally unpleasing and hard of cure.

With the waning of the hot weather of 1916 things began to move in Mesopotamia, and the operations which were to follow were not to be entirely restricted to the Tigris front. Sir Stanley Maude had taken over command on August 28th and immediately devoted his high organizing ability and tireless energy to preparation for the forward movement against the Turks, which was to commence that winter.

[1] *Vide* Part IV, p. 368.

On the Euphrates, fighting started as early as September, though it was not against the Turks, who then had only a small regular detachment on that front at Samawa. Arab irregulars, allies or foes of either side as opportunity offered, had begun to give trouble, and our comparative inactivity in the summer had rendered them more truculent; so that patrols and camps in the vicinity of As Sahilan were being subjected to an annoying series of minor depredations. Steps had to be taken to deal with the matter before these guerrilla concentrations attained formidable dimensions.

Action Against Arabs, September 11th.
On September 11th, at dawn, the 15th Division moved out with the 42nd Brigade on the left and the 12th on the right. The 2/5th, under the command of Major Harington, had two companies with the main body. "B" Company (Captain Wellesley) formed the left flank guard, and Second-Lieutenant Fisher, with two platoons of "A," was on the right flank. Lieutenant Maconchy, with "A" Company's two remaining platoons, acted as rear-guard. Except for the deep irrigation channels, which proved such annoying obstacles all over riverain Mesopotamia, the ground was comparatively open for the first two miles. Shortly after moving off the sound of heavy firing from the right indicated that the 12th Brigade had come into action. At 6.15 a.m. the advanced guard (1/4th Dorsets) got into very awkward country broken by deep *nullahs* and covered with high camel-grass, in which it was evident that the Arabs were holding a position, for heavy fire was opened on the leading troops of the Dorsets. The Kohat Mountain Battery came into action and soon brought fire to bear on the enemy line, while "C" Company of the 2/5th (Second-Lieutenant Gladstone) was ordered to the support of the advanced guard. It was not long before the enemy was dislodged, and when signs of his withdrawal were noticed, "B" Company was pushed forward on the left with a view to intercepting his retreat. This movement was, however, shortly afterwards cancelled, as masses of Arabs were seen to be collecting on the left flank of the brigade, evidently trying to work round the rear; but the advance already made by "B" Company had opened a gap between it and the rear-guard. This "D" Company sent a platoon to fill. As the situation now developed the 42nd Brigade became a left flank guard to the 12th, and General Brooking decided to make no further advance until the position on this flank was cleared up, calling a halt accordingly. It was in this phase that the Battalion incurred most of its casualties. The units on our left flank were very heavily engaged with Arabs of a strength estimated at 2,000, who kept up a continuous covering fire, under which their advanced troops pushed forward to within forty yards of our firing-line, making very skilful use of the broken ground. Major Harington was twice wounded—first in the chest and half an

hour later in the head. Notwithstanding his hurts he insisted on carrying on, and was able to ride his horse out of action in the subsequent withdrawal. Captain Wellesley and Lieutenant Bruce were slightly wounded.

At noon divisional headquarters issued orders for the withdrawal, and "B" Company retired on "C," which was supporting it. The fact that they moved at the double apparently gave the enemy some encouragement, for they left their position and came out into the open in hurried pursuit. Retribution for their temerity followed swiftly, as the machine-guns were not slow in taking advantage of the excellent target thus offered. The cover afforded by the Wusman Nullah was utilized to reform the Battalion, and from here the retirement was conducted by wings, "D" Company being detached in the final stages to support the 12th Cavalry, who were seen to be in close engagement with enemy on the left. The Arabs, according to the usages of savage warfare, followed up the retirement very closely, but most effective covering fire was afforded by two guns of the mountain battery and a section of the machine-gun company.

At 3 p.m. the Battalion was back in camp, having lost in this action fourteen rank and file killed. In addition to the three British officers already mentioned, Subadar Pahalsing Rana and twenty other ranks were wounded. According to an official despatch dated April 10th 1917, the enemy had lost 436 killed and some 800 wounded out of a total strength of about 5,000. The operations were said to have had an excellent effect round Nasiriya, and the steady behaviour of our troops was commended. The day after the engagement the work of the Battalion was favourably commented on in messages from divisional and brigade headquarters, and the following immediate awards were made:—

    Major W. G. Harington—D.S.O.
    Captain R. W. G. Hingston, I.M.S.—M.C.
    Lance-Naik Dhansing Gurung—I.D.S.M.
    Rifleman Gambirsing Mal—I.D.S.M.
    Rifleman Balbir Rana—I.D.S.M.
    Rifleman Dalbahadur Thapa—I.O.M. (2nd Class).

No further operations took place on the Euphrates, and the remainder of 1916 passed quietly enough. Arabs gave no more trouble except for occasional and rather futile sniping from which, one night in October, the 2/5th had a sentry wounded. Till December two companies were on detachment at Safah, nine miles from Nasiriya and close to the famous ruins of Ur of the Chaldees. Life at Nasiriya was monotonous, varied only occasionally by the despatch of a company on escort to the monitors which used to patrol the river towards

Samawa, but this duty never resulted in an encounter with the Turkish detachment stationed there. Days not thus occupied were devoted to training, and the daily work on the defences still went on. Detachment duty at Safah was welcome, not only as providing a change of scene, but also because the shooting was exceptionally good. Some very fine bags of sand-grouse were recorded. According to descriptions these birds were so plentiful that the sky was, on occasions, literally darkened by clouds of them round the water-holes.

A divisional assault-at-arms was organized in December, in which the Battalion succeeded in carrying off a few prizes. Naik Goria Rana and Lance-Naik Jamansing Gurung won the swimming and obstacle races respectively, and second place in the long jump went to Naik Birjlal Thapa. In the divisional point-to-point two teams of four officers each were entered; but neither managed to score a win, though Captain Duncan came in third and Second-Lieutenant Marindin secured fourth place.

During the year Lieutenant-Colonel Holdich had received a D.S.O. for distinguished service on the Staff. The following officers joined from the depot: Second-Lieutenants C. W. Cousins, J. F. Marindin, G. G. Crawford, C. P. Gouldsbury, and R. M. Banks. Major Sanders was invalided to India in September, and Captain C. A. Gouldsbury took up a Staff Captain's billet at Advanced Base, M.E.F. Early in 1917 Captain A. N. Rolfe and Second-Lieutenant A. U. Spottiswoode arrived from the depot in India.

1917.

No change in the Euphrates situation developed during the first three months of the new year. Practically the only event of any interest was the sudden appearance of two enemy aeroplanes, which circled over our camps, causing some excitement and inflicting a few casualties by bombing. It was like life in Abbottabad again, only in less pleasant surroundings. Pessimists began grimly to prophesy that the end of the war would find the 2/5th still doing duty in this unpleasing desert town. There are indications, however, that the gloomy spirits did not entirely control the situation, and congenial company helped to make the best of the existing state of affairs. As in all quarters, the war had brought together individuals of many different temperaments and varying political ideals. In the Battalion this lent considerable interest to the discussions which are inevitable whenever Anglo-Saxons, in their twos and threes, foregather in odd corners of the world. The mess could produce ardent supporters of every political creed ever represented on the benches of Westminster: Gladstone, of course, a Liberal of Liberals by tradition and training; Banks, a Tory, hoping some day to represent his Party; and Hingston, a red-hot Irish Nationalist. When other topics failed during the post-prandial hour, all or any of these could be relied on to initiate an argument which, without becoming acrimonious, was sufficiently heated to keep the onlookers entertained.

Early in March a stir in the Headquarters Staffs appeared to presage an advance on Samawa by the whole division, but, though orders for a move were actually issued, they were shortly afterwards cancelled. The successful operations on the Tigris had in the meantime rendered the position of the Turks on the Lower Euphrates untenable, and the advance became unnecessary. General Maude's offensive had proceeded with signal success. The recapture of Kut, after severe and prolonged fighting against entrenched positions tenaciously held, was followed by a swift advance up the river, delayed only by a halt to reorganize communications; and the British colours were hoisted in the citadel of the City of the Caliphs on March 11th. Our hold on Lower Mesopotamia was thereby secured, the Turkish forces being driven on divergent lines beyond Baghdad.

General Brooking's division was thus able to make its forward move without anticipating opposition, and on March 28th it received welcome orders to join the victorious Tigris Corps, whose rôle was now consolidation of the advanced position gained; the completion of the defeat of the scattered enemy; and union, if possible, with the Russian troops operating in East Persia.

CHAPTER III

DEPARTURE FROM NASIRIYA—BAGHDAD—RAMADI—HIT AND KHAN BAGHDADI—GARRISON DUTY IN IRAQ—RETURN TO INDIA

Departure from Nasiriya, March 28th, 1917.
THE move to Baghdad, made under what amounted to peace conditions, was devoid of any excitement, but a change of scenery and the very fact of movement were welcome to everyone after the monotony of the past few months. There was no practicable line of advance along the Euphrates, and so the circuitous route by Basra and thence up the Tigris was utilized for the movement of the 15th Division. By this time Nasiriya had been linked to Basra by a line of railway, and the transfer therefore involved passage by rail, road, and river. The Battalion entrained at Nasiriya in two parties on March 28th, the right wing, under Captain Duncan, leaving at 5.80 p.m., and headquarters and the left wing about two hours later. Magil was reached early the next morning, and there the railway was abandoned and the troops transferred to the river-steamer P.S. 50, moving up the Tigris the same evening. At Magil they met again the 1st Battalion of the Regiment, which had just arrived by way of India from the Dardanelles and Egypt. It was a very great pleasure to all to learn that both battalions were to serve henceforth side by side in the 42nd Brigade, and it was an additional stroke of fortune which gave them as Brigade Commander one of their own people, Brigadier-General F. G. Lucas.

Passage up the Tigris against the current was slow, and P.S. 50 had several times to draw into the bank to admit of the passing of other vessels. Leaving Qurnah behind during the night and Ezra's Tomb in the early hours of the 29th, Amara was not reached till 10.80 on the evening of March 80th. Here a twenty-four-hour halt was made, during which the men took the opportunity, very welcome, of bathing. After a short march the next day the voyage was resumed, past Ali Gharbi, Sheikh Saad, and Kut—all historic names by now—as far as Hinaidi, four miles south of Baghdad, where the Battalion disembarked and made camp in an orange-grove on the left bank of the river. It sounds a pleasant enough resting-place; but, alas! brother Turk had been there before and, with his conservative views in matters of sanitation, had left it very redolent of his presence. Enemies of flesh and blood we had been trained to cope with, but no measures gleaned from study of any manual could withstand the army of fleas, voracious and of an activity really startling, with which that balmy spot was infested. Recognition of superior adverse forces was the only course, and discretion counselled an orderly withdrawal to fresh ground in the open. This latter was close to the Tel Muhammad position, where the Turk had made his final stand before Baghdad. There still existed evidences of the fighting, and the Battalion had to furnish fatigue parties to clear the battlefield and give decent interment to the corpses which lay scattered on the scene of the action.

When the 15th Division was ordered to the Tigris front, hopes ran high, as it was natural to expect that after their comparatively easy time in Nasiriya they might be employed in some of the important movements which were afoot to the north of Baghdad. Apparently, however, General Maude preferred to carry these out with troops already on the spot, who had helped him to bring to such a successful issue his plans for the attack on and advance from Kut-el-Amara. General Brooking's command remained in the vicinity of Baghdad as a sort of reserve, and was not called on to participate in any engagement for some time.

Baghdad.
Baghdad was universally regarded as an improvement on Nasiriya, though indeed but little evidence remained of the glory ascribed to it in the tales of Haroun the Bountiful Caliph. Only its size distinguished it from any other insanitary Mesopotamian town, though the energetic efforts of its British occupants were beginning to bear, even then, some fruit. Opportunity was taken to march the men through the streets, and its history, with the fact that British and Indian troops alike had striven for its capture since the early days of the war, invested it with a certain measure of importance and interest. The stay here was comparatively brief, for less than a week after its arrival the Battalion had to move farther up the Tigris and was distributed in four posts for the protection of the river from marauding bands of Arabs and small bodies of Turks. At this time the danger of floods is known to have caused considerable anxiety to General Maude. The river lies in many places above the level of the surrounding plain and is confined to its course by artificial works. Were these to be washed away, or severed by enemy action during the flood season, the country would be inundated over a very large area, and bodies of troops would be cut off, tactically and administratively, by miles of water.

The Tigris Posts.
The 2/5th marched out of Hinaidi at 6 a.m. on April 10th on operation scale, which means no tents, twenty pounds of baggage each for the officers, and only one blanket and a waterproof sheet each for the men. By the

evening it had reached Al Minar, 15 miles distant, where it bivouacked for the night. "D" Company, under Captain Rolfe, was left as garrison here, and the remainder resumed the march the next morning to Yahaudie, dropping "C" Company (Major Harington) *en route* at Daudie. Though the distance was but eight miles, it was an uncomfortable and trying march through deep dust and in very severe heat. Captain Wellesley, with "B" Company, remained in occupation of Yahaudie, and Captain Duncan took "A" Company forward, on the 12th, five and a half miles to Kasirin. Thus distributed in these four posts the Battalion remained for the next month. Temperatures ran high during this period, but the men, except in Yahaudie, where they occupied Arab houses, were able to camp in palm-groves, which afforded some protection from the sun, so were not unduly uncomfortable. Nothing of interest happened, and the only duties were the daily patrolling of the river banks and frequent measuring of the height of the water in the Tigris. The apprehension in higher quarters of the danger of floods is evident from the fact that the officer commanding was held responsible for taking a reading of the water level three times a day, and for forwarding the results to force headquarters, with copies to all and sundry who might be interested in this class of information. History is silent as to whether the Local Audit Officer punctually received the statements on the subject, to which he must surely have been entitled.

In May orders were received to return to Hinaidi, and the Battalion started the march on the 13th, arriving on the 17th.

Karradah. The whole brigade (42nd) moved on June 3rd to Karradah, a suburb of Baghdad, where it settled down for the summer. The 1917 hot weather broke records, being the most trying Baghdad had experienced for some years. One hundred and twenty-eight degrees in the shade was the highest temperature touched. Everything considered, the health of all ranks remained good, and it was possible, in spite of adverse conditions, to carry out a considerable amount of training for the operations, which were expected to take place as soon as the cooler season set in. Practice in trench warfare played a large part.

In July, Lieutenant-Colonel Johnson was invalided to India, and was posted to the depot in Abbottabad on again being pronounced fit for duty. Command of the Battalion devolved on Major Harington.

September brought weather sufficiently cool for marching and fighting, and a series of operations began, in which the 15th Division participated. These are summarized in the following extract from Callwell's " Life of Sir Stanley Maude ":—

" During the closing days of September two important operations were carried out with a view partly to extending the area under the control of the Anglo-Indian forces, and partly to depriving the enemy of valuable sources of supply. The first was the occupation of Mendali, on the Persian frontier, about fifty miles east of Baqubah, which was effected on the 29th by a force after a sharp skirmish. The second, a much more serious enterprise, was a carefully prepared attack by General Brooking, with his 15th Division, upon Ramadi on the Euphrates above Felujah, where a Turkish force had been in position all the summer. This undertaking proved a signal success."

15th Division Move to Euphrates Front, September 16th.

The latter operation demanded very careful preparatory work on the part of the Staffs concerned. Ramadi lay at a considerable distance from Baghdad, and communications between the two places were in a wretched state. The Turkish garrison of the former had been reinforced as a result of our operations in July, and its capture now necessitated the employment of a force of some magnitude. It was not until September 26th that a column of adequate size could be concentrated within striking distance of the objective.

The 2/5th left Karradah at five o'clock in the morning of September 16th. Marching by Khan Nuktah, Faluja, and Tel-el-Dhibban, they reached, on the 29th, a place called Madhij, where the river had been bridged. Two days later they relieved the 1/4th Dorsets in the outpost line, which extended from the river bank in a semicircle west and south of the camp, at a distance from it of about a mile and a half.

General Sir Stanley Maude's despatch, from which the following is extracted, gives a general account of the operations which followed:—

Preparations for the Battle of Ramadi.

" The enemy held an advanced position four miles east of Ramadi, on the Mushaid Ridge, which runs north and south and rises sixty feet above the plain. To the north of the ridge lies the Euphrates River, and to the south the Habbaniyeh Lake. The Turkish main position was semicircular in outline, and was sited about one mile to the east and to the south of Ramadi. The eastern front ran along, but behind, the Euphrates Valley Canal to the Aziziyeh Canal, which leaves the Euphrates one mile west of Ramadi and flows southwards.

"The plan of the operations was to turn the southern flank of the Mushaid Ridge, secure a crossing over the Euphrates Valley Canal, and attack Ramadi from the south with the bulk of the column; whilst the Cavalry, operating west of the Aziziyeh Canal, threw themselves across the enemy's communications with Hit by blocking the Aleppo Road. Steps were taken to induce the enemy to expect the main attack against his left on the Euphrates, and with this intent the river was bridged at Madhij, and a road was constructed thence up the left bank, whilst supplies were also collected there. The distribution of the troops until the night of the 27th–28th was also designed to give colour to such a movement.

"At 6 p.m. on the 27th two Infantry columns, with the Cavalry, moved from Madhij to the position of assembly some five miles in front of our outposts, and the Infantry subsequently made a night advance some two miles in a westerly direction to a position of deployment, whence an attack on Mushaid Ridge could be delivered at dawn."

Battle of Ramadi, September 27th and 28th

Before the operation began the designation of the formation to which the 2/5th belonged (42nd Brigade) was changed to "Lucas Column," and on September 27th, in the morning, orders were issued for the advance against the enemy position. The first objective was the Mushaid Ridge, to the west and slightly north of Madhij. The 12th Infantry Brigade was to attack the northern end of the ridge and Lucas column the southern extremity. The latter moved out the same evening along the Aleppo Road, turning half-left across the hills to the position of assembly. Here the column formed up as under, each battalion in mass.

```
    2/6 G.R.              1/4th Dorsets
     [  ]                    [  ]

    1/5 G.R.              2/5th G.R.
     [  ]                    [  ]

         30th M.G. Company
              [  ]

         44th Field Company R.E.
              [  ]
```

First Knoll, the first objective, was taken without difficulty, and the 2/5th were then pushed forward in a westerly direction to occupy Lower Knoll and the dam over the Euphrates Valley Canal. Captain Wellesley, with "A" and "B" Companies, dug in and consolidated the position here, while "C" and "D" Companies, under Major Harington, supported the 1/4th Dorsets, who were in the meantime advancing against Mushaid Ridge. "C" and "D" made an advance of about one thousand yards and then consolidated in support of the Dorsets on what was then believed to be the ridge itself. The Battalion remained in these posi-

Preparing to Advance.

In Action.
2/5th Lewis Guns at Ramadi, Mesopotamia, 1917.

tions till dawn on the 28th, when the Turkish guns reopened fire, but good cover had then been constructed and little loss was sustained.

By 8 o'clock on the morning of the 28th, Mushaid Ridge proper had been captured and the Turks had fallen back. The 2/5th were then directed to advance and capture a feature of the Ramadi position known as Double Hill. They moved forward at 9 a.m. and crossing the dam occupied Tel al Rayan. From here onwards the attack on Double Hill was under shell and rifle fire. Captain Wellesley, with "A" and "B" Companies, took the first ridge and then moved west to occupy another feature, the ground he thus vacated being taken over by "C" and half of "D" Company. The other half of "D," under Lieutenant Gouldsbury, was sent to guard the left flank, where some bodies of Arabs appeared to be collecting in the neighbourhood of the Aziziyeh Canal. While digging in on Double Hill the Battalion was subjected to enemy fire of considerable intensity and sustained several casualties. Amongst others, Lieutenant J. F. Marindin and Jemadar Chintram Bura were wounded.

About 1.30 in the afternoon a unit of the 12th Brigade took over the position on Double Hill. The 2/5th were then ordered to attack the Ramadi Ridge in conjunction with the 1st Battalion, which advanced from Middle Hill. As they moved forward they came under very heavy shell fire from the Turkish guns on the left flank, and this grew more and more severe as the attack swung to the left and drew nearer to Ramadi Ridge. At about two o'clock in the afternoon Major Harington received the mortal wound from the effects of which he died within a very few minutes. Captain Wellesley was the next senior officer on the spot, and he accordingly assumed command of the Battalion. The foremost troops had reached the crest of the Ramadi Ridge, but every effort to push farther forward was frustrated by the overpowering machine-gun and rifle fire which came over perfectly flat and open ground from the Turkish trenches no more than 800 yards away. Digging in just below the crest of the ridge was therefore resorted to, and fresh supplies of ammunition were brought up during the afternoon which enabled a steady fire from Lewis guns and rifles to be kept up on the enemy.

Communication was established and maintained by helio with Lucas column headquarters established at Tel-al-Rayan.

By seven in the evening there appeared to be a considerable slackening in the fire from the Turkish position. The various commanding officers concerned held a conference, at which it was decided to utilize the cover of darkness to withdraw to Middle Hill, about a thousand yards to the rear. This withdrawal was begun at once, and completed by 8 p.m. Command of the troops in the forward position was assumed by Lieutenant-Colonel Nightingale, who had under him the 1/5th

Gurkhas on the right, the 2/5th in the centre, and the 1/4th Dorsets on the left. This line was held throughout the night of September 28th–29th, and, as no water could be brought up, the men suffered severely from thirst. Before dawn on the 29th, Lieutenant Gladstone went forward with a strong patrol towards Ramadi Ridge and found that the enemy were still in occupation of the same trench line that they had held the previous evening. Later in the morning, however, the results of the turning movement by the Cavalry Brigade and the 12th Infantry Brigade became apparent. This had been successfully completed, and the Turkish right flank was turned so that their line of retirement westwards was jeopardized. At 10 a.m. Lucas column again advanced and attacked the Ramadi Ridge, the 2/5th being on the left of the line. The movement had scarcely developed when a body of some three hundred Turks was noticed coming forward in close formation and without arms. These were at once sent to the rear under escort.

The ridge was occupied without opposition, and the advance continued up the river, reaching a point just beyond the building known as Jackson's House. As it approached the river the Battalion was fired on by a small body of Arabs pursuing their usual guerrilla tactics, but these were speedily dispersed without difficulty. By noon all firing in the quarter with which we are concerned had died down, and the capture of the Ramadi position, involving the surrender of the whole Turkish force which had been in occupation of it, was complete.

"Throughout these operations, which were continuous," wrote General Maude in his subsequent despatch, "the endurance and fine fighting spirit of the troops were conspicuous, whilst the night operations so successfully carried out testified to the excellence of their discipline and training. During the daytime the heat was considerable, and these operations, which were conducted at some distance from the river, were only rendered possible by the excellence of the arrangements for water supply."

On the morning of the 30th, Captain Neville Rolfe took over the Battalion. As second-in-command at the beginning of the action he had, in accordance with the arrangements then in force, been left out of the actual battle, and had remained behind at Madhij with the usual nucleus. During the night the right wing, under Captain Wellesley, provided piquets along the river bank, while headquarters and the left wing went into bivouac close to Jackson's House.

Casualties in the Battle of Ramadi in the 2/5th were as follows:—
Killed, one British officer and thirteen rank and file.
Wounded, Lieutenant J. F. Marindin, Subadar Pahalsing Rana, Jemadar Chintram Bura, and sixty-five other ranks.

It is not easy to find words in which to assess the loss sustained, not only by the Battalion but by the Regiment, in the death of Major

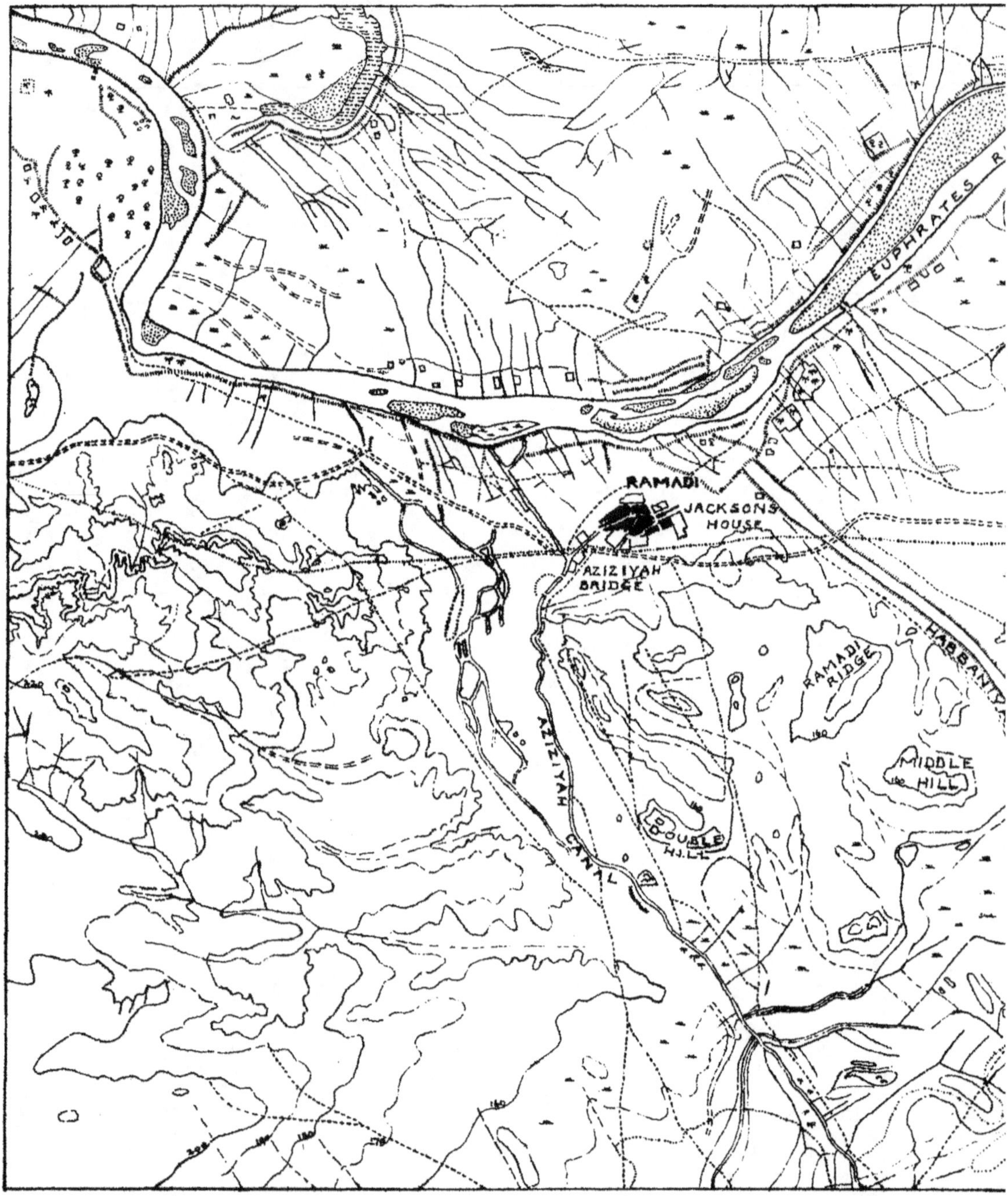

RA

ENLARGED FROM MAP 7

SCALE 1:70,400 or

MILES 1 ¾ ½ ¼ 0 1

(Based on Map No 34 of The Campaign in Mes

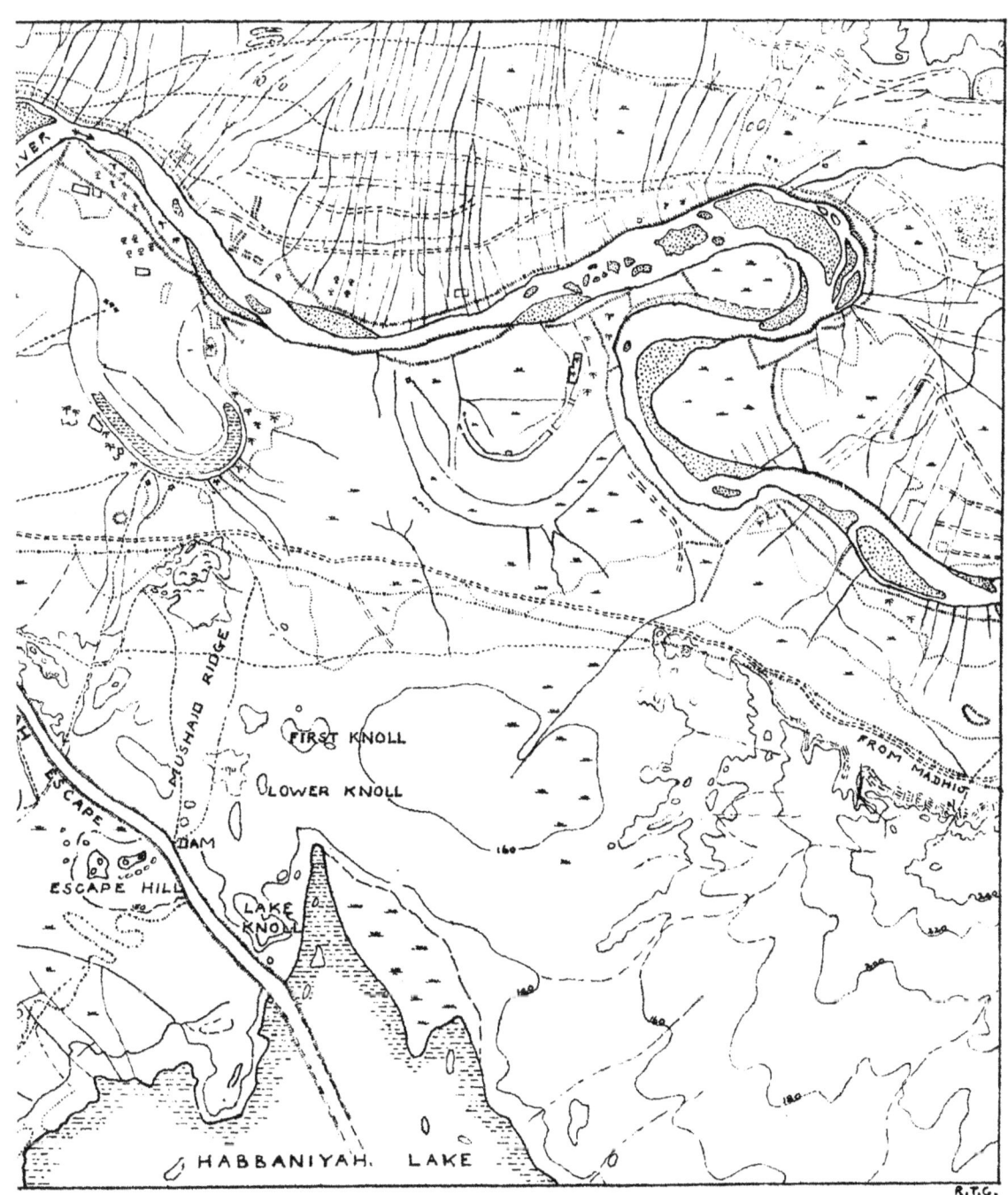

MADI

T.C. 101 (G) DATED 7.2.1918.

1 INCH = 1·11 MILES.

(...spotamia by permission of H.M. Stationery Office.)

Harington. A most accomplished officer and a great leader, he was loved by all, especially those with whom he had shared the perils and hardships of so many battles. The capacity for doing the right thing, apparently by intuition, though actually through intimate knowledge of his profession and exceptional personal courage, was his to a marked degree, and this had been manifested in many a hazardous situation. Good at all games, he was especially distinguished as a polo player of exceptional promise. As already recorded in these pages, his experience of active service had been practically continuous from the beginning of the war, and he had three times been wounded in action. His untimely death undoubtedly cut short a very brilliant career, and his passing left a gap in the Battalion which, it was universally recognized, would prove very hard to fill.

For its services at Ramadi the Battalion was warmly congratulated by the Divisional Commander, Major-General Brooking.

The few days immediately following the action at Ramadi were spent in clearing the battlefield. A handsome collection of arms, ammunition, and equipment was gathered in and duly handed over to the representatives of the ordnance department. On October 4th the Battalion moved to Madhij and remained there employed in the preparation of a defensive position till November 18th. Major G. P. Sanders arrived from the depot in India on November 15th and took over command from Captain Rolfe. On the 18th there was a further move back again to Ramadi, and here they went into camp at the Narrows, three miles below the town on the right bank of the river. Further defensive works had to be taken in hand, and road-making, too, occupied much of the available time. On the same day the infinitely sad news was received of the death of General Maude, after a few days' illness, from cholera. He was succeeded by Lieutenant-General Sir W. R. Marshall. On December 14th the Battalion returned to Madhij. Two new subalterns joined here, Lieutenant R. D'Oyly Hughes and Lieutenant T. H. Denny.

Madhij, 1918.
The stay in Madhij was prolonged into the new year, and during this period there were several changes in the British officer personnel. Captain R. M. Bruce went to Baghdad on January 8th to take up an appointment as Staff Captain, General Headquarters.

On January 12th, Lieutenant-Colonel C. E. Bateman-Champain arrived and assumed command from Major Sanders. On the 19th, Captain Neville Rolfe was appointed Staff Captain to the 53rd Infantry Brigade. Major Duncan changed over on January 21st from the 7th to the 42nd Brigade, still in the appointment of Brigade Major. During this period the command of the forces in Mesopotamia had also changed hands.

On February 5th the Battalion moved again—back to Ramadi once more. Their stay here was brief, for on the 17th orders were received for the brigade to march early the next day on operation scale to Khan Abu Rayat. The object of the move was the capture of the Turkish post at Uqbah, some eight miles to the north-west of the brigade's destination, and the operation is referred to as follows in General Marshall's despatch of April 15th, 1918:—

"During December and January it was evident that the Turks were being reinforced, the bulk of their troops being near Hit, and as their strength grew, their patrols were pushed downstream as far as Uqbah and Nafata. I accordingly issued orders to Major-General Sir H. T. Brooking, K.C.B., K.C.M.G., commanding the troops on the Euphrates front, to capture Hit and its garrison as soon as his arrangements were completed and the state of the ground permitted. My opinion was that there would be no difficulty in capturing the town and driving the Turks out of their position, but that the capture of the Turkish force would be a matter of extreme difficulty in view of their previous experience at Ramadi."

Khan Abu Rayat and Uqbah.

On February 18th a small column moved out of Ramadi at 7.45 a.m. under Brigadier-General Lucas. Included in it were the 2/5th Gurkhas, less "A" Company. They arrived at Khan Abu Rayat at two o'clock in the afternoon and halted there till 8 p.m., when they resumed their advance on Uqbah. Having come within a mile of the post, the column halted, and "B" and "D" Companies were sent round on an encircling movement by the left flank. This effected, they were to advance on Uqbah at dawn in conjunction with the frontal attack by the rest of the column. The plan materialized as was intended, but the post was found to have been vacated by the garrison, so the column returned to Khan Abu Rayat.

Reconnaissances of the Hit Position.

On the day following the whole battalion, with attached troops, all under the command of Lieutenant-Colonel Champain, moved to Uqbah for the purpose of carrying out a reconnaissance for the brigade of the Turkish position at Hit. Marching at 6 a.m. on the 21st, preceded by Cavalry and armoured cars, they quickly came in contact with the enemy. Some thirty prisoners were captured, and, success achieved, they returned to camp at Uqbah. A similar reconnaissance was carried out on the 22nd. On this occasion the column advanced to within a mile and a half of the Turkish position at Hit, but encountered no opposition whatever, though during the day two enemy aeroplanes circled overhead, dropped some bombs and opened machine-gun fire, without, however, inflicting any casualties. Captain Wellesley, with the flank guard, engaged a Cavalry patrol at long range, but the fire of our guns failed entirely to elicit any reply from the Turks. On returning

Sections of 2/5th in Battle Formation, Ramadi, Mesopotamia, 1917.

A Runner, 2/5th, Mesopotamia, 1917.

to camp at Uqbah in the evening it was found that the whole of the 42nd Brigade had closed up there from Khan Abu Rayat. During the night (22nd–23rd) the enemy suddenly opened rapid fire on the camp—evidently a hostile patrol which had managed to creep from Hit unobserved down the left bank of the river. Two men of the 2/5th were seriously wounded and several mules were hit. On February 25th the brigade marched back again to Khan Abu Rayat and went into camp half a mile from the river on the right bank. Here they remained for several days, during which there was considerable aerial activity on both sides. On one or two occasions the enemy machines dropped bombs, but the results were insignificant.

From these various reconnaissances, and from the reports sent in by our airmen, the fact had been definitely established that the main Turkish position had at the outset been taken up some two miles above Hit behind a depression known as the Broad Wadi. Two-thirds of their force was some fifteen miles upstream at Sahaliya. By the end of the first week in March, however, it was discovered that they had vacated the Broad Wadi and were falling back on Sahaliya. General Marshall now decided to press this withdrawal as much as possible and to endeavour to inflict damage on the Turkish columns and transport as they fell back.

In pursuance of this object the 42nd Brigade marched at very short notice on March 18th to Uqbah. On arrival they received orders to the effect that they were to move forward again at 6 o'clock the following morning to support the 50th Infantry Brigade, which had been detailed to attack the Turkish position at Hit. This advance was carried out according to plan on the 19th, and both the Hit and Broad Wadi positions were occupied practically without a shot having been fired. The 50th Brigade then advanced on Sahaliya, and the 42nd, following in support, reached Hit at 3 p.m., where they went into camp half a mile below the town. Here, till the 23rd, the Battalion was employed on road-making and the salving of wire, wood, and such other commodities as could be gathered in from the position recently held by the Turks in front of Hit. The work was laborious and monotonous to a degree, but all applied themselves cheerfully to the task and worked well. On March 11th the Adjutancy was taken over by Lieutenant D'Oyly Hughes, and he held this appointment during the remainder of the stay of the Battalion in Mesopotamia.

Sahaliya. Plans for further operations against the enemy, who after our occupation of Hit and Sahaliya had withdrawn to Khan Baghdadi, were in course of preparation. General Marshall's despatches may again be quoted to illustrate the course of events. After referring to the Turkish withdrawal he continues:—

z

"I then issued orders to drive the enemy as far as possible from Hit and to inflict all possible damage upon him. To assist in this object additional mobile troops, including a Cavalry brigade and light armoured motors, were ordered to Hit, with instructions to move by night and conceal themselves by day, so that the enemy might think that no further advance by my troops was intended; in many ways efforts, apparently successful, were made to deceive the Turks as to our intention.

"On the 26th the plan of operations was to make an attack in strength against the enemy's left, and to send the Cavalry and armoured motor-cars round his right flank. Preparations for this attack were nearing completion when it became evident that the enemy had already begun to withdraw from their forward positions, but intended to make a stand north-west of Khan Baghdadi. Arrangements for assaulting this position were accordingly made, and under cover of an effective barrage it was carried out at 5.30 p.m. with slight loss."

Battle of Khan Baghdadi, March 26th.

On March 23rd the 42nd Brigade made a night march to Sahaliya, where it arrived in the early hours of the following morning, going into camp on the river bank two miles in advance of the 50th Brigade. On the afternoon of the 25th orders were received to march at eleven o'clock the same night, following in rear of the 50th Brigade, with a view to attacking and destroying the 50th Turkish Division, which held Khan Baghdadi and its environs. The movement began at the hour laid down, and after a few miles had been traversed, at about 2.15 in the morning the enemy guns opened fire, their shells bursting about 600 yards ahead of the front of the column. A halt was made while a Staff Officer was sent forward to make inquiries regarding the situation. He returned shortly and reported that the 50th Brigade was in contact with the enemy's forward troops, but that the Brigade Commander was in no immediate need of support, and his intention was to push the Turks from their advanced position, when he would halt and await further orders from divisional headquarters. The 42nd Brigade therefore remained halted in a *wadi* two miles in rear of the 50th Brigade.

At 8 a.m. it was ascertained by means of air reconnaissance that the enemy was holding the Khan Baghdadi position in strength and the northern position but lightly. Our Cavalry were successfully working round the southern end of the Turkish line, and the 15th Division received orders to attack. The 12th Brigade was held in divisional reserve, while the 42nd made a frontal attack, advancing on both sides of the Aleppo Road. The 50th Brigade was to move west and attack the Turkish right flank.

The order in which the 42nd Brigade moved forward was:—

First Line.—The 1/4th Dorsets on the left and the 2/6th Gurkhas on the right. Each battalion had a front of four hundred yards.

Second Line.—The 2/5th Gurkhas, with a section of machine-guns on each flank.

Third Line.—The 1/5th Gurkhas forming brigade reserve.

Considerable shell fire was encountered during the advance, but our forward movement continued unchecked as far as the Wadi Baghdadi. Here there was a halt and the brigade reorganized.

It continued its advance at 5.30 p.m., again under heavy Artillery fire, to attack the Turkish northern position, and during this phase the 2/5th were withdrawn into brigade reserve. When our forward troops arrived at the foot of the small hill, the crest of which had been held by the Turks, the enemy surrender had already commenced. All along the position there was a gay fluttering of white flags and, where the supply of these ran short, of shirts in as white a condition as ever pertains to that intimate garment when in Oriental wear. About 6.30 p.m. all firing in this part of the battlefield had died down, and it was an inspiring sight to witness the Turks being marched in as prisoners—even whole battalions of them.

The enemy losses were heavy during the battle, and in the pursuit which followed it—which was continued by the armoured cars for over seventy miles along the Aleppo Road—there fell into our hands, in addition to the Commander and Staff of the 50th Turkish Division, the Commandant of Ana, the Commandants of two regiments, 213 officers, and 5,022 non-commissioned officers and men. Captured material included 12 guns, 47 machine-guns, and a great quantity of rifles, ammunition, and stores of all kinds. "The complete success of this operation," wrote General Marshall in his despatch, "I attribute to the masterly way in which the force was handled by Major-General Sir H. T. Brooking, and his very complete preparatory arrangements. The endurance of the troops and their determination to get at the enemy were worthy of all praise, whilst the tactical ability of their Commanders was of a very high order." As already recorded, the 2/5th were not heavily engaged, and their casualties were slight. One man only was killed and three wounded during the course of the action.

The night following the close of the fighting was spent in bivouac in the Wadi Baghdadi. Early next morning the Battalion left for Jubbah, and was employed in clearing the battlefield *en route*. This work continued during the next few days.

On March 31st, being Easter Sunday, a thanksgiving service was held for the victory of Khan Baghdadi. The next day the Battalion started to march to Alus, but the Wadi Hauran was at this time in flood and proved to be impassable. A halt was made, and the troops camped on the south bank of the Wadi till April 5th, when the floods had subsided, and the march to Alus was continued.

Here an Inland Water Transport Salvage Party was busily engaged in raising two gun barges which had on board eleven 5-cm. naval guns, and two German launches. The enemy had sunk these in the hope of preventing their falling into British hands. A few days were spent in Alus, and a move was made back to Khan Baghdadi again on April 10th. Two days later the Battalion marched once more to Ramadi, where it arrived on the 16th and reoccupied its former camp on the right bank of the river. This was the last move for the moment, and arrangements were made for settling down in Ramadi for the hot weather. Training was resumed, and a percentage of all ranks was granted six weeks' leave to India.

During the next few months some changes occurred. "D" Company proceeded, on May 15th, under Major Sanders, to Amara, where they were to become part of the 1st Battalion 11th Gurkhas, which was to be raised there on the 18th of the same month by Major A. E. Johnson, 1st Gurkhas. Captain Neville Rolfe returned from Staff employ during May, and the following joined from India:—

"D" Company join 1/11th Gurkhas, May 15th.

Lieutenant R. N. D. Broad.
Second-Lieutenant K. C. Garvie.
Second-Lieutenant L. A. Alexander.

Lieutenant Broad came from the Indian Army Reserve of Officers, and the other two were posted from the Unattached List. During the course of the summer, detachments were furnished at Uqbah and Khan Abu Rayat.

During the waning summer nothing more was seen of the Turks. Their day in Mesopotamia was done, and on November 1st came the news of the cessation of hostilities, celebrated with legitimate jubilation by the troops which had helped to win the victory. Eleven days later information of the conclusion of the armistice with Germany was received. The Great War was ended. A firework display of unusual magnificence marked the occasion in Ramadi. On the 19th, Major-General Brooking read a proclamation to the Arab inhabitants of the district, and selected ranks of the 2/5th shared the privilege with representatives of the 451st Company Royal Engineers of mounting the Guard of Honour for the occasion. The Divisional Commander expressed himself in most congratulatory terms on the appearance and turn-out of the Guard.

Cessation of Hostilities, November 1st.

On November 30th a memorial, which had been erected on Ramadi

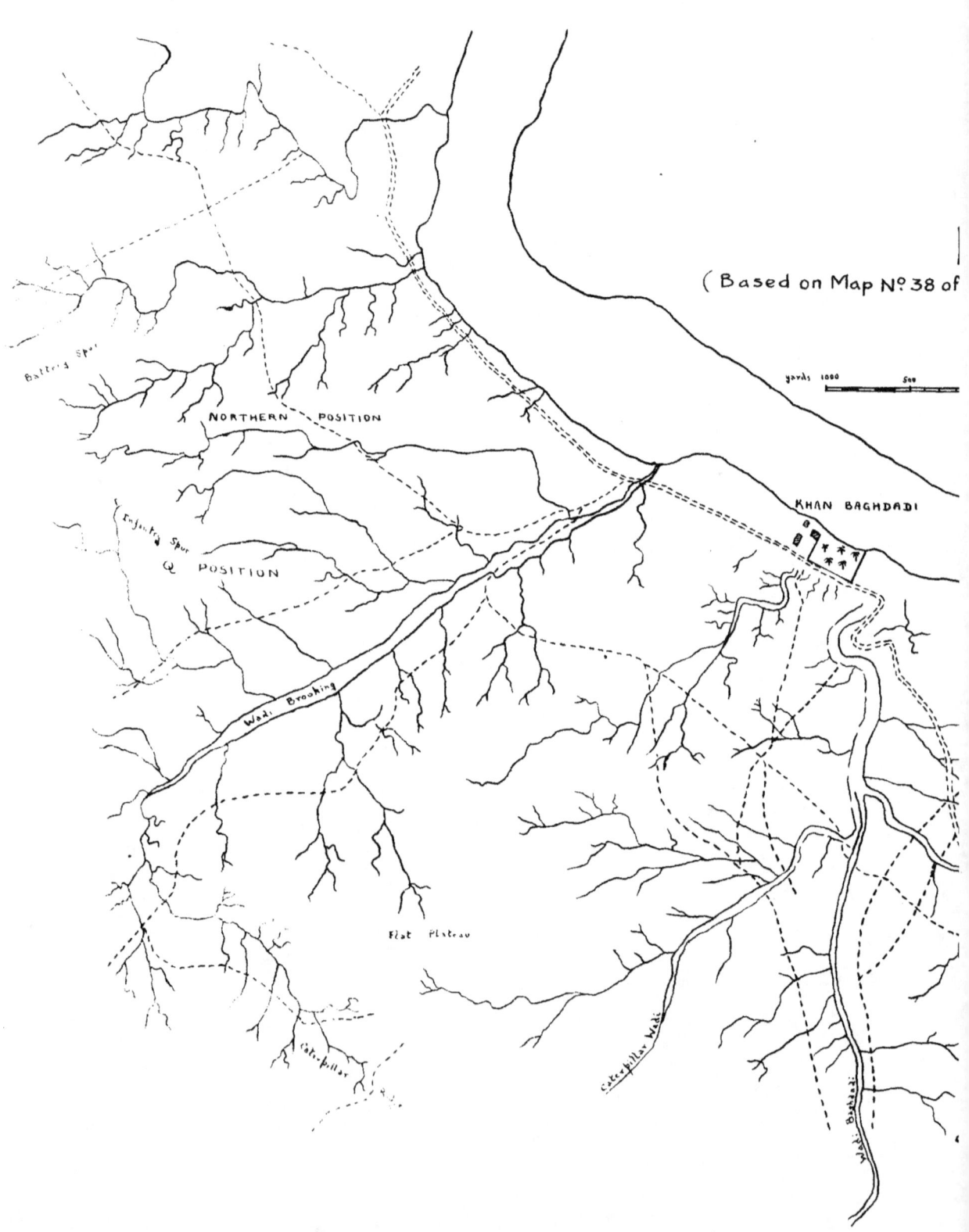

SKETCH MAP
KHAN BAGHDADI
("The Campaign in Mesopotamia" by permission of H.M. Stationery Office)
SCALE 3 INS. TO 1 MILE

Unveiling of Memorial on Ramadi Ridge, November 30th.

Ridge to the honour of those who had fallen in action on September 27th, 28th, and 29th, 1917, was unveiled by General Brooking.

Relieved of the anxieties and uncertainties of war the garrison at Ramadi were able to enjoy the limited pleasures afforded by the locality. Life was bearable as the cold weather set in. The neighbourhood afforded excellent facilities for *shikar* in a small way, and shooting-parties made good bags of black partridge, sand-grouse, etc. The troops made the most of a rest truly well-earned.

In January, 1919, information was received that the 2/5th were to form part of the post-war garrison of Mesopotamia, or, as it should now be referred to, Iraq. Its station was to be Baiji on the Tigris north of Baghdad. This involved a parting from the 15th Division, in which it had served uninterruptedly since its arrival in the theatre of war. The prospect held regrets for all. Major-General Sir H. T. Brooking, who had led the division during the whole period, was exceedingly popular, liked and thoroughly respected by all ranks, so that sorrow at passing out of his command was universal. His name will not be forgotten in the Regiment for many a year. Before they moved, General Brooking held an inspection of the Battalion, at the close of which he made the following farewell address:—

Departure from 15th Division, Feb. 2nd, 1919.

"To-day is for me a sad day, a day on which one has to say goodbye; it must be a sad one especially when it is to old and tried friends, friends who have been serving with me for three years of active service. Three years ago, when I heard that the 2/5th were coming to my division, I was delighted, as they were old friends.

"I have tried you hard, have called on you to do many duties outside that of soldiering—such as brick-making, road-making, etc.; these duties you have always carried out willingly, smartly, and cheerfully. As regards your fighting qualities, these were well known before you came under my command; in all actions under shell, rifle, and machine-gun fire you have fully maintained your great reputation.

"I congratulate you to-day on your turn-out, which is very good, and still more do I congratulate you on your steadiness in the ranks; my inspection has been slow—I made it purposely slow in order to test that steadiness. I knew I should not be disappointed, and I was not. Turn-out and steadiness such as I have seen to-day shows that a high state of discipline has been reached and maintained. Should I have any further command given me I hope that the 2/5th will be in it, and I shall certainly ask for them. I wish you good luck and good fortune, and hope that soon you will all return to your homes."

The 2/5th left Ramadi on February 2nd and arrived six days later

Baiji. at Baiji, where they joined the 55th Infantry Brigade, under the command of Brigadier-General G. M. Morris, D.S.O. They occupied, at first, a temporary camp near the railway station, moving shortly afterwards to one more permanent on the bank of the river. This latter proved to be a very pleasant spot clothed in soft green turf. Steps were taken at once to ensure as comfortable a time as possible for everyone during the coming hot weather. E.P. tents were issued to live in, permanent cooking-places were built, and gardens were even laid out. A club was established where the pre-prandial vermouth could be consumed in comfort, and Colonel Champain was instrumental, with the expert assistance of a man of the East Surrey Regiment who had been a golf professional in pre-war days, in providing a course for devotees of the royal and ancient game. Tennis courts made their appearance, and orders went to India for consignments of rackets and balls. Despite the heat football was very popular, and the weekly matches with the various teams from British units in the garrison attracted quite large crowds of enthusiastic supporters. It was not long before Baiji assumed all the more pleasing attributes of a peace-time cantonment, and all looked forward to a summer very congenial compared with those just gone by.

The illusion was abruptly shattered as far as the 2/5th were concerned. On May 12th they received unexpected orders to return at once to India. Though the "war to end war" was over, there was still the aftermath to be reckoned with. All was by no means well in India, where an internal rebellion in April, of a magnitude unprecedented since the Mutiny, was followed by a war across the border. Afghanistan during the Great War had been held well in hand by the old Amir, but he had met his death at treacherous hands. His successor, the reins hardly yet firm in his hands, sought to secure his somewhat precarious seat by creating a diversion which might serve to unite opposing factions against a common enemy.

Return to India, May 13th.

It was a gambler's throw, being of no less hazardous a nature than open rupture with the power which had just emerged victorious from the greatest conflict known to history. His move towards the frontier outposts opened hostilities which involved the mobilization of the Field Army in India, and units had to be gathered in even from as far afield as Baiji.

On May 13th the 2/5th left their pleasant station for Baghdad on the river steamer No. 51. Reaching Basra they occupied barracks at Makina Masus, close to the spot where just over three years previously they had camped on a desert. Miles of buildings stretched now where only sand had been. On the 23rd they embarked on the

Arrival in India, May 27th.

2/5th marching to Docks from Rest Camp, Basra, to embark for India.

2/5th embarking at Basra for Karachi, on s.s. "Bankora," May 23rd, 1919.

Bankora and sailed for Karachi, which they reached, after a smooth voyage, on the 27th. Here they were accorded an organized reception by the local Welcome Committee. Speeches were made, and all ranks were entertained before moving to the rest camp. This stage of the proceedings was not so pleasant. The heat was great and no transport was ready. In the camp the tents intended for the Battalion were found to be in the hands of a labour corps, which had to be evacuated before the allotted accommodation could be occupied. Comment was rather bitter.

The names of the officers who returned to India with the Battalion are given below:—

    Lieutenant-Colonel C. E. Bateman-Champain.
    Brevet-Major R. C. Duncan.
    Captain A. Neville Rolfe.
    Captain G. A. Maconchy.
    Captain C. S. Baker.
    Captain K. J. Mackintosh, M.C.
    Captain R. D'Oyly Hughes (Adjutant).
    Captain J. C. March.
    Lieutenant N. Macdonald (Quartermaster).
    Lieutenant S. K. Bradford.
    Lieutenant J. McGarry.
    Lieutenant K. C. Garvie.
    Captain A. W. Panton, I.M.S. (Medical Officer).
    Subadar-Major Amarsing Thapa.
    Subadar Sahabir Gurung.
    Subadar Maidhar Gharti.
    Subadar Chintram Bura.
    Subadar Narbahadur Gurung.
    Subadar Bhawansing Thapa.
    Subadar Amarsing Thapa.
    Jemadar Nainsing Thapa.
    Jemadar Chandrasing Gurung.
    Jemadar Manbahadur Rai.
    Jemadar Jitbahadur Thapa.
    Jemadar Balbir Rana.
    Jemadar Indrabir Khan.
    Jemadar Ransur Pun.
    Jemadar Harkasing Gurung.
    Jemadar Puransing Thapa.
    Jemadar Hastadal Thapa.

Major Duncan had come back from the Staff and taken over second-in-command on February 19th. Captains Baker and Mackintosh had been transferred to the 2nd from the 1st Battalion when the latter was recalled to India in March.

PART IV.

THE THIRD BATTALION

CHAPTER I

NOVEMBER 28TH, 1916, TO MAY 15TH, 1919.

Origin and Constitution, November, 1916

THE third battalion of the Regiment was a product of the Great War, and enjoyed a brief existence from its raising on November 28th, 1916, until its disbandment in June, 1921. The story of its doings is, perhaps, worth the telling, not only because it deals with two minor wars of which the names are now borne among the other battle honours of the Regiment, but also as serving to throw some light upon the exceptional conditions which obtained in India during that period. The birth-place of the Battalion was Ferozepore, and the task of raising it was entrusted to Lieutenant-Colonel C. A. Roosmale Cocq of the 1/8th Gurkhas. He was so far fortunate that he was under no necessity to start from the very beginning, since between December 4th and December 22nd, 1916, there were sent to him four companies of trained soldiers. Of these, one came from the 2/1st Gurkhas at Dharamsala, one from the 1/4th Gurkhas at Bakloh, one from the 1/9th Gurkhas at Dehra Dun, and one from the 2/10th Gurkhas at Maymyo. When these had all concentrated from their widely distant places of origin the strength of the Battalion reached the respectable total of 16 Gurkha officers and 1,031 Gurkha other ranks. This number was augmented during the month of December by the enlistment of 51 recruits.

The British officers appointed to the Battalion were as follows:—

Commandant.
Lieutenant-Colonel C. A. Roosmale Cocq, 1/8th Gurkhas.

Wing Commanders.
Major D. H. R. Giffard, 1/8th Gurkhas.
Major A. B. Rombulow Pearse, 2/6th Gurkhas.

Adjutant.
Second-Lieutenant L. G. W. Hamber, 2/1st Gurkhas.

Quartermaster.
Second-Lieutenant R. D'Oyly Hughes, 2/1st Gurkhas.

Company Officers.
Second-Lieutenant P. D. Burch, 2/1st Gurkhas.
Second-Lieutenant J. H. C. Woolley, 2/1st Gurkhas.
Second-Lieutenant W. R. Ransford, I.A.R.O., 2/10th Gurkhas.
Second-Lieutenant W. W. T. Moore, I.A.R.O., 2/10th Gurkhas.

The composition of the infant unit was peculiar and merits a moment's consideration. The 2/1st and 1/4th Gurkhas sent Magars and Gurungs, the 1/9th Gurkhas sent Thakurs and Khas, and the 2/10th Gurkhas sent Limbus and Rais. It comprised, therefore, all classes enlisted in the twenty battalions of Gurkhas which existed before the war. The procedure followed was to group the men into companies on the basis of their origin. Thus it came about that "A" Company was composed of the draft from the 2/1st Gurkhas, "B" of that from the 1/4th, "C" of that from the 1/9th, and "D" of that from the 2/10th. That this method of organization was adopted is in no way surprising; it would appear at first sight to be the most natural and desirable. The result, however, was to retard progress in the inculcation of *esprit de corps*. Slightly to modify a favourite Kipling saying: "When you come to think of it you will see how it must have been so." Lacking a common tradition, each company fell back on that of its parent battalion, and this state of affairs only found a remedy in active service. No great harm was done, but it is possible that homogeneity would have been established more quickly by dividing up the drafts and fixing the composition of each company at two platoons of Magars and Gurungs, one of Khas, and one of Limbus and Rais.

Designation. When first raised the Battalion was given the designation "2nd Reserve Battalion Gurkha Rifles." On May 30th, 1917, the title was changed to 3rd Battalion 5th Gurkha Rifles, and this was followed up by an army department notification dated October 9th, 1917, which bestowed on it the title 3rd Battalion Fifth Gurkha Rifles (Frontier Force). It was unfortunate that at the time of the first change in designation the newly named 3/5th Gurkhas contained not a single representative of either of the older battalions of the Regiment, with the exception of one re-enlisted man who had taken his discharge from the 2nd Battalion before the war. Still, this rechristening of Gurkha units raised since the outbreak of war was completely sound. In the case of those more fortunately placed than the 3/5th Gurkhas it provided them with matured traditions, and helped to link them up with the established order of things.

The record of the first year or two of the Battalion's existence need

Early Days, 1916, 1917. not long detain us. The original drafts were composed for the most part of very young soldiers, and recruiting was proceeding apace, so that the chief need was time in which to train and to smooth out kinks in the arrangements for organization and interior economy. So long as the Battalion remained in Ferozepore, ample time was available, for the Brigadier, General Crocker, realizing the necessity, excused it from the performance of all station duties, and gave a free hand to Colonel Roosmale Cocq.

These advantages were lost when on April 18th, 1917, a move was made to Rawalpindi, which was to prove far from ideal as a station for a newly raised Gurkha unit. *Move to Rawalpindi, April, 1917.* The men—and to a far greater extent the women and children—suffered from the heat, duties were heavy, and the obligation to provide large fatigues at the arsenal, rest camp, and other places, interfered with training. Still, such disabilities were as nothing compared with the real hardships which were being borne with fortitude at that time by millions of soldiers in many theatres of war, and so everybody settled down in the Edwardes lines, prepared to make the best of things.

In July, 1917, Lieutenant-Colonel A. C. Wall took over command of the Battalion from Lieutenant-Colonel C. A. Roosmale Cocq, who proceeded to join the 1/8th Gurkhas, then on active service in Mesopotamia. *Changes Amongst British Officers.* In the same month Major D. H. R. Giffard left, to be replaced as a Wing Commander by Captain H. R. C. Lane of the 2/5th Gurkhas, who joined in September. Of the numerous other changes amongst British officers, considerations of space will only permit a reference to the arrival of Lieutenant (Acting-Captain) A. E. Barlow, M.C., and Lieutenant (Acting-Captain) P. C. Tudor Craig in October. These two officers served with the Battalion until its disbandment in 1921. One incident in which the Battalion was concerned during its stay at Rawalpindi is perhaps worthy of record. It concerns an unusually trying march.

After undergoing battalion training at Usman Khattar, and brigade training at Khanpur, the Battalion took part in inter-brigade manœuvres, which led it via Panian and Hasan Abdal to Fateh Jang. *A Strenuous March, December, 1917.* Here, on December 21st, the exercise terminated, and simultaneously the usual manœuvre rains set in in earnest. Orders were received to make Rawalpindi next day, the 22nd. This entailed a march of twenty-eight miles. Dawn broke on a very cheerless prospect; owing to wind and rain hardly a bivouac shelter had survived the night, and the camping-ground was a sea of mud. Orders and counter-orders caused some delay, but eventually a start was made. The wind which blew cut like a knife and appeared to come straight off the snows, and the first fifteen miles were accomplished for the most part in a pelting downpour of hail. The precaution had been taken of sending on overnight a half-road meal of *chupatties* and the wherewithal to make tea, but the tea did not materialize, and the *chupatties* were sodden lumps of dough. The driver of the A.T. cart provided for the mess, died of exposure as he drove, the mules ran away, and the contents of the cart were looted by the local inhabitants. Fortunately the coffee-shop contractor of the Durham Light Infantry was encountered by the way and proved to be in a position to provide hot tea. By that time hands were so numb as to be incapable even of holding a mug securely, but means were taken to restore circulation, everybody was served, and the march resumed. Darkness had fallen some time before West Ridge was reached, so no regrets were expressed when at that point a string of lorries was encountered, which conveyed the weary troops over the remaining two and a half miles of the journey to barracks.

Marri Expedition, February, 1918.
In February of 1918 an expedition was sent against the Marris, a Baluchi tribe inhabiting a tract of country to the east of Sibi. A small draft of the Battalion under Jemadar Kabir Thapa was attached to the 2/2nd (K.E.O.) Gurkhas for this expedition, and it rejoined on the conclusion of operations in May.

Peshawar, 1918.
On March 19th, 1918, the Battalion was transferred to Peshawar, where it took up its quarters in the Nicholson lines. Here the hot weather proved very trying; there was much sickness, which culminated in an outbreak of influenza attended by many deaths, and heavy duties interfered with training.

During the previous hot weather in Rawalpindi the mortality among the women and children had been very heavy, and it was felt that every effort must be made to ensure their escape from the more trying climate of Peshawar. Sanction having been given, in June the families were transferred to Bakloh, where they occupied a part of the married lines of the 1/4th Gurkhas. Successive Depot Commanders of that battalion did everything in their power to make things easy for them, and there, in charge of a Gurkha officer and twelve married G.O.R.'s, they lived happily for more than a year.

It would be difficult to imagine conditions less favourable for the training of Gurkha recruits than those attaching to the Peshawar hot weather. The Battalion was not alone in voicing its troubles in this connection, with the result that in July orders were issued for the formation of a camp at Kalabagh, where the recruits of all Gurkha battalions stationed in the plains were to assemble for training. The charge of the camp was given to Captain Lane, who found himself by the end of August responsible for the training and administration of two thousand men drawn from seven different battalions. Those acquainted with the locality do not need to be told that flat ground is hard to find, and such as exists being beyond rubies in value for parade purposes, the provision of tent sites for the accommodation of so large a number of men presented certain difficulties. However, Subadar Karbir Gurung of the Battalion, who acted as Subadar-Major of the camp, proved himself equal to every emergency, and carried through some astonishing feats of engineering in his successful endeavour to house each detachment as it arrived. The recruits improved enormously in physique, and progressed in their training at a rate more rapid than that attainable in the plains. It was perhaps a mistake to retain them in Kalabagh as late as the middle of December, since 160-lb. tents, even though reinforced with uprights and cross pieces of cut pine branches, form a poor protection against heavy snowfalls and biting winds. There were a few cases of frostbite, and influenza—which that year drove through the world as a scourge—claimed a number of victims. To the great regret of all ranks Captain Newcome of the 3/2nd Gurkhas contracted the disease, and after being sent to Abbottabad, died in hospital there a few days later. On the whole, however, the outcome of the establishment of the camp may be written in the account as nearly all gain, and the experiment would doubtless have been repeated in subsequent years had not other means been found to provide escape for Gurkha recruits from the rigours of the hot weather in the Punjab plains.

On July 28th, 1918, Lieutenant-Colonel A. C. Wall left to take over command of the 2/8th Gurkhas, and was succeeded by Lieutenant-Colonel C. P. Barlow of that battalion. Other British officers who joined the Battalion during the year and who were destined to remain with it until its disbandment were Second-Lieutenant D. Campbell, I.A.R.O.; Second-Lieutenants A. R. Gray and R. G. Leonard, from Wellington Cadet College; Lieutenant B. A. Ryan from the 1/4th Gurkhas; Second-Lieutenant T. R. Harrison from the R.M.C., Sandhurst; Lieutenant A. G. Pinches from the Australian Imperial Forces; and Second-Lieutenant C. R. Wilkinson.

Move to Murree Hills, 1919.

After a month of battalion training carried out at Dag on the road to Cherat in January, 1919, the Battalion returned to Peshawar to prepare for a move to the hills. Its destination was Chamiari, a camping-site six miles north of Murree on the long spur which stands above the right bank of the Jhelum, and drops gradually to river level at Kohala. The whole Battalion was concentrated there by March 11th, but arrangements had hardly been put in train for the spending of a profitable summer when news was received of serious disturbances in Amritsar, Gujranwala, Lahore, and other places in the Punjab. The arrival shortly afterwards in Murree of harassed refugees from the plains showed how gravely the situation was viewed by those in authority, It became necessary to take precautionary measures on the spot, entailing the dispersal of the Battalion for the safeguarding of certain localities in and around Murree.

Mobilization for Third Afghan War, May, 1919.

Such was the situation when, at about 2 a.m. on the night of May 6th–7th, a telephone message was received from brigade headquarters directing the Battalion to be ready to move in an hour. Move whither and on what mission? The telephone having functioned, remained from that moment dumb, and time being precious, efforts to glean further information were abandoned. It was a pitch-dark night, and under the best of circumstances a hill camp affords few facilities for rapid preparation. Thanks, however, to the almost uncanny faculty of the Gurkha for avoiding, in the dark, " pitfall and gin "—in this case tent ropes, ravines, and terraces, these last in some places giving a drop of twelve feet or even more—all was in readiness in advance of the appointed hour. Camp guards had been detailed, ammunition and rations issued, Lewis-gun mules loaded, and companies fallen in. As was only natural, the sudden order was attributed to fresh developments of the internal security situation; actually it was occasioned by external affairs. When, the telephone active once more, information to this effect had been communicated the Battalion was dismissed, and lamps were lighted in the office tents as a preliminary to mobilization for a war against Afghanistan.

With detachments scattered all round Murree, and with its stores and clothing nearly fifty miles away in a redoubt of the outer line of the Rawalpindi defences, the Battalion found many stumbling-blocks in the path of rapid mobilization. By noon on May 8th all that it was possible to accomplish in Chamiari had been done, and at 4 p.m. on that date the Battalion marched for Rawalpindi. The distance of forty-two miles was covered in about thirty-six hours, dawn of the 10th discovering the small column, by now a little footsore owing to the constant downhill gradient, halted just north of the city, while it awaited the decision of higher authority regarding its exact destination. Soon it was on the move again, and making for the Chamberlain lines. Here five days were spent in completing mobilization, and on the night of May 15th–16th the Battalion entrained for Peshawar to gain its first experience of active service.

At Serai Kala a draft was met composed of about 150 men of the 2nd Battalion under Jemadars Ransing Thapa and Goria Thapa. They were destined to serve with the 3rd Battalion for many days to come, and their presence did much to foster the regimental spirit which had only lately shown signs of growth.

CHAPTER II

Third Afghan War—The Battalion in Mardan.

May, 1919, to September, 1920.

General Situation, May, 1919.
The attitude of Afghanistan during the Great War had more than once given cause for anxiety. So long as the Amir Habibulla remained alive, however, despite conflicting interests, he conducted the affairs of his country with circumspection. A Turco-German Mission, which went to Kabul in October, 1915, returned home again without effecting its object, but left behind certain Indians who had accompanied it. Whether by their efforts or through some other agency, a definitely anti-British party was formed, which found influential leaders in Nasrulla—brother of Habibulla, Amanulla—the third son of the Amir, and Nadir Khan—the Commander-in-Chief.

In February, 1919, Habibulla was murdered, and Nasrulla, with the support of the army, had himself proclaimed Amir in his stead. His position none too secure, and anxious to divert attention from the murder of his brother, he decided to attack India. As a preliminary he entered into negotiations with the revolutionary party in India, and it is probable that his activities in that direction were in a measure responsible for the outbreak of serious disturbances in the Punjab in the following April. The first act of aggression on the part of Afghanistan was the seizure, on May 3rd, 1919, of the Bagh Springs over against Landi Khana. On May 5th two companies of Infantry were sent from Peshawar in lorries to reinforce the Khyber Rifles at Landi Kotal, and on May 6th war was formally declared. At that time the Afghans had three battalions of Infantry with two guns at Bagh, 350 Infantry with two guns at Spinatsuka, and five battalions of Infantry with 200 Cavalry and six guns at Dakka. To oppose this force the British had immediately available only two companies of Infantry and 500 bayonets of the Khyber Rifles at Landi Kotal. On May 7th the 2nd Battalion Somerset Light Infantry with two sections of No. 8 Mountain Battery were rushed up the pass in lorries, but as an offset to this the internal situation was complicated by a serious rising in Peshawar City. This, however, was successfully suppressed, and on May 8th the 1st Indian Infantry Brigade, under Brigadier-General Crocker, arrived at Landi Kotal. There followed in quick succession the unsuccessful attempt of the

1st Brigade to recapture Bagh Springs on May 9th, the arrival of the 2nd Brigade on the 10th, and its successful effort against the same objective on May 11th. After reconnaissance of the Tor Tsappar and Spinatsuka positions on May 12th the advance to Dakka began next day. May 14th and 15th saw three brigades concentrated at Dakka, with the surrounding heights still unsecured, and the Cavalry engaged in an unsuccessful attempt to locate the Afghan Army. On May 16th the Afghans themselves saved further trouble on this score, for a reconnaissance sent out under Colonel Macmullen found them preparing for an attack in force on Dakka itself. In the fighting which ensued the Afghans succeeded in gaining a footing on the unpiquetted hills overlooking the camp, so creating a very awkward situation for the British force. Meantime there was considerable activity on other fronts. Nadir Khan himself was preparing for an advance through Khost, which culminated in the investment of Thal Fort, while at many places on the long line of frontier, notably the Tochi and Tank Zam, the tribes were openly hostile.

This was the situation when on May 16th the 3/5th Gurkha Rifles arrived in the area of operations. Before confining the narrative to their part in the campaign it is convenient to mention here that subsequent operations at Dakka took the form of attacks on the surrounding hills, and these secured, of scouring the country in the vicinity; that Thal was eventually relieved by a force under Brigadier-General Dyer; and that in Waziristan the tribes persisted in their hostile attitude, demanding the dispatch against them of the expeditions of 1919–20 and of 1922–23. From every point of view it was to prove a most unsatisfactory campaign. Afghanistan could hope for nothing in opposition to a first-class power; while on her side, India, with her heavy overseas commitments, was in no position to force a decisive issue to the contest.

Experiences on L. of C., May to July, 1919.
It is not proposed to give a day-by-day chronicle of the doings of the Battalion during these operations, since it would serve no good purpose and would prove as wearisome to read as it would be toilsome to record. Instead, a few typical incidents will be described in detail, from which it will be possible to form a fair idea of the kind of existence it was called upon to lead.

From May 16th until July 31st the Battalion was employed on the lines of communication between Kacha Garhi and Ali Masjid. Its duties were to furnish piquets, to escort convoys, to patrol the Kajuri Plain, or merely to swelter in tents and wait for something to happen. The intense heat was undoubtedly the worst enemy encountered. Judging by the event it would appear that the hearts of the Khyber Pass Afridis were not in the game, since their unenterprising attitude on most occasions can hardly be ascribed to lack of opportunity. In proof of this assertion one incident will suffice. During the latter half of May the Battalion was split into detachments at Ali Masjid, Shagai, Fort Maud, and Baghiari. These detachments provided route piquets for the protection of the line between Ali Masjid and Jamrud. The security scheme on which protective arrangements were based fixed the strength of a number of piquets at one and six. They were required to go out to their positions before dawn, often unsupported and in some cases separated from the road by a mile of broken country. They were withdrawn at dusk. And yet it was not until the day succeeding that on which the Battalion handed over these duties to the 2/8th Gurkhas that a piquet was molested. Then, of course, it was wiped out.

On two occasions large convoy escorts were called upon to march from Jamrud to Ali Masjid and back in the day, a distance of twenty-two miles. The maximum day-temperature was in the neighbourhood of 120°—but on neither ocasion did a single man fall out.

Affair of Shamgakki Pass, July, 1919.

The greatest test of endurance, however, was furnished in the experiences of July 21st and 22nd. A considerable force of the enemy had previously moved against the Khyber communications from the south. After meeting with some success, notably in the complete annihilation of a piquet on Bali Hill, they were driven off, and during their retirement left strong detachments on the Besai Ridge. A column, of which the 3/5th Gurkhas formed part, was organized at Kacha Garhi, with orders to march at midnight of July 21st–22nd, with the object of surprising these detachments at daylight. The Battalion fell in at 11.30 p.m., and proceeded to the rendezvous, the west gate of the camp. The night was intensely dark, and on the way two ammunition mules walked straight into a deep borrow pit, from which they were extricated with considerable difficulty. Arrived at the rendezvous there was no sign of any other unit, nor yet of column headquarters. The Adjutant, being sent to find them, ran them to earth in bed, and it only then transpired that the starting-hour had been postponed until 1.30 a.m. Through an oversight the only complete unit in the column had been left in ignorance of the change, and the men had missed half a night's precious sleep for nothing—truly a bad beginning for what was to prove a most trying operation.

In due course other units began to arrive at the rendezvous, and at 2 a.m., with the Battalion leading and furnishing the advance guard of one company, the column began its march. Its immediate objective was the Shamgakki Pass connecting the long low ridge of Besai with the higher hills on the south of the Khyber Pass. It was a most oppressive night, but there were no obstacles to progress, and it was possible to maintain a comparatively rapid rate of marching. About seven miles had been covered by 5 a.m., when a halt was called, and protected by "D" Company of the 3/5th Gurkhas the column waited for the day. With dawn came realization that it had approached rather too closely the mouth of the pass in march formation. Before deployment could be effected a brisk fire was opened by the enemy in occupation of the heights on either side of the pass. Probably owing to the poor visibility, however, casualties were few; shelter for the animals was found in a convenient *nullah*, and "D" Company of the Battalion, with "C" Company in support, advanced to the attack. Reluctant to abandon so tempting a target as that presented by the main body of the column, the enemy at first showed little inclination to withdraw, but the near approach of our men, and the fire of a section of guns which opened on them at a range of less than 1,000 yards, presently convinced them that to wait longer might be unsafe, and they melted away to the southward. "C" and "D" Companies then moved forward on either side of the pass, dropping piquets as they went, and soon after 9 a.m. the available Cavalry was pushed through to scour the Kajuri Plain on the far side.

While this operation was in progress Major Lane, who commanded the Battalion in Colonel Barlow's absence, was summoned by the Column Commander. He was informed that numbers of the enemy were reported to have made good their escape along the Besai Ridge in the direction of Bara Fort, and that orders had been received from the General Officer Commanding at that place to detach a part of the Kacha Garhi column to go after them. The 3/5th Gurkhas having been selected for the task, moving as quickly as possible were to make a thorough search of the Besai Ridge throughout its length, endeavour to round up the enemy party, and return to Kacha Garhi independently of the rest of the column on completion of the operation. A distinguished General, commenting afterwards on this move, said that the order had obviously been given "off the map."

Just twelve hours after falling in at Kacha Garhi the Battalion started on this, which was to prove the most arduous part of a prolonged effort. The ground was known to be quite impracticable for mules, so extra burdens were imposed on the men. *Chaguls* and water-bottles were refilled, Lewis gun loads were distributed to the sections, and expended ammunition was replaced. The distance to be traversed along the hills was not more than seven miles as measured on the map, but the ground was rocky and difficult, the crest of the ridge was found to bend and double on itself like a winding river, and often during that painful journey in search of an elusive enemy it was necessary to climb steeply several hundreds of feet, only to drop precipitously an equal distance on the other side. The heat was intense, and as one man after another showed symptoms of heat exhaustion it became advisable to remove all restrictions regarding the drinking of water. As a result of this, after several hours the supply began to fail. At 3.30 p.m. a few shots were fired, disclosing the position of two or three of the enemy on the northern face of the ridge. They disappeared almost immediately, and the task of locating them again, as was bound to be the case, was beyond the power of exhausted men. This led to the decision to descend from the ridge by two parallel spurs under cover of a rear-guard, and to make for Kacha Garhi, in accordance with the original orders. By the time the Battalion had concentrated in the plain two men were dead from heatstroke and some twenty others were unconscious, of whom three died on the way. Many more were on the verge of collapse, and but for the providential arrival of the weary column at the Bara Reservoir while still some distance from its destination, the tale of deaths would have been much longer. The necessity for frequent halts to pour water over those who had succumbed to the heat and the severe tax on the flagging energies of the carrying parties made progress very slow, and it was 7 p.m. before the Battalion arrived in camp.

Lest a false impression should be given by the record of these twenty hours, a few words of comment are advisable. There can be no question that the men were fit—they had proved it on more than one occasion by their marching prowess, and, when operating in brigade, they had withstood the heat as well as other classes of soldiers. That there were so many victims of heat exhaustion on this occasion can only be accounted for by conceding the exceptionally arduous nature of the task which the Battalion was called upon to perform. When due weight is given to such factors as lack of sleep and number of hours under arms; the extreme difficulty of the country traversed; the extra weight imposed by lack of transport for ammunition, Lewis guns, and water; the intense heat, and, during the last few hours on the ridge, the scarcity of water, ample cause is forthcoming for the collapse of so many men.

Patrol Work, July, 1919. As an example of the patrol work on which the Battalion was frequently employed—work, incidentally, which accounted for most of its casualties—the following will serve. On July 11th news was received at Kacha Garhi towards evening that a railway engine on its way from Jamrud to Peshawar had been fired on near Windy Corner, the fireman being hit. Lieutenant Harrison was detailed to lead a patrol of forty men in an attempt to round up the enemy party responsible. For the proper understanding of what ensued it is necessary to mention that patrols moved out on alternate evenings from Jamrud and Kacha Garhi to search the ground in the vicinity of Windy Corner, the name given to a road and *nullah* junction east of Jamrud, where enemy parties, bent on making themselves unpleasant, were wont to resort at dusk

On this particular evening it was the turn of Jamrud to send out a patrol. On nearing Windy Corner with his small force Lieutenant Harrison noted a body of men of the approximate strength of a company, and dressed as Indian Infantry, moving towards him in open order from the direction of Jamrud. He very naturally concluded that he was about to meet the Jamrud patrol, and when the khaki figures suddenly changed direction across his front, and began to double, he made haste to conform to their movement, under the impression that they were after the enemy party, which was the object of his search. Disillusionment, then, came somewhat suddenly, when the supposed patrol disappeared behind the cover of previously constructed sangars and opened a heavy fire at a range of two hundred yards. Lieutenant Harrison was wounded seriously, and two of his men were also hit. Despite shattered bones and a severed artery, with the help of his orderly he succeeded in tying up his wound and continued to direct operations. The enemy having been evicted from his first position, maintained a running fight in the direction of the Shamgakki Pass, Lieutenant Harrison and his party following closely and endeavouring to work round his flank and intercept him. For over an hour the pursuit was sustained, and then darkness intervened. Lieutenant Harrison called a halt, collected his command, and conducted it safely back to camp. At the very entrance to the perimeter he himself lost consciousness from shock and loss of blood. For his conduct on this occasion he was recommended for the award of the Military Cross, the recommendation receiving warm support from General Sheppard, the Brigade Commander. Despite his efforts, however, the award was not made.

The Lighter Side, 1919.
Even a hot-weather campaign at the wrong end of the Khyber has its humorous side. When the Battalion arrived in Peshawar on May 16th one wing entrained immediately for Jamrud. Only after three unsuccessful attempts did the engine succeed in taking the final gradient, each successive failure necessitating a longer run at the slope, so that at one time the half-battalion found itself back at the Islamia College. The nine-mile journey occupied nearly three hours, and Jamrud was attained only at 1 a.m. There the officer in command made his way into the fort to collect information. There had been fighting in the pass, and it may be that nerves were a little overwrought. He was asked how many men he had brought with him, and on replying, "About four hundred," was somewhat surprised at the fervent, "Thank God, we are saved" of his interlocutor. Expecting to be required for convoy duty up the pass in the morning he asked for orders on the subject. "Convoys! My dear young man, can't you understand? We've lost the pass!" After that it only remained to go to bed, so he asked where

Kacha Garhi, 1919: Corner of 3/5th Camp.

Relief of Samawa: Samcol on the March with Armoured Construction Train.

he and his command should bivouac. He was told that there was no room inside the defences, that an attack of 5,000 tribesmen was expected from the *north-east* at any moment, that the perimeter was fully manned and everybody ready for instant action, but that his half-battalion could settle down *outside the north-east face* of the perimeter. This they did, undisturbed till the early morning, when they went up the pass with their convoy.

Then there was the occasion when a large and strong Lama of the Battalion held up the entire watering arrangements of the brigade by taking forcible possession of the standpipes and driving away all who approached, because, though he understood no language but his own, he was convinced that an insult had been offered to his Regiment by one drawing water for another unit.

There was an enterprising Quartermaster, who shall be nameless. When awaiting his turn to draw rations he set his working party to occupy the attention of a distracted Conductor by a pretence of pilfering, while with the help of two trusty henchmen, from the other side of the pile he removed a large ice-chest, which found its way to the mess.

Finally there was the incident of the nightmare, which, it is to be feared, was not viewed humorously by the victim. On one occasion a British machine-gun detachment was sent to reinforce one of the Battalion piquets at a salient of the perimeter. During the night a gunner of the detachment had a bad dream, sprang up with a shout, forced the exit, and fled shrieking in the direction of enemy country. Before anybody else could act a youngster who had been sworn in at Chamiari only a few days before the Battalion marched, still dazed with sleep, with a muttered " lo, kha ! " fired two rounds rapid in the direction of the noise. Both found their billet in the dreamer, who, however, made a rapid recovery.

End of the Campaign.
After July 22nd the Battalion was engaged in no affair of interest or importance; as far as Afghanistan was concerned, hostilities had come to an end, and on the 31st a move was made to Peshawar.

The Battalion casualties during the campaign had been:—

Killed, 1 G.O.R.
Died of heatstroke, 5 G.O.R.'s.
Wounded, 1 B.O., 7 G.O.R.'s.

In June, Major A. B. Rombulow Pearse had left to take over command of the 3/1st Gurkhas. He was at that time the only survivor of those British officers who joined the Battalion on its formation; as second-in-command his experience, and more especially his knowledge of interior economy, had proved of the greatest value, and while rejoicing at his promotion, the 3/5th Gurkhas could not but regret the loss of a true friend.

The sojourn in Peshawar was not of long duration, for on September 9th the Battalion found itself in Mardan, the stronghold of the Guides. Here for a short time it was accommodated in temporary structures which formed a kind of annexe to the Cavalry lines, but before long a change for the better was made to the Bagdada lines at the northern limit of the cantonment. The depot remained at Chamiari until October, when it was transferred to Kakul, near Abbottabad.

Mardan, 1919–20.

On September 22nd, Lieutenant-Colonel Barlow proceeded on leave to England, and for a year Major H. R. C. Lane officiated for him in command of the Battalion. Captain H. N. Irwin from the 2/3rd Gurkhas, Lieutenant L. G. Watts from the 2/1st Gurkhas, and Lieutenant W. B. Whitaker from the 1/1st Gurkhas all joined during August and were destined to remain until disbandment.

The year in Mardan was both pleasant and profitable. Almost for the first time since leaving Ferozepore the Battalion was left free to work at a progressive scheme of training without the interference of heavy duties and a high sick-rate. The men were contented and fit, they could fish and shoot to their hearts' content, facilities for games were greater than had previously existed, and except for mountain warfare there was excellent training-ground. Furlough was opened for 30 per cent. of the establishment at a time for a period of four months, and this factor governed the training-programme, all furlough vacancies being filled from one half-battalion, which furnished all duties from the remainder of its strength, so leaving the other half-battalion intact to carry out four months of individual training. At the end of the first period of four months the half-battalions exchanged rôles. India at this time boasted a great number of schools of instruction, and on the whole the results achieved at them were surprisingly good. One of the most gratifying features of this period is the number of first-class instructors that materialized.

It was in the summer of 1920 that a zeal for education was born. Spurred on from above, the Battalion tackled the problem by limiting the attendance at the Battalion school to those reading for 1st and 2nd Class certificates of education, and shifting on to Company Commanders the responsibility for education up to the 3rd Class standard. The Company Commander, in his turn, organized seven classes under selected N.C.O.'s or well-educated riflemen. Of these four parallel classes were for complete illiterates, two parallel classes for those with some knowledge of reading and writing, and one class for those about to take the 3rd Class school examination. This will give some idea of the large proportion of men unable to read and write in the new battalions.

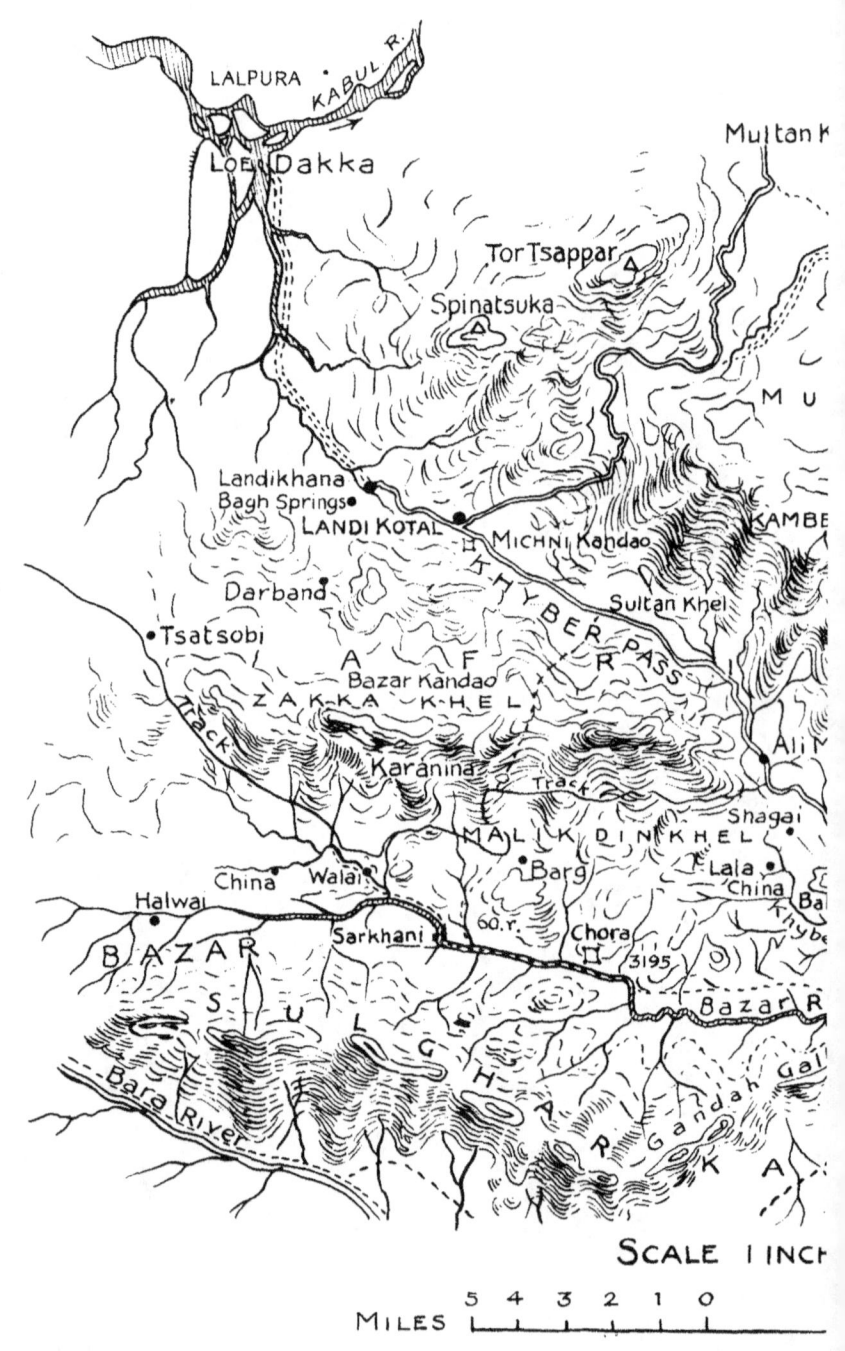

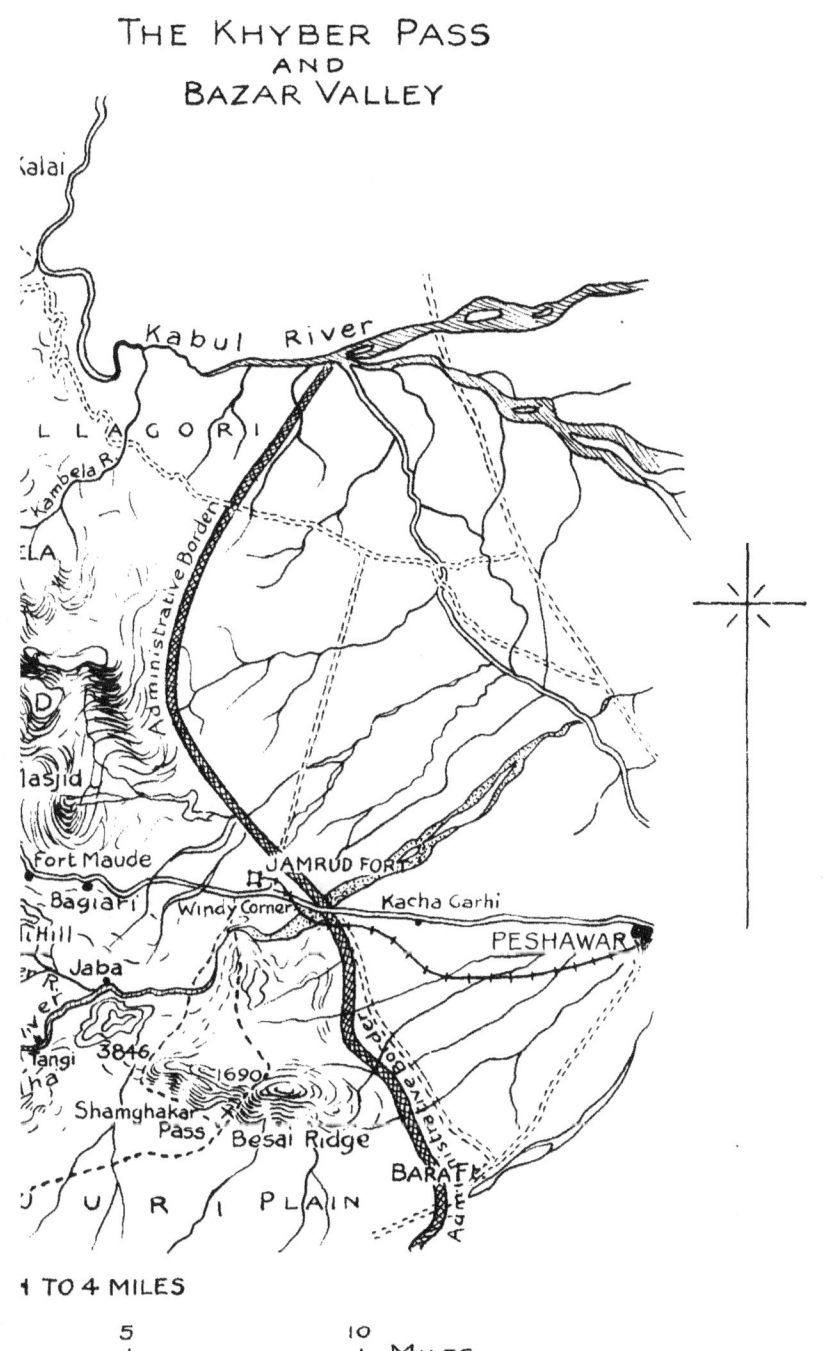

Such was the impetus of the progressive spirit that an English Class was conducted for Gurkha officers; but, after trial, the effort was abandoned as they simply would not play.

While in Mardan the British officers enjoyed the hospitality of the famous Guides Mess, and to mark their appreciation they subscribed for a silver statuette of a Gurkha, to take its place with those of other classes enlisted in the Guides which stand around the big centre-piece. Unlimited polo, good riding-country, excellent shooting in the cold weather, the swimming-bath and all the usual games, made life very pleasant.

In April, 1920, Mardan was honoured with a visit by His Excellency the Commander-in-Chief in India, General Sir Charles Monro, who inspected the garrison on parade, and in his speech, referring to the Guides and the 5th Gurkhas, spoke of them as " the two most famous regiments of the Indian Army." Others who inspected the Battalion were the G.O.C. 1st Cavalry Brigade and the G.O.C. 1st Peshawar Division. The reports of both were very complimentary.

Move to Kakul for Mobilization, August, 1920. During the summer of 1920 orders were received to prepare for disbandment. This was a great disappointment, but fortunately preparations in that direction were not very far advanced when the instructions were cancelled, and instead the Battalion was directed to proceed to Kakul, the station originally chosen for disbandment, there to mobilize for active service in Mesopotamia. The move took place on August 27th, and mobilization was completed by September 12th. On September 13th, Lieutenant-Colonel C. P. Barlow rejoined from leave and took over command from Major Lane. A few days previously Captain H. N. Loch, D.F.C., and Lieutenant M. A. Platts had been transferred from the 2nd Battalion of the Regiment.

The stage is now set for the final appearance of the 3/5th Gurkhas, and the curtain will shortly lift on the sands of Mesopotamia and the River Euphrates.

CHAPTER III

THE ARAB RISING—DISBANDMENT.

SEPTEMBER, 1920, TO JULY, 1921.

Active Service in Mesopotamia, 1920.

The Battalion marched out from Kakul on September 14th, 1920, with a strength of 12 British officers, 1 Sub-Assistant Surgeon, 742 Gurkha other ranks, and 59 followers. The British officers who accompanied the Battalion were:—

Lieutenant-Colonel C. P. Barlow.
Major H. R. C. Lane.
Captain H. N. Loch, D.F.C.
Captain A. E. Barlow, M.C.
Captain H. S. Burgess.
Captain F. E. C. Hughes.
Lieutenant M. A. Platts.
Lieutenant T. R. Harrison.
Lieutenant R. G. Leonard.
Lieutenant D. Campbell.

In Karachi, Captain Dobbs and Captain G. E. R. S. Hartigan, M.C., reported for duty, but as only one additional officer could be taken the former, by virtue of his seniority, came with the Battalion, and the latter, to his justifiable chagrin, was obliged to betake himself to the depot.

On September 15th the Battalion entrained at Havelian, and arrived at Karachi on the 18th. One night was spent in the rest camp, and on the 19th, headquarters and three companies embarked on the s.s. *Bandra*, a B.I. ship of some 3,500 tons. Owing to lack of space "D" Company under Captain A. E. Barlow, M.C., remained behind, to be brought on a day or two later by the s.s. *Chakdara*. Embarkation completed, the *Bandra* weighed anchor, and it soon became apparent that, at sea, monsoon conditions still prevailed. The men suffered accordingly, but good weather and calm water—encountered in the Persian Gulf—coming to the rescue of their rebellious stomachs, recovery was rapid. Physical training and bathing-parades helped them through the day, and by the time the ship had reached the bar at the mouth of the Shatt-el-Arab they were sleeping well, and eating well, and willing even to work.

The *Bandra* arrived at Basra on September 24th. Disembarkation began at once, and the Battalion went into camp at Makina. Here two days were spent in drawing certain articles of equipment required to complete to Mesopotamian scale, as well as Lewis-gun mules and officers' chargers. These last, on the whole, were a very good lot, but there was one exception. He was a chestnut and a brute, and with him it was a case of, " Why pay to see the rodeo when our Captain Barlow gives two performances daily, entrance free? " Information given in Basra regarding the future movements of the Battalion was to the effect that it would form part of Samcol, a column organized for the relief of Samawa on the Euphrates, where the rebellious Arabs had succeeded in isolating a small garrison of Indian troops. The command of the column was to be given to Brigadier-General F. S. Coningham, C.M.G., D.S.O., himself an officer of Gurkhas, and the stormy petrel of the rebellion, since his appearance anywhere—and he was employed everywhere—invariably presaged trouble for the Arab.

General Situation, 1920.
Before going further it seems advisable to describe briefly the situation in Mesopotamia at this time. The Turk, having been ousted from the Iraq during the Great War, the country had come under the administration of British political officers. These, until early in 1920, had been backed by a strong garrison of British and Indian troops, but then, in response to the universal cry for economy, a number of units were sent out of the country. The British way was not the Turkish way. Where the Turks bled white those from whom they need not fear retaliation, and exacted nothing from those who might give trouble, the British administrators attempted to relieve the burden of the former class, and to impose on the latter a tax, light enough, but the payment of which had not till then been demanded of them. In this way the seed of discontent was sown, and there were not wanting those eager to nurse it into growth whenever the season should serve. The reduction of the garrison gave them their opportunity. Turkish and, there is reason to believe, Bolshevist agents instigated an anti-British agitation, which had for its main field of activity Nejef, the centre of the religious life of the community. Tended and watered, the seed grew into a flourishing plant, and in July began to bear fruit. All along the course of the Euphrates, as well as to the north and east of Baghdad, railways were torn up, telegraph lines destroyed, British garrisons isolated, and British officials murdered. To restore the situation an urgent call was made on India for reinforcements. These on arrival were formed into columns for the relief of beleaguered garrisons, the punishment of the insurgents, and the repair of railways and telegraph lines. During the interval between the outbreak of the rebellion and the arrival of reinforcements there were many regrettable incidents illumined only by

that heroism which, in British history, seems always to respond to the urge of peril or disaster. The series of gallant acts performed by Captain G. S. Henderson, north of Kifl on July 24th, which earned for him a posthumous award of the Victoria Cross, deserve their place in any scroll of fame. The situation would have been even more serious but that the powerful Muntifik tribe, settled mainly between the lower courses of the two rivers, gave no help to the insurgents, and the Tigris remained open for navigation throughout the operations.

Advance on Samawa, October, 1920.

The Battalion detrained at Nasiriya on September 28th, and there Samcol was formed. The fighting troops consisted of:—

10th Lancers (less 2 squadrons).
10th (How.) Battery R.F.A.
13th Battery R.F.A.
" D " Coy. 8th Battn. M.G.C.
1st Battn. K.O.Y.L.I.
3/23rd Sikh Infantry.
3/5th Gurkha Rifles (F.F.).
3/8th Gurkha Rifles.
1/11th Gurkha Rifles.

Though the column was intended to effect the relief of the Samawa garrison it has to be borne in mind that this was not its only task. The restoration of communications was an object of primary importance— an object entailing the reconstruction of railway and telegraph lines, and arrangements for their protection on completion of the work by the erection, provisioning, and garrisoning of blockhouses. From Nasiriya the railway, now completely wrecked, ran S.S.W. for eight miles to Ur of the Chaldees, and thence followed a westerly route to Samawa, touching the river on the way only at Khidhr, about seventeen miles short of Samawa. It was no case of marching gaily along the river, untroubled by considerations of water supply and with all the comforts of civilization in "mahelas" alongside. The force had to betake itself to the desert and to accommodate its pace to the rate of progress of railway reconstruction.

The following system had been devised to meet the requirements of the situation.

Two trains accompanied the column on its day's march, of which No. 1 was a railway construction train and No. 2 carried water and supplies. No. 3 train, running daily between railhead and the advanced base, was used for the replenishment of supplies, and No. 4 train, moving generally close behind the column, carried personnel and material for the construction, provisioning, and occupation of blockhouses. The protective needs of trains 3 and 4 being supplied by the blockhouses already completed, it was the combined length of trains 1 and 2 which governed the dispositions of the column on the march and the frontages of the bivouac area at night. Protection on the march was afforded by a battalion of Infantry at each of the four points of a diamond, in the centre of which moved the main body and trains. Each protective body was again disposed in diamond formation, distances and intervals being adjusted to leave lanes of fire for Artillery and machine-guns at the front and rear of the main body. When at rest, because the length of the trains dictated the occupation of a large area for their protection, battalions established strong posts at intervals on their frontages, with supports and reserves in rear to fill the gaps.

On October 1st, Samcol marched from Nasiriya. Ur was passed in the course of this first day's journey in the wilderness. At that time excavations, if they had been begun had made very little progress; nothing showed of its former greatness. There was but a mound rising above the desert, and the conditions of the day, emphasizing the desolation of the scene, seemed to afford complete justification for Abraham's action in leaving the place. Though the season was so far advanced, the proverbial heat of Mesopotamia showed as yet little sign of abatement, the maximum temperature from October 1st until the middle of the month varying between 115° and 119°. The supply of water carried on the train gave a nominal allowance of two gallons per man daily for cooking and drinking. Under the prevailing conditions this was little enough, but much of the precious liquid was spilled as the trucks jolted over the newly laid track, bumped buffer to buffer when the engine came suddenly to a standstill, or jerked against the strain on restarting, so that the men had to subsist on considerably less. The supply available for the march was insufficient to keep their pores working, with the inevitable result that a certain number succumbed to heat exhaustion. Except from this one cause there was no case of a man falling out on the line of march.

For three days nothing happened, and the only anodyne for too active imaginations which tantalized with pictures of liquid refreshment was provided by observation of the long lines of trucks as they changed from one fantastic shape to another, worked on by the wizardry of the mirage. The enemy was first encountered on October 4th, near Deraji, where shots were exchanged. Railway and river at this point are separated by a bare two miles of desert, a fortunate circumstance which led to the decision to send the suffering animals of the column to drink their fill.

To give effect to the decision it was necessary first to secure the ground in the vicinity of the watering-place. The task was entrusted to the 3/5th Gurkhas and the 1/11th Gurkhas, who had no difficulty in dealing with the slight opposition encountered. With piquets posted and patrols at work, the animals were allowed to approach, and it is hardly an exaggeration to say that they changed shape visibly as they drank. One pony, a grey, decided that he had had enough of trekking with a waterless column. He began to drink, desisted suddenly and gazed steadfastly at the farther bank. Then, without warning given, he entered the water, swam across and made straight for the enemy, who could still be seen, well out of range, trying to round him up when the time came to leave the river bank and make for the bivouac.

At Deraji news was received of a large enemy concentration before Khidhr, the principal stronghold of the Sowabi tribe. Consequently October 5th was spent in reconnaissance and in laying the railway ahead as far as considerations of safety allowed, as a preliminary to attacking and dispersing the enemy concentration.

Action at Khidhr, Oct. 5th, 1920.

At 7 a.m. on October 5th the force detailed for the attack was concentrated east of the Nahr-al-Ghulaidh, a name given to a small irrigation channel which, like others in the vicinity, at this time held no water. The direction of the projected attack was nearly due west. The railway bisected the frontage of the attacking troops nearly at right angles. To the north was the Euphrates, running, not parallel to the railway, but curving in towards it from the north-east. Southwards was desert. About three miles to the west of the Nahr-al-Gulaidh, and filling the space between the river and the railway, was the village, of Abu Risha. The ground before the village had been chosen by the enemy for his stand. His left flank rested on the river, and his line was carried across the railway to a point in the desert beyond. There was no cover for the attackers with the exception of borrow pits on either side of the permanent way. In the dispositions for the attack the forward bodies consisted of the 3/5th Gurkhas and the 3/23rd Sikhs. The former were given a frontage of about five hundred yards immediately north of the railway, their flank protected by one company of the 3/8th Gurkhas and a section of machine-guns moving in echelon on their right. South of the railway the 3/23rd Sikhs were similarly disposed, and given protection for their outer flank.

Soon after 7.30 a.m. the advance began. The first objective was the Nahr-as-Suwaili, an irrigation cut running at right angles to the line of advance and so diminutive that the forward companies were in danger of overshooting their mark. It was reached at 8.5 a.m. and here, in accordance with the time programme, a prolonged halt was made for the benefit of the construction train, which could otherwise have been left outside the safety area. It was during this phase that the opposing forces joined issue. The Battalion was disposed with "B" Company under Captain Loch on the right and "C" Company under Captain Dobbs on the left nearer to the railway. The two companies divided the frontage of five hundred yards and occupied about four hundred yards

Lining Bank of Euphrates: Action at Khidhr.

The Defence Vessel F2, near Khidhr.

in depth. "A" and "D" Companies were in reserve. It soon became evident that the enemy had mustered a considerable force to oppose the advance. The official estimate of his strength was 2,800, and thirteen standards could be counted north of the railway alone. This habit of displaying standards showed rather a touching lack of sophistication. Before long the Arabs abandoned the custom, and either left the standards at home or planted them firmly in the ground and themselves sought cover elsewhere, but while it was in vogue it provided hitherto undreamed-of opportunities for the gunners, who more than anybody bemoaned its falling into desuetude. The forward companies had no sooner halted than they came under fire. Encouraged by the lack of movement the enemy dribbled men forward from borrow pit to borrow pit, and sent parties round to intervene between "B" Company's outer flank and the river. For the waiting companies there existed no vestige of cover, since the irrigation cut, despite its sonorous title, would hardly have sheltered a rabbit, and the enemy's fire making up in intensity for what it lacked in direction, they were faced with the prospect of an uncomfortable half-hour. Luck serving, however, nobody was hit, and on the near approach of the construction train, the advance was resumed.

The second and final objective of the Battalion was the line Khidhr railway station–Abu Risha Village, both inclusive. Stress had from the beginning been laid on the necessity of pressing forward until the incidence of casualties should make it imperative to open fire. This contingency did not arise; the enemy's fire, though heavy, was most inaccurate, and its objective now clearly in view, the Battalion swept on. Appearing to lose heart as a consequence of this steady advance, and probably influenced by the number of casualties sustained as the result of the fire of the two field batteries, the enemy downed standards when the Battalion was still three to four hundred yards distant from the main position, and melted away. The clearing of Abu Risha occasioned some delay, a few diehards having remained in the village, presumably to act as a rear-guard. Here the hand-grenade came into its own. Once he realizes the situation, it takes a very brave Arab to continue lurking in a courtyard when at any moment two or three Mills bombs, impelled by unseen hands, may drop in to bear him company.

By noon the railway station and the village of Abu Risha had been occupied by the Battalion, and it was next employed in support of the 3/23rd Sikhs, who were given the task of clearing the hamlet of Ibrah beyond, and of securing the bivouac site against sniping from the left bank of the Euphrates, on which was situated the town of Khidhr. By 6 p.m. all had been reported clear, and the Battalion was withdrawn to the bivouac. The Cavalry was given no opportunity owing to the wisdom of the enemy, who, once he had decided on abandoning his position, disappeared at speed through the palm-groves and enclosures bordering the river for some distance to the west of Abu Risha, and then crossed over to the far bank. During the course of the action a number of enemy Cavalry could be seen from time to time. Their rôle was confined to aimless galloping well outside the danger area, and to shouting. The good luck enjoyed by the Battalion in this, its first serious engagement in Mesopotamia, is worth passing comment. One mule driver, far to the rear, was hit through the eye, but, though a few of the fighting men could show the marks of bullet grazes, and others had their clothing or accoutrements perforated, this was the only casualty.

Punitive Measures Around Khidhr, October, 1920.
The damage to the railway at Khidhr was very extensive. This was not due only to the destructive propensities of the Arabs, even greater havoc than they had the means to effect having resulted from a serious collision at the time of the partial evacuation of the post in July. Further progress towards Samawa could be undertaken only after the damage had been repaired. It was decided to take advantage of the few days' halt imposed by this necessity, and to inflict punishment on the villages concerned for their share in the tragedy of the *Greenfly*. This vessel was a river gunboat which had run aground some miles upstream of Khidhr soon after the outbreak of the insurrection. All attempts to refloat her proved unavailing, but at the time Samcol left Nasiriya she was known to be holding out, despite the hostility of the local Arabs, and the hope had been entertained of rescuing her occupants on the arrival of the column at Khidhr. It was not to be, however; the Arabs succeeded in boarding her, and put to death the officers and all her crew with the exception of some of the Indian personnel. Subsequently conclusive proof was forthcoming that the treachery of these same Indians had played a great part in the disaster.

Some of the villages to be visited were situated on the far side of the Euphrates, so on October 6th the sappers were hard at work devising means of crossing, while the rest of the force was left free to drink, wash, and fish. This nearly proved the undoing of several officers of the 1/11th Gurkhas. Like everybody else after their waterless journey, they found the spell of the river irresistible, and they wandered along it rather farther than was safe to a place nearly a mile downstream of the spot where the sappers were at work. There they bathed, and the day being hot, they did not trouble to dress again fully, but donned their shorts, draped large towels picturesquely about their persons, and started to wander back. Some sapper at this juncture must have looked downstream to see, as he thought, a party of Arabs advancing to the attack. A series of alternate long and short blasts on the whistle sent everybody running for their rifles. A machine-gun materialized from a palm-grove, and armed men arriving from every direction, those officers were subjected to such a volume of fire as they were destined never to experience again during the campaign. Their draperies flapping, they ran as they had never run before, but cover was scarce. Luckily the range was long, and the fusillade had lasted for only a short time when somebody looking through glasses, recognized them for what they were. They returned to camp by a very roundabout way.

By the evening of October 6th the river crossings were ready, and the next two days were occupied in visiting the *Greenfly* and in burning villages. On October 8th it fell to the Battalion to destroy the village of Dhuwairah, which had obviously been deserted only as the avengers came in sight. Here were found quantities of clothes, piles of carpets, brass vessels of every size and shape, many *maunds* of grain, together with movable fittings of the *Greenfly* and some hundreds of rounds of gun ammunition. Owing to lack of transport but little could be carried away, so a few articles, including parts of the *Greenfly*, were retained as mementoes and the rest destroyed. The behaviour of the Arabs during these expeditions seemed to indicate that their *moral* had been considerably shaken by the action of the 6th. Though the forces sent out were small, they allowed their villages to be entered without opposition, and contented themselves with a desultory, ill-aimed fire directed on the flank and rear-guards of the retiring columns.

The Relief of Samawa, October 10th to 14th, 1920.
The advance was resumed on October 10th, when it was found that the railway had been so badly damaged between Khidhr and Samawa as to necessitate progress by short stages. The opposition encountered during the first two days was negligible. As Samawa was approached, however, the column gained touch with a large concentration of tribesmen, whose strength on the basis of data which became available later—was calculated at 7,500. In the action which followed the Battalion took but little part, its rôle being confined to the protection of the left, or desert flank of the column.

From a point distant about six miles from Samawa the railway and river again converged. The right bank of the Euphrates throughout the whole of this reach was lined with a succession of palm-groves and gardens. Each garden was bounded by thick mud walls from ten to twelve feet high, and being proof against anything except a direct hit by a high-explosive shell, they not only proved serious obstacles for negotiation by attacking troops but also provided perfect cover for the defenders. Here, then, was the scene of the enemy's main effort at resistance. On October 12th, the march of the column having brought it within striking-distance of the river banks, the 1/11th Gurkhas were given the task of ejecting the enemy from the palm-groves. As Samawa was approached the resistance became more stubborn, and on October 13th the 1/11th Gurkhas were reinforced by the King's Own Yorkshire Light Infantry, who co-operated on their inner flank. Advancing by bounds, in the face of stout opposition they drove the enemy from one strong wall to the next, and more than once were given the opportunity to inflict severe casualties. Our own casualties were the heaviest yet sustained, and included several British officers of the two battalions engaged; but that the losses were not in vain is attested by the fact that the insurgents were busily occupied during the night in removing their dead and wounded, and subsequently admitted a total of eighty-five men killed.

The troubles of the Samawa garrison were now at an end. Samcol took over the town and its defences on October 14th, the relieved troops in their clean khaki and with their general air of well-being presenting an odd contrast to their dusty and travel-worn rescuers. This is not to belittle their achievement, for during their isolation they had passed through a period of acute anxiety, had undergone much real hardship, and with it all had maintained an unbroken front. The Battalion went into camp at the railway station, a most unsavoury spot, where there was still ample evidence of the disastrous attempt made some two months previously to evacuate the post which had been established there. On that occasion, after the garrison of the post had entered the train which was to bear them to the safety of the main defences the engine broke down, and the Arabs in the cover of the neighbouring enclosures rushed the motionless trucks and fell upon the almost defenceless occupants.

The railway, after passing Samawa, turns north and crosses the Euphrates by the Barbuti Bridge. The insurgents had succeeded in setting fire to the bridge, destroying completely several spans and imposing a delay of about three weeks for its repair before a further advance could be undertaken. The enemy's heart was still hardened. So to bring him to terms a series of offensive operations was planned, which had as their object the undermining of his will to resist by inflicting casualties and destroying property. All villages in the vicinity of Samawa were visited in turn. It would be wearisome to chronicle each day's doings in detail, and the accounts which follow of the occurrences at Artaubari and Dabbus may be taken as representative. Generally speaking the enemy would collect to the sound of firing as the objective was approached, after slight opposition would remain hidden while the work of destruction was in progress, and with the first indication of withdrawal would awake to renewed activity, displaying a wonderful power of rapid

Operations Around Samawa, October 15th to November 10th, 1920.

movement and great natural ability in the use of ground. To get clear away without a disproportionate number of casualties called for a skilfully planned and rapidly executed retirement.

Reconnaissance of Imam Abdulla Bridge, Oct. 20th, 1920.
Some four miles north of Samawa the railway is carried across an arm of the Euphrates, known as the Shatt-Abu-Shuraish, by the Imam Abdulla Bridge. On October 20th the column moved out of Samawa under the command of General Coningham to reconnoitre the bridge with a view to ascertaining the extent of the damage it had sustained and to destroy villages in its vicinity. The Battalion on this occasion formed part of the main body. Marching at 8 a.m. with the 3/23rd Sikhs as advance guard, touch was soon gained with a considerable force of the enemy, who began to snipe from well-concealed positions on the left bank of the Shatt-Abu-Shuraish. It was no part of the rôle allotted to the Battalion to deal with the snipers, but a *mauvais quart d'heure* was spent sitting in the open, because no cover was available, while bullets aimed at the advance guard kicked up the dust between the waiting ranks. It was a relief, therefore, when orders were received to destroy the villages of Siyaah, Artaubari East, and Artaubari West. These were three small villages lying eastwards of the bridge and close to the right bank of the river. Siyaah was found to consist only of one ruined tower, so Major Lane, who had with him "B" Company under Captain Loch and "D" Company under Captain Barlow, directed the former on to Artaubari East, and the latter on to Artaubari West. While still advancing towards its objective, "B" Company was fired on by a body of tribesman, consisting of mounted men and men on foot, which appeared to be working round its right flank. "B" Company was consequently diverted from its objective to take up a position south of the village, whence it could secure the right flank of the Battalion, while "A" Company under Captain Burgess was detached from the local reserve under Colonel Barlow and sent through to deal with the village.

Meantime "D" Company had reached its objective, where it was subjected to the attentions of a number of enemy snipers posted in the broken ground across the river to the north-east. To ensure their maintaining a more respectful distance during the work of demolition it was necessary to push on, so Captain Barlow, after setting light to the village and reporting the find of a 13-pr. gun, moved forward and occupied positions beyond. The destruction of the villages completed as far as the available means allowed, preparations were begun for a withdrawal to the railway. "C" Company on the left, under Captain Dobbs, took up a position with its left flank resting on Artaubari West, and facing north-east, while "A" Company, withdrawn from Artaubari East, halted on approximately the same alignment, but at some distance to the south-east, ready to cover the withdrawal of "B" Company. Assisted by the fire of "C" and "A" Companies, "D" Company withdrew through the gap and "B" Company round the right flank, and prepared to cover the further withdrawal from a broken line about six hundred yards in rear. It was unfortunate that at this juncture a limber should arrive, sent up by column headquarters, without previous warning given, to remove the 13-pr. gun found by "D" Company in Artaubari West. The weight to be manipulated ran to nearly half a ton, and its transference to the limber consequently entailed the crowding of a number of men in one place. Helped by the broken nature of the country on the far bank the Arabs were quick to seize their opportunity and concentrated a hot fire on the luckless workers. It will have been realized, ere this, that the Arab is no marksman, and fresh proof of the fact was afforded in the present instance; for despite the Allah-given chance there were only two casualties, while the horses went untouched. Without tackle it was found impossible to shift the gun, so an attempt was made to get it away in the captured A. T. cart in which it had been found reposing. The cart bore up nobly for a considerable distance, but with nearly half its journey done both wheels collapsed simultaneously. The circumstances were represented to column headquarters, who ordered the abandonment of the gun, which was regretfully left behind when the withdrawal was resumed. Whether lured by the bait of the derelict gun, or influenced by some other cause, the enemy followed up the withdrawal more persistently than usual, and was still active when the Battalion, now left flank guard to the column, came under the protection of the camp piquets.

Operations Near Dabbus, October 29th and 30th, 1920.

Towards the end of October all villages east of Samawa which could be reached in a single day from that place had been punished. It was therefore decided to go farther afield in that direction, camping for one or more nights at Dabbus, eight miles from Samawa on the left bank of the Euphrates, and operating thence against the nearer villages.

On October 29th the column left Samawa at 8 a.m., the Battalion on this occasion acting as advance guard. The usual diamond formation was adopted, "C" Company being in front, "B" Company on the right, taking in all ground up to the river bank, "D" Company on the left, and "A" Company with battalion headquarters in rear. When about six miles had been covered, "D" Company came into touch with a party of the enemy who had established themselves in somewhat broken ground to the north of Imam Jaubah, and shots were exchanged. Two platoons were posted to keep them occupied until the left flank guard of the column should arrive, and the advance was resumed. On approaching Dabbus the squadron of Cavalry (37th Lancers, which had replaced the 10th Hodson's Horse in the force on the previous day), which had preceded the advance guard, was found to be in action against a number of the enemy occupying old Turkish trenches situated a few hundred yards eastwards of the village. The Cavalry had already sustained several casualties and their horses were attracting much unwelcome attention. The Squadron was consequently withdrawn to perform a task better suited to its attributes, while " C " and " D " Companies of the Battalion at once took up the running. A rapid survey showed that whereas the ground in front of " D " Company was entirely devoid of cover, " C " Company in its advance would be reasonably well served in that respect. The latter under Captain Dobbs was therefore sent forward to Albu Muhar, where it would be in a position to enfilade the enemy's trenches, while Captain Barlow was instructed to make for his objective as soon as the progress of " C " Company should justify the onward move. Though under fire from the front and from the right flank, both companies succeeded in reaching the trenches with only one or two casualties, the enemy retiring to a second line of trenches about six hundred yards to the east.

Major Lane, who was with the two forward companies, was now called upon to decide whether to advance against the next line of trenches or to remain in the position just won. It appeared to him that the ground on which the force was to bivouac for the night was now secure from the east, and that the shallow *nullah* in which the two companies lay, bending round as it did to the west, was admirably adapted to form a strong post for defence by the Battalion during the night. On the other hand, the ground in front being very open and no support forthcoming from the rear, a further advance might expose the Battalion to avoidable loss while leaving it in the air, and so allowing the Arabs to interpose between the outposts and the main body. He therefore decided to remain, and Colonel Barlow, who soon afterwards arrived with Battalion headquarters, agreed with these views. Just at this time a message arrived from column headquarters, who were not yet fully acquainted with the situation, directing a further advance " provided serious casualties could be avoided." On the situation being represented, however, the order to advance was cancelled, and instructions issued instead for certain protective measures to be undertaken at once. Frontages were allotted, and companies began to dig themselves in. The enemy meantime kept up a brisk fire, which continued till nightfall, but cover was good, and fortune proving kind, there were no further casualties.

During the night operation orders were received, making provision for a further advance in the morning. The 3/5th were given, as their first objective, the old Turkish trenches to their immediate front, and as their second objective, the village of Nukhailah. The 3/23rd Sikhs, working on the right of the 3/5th, were directed on the village of Khunainiyah. After a very cold night, the peace of which was disturbed by firing from the main camp, " A " and " C " Companies crossed the starting-line at 7 a.m. and made for the Turkish trenches. These had been deserted during the night, and, the advance continuing, Nukhailah was reached almost without opposition. Shortly afterwards the Sikhs reached Khunainiyah, whereupon the destruction of both villages was begun. North and north-east of Nukhailah, just beyond Saiyid Nasir, and at Radhi, Birshan, Atawah, and Kausah, considerable numbers of the enemy could be seen awaiting the opportunity which they hoped would come with the initial withdrawal of the force. On this occasion they were to be disappointed. Experience had shown that a number of casualties was only to be avoided in a withdrawal before fast-moving Arabs over a flat plain by (*a*) keeping the enemy at a distance before the retirement began; (*b*) making very thorough preparations beforehand, including the early winding up of telephone lines, previous registration of hostile lines of advance by the Artillery, agreement with the Artillery and machine guns, as far as possible, regarding targets to be engaged, and the arrangement of a system of simple signals to be used in default of telephone communication to inform those concerned when covering fire was wanted; (*c*) keeping the enemy guessing regarding the first movement to the rear; and (*d*) moving successive lines all together at a given signal with the object of putting between the rear-guard and the enemy as great an extent of ground as possible before he could realize the situation. Should the evacuation of casualties or any other untoward incident then compel a halt, all was in readiness for the adoption of the system of the successive withdrawal of forward bodies covered by the fire of those in rear. By adopting these tactics on the present occasion the 3/23rd Sikhs arrived at the original line with only one casualty, and the Battalion, retiring later than they, and more on the threatened flank, had only one man wounded.

Punitive measures from Dabbus were now completed, and the force returned to Samawa. The Battalion acted as advance guard. During the march the rear-guard became involved through pursuing a " coat-trailing " policy, sustained a number of casualties, and arrived late in camp.

Action Near Imam Abdulla, Nov. 11th, 1920. The repairs to the Barbuti Bridge having been completed, orders were issued for the next forward move to be undertaken on November 11th with the object of seizing the crossing of the Shatt-Abu-Shuraish at Imam Abdulla. Strong opposition was expected, and the Arab being notoriously fond of his bed, the force fell in in the dark at 5.30 a.m. in the hope of gaining a footing on the far bank of the river before the enemy should become fully alive to the situation.

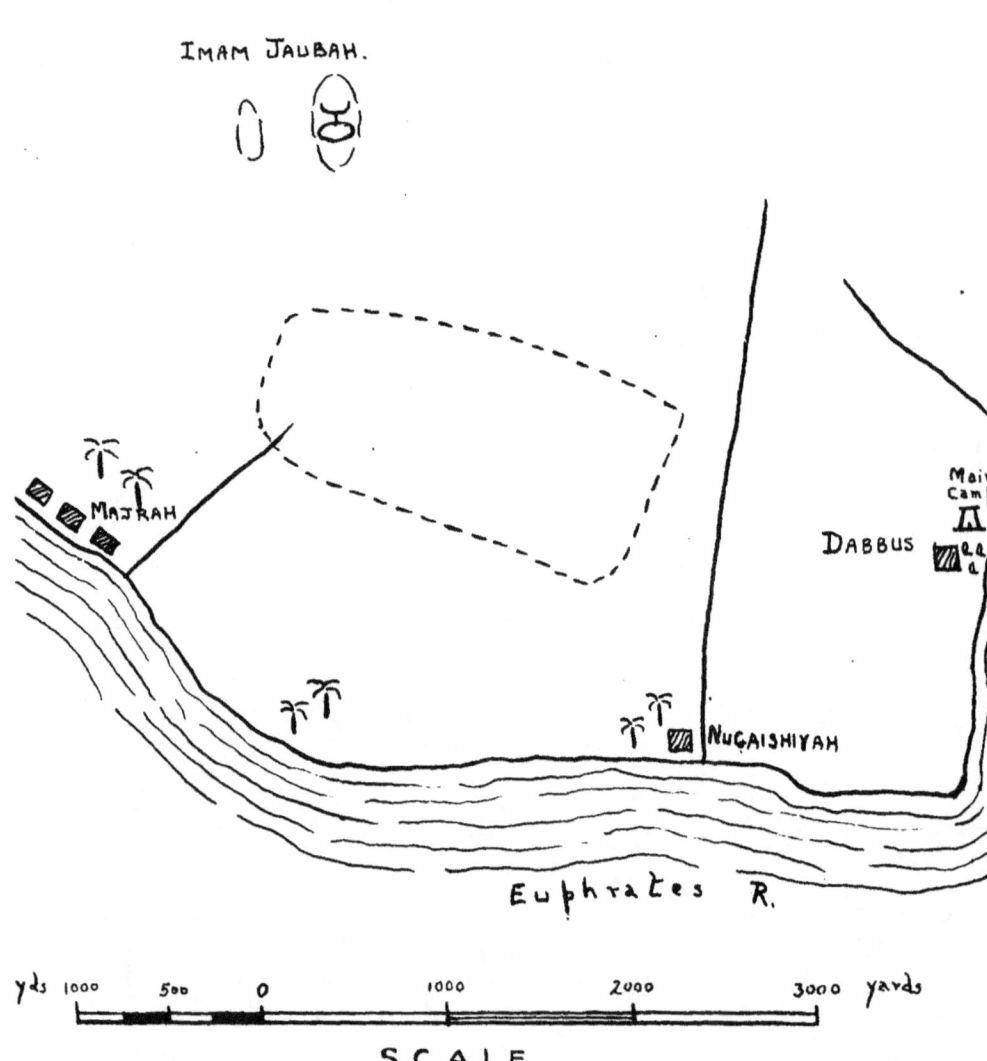

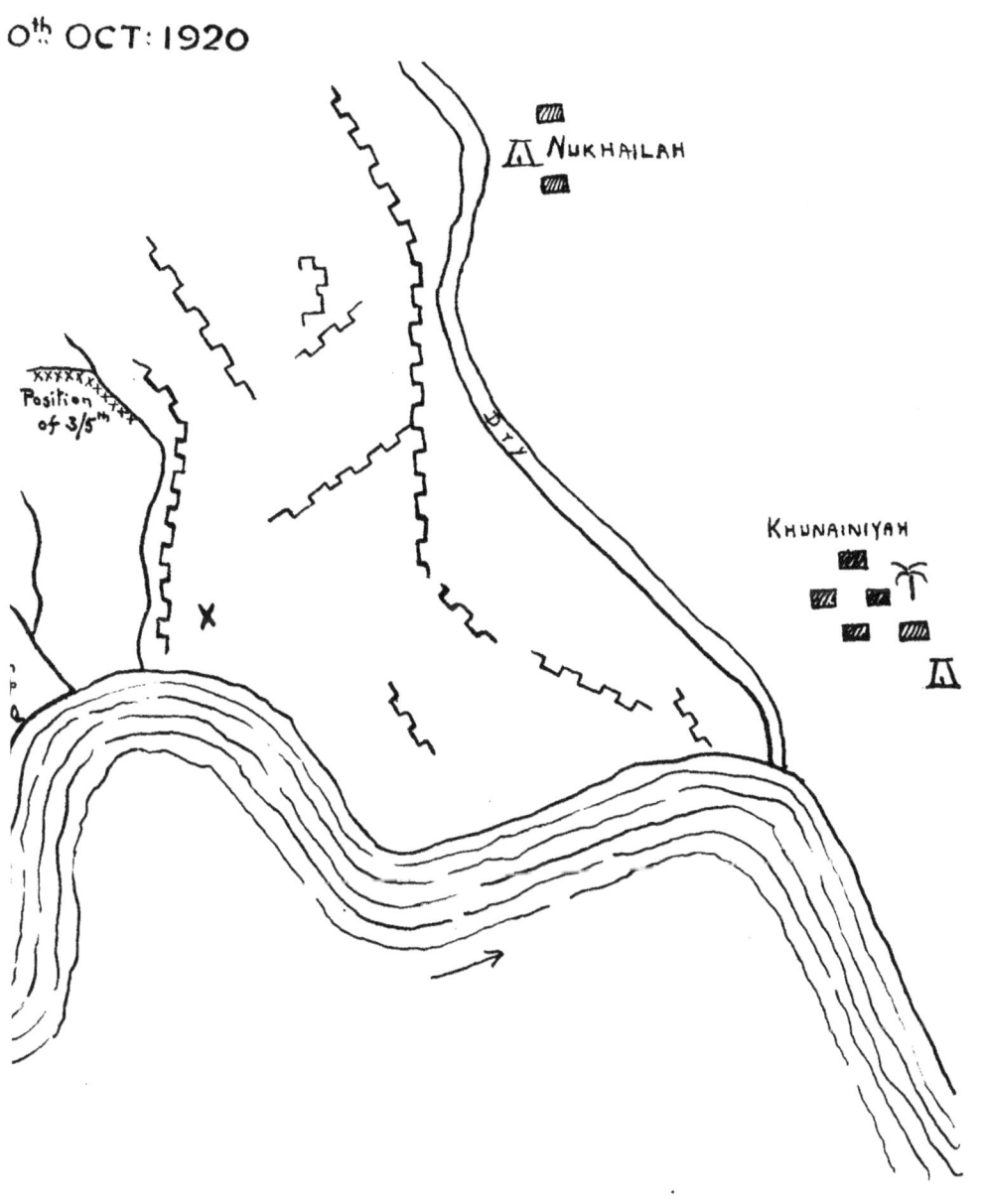

The Imam Abdulla Bridge is thrown across at the most salient point of a sharp bend in the Shatt-Abu-Shuraish, which approaches it from the north-west and leaves it in a north-easterly direction. As a result of this conformation, water cuts and *nullahs* suitable for use as fire positions situated on the farther bank, and each forming, as it were, a cord of this arc, could be enfiladed from positions on the near side of the river, situated well up either arm of the bend. This factor was taken into consideration in framing the orders for the attack.

The 3/23rd Sikhs, starting as advance guard to the column, were to cross by a ford two hundred yards downstream of the bridge. The 37th Lancers, moving independently, were to seize ground to the north-west of the bridge, from which they could enfilade the enemy positions on the far bank. The 3/5th Gurkhas, starting as right flank guard, when the Sikhs should arrive at the ford were to move down the right arm of the bend and occupy positions near Artaubari West, from which to support their crossing.

The Cavalry were soon in action, and the 3/5th, on approaching Artaubari West, came under fire from the ruins of Artaubari East, and from broken ground near a single tower on the far bank, which appeared to have no claim to its imposing name of Mizaihar-al-Jarudh-al-Shinabirah. As a result of the diversions north-east and north-west of the ford, the 3/23rd Sikhs were enabled to cross the river unopposed. On advancing, however, to establish a line astride the railway near Falbah, they encountered stout resistance, and sustained a number of casualties. The enemy in the course of this action showed greater enterprise than on any previous occasion, and that he was not devoid of fighting qualities the following incident will show. A company of the 3/23rd, in a somewhat unfavourable position, ran short of ammunition. A strong party of the enemy, apparently realizing the situation, charged the company with swords and fixed bayonets, the latter presumably captured during the previous months. The Sikhs were mostly young soldiers, the Arabs were ugly and appeared very formidable, and there were signs of wavering. Fortunately Major Campbell, the second-in-command of the 3/23rd, was on the spot, and showed himself equal to the occasion. Mere encouragement, couched in the language ordinarily employed between British officers and soldiers of the Indian Army, would almost certainly have failed of its effect. He was inspired to shout the Sikh war cry, which acted like magic. In his men the offensive spirit revived, and placing himself at their head he led a counter-charge which had an immediate success. The slowness of some amongst the Arabs to sense the change in the psychological atmosphere proved their undoing and was instrumental in giving to the young Sikh soldiers the opportunity themselves to use their bayonets. Major

Campbell received an immediate award of the Distinguished Service Order for his part in the affair.

Meanwhile "C" and "D" Companies of the 3/5th occupied positions on the right bank of the Shatt-Abu-Shuraish, which faced generally north-west, to enable them to fulfil their mission of supporting the 8/23rd Sikhs, but having detachments posted in echelon from the right for their own protection against the enemy across the river and at Artaubari East. The ground was very open, the Arabs, concealed in deep pits and in dug-outs cut into the river bank, kept up a continuous fire, and any movement on the part of our men was the signal of a burst of some intensity. The men, however, worked well; the fire control was good, and when the need arose, not the smallest hesitation was shown in crossing long stretches of open ground for the purpose of replenishing ammunition or bringing up Lewis gun spare parts. During the early afternoon the decision of headquarters was communicated regarding the permanent occupation of the Imam Abdulla position. The scheme provided for a main camp close up to the railway just to the south-east of the bridge, and outlying positions provided with a system of all-round defence, to be occupied by the 8/23rd Sikhs and the 8/5th Gurkhas. For the former the situation selected was immediately west of the railway, near Falbah, and for the latter, near Artaubari West. This left a big gap to the north-east of the main camp, which was filled by the 1/11th Gurkhas, who were held back north of the river, covering the ford.

By this time the enemy was displaying less activity. The position to be occupied by the 3/5th had been surveyed by Colonel Barlow, who had decided on his dispositions, so Major Lane, with the object of expediting the work of preparation, took advantage of the lull to order the withdrawal of the forward platoons of "C" and "D" Companies to positions in which they would be more favourably placed to cover the working parties, intending to release some of the supporting platoons for digging the defences. The first platoon to move, however, attracted so heavy a fire—accurate for the nonce, and causing several casualties—that it was deemed advisable to postpone further movement until dusk. Meantime "A" Company, which had acted as battalion reserve, and "B" Company, which had been used to protect the right rear of the Battalion, were brought up and started to entrench.

It was just as the light began to fail that the most dramatic incident of the day occurred. It would appear that the Arabs had noted the gap between the 3/23rd Sikhs and the 3/5th Gurkhas, and had concluded that through this avenue of approach they could reach the main camp and strike a decisive blow. Be that as it may, while it was still possible to see figures up to a distance of four hundred and fifty yards, a large body of the enemy, estimated at four hundred to five hundred,

Samcol Headquarters at First Action of Imam Abdulla.

Railway Bridge at Imam Abdulla, destroyed by the Arabs.

in close formation, appeared in the gap. Fire was opened immediately from the partially prepared entrenchment near Artaubari West, and great execution was done. Mention must be made here of the subsection of "D" Company, 8th Machine Gun Corps, which, not for the first time, had been attached to the Battalion for the day, and rendered good service. The two guns were posted on the river bank near the tower at Artaubari West, and helped to swell materially the tale of casualties inflicted on the enemy. The Arabs had obviously worked themselves up to a standard of courage beyond that which they had hitherto been wont to display. Their skirts tucked higher than was seemly, and calling loudly on Hasan and Hussein, they dashed from point to point and fired with the greatest energy, their bullets of every shape and make falling thickly on the parapet and interior of the entrenchment. To such an extent had digging progressed, however, that no material damage was sustained. Meanwhile the covering platoons of "C" and "D" Companies were endeavouring, under circumstances of the utmost difficulty, to carry out their orders to retire at dusk. They were No. 9 Platoon (Subadar-Major Lalitbahadur Mal), No. 10 Platoon (Jemadar Himlal Khattri), No. 13 Platoon (Subadar Kabir Thapa), and No. 14 Platoon (Jemadar Shamsher Gurung). The two first-named had been posted on and near the river bank about four hundred yards north-east of the tower at Artaubari West; No. 13 Platoon had been south of No. 10, at about the same distance from the entrenchment; and No. 14 to the right rear of No. 13, some two hundred yards from the main position. To help the retirement of the two "C" Company platoons, two Lewis guns had been posted slightly to the north-east of Artaubari West, and farther to the right similar support had been arranged for "D" Company.

The retirement of the covering troops had hardly begun when there occurred the irruption of the enemy into the gap across the river. Several hundred Arabs, seeing the movement of what they took for small isolated bodies of our men, crossed the river near Mizaihar-al-Jarudh-al-Shinabirah, where till then it had been regarded as unfordable, and yelling demoniacally, gave chase. Though vastly outnumbered the Gurkha officers handled their platoons with the greatest gallantry, and showed judgment and coolness in the tactics they adopted, while the N.C.O.'s in charge of the Lewis guns placed to cover the retirement, rendered great assistance. The Arab rush was made at topmost speed, so it was essential to administer a check from time to time to ensure the safe evacuation of casualties. To effect this the principles of mutual support were applied, Lewis guns again doing good work. That in the circumstances described all four platoons should have reached the entrenchment with only five casualties, and with the rifles, ammunition, and equipment of these complete in every detail, is a tribute to the discipline of the men and to the control exercised by their leaders. Subadar Kabir Thapa on this occasion appears to have owed his life only to very special exertions on the part of his guardian angel. Early in the withdrawal he had loaded himself with the rifles, equipment, and felt hats of three wounded men, and the burden exceeded his carrying capacity to the extent of just a single felt hat. During one rush between positions, do what he would it evaded his grasp. Three times he dropped it, three times he turned and stooped to retrieve it, and on each occasion, as he stooped, an Arab knelt on the sand within a few feet of him, took careful aim and pressed the trigger. Three times a misfire resulted.

The closeness of the pursuit is attested by the fact that an Arab was killed within fifteen yards of "D" Company's perimeter in the main entrenchment. Very lights sent up throughout the night disclosed the enemy removing his dead, but, despite his efforts, sixteen bodies were found next morning.

The action was followed by the bestowal of some well-merited decorations. Subadar Kabir Thapa received the Indian Order of Merit (2nd Class), and the Indian Distinguished Service Medal was awarded to No. 816 Naik Sanman Sunwar, No. 636 Naik Punaram Khattri, and No. 720 Lance Naik Dhanbahadur Khattri.

Armistice. November, 1920. During the days succeeding the action at Imam Abdulla retribution was exacted from the neighbouring villages for the part taken by them in the insurrection. Each day's operation concluded with the usual rear-guard action, but the Arabs displayed markedly less activity than before, and on November 18th hostilities were suspended for three days to allow them to consider terms. On November 21st an armistice was declared, imposing certain conditions by which all the principal sheikhs in the neighbourhood agreed to be bound. Like results had already been achieved by columns operating in other parts of the country, and though subsequently it was necessary to show the flag in certain localities to ensure compliance with the terms of the armistice, there was no further bloodshed.

The total casualties in the Battalion during the campaign are given in the appropriate appendix.

Move to Rumaitha, December, 1920. On November 30th the column concentrated near Falbah to the north of the bridge, and next day began its march to Rumaitha. That town had been the scene of an earlier achievement of General Coningham's, when in July, in the face of very strong opposition and at the cost of a number of casualties, he had succeeded in extricating safely the hard-pressed garrison. On arrival there on December 6th it was found that the railway station and rolling-stock had sustained

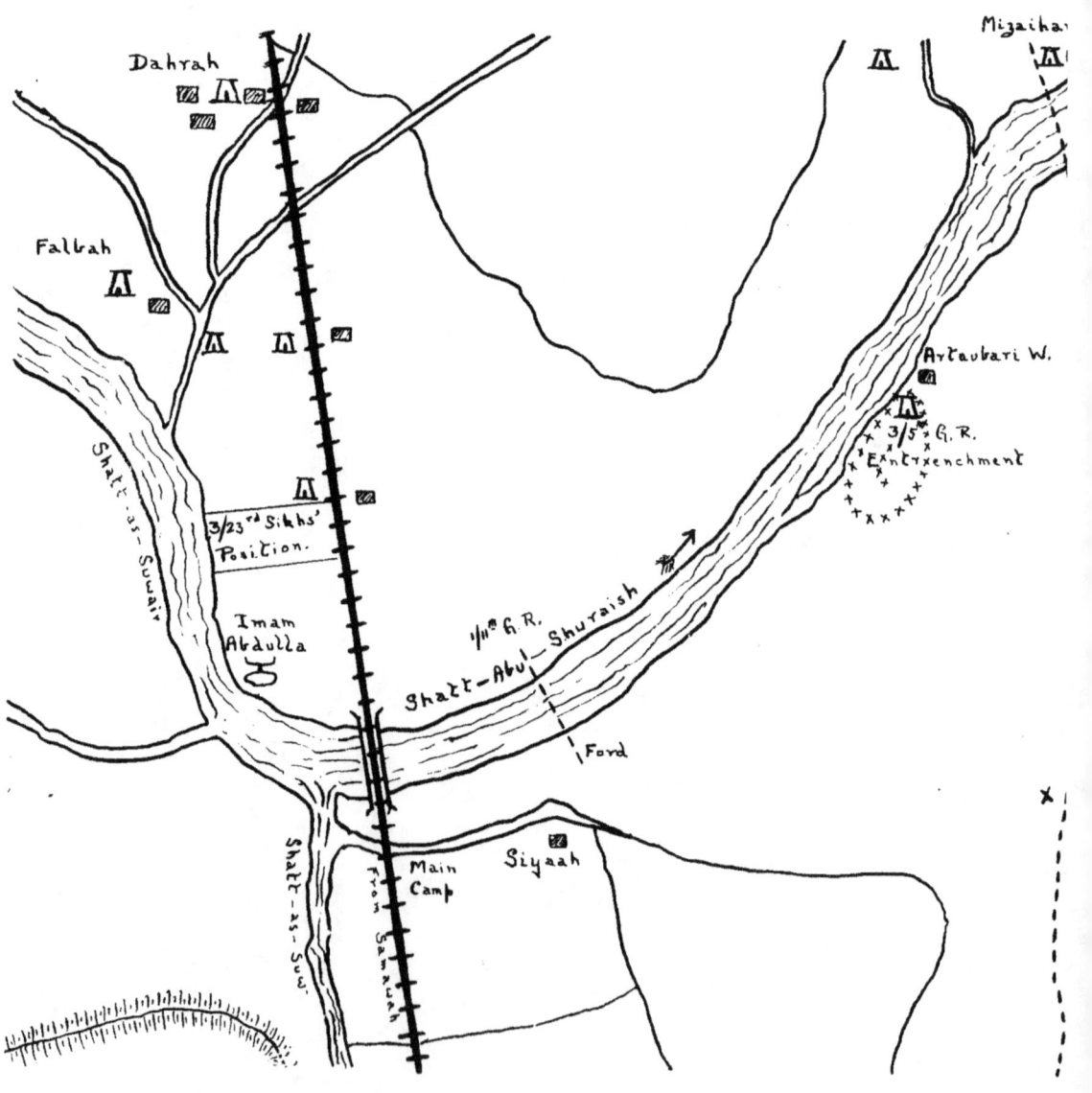

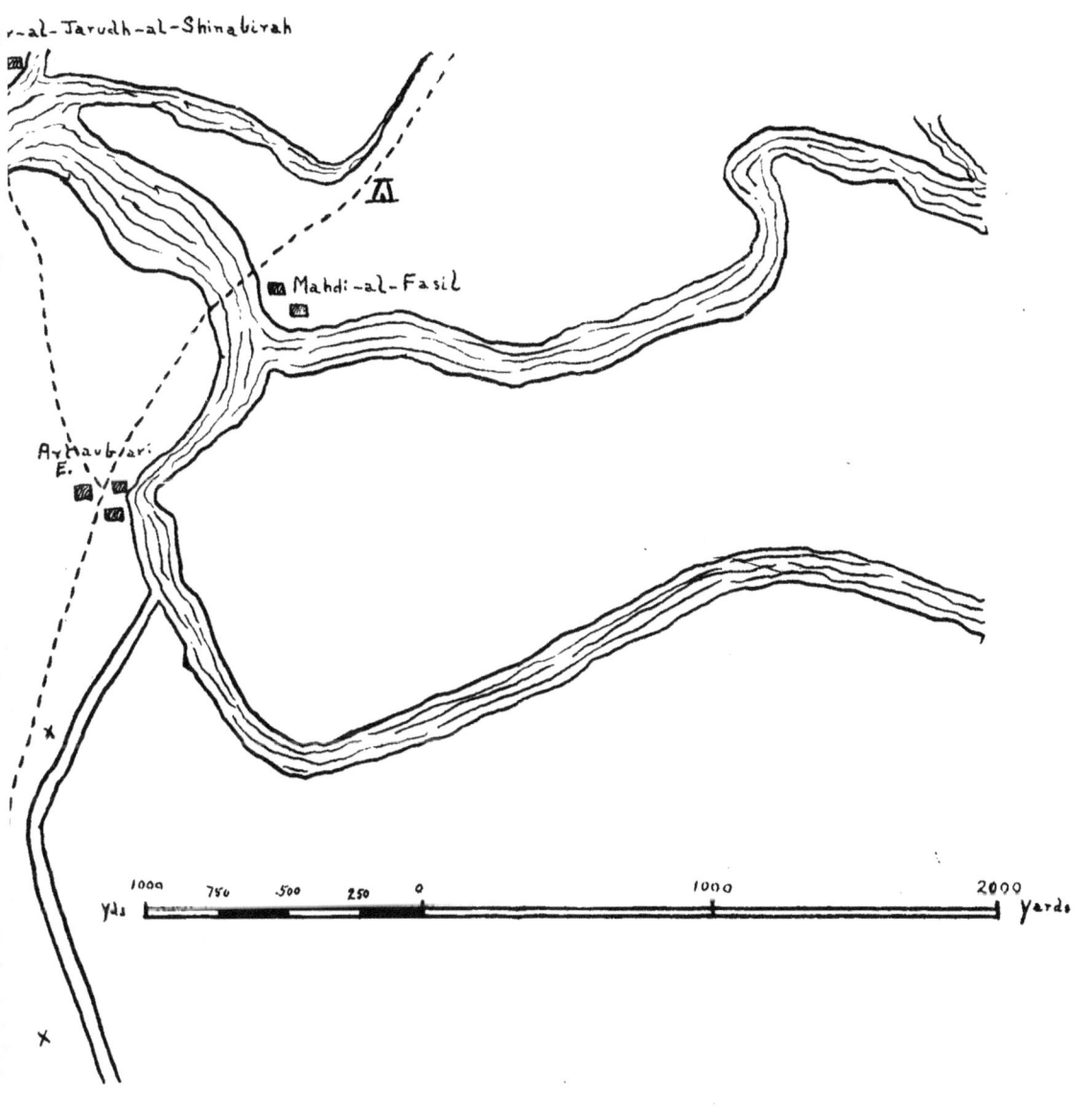

very serious damage, and this, coupled with the wrecking of the bridge and line, necessitated a long halt for purposes of repair. Conditions during the whole of this period were entirely peaceful, and the number of duck, snipe, sand-grouse, and black partridge which could be killed was only limited by the number of cartridges available and the proficiency of the sportsmen. It is only fair to qualify the description of the country—attributed to the British soldier, which begins " miles and miles and miles," and which, though not to be bettered for accuracy and expressiveness in its application throughout eight months of the year, is not for publication *in extenso*—by recording that there are worse places in the world than the middle Euphrates in the cold weather.

Return to Samawa, December, 1920.

With the approach of Christmas began the disintegration of Samcol, which had lately lost its identity with the removal of certain units and the addition of others, the resulting formation being known as the 34th Brigade Column, and on December 24th the Battalion found itself back in Samawa. Here it guarded the Barbuti Bridge and fell back for occupation on a course of peace-time training, while the British officers added to the sport of shooting the pastime of jackal sticking, introduced by the 37th Lancers. It led to many gallops over the sand, but helped no whit to reduce the number of jackals living in the vicinity of Samawa.

Last Days in Iraq, and Return to India, 1921.

The last service performed by the 3/5th Gurkhas in Mesopotamia was the holding of the blockhouse line from Wawiyah to Deraji, with battalion headquarters at Khidhr. Taking them over on January 11th they remained in occupation until the second week in February, when a move was made to Basra preparatory to embarkation for India. While there news was received of the announcement, made by the Duke of Connaught at Delhi on February 10th, to the effect that the 5th Gurkha Rifles (Frontier Force) was one of those selected to bear the title of Royal by command of His Majesty the King Emperor.

Embarking at Basra on the s.s. *Purnea* on February 24th the Battalion reached Karachi on March 1st. Part of the short stay made at that place was taken up by an inspection carried out by the G.O.C. Sind and Rajputana District, and the journey was then continued to Dehra Dun, which was reached on March 3rd.

At Dehra Dun, to the poignant regret of all ranks of the Battalion, orders were given to proceed with disbandment as soon as the Pani Patiya ceremonies should be completed. Almost the last military function in which the Battalion took part as a battalion was an inspection by His Excellency the Commander-in-Chief in India, General Lord

Rawlinson, who complimented it on the part it had played during its brief existence.

Not always is parting "such sweet sorrow," and those last days, involving the scrapping of so much excellent material, were sad days, unalleviated by thoughts of a "morrow," for all connected with the 3rd Battalion 5th Royal Gurkha Rifles (Frontier Force). Out of a total of 950 fighting men, 136 to whom the Battalion owed much, were retransferred to the 2nd Battalion of the Regiment, room was made for 46 in the 1st Battalion, and another 84 found places in one unit or another of the Gurkha Brigade. All the rest were lost to the Army.

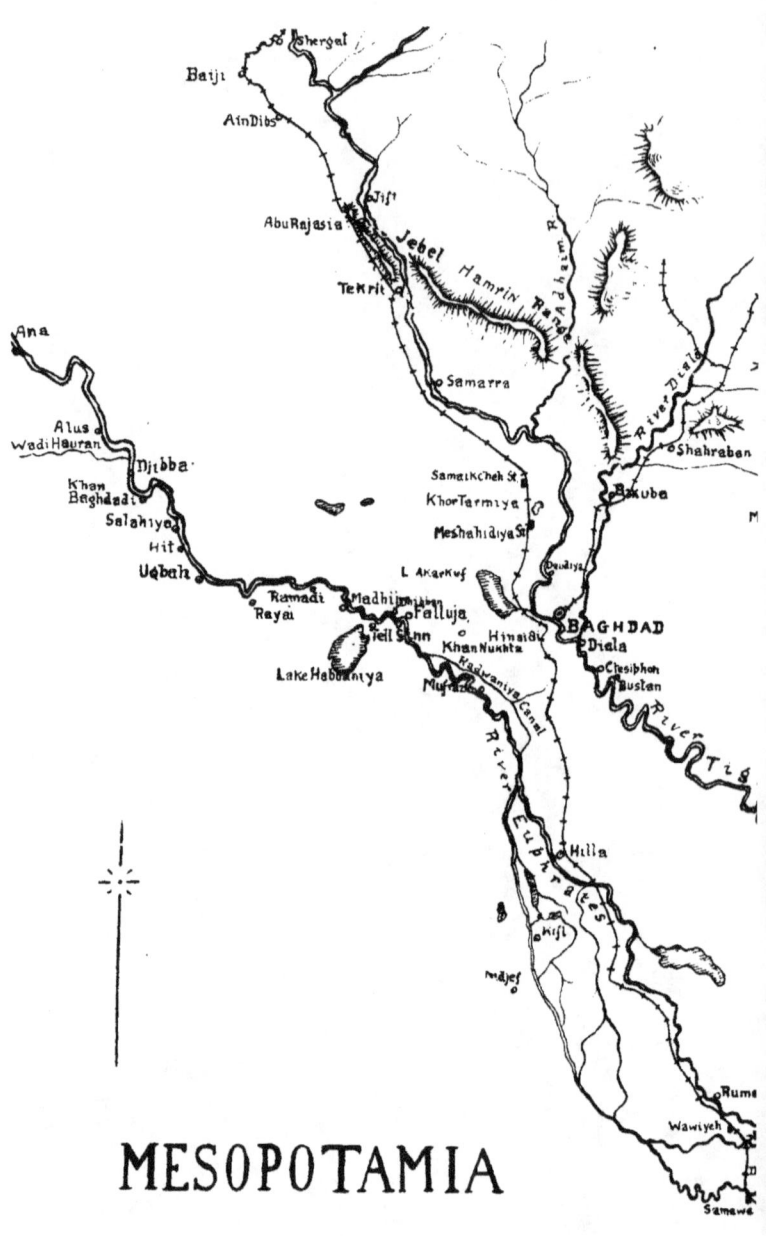

MESOPOTAMIA

Scale 1:2000000 or 1 Inch = 31.56 Miles

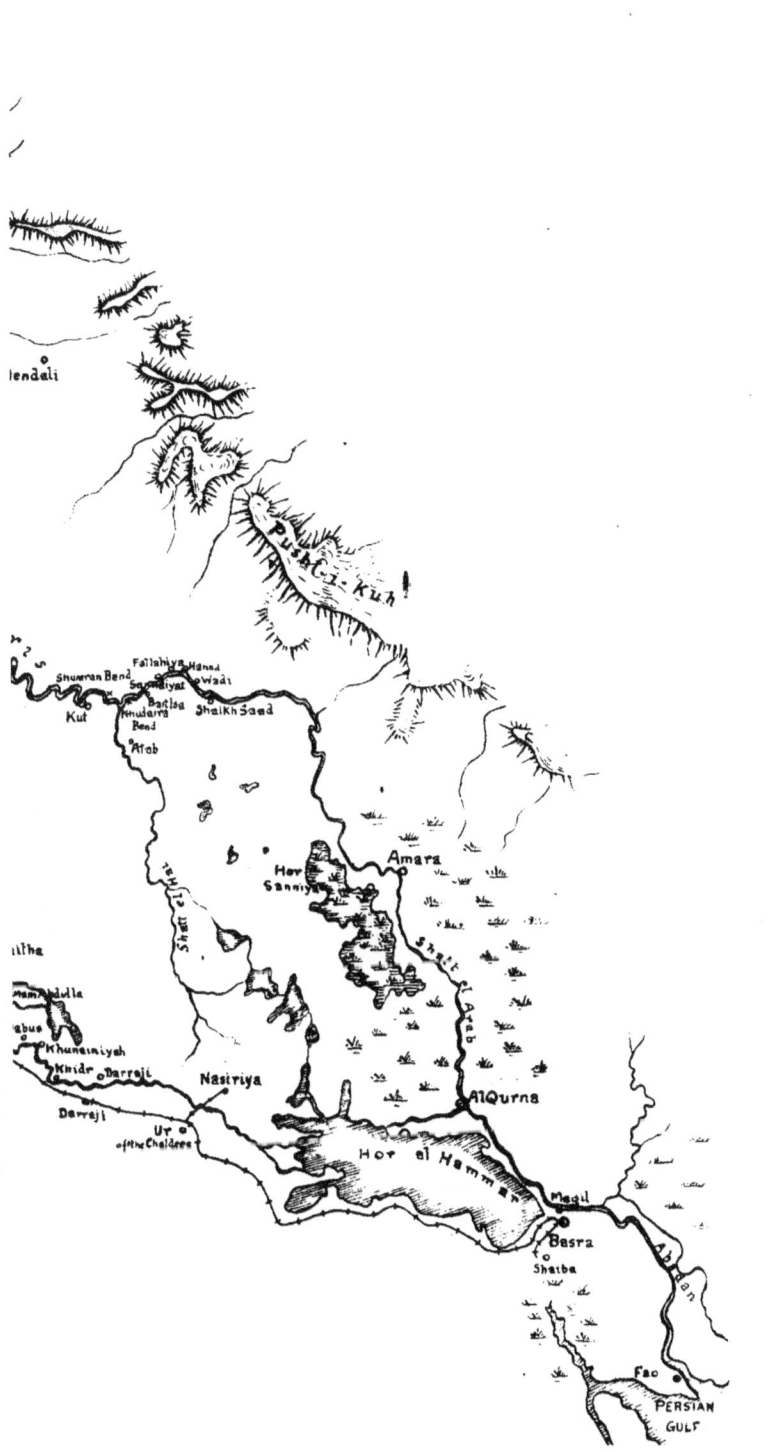

PART V

THE REGIMENT AFTER THE GREAT WAR

CHAPTER I

THE 1ST BATTALION, 1919 TO 1928.

Conditions in India in 1919.

WHEN the 1st Battalion returned to Abbottabad on March 27th, 1919, it was looking forward to a period of quiet. After more than four years of stress, it had need of a breathing space which it might use for the purpose of adjusting itself to the altered conditions of post-war existence. Instead it was hurried away to take its part in meeting the dangers, first of internal disorder and later of grave unrest on the frontier.

At the end of March, however, the storm had not yet broken, and the Battalion at once embarked on its task of reorganization. Before anything else could be done the men must undergo the " Pani Patiya " ceremony—purification after travel overseas. By a special dispensation of the Maharaja of Nepal, this was performed in Abbottabad, and then a beginning was made with the work of demobilization. Included in the ranks of the Battalion at this time were numbers of men who had enlisted only for the period of the war, and these, ever since the cessation of hostilities, had eagerly anticipated their early quittance which would allow them to go to their homes and look after their neglected lands. Many others were hoping for a well-earned period of furlough. Few, probably, realize even now the extent of the sacrifices made by Nepal, and many are still unconscious of the hardships entailed on her yeomen and their dependents by the prolonged absence on active service of a very large proportion of the manhood of the country.

A very distinguished soldier once said of the Battalion that it was " pervaded by a great spirit." At no period in the history of the Regiment has that spirit been more finely displayed than at this time by those who, experiencing such bitter disappointment in the matter of demobilization and furlough, yet served with goodwill and zeal during a hot weather in the plains, and gave of their best under the uncongenial conditions imposed by the necessity of enforcing martial law.

Mr. Gandhi's campaign of *Satyagraha* with its accompaniment of civil disobedience, launched as a protest against the passing of the Rowlatt Act, had resulted in a state of serious unrest. On April 10th there were outbreaks of mob violence at several towns in the Punjab. At Amritsar three English bank managers were killed, a European railway guard was beaten to death, and a lady missionary going her rounds was struck off her bicycle, beaten repeatedly and left for dead. The trouble spread rapidly, and in addition to the repressive measures demanded by the situation, special arrangements became necessary for the safeguarding of communications. In this way it came about that, in the middle of April the Battalion was called upon to find detachments for the protection of the railway from the Margalla tunnel to Lawrencepur. Efforts at reorganization were rudely interrupted, and men on the point of going light-heartedly to their homes were retained for a further unwelcome spell of service. Posts were established at Havelian, Taxila, Hasan Abdal, the Cheblat Bridge and Burhan, and a detachment was also provided for the manning of an armoured train which, based on Rawalpindi, patrolled the line between Lala Musa and Lawrencepur. The work required of the posts was not of a kind to appeal to men but lately returned from active service, and when, in May, the swashbuckling attitude of Afghanistan made war inevitable, hopes ran high that the 1/5th Gurkhas would be allowed to exchange its role of caretaker for one less tedious and passive. The outbreak of hostilities did indeed bring a change of occupation, though not in the desired direction, for on May 18th orders were received that the Battalion would move south next day to garrison the disturbed areas in the Punjab.

Railway protection, April 1919.

Accordingly, on May 19th there began for the 1/5th a series of movements which left it widely scattered over the face of the province. "A" company was quartered in the Lahore Civil Area, "B" Company was at Amritsar with a detachment of two platoons at Ferozepore, "C" Company, on being relieved at Attock, went to Multan, and "D" Company and headquarters were accommodated in the Lahore Cantonment. Martial law, which had been instituted in April, was still in force, and in Lahore its administration was in the capable hands of Colonel Frank Johnson. A company was at his immediate disposal, but the measures previously devised by him to cope with the tide of rebellion proved effective, and from May to November it was not once found necessary to call out the troops in aid of the civil power. For all the detachments duties were heavy; they lived in an atmosphere of tension, and serving as they were throughout the hot weather in some of the hottest stations of the plains, their lot was a hard one. With others similarly situated the Battalion earned the high praise bestowed by the Commander-in-Chief in the following Army Order :—

Move to disturbed areas, May, 1919.

"It is with profound satisfaction that I am able to record the valuable services rendered by all ranks of the Army in India, both British and Indian, during the recent disturbances in various parts of India. The high standard of discipline which animates the Army has been shown by the patience, forbearance and restraint with which the arduous and irksome duties in connection with the restoration of public order have been performed."

A few days only after the arrival of Battalion Headquarters in Lahore, Lieut.-Colonel F. Skipwith was given the command of the 2/10th Gurkhas, and left to take up his new duties. His place was taken by Major G. P. Sanders, who, in the absence of Lieut.-Colonel Villiers-Stuart, continued to command the Battalion throughout the harassing eighteen months which followed. It was the fate of Colonel Villiers-Stuart to be called upon to fill a succession of important appointments, and as soon as he had begun to see the results of his labours in one, to be moved on to another. At this time he was commanding the 3rd Battalion of the Guides, which he had himself raised, and finding himself short of Gurkha officers for his two Gurkha Companies, he called on the 1/5th for assistance. Six senior non-commissioned officers were accordingly transferred to the new battalion, where they were at once promoted.

Return to Abbottabad, November, 1919. It was without regret that, in November, 1919, the companies of the Battalion quitted the cities of the plains and concentrated in Abbottabad. There the men fell a prey to a mild outbreak of influenza and, being segregated in their own lines, were debarred from intercourse with the rest of the garrison. That trouble at an end, there was great uncertainty regarding future movements. First the Battalion was directed to provide demonstration troops for the Mountain Warfare School, about to re-open under the direction of Colonel Villiers-Stuart. Without any cancellation of that order it was next warned, on January 16th, 1920, to be ready to move at short notice to Waziristan, where the 2nd Battalion had already begun to distinguish itself in the hard fighting which followed the earlier set-backs about Palosina. Finally, on February 12th, doubts were set at rest by the receipt of definite instructions to leave Abbottabad on the 15th preparatory to joining the Kohat-Kurram Force. It is relevant at this point to refer to the excellent work done by the Depot during this difficult period. Each new order added to the labours of Captain Watt and his staff, and complicated as these already were by the administration of field service accounts, war gratuities, demobilization concessions, pensions and the like, it is greatly to their credit that they were found equal to every emergency.

Reaching Kohat on February 17th, the Battalion went into camp near the railway station, to spend nearly three weeks in a wearisome round of duties. On March 8th it set out to join the Kohat—Kurram Force at Darsamand, and moving by Ustazai, Hangu, Togh and Doaba, arrived at its destination on the 12th. Active operations at this time were confined to Waziristan, but the proximity of Khost made it necessary to keep a watch on this portion of the Frontier, and this was sufficient reason for the existence of the force and for its location at Darsamand. On the whole the period of the Battalion's sojourn there was uneventful, but the presence in the neighbourhood of large gangs of raiders made it necessary to take all precautionary measures usually associated with warfare against the tribes. Numbers of men were constantly employed on perimeter defence and in providing the garrisons of the piquets around camp, so that nights in bed were few. As the hot weather advanced a peculiarly devastating form of malignant malaria became very prevalent and took an increasingly large toll of the ranks of the Battalion. Those attacked by the malady failed to rid themselves of its effects until long after their return to Abbottabad.

With Kohat-Kurram Force, February to September, 1920.

As the year passed conditions became more stable, both internally and on the frontier. A move was therefore made in the direction of reducing establishments to the normal, and demobilization became general. The step was inevitable, but nonetheless it was impossible to regard without a keen pang of regret the loss to the army of so much excellent material.

On September 9th the Battalion returned to Abbottabad, and Darsamand had become but an unpleasant memory. The sojourn there, however, had left its mark, for the daily attendance at sick parade for several weeks numbered between two hundred and three hundred men. In Hazara there were few signs of that general improvement in the situation which had seemed to justify a reduction in the strength of the army. Kakul was full of young battalions—including the third battalion of the Regiment—all mobilizing busily for service in Mesopotamia. Large bands of *musalmans*, sullen and somewhat bewildered in appearance, moved from village to village at the behest of fanatical mullahs who were out to stir up trouble in connection with the *Hijrat* campaign of the brothers Ali. After many years Oghi in Agror had once more been occupied by regular troops, who had lately been called upon to repel the attacks of several thousand misguided tribesmen. Included in the small force at Oghi were the 3/6th Gurkhas, who had previously been employed as demonstration troops for the Mountain Warfare School. Their hurried despatch towards the frontier had hampered the work of the school,

Trouble in Agror, September, 1920.

Darsamand Camp, 1920 : Part of 1/5th Perimeter Wall.

Parachinar Fort, 1922.
Showing the North-East Bastion, built by the 1/5th in 1897 during the Chamkani Blockade.

and the 1/5th were therefore called on to take their place. They had continuously provided a detachment for demonstration purposes from among those left in Abbottabad during the hot weather, and their total contribution to the success of the mountain warfare classes was later acknowledged by the Chief of the General Staff in the following terms :—

" I am directed to request that you will convey to the demonstration troops, 1/5th Gurkha Rifles (F.F.), the appreciation of H.E. the Commander-in-Chief of the assistance given by this unit to the Mountain Warfare School. The trouble taken in training the men for demonstrations, the keenness displayed in carrying them out and the excellent results obtained, reflect the greatest credit on all concerned, and have been of undoubted benefit to the Army."

Meanwhile, it was still necessary to keep a small column composed of regular troops in Agror, and with the closing down of the Mountain Warfare School, the Battalion became available to take its part in the occupation of Oghi. By the middle of November the strength of detachments sent there from the 1/5th numbered about four hundred rifles, and a platoon of "D" Company was at Mansehra. A month later the situation on the Agror frontier and throughout the district had become normal, and the Oghi column returned to Abbottabad.

One other important event of 1920 was the return of Lieutenant-Colonel W. D. Villiers-Stuart to take over command on November 1st.

Visit of H.R.H. the Duke of Connaught, February, 1921.

During the cold weather of 1920-21 His Royal Highness the Duke of Connaught visited India. A soldier himself, and the friend of soldiers, he was probably but little troubled by the boycott organized by the civilian population of some of the garrison towns which he honoured. His first big review of troops was held at Delhi, and there the Battalion was represented by Subadar Sasidhar Thapa, Havildar Balwant Thapa and the oldest serving soldier, No. 4144½ Rifleman Badal Sing Gurung. Rawalpindi was to be the scene of a similar function in February, and both battalions of the Regiment left Abbottabad to take their part in it on January 30th. They arrived at Chaklala, where they were to camp, in a heavy storm of wind and rain, on February 3rd. His Royal Highness made his formal entry on the 15th, and to the 1/5th Gurkhas was given the task of lining the roads in the vicinity of the jail. Very smart they looked in well-fitting khaki drill, a fact which did not escape the notice of the Duke's staff, who complimented the Commanding Officer on their appearance. Then came the divisional practice parade for the great review. It was to be a red-letter day in the history of the Regiment, for the Brigade had no sooner formed up than a telegram was handed to the Commanding Officer. After a preliminary glance he read it out to the Battalion :—" His Majesty the King has been pleased to confer the title of 'Royal' on the Regiment on account of distinguished services rendered in the recent war."

Title of " Royal" conferred. Not one of the Regiment but felt intensely proud of the honour done to it, and thoughts naturally turned to those of all ranks no longer with it, whose courage and self-sacrifice had gained for the 5th Gurkhas this signal mark of recognition.

On February 18th the review was held. His Royal Highness expressed his pleasure at the manner in which the troops had borne themselves on parade, and added :—

" Many of the regiments are young, especially in the Artillery and in the British battalions as well as amongst the Gurkhas, but I have rejoiced to see them shaping so well, and I have every confidence in their future efficiency."

The return march began next day, and on February 24th the Battalion arrived back in Abbottabad. Messages of congratulation on the honour lately done to the Regiment continued to come in, and it was pleasant to find so many well-wishers among the higher commands and throughout the Army. On February 28th the following Battalion Order was published :—

" The Commanding Officer is proud to publish for the information of all ranks, the contents of a letter received from General Sir Baber Sham Sher Jang Bahadur Rana, K.C.S.I., K.C.I.E., Inspector-General, Nepalese Army, Singha Barbar, Nepal, February 16th, 1921 :—

'THE OFFICERS COMMANDING,
   1ST AND 2ND BATTALIONS
      THE ROYAL 5TH GURKHA RIFLES.

'MY DEAR COLONELS,

'I have received with great pleasure the telegram sent by you asking me, on behalf of all ranks of the 5th Gurkha Rifles, to convey their respects to General His Highness the Maharajah, Sir Chandra Sham Sher Jang, and to inform him of the distinguished title which has been conferred on the Regiment. His Highness is now on his way back from Calcutta and I shall be proud to convey to him your kind message. May I take this opportunity of expressing the great gratification which I myself felt at the great honour which a Regiment formed of my fellow-countrymen has received. I beg sincerely to offer my congratulations to all ranks of the gallant Regiment who, together with their comrades of the other Gurkha Battalions, covered themselves with glory, and so nobly upheld the high traditions of the Gurkha nation during the greatest of wars.

'Before concluding, allow me to say how greatly I appreciate and value the sentiments of friendship and comradeship which prompted you to send me the telegram.

'Yours sincerely,

'BABER SHAM SHER JANG BAHADUR RANA,
'*General, Nepalese Army.*'"

Change of Command, February, 1921.

On the same date (February 28th) the change in the command of the 1/5th was officially notified. Although Colonel Nightingale had left to take up a higher command in December, 1917, his name had remained on the books of the Battalion as Commandant. Now his tenure was at an end, and a few days later his farewell message reached the men with whom he had served with distinction in several theatres of war.

"Though it has not been my good fortune to be with the Battalion for over three years, still my thoughts have always been with it, and it has always been an intense pride to me to remember that I have served with it in Egypt, Gallipoli and Mesopotamia, where the daring and gallantry of all ranks was beyond praise. Now, on completion of the tenure of my command, I desire to express my thanks to all who so loyally helped me when I was there with them, and to send my greetings and best wishes to everyone in the Regiment, who in future will, I know, carry on the same traditions in the same spirit which, in the past as in the present, have made the 1/5th Gurkhas second to none other in India. Good-bye and good luck."

Soon after Lieutenant-Colonel Villiers-Stuart was given the substantive appointment of Commandant, Major G. P. Sanders left to take over command of the 3/11th Gurkhas in Waziristan. Major H. R. C. Lane, from the 3rd Battalion, became officiating Second-in-Command in his place, and joined in December.

Death of Sir John Sym.

On June 28th, 1921, the Colonelcy of the Regiment fell vacant through the death of Major-General Sir John Munro Sym, K.C.B. He was succeeded by that distinguished soldier and devoted son of the Regiment, Lieutenant-General Sir A. R. Martin, K.C.B.

The remainder of 1921 passed uneventfully, but we may note one important change in organization brought about by the creation of the Headquarter Wing. Previously specialists such as signallers, machine gunners, transport staff, clerks, bandsmen and artisans had been distributed through the companies. Now they were all collected into the Headquarter Wing, within which they were grouped according to their several occupations.

Early in 1922 the Regiment was again brought in contact with a member of the Royal House, when the Prince of Wales visited Rawalpindi in the course of his Indian tour. Each battalion provided 1 Gurkha officer and 62 Gurkha other ranks to form the guard of honour under the command of Captain K. C. S. Erskine, M.C., and they deservedly received very high praise for their smartness and for the perfection of their turn-out during the time that they were on duty.

Move to Parachinar, May, 1922.

A month later the Battalion was warned for another spell of service away from Abbottabad. On this occasion it was necessary to evacuate the lines, as they were to be occupied by the 1/6th Gurkhas, and preparations went forward accordingly. In April Colonel Villiers-Stuart went to England, and it fell to Major Lane to take the 1/5th Gurkhas to their new destination, Parachinar, at the head of the Kurram Valley.

The journey, which began on May 5th, was made by train as far as Thal. There was a halt of some hours at Kohat, and there, with the traditional hospitality of the old Frontier Force, the Battalion was made welcome by the 51st and 53rd Sikhs. Tea was provided for the Gurkha ranks, band and pipes discoursed sweet music on the platform and the British officers were taken off to the Mess. From Thal the Battalion marched up the Kurram Valley by the usual stages, and on arrival in Parachinar on the 10th was incorporated in the newly formed 5th Indian Infantry Brigade under the command of Colonel-Commandant F. E. Coningham, C.B., C.M.G., C.S.I., D.S.O. Just why the Brigade had been called into being at this time was, at first, matter for speculation. Later it became known that Government had decided on the policy of " roads and permanent occupation " as the only means of solving the Mahsud problem, and that in the autumn the 5th Brigade would be used with others to give effect to that policy.

It would be hard to find a better place than Parachinar for training of the kind needed by a battalion expecting soon to fight in Waziristan, and having made their camp among delightful surroundings, the 1/5th settled down to fit themselves for the work before them. At first there was no rifle range, but by dint of very hard work, and with help from the 56th Rifles (F.F.), the deficiency was soon supplied. With the completion of the range the last obstacle to a successful course of training was removed. The climate was excellent, duties were light, the men were in the best of health and spirits, and the ground available was exactly of a type to meet requirements. Except for one very bad dust-storm which raged throughout forty-eight hours, ripped

Clearing after a Duststorm.

The 1/5th Camp at Parachinar, 1922; and the Peiwar Kotal (extreme left skyline).

up tents and tore off the galvanized iron roofs of the cookhouses like so much cardboard, the stay at Parachinar holds no memories which are not pleasant. Others who shared the amenities of the place were the Kurram Militia—the only permanent residents—the 1st Battalion Border Regiment, the 56th Rifles (F.F.), the 108th Pack Battery, a company of Sappers and Miners, and a squadron of the Royal Air Force.

Battalion training had been completed by the middle of October, and a few days later Colonel Villiers-Stuart rejoined from leave. On October 28th the Brigade marched for Thal, and arrived there early in November. Notoriously unhealthy, the placed lived up to its reputation, and fever was very prevalent. An aftermath of the troubles of 1919, when Thal had been besieged and bombarded by an Afghan army, the camping grounds were still unsanitary, and flies bred in noisome hordes. The month of November was spent in Brigade training, and on December 6th, 1922, the Brigade set out for Waziristan.

March from Thal to Waziristan, December, 1922.

During the first two days a cross-country route was followed via Gurguri and Bahadur Khel, to meet the Kohat—Bannu Road, two and a half miles west of the latter place. The track was narrow and winding, sometimes with a cliff on one side and a steep drop on the other, so that camels with bulky loads could only just scrape past, and progress was very slow. From Gurguri to Bahadur Khel the distance was eighteen miles, and the rearguard, provided by the Battalion, only arrived in camp at 11.30 p.m. Owing to scarcity of water—brackish at that—food was not ready until some hours later, and few of the men had any sleep. Bannu was reached on the 9th after a long march of twenty-one and a half miles from Latamber, and quarters were found in the rest camp.

Situation in Waziristan.

The road which was to bring peace and settled conditions to the Mahsud tribes of Southern and Central Waziristan, had been begun early in the year. Branching from the main Tochi Road at Thal-in-Tochi, it was designed to strike the Khaisora at Asad Khel, running thence via Tamre Oba and Razani to the Razmak Narai, and on down the Tauda China to meet its counterpart under construction from the Tank Zam side. The peaceful influence of the road was to be helped and consolidated by the establishment of a strong brigade in occupation of the Razmak Plateau, a short distance north of Makin. The Mahsuds presently showed their disapproval of Government's well-intentioned plans for their reclamation. Attacks on British troops located in the Tank Zam sectors became very frequent, stout opposition was offered by the Abdullai clan to the establishment of a *khassadar* post at Tauda China, near Makin, and on December 12th Lieutenant Dickson, Royal Engineers, was murdered not far from

Razani while superintending road-making by local labour under the escort of *badraggas*.

To carry through the project of road construction and permanent occupation in the face of opposition, the following plan of campaign was decided on. The 5th Brigade would first enter the Khaisora Valley and establish permanent piquets nearly as far as Razani. The 7th Brigade would then go through, halt at Razani long enough to secure the Razmak Narai and the road to it, and after relief by the 5th Brigade, join hands with the 9th Brigade near Makin. From a standing camp at that place, operations would be undertaken with the object of breaking down Mahsud opposition, and once the tribesmen had been induced to accept the inevitable, occupation, more or less peaceful, would follow.

Asad Khel, December, 1922.

In accordance with the plan just outlined the 5th Brigade left Bannu on December 11th, and reached Asad Khel on the 16th. The march was almost without incident; opposition which had been expected on the last stage from Thal-in-Tochi to Asad Khel, did not materialize. The camp was situated on the left bank of the Khaisora at a point where the new road—already partially constructed—turned westwards up the valley. The work of securing the road was begun next day, and continued almost without interruption until December 31st. Nearly every day the Battalion was engaged in the work of piquet construction, nine permanent piquets being required to ensure the safety of the route between Asad Khel and Tamre Oba.

An overcrowded memory, when called on for incidents of this period, produces little more than two pictures : one, constantly repeated, of the Battalion shivering in the dark in the bed of the stream as it waited to start on the day's work ; the other, of scores of Mongolians, all pink and smelling of soap, emerging from the weekly hot bath which was a feature of the place. Besides these there persists only the memory of the narrowly averted tragedy of Christmas Day.

It was an off-day, with neither piquet construction nor convoy escort duty to mar its restful calm. It was known that the Mess President had made a special effort, and as dinner time approached, one officer after another stumbled down the ill-lit steps into the deeply dug-down Mess, until all were present and ready to enjoy the seasonable fare provided. The Mess cook of that time was a Goanese, an expert in his trade, but not strictly a teetotaller. He had been nicknamed " Jack Johnson," partly on account of his burly physique and bellicose disposition, but chiefly because his clothes savoured of the ring-side— thick sweater, flannel trousers and sand shoes. At the appointed time the order was given to serve dinner. Nothing happened. Fifteen minutes passed, and there were signs of impatience. Half-an-hour passed, and unable to get a satisfactory explanation from the waiters, the Mess President himself went to see. He was a boxer much above the ordinary amateur class, and presently returned, humouring his knuckles, with the announcement that all would yet be well. The cause of the delay had been Jack Johnson's intense admiration for the beauty of his own handiwork. To expose the masterpiece which was the dinner he had prepared to the desecrating touch of knives and forks was more than he could bear. Armed with his largest soup ladle he had defied all attempts on the part of the other servants to get within reach of his dishes, and in the end it was only the entry of the Mess President with his persuasive methods which had saved an excellent dinner from the fate of Alfred's cakes.

By the end of December, 1922, the greater part of the 7th Brigade had concentrated at Asad Khel, and on January 1st, 1923, they went on to Tamre Oba. The arrival of the 2/8th Gurkhas to augment the strength of the 5th Brigade, enabled that formation to prolong the line of piquets already held, and on January 4th the 7th Brigade reached Razani. From there, meeting occasionally with slight opposition, they secured the forward route step by step until their piquets at last dominated the Razmak Narai itself. That done, they were ready for their next bound over the pass and on to the plateau north of Makin, but first the 5th Brigade must in turn move forward. Accordingly, on January 21st, " B " and " C " Companies of the 1/5th marched to Razani and took over the camp piquets. A day or two later the 7th Brigade advanced. On the preceding night there had been a heavy fall of snow, and when dawn broke the storm became a blizzard. As far as Razani the road had been aligned and levelled, though it was as yet unmetalled, but beyond there was nothing but a winding, narrow track leading up the Kupiri Algad, with an abrupt rise to the crest of the pass. Difficult at the best of times, under prevailing conditions it was only just negotiable, and although the leading troops left Razani at dawn, it was nearly 11 p.m. when the last of the 1,100 mules and 1,500 camels which formed the transport train, slithered wearily into the new camp. Fortunately the Mahsuds had shown small liking for the hard weather, and the few who had ventured abroad offered but a feeble resistance.

Advance to Razani and Razmak, January and February, 1923.

The remainder of the Battalion joined " C " and " D " Companies at Razani on the 29th, to be followed in due course by the other units of the Brigade. Piquet construction and convoy work were again the order of the day. Meantime, the 7th Brigade had made all ready for a further advance towards Makin. To enable them to go forward the 56th Rifles were pushed up to Razmak (old) camp on February 3rd, to be followed by " C " and " D "

Companies of the 1/5th under Major Lane on the 4th. The rest of the Battalion was collected there by the 6th.

Shortly afterwards offensive operations began against Makin. On February 4th the 7th Brigade had joined hands with the 9th, which had previously withdrawn to Piaza from Ladha in a heavy snowstorm, and the force then came under the command of Major-General Sir Torquhil Matheson, K.C.B., C.M.G. For some weeks the Mahsuds around Makin offered a stout resistance to the offensive launched with the object of bringing them to terms, but the 5th Brigade was engaged only on the outskirts, and in its almost daily excursions towards Makin met with no serious opposition.

Razmak Camp — Razmak Camp, as it existed at this time, was sited in a depression, which had the advantage of defilading it on three sides and so reducing the number of the camp piquets. During dry weather this was ideal, but later, when heavy snow came, it was to prove a mixed blessing, for the ground in the hollow became a sea of mud, feet deep in places, in which a bundle of *bhoosa* could be lost for ever. To the north of the camp, about a mile away, was the Narai, some 1,200 yards in breadth and flanked on both sides by high hills; to the west Shuidar, 10,948 feet, and on the east a ridge, 1,000 feet above the Narai, running northwards towards Razani. This ridge, of which more will be heard anon, was named Alexandra Ridge, after the 3rd (Q.A.O.) Gurkha Rifles, who had first held the piquets established on it. The crest of the Narai was reached by a winding track in these early days and the whole of Alexandra Ridge and of the Kupiri Algad, between the ridge and Shuidar, as well as Shuidar itself, were covered with thick scrub.

Once on the Narai the country opened out into a plateau. The Alexandra Ridge was continued southwards, but Shuidar on the west receded, merging into the Spin Kamar Range which trended southwards to Khawaba Sar, 9,236 feet, and Mandach Narai, and culminated in the imposing peak of Pir Gul, 11,517 feet. From these high hills to the west numerous big *nullahs* ran down, intersecting the Razmak plateau and joining a main *nullah*, the Tauda China, which descended from the Narai southwards past the foot of the hills bounding the plateau on the east.

Between these *nullahs*, and running on a general south-westerly line, were ridges which marked the bounds of convoy-escorting troops. All these ridges, as also the bank of the Tauda China and the eastern hills, were covered with scrub, the whole forming a terrain which everywhere gave opportunities for enemy ambuscade.

Two such ridges affect this story most. The first was called " Gun Ridge," three miles from Razmak Camp. During operations towards Makin this was the position usually occupied by Column Headquarters

Razmak (Old) Camp: 1/5th Perimeter after the Blizzard, February 7th, 1923.

1/5th on Convoy Escort Duty, closing on Razmak (Old) Camp.

and by the artillery which supported the further sweeping of the route to "Green Ridge," two miles further south. Opposite Green Ridge on the east was the Engamal re-entrant, so broken with scrub and pinnacles of rock that connection could only with great difficulty be maintained. When working through this difficult country, the Battalion found that Vickers guns and artillery could give little help to forward troops, for once committed to the scrub, they disappeared from view for long periods, and it became impossible to follow their movements. To cope with these conditions the tactics adopted were for the Vickers guns and the artillery to deny, whenever possible, those areas of ground which appeared to be most dangerous, whilst the forward troops fended for themselves. For them the most suitable formation was found to be successive lines of sub-units, the line in rear working close enough to that in front to ensure effective support, yet not so close that it would become simultaneously embroiled should the enemy attempt an ambush. That it was necessary, between Gun Ridge and Green Ridge, to have the lines, on occasion, as close as fifteen yards to each other, indicates the density of the scrub.

Tactics at Razmak.

Such then were the conditions in which the Battalion was to work whilst the 7th Brigade, joined by the 9th Brigade from the Ladha line, were engaged in the burning of the villages around Makin.

On the night of the 6th-7th snow began to fall heavily and continued throughout the 7th. Conditions in the camp soon became extremely unpleasant. Tent-poles could not support the weight of snow and broke; snow and sleet were churned into a mass of liquid mud. The camels' lot was perhaps the hardest, for they became frozen in, and much labour was required to get them dug out and loaded for the convoy which was to proceed to the 7th Brigade that day. Conditions at 7 a.m., when the escorting troops were due to leave camp, could hardly have been worse. The driving snow and sleet made visibility extremely poor, and signalling communication, when possible, could be maintained only with Lucas lamps, and was often lost for long periods at a time.

Snowstorms.

The column this day consisted of :—

The operation of February 17th, 1923.

Colonel W. D. Villiers-Stuart, C.B.E., commanding column.
1/5th Royal Gurkhas, F.F. (Major H. R. C. Lane, O.B.E., commanding).
108th Pack Battery.
56th Rifles, F.F. (less one and three-quarters companies and one sub-section vanguard).
One company, 32nd Sikh Pioneers.
Two troops, 16th Light Cavalry.
Brigade Signal Section.

The 56th Rifles were responsible for establishing piquets beyond the furthest permanent piquet, known as "Bakshi's," on the left bank of the Tauda China, as far as, and inclusive of, the Engamal re-entrant. They successfully achieved their task with the result that the left flank of the route was denied to the enemy throughout the day.

The advanced guard for the right bank, on which no permanent piquets existed, was composed of "B" Company (Captain Cosby, M.C.) with its left on the *nullah*. "C" Company (Captain Cameron) was echeloned back from the right of "B," and "D" Company (Major Erskine, M.C.) again in echelon from "C," with its right across the Shuran Algad, covered column headquarters on Gun Ridge. "A" Company was on Gun Ridge in column reserve. The right flank of the route up to Gun Ridge was blocked by a series of stops provided by the company of Pioneers, whilst the 56th Rifles' permanent road piquet was watching the left flank from opposite Gun Ridge back to camp.

The Column had secured the area by 9.15 a.m., but a long delay ensued. Communication with the 7th Brigade could not be obtained, nor was there any sign of the advance of their convoy from Shingi, where it could be seen parked in the broad bed of the Tauda China. It was not until the 5th Brigade Column Headquarters got a message through to the 1/5th forward troops to order the convoy to advance, that at last it did so. As soon as it was safely past the liaison point, the 5th Brigade forward troops retired according to the pre-arranged plan. By this time it had become evident that there were hostile Mahsuds in the vicinity, and that they intended to follow up the withdrawal. "B" Company, after exchanging shots with them on Green Ridge, helped by the scrub, retired inside "C" Company. "C" Company, in its turn, found the enemy working round its right flank, did some execution with its Lewis guns, and then got clear. It was now for "D" Company to act. Hitherto they had lain low and said nothing, with the result that a party of Mahsuds, still intent on their outflanking movement, blundered straight into them. Two were shot at close quarters, there was some spirited firing, the guns found a target and, in a little more time than it takes in the telling, "D" Company, too, had effected its withdrawal. This success made the enemy so wary that the Column was enabled to jump clear, and arrived in camp without further incident.

Our only casualty was one Signal Section Gurkha slightly wounded in the foot.

This small operation has been given at some length for surprise, speed and initiative had all contributed to its successful conclusion, and it led to the comforting conviction that doubts entertained at Parachinar regarding the young riflemen and non-commissioned officers, none of them conversant with frontier fighting, could now be laid aside for good.

From now onwards the Battalion was engaged in convoy escort duties down to the 7th Brigade, and backwards towards Razani. At all times it was necessary to maintain a never-flagging vigilance as several bands of enemy were reported to be in the vicinity. One such band scored a small success on February 10th. While the 1/5th cleared the right bank of the Tauda China, the 56th Rifles, F.F., were called upon to piquet a hill overlooking the Engamal *nullah* from the south. The scrub here was exceptionally thick and high, and as must happen now and again, their leading men were fired on at a distance of a few yards. One Indian other rank was mortally wounded, and the enemy got clear away.

Snow-blindness, February, 1923.

More snow fell on the 14th, and at last the glare from long stretches of dazzling whiteness began to have its effect, and snow-blindness became prevalent. By the 16th so many men were suffering from it that an issue of surgical gauze was made. This was tied across the eyes to form eye-bands, but the irritation caused by the constant friction added if anything to the trouble. It was only with the arrival on February 22nd of proper glare glasses that, to everybody's relief, the difficulty was finally solved.

Whilst on the subject of equipment, it should be mentioned that all troops were now in possession of splendid leather jerkins. These kept the men warm during the long halts which took place when convoys were passing through an area, and did much to maintain the general health of the troops. This remained excellent, under extremely severe winter conditions, except for two complaints—the snow-blindness already referred to, and sore feet caused by the continuous wearing of boots which were never dry.

Mahsuds accept terms.

Meantime, the destruction of Makin had induced the vast majority of the Mahsuds to accept terms, and it remained to complete the arrangements necessary for the furtherance of the new "Forward Policy," now to be initiated. This entailed the withdrawal of the striking force to Razmak New Camp, situated between Gun Ridge and Green Ridge, and the transfer of the 5th Brigade to points on the lines of communication from Damdil to Razmak Narai, with headquarters at Razani.

The evacuation of Razmak Old Camp by the 5th Brigade thus began with "A" Company, under Major Lane, leaving for Razani on the 10th, and unexpected orders resulted in "B" Company, under Captain Cosby, following the next day. The remainder of the Battalion was kept busy in providing working parties on stores, whilst all details of the 2/3rd and 1/9th Gurkhas were despatched to join their units in the new camp.

On the night of March 14th-15th the wire surrounding the transport enclosure was cut by the enemy and eight camels were stolen from the camp.

Operation of February 15th, 1923.

On the 15th the Battalion, less "A" and "B" Companies took part for the last time in an operation down the Tauda China, when it formed part of an escort to a convoy conveying the last of the dump at the old camp to New Razmak. It was given the additional task of covering the relief by troops of the 7th Brigade, of No. 1 Piquet, Razmak—Tauda China sector. Owing to a misunderstanding, the Battalion's withdrawal was started too soon, and it became necessary for the units of the column to re-occupy their original positions in order to safeguard the passage of a number of empty mules proceeding to Tauda China in accordance with a belated decision. At last the second withdrawal began, and at once fire was opened by an enemy party on the cavalry securing the low hills on the right flank of the column. The withdrawal went according to plan until "C" and "D" Companies were clear of Gun Ridge, when a message came through saying that the cavalry had had a casualty. The withdrawal immediately stopped and dispositions were made ensuring that the enemy should not creep round the flank and give trouble from that direction on the resumption of the movement. Stretcher bearers from the 1/5th were hastily despatched to cavalry headquarters, and thanks to good work by Lieutenant Hillyard, commanding the squadron, whose horse was shot under him, the wounded man was quickly brought into safety without other mischance. A fresh start having been made, the Column reached camp without further incident.

Camel thieves ambuscaded by the 1/5th, February 16th, 1923.

That night special precautions were taken by the Battalion to ensure that no further theft of camels would be possible. The usual guards for the camel camp had been two piquets, but on this night an extra two were posted, the new positions being taken up stealthily after dark. The night was a black one.

About 2.30 a.m. a sentry of one of the new piquets perceived men cutting the wire. The rest of his piquet were immediately aroused and, having taken up their positions, simultaneously opened fire on the three men who could just be discerned. Then Véry lights were fired and a final volley, by their aid, was sent after the enemy who were now making off. Next morning a patrol followed blood-stains from the wire, and discovered a wounded man in a *nullah* 400 yards away. He was identified as an Abdullai Mahsud. He died in the camp hospital that day from the effect of his wounds.

On March 15th further details of the evacuation of Old Razmak

1 5th Advance Guard opening out on Right Bank of the Tauda China.

Camel Convoy in Tauda China passing Liaison Point between Old and New Razmak.

Camp were made known. On the 16th, the 5th Brigade was to move to Razani; at the same time the 1/5th were to take over from the 51st Sikhs all permanent piquets from Razani to the Narai, and the 7th Brigade was to hold the remainder onwards as far as their new camp. That night sniping at the camp took place for the first time, but there were no casualties. According to plan Old Razmak Camp was evacuated the next day, and Battalion Headquarters, after covering " D " Company up to Nos. 4, 6 and 8 Piquets on Alexandra Ridge, " C " Company on to the Narai Piquet (Duncan's) and Nos. 2, 5, 7 and 9 on the west of the road, made their way to Razani. The relief of these piquets occurred without a hitch, although the road on the top of Alexandra Ridge from No. 8 Piquet (Simpson's) to No. 6 and No. 4 was extremely rough, entailing light loads for mules and single leading.

Old Razmak Camp vacated.

When the Battalion arrived in Razani, much work was needed in the camp. Tents had to be defiladed as much as possible from all sides, and while this work was progressing the never-ending convoy escorts had to be found, and the piquets held by the Battalion rationed and watered. Alexandra Ridge was still covered in dense scrub and until it could be cleared the safety of the route could not be guaranteed. At the same time the security of piquets themselves entailed much renovation and remodelling of their defences, whilst practically the whole of Duncan's and No. 9 Piquet below it had to be remade. There was, therefore, no lack of occupation during this period.

Back to Razani.

The story of the 1/5th in Waziristan would be incomplete without some attempt to describe life in a permanent piquet. From Asad Khel up to the time the Battalion left Razani the strengths of piquets varied. The smallest had a garrison of only two sections, while the largest, such as Simpson's on Alexandra Ridge, and Duncan's on the Narai, held a company headquarters and two platoons, with or without the addition of Maxim guns.

Piquet life, 1923.

At dawn the mobile portion of the garrison would sweep the area around the piquet to make sure that all was clear, dropping what were termed " day groups " at tactical points. In this way enough ground was put under constant observation to obviate surprise and to allow of limited movement outside the piquet defences during the day. It was felt that some such system was essential, chiefly from the standpoint of morale, which must suffer if men are cooped up for ten days at a time in a confined space, waiting for something to happen. But it had the additional advantage that cooking and sanitation could be arranged for outside, thus giving a minimum length of perimeter to be manned in case of necessity.

When the road was closed a piquet was responsible for its own protection alone, but when the road was opened it undertook to help the convoy escort by using its mobile reserve to clear ground intervening between the permanent piquets. From a main piquet, such as Duncan's or Simpson's, the sweep made by the mobile troops was comprehensive, and as time went on and the scrub became gradually thinned down, it was found possible progressively to reduce the strength of convoy escorts.

When the piquet had finished its work for the day groups were recalled, either by the help of another sweep or under adequate covering fire arrangements from the piquet itself. Each day the piquet commander had to devise some new method of sweeping, and to ring the changes on the various tactical points suitable for day groups.

As the summer progressed the 1/5th made many changes and improvements. The clearing of scrub took much time. This consisted mainly of bushes of holly-oak, growing very closely together to a height of about twenty feet. Gradually the clear areas round piquets were extended, and broad lanes were cut beyond, allowing fire to be brought on to avenues of approach. In time these lanes were extended until those radiating from any one piquet met others, forming lines of fire for the piquets on its right and left. Roads were improved between piquets so that reliefs were not the tiresome business they had been. Piquets were able to obtain water themselves when once springs had been discovered and roads made to them. Later came other achievements, and the most unexpected was the construction of a basket-ball ground and a rifle range, complete with shelter trench and up and down targets, for every piquet. It is easy to picture what a difference this made to the garrisons. It is true that when games were in progress or the ranges in use, it was necessary to post extra groups, but the results made this well worth while. Down in Razani basket-ball became the rage and to this day the Battalion is the proud possessor of two trophies won in 1923. One is a silver cup presented for an inter-platoon competition open to the whole Brigade, which was borne off by No. 1 Group of the Headquarter Wing, and the other, a gigantic tin mug made from kerosene tins, the fruits of the prowess of a team of British officers of the Battalion.

As time went on means were found to add to the comfort of the men's quarters. Very early in the day, bivouac shelters were replaced by tents. Later thatched roofs were made during spare hours, and mud walls being added reaching well up under the eaves, the accommodation in piquets became almost palatial. The acme of comfort was attained with the provision of central heating. A mud flue, lined with tin, was run through the centre of each tent. Its opening was at one end and at the other it terminated in a chimney, made by the armourers from kerosene oil tins. It was only necessary to light a fire well inside the opening and the flue did the rest. Only by such expedients was it possible to cope with the intense cold of the winter at that altitude.

Two British officers lived in piquets, one each in Duncan's and Simpson's, when their companies were on piquet duty, and each tour of duty lasted ten days. Ten days in Razani, followed by ten days in a piquet sector was the routine, and companies never occupied the same sector on two successive tours. Simpson's and Duncan's piquets started three rival periodicals, a shooting diary—for chikor and pigeon and an occasional hare were to be had for straight holding and much climbing and scrambling over the slopes of the ridge; a poetry-file in which many weird verses could be perused; and lastly, a botanical record of wild flowers noticed by successive British officers. So outrageous were some of the names ascribed to the most common flowers, and so acrimonious the comments of successive incumbents on the efforts of their predecessors, that in the interests of amity the record had abruptly to be closed.

Of the Battalion's sojourn in Waziristan there is little left to tell. The spring and summer passed most pleasantly, especially during the time spent on piquet duty, for then the Alexandra Ridge and the Narai were at their best. A perfect climate, scenery of the finest, green turf, woodland, and wild flowers in abundance. Sweeping operations from Razani were extended to include new ground, new ideas for the greater security of convoys were conceived and tried out, a pipe water supply was provided for the camp, the road was opened regularly on the appointed days with never a mishap, and despite the numerous calls on their time, companies managed to complete a comprehensive course of individual training which included the range practices of the annual courses for rifles, Lewis guns and Vickers guns.

Constant reminders were given by raiding gangs of their presence in the vicinity, and these provided an incentive to remain always on the *qui vive*. Occasionally a bomb trap would be exploded, though it was never found that a "hostile" had been damaged; more than once it was discovered that elaborate arrangements had been made to ambush a patrol, the attempt being abandoned, perhaps because the patrol failed to act as anticipated; wire was cut with moderate frequency; once a number of mules was stolen from the watering place whither they had been taken in an hour not authorized, and once a few desperadoes were flushed from inside the camp at night, but managed to make good their escape without harm to either side.

The new road to Razmak was completed in August. Its alignment being several hundred feet above the Kupiri Algad, it became unnecessary to hold the piquets on the far side of the *nullah*. At the same time, danger to convoys was to be feared from certain points below the road and these could not be dealt with by the piquets sited on the crest of the ridge. This led to an interesting experiment in building on the part of the Battalion. Any variation of the normal type of sangar would have been useless, the ground being so steep that defilade could not be ensured. Resort was had to two blockhouses with bombproof roofs, constructed entirely of unfaced stone and holly-oak timber, and these were found to serve their purpose.

Completion of road, August, 1923.

It was at this time that the 1/5th had the pleasure of renewing its connection with an old friend and brother officer, in the person of Brigadier-General M. R. W. Nightingale, who took over command of the 5th Brigade, which, after Brigadier-General Coningham's departure early in the summer, had been commanded temporarily by Colonel Villiers-Stuart.

On October 4th the Battalion lost its Subadar-Major who proceeded to the Depot prior to retirement. Subadar-Major (now Honorary Captain) Kulbahadur Gurung, I.D.S.M., had an honourable career in the 1/5th. During the Great War he saw much active service with the Battalion in Gallipoli, where he won his I.D.S.M., and again throughout the Battalion's period in Mesopotamia. It was with genuine regret that all ranks bade him farewell, after his twenty-six years' loyal service in the Battalion.

On December 8th occurred the only regrettable incident of the campaign as far as the Battalion was concerned. On this occasion a strong band of raiders was successful in wounding, mortally, a rifleman, and in getting away with his rifle. Up to 5 p.m. the day had passed normally in the sector held by "A" Company. Headquarters and two platoons occupied Duncan's Piquet, and thence a wide sweep had been carried out in the course of the morning, embracing the heads of all the tributary *nullahs* running down from Shuidhar, which joined to form the Kupiri Algad. There was no sign of an enemy. For a proper understanding of what happened it is necessary to explain that 300 yards west of the piquet the ground dropped abruptly to a big re-entrant measuring 450 yards across, and the bottom being thickly wooded, it was very necessary to keep it under observation during the daytime. The slope being convex the group in observation was just out of sight of the piquet, and for this reason, two additional groups were posted for its protection, one on a small spur to its right rear, the other on its left, some fifty yards nearer to the head of the re-entrant. The fire of the additional groups crossed about seventy yards in front of the observation group.

The Affair at Duncan's Piquet, December 8th, 1923.

From the little piles of empty cartridge cases left on the ground, as also from other evidence, it was possible to reconstruct exactly the tactics of the raiding gang. It was distributed in no less than seven parties, which took up covering positions on the far side of the re-entrant, and also in prolongation of the spur occupied by one of the protective groups. In addition a few daring men hid in the bushes in the bottom of the re-entrant immediately below the observation group. Apparently on a preconcerted signal a heavy fire was opened from right and left on the protective groups, which at once turned to face the aggressors. The observation group, on being shot at, withdrew a short distance to a fire position at the top of the slope and from there returned the enemy's fire. All, that is, except one rifleman, Bhimbahadur Gurung, whose thigh was shattered at the first scattered volley. While he was crawling to shelter he was again wounded, and at that moment three men appeared from the *nullah*, seized his rifle, and made off with it. They were in view of the remainder of the group for only a second or two, and though fired on, appear to have escaped unharmed.

When the first shots were heard, soon after 5 p.m., the men of the piquet had returned from their afternoon game of basket-ball, and were preparing for evening stand-to. All available Lewis guns and rifles were at once turned out, and manœuvred rapidly to positions from which they could deal with the enemy's fire. By this time the piquet itself had become the object of the enemy's attention, while the ground intervening between the sangar and the day groups was swept by bullets. Some time elapsed while the company commander carried out a reconnaissance, the location of the several enemy parties proving a matter of some difficulty in the fading light. It became evident that any attempt to round up the raiders in the few minutes of daylight which remained, would inevitably fail, and that the only course open was to neutralize their fire, so that the wounded man could be brought in with a minimum of further casualties. The shooting ability of our men proved equal to the task, and just before darkness fell, all were safe once more within the piquet. The wounded rifleman died early next morning.

The 1/5th leave Waziristan.

It had already been made known that both the 1/5th and the 2/8th Gurkhas were to be relieved and would leave the Waziristan Force, the Battalion's destination being the Samana. On the 18th a move was made across the *nullah* to the Pioneer Camp, and therewith the Battalion ceased to be an entity of the 5th Brigade. The 1/5th finally said good-bye to Razani on December 20th when, in company with the 121st Pack Battery, it marched for Asad Khel. The usual march stages—Thal, Idak, Saidgi and Bannu—were completed on successive days without incident and on Christmas Day, 1924, the 1/5th left Wazir Force for good.

Arrival at the Samana.

The journey to the Samana was accomplished by three echelons moving by train to Mari Indus, and arriving during the early hours of Boxing Day. Apparently the Battalion was not expected and no arrangements existed to transport it across the river, so that it was not till late that evening that the last party arrived in the Kala Bagh Camp. Kohat was reached on the 28th, and there the Battalion was split up. "B" Company, under Captain Nepean, proceeded direct to Thal-in-Kurram; "A" and "D" Companies took over Fort Lockhart, Gulistan and Sangar on the Samana Ridge; and Headquarters and "C" Company took over Hangu, in all cases relieving the 56th Rifles, F.F.

At this time, Ajab, notorious in connection with the kidnapping of Miss Ellis from Kohat, was still at large, and extraordinary precautions were considered necessary to guard against any attempted repetition of his ill-doings. The possibility of his sudden appearance on the scene remained as a bugbear to cramp the activities of officers and men throughout their stay in the Samana area. There were piquets around Hangu Camp on this account and the detachment there was kept busy in rebuilding them. None could move anywhere without an escort, while convoy duties entailing the wearisome march to Patdarband and back, with protection on a scale suited to active service conditions, proved particularly irksome.

1924.

Shortly after arrival at Hangu the Commanding Officer received the following message from the G.O.C. Wazir Force (Major-General Matheson):—

"Now that you are leaving the Force, I wish to say good-bye to you and all ranks of the Battalion under your command, and to thank you for the excellent work you have done.

"During the year you have been in Waziristan you have served at Asad Khel, Razani, Old Razmak and again at Razani.

"In your encounters with the enemy you have fully maintained the fine record of your Regiment. I regret that you have lost 2 Gurkha other ranks killed and 3 by disease.

"You have experienced to the full the discomforts of the Waziristan winter, but at all times your discipline, behaviour and vigilance have been exemplary and in accordance with your high traditions.

"I wish you each individually good-bye and good luck wherever you may be called upon to serve."

Major H. E. Weekes, O.B.E., reported his arrival from Army Headquarters on February 26th, 1924, having been posted as second-in-command to the Battalion from the 2/10th Gurkha Rifles.

The Battalion earned two distinctions shortly after arriving in the Kohat District. Firstly, Battalion teams were successful in securing

The 15th Quarterguard over the Main Gate,
Fort Lockhart, 1924.

The Unveiling of the Frontier Force Memorial, Kohat, October, 1924.

the Kohat Musketry Shield at a rifle meeting held there on April 4th. The aggregate points obtained at the meeting by Battalion, company, Lewis gun and pistol teams amounted to 3,219 in all, and gave the Battalion seventh place in the competition for the King Emperor's Cup, open to similar teams from all units of the Indian Army. Much jubilation was felt over this success, as this was the first occasion on which the 1/5th had entered for a competition fired under the auspices of the Army Rifle Association (India). At a later place mention of progress in the standard of rifle shooting will be made.

Rifle and Football Successes at Kohat, 1924.

Secondly, in football, the 1st XI succeeded in carrying off the Piffer Cup, which had been won previously on only one solitary occasion, in 1912. Playing when that success was gained were Turner and Beddy, killed on the same day in Gallipoli, and an elder brother of each was spectator of this victory.

On April 10th, 1924, it was with the greatest regret that the Battalion had to say good-bye to Colonel W. D. Villiers-Stuart, C.B.E., on the expiry of his tenure of command, after twenty-eight years' service in the Battalion. He was succeeded by Lieut.-Colonel H. E. Weekes, O.B.E.

On April 28th "B" Company was relieved in Thal by the 1/9th Jats and, with headquarters and the Headquarter Wing, went to Fort Lockhart. Here much work had been done by "A" and "D" Companies in preparing a perimeter wall round the summer camp of Kohat District Headquarters, and in digging tent-sites.

Among other changes in dress and equipment made at this time, was the discarding of the green and black whistle cord. It had become superfluous owing to the introduction, by command of His Majesty, of a "Royal" cord, red in the case of regiments whose uniform is green, and worn on the right shoulder. No unattested recruit may don it; he receives it on the day he is "sworn in," personally from the hand of the Commanding Officer. A rifleman is deprived of his Royal Cord for such unrifleman-like behaviour as letting off a round through carelessness; and naturally, no man undergoing a sentence on account of a military crime is allowed to wear it.

The "Royal" Cord.

During the summer the detachment at Hangu was changed round every two months, this being necessary on account of the heat and because a good deal of fever was to be expected there.

During the first part of the stay of the 1/5th in Samana, the Kohat District was commanded by Major-General A. le G. Jacob, who had also been their Divisional Commander for a time in Waziristan. When, towards the end of the summer, he left the district, he requested the

Commanding Officer to convey to all ranks his very great appreciation of their excellent work under him both in Waziristan and in the Kohat District.

The General Officer Commanding stated that in all his long service with the Indian Army he had never known a finer battalion than the 1/5th Royal Gurkhas. This was praise indeed from one in his position, and it served to harden the determination of all ranks serving in the Battalion to maintain its reputation at that high level.

About the same time, with great regret, the Battalion had to say good-bye to their old Commandant, Colonel M. R. W. Nightingale, on his ceasing to command the 5th Indian Infantry Brigade.

The Samana Posts Vacated, October, 1924. The evacuation of the Samana by the Battalion began on October 10th, 1924, when " A " Company moved to Hangu and was followed by headquarters and the recruits on the 12th. " A " and " D " moved into camp at Hangu on the 24th to make room for the incoming battalion, the 2/8th Gurkha Rifles.

Unveiling of the Kohat War Memorial. On the 23rd the Battalion, less " B " and " C " Companies, was inspected by the Commander-in-Chief, after his unveiling of the Frontier Force War Memorial at Kohat. The Commanding Officer and the Adjutant represented the Battalion at the ceremony, and the following order was published :—

" This Regiment in Gallipoli, Egypt and Mesopotamia lost 26 British officers, 17 Gurkha officers and 478 Gurkha other ranks, many more than any other unit of the Frontier Force, and a bronze plaque with the crest and name of the Regiment records this glorious total on the Memorial at Kohat. His Excellency the Commander-in-Chief, in the presence of the 57th Rifles and 53rd Sikhs and of representatives of all Frontier Force units, unveiled the Delhi sandstone pillar which has been erected. The troops present on parade there presented arms and marched past the Memorial, each unit saluting the memory of their dead comrades."

" B " Company left Fort Lockhart on the 27th, and after handing over to a detachment of the 2/8th Gurkhas, " C " Company completed the reunion of the whole Battalion at Hangu on the 29th, after it had been split up for ten months.

Abbottabad once again, November, 1924. The Battalion eventually left Hangu on November 1st, and on the 2nd, after a not uneventful absence of two and a half years, found itself back in its old home, the Martin lines.

On its departure, Major-General G. McK. Franks, C.B., placed on record the appreciation of the commanders under whom the Battalion served of the good work done on field service in Waziristan and under peace conditions at Kohat. He added his congratulations on the maintenance of a high standard of all-round efficiency " for which the Battalion was noted when he served alongside them in the past."

The sister battalion was absent from the station, exiled for two years to the Malakand, and throughout that time it was to be the fate of an ever dwindling band of bachelors returned from banishment to populate the old mess house without their help. A bare week or two had elapsed when the Battalion found itself passing once again the remembered landmarks of the Hasan Abdal Road, *en route* to manœuvres. " The Donkey's Grave," Sultanpur camping ground with the high hill of Baz Man away to the right, Maksud Bagh and its well-fed *mahseer*, Serai Saleh and the orchards of Haripur were left behind, and the Brigade took the road to Kot Najibullah. As the training proceeded it was seen that the time spent on the frontier had not affected adversely the marching and digging powers of the Battalion, while tactics had actually benefited, despite altered conditions, by the recent necessity to apply principles to the more difficult conditions attaching to work in the hills. Christmas was fast approaching when the 1/5th found themselves back in Abbottabad, and the festivities over, a serious effort was made to put the house in order.

1925.

Changes introduced at this time had generally as their object the conversion, to meet the requirements of life in cantonments, of details of kit, equipment and interior economy hitherto found most suitable for existence in frontier posts. As examples, the universal type of rifle button gave way to a pattern bearing the regimental crest, and kilmarnock caps, which had been discarded during the Great War, were again brought into wear.

The rank and file were intimately affected by the abolition of slavery in Nepal. Asked their views before a definite pronouncement had been made, they expressed themselves as in favour of the proposal, and this opinion being communicated to Maharajah Sir Chandra Sham Sher Jang Rana Bahadur, he gave proof of his gratification in the following letter :—

" DEAR COLONEL WEEKES,

" Allow me to express my thanks to you for your kind communication of the 1st instant, conveying the views of the Gurkha officers and Gurkha other ranks of the Battalion under your command on the subject of my move directed towards the abolition of slavery in Nepal. I am indeed very glad to have expressions of sympathy from those gallant officers and men, and beg of you kindly to tell them that I very much appreciate them."

A noticeable success was scored in the Rawalpindi District Military Tournament, when the Battalion took first place in two events, the Dismounted Assault Course and the Alarm Race. In the Individual Rifle Championships, held in February, two out of the three representatives sent to Meerut obtained places in their respective classes, of whom one, Havildar Balbahadur Thapa, I.D.S.M., earned the Army Rifle Association's bronze medal. A few weeks later were fired in Abbottabad the five team matches counting for the award of the King Emperor's Cup, and, with an aggregate of 4,924 points, the Battalion obtained third place among units competing from the whole of the Indian Army.

The Rawalpindi District Military Tournament. A.R.A. Successes.

Progress in normal training is marked by the achievement of the signallers, who obtained a figure of merit in their annual test of 99.19 per cent.—a figure which placed them amongst the first five units in the Army, and by the results of the annual classification in rifle and Lewis gun shooting, which surpassed all previous records.

With the close of the year came manœuvres on the grand scale. The experiences of a single battalion read so differently from the official review published later in the light of all the facts, that it may be worth while to summarize the doings of the 1/5th in this " great war."

The 1925 Manœuvres.

On the outbreak of hostilities left Haripur Horse Show ground at dusk, and marched twenty miles during the night. Reached a point one mile south of the Haro River at 3 a.m. and waited for transport till just before dawn. A hard frost and very cold. On arrival of transport dispersed to water-worn areas and spent the day hiding from aeroplanes. Marched again at nightfall, and at 3 a.m. reached Pir Gumat Shah, a big ziarat on the south of the Grand Trunk Road about two miles west of the bridge over the Haro. Provided piquets on the crossings of the Haro and Chablat. With daylight hostile aeroplanes became very active. Concentrated at 2 p.m., and at dusk reached Lawrencepur. Thence a night march to the north, through Hazro, deployed beyond the village, turned west and then south, bumping parties of enemy cavalry at intervals, and taking prisoners. Movement continued till dawn. Apparently successful attack on a big village just before full daylight, defeated by umpires. Out of action for two hours, but no means of bringing up food. Moved again, deployed, and went on till late afternoon. Brigade attacked by Brigade of cavalry which concentrated in the open 1,800 yards away under fire from our artillery and machine guns. Came at a trot for 1,800 yards, fired at by every weapon in the Brigade. Broke into a canter, still shot to pieces, then galloped through our infantry. Much recrimination. Previous movement continued till nightfall. Cease fire and dismiss sounded at 8 p.m.

Marched back to Hatti, reaching the camping ground at 1 a.m. Food at last, and then rest.

It was pleasing to read, some months later, in the report on the Northern Command manœuvres, that a number of useful lessons had been learnt.

1926,
The Regiment's
Battle Honours
for the
Great War.

The belated announcement of Battle Honours for the Great War was made in a Gazette of India notification dated February 20th, 1926. The Regiment's share comprised the following : — " Helles," " Krithia," " Suvla," " Sari Bair," " Gallipoli, 1915," "Suez Canal," " Egypt, 1915-16," " Khan Baghdadi," " Mesopotamia, 1916-18," " North-West Frontier, India, 1917."

A year later was added " Afghanistan, 1919," an honour earned by the 3rd Battalion of the Regiment, disbanded in 1921.

The " Training
Company "
created.

The year 1926 passed quietly in peace training, but one important change in organization has to be recorded in the institution of a Training Company for Gurkha Battalions. A year or two before, the rest of the Indian Army had been organized into regiments consisting generally of four or five battalions, and Training Battalions had been formed to serve the needs of each regiment in such matters as recruiting, training of recruits and the formation of a depot in the event of mobilization. For various reasons, chief among them the desire to meet the wishes of the Nepalese Durbar by limiting recruitment, this could not be done in the case of Gurkha units, and the new departure was an attempt to bring their organization more nearly into line with that of the rest of the infantry of the Indian Army. Instead of a Training Battalion to serve a regiment, they were given a Training Company to serve a battalion. It is the intention, on mobilization, to amalgamate the Training Companies of a group of four battalions into a group centre—the equivalent of a Training Battalion—but rocks are discernable ahead from the fact that financial stringency has precluded the provision in peace time of the necessary staff.

Death of
Field-Marshal
Sir Arthur
Barrett.

It was with a deep sense of loss that towards the close of the year the news was received of the death first of Field-Marshal Sir Arthur Barrett, and, a few weeks later, of the death of the Colonel of the Regiment, Lieut.-General Sir Alfred Martin. An attempt was made in Battalion Orders to bring home to those then serving the degree of their indebtedness to these two distinguished officers. Sir Arthur's death was made known in the following words :—

"It is with very great regret that the Commanding Officer announces the death in England recently of Field-Marshal Sir Arthur Barrett. Joining the Regiment soon after the conclusion of the Afghan War of 1878-80, Sir Arthur continued to serve with it till 1904, when promotion took him elsewhere. His fine soldierly qualities brought him honours which reflected renown on the Regiment in which he served, while his sympathy and kindliness as a private individual caused him to be very warmly regarded by all with whom he came in contact. His deep interest in the Battalion which he had commanded was maintained to the end, and his death leaves a gap which may not easily be filled. Mindful of his achievements as a soldier, and his attributes as a man, those who succeed him in maintaining the good name of the Regiment will long hold him in affectionate remembrance."

A few weeks later came the announcement of a further grievous loss.

Death of Sir Alfred Martin.

"The Commanding Officer deeply regrets to announce the death of Lieut.-General Sir A. R. Martin, K.C.B., Colonel of the Regiment. Joining the Regiment on April 2nd, 1877, he served with it in the Jowaki operations of 1877-78, and then in the Second Afghan War. He was with the Regiment on the famous march from Kabul to Kandahar, was many times mentioned in despatches, and received the medal with four clasps, as well as the bronze star. Among other expeditions, General Martin was present with the Regiment in the Hazara Expedition of 1888 and the second Miranzai Expedition of 1891. He was Adjutant of the 1st Battalion from September 27th, 1878, to December 21st, 1885, and commanded it from June 3rd, 1896, to May 6th, 1899, when he left to take up an important post in Simla. After a long and distinguished career Sir Alfred finally retired from the Service in 1912."

Sir Alfred was succeeded as Colonel of the Regiment by Major-General Sir J. M. Stewart, K.C.B., K.C.M.G.

1927 and 1928.

The Battalion was destined to spend a further two years in Abbottabad before again proceeding in relief to one of the outposts of Empire. They were pleasant years for those who served through them, and marked by steady progress in work and play, but so unbroken was their calm that little can be recorded of them beyond successes in shooting and football.

Football.

Taking football first, in 1927 the Battalion reached the final of the Gurkha Brigade Cup, and won the District Tournament. It was unfortunate that the P.F.F. Tournament clashed with the latter rounds of the Gurkha Brigade football, necessitating the despatch of a second eleven

Field-Marshal Sir Arthur Barrett, G.C.B., G.C.S.I., K.C.V.O.

to Kohat to battle for the honours of retaining the trophy. Though they put up a gallant fight, they were unsuccessful.

However, with the first eleven able to enter in 1928, the P.F.F. Cup was won once again, and again the team reached the final of the Gurkha Brigade Tournament. But for serious casualties in the semi-final, there was every prospect of their bringing the cup to Abbottabad.

Competitive Rifle Shooting Results.

In shooting there were some notable feats. In 1927, in the competition for the King Emperor's Cup, fourth place was secured. In 1928 the Battalion, with an aggregate of 5,569 points, was placed second, thus securing the 56th Rifles' Cup—an understudy, as it were, of the King Emperor's—and scored outright wins in more than one of the five matches in which the points obtained go towards the aggregate which counts for the award of the major trophy. These wins included the 88th Carnatic Infantry Gold Cup, competed for by battalion teams, and the Cawnpore Woollen Mills Cup, for which platoon teams of sixteen men are eligible to compete. Further, second place was gained in the shoot for the Rawlinson Trophy, open to company teams. Lastly, the machine gunners of the Battalion succeeded in carrying off the Mother Country Cup with a record score, the sister battalion being placed second only a few points behind.

In the Individual Championships held at Meerut, the Bisley of India, the outstanding figure was Lance-Naik Nandabahadur Thapa. In 1927 he won the Priestly Memorial Medal, given to the Gurkha soldier making the highest score in the championship match, the special medal given by the Army Rifle Association (India) for the highest score made on any one day of the meeting, and the bronze medal of the Association for securing second place in his class. In 1928 he did even better. The standard of marksmanship this year proved higher than ever, and a record score was established by the winner of the King's Medal, Rifleman Lewis, of the K.R.R.C., who in the two days of the meeting scored 313 points. On the first day of the meeting Lance-Naik Nandabahadur Thapa had trouble with his rifle and, as a result, he appeared to be out of the running. Nothing daunted, however, on the second day he shot as one inspired, and with the magnificent score of 175 points—12 points better than the previous record for a single day—he finished up only one point behind the winner. This performance earned for him the title of Champion Shot of the Indian Army, an honour carrying with it the award of the Magdala Gold Medal. He also won the Priestly Memorial Medal for the second successive year—a feat never before achieved; the special medal for the best shoot on a single day of the meeting; the championship medal for the first place in his class; and the John Pinches Marksmanship Medal, given for the best aggregate score compiled by a non-European domiciled in India. As minor awards he was given a silver spoon for the best performance in the fire-and-movement practice on the first day, and another for a similar achievement in the snapshooting practice on the second day.

In April, 1928, Colonel Weekes's period of command came to an end. He had left shortly before to take up an acting appointment as Brigadier, General Staff, Western Command, but it is pleasant to remember that these successes, which his keenness had done much to ensure, were recorded before the passing of the years severed his direct connection with the Battalion. He was succeeded by Lieut.-Colonel F. S. Massy.

But little remains to be added to the record of this period. Facilities for football were increased by levelling the recruits' parade ground—which a previous generation will remember as a gravelly surface broken by runnels and rivulets sloping down to the road—grassing it over and thus converting it into a first-class football ground.

New Regimental Crest, 1927.
Yet one other change is worthy of mention. When the 5th Gurkhas became a Royal Regiment, a Tudor Crown was superimposed on the five of the regimental crest. Later, because the crests of half the regiments, royal or otherwise, of the Indian Army bear a similar crown, it was felt that the addition failed to meet the case. Permission was therefore sought to replace the crown by the Imperial Crown and Lion, and in August, 1927, it was intimated that His Majesty had been graciously pleased to sanction the change. The result can be seen on the cover of this book.

Move to the Malakand.
November, 1928, saw the Battalion taking part in manœuvres on a grand scale between Gujrat and Jhelum. On their conclusion, entrainment was effected at Lala Musa on December 7th, and Abbottabad was reached in time to allow everything to be packed in a hurry before marching out, on the 17th, for a two years' tour in the Malakand.

In that fastness, until the time comes to write a second volume of the History of the Regiment, we leave the 1st Battalion, wondering a little how efficiency is to be maintained in face of the paucity of men available for training, but confident that a way will be found.

CHAPTER II

THE 2ND BATTALION, 1919 TO 1928

Return to India, 1919.
As recorded in a previous chapter the Battalion was ordered back to India from Mesopotamia on the outbreak of the Third Afghan War. The journey from Baiji, north of Baghdad, to Basra and the voyage thence to Karachi were carried out without a hitch. The Battalion, on arrival in India, was ready for war, being at mobilization strength in officers, men, animals, arms and equipment.

Orders were received to proceed to the Rawalpindi Divisional Area as Divisional troops, so in this capacity the Battalion returned to Abbottabad, its permanent peace station, for the first time since December, 1915, to find that orders were waiting there for the immediate despatch of one company to Attock. Accordingly "A" Company, under Captain G. A. Maconchy, marched out the following morning, June 6th, 1919.

The Battalion, less "A" Company, remained at Abbottabad for three weeks, but as a state of mobilization had to be maintained, the Depot was not amalgamated.

On June 19th "D" Company, under Captain A. N. Rolfe, proceeded to Sialkot to take over the duties of the British troops there. Headquarters and the two remaining companies, under Lieutenant-Colonel C. E. B. Champain, moved to Rawalpindi for a similar purpose on June 26th, whilst the Depot, under Lieutenant-Colonel C. R. Johnson, stayed at Abbottabad.

The Battalion remained thus distributed, carrying out its own reliefs of the two detached companies until December. During this period there were no British battalions in the area and the 2/5th were called upon to find practically all the guards normally furnished by British troops. The men were thus fully employed and it was impossible to carry out parades or training. The number of British officers was depleted owing to the employment of some on various duties in India and to the absence of others on leave in England. Among these latter was Lieutenant-Colonel Champain. Captain G. A. Maconchy was in temporary command of the Battalion, Major R. C. Duncan having been appointed Brigade Major, 69th Infantry Brigade, and Captain A. N. Rolfe, Brigade Major, Lahore Brigade Area. During December the company at Sialkot was relieved and rejoined Headquarters at Rawalpindi.

Battalion ordered to Waziristan. December, 1919.
On December 22nd the Battalion, then stationed at Rawalpindi, with "B" Company at Attock and the Depot at Abbottabad, received orders to mobilize for field service in Waziristan, but no definite date was fixed, and conditions remained unchanged; the numerous station guards were not relieved and there were only six British officers present.

On Christmas Eve at about 5 p.m. Divisional Headquarters made urgent inquiries, and were informed that the Battalion would be ready to move twenty-four hours after the company at Attock rejoined Headquarters. Later the same evening information was received that the situation in Waziristan was such that the move would have to be carried out on the morning of December 26th. The message added that every facility would be given on Christmas Day for drawing field service clothing and ammunition, and that the company at Attock would follow separately to Waziristan when a relief had been arranged. Mobilization was completed with difficulty owing to the Christmas holidays. On the evening of December 25th Major J. D. Crowdy, D.S.O., rejoined very unexpectedly and assumed command, having been away since 1913, and it was a great surprise for him to find that the Battalion was proceeding on active service the following morning.

The mobilization was carried out in heavy rain and the issue of field service serge clothing in place of khaki drill was only completed at 4 a.m. on December 26th. No time was available to fit the clothing properly and some amusing misfits were to be seen as the Battalion marched to the railway station in the early hours of the morning.

Entrainment was delayed for some hours by the unexpected arrival of an ambulance train, and from the stories told by the wounded it appeared that the morale of the troops in the field was in a very low state.

The move up the line proceeded according to programme, as follows:

December 27th	...	Detrained at Darya Khan.
December 28th	...	Marched to Dera Ismail Khan.
December 29th	...	Marched to Potah.
December 30th	...	Marched to Hatala.
December 31st	...	Marched to Tank.

At Tank a halt was made for one day to complete field service equipment and clothing. Here, too, "B" Company from Attock rejoined and was issued with war equipment. A dump of surplus kit was formed and loads were worked out to suit the pack transport now allotted.

THE 5TH ROYAL GURKHA RIFLES (F.F.)

Arrival at Khirgi, January 2nd, 1920.

On January 2nd, 1920, the Battalion marched to Khirgi. The transport mules being new to pack work gave a great deal of trouble. Palosina Camp was reached on January 3rd and the Battalion joined the 67th Brigade, commanded by Brigadier-General F. G. Lucas, C.B., C.S.I., D.S.O., a former commandant of the Battalion. The other units in the Brigade were :—1/55th Coke's Rifles, F.F., 1/103rd Mahratta Light Infantry, 2/112th Infantry; the two latter were afterwards relieved by 2/9th Gurkha Rifles and 4/3rd Gurkha Rifles on January 10th and February 12th respectively.

The morale of the troops with the Derajat Column was at this time very low. Hair-raising stories were being constantly circulated, and a cheerful face was hardly ever seen. The site of this camp was the same as that used in 1894 when the 1st Battalion was present.

Advance to Kotkai, January 6th, 1920.

The Brigade remained at Palosina until January 6th, when they moved forward to Kotkai and joined up with the Derajat Column. This column consisted of:

Major-General A. Skeen, C.M.G. (Commanding).
Column Headquarters.
Column Troops (2 battalions Infantry, 1 battalion Pioneers, Sappers and Miners, etc.).
43rd Infantry Brigade.
67th Infantry Brigade.

By this time the Battalion which had mobilized at Rawalpindi, with only six British officers, had been reinforced and the following were now present :—

Major J. D. Crowdy, D.S.O.	Commanding.
Captain C. P. Blackett	2/6th Gurkha Rifles.
Captain G. C. Strahan, O.B.E.	2/6th Gurkha Rifles.
Captain G. A. Maconchy	"A" Company.
Lieutenant J. M. Hobbs, M.C.	"B" Company.
Lieutenant J. C. March	"C" Company.
Lieutenant K. J. Macintosh, M.C.	Adjutant.
Lieutenant P. E. Cayley	"D" Company.
Lieutenant N. Macdonald	Quartermaster.
Lieutenant P. R. Broadway	1/5th Gurkha Rifles, F.F.
2/Lieutenant E. J. Edser	10th Gurkha Rifles.
Captain N. M. Dotivala	I.M.S.

The task before the Column was the capture of, and passage through, the Ahnai Tangi. The latter is about four miles from Kotkai Camp. The actual gorge is about eighty yards long and only thirty yards wide; its sides are precipitous and rise to a height of 150 feet above the river bed. Of the country beyond this Tangi very little information was available.

Passage of Ahnai Tangi, January 7th to 14th, 1920.

On January 7th an attempt to pass through the defile was made, the 43rd Brigade making good the left bank for a distance of some three miles, thereby protecting the advance of the 67th Brigade which moved along the plateau on the right bank. By 1 p.m. it became evident that the enemy were in force and fully intended to oppose any further advance by the Column. There were not sufficient hours of daylight left in which to complete the operation, so General Skeen decided to defer the attack on the Tangi and ordered a withdrawal to Kotkai Camp.

On January 9th the 67th Brigade advanced, without casualties, some three miles to a small bivouac camp called Gurlamah Kach, and the next day the Column carried out operations which led to the capture of the actual gorge of the Ahnai Tangi. Permanent piquets were then established on the heights on both sides. These were named Ahnai Right and Ahnai Left, that is, when facing upstream. At the same time the 67th Brigade formed a new camp at Zeriwam, about one mile below the Tangi, on a plateau on the right bank. "D" Company sustained the only casualties, one rifleman killed and one wounded. Major H. Exham, 7th Gurkha Rifles, now joined the Battalion and took over the duties of second-in-command from Captain Blackett. On January 12th and 13th further operations were carried out with the object of consolidating the ground already gained. Two riflemen of the Battalion were wounded, one in "B" and one in "C" Company.

Action at Ahnai Tangi, January 14th, 1920.

On January 14th the advance through the Ahnai Tangi was accomplished. Running north from the Tangi on the east bank of the Tank Zam is a long narrow spur culminating in a flat-topped hill known as Flathead Left (later renamed Flathead Right). This hill towers 900 feet above the Tank Zam and completely dominates the river bed and right bank.

Farther upstream the advance is threatened from a mass of cliffs known as Marble Arch and more to the east by a hill which is separated from Flathead Left by a steep and precipitous *nullah*. This second hill was known as Flathead Right. The ground was extremely difficult and the Column Commander decided that the most important tactical feature was the ridge on the left bank culminating in Flathead Left. With this decision in mind it is hard to understand why a stronger force, with adequate artillery support, was not detailed to protect this dangerous flank.

The Battalion, less "C" and "D" Companies, was detailed as a special flank detachment, to start from Ahnai Right Piquet at

7.30 a.m. and move along the spur to secure Flathead Left, with Flathead Right as the ultimate objective. Meanwhile, " C " Company was detailed as vanguard to the column, while " D " Company marched at the head of the main guard. Lieutenant-Colonel Herdon, 1/55th Coke's Rifles, was in command of the advanced guard.

The flank detachment made good progress; " B " Company was dropped to make good a position half-way along the ridge and to build a piquet at that point, whilst Battalion Headquarters, with " A " Company, moved forward along the ridge to select a site for and construct a piquet on Flathead Left. At 10 a.m. " B " Company was ordered forward to Flathead Left, leaving two platoons to hold their original position.

Headquarters and " A " Company had meanwhile reached Flathead Left and Lieutenant-Colonel Crowdy selected the piquet site, but as it was overlooked by, and also under heavy rifle fire from Flathead Right, he ordered Captain G. A. Maconchy, with " A " Company, less two platoons, to advance to capture that hill. This party moved off and were very soon out of sight in the dead ground between the two hills. Here, it is believed, they were rushed by a strong party of the enemy concealed there and quickly overwhelmed. This account is based on the report of a rifleman who was wounded in the first enemy rush and left for dead by them; he finally crawled into Kotkai Camp that night. It has been reported that some few men reached the top of Flathead Right, but were immediately forced to withdraw in the face of vastly superior numbers of the enemy.

Battalion Headquarters, with two platoons from both " A " and " B " Companies, on Flathead Left, were at this time heavily attacked twice by a party of the enemy who crawled close up to the position covered by deadly accurate fire provided by their fellow tribesmen on Flathead Right, and as a shortage of ammunition was now making itself felt, Lieutenant-Colonel Crowdy gallantly led a charge which beat off the second attack, but in doing so he unfortunately lost his life. Lieutenant Broadway was wounded in this same charge. Major Exham was now called up and assumed command of the Battalion.

Meanwhile, the vanguard had advanced without serious opposition to a point in the bed of the Tank Zam slightly in advance of Flathead Left. Suddenly a small piquet found by the piquetting troops with the main guard, was rushed and overwhelmed by large numbers of tribesmen. This party of the enemy continued their headlong rush right into the river bed where they cut in in rear of " C " Company, the vanguard. " C " Company had to fight their way back and in the heavy hand-to-hand fighting which ensued the company commander, Captain J. C. March, was killed. This party of the enemy, it is believed, were making good their escape from the charge led by

Lieutenant-Colonel Crowdy on Flathead Left, and this fact would account for their determination to break away through the piquet line. The advanced guard was now held up and no further progress was made on account of the situation on the right flank.

The flank detachment meanwhile found any further advance impossible except at great cost, so immediate action was taken to strengthen the defence of the ground already held. By 11 a.m. ammunition and grenades had been replenished from the Battalion reserve which had by this time arrived, with the transport of the column, in the bed of the Tank Zam below Flathead Left.

During the day the enemy made six separate and determined attacks against the covering position now held on the forward slopes of Flathead Left, all of which were successfully driven off, but not without heavy casualties. At approximately 1 p.m. the 2/76th Punjabis advanced through this position with the object of reaching the high ground, Flathead Right, some 800 yards ahead. They immediately sustained heavy casualties and were forced to retire.

The Battalion was now reinforced by two platoons from the 2/9th Gurkha Rifles, but these platoons were shortly called back to assist in the construction of a permanent piquet at Battalion Headquarters on Flathead Left.

During the sixth and last enemy attack which took place at about 7 p.m., the position was strengthened by the arrival of the 2/9th Gurkhas and the enemy was beaten off, having suffered heavy casualties. The Adjutant, Lieutenant K. J. Macintosh, who had gone forward to the covering position, was severely wounded during this attack, and died in hospital two days later.

At 7.30 p.m. Flathead Left piquet having been established and manned, the covering position was vacated and the Battalion withdrew to the column camp in the river bed below.

By its action throughout the day the Battalion earned great distinction. The possession of Flathead Left was essential for the safety of the column, massed as it was in the *nullah* below. The loss of this important point, for which the enemy fought so desperately, might have meant the total destruction of the column, trapped with the narrow Ahnai gorge immediately in rear.

The main feature of the fighting was the enemy's clever employment of our own tactics. In his ranks were many ex-soldiers from our army and hundreds of trained Militia deserters. Every movement he made was carried out under a deadly accurate covering fire, every shot being carefully aimed.

Our own artillery was unable to assist the right flank detachment from its position in the bed of the Tank Zam as all fire was masked by the precipitous slopes of Flathead Left rising sheer some 900 feet above the gun positions.

"Flathead Left" from Asa Khan Camp.

Makin.

That night every officer and man was posted on the perimeter; it was a disturbed night, but the enemy made no further attacks.

By Colonel Crowdy's death the Battalion lost one whom they could ill spare. It was but a short time since he had returned from several years of distinguished service on the Staff, but in that brief period he had shown that he was a fine leader and a capable commander. It seldom happens in frontier warfare that a Commanding Officer must sacrifice himself in leading a charge, and that one so experienced and well balanced should have found this course necessary is sure evidence of the gravity of the situation with which he was faced. Gallantly he rose to it, and bravely he met his death.

The total casualties during the day were :—

Lieutenant-Colonel J. D. Crowdy, D.S.O.	Killed.
Captain G. A. Maconchy ...	Killed.
Captain J. C. March ...	Killed.
Lieutenant K. J. Macintosh	Wounded (died in hospital on January 16th, 1920).
Lieutenant P. R. Broadway	Wounded.
Subadar Bhawansing Thapa	Killed.
Jemadar Chandersing Thapa	Wounded.
Gurkha Other Ranks ...	25 killed, 53 wounded.

Preparations for further advance January 15th to 17th, 1920.

On January 15th the piquets established on the previous day were strengthened, the camp in the *nullah* bed at Asa Khan was improved and the construction of the perimeter completed. Major C. D. Roe, D.S.O., 4th Gurkha Rifles, reported his arrival and assumed command of the Battalion, and 2/Lieutenant French rejoined.

On January 16th operations were resumed; a permanent piquet was constructed and an effort was made to recover the bodies of Lieutenant-Colonel Crowdy and Captain Maconchy. The former was successfully brought into camp, but the latter again had to be abandoned owing to very heavy sniping fire.

The following day Brigade operations were carried out, covering the construction of permanent piquets on Marble Arch and on the slope above that hill, known as Park Lane. These operations lasted from 7.45 a.m. until 4 p.m., but were carried out without casualties. In spite of the heavy casualties sustained by the column on the 14th, it was evident that the enemy had not escaped without heavy punishment, as he showed no further desire to come out into the open. In fact, from this time onwards the nature of the fighting changed, the enemy remained concealed from view and his action was restricted mainly to sniping fire.

That evening there was a funeral service attended by all available officers with the column. The bodies of Lieutenant-Colonel J. D. Crowdy, D.S.O., and Captain J. C. March were buried together close to the camp at the foot of a cliff. A huge mass of rock now marks the grave.

The same evening, after dark, the body of Captain G. A. Maconchy was recovered and in the early hours of January 18th, before the column moved away from Asa Khan, a short funeral service was held. The grave is situated on the slopes of the hill close to Flathead Piquet.

Advance to Sorarogha, January 18th, 1920.

This was to be a long and arduous day. The Battalion marched up the bed of the Tank Zam at the head of the column to a new camp on the Sorarogha Plateau, some three miles upstream. It was engaged in making good the actual plateau and in taking up a covering position to the north-west. The construction of two piquets was commenced, one for sixty rifles and the other for thirty rifles. The party which was covering the construction of one of these piquets was attacked and the Naik in command of the party was wounded. " A " Company was sent to assist and " C " Company remained in support, whilst two further attacks were beaten off. Work on the piquet was completed by 6.30 p.m., " D " Company remained as its garrison and the remainder withdrew to camp. The smaller piquet, not having been completed, it was decided not to occupy it that night. The Battalion reached camp at 8 p.m. after an extremely long day's work of some fifteen hours' duration. After this the camp perimeter had to be sited and constructed in the dark and preparations were made to meet a night attack which was expected but did not materialize.

The column halted at Sorarogha until January 27th. During the intervening period the existing piquets were strengthened, reserves of ammunition, stores and supplies were replenished and firewood collected from the neighbouring villages. An urgently needed draft arrived from the Depot.

About one-and-a-quarter miles north of Sorarogha the Tank Zam cuts through the Sarkai Ghar, forming a gorge called the Barari Tangi. The latter is some 300 yards long and 60 yards wide with sides which rise precipitously to an average height of 100 feet. The bed of the river here turns almost due west and is joined by the Barari Algad from a north-easterly direction. After passing through the Tangi further advance is obstructed by a hill known as Barari Centre. Before attacking Barari Centre it was necessary to secure Sarkai Ghar. The ridge on the right bank known as Barari Left was the most

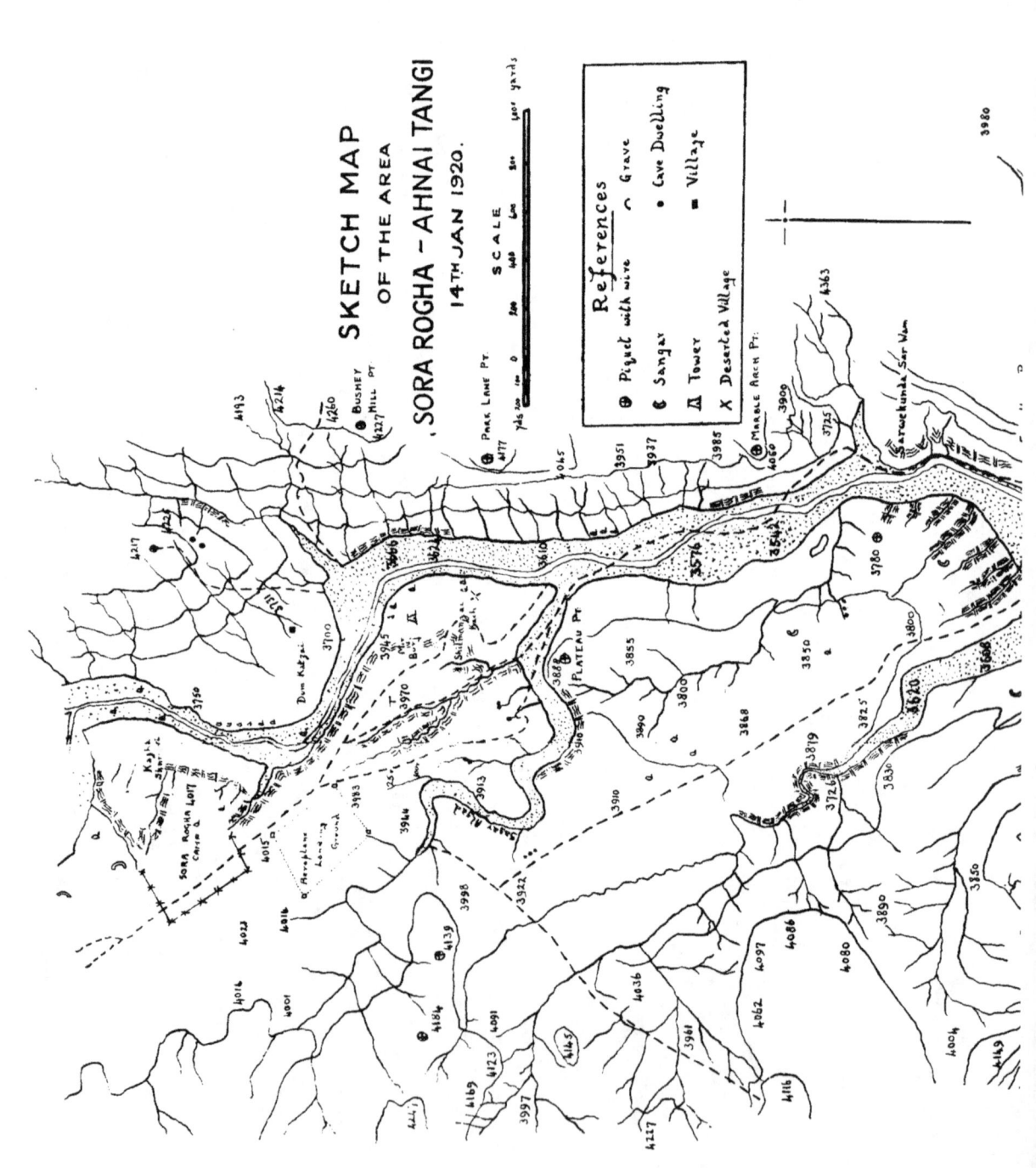

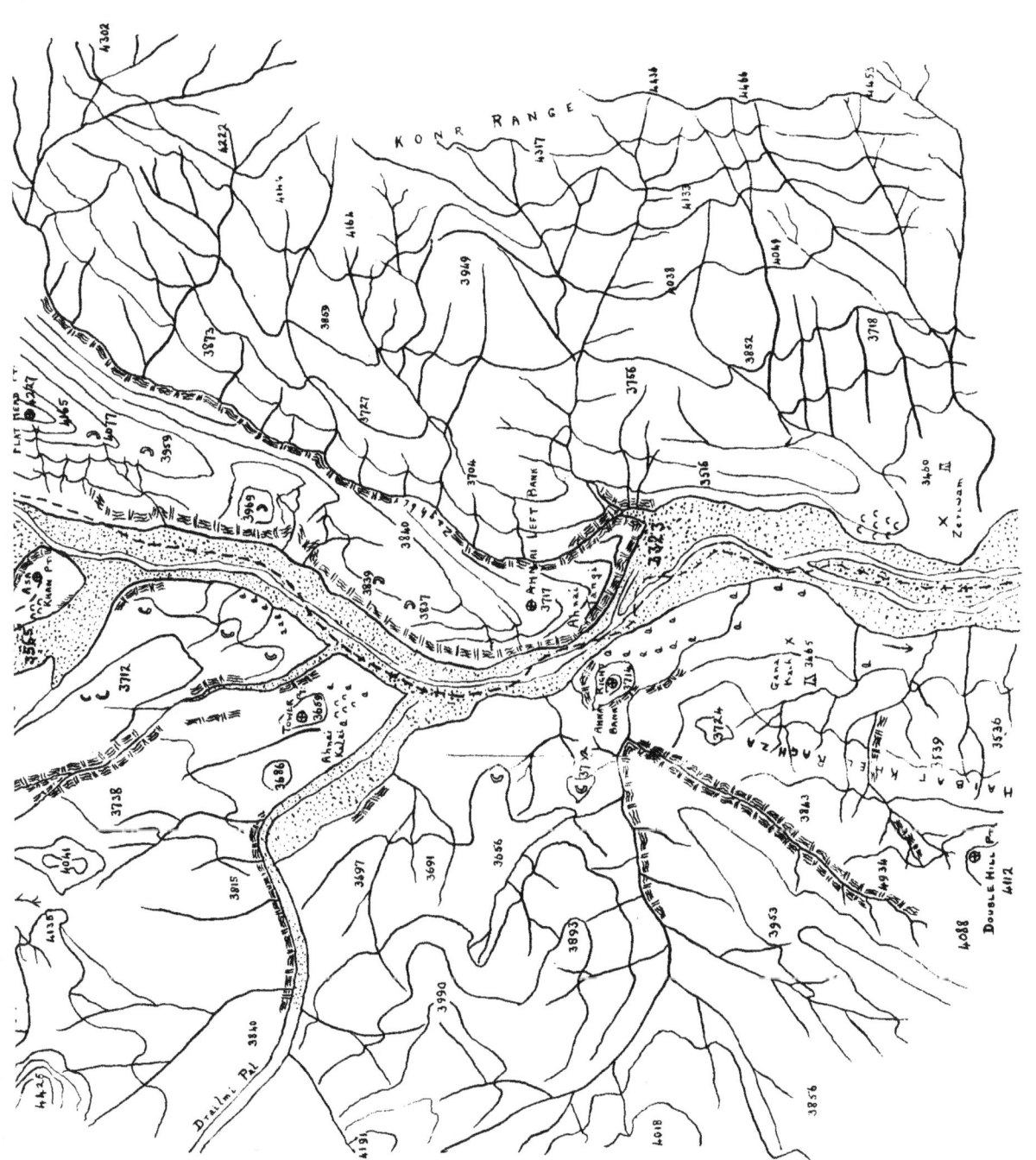

formidable, but higher and less exposed than the part on the left bank known as Barari Right, and gave observation over the latter and its surroundings. As the column penetrated the enemy country the terrain became more and more cut up by small ravines and hills thickly covered with bush and scrub, which gave good cover to enemy snipers.

On January 23rd, at 5.30 a.m. the 67th Brigade moved out from camp, traversed the intricate *nullahs* and bush that lay north of the Sorarogha Plateau, ascended the precipitous slopes of Sarkai in the dark and established itself without loss in positions covering the site selected for the construction of a permanent piquet on Barari Left, subsequently named " Bluff Piquet." The only opposition met during this advance was a small Mahsud piquet which was surprised at the top of the ridge and retired abandoning several *charpoys*.

During the day " C " Company in a forward covering position, was attacked and had two Gurkha ranks killed and seven wounded. Bluff Piquet, when established, was taken over by the 2/9th Gurkhas. The withdrawal was heavily sniped and the 2/9th suffered some casualties.

On January 25th operations had to be suspended owing to a fall of snow followed by heavy rain. The early hours of the night were somewhat disturbed by a party of the enemy who first collected round one of our camp piquets and were later located close to the camp perimeter, but they did not attack the camp.

The next day the 67th Brigade moved out again and established a permanent piquet on Barari Right. The 2/5th were given the task of holding the right sector of the forward covering position. The situation throughout the day was extremely difficult and the Battalion was lucky to complete the task with only Captain C. P. Blackett slightly wounded, one Gurkha rank killed and six wounded. The opposition was provided by from 300 to 400 of the enemy who attempted to work round the right flank and at one period, about 11 a.m., nearly succeeded. Sniping fire throughout was heavy, and with a more resolute enemy things might have been nasty. On this occasion the Mahsuds are reported to have used captured Lewis guns against our troops.

On January 26th there were several changes in the Battalion. Lieutenant-Colonel D. M. Watt, D.S.O., of the 2/2nd Gurkhas, arrived and took over command from Major Roe. Major H. Exham, O.B.E., was transferred to the 2/9th Gurkhas as second-in-command. Lieutenant J. V. Bell, 9th Gurkhas, and Lieutenant C. C. Power, 6th Gurkhas, joined the Battalion.

The 43rd Brigade marched up from Kotkai and camped alongside the 67th Brigade.

During the next two days the Battalion was employed on covering duties, which were carried out without casualties.

From January 29th to 31st, owing to continued bad weather, active operations were impossible and the Battalion was employed on convoy work and the strengthening of camp piquets. A draft consisting of 1 Gurkha officer and 77 other ranks arrived from the Depot.

On the evening of the 31st information was received that the 43rd Brigade were in difficulties and the Battalion, together with the 2/9th Gurkhas, was ordered to join the column at their forward camp, as column troops. They marched on February 1st, at 6 a.m., before daylight, in order that the column at Ahmedwan might be reached before 7.30 a.m. when operations were due to commence. The Battalion moved up the bed of the Tank Zam and on joining the column was placed in reserve. In this capacity companies were distributed under column orders at various points throughout the day. There were no operations of special interest except that Lieutenant-Colonel Watt carried out a reconnaissance with a view to the future capture of the hill known as Cloud End. Camp was reached at 6.15 p.m. Jemadar Ganjagir was wounded twice and two other Gurkha ranks were wounded.

On February 2nd the column rested and preparations for the night operations to follow were made. The next morning these started at 1 a.m., at which hour the Battalion marched from camp bound for Cloud End with orders to establish a permanent piquet there. Immediately rain began to fall and this, combined with the frequent crossings of the Tank Zam, soon caused every man to be wet through. This was nothing compared with what was still to come. In some places stepping stones had been provided to make the crossing of the stream easy, these were covered with ice which caused the leading files to land in a sitting position up to their necks in icy cold water. After wading through the stream the water in the men's clothes quickly froze. Still, the actual advance to the ridge was carried out with success in spite of the very difficult nature of the country. "A" Company, on the right, encountered what was either an enemy sniper or a piquet, who fired some half-dozen shots and then vanished. "A" and "B" Companies took up positions high on the ridge to the north-east, while "C" Company proceeded lower down the spur with the main object in view of starting the construction of the piquet. "D" Company and Battalion Headquarters were 100 yards lower down the slope.

Night Operation from Sorarogha, February 3rd, 1920.

At 3 a.m. snow began to fall and conditions soon became very bad. Work was much impeded, the men becoming quite numbed and covered with snow from head to foot.

At 6 a.m. column headquarters at last made a decision that conditions were too bad for any advance to take place, and ordered the Battalion back to camp. The withdrawal began without delay through Cliff End village, where the 3rd Guides had taken up a covering position, and company by company, wet and bedraggled, the Battalion finally reached camp, once more in thick snow, at 8 a.m. Several men had to be assisted back, as they had become practically senseless with cold. Many had nasty falls in the dark on the slippery hillside, but only one had been slightly wounded by the fire from the enemy piquet. It was a very severe night's experience, but after an issue of rum the men's spirits were as high as ever.

Meanwhile rain and snow had made a morass of the camp site, and tents had been struck prior to a move to a new camp. Tents were repitched further up the hillside and the day was spent in draining the camp and constructing stone paths and roads.

During these operations the enemy was assisted by two Afghan guns with their teams. The Mahsuds put great faith in them and expected far-reaching results, which, however, never materialized.

During this day Lieutenant G. de la Rue Browne, 6th Gurkhas, joined the Battalion.

The next day, to quote Column Orders, was "A day of rest and destruction." Road-making within the camp was continued by tearing down the retaining walls of the fields and using this material as road metal. One man was unfortunately killed and another wounded by sniping fire into the camp. February 5th was a remarkable day, as very few shots were fired.

Further Advance.
The column proceeded on its way from Aka Khel, and instead of merely accomplishing the usual mile and a half or so with difficulty, actually reached Janjal, a distance of over three miles, by 1 p.m. with no opposition. It seemed too good to be true, as considerable opposition had been expected. The particular role of the Battalion was a repetition of the operations on Cloud End on February 3rd, only on this occasion they left camp at 2.30 a.m. and weather conditions were more favourable. The following extract from the official account is of interest :—

"The heavy rain and snow had ceased, but the cold was very severe, and the night march ranks as a very high feat of endurance on the part of all ranks. Not only was the temperature twenty-five degrees below freezing point, but a strong bitter wind added to their discomfort. The Tank Zam had to be forded many times, each time the troops emerged from the river their boots and putties were encased immediately in ice. Icicles formed on the cables where they crossed and were struck by the stream, and all channels of the Tank Zam, except a very narrow strip of the main stream, were thickly crusted with ice. The men working in the dark on the construction of defences on the high ground had first to wrench up the stones, which were frozen fast to the ground, and then handle this icy material without respite or means of warming themselves. In spite of the hardships so bravely endured by the troops, the operation proved a most signal success and so thoroughly disheartened the enemy that he offered no combined opposition."

The left wing was later included as part of the advanced guard, and finally reached camp at 5.30 p.m. after spending several hours covering the construction of camp piquets. On February 6th the column advanced approximately one and a quarter miles to Piaza Raghza, where a splendid camp was formed.

A halt was made at this place until February 14th in order to build up a reserve of supplies and to improve the roads leading from the river bed into the camp. During this period the destruction of several villages was carried out, and the roof beams collected as firewood for the troops. No opposition was met, and after the experiences of the last month it seemed strange to be able to move about without being under fire. The weather remained appallingly cold, and snow continued to fall at intervals. This camp was made thoroughly comfortable, a fireplace was constructed in the mess tent, also a mud sofa with cushions stuffed with straw. A badly needed reinforcement in the form of seven signallers arrived from the Depot. Some training was carried out, and the men even enjoyed the luxury of a badly-needed hot bath.

Major C. D. Roe, D.S.O., left to take over command of the 3/11th Gurkhas, who at this time joined the column, and in his place Captain Goodall came across from that battalion. On February 15th the column resumed the march into the heart of the Mahsud country and reached the village of Marobi. The Battalion forming the advanced guard, under Lieut.-Colonel Watt, left camp at 6 a.m. under cover of darkness. On entering the narrow Dwa Toi defile at daybreak, considerable opposition from snipers on all sides was experienced. The Commanding Officer, Jemadar Dhanbar Gurung and one rifleman, the Adjutant's runner, were almost immediately wounded, but when the surrounding heights had been made good the opposition ceased. The Battalion reached camp at 6 p.m. Lieut.-Colonel Watt's wound luckily was only slight, a bullet having pierced the flesh of his heel, but he was confined to camp and unable to command the Battalion for some days.

On February 16th one of the main objectives of the column was reached at long last. An advance was made from the temporary overnight camp at Marobi village to the Tauda China Raghza, a plateau within two miles of Makin town, and less than that distance from the other villages in the area.

The Battalion was at the head of the main body in the early stages of the advance, and finally had to push forward over the *raghza* and make this good by taking up a covering position on the north-west edge. Opposition was not great, but the usual sniping caused us five casualties :—Lieutenant G. de la Rue Browne (wounded), Subadar Sahabir Gurung (slightly wounded), 3 Gurkha ranks (wounded).

Captain G. C. Strahan was in temporary command of the Battalion.

Operations about Makin, February 17th to 25th, 1920.
During the afternoon of the following day the Battalion was called out to cover the withdrawal of the 4/3rd Gurkhas, who had got into difficulties whilst collecting firewood from a village close to camp. During the retirement, which could not be completed until after dark, the 4/3rd Gurkhas had some fifty casualties, whilst our own were :—Jemadar Hastadal Thapa (killed) and one rifleman wounded.

This rifleman, Tilchand Thapa, was awarded the Indian Order of Merit for his bravery. Whilst acting as runner to his company commander he, though badly wounded in the leg at the time, delivered a message to one of the forward platoons under heavy sniping fire.

February 18th was given up to convoy work and the replenishment of supplies, but the next day the Battalion marched from camp, as part of General Lucas's Force, to destroy the town of Makin and houses in the neighbouring areas. At about 8 a.m., after they had advanced about a mile, it became evident that all had not gone according to plan. The 4/3rd Gurkhas who were directed on Tree Hill had missed their way in the dark, and did not reach this position until daylight. The Battalion therefore did not advance beyond Tree Hill, where they took up a position to cover the 2/9th and 3/11th Gurkhas. Tree Hill piquet was completed and garrisoned, but whilst this was going on constant sniping took place from the opposite bank of the river in direct enfilade of our position. Owing to the maze of villages it was extremely difficult to discover the exact whereabouts of the many snipers, but the Lewis gunners were successful in keeping this fire down. After a great deal of destruction had been done the retirement was ordered, and the Battalion held its position until the 2/9th and 3/11th Gurkhas had fallen back and were clear. Its share in the retirement was uneventful until the final covering position was reached, some 600 yards from the camp. At this point some snipers from Musa Khan's village on the spur on the opposite bank hit two of our men. One of these fell hit in the knee, and for a moment was unseen by his comrades, but a few moments later when he was spotted three men very gallantly went back while the retirement was stopped for a period.

Major Exham, 2/9th Gurkhas, was loaned to the Battalion for the day to act as commanding officer.

Information was afterwards received that the force had inflicted heavy casualties on Musa Khan's Abdullai tribes, and as some half dozen towers and many houses had been destroyed, the results of the day's operations were good.

February 20th was a day to be remembered and very reminiscent of January 14th at Ahnai Tangi. The Battalion marched out at 6.30 a.m. as part of a force under Brigadier-General Lucas, and then proceeded to Split Hill spur with a view to taking part in further work of destruction. Until Split Hill was reached the task was easy, but from there the Battalion was sent forward to Brown Tower and White Tower villages, to enable the pioneers to blow up more towers and destroy more houses. " D " Company advanced first to Brown Tower, followed by " C " Company, who took up a central position, enabling " B " Company to reach a third position further forward at White Tower village. " A " Company was in reserve at Battalion headquarters. Immediately the first village was approached a heavy sniping fire opened from the left flank and from some houses in rear. In such an advance and in village fighting it seems impossible to find out where the bullets come from ; more especially when the first comes from the front, the second from a flank and the third from the rear. Both " D " and " B " Companies managed to reach their objectives, but " C " Company experienced serious opposition, and was unable to reach White Tower spur. Accurate sniping fire continued from all sides. Casualties at once began to mount up, and in making gallant endeavours to get these back to safety more men fell. Captain Hobbs, with " B " Company, was hit in the leg but managed to carry on. Communication from headquarters to the forward companies became a matter of considerable difficulty, and in fact visual signalling was abandoned in most cases, messages being sent by means of runners. The latter were magnificent, and though some fell, the messages always got through, and in the end the retirement was co-ordinated far better than had been expected. The three or four hours spent in these villages will not easily be forgotten by those who were there. Subadar Sahabir Gurung, of " D " Company, was wounded, as also were Jemadars Tekbahadur Mal and Lalbahadur Rana, of " B " Company—all somewhat seriously. Other casualties amounted to 23 Gurkha ranks killed and missing and 47 wounded.

The retirement was well covered by the 55th Coke's Rifles and 2/9th Gurkhas in rear, and by the 4/3rd Gurkhas on the other bank of the river. Had it not been for their well-directed fire our passage from the villages across the 800 yards of open fields would have been much more difficult. This was probably one of the most difficult situations that the Battalion has ever found itself in, owing to the accurate and incessant fire from all sides. Had it not been for the magnificent behaviour of the men, it would have been impossible to hold the ground while 17 towers and

160 houses were destroyed and the retaining walls of many fields removed. News was afterwards received that some bombs, thrown into some houses in circumstances demanding great gallantry, by Havildar Naine Bura, of "C" Company, who was awarded the Indian Distinguished Service Medal for his bravery, killed one, Zer Khan, the most noted fighter of the Umar Khel, and three of his companions. This act brought about the surrender of the Umar Khel tribe the following day.

Major Exham, 2/9th Gurkhas, again commanded the Battalion on this occasion.

All the wounded were brought back to camp, but some ten dead had to be left behind owing to difficulties of evacuation.

The Brigade Commander issued a congratulatory order on the work carried out by the Battalion.

On February 21st Major-General S. H. Climo, C.B., D.S.O., the G.O.C. Waziristan Force, visited the column and saw each Battalion in its own area. He made a point of meeting all men who had been granted awards for bravery in action. These were Subadar Indrabir Khan, awarded the Indian Order of Merit, and Lance-Naik Nainsing Rana, "A" Company, the Indian Distinguished Service Medal, for gallantry on January 14th at Ahnai Tangi, and Havildar Bahadur Thapa, "D" Company, the Indian Distinguished Service Medal, for his conduct at Sorarogha on January 18th. General Climo was astonished to find that most of the men had had no leave to their homes since before the Great War.

On February 22nd the left wing, assisted the 4/3rd Gurkhas to retake Tree Hill piquet, while the right wing took up a position covering the withdrawal of a small force which had been detached to Marobi to carry out the destruction of that village. Both these operations were completed without casualties.

The Battalion took part, on February 23rd, in operations to complete the destruction of Makin town. Captain Strahan was in command.

An early start was made, the column leaving camp at 5.30 a.m. Dispositions on this occasion were the same as on February 19th. The only enemy seen were small parties, about forty in number, almost out of rifle range.

The next day the Battalion, with Captain Strahan in command, covered the destruction of the villages under Brown Tower. The dispositions were as described for February 20th. There was very little opposition, only a few shots being fired during the retirement, which was carried out without casualties.

On February 25th, at 4 a.m., the Battalion moved out independently, as part of a force under Brigadier-General Lucas, to cover the destruction of the two villages, Auburn and Brompton, and the surrounding towers.

The task given to the Battalion was to protect the right flank of the operations by taking up a position on the high hills to the east of Auburn. The night was very dark, there being heavy clouds in the sky and no moon. The foothills were reached without difficulty. "B" and "C" Companies were detached to move off to the right along a spur leading to a higher and more forward position. Battalion headquarters, with "A" and "D" Companies, moved across this spur and made for a lower hill known as Half Way. The route was extremely difficult, as the hills were merely precipitous knife edges. "A" Company was in position by 6.30 a.m., closely followed by "D." "C" Company reached their objective, named Sniper's Nest, by 7 a.m., but "B" Company was unable to ascend to the highest point, Kenny Peak, as the approaches were precipitous. The only possible route, on the far side of the hill, was already in the hands of the enemy. "B" Company was therefore forced to take up a position below this feature, with the result that the Mahsuds were able to hurl stones and rocks at the company beneath. Snipers also gave some trouble; three men in "B" Company were grazed by bullets, and a Lewis gun was hit and put out of action. Work in the villages was completed by 10 a.m., at which hour the pioneers set fire to the houses and the withdrawal began. It was entirely due to the excellent support given by the 27th Mountain Battery, who kept up an accurate fire on Kenny Peak, that the retirement was effected without casualties.

From February 26th to the 29th operations were discontinued, and the men obtained a well-earned rest. Secret preparations were made for the withdrawal of the column from Makin.

Withdrawal from Makin, March 1st, 1920.
On March 1st the destruction of Makin having been carried out, a new phase of operations opened. The first stage was the withdrawal from Tauda China camp to Dwa Toi, the junction of the Dara Toi and Badder Toi streams, about a mile up-stream from Piaza Raghza camp.

Captain Strahan remained in command of the Battalion, as Lieutenant-Colonel Watt was still suffering from his wound. Camp was struck and transport loaded by 5.30 a.m. in complete silence and under cover of darkness. At 6.15 a.m. the Battalion moved into a series of successive positions to cover the withdrawal of the column from camp. The enemy was taken by surprise, and did not follow up the retirement at first. He, however, kept up a fairly steady fire down the river bed. Most of his energy was wasted in the search for loot and food in the deserted camping ground. This action had been anticipated and several "booby traps" arranged, the principal being a sham grave containing a charge of 50 lbs. of guncotton, which was later reported to have caused eight casualties, seven men being blown to pieces.

Lieutenant L. A. Alexander, one Gurkha officer and 146 Gurkha ranks joined the Battalion from the Depot.

Advance to Kaniguram, March 3rd to 6th, 1920.
On March 2nd preparations were made for an advance up the Badder Toi on Kaniguram, and on March 3rd this advance began, with the Battalion as part of the main body. A spur, known as the Dam, was reached without incident, and from this point the Battalion was sent forward to take over the duties of the advanced guard. On reaching Ladha, which had been fixed as the limit of the day's advance, the surrounding heights were made good. Camp was reached at 5 p.m. without casualties, in spite of the steady sniping fire kept up by the enemy throughout the day.

During March 4th and 5th a strong point was constructed at Ladha for occupation by the 3rd Guides during the period of the operations up the Badder Toi.

On March 6th the column advanced to Kaniguram. The left wing under Captain Strahan, was attached to the 2/9th Gurkhas as advanced guard, moving from camp at 5.30 a.m. Headquarters and the right wing were the leading troops of the main body. All went well until a hill known as Bar Spur was reached. Here the river bed was too rough for the camel transport, so the advance was delayed until roads had been made over the hill. The advanced guard shortly called for more troops, and the remainder of the Battalion was sent forward to join the left wing.

"C" Company, acting as a flank detachment, moved along the plateau on the right bank clearing it as they went. "A," "B" and "D" Companies were used up as route piquets. Camp was formed on the plateau some 800 yards east of Kaniguram. The Battalion was allotted a long spur running along the east face and high above the main camp. The nature of the site allotted necessitated an enormous amount of work on the perimeter. This isolated situation of our camp was the cause of much annoyance, but, as will be seen, in the weather that was to follow it had its advantages.

Kaniguram is, properly speaking, the only town in Mahsud country, and is regarded as the capital. The town is built in terraces on the south side of a steep spur about a mile in length flanking the left bank of the Badder Toi, and consists of about 1,000 houses and five towers. It is the chief commercial centre of the country, and contains a large bazaar and several rifle and knife factories. Here all important Mahsud national assemblies take place.

It was evident that our advance up the Badder Toi had again taken the Mahsuds by surprise, as there were signs of a hasty evacuation of the villages. Although Kaniguram had been subjected to heavy bombing by the Royal Air Force for several months, very little damage had been done.

From March 7th to the 25th the column remained in this camp, and except for some sniping at night the enemy gave little trouble. On the night of March 11th-12th heavy snow fell and continued throughout the day, and convoys were cancelled as the camels were unable to move. In its camp on top of the hill the Battalion was well off; but conditions in the main camp were dreadful, especially in the transport lines. The melting snow formed deep slush and mud. Attempts made to drain the camp resulted only in water passing on into a neighbour's camp. In this respect the 55th Coke's Rifles were the most unfortunate, as their camp was the most low-lying, the entire drainage from the column camp and transport lines being diverted into their area.

Some minor operations covering a survey party at work were carried out without casualties.

On the 21st of this month Major-General Climo again visited the column and interviewed the undermentioned men who had been granted awards since his last visit :—Jemadar Bahadur Thapa and Rifleman Harkoman Newar, awarded the Indian Order of Merit, and Havildar Naine Bura, Rifleman Nandlal Pun and Rifleman Santabir Ale the Indian Distinguished Service Medal.

During this period the following officers joined the Battalion :— Lieutenant R. D'Oyly-Hughes, from leave in England; Lieutenant K. C. Garvie, as a reinforcement from India; and 2/Lieutenant A. F. C. Tainton, from the 3/11th Gurkhas; while Captain L. M. Goodall was transferred to the 3/11th Gurkhas. About this time, too, a number of officers from the British Service were attached to the various units of the Derajat column for instruction, of whom six came to the Battalion. These attachments were commonly known as " Cook's Tours."

On March 26th the column moved to a new camping ground on the opposite bank of the stream, the old site having been pronounced unsuitable by the medical authorities.

This new camp, constructed more or less under peace conditions, was to have been a model for the instruction of the " Cook's Tourists." Under the direction of column headquarters splendid broad roads were made; but, unfortunately, after this had been done there was barely sufficient space left for the troops, with the result that these new quarters proved far from comfortable.

A slight diversion was caused by the arrival of " sparklets " in the Mess for the manufacture of soda water, with the result there was a constant stream of visitors at the Mess every evening.

During the remaining period up to April 5th there were no operations of any importance with the exception of those carried out to cover the

The Blizzard at Kaniguram. [Photo by Holmes, Peshawar.

"Jirga" discussing Peace Terms, Kaniguram. [Photo by Holmes, Peshawar.

working of the survey party, but a lot of heavy work was done in the construction of a motor road between Kaniguram and Ladha.

On March 30th Captain J. D. Ogilvy, 1st Gurkha Rifles, joined as second-in-command.

Operations against Abdur Rahman Khel, April 6th to 8th, 1920.

On April 6th the Battalion moved out at 5.50 a.m. at the head of the main body of a small column despatched with the object of coercing the Abdur Rahman Khel, the inhabitants of the upper valleys of the Badder Toi, who believed themselves to be out of reach of our troops. Their country had not been entered by any previous expedition into Waziristan. At a point where the Badder Toi bends to the north-west, about three miles west of Kaniguram, a road had to be cut across the hills, as the bed of the stream now became too narrow and rough for the transport. In order to carry out this operation with as little delay as possible, only five battalions went with the column, with a reduced scale of kit and transport. "A" Company was used up as route piquets, while "B" Company pushed forward across the camping ground to the opposite bank of the stream in order to cover the concentration of the column and establish camp piquets. From this position a splendid view of the Wana Valley was obtained, on the far side of a mass of hills. The only opposition during the day was from some snipers who worried "B" Company. On this occasion Lieutenant-Colonel Watt commanded the Battalion, having quite recovered from his wound.

The next day the Battalion was advanced guard to the column, which moved out at 8.30 a.m. to destroy the Abdur Rahman towers above the village of Giga Khel. "C" Company was vanguard, and on their reaching a point close to Giga village, the enemy opened heavy sniping fire from the hills on the right flank above Giga. "C" Company quickly captured Giga Hill when one company of 55th Coke's Rifles moved forward to Brown Hill beyond, covered by "C" Company. At the same time "D" Company moved forward to capture a lone tower further up-stream, but was held up by fire from all sides. "A" Company, and two platoons of "B" Company, were sent to secure the left flank of "D" Company.

After the company of 55th Coke's Rifles had reached their objective, "C" Company again moved forward through their position and made good a further and higher peak of the same hill. The capture of the lone tower by "D" Company was not considered worth the sacrifice of additional casualties, so it was decided to carry out the destruction by gun fire. Two more towers close to Giga village were rushed by a party of sappers and miners and blown up.

The retirement commenced at 2.30 p.m., but so far as the Battalion was concerned was not strongly followed up. A piquet of the 4/3rd Gurkhas was, however, rushed and wiped out.

Our total casualties during the day were :—

Lieutenant H. C. M. Davis ...	Killed.
Subadar-Major Arjun Thapa, I.D.S.M.	Wounded.
Subadar Narbahadur Gurung, I.D.S.M.	Wounded.
Subadar Indrabir Khan, I.O.M.	Wounded.
4 Gurkha ranks	Killed.
16 Gurkha ranks	Wounded.

After the operations at Sorarogha the Commanding Officer adopted the expedient of withdrawing one Lewis gun with its team from each company, and combining them into one Lewis gun platoon with headquarters. As there were no machine guns in the Waziristan Force, these Lewis guns proved most valuable, especially in retirements when it was possible to provide covering fire to the forward troops as they withdrew.

On April 8th the column returned to Kaniguram. The 67th Brigade was rearguard, with battalions occupying successive areas through which the column retired. The 2/5th were in rear of the 2/9th Gurkhas, and the area allotted included both banks of the river. The right wing with Battalion headquarters, held this area, whilst the left wing remained in Brigade reserve. All was fairly quiet and the transport passed through safely, but as the 2/9th Gurkhas withdrew they were rushed by a strong party of Mahsud swordsmen, who were covered by fire from the hills. The 2/9th Gurkhas were forced to retire leaving several casualties in the river bed. Lieutenant-Colonel Watt immediately ordered the retirement to stop, and while "A" Company were moving forward to retake a hill on the left bank, the Battalion stretcher-bearers brought in all the wounded. Meanwhile, "C" and "D" Companies were brought up from brigade reserve and covered the withdrawal of the right wing. Lieutenant-Colonel Watt had by this time assumed command of the rearguard, and after all casualties had been cleared, the Battalion retired through the 2/9th Gurkhas. By this time the enemy had been driven off and made no further effort to follow up the retirement. Our casualties were only two Gurkha ranks wounded.

The period from April 9th to the 17th was entirely taken up with road-making and convoy work, but on April 18th the column withdrew from Kaniguram to Ladha camp. The Battalion was allotted a sector of the route through which the column retired in safety. Large numbers of Mahsuds followed up the retirement, but showed no signs of hostility and accordingly were not fired at. The operations from this time onwards assumed a rather one-sided aspect ; the Mahsuds having

Battalion Aid Post at Giga Khel.

General Lucas bidding Farewell to the 2/5th on its leaving "Skeencol."

accepted our terms were now at peace, but treacherous acts were to be expected. Every man was treated as a friend until he proved himself to be an enemy. The Mahsud therefore had the advantage of being able to strike the first blow in an encounter.

On April 19th Ladha camp was prepared for permanent occupation by the column. The Battalion received orders to move forthwith to Kotkai.

Move to Kotkai, April 20th, 1920.
On April 20th Major-General A. Skeen, C.M.G., the G.O.C. Derajat Column, said good-bye to all officers, and at 1.45 p.m., after an inspection by Brigadier-General F. G. Lucas, C.B., C.S.I., D.S.O., G.O.C. 67th Brigade, the Battalion marched away from Ladha and the Derajat column, and so its connection with the 67th Brigade was severed.

Kotkai was reached on April 23rd, and then followed a period of stagnation, during which the Battalion occupied a number of permanent piquets and the remaining men were constantly employed escorting the daily convoys up the line. Such work after the previous months of hard fighting was extremely tedious, more especially as the weather was now getting hot.

Lieutenant-Colonel D. M. Watt, D.S.O., left the Battalion on April 29th to take up his new duties as A.A. & Q.M.G., Meerut, and Major J. D. Ogilvy took over command. Lieutenant-Colonel Watt joined at an extremely difficult time, when the heavy casualties amongst all ranks during the Ahnai Tangi fighting were badly felt. Most of the officers had then only recently arrived, and only three of those who had started with the Battalion from Rawalpindi were left. Colonel Watt had made himself beloved by all ranks, who were inspired with the utmost confidence in his judgment and leading. Those who served under him appreciated his exceptional qualities, and sincerely regretted his departure.

Return to Abbottabad, May 24th, 1920.
On May 18th the Battalion left Kotkai to return to Abbottabad, where it arrived on the 24th of that month. Major-General S. H. Climo, C.B., D.S.O., G.O.C. Waziristan Force, at his farewell inspection addressed the Battalion to the effect that there had been some very dark days, but after the Gurkhas and Garhwalis arrived, the Mahsuds knew they were fighting a lost cause. The Battalion had suffered severe losses, but it must please them to know that they had broken the back of the Mahsud resistance at Ahnai Tangi.

In concluding the account of these operations the following extract from the last pages of the official account will not be out of place :—

" The operations in the Badder Toi closed the active work of the Derajat Column . . . The headquarters of the Derajat Column were dispersed on May 7th, and their dispersal brought the operations to an end. Thus ended a frontier campaign of unparalleled hard fighting and severity. The enemy fought with determination and courage which has rarely, if ever, been encountered by our troops in similar operations. The character of the terrain, combined with trying and arduous climatic conditions, alone presented difficulties before which the most seasoned troops might well have hesitated. The resistance of the enemy was broken and the difficulties successfully overcome by a force composed almost entirely of young Indian troops. No British troops, except from the Royal Air Force and a British battery of Mountain Artillery, were employed. This fact has, without doubt, considerably raised the prestige of the Indian Army on the Frontier and increased the *esprit de corps* of the troops engaged."

1920. Under the scheme of demobilization lately brought in force, the Battalion, on return from Waziristan, was at once reduced to the post-war peace establishment. At the same time a large party was sent off on leave.

Colonel H. J. P. Browne was appointed commandant on his return from the staff.

In August considerable civil unrest, largely connected with the Hijrat movement to Afghanistan, broke out in and around Mansehra. The disaffected population of Mansehra and the Pakhli Plain set up a local government, even appointing their own civil officials, including a judge. The latter's appointment was popular until he endeavoured to enforce his sentences, when several shots fired in the court caused the proceedings to come to a premature end.

This unrest caused considerable anxiety to the civil authorities in Abbottabad, and when the self-appointed Mansehra Government invited the Black Mountain tribesmen to cross the border, capture Oghi Fort from the Frontier Constabulary and drive the British from Abbottabad, the intervention of troops was clearly necessary.

Trouble in Agror, August and September, 1920. At 4 p.m. on August 24th Colonel H. J. P. Browne, who was then in officiating command of the Abbottabad Brigade, ordered the Battalion to bring one company up to a strength of 200 rifles and despatch it to Mansehra by lorry the following morning. This company was to form part of a column to overawe the population of that place and then march on to Oghi to intercept the expected attack of the Black Mountain tribesmen on the fort.

Owing to the large number of men away on leave, it was only possible to find sufficient men by detailing one platoon from each company of the Battalion, and even then the number was only attained by the inclusion of the band.

This company, under Captain R. D'Oyly-Hughes, proceeded next day by lorry in advance of the main column, which assembled there by evening.

The composition of the column was :—

Commander	...	Major Snowdon, D.S.O., R.A.
Staff Officer	...	Captain J. F. Marindin, 2/5th Gurkhas.
Troops ...	...	One company 2/5th Gurkha Rifles, F.F.
		One company 2/6th Gurkha Rifles.
		One battery Mountain Artillery.

The arrival of this column caused considerable local excitement, but no untoward incidents occurred. At 11 p.m. on August 26th they marched on and at noon the following day reached Oghi. A perimeter camp was established which, in accordance with instructions, was sited some 1,500 yards to the west of the Constabulary Fort. The large number of animals to be accommodated necessitated so large a camp that a continuous perimeter was impossible and the available troops had to be eked out in a string of disconnected posts affording each other as much support as the ground would allow. Firewood was sacrificed to provide supports for one low trip wire round the camp.

The situation was an anxious one, as the Civil Authorities predicted an immediate attack by several thousand tribesmen. A peaceful night, however, was passed, and the next day the perimeter was considerably strengthened. The fort was ransacked for barbed wire and by evening a double apron entanglement nearly surrounded the camp.

At dusk a large collection of tribesmen was seen waving standards and brandishing swords on a ridge some two thousand yards to the north. The mountain guns were trained on them, and to the great delight of the men, who had an excellent view, four rounds of shrapnel were burst right over the standards. The tribesmen hurriedly disappeared because, as was later ascertained, the shells inflicted very heavy casualties. Even a priestess who had guaranteed to turn our bullets to water, was killed by the first shell, much to the consternation of her followers. The camp settled down in the expectation of an active night, bomb traps were laid after dark on likely lines of approach, luminous sights fitted to the Lewis guns and the mountain guns set their shrapnel to burst at point blank range.

At about 11 p.m. a volley was fired into the camp from close range. The troops immediately stood to their alarm posts and after a long silence spasmodic sniping began at ranges from fifty to two hundred yards. No reply was made to this fire, but as the snipers advanced closer they were engaged with controlled Lewis-gun fire. Several bomb traps now exploded to the accompaniment of howls of pain and anger, making it clear that considerable numbers of the enemy were collecting, under cover, to launch an attack on the camp. Suddenly a Mullah began a long harangue at the top of his voice, which was responded to by frantic yelling on all sides. The men completely discounted the moral effect of this by howling back in imitation of a pack of jackals. In due course the attack came, fortunately only in driblets, as over three thousand tribesmen were collected round the camp and had they attacked *en masse* the column might have fared badly. Luckily never more than a hundred attacked at once and frequently small parties of fanatics charged towards the wire. There was a brilliant moon providing excellent visibility up to fifty yards. The Lewis gun and rifle fire was more than sufficient. No attack got home; few attackers even reached the wire, and those that did met their death there.

One camp piquet, thirty yards outside the perimeter, held by the 2/6th Gurkhas, was hard pressed. They beat off seven attacks and then ran out of ammunition, but were replenished and reinforced at considerable risk in the dark. The Havildar in command of this piquet was awarded the I.O.M.

Sniping and attacks continued until just before dawn when the enemy dribbled away towards the Black Mountain, leaving several corpses behind, and the pools and trails of blood gave ample proof that they had lost heavily. Their bravery had been amazing and their armament pitiful; even muzzle-loading rifles were scarce and many had attacked with clubs and knives only.

Our own casualties totalled two gunners, one man of the 2/6th Gurkhas and several mules wounded.

Two days later the 3/6th Gurkha Rifles arrived from Abbottabad and occupied the constabulary fort. On the night of their arrival the enemy again attacked, but showed little determination. Close-range sniping caused casualties to animals, but none to personnel, and at dawn the enemy dispersed finally.

The Air Force continued the offensive by bombing the enemy villages in order to enforce our peace terms.

According to reliable information the total casualties suffered by the tribesmen in their attacks on the camp exceeded three hundred.

The Battalion, in conjunction with the other battalions in Abbottabad, maintained two companies at Oghi for some time longer, but in December all troops were withdrawn.

Colonel H. J. P. Browne, who had commanded the Abbottabad Brigade throughout this period, was awarded the C.B. for his conduct of the operations.

In February, 1921, both battalions of the Regiment took part in the review held by H.R.H. The Duke of Connaught at Rawalpindi, and it was on this occasion that the announcement was made that the title of "Royal" had been conferred on the 5th Gurkhas in recognition of distinguished services during the Great War.

1921.

On March 12th Lieutenant-Colonel C. E. B. Champain relieved Colonel H. J. P. Browne, C.B., in command of the Battalion when the latter was appointed a Brigade Commander.

During the year General Sir A. A. Barrett, G.C.B., K.C.S.I., K.C.V.O., A.D.C., was promoted to the rank of Field-Marshal, and Lieutenant-General Sir A. R. Martin, K.C.B., became Colonel of the Regiment. Details of the services of these two distinguished officers have been included in the 1st Battalion account.

Other happenings during the year which are not without interest are given shortly below.

A recruits' summer camp was formed for the first time since the war, at Nimbal.

A chicken farm was started with the object of helping the married families. The experiment was a failure, so the farm was disbanded about twelve months later.

Memorial boards, giving the names of all ranks killed since 1914, were put up on the Quarter Guard verandah. Two captured Turkish guns and other war trophies were also placed in front of the Quarter Guard.

The Battalion football team won the P.F.F. Tournament, beating the 58th Rifles in the finals.

Great efforts were made to get polo going again and a team took part in the Murree Brewery Tournament at Rawalpindi.

1922.

A reference to the Indian Army Lists of the years following the Great War shows how far in excess of the normal establishment was the number of British officers borne on the strength of units of the Indian Army. For some time past regiments had been engaged in mustering out their superfluous rank and file, and at the beginning of 1922 it was ordained by those in authority that the same process must be applied to British officers. Some there were amongst them who had never intended to make the Army their profession, and these, though feeling the wrench entailed by the severance of their connection with their associates of several years, yet welcomed the chance to make a start on work of their own choosing. Of the rest, there were many in excess of the number to be retained who wished above everything to remain in the Service, and the task of Commanding Officers, called upon to judge between the claims to retention of their young officers, was difficult and delicate. Of those who left the Battalion at this time were Captains

Silberbauer and Cayley and Lieutenants Paterson, McGarry, Diack and French. On completion of the mustering-out process—known throughout the Army as " the axe "—other young officers, who had hitherto only been attached to the Regiment, received their long overdue and very welcome posting orders.

In October came the sad news of the death in England on the 5th of the month, of Brigadier-General F. G. Lucas, C.B., C.S.I., C.I.E., D.S.O. The chief incidents of his long and distinguished career as a soldier are set out in the appropriate appendix, but the Battalion is indebted to him for more than his contribution to its welfare as Adjutant and Commanding Officer, as also for more than the fame he brought it through his handling of the Gurkha Scouts and, later in his service, in various responsible appointments. His knowledge of the men and of their language was an incentive to younger officers to cultivate those happy relations with the men serving under them without which hard work and earnest endeavour are often barren of result; his encouragement of football was a boon conferred, not only on the Regiment, but on the whole of the Gurkha Brigade. His example of activity on the hillside went far towards establishing a standard of speed and elasticity entirely in accord with 5th Gurkha tradition ; and lastly, his love of music and his informed appreciation of all that was best in it ensured something of merit in the performance of band and bugles even when conditions were unfavourable.

A little later in the year all ranks of the Battalion were grieved to learn of the death of Honorary Captain Amar Sing Thapa, M.C., Sardar Bahadur. Enlisting in 1886, he rose to become Subadar-Major in 1905. He held that appointment until 1919, when he was made an Aide-de-Camp to the Viceroy. When the Great War broke out he had already several campaigns to his credit, and the distinguished service rendered by him with the Battalion in Mesopotamia was recognized by the award of the M.C. Unusually well educated, his outstanding ability, his tact and his loyalty gained for him a reputation as one of the finest Gurkha officers who ever served in the Regiment.

On October 17th an impressive ceremony was held to mark the completion of one of the war memorials in Abbottabad. This particular memorial takes the form of a stone wall with an imposing archway leading through it, erected round the Gurkha cemetery to perpetuate the memory of the 21 Gurkha officers and 841 Gurkha other ranks of the 5th and 6th Gurkhas who were killed in the war. The criticism is sometimes made that it serves its purpose ill because few ever see it. The answer is to be found in the attitude of the men of both regiments, who, when the question was first mooted, gave preference to this form of memorial over any other then suggested, and now that it is completed, show great appreciation of a work which adds dignity and seemliness to their funeral rites.

A few days later were unveiled the bronze tablets placed in St. Luke's Church in memory of the 43 British officers of the 5th and 6th Gurkhas who were killed on active service between 1914 and 1921.

Earlier in the year the Regiment was threatened with a most unwelcome change of designation. With the exception of Gurkha battalions the whole of the infantry of the Indian Army was then undergoing a metamorphosis, which when completed left units with titles no longer to be recognized and often with a class composition greatly different from that which had previously filled their ranks. In their case the change was logical, and followed on the newly initiated organization into regiments consisting of four or five active battalions and one training battalion. Gurkha battalions, however, had not been affected by that change; they had no training battalions, and their composition remained the same. When, therefore, the announcement was made that they too would be renumbered, and when the 5th and 6th Gurkhas were asked to choose between 4th and 24th as their future designation, a strong protest was lodged. To the relief of both regiments that protest was successful, and each has retained the number under which it earned fame and with which its traditions have become inalienably associated.

The guard of honour provided by the Regiment for H.R.H. The Prince of Wales has already been mentioned. The 2nd Battalion contingent was under the command of Subadar Indrabir Khan.

In the field of sport the fine performance of the Battalion polo team at Rawalpindi in March merits record in these pages. The occasion was the Tradesmen's Cup Tournament, and the team consisting of Duncan, Gouldsbury, Wellesley and McGarry, found itself drawn against a very strong side of the P.A.V.O. Cavalry, which eventually won the cup and which included one International player in the person of Jack Denning. In a fast and very exciting game the Battalion representatives actually led at half-time, but then the pace began to tell on their ponies, and they were beaten in the end by 6 goals to 4. Far more meritorious was this defeat than would have been a victory over one of the weaker teams, and it was a great encouragement to those who had spent much time and trouble in an attempt to revive polo in the Regiment.

1923.   Very early in 1923 a part of the Battalion was again on active service. In the 1st Battalion account will be found a reference to events in Waziristan during 1922-23. With the 9th Brigade at this time were the 2/6th Gurkhas commanded by an old 5th Gurkha officer, to wit, Lieutenant-Colonel G. P. Sanders, D.S.O. They were under strength, and to complete their numbers before they should be called upon to engage in the serious fighting expected about Makin, "B" Company, under

Lieutenant R. C. O. Hedley, was despatched from Abbottabad on January 16th, and joined the 2/6th Gurkhas at Ladha some days later. They took part in the operations around Makin, and on the Razmak—Marobi road during February and March. In April, when the Mahsuds had accepted terms, a strong brigade was located at new Razmak Camp, whence the 6-inch howitzers could shell Makin should the need arise, and a second column was sent up the Wana line to carry out the evacuation of the Wana post which, till then, had been occupied by the South Waziristan Scouts. With it went the 2/6th Gurkhas and " B " Company. The evacuation successfully completed, the column returned to Jandola on April 17th, and on May 3rd " B " Company arrived back in Abbottabad. Their casualties in action were one man killed and one wounded. For gallantry displayed in action near Makin, Lance-Naik Kulbahadur Rai was awarded the Indian Distinguished Service Medal.

At headquarters in Abbottabad there were a few occurrences of permanent interest. In October the command of the Battalion changed hands; Colonel C. E. Bateman-Champain, who had been promoted in February, retired from the service, and was succeeded by Lieutenant-Colonel H. St. G. Scott, D.S.O., who came from the 4th Gurkhas. The Battalion football team had a successful year; they won the P.F.F. Cup, defeating the 1st Battalion in the finals, and in the Gurkha Brigade Tournament, of which the concluding rounds were played in Abbottabad, they only lost by a narrow margin to the eventual winners—the 2/8th Gurkhas.

Later in the year the Regiment was honoured with a visit by the Countess Roberts. Welcome for the sake of her illustrious father, when she came she was doubly welcome for her own sake. She inspected the Battalion on parade, and accepted an invitation to dine in the Officers' Mess. She charmed everybody by her deep interest in the Regiment, and by her knowledge of matters affecting it. A valued memento of her visit survives in her generous gift of a magnificent silver cigar box, which had many years before been presented to Lord Roberts.

1924—1926, *The Malakand.*

The days have gone by when the Regiment remained continuously in Abbottabad except when called out for active service or for the purpose of training. Nowadays every Gurkha " group " is responsible for manning one or more of the frontier outposts, and so it happens that, out of a group of four battalions, there are never more than three present simultaneously at the home station. In the case of the 5th and 6th Gurkhas they may be sent to Razmak, the Khyber or the Malakand. In 1924 the 2/5th received orders to leave Abbottabad for a two years' tour of duty in the Malakand.

Before the Battalion marched out Colonel-Commandant F. E.

Photo by Melaram, Nowshera.]   **Malakand from "Guides Piquet," 1925.**

Photo by Melaram, Nowshera.]
Chief Commissioner's Durbar, Chakdara, 1926: "A" Company, 2/5th, Guard of Honour.

Coningham held a farewell parade and made it the occasion to issue the following message :—

"On the departure of the 2/5th Royal Gurkha Rifles the Brigadier wishes to place on record his appreciation of the excellent work and behaviour of all ranks of the Regiment during the period they have been in his command. He only wishes he had the opportunity of taking the Regiment on active service, as he is confident that they would have added to the already high reputation they have for all-round excellence."

On September 13th the Battalion entrained at Havelian, and arrived at Dargai—now served by a broad-gauge line of railway from Nowshera—early the following morning. The relief of the Malakand posts is usually carried out in combination with the relief of Chitral, and it was so on this occasion. Consequently, before taking over from the 1/6th Gurkhas at Malakand and Chakdara, the 2/5th found themselves forming part of a movable column which remained at Chakdara under the command of Colonel Scott, while the Chitral relief was being effected. It was not until October 12th that they were free to embark on their new duties.

The Malakand Fort, where three companies and headquarters were stationed, is sited above the pass, and commands a fine view over the Yusafzai plain to the south, and up the beautiful Swat Valley to the north. Chakdara, where the remaining company was accommodated, is about nine and a half miles distant, and its object is the safeguarding of the bridge which crosses the Swat River at that point. In winter the climate of both places is excellent; there is good shooting, and fish are plentiful, though generally it takes a good man to catch them. At that time of year the only drawbacks to existence are the high wind which blows coldly from the north through the funnel of the Pass, and the scarcity of men for training owing to the heavy duties. In the autumn Chakdara becomes very unhealthy for the reason that rice is extensively cultivated to within a short distance of the fort walls, and it then becomes necessary to adopt every precautionary measure known to man in the attempt to cope with the hordes of malaria-bearing mosquitoes. Despite these disadvantages the Malakand is a pleasant place enough, and during the two years spent there much useful work was done. Regarded as one of the show places of the frontier, it is often visited by well-known people, but it can seldom have happened that the unit stationed there has been given the opportunity of receiving a reigning king and queen. This unusual experience did actually fall to the lot of the Battalion which, on October 13th, 1925, had the honour of welcoming the King and Queen of the Belgians. During the same year an interesting ceremony was held in connection with the proclamation of Shah Jahan Khan as

Nawab of Dir. A great Durbar was held at Chakdara; all the frontier notables from miles around attended, and "A" Company, under Captain Marindin, formed an armed guard of honour for the Chief Commissioner.

Although the tribes of the Swat Valley are well disposed, and the Wali himself is a staunch upholder of British influence, the mere proximity of the post to tribal territory gives rise occasionally to "incidents." Two such befell the Battalion during its tour of duty. On October 19th, at Chakdara, a trans-border Pathan fired on an unarmed party of "D" Company as it was returning to the fort from fatigue duty on the range. On this occasion the aggressor was killed by rifle fire from the detachment piquet on Signal Hill. Again, on the night of May 15th-16th, 1926, while on patrol duty at Chakdara, a rifleman was shot dead by a prowling tribesman whom he was gallantly attempting to capture.

The good work done in the Malakand is attested by the fact that in 1926 the Battalion was awarded the Barrow Cup, open to all units in the district, and only to be won by that which is adjudged to excel in all-round efficiency. The following letter received from the District Commander will help further to explain this achievement:—

"I write to offer you and all ranks of your Battalion my warm congratulations on winning the Barrow Cup this year. As you doubtless know, the test is spread over a long range of subjects and is operative throughout the year, and consequently the winning battalion must have made a sustained effort over a long period. To be able to do this is in itself a matter for congratulation, since in this way alone can real efficiency and readiness for war be reached."

On May 31st, 1926, Subadar-Major Arjun Thapa, I.D.S.M., who had lately been promoted to the 1st Class of the Order of British India, retired on pension with the rank of Honorary Captain. He had a distinguished record in the Battalion. After spending a number of years on the drill staff he became Jemadar Adjutant. For gallantry in action at the Battle of Ramadi he received the Indian Distinguished Service Medal, and during the Waziristan Campaign of 1920, when he was Subadar-Major, he more than once commanded a company in action with distinction. For his services during that campaign he was made a Companion of the 2nd Class of the Order of British India. His son has lately (1928) joined the Battalion as a recruit. Mention has already been made of the great loss sustained by the Regiment in the deaths during 1926 of Sir Arthur Barrett and Sir Alfred Martin. Major-General Sir James Marshall Stewart, K.C.B., K.C.M.G., was then appointed Colonel of the 5th Gurkhas. The details of his distinguished career are given in the appropriate appendix, but it is not out of place to record here that his period of command of the 2nd Battalion increased

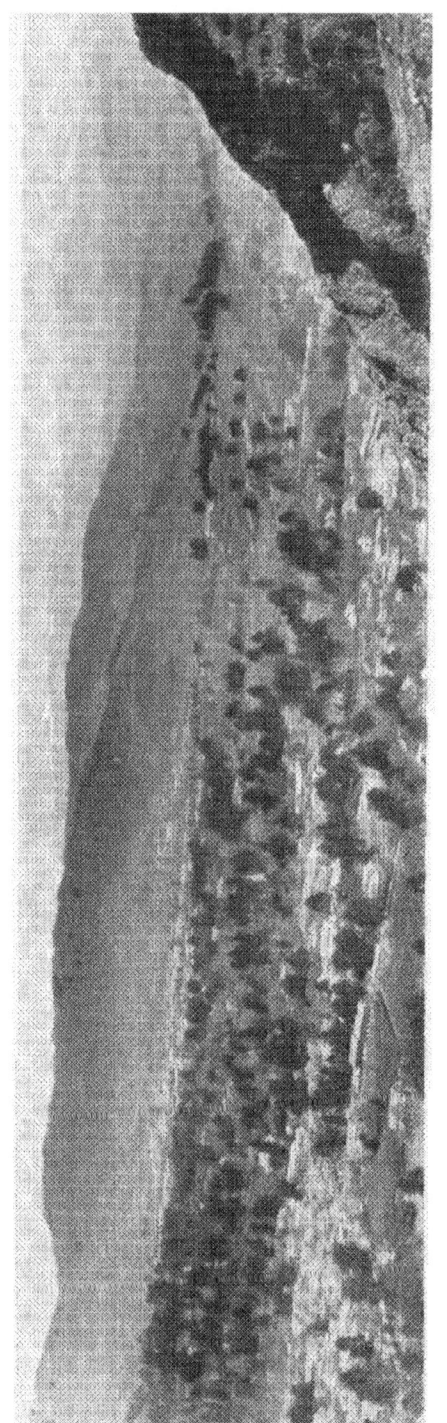

Looking North from Sarban.

[*Photo, Holmes, Peshawar*]

The View from the Terrace, Officers' Mess.
[The 6th G.R. Mess in Foreground.]
ABBOTTABAD, 1928.

its reputation, already great, and was marked by the introduction of many amenities directed towards improving the lot of those whom he commanded. His interest in all that affects the welfare of the Regiment appears to be only intensified by the passing of the years.

One noteworthy event of the stay in the Malakand was the revival of the pipe band. Before the war the pipers of the 2/5th, coached by their comrades of the Seaforth Highlanders, had always maintained a creditable standard, but, like so many other good things, they had disappeared during the upheaval. Now, to start them on their way, they were again sent for tuition to the Seaforths and at the time of writing, two years later, both pipes and drums show promise of becoming as good as ever.

Of this out-station tour it only remains to record successes in football and shooting. In 1926 the Battalion team again won the P.F.F. Cup, and in the competition for the 5th Fusiliers Cup the Headquarter Wing beat " A " Company of the 1st Battalion in the finals. In the contest for the Mother Country Cup two teams entered from the Machine Gun Platoon obtained second and third places.

Return to Abbottabad, 1926. In September the Chitral Relief Column passed through the Malakand, and on its return the 2/5th, having handed over to the 2/6th Gurkhas, concentrated at Dargai on October 9th. Next day they arrived back in Abbottabad.

1927—1928. Since the return of the Battalion to its peace station the only event of importance has been the change in command. Colonel Scott's tenure came to an end in November, 1927, and he was succeeded by Lieutenant-Colonel F. S. Massy from the 1st Battalion. In April, 1928, the latter was retransferred to the 1st Battalion, and Lieutenant-Colonel H. T. Molloy became Commandant of the Battalion which his father had raised and commanded many years before.

Meantime, the 2/5th Royal Gurkhas go happily on their way, striving, successfully it is hoped, to maintain their efficiency and to keep pace with modern developments, but always holding fast to those great traditions which have set their name so high.

EPILOGUE

The account has now been completed of events which have had their influence on the development of the 5th Gurkhas during the seventy years of the Regiment's existence. The writing has necessarily been entrusted to unpractised hands, but whatever the manner of the narrative may be found to lack, the matter of it has merit to save from oblivion those things of which it speaks, and to serve as an inspiration to those who come after. For its concern is with the soldierly virtues—discipline, courage and self-sacrifice; here and there its pages reflect, however imperfectly, the glory of great deeds, and the score or so of campaigns with which it deals, are for the Regiment an unbroken record of success in war. If a further period of seventy years is to elapse before the next volume is added, it will be written, perhaps, under circumstances so changed that no man may now foresee them. Yet whatever of new invention comes to complicate existence for the rifleman of the future, there need be no misgiving as to the spirit in which he will set about his task. The old traditions will persist and the soldierly attributes of the Gurkha will prove equal to every demand.

For all that the Regiment is it owes to the Gurkha and to his inherent qualities of cheerfulness in good times and bad, of simplicity and straightforwardness, of vigour and activity, of courage and endurance, of quick response to sympathy and fair dealing and of ready acceptance of an ideal for which to work. None who has known him but has felt a very genuine affection for the sturdy little man from the hills, and those to whom he has given his confidence, he has never failed.

1865
Fighting Order
Short Smooth-bore Fusil
(issued 1858).

1882
Fighting Order
Short Enfield Rifle
(issued 1874).

NOTES:—i. The Tilt of the Head-dress was changed from Left to Right immediately before Peiwar Kotal, 1878.

KIT AND SMALL ARMS ARMAMENT, 5th ROYAL GURKHA RIFLES (FRONTIER FORCE).

1896
Quarter-Guard Commander
Martini-Henry Rifle
(issued 1888).

1902
**Boer Prisoner Sentry
(Winter)**
Long Lee-Enfield Rifle
(issued 1901).

ii. Before 1865, the Head-dress was a Turban and the Rifle the "Two Grove." No photograph of the Kit of 1858 exists.

1907
Fighting Order
Maxim Gun (issued 1902).

1906	1914
Drill Order	**Fighting Order**
Short Lee-Enfield Rifle (issued 1905).	Short Lee-Enfield (charger-loading).

iii. Kilmarnock Hats were sanctioned 14th July, 1865, and Felt Hats for Fighting Order came in 1903, being first worn on the March to Chitral. The Double Green Band in the Pagri, as the distinguishing mark of the 5th, was adopted in 1907.

1928
Fighting Order (2nd Battalion)
Lewis Gun, Mk. I (issued 1917).   Webley Revolver (issued 1918).

1919
Fighting Order
H.V. Short Lee-Enfield, Mk. III
(issued 1917).

1928
Fighting Order
H.V. Short Lee-Enfield,
Mk. III*.

iv. Mackenzie Equipment received to replace Old Accoutrements in December, 1887. Bandolier Equipment received in 1905, and Web in 1920.

1928
Fighting Order, Hill Warfare (1st Battalion)
Vickers Gun, Mk. II (issued 1920).

APPENDICES

THE 5TH ROYAL GURKHA RIFLES (F.F.)

APPENDIX I
(Relating to the Raising of the Regiment).

A.—The established complement of the Regiment when raised was as follows:—

- 1 Commandant.
- 1 Second-in-Command.
- 1 Adjutant and Quartermaster.
- 1 Officer Doing Duty.
- 1 Assistant Surgeon.
- 2 Native Doctors.
- 10 Subadars.
- 10 Jemadars.
- 1 Native Adjutant (included in the commissioned officers).
- 60 Havildars.
- 60 Naiks.
- 20 Buglers.
- 800 Sepoys.
- 1 Tindal.
- 10 Khalasis.
- 20 Bhistis.
- 10 Sweepers.
- 3 Ghunta Pandies.
- 1 Munshi.
- 1 Chaudri.
- 1 Matsaddi.
- 3 Weighmen.
- 1 Jemadar and 33 Syces for mules.
- 1 Mate and 30 Dooly Bearers.
- 2 Hospital Cooks, 1 Dresser, 1 Bhisti, 1 Sweeper, 1 Goorga.

The Regiment had 10 companies.

B.—The transfers sent from other regiments to form the nucleus of the Hazara Goorkha Battalion were as follows:—

REGIMENTS.	Subadars.	Jemadars.	Havildars.	Naiks.	Buglers.	Sepoys.	TOTAL.	Nepal.	Dotee.	Kumaon.	Garhwal.	Other District.	TOTAL.
Guides Infantry	1	4	18	16	—	63	102	97	—	—	5	—	102
2nd Sikhs	3	6	15	11	6	210	251	112	14	42	69	14	251
3rd Sikhs	—	1	2	7	1	60	71	41	4	15	9	2	71
4th Sikhs	—	—	—	2	2	58	62	19	13	10	19	1	62
H.M. Battery	—	—	—	—	—	1	1	—	—	—	—	—	1
4th Punjab Infantry	—	—	—	—	—	3	3	1	1	1	—	—	3
8th Punjab Infantry	—	1	—	—	—	2	3	1	—	1	1	—	3
10th Punjab Infantry	—	—	—	—	—	40	40	4	30	5	1	—	40
11th Punjab Infantry	1	—	1	—	—	—	2	2	—	—	—	—	2
12th Punjab Infantry	—	1	5	5	2	9	22	4	—	5	6	7	22
13th Punjab Infantry	—	—	3	3	—	64	70	1	8	10	41	10	70
16th Punjab Infantry	—	1	—	—	—	1	2	—	—	2	—	—	2
18th Punjab Infantry	—	—	—	1	—	7	8	3	1	3	1	—	8
19th Punjab Infantry	1	—	3	2	—	7	13	7	—	1	4	1	13
20th Punjab Infantry	2	1	2	3	—	2	10	6	—	1	2	1	10
23rd Punjab Infantry	—	—	5	3	—	93	101	2	2	14	66	17	101
2nd Police Battalion	—	—	—	—	—	3	3	3	—	—	—	—	3
3rd Police Battalion Kuttamookhees	4	1	1	1	1	9	17	12	1	3	1	—	17
4th Police Battalion or Soorujmookhees	—	—	1	1	—	—	2	1	1	—	—	—	2
5th Police Battalion or Soorujmookhees	—	—	1	2	—	53	56	45	1	4	5	1	56
7th Police Battalion or Soorujmookhees	1	1	—	—	—	5	7	3	1	3	1	—	7
Total, 21 regiments	13	17	57	57	12	690	846	364	77	120	231	54	846

APPENDIX II

Honours and Awards

1st BATTALION.

1858. Captain H. F. M. Boisragon gazetted Brevet Major for services in the Indian Mutiny, dated January 19th, 1858.

1860. Mentioned in despatches, Mahsud Waziri Expedition:

Major O. E. Rothney. (Twice).
(Colonel Lumsden's despatch dated April 25th, 1860. Brig.-General Sir N. Chamberlain's despatch, dated July 7th, 1860.)

1863. Awarded the Indian Order of Merit, 3rd Class, for acts of gallantry during the Ambela Campaign:

Havildar Ramsingh Kaintura	October 30th, 1863.
Havildar Balbahadur	November 6th, 1863.
Sepoy Narsingh Mohat	,, ,,
Sepoy Daulat Singh Bhandari	,, ,,
Sepoy Dansing Pajai	,, ,,
Sepoy Jangbir Thapa	,, ,,
Sepoy Balbahadur Khanka	,, ,,
Jemadar Ratan Singh Aswal	December 15th, 1863.
Sepoy Kalian Singh Negi	,, ,,

1878. Mentioned in Sir F. Roberts's despatch, dated December 18th, 1878:

Major A. Fitzhugh.
Captain J. Cook.

Sir F. Roberts's despatch, dated December 31st, 1878:

Captain C. F. Powell.
Lieutenant A. R. Martin.
Lieutenant C. C. St. E. Lucas.
Surgeon-Major G. Farrell.

1879. Captain J. Cook awarded the Victoria Cross for gallantry in the action of Peiwar Kotal.

Awarded the Indian Order of Merit, 3rd Class, for gallantry in the actions of Peiwar Kotal and Mangiar Defile.

Subadar Ragobir Nagarkoti.
Havildar Parsu Khattri.
Havildar Jagat Singh Rana.
Sepoy Hastabir Khattri.
Sepoy Kishenbir Nagarkoti.

1879. Bugler Surbir Damai.
Naik Wazir Singh Adikari.
Sepoy Manraj Pun.
Hospital-Assistant Shankar Das. (Attached.)

Appointed a member of the 2nd Class of the Order of British India :
Subadar-Major Bhagiram Gurung.

The following promotions were conferred in recognition of services rendered during the campaign, 1878-79 :—

To be Brevet Lieutenant-Colonel :
Major Alfred Fitzhugh, B.S.C.

To be Major :
Captain John Cook, V.C.

Promotions to the Indian Order of Merit for conspicuous gallantry in the action at Charasia on October 6th, 1879 :—

To the 2nd Class :
Sepoy Kishenbir Nagarkoti.

To the 3rd Class :
Subadar Hurri Dewa Jaicie.

1880. Promotions to the Indian Order of Merit for conspicuous gallantry at Kabul on December 12th, 1879 :—

To the 1st Class :
No. 1212 Naik Kishenbir Nagarkoti.

To the 3rd Class :
No. 593 Havildar Kurrun Singh Negi.
No. 1771 Sepoy Dammursingh Negi.

Mentioned in Lieut.-General Sir F. Roberts's despatch, dated October 12th, 1880 :—

Lieut.-Colonel A. Fitzhugh.
Major J. M. Sym.
Captain E. Molloy.
Lieutenant A. R. Martin.
Lieutenant C. C. Chenevix-Trench.
Lieutenant C. C. St. E. Lucas.

1881. Subadar-Major Balbahadur Negi was appointed Aide-de-Camp on the Personal Staff of His Excellency the Viceroy and Governor-General in recognition of the services of the Regiment during the Afghan Campaign.

"London Gazette Supplement," dated March 1st, 1881 :—

"The Queen has been graciously pleased to give the following promotions and appointments to the Most Honourable Order of the Bath :—

"To be Ordinary Members of the Military Division of the 3rd Class—
Lieut.-Colonel Alfred Fitzhugh."

1881. The following promotions were gazetted in recognition of services rendered during the late Afghan Campaign :—
To be Brevet Lieutenant-Colonel :
Major John Munro Sym.
To be Major :
Captain Edward Molloy.
Surgeon-Major G. Farrell appointed Honorary Surgeon to His Excellency the Viceroy, dated September 9th, 1881.

1883. Admitted to the Order of British India :—
Subadar-Major Ram Singh.
Subadar Balbahadur Negi.

1886. Appointed to be a Companion of the Most Honourable Order of the Bath :—
Brigade Surgeon George Farrell.

1888. The following were admitted to the Indian Order of Merit for conspicuous gallantry in the Black Mountain on June 18th, 1888, on the occasion of the death of Major Battye and Captain Urmston :—
To 1st Class (2nd time) :
Subadar Kishenbir Nagarkoti.
To 3rd Class :
No. 2684 Sepoy Indrabir Thapa.
No. 2685 Sepoy Motiram Thapa.
Mentioned in General McQueen's despatch for services rendered in the Black Mountain Expedition :—
Colonel J. M. Sym.

1889. Appointed Companion of the Most Honourable Order of the Bath :—
Colonel J. M. Sym.

1891. Mentioned in Sir William Lockhart's despatch, dated July 3rd, 1891, for services rendered in the Miranzai Expedition :—
Colonel J. M. Sym, C.B.
Lieutenant the Hon. C. G. Bruce.
Captain A. R. Martin.
Appointed Companion of the Most Honourable Order of the Bath, dated November 24th, 1891 :—
Lieut.-Colonel Alfred Gaselee.
Promoted Major, vide "London Gazette," dated November 24th, 1891 :—
Captain Alfred Robert Martin.
The following were admitted to the Indian Order of Merit for conspicuous gallantry at the Storming of Nilt on December 2nd, 1891, during the Hunza-Nagar Expedition :—
No. 2994 Sepoy Kamansing Burathoki.
No. 2173 Sepoy Bhagtabir Thapa.

THE 5TH ROYAL GURKHA RIFLES (F.F.)

1891.
No. 75 Bugler Nandia Thapa.
No. 2940 Sepoy Gokal Gurung.
No. 2150 Sepoy Dilaram Kunwar.
No. 2495 Sepoy Damarsing Gurung.
No. 2552 Sepoy Manjit Pun.
No. 2410 Sepoy Balbir Thapa.
No. 2211 Sepoy Bandhu Pun.
No. 2967 Sepoy Harkabir Thapa.

1892. "London Gazette," dated July 12th, 1892 :—

The Victoria Cross conferred upon Lieutenant Guy Hudlestan Boisragon for conspicuous gallantry at the Storming of Nilt on December 2nd, 1891.

Lieutenant Francis Frederick Badcock to be a Companion of the Distinguished Service Order for gallant conduct at the same action.

1893. Colonel A. Gaselee, C.B., appointed Aide-de-Camp to the Queen.
Subadar Parsu Khattri admitted to the 2nd Class of the Order of British India.

1895. Mentioned in the Waziristan despatches by Lieut.-General Sir William Lockhart, dated May 10th, 1895 :—
Major A. R. Martin.
Colonel A. Gaselee, C.B.

Honours and awards for services in Waziristan published in the "London Gazette," dated September 20th, 1895 :—
To be Brevet Lieutenant-Colonel :
Major Alfred Robert Martin.

1896. Subadar-Major Parsu Khattri was admitted to the 1st Class of the Order of British India.

1898. General Sir William Lockhart's despatches after the Tirah Campaign :
Lieut.-Colonel A. R. Martin.
Lieutenant the Hon. C. G. Bruce. (Twice.)
Captain I. Philipps.

The following were admitted to the Indian Order of Merit for conspicuous gallantry when employed as scouts during the Tirah Campaign :—

Promoted from the 3rd to the 2nd Class :
No. 2984 Havildar Kamansing Burathoki.

Admitted to the 3rd Class :
No. 2995 Lance-Naik Karbir Burathoki.
No. 3462 Rifleman Maniram Pun.
No. 2497 Lance-Naik Goria Rana.
No. 3220 Rifleman Goria Gharti.

THE 5TH ROYAL GURKHA RIFLES (F.F.)

1898. Captain the Hon. C. G. Bruce was promoted to a Brevet Majority in recognition of his services on the North-West Frontier, 1897-1898.

1899. The following were admitted to the Indian Order of Merit in recognition of their conspicuous gallantry in the Chamkanni country, December 1st, 1897 :—
Promoted from the 3rd to the 2nd Class :
Subadar-Major Parsu Khattri Sardar Bahadur.
Admitted to the 3rd Class :
No. 1846 Havildar Birsing Gurung.
No. 2848 Rifleman Birkhdhoj Khattri.

1900. Subadar-Major Jangia Thapa admitted to the 1st Class of the Order of British India.

1901. Subadar Pirtilal Limbu admitted to the 2nd Class of the Order of British India.

1905. Subadar-Major Bishnu Thapa admitted to the 2nd Class of the Order of British India.

1907. Subadar-Major Bishnu Thapa was admitted to the 1st Class of the Order of British India.

The following refer to Gallipoli and Egypt, *date of Gazette* being entered on left :—

25/8/15.	Distinguished Service Order : Major M. R. W. Nightingale.
10/6/20.	Captain H. T. Molloy.
14/1/16.	Military Cross : Lieutenant K. C. S. Erskine.
8/6/16.	Lieutenant N. R. C. Cosby. Jemadar Dhanlal Gurung.
8/6/16.	Order of British India, 2nd Class : Subadar-Major Harkbir Thapa, I.O.M.
17/9/15.	Indian Order of Merit, 2nd Class : Subadar Dhanjit Gharti. Subadar Dhanraj Gurung.
1/1/16.	Jemadar Tejbir Thapa.
20/3/20.	Jemadar Biraj Gurung. No. 4485 Naik Gangaraj Thapa. No. 4799 Naik Birbahadur Thapa. No. 4130 Havildar Dandbir Thapa.
17/9/15.	Indian Distinguished Service Medal : No. 4544 Lance-Naik Ratanbir Thapa.

THE 5TH ROYAL GURKHA RIFLES (F.F.)

16/6/16.	No. 7824 Havildar Chintram Bura (2/5th). No. 1489 Naik Narbahadur Gurung. No. 4766 Rifleman Dalbir Chand.
26/6/16.	Subadar Dhansing Gurung.
20/3/16.	Subadar Partiman Rana. Jemadar Budhichand Bura. Jemadar Biraj Gurung. No. 4324 Naik Narbahadur Thapa. No. 4929 Rifleman Shamsher Gurung. No. 4159 Havildar Budhsing Gurung. No. 4332 Havildar Lokbahadur Thapa. No. 3694 Havildar Bahadursing Gurung. No. 3712 Havildar Kulbahadur Gurung. No. 4878 Rifleman Balbahadur Gurung. No. 4649 Rifleman Kamansing Gurung. No. 4627 Rifleman Gopalsing Pun. No. 4769 Naik Bhairabsing Gurung. No. 4818 Naik Debiram Thapa. No. 3756 Rifleman Ratansing Gurung. No. 4220 Rifleman Manbir Roka. No. 3807 Rifleman Mahabir Gharti. S.A.S. Shankarlal, I.M.D.
20/3/20.	Meritorious Service Medal : No. 4807 Naik Khambasing Thapa.
29/10/15.	Special Promotions and Brevets : To be Brevet Colonel : Lieut.-Colonel G. H. Boisragon, V.C.
29/9/16.	To be Captain : 2/Lieutenant N. R. C. Cosby, M.C. To be Lieutenant : 2/Lieutenant H. E. Winn.
22/9/15.	Mentioned in Despatches :— Major M. R. W. Nightingale, D.S.O. Lieutenant K. C. S. Erskine, M.C. Subadar Dhanjit Gharti. Subadar Dhanraj Gurung. No. 3678 Havildar Sherbahadur Gurung. No. 4544 Lance-Naik Ratanbir Thapa, I.D.S.M.
10/3/16.	Lieut.-Colonel R. A. Firth. Captain P. M. Rennie, I.M.S. Lieutenant K. C. S. Erskine, M.C. Lieutenant N. R. C. Cosby, M.C. Subadar Dhansing Gurung. Subadar Mansaram Pun. Jemadar Tejbir Thapa.

THE 5TH ROYAL GURKHA RIFLES (F.F.)

10/3/16.
: No. 7824 Havildar Chintram Bura (2/5th).
No. 1489 Naik Narbahadur Gurung.
No. 4766 Rifleman Dalbir Chand.
No. 3756 Rifleman Ratansing Gurung.
No. 4220 Rifleman Manbir Thapa.
No. 3837 Rifleman Mahabir Gharti.
No. 2629 Rifleman Dhanbir Rana.
No. 2783 Rifleman Kalia Gurung.

18/8/16.
: Major A. B. Tilliard, D.S.O.
2/Lieutenant N. R. C. Cosby, M.C.
Subadar Dhansing Gurung.
Subadar Mansaram Pun.
Jemadar Dhanlal Gurung.
No. 4646 Naik Narbahadur Gurung.
No. 2702 Lance-Naik Chandrabir Ale (2/5th).
No. 2783 Rifleman Kalia Gurung.
No. 2529 Rifleman Dhanbir Rana.
No. 4766 Rifleman Dalbir Chand.
No. 7824 Havildar Chintaram Bura (2/5th).

11/5/17.
: Major H. M. Battye.
Lieutenant R. L. Beddy.
Lieutenant E. Birkbeck (128th Pioneers).
Captain W. K. Brown.
Lieutenant H. J. Cummins.
2/Lieutenant A. S. Fletcher.
Major D. M. Govan.
2/Lieutenant E. H. Hunter.
Lieutenant D. I. B. Lloyd.
Captain M. F. Reaney, I.M.S.
2/Lieutenant G. E. V. Roberts.
Captain G. Turner.
Captain A. B. H. Webb.

11/8/16.
: Brevet Colonel G. H. Boisragon, V.C.
Lieut.-Colonel E. B. C. Boddam.
Lieutenant K. C. S. Erskine, M.C.

FOREIGN DECORATIONS.

Egyptian Order of the Nile, 4th Class :—
Colonel G. H. Boisragon, V.C.

French Legion of Honour, Croix de Chevalier.
Captain K. C. S. Erskine, M.C.

Medaille Militaire :—
No. 4485 Havildar Gangaraj Thapa.

The following refer to Mesopotamia :—

1/1/18.
: Order of St. Michael and St. George :—
To be a member of the 3rd Class, or Companion :
Lieut.-Colonel M. R. W. Nightingale, D.S.O.

THE 5TH ROYAL GURKHA RIFLES (F.F.)

30/4/20.   Order of the Indian Empire.
        To be a member of the 3rd Class, or Companion :
          Colonel M. R. W. Nightingale, C.M.G., D.S.O.

12/7/18.   Distinguished Service Order :
        Lieutenant (Acting Captain) H. D. H. Y. Nepean.

25/10/18.   Major J. D. Crowdy.

23/3/18.   Military Cross :
        Lieutenant K. J. Macintosh.

3/5/18.   Indian Order of Merit, 2nd Class :—
        No. 4475 Havildar Jabarsing Thapa.
        No. 175 Rifleman Ramsing Gurung.

11/1/19.   No. 4683 Naik Anaram Pun.
        Subadar Dhansing Gurung, I.D.S.M.

1/1/18.   Indian Distinguished Service Medal :—
        No. 980 S.A.S. Ghulam Haider, I.S.M.D.

3/5/18.   No. 4250 Naik Amarsing Ale.
        No. 758 Rifleman Balbahadur Thapa.
        No. 1 Lance-Naik Manbahadur Gurung.
        No. 502 Rifleman Sarbu Gurung.
        No. 763 Rifleman Urbahadur Gurung.

16/8/18.   No. 4367 Havildar Damarsing Gurung.

11/1/19.   No. 4543 Rifleman Parbir Rana.
        No. 4227 Colour-Havildar Kharaksing Gurung.
        No. 4518 Naik Bagbir Thapa.
        No. 4749 Lance-Naik Chandrasing Thapa.
        No. 426 Rifleman Tekbahadur Thapa.
        No. 4604 Lance-Naik Tularam Thapa.

1/1/18.   Meritorious Service Medal :—
        No. 275 Rifleman Mangaljit Newar.

25/10/18.   No. 4927 Rifleman Shamsher Mal.
        No. 4307 Naik Khambasing Thapa.
        No. 4332 Havildar Lokbahadur Thapa.
        No. 4889 Havildar Tilbir Thapa.
        No. 4056 Havildar Bhimlal Rana.
        No. 4693 Rifleman Kesar Pun.
        No. 4345 Lance-Naik Harkabahadur Thapa.
        No. 4649 Rifleman Kamansing Gurung.
        No. 4799 Naik Birbahadur Thapa.
        No. 4818 Naik Debiram Thapa.
        No. 4683 Naik Anaram Pun.
        No. 4362 Naik Napa Girth.

25/3/20.   No. 4634 Naik Bhimraj Gurung.

30/12/16.   Special Promotions and Brevets :—
        To be Brevet Colonel :
          Brevet Lieut.-Colonel H. J. P. Browne.

THE 5TH ROYAL GURKHA RIFLES (F.F.)

2/5/19.   Lieut.-Colonel (tempy. Brig.-General) M. R. W. Nightingale, C.M.G., D.S.O.

27/8/17.   Mentioned in Despatches :—
Major J. D. Crowdy, D.S.O.
Lieut.-Colonel M. R. W. Nightingale, C.M.G., D.S.O.,
Captain N. R. C. Cosby, M.C.
Captain H. D. H. Y. Nepean, D.S.O.
Jemadar Kansbir Rana.
No. 4381 Havildar Keharsing Thapa.
No. 4245 Colour-Havildar Kharjit Gurung.

27/8/17.   Mentioned in Despatches :—
No. 4808 Rifleman Tulbir Thapa.

18/4/19.   Lieut.-Colonel M. R. W. Nightingale, C.M.G., D.S.O.

18/7/19.   No. 4263 Rifleman Sirilal Gurung.

5/6/19.   Lieut.-Colonel M. R. W. Nightingale, C.M.G., D.S.O.
Major (Acting Lieut.-Colonel) F. Skipwith.

FOREIGN DECORATIONS.

Serbian Order of the White Eagle, 3rd Class (with Swords) :—
Brevet Lieut.-Colonel H. J. P. Browne.

The following refer to India :—

8/10/18.   Mentioned for services rendered in India during the Great War, N.W.F.P. *Gazette*, October 8th, 1919 :—
Major G. P. Sanders.

7/12/18.   Mentioned in Despatches :—
Major (tempy. Brig.-General) W. D. Villiers-Stuart.
Captain H. R. C. Lane.
(Officiating Commandant, Lakhimpur Battalion, Assam Military Police.)

19/12/18.   Special Promotions and Brevets :—
To be Brevet Lieutenant-Colonel :
Major (tempy. Brig.-General) W. D. Villiers-Stuart.

8/6/19.   Brought to the notice of the Secretary of State for War for valuable services rendered in India in connection with war :—
Lieut.-Colonel W. D. Villiers-Stuart, C.B.E.
(G. of I.A.D., No. 1426, dated July 16th, 1920.)

1920.   "Gazette of India," No. 801, dated April 30th, 1920 :—
"The Governor-General in Council is pleased to sanction the grant of the following awards for services in India during the War :—
" Indian Meritious Service Medal (without annuity).
" 1/5th Royal Gurkha Rifles (F.F.) :—
" No. 4577 Havildar Mir Hussain.
" No. 3774 Havildar Babulal Mathuria.
" No. 3749 Havildar Narsing Thapa.
" No. 4766 T./Havildar Dalbir Chand.
" No. 949 Naik Ghulam Rasul.
" No. 4247 Rifleman Goria Gurung."

THE 5TH ROYAL GURKHA RIFLES (F.F.)

11/12/20. Order of the Star of Nepal, conferred by H.M. the Maharaja of Nepal :—
Lieut.-Colonel W. D. Villiers-Stuart, C.B.E.
("Gazette of India," A.D. No. 2454, dated December 11th, 1920.)

12/4/21. Promoted Field-Marshal :—
Sir Arthur A. Barrett, G.C.B., G.C.S.I., K.C.V.O.

28/6/21. Appointed Colonel of the Regiment from June 28th, 1921 :—
Lieut.-General Sir Alfred R. Martin, K.C.B.

23/3/22. Special and Brevet Promotion :—
Lieut.-Colonel W. D. Villiers-Stuart, C.B.E., I.A., to be Colonel, March 22nd, 1922.
("Gazette of India," A.D. No. 767, dated April 28th, 1922.)

1923. Captain K. C. S. Erskine, M.C., to be Brevet Major, dated January 3rd, 1923. ("Gazette of India," No. 221, dated February 29th, 1923.)
Major H. E. Weekes, O.B.E., to be Brevet Lieut.-Colonel, dated December 29th, 1923. ("Gazette of India," No. 154, dated February 2nd, 1923.)

1924. Waziristan, 1921-24 :—Mentioned in despatches for distinguished service during the operations in Waziristan, January, 1922, to April, 1923. Lord Rawlinson's despatch, dated July 25th, 1923 (published in "London Gazette," dated February 27th, 1924) :—
"1/5th Royal Gurkha Rifles (F.F.) :
"Captain and Brevet Major K. C. S. Erskine, M.C.
"Subadar Budhsing Gurung, I.D.S.M.
"Subadar-Major Kulbahadur Gurung, I.D.S.M.
"Subadar Sasidhar Thapa.
"No. 4480 Company Havildar-Major Baliram Pun.
"No. 4995 Company Havildar-Major Dhanbahadur Gurung.
"No. 4792 Company Havildar-Major Humansing Thapa.
"No. 4828 Havildar Narbahadur Thapa.
"No. 4920 Havildar Partiman Gurung."

1925. "London Gazette," dated March 13th, 1925 :—
"The King has been graciously pleased to approve of the undermentioned awards for distinguished service rendered in the field in connection with military operations in Waziristan, April 21st, 1923, to March 31st, 1924 :—
"Awarded the Distinguished Service Order :
"Major Hugh Robert Charles Lane, O.B.E., 1/5th Royal Gurkha Rifles, Frontier Force, Indian Army.
"Colonel William Desmond Villiers-Stuart, Indian Army."
Mentioned in despatches for distinguished service during the operations in Waziristan, April 21st, 1923, to March 31st, 1924, in Lord Rawlinson's despatch, dated June 11th, 1924. ("London Gazette," dated March 13th, 1925) :—

1925.
"1/5th Royal Gurkha Rifles (F.F.)—
"Major H. R. C. Lane, O.B.E.
"Colonel W. D. Villiers-Stuart, C.B.E.
"Subadar Dandabir Thapa, I.O.M.
"No. 4792 Colour Havildar-Major Humansing Thapa.
"No. 4722 Havildar Karnasing Pun.
"No. 4828 Colour Havildar-Major Narbahadur Thapa.
"No. 4923 Colour Havildar-Major Pahalman Gurung.
"Subadar-Major Udebir Gurung."

1927. Lieut.-Colonel H. E. Weekes, O.B.E., to be Brevet Colonel, dated January 1st, 1927. ("Gazette of India," No. 171, dated February 11th, 1927.)

1928. Major H. R. C. Lane, D.S.O., O.B.E., to be Brevet Lieutenant-Colonel, dated July 1st, 1928. ("Gazette of India," A.D. 1152, of 1928.)

2ND BATTALION.

Year.	Name.	Award.	Remarks.
1892	Sub.-Maj. Bhimal Sahi	O.B.I., 2nd Class	—
1894	Sub. Parsaram Thapa	O.B.I., 2nd Class	—
1895	Lt.-Col. E. Molloy	C.B.	—
1898	Maj. A. A. Barrett	Brevet of Lt.-Col.	For services with Tirah Expeditionary Force.
	Capt. A. H. G. Kemball	Brevet of Major	
	Capt. F. G. Lucas	Brevet of Major and D.S.O.	
	3 Gurkha other ranks	I.O.M.	
1901	Sub. Thamansing Mahat	O.B.I., 2nd Class	—
1908	Lt.-Col. J. M. Stewart	Men. in Despatches, appointed A.D.C. to H.M. The King	For services with the Zakka Khel Expedition.
	Maj. F. G. Lucas	Men. in Despatches	
	Sub.-Maj. Amarsing Thapa	O.B.I., 2nd Class	
1911	Lt.-Col. J. M. Stewart	C.B.	—
	Sub.-Maj. Amarsing Thapa	O.B.I., 1st Class	—
1913	Sub.-Sankhbir Thapa	O.B.I., 2nd Class	—
1915	Maj. H. A. Holdich	Brevet of Lt.-Col.	For services in Mesopotamia.
	Maj. H. T. Molloy	D.S.O.	For services in Gallipoli.
	Sub. Mansaram Pun	I.D.S.M.	For services in Gallipoli.
	Jem. Tejbir Thapa	I.O.M.	
	Jem. Chintaram Bura	I.D.S.M.	
	1484 Col.-Hav. Narbahadur Gurung	I.D.S.M.	
	2573 L./N. Gore Thapa	I.D.S.M.	For services in France.

THE 5TH ROYAL GURKHA RIFLES (F.F.)

Year	Name	Award	Remarks
1916	Lt.-Col. H. A. Holdich	D.S.O.	For services in Mesopotamia.
	Capt. W. G. Harington	D.S.O.	For services in Mesopotamia.
	2455 Rfn. Dalbahadur Thapa	I.O.M.	⎫ Immediate awards for action of 11th September in Mesopotamia.
	2068 Rfn. Balbir Rana	I.D.S.M.	
	2298 L./N. Dharamsing Gurung	I.D.S.M.	
	2627 L./N. Gambirsing Mal	I.D.S.M.	⎭
1917	2702 L./N. Chandrabir Thapa	⎫ Serbian Order of Karageorge in Gold	⎫ For services in Gallipoli.
	2661 L./N. Jamansing Gurung		
	2876 Rfn. Kharakdhoj Gurung	⎭	
	2896 Rfn. Munesor Thapa	⎫ Order of Karageorge in Silver	
	2610 L./N. Naran Thapa	⎭	
	2529 Rfn. Bhanbir Rana	Cross of St. George, 3rd Class	
	2385 Rfn. Lalsing Pun	Medal of St. George, 2nd Class	
	2818 Rfn. Mansing Bura	Medal of St. George, 3rd Class	⎭
	Capt. H. A. Wellesley	M.C.	For services in Mesopotamia.
	2960 Rfn. Dhanbir Gurung	Medal of St. George, 4th Class	⎫
	3351 Rfn. Budhibal Gurung	M.S.M.	
	Sub. Mansaram Pun	O.B.I., 2nd Class	
	Bt. Col. H. J. P. Browne	⎫ Men. in Despatches by Lt.-Gen. Sir Stanley Maude, K.C.B.	For services in Mesopotamia.
	Maj. J. D. Crowdy		
	Capt. W. G. Harington		
	Capt. H. A. Wellesley		
	Lieut. A. C. Gladstone		
	Sub.-Maj. Amarsing Thapa		
	Sub. Arjun Thapa		
	Jem. Chintaram Bura		
	2439 L./N. Shamsher Gurung		
	2818 Rfn. Mansing Bura	⎭	
1918	Col. F. G. Lucas	Croix de Guerre (Officier) and C.B.	⎫ For services in Mesopotamia.
	Maj. J. D. Crowdy	D.S.O. and Mention	
	Capt. R. C. Duncan	Brevet of Major and Mention	
	Capt. C. A. Gouldsbury	Brevet of Major, Croix de Guerre and Mention	
	Capt. H. A. Wellesley	Bar to M.C. and Mention	
	Capt. R. M. Bruce	M.C.	⎭

Year	Name	Award	Remarks
1918	Sub.-Maj. Amarsing Thapa	M.C.	
	Sub. Arjun Thapa	I.D.S.M. and Mention	
	Sub. Chintaram Bura	I.O.M.	
	Sub. Narbahadur Gurung	Bar to I.D.S.M.	
	1883 Hav. Budhibal Pun	I.D.S.M.	
	1973 Hav. Harkasing Gurung	I.D.S.M.	
	2039 Hav. Birjalal Thapa	M.S.M.	
	2802 Hav. Harising Thapa	M.S.M.	
	2619 Naik Shamshersing Sahi	M.S.M.	For services in Mesopotamia.
	2529 Naik Bhanbir Rana	M.S.M.	
	2880 L./N. Manraj Gurung	I.D.S.M.	
	2701 L./N. Chandrabir Ale	M.S.M.	
	Maj. C. E. B. Champain		
	Lieut. A. C. Gladstone		
	Capt. R. D'Oyly-Hughes	Mentioned in Despatches	
	Sub. Sukbir Gurung		
	1487 Hav. Aimansing Rana		
	2256 Naik Rudrabir Pun		
1919	Maj. C. E. B. Champain	Brevet of Lt.-Col. and Mention	
	Capt. H. A. Wellesley	Bar to M.C.	
	Capt. R. M. Bruce	Brevet of Major and Mention	
	Capt. A. C. Gladstone	M.B.E.	
	Sub. Bilbikram Rana	O.B.I., 2nd Class, and Mention	For services in Mesopotamia.
	Jem. Puransing Thapa	I.D.S.M.	
	2208 Hav. Madhoram Thapa	M.S.M.	
	1568 Naik Ranbahadur Mal		
	1474 Rfn. Mohansing Sahi	Long Service Medal	
	1501 Rfn. Aimansing Gurung		
	2848 Rfn. Ujirsing Thapa	Medaille D'Honneur (avec glaves)	
1919	Maj. J. D. Crowdy		
	Capt. and Bt. Maj. R. C. Duncan		
	Capt. and Bt. Maj. C. A. Gouldsbury	Mentioned in Despatches	For services in Mesopotamia.
	Capt. A. N. Rolfe		
	Lieut. C. W. Cousins		
	Sub.-Maj. Amarsing Thapa	Appointed A.D.C. to H.E. The Viceroy and Hon. Captain	

THE 5TH ROYAL GURKHA RIFLES (F.F.)

Year.	Name.	Award.	Remarks.
1920	Lt.-Col. D. M. Watt, D.S.O.	C.I.E.	
	Maj. H. Exham (2/7th G.R. attached)	D.S.O.	
	Maj. R. C. Duncan	O.B.E.	
	Capt. G. S. Strahan (2/6th G.R. attached)	Brevet of Major	
	Capt. J. M. Hobbs	Bar to M.C.	
	Capt. N. M. Dotiwala, I.M.S. (Medical Officer)	M.C.	
	Capt. P. E. Cayley	Chevalier, Order of Star of Roumania	
	Sub.-Maj. Arjun Thapa	O.B.I., 2nd Class	
	Sub. Indrabir Khan	I.O.M.	
	Jem. Tekbahadur Mal	I.D.S.M.	
	1491 Hav. Bahadur Gurung	M.S.M.	
	2216 Hav. Bahadur Thapa	I.O.M. and I.D.S.M.	
	2612 Hav. Hargobind Rana	M.S.M.	
	2546 Hav. Ranjasing Gurung	I.D.S.M.	
	2825 Hav. Naine Bura	I.D.S.M.	
	1610 Hav. Bhabesor Gurung	M.S.M.	
	2800 Naik Kulbahadur Rana	I.D.S.M.	
	2822 Naik Balbir Gurung	I.D.S.M.	For services in Waziristan.
	2844 Naik Jagbir Roka	I.D.S.M.	
	2833 Naik Birbahadur Gurung	M.S.M.	
	3104 L./N. Debising Thapa	I.O.M.	
	3351 L./N. Budhibal Gurung	I.D.S.M.	
	3340 L./N. Nainsing Rana	I.D.S.M.	
	2067 Rfn. Narbir Thapa	I.O.M.	
	3098 Rfn. Tilchand Thapa	I.O.M.	
	3226 Rfn. Hastabahadur Thapa	I.O.M.	
	3938 Rfn. Kumansing Gurung	I.O.M.	
	4357 Rfn. Harkaman Newar	I.O.M.	
	4373 Rfn. Santabir Ale	I.D.S.M.	
	4392 Rfn. Mohansing Thapa	I.D.S.M.	
	4412 Rfn. Sonbir Thapa	I.D.S.M.	
	4456 Rfn. Jitman Bura	I.D.S.M.	
	4653 Rfn. Harde Bura	I.D.S.M.	
	4807 Rfn. Nandalal Pun	I.D.S.M.	
	106 Rfn. Manbir Gurung	I.D.S.M.	
	122 Rfn. Kharakbahadur Ghale	I.D.S.M.	
	2763 Rfn. Dhanbir Thapa	Roumanian Cross for good Service, 2nd Class	—

THE 5TH ROYAL GURKHA RIFLES (F.F.)

Year.	Name.	Award.	Remarks.
1920	2110 Hav. Ramkishan Thapa	M.S.M.	For services in Mesopotamia.
1920	Lt.-Col. D. M. Watt, D.S.O. Maj. R. C. Duncan, O.B.E. Capt. P. E. Cayley Sub.-Maj. Arjun Thapa, I.D.S.M. Jem. Birjalal Thapa Jem. Indrabir Khan Sub. Ransur Pun Jem. Rudrabir Pun Jem. Tekbahadur Mal 1610 Hav. Bhabesor Gurung 2116 Hav. Bahadur Thapa 2822 Naik Balbir Gurung 2883 Naik Birbahadur Gurung 3851 L./N. Budhibal Gurung 4476 Rfn. Chandrabir Gurung 4812 Rfn. Daljit Thapa 8104 L./N. Debising Thapa 2963 Rfn. Dhanbir Thapa 4071 L./N. Digbahadur Karki 2679 Hav. Ganjasing Gurung 2612 Hav. Hargobind Rana 4857 Rfn. Harkaman Newar 3226 Rfn. Hastabahadur Thapa 5463 Rfn. Hirde Bura 2844 Naik Jagbur Roka 4456 Rfn. Jitman Bura 122 Rfn. Kharakbahadur Ghale 2800 Naik Kulbahadur Rana 8938 Rfn. Kumansing Gurung	Mentioned in Despatches	For services in Waziristan.
	Jem. Sheolal Chandor	M.S.M.	For services in India during the war.
1923	8736 L./N. Kulbahadur Rai 8994 Rfn. Harkasing Thapa	I.D.S.M. Mentioned in Despatches	For services in Waziristan with 2/6th G.R.

THE 5TH ROYAL GURKHA RIFLES (F.F.)

3RD BATTALION.

3rd Afghan War.

Brought to notice for distinguished service in operations against Afghanistan. (G. of I. Army Dept. Notification 1846 dated 10.9.20.)

Captain T. R. Harrison.

Mesopotamia, 1920.

Awarded the Indian Distinguished Service Medal for gallantry in action at Imam Abdullah on November 11th, 1920. (M.E.F. Order of day dated 7.1.21.)

No. 636 Naik Purnaram Khattri.
No. 816 L./Nk. Sanman Sunwar.
No. 720 L./Nk. Dhanbahadur Khattri.

Awarded the Indian Order of Merit, 2nd Class, for " conspicuous gallantry and skilful handling of his platoon " at the action of Imam Abdullah on November 11th, 1920. (M.E.F. Order of the Day dated 27.1.21.)

Subadar Kabir Thapa.

To be an Officer of the Military Division of the Most Excellent Order of the British Empire for valuable services rendered in connection with Military Operations in Mesopotamia. (G. of I. Army Dept. Notification 2051 dated 9.9.21.)

Major Hugh Robert Charles Lane.

Mentioned in Despatch of Lieutenant-General Sir J. A. L. Haldane, Commanding-in-Chief Mesopotamian Expeditionary Force, dated February 7th, 1921.

Major (Acting Lieutenant Colonel) C. P. Barlow.
Major H. R. C. Lane.

APPENDIX III

CASUALTIES SUSTAINED BY 5TH ROYAL GURKHA RIFLES, F.F., ARRANGED BY CAMPAIGNS.

1ST BATTALION.

The Mahsud Waziri Expedition of 1860.
    Died of wounds ... ... 2 other ranks.
    Wounded ... ... 13 other ranks.

The Yusafzai—Ambela Campaign of 1863.
    Killed ... ... 1 Gurkha officer.
                                                       27 other ranks.
    Wounded ... ... Lieutenant J. S. Oliphant.
                                                       37 other ranks.
Lieutenant Oliphant subsequently died of his wounds.

Operations against the Black Mountain tribes in 1868.
    Wounded ... ... Colonel O. E. Rothney.
                                                       2 other ranks.

Operations during the blockade of the Jowaki Afridis in 1875.
    Wounded ... ... 1 subadar.
                                                       3 other ranks.

The Afghan War of 1878 *to* 1881.
    (*a*) The Assault on the Peiwar Kotal.
        Killed ... ... 5 other ranks.
        Wounded ... ... Captain C. F. Powell.
                                                      30 other ranks.
    (*b*) The Action of Charasia.
        Killed ... ... 3 other ranks.
    (*c*) The Explosion of the Bala Hissar.
        Killed ... ... Subadar-Major Bhagiram Gurung.
                                                      11 other ranks.
    (*d*) The Action of Mir Karez.
        Killed ... ... 1 other rank.
        Wounded ... ... Major A. Fitzhugh.
                                                      3 other ranks.
    (*e*) The Attack on the Takht-i-Shah Hill.
        Killed ... ... 1 other rank..
        Wounded ... ... Captain J. Cook, V.C.
                                                      6 other ranks.
Captain Cook subsequently died of his wounds.

(f) The Retirement to Sherpur Cantonment.
    Killed ... ... Subadar Ragobir Nagarkoti.
                                                      2 other ranks.
    Wounded ... ... 2 other ranks.

(g) The Action of Kandahar.
    Killed ... ... 1 other rank.
                                                        2 followers.
    Wounded ... ... 2 other ranks.

The Black Mountain Expedition of 1888.
    Killed ... ... 1 other rank.
    Wounded ... ... 4 other ranks.

Operations in Miranzai Valley, 1891.
    Wounded ... ... 2 other ranks.

The Hunza—Nagar Campaign, 1891.
    Killed ... ... 2 other ranks.
    Died of wounds ... ... 2 other ranks.
    Wounded ... ... 20 other ranks.

The Mahsud Expedition, 1894.
    Killed ... ... 1 other rank.

Tirah, 1897.
    Killed ... ... 5 other ranks.
    Wounded ... ... Lieutenant W. D. Villiers-Stuart.
                                                     4 other ranks.

THE GREAT WAR, 1914-1918.

(a) *The Gallipoli Campaign.*
    Killed ... ... Major H. M. Battye.
                                                     Major D. M. Govan.
                                                     Captain A. B. Hay-Webb.
                                                     Captain W. K. Brown.
                                                     Captain G. Turner.
                                                     Captain M. F. Reaney, I.M.S.
                                                     Lieutenant R. L. Beddy.
                                                     Lieutenant E. Birkbeck.
                                                     Lieutenant H. J. Cummins.
                                                     Lieutenant D. I. B. Lloyd.
                                                     Lieutenant G. E. V. Roberts.
                                                     9 Gurkha officers.
                                                     284 Gurkha other ranks.

Died of disease when on active service	24 other ranks.
Wounded	Lieut.-Colonel G. H. Boisragon, V.C.
	Lieut.-Colonel E. B. C. Boddam.
	Lieut.-Colonel M. R. W. Nightingale.
	Captain F. M. Bailey.
	Lieutenant K. C. S. Erskine
	Lieutenant J. D. H. Cook.
	2/Lieut. N. R. C. Cosby.
	2/Lieut. G. K. Knowles.
	2/Lieut. H. D. H. Y. Nepean.
	9 Gurkha officers.
	559 Gurkha other ranks.

(b) *The Campaign in Mesopotamia.*

Killed and died of wounds	Lieutenant J. D. H. Cook.
	3 Gurkha officers.
	87 Gurkha other ranks.
Missing (presumed killed)	Lieutenant J. H. Stables.
	4 other ranks.
Died of disease when on active service	16 other ranks.
Accidentally killed when on active service	Lieutenant R. F. D. Plunkett.
Wounded	Captain K. C. S. Erskine.
	Captain H. D. H. Y. Nepean.
	Lieutenant W. B. O. Fox.
	Lieutenant C. S. Baker.
	Lieutenant G. S. V. Paterson.
	Lieutenant K. J. Mackintosh.
	3 Gurkha officers.
	149 other ranks.

2ND BATTALION.

Hazara Campaign, 1888.

Died of disease	5 other ranks.

Hazara Expedition, 1891.

Killed	1 other rank.

Zakka Khel Expedition, 1908.

Wounded	1 other rank.

THE 5TH ROYAL GURKHA RIFLES (F.F.)

THE GREAT WAR, 1914-1918.

France and Gallipoli, 1914-1915.

Killed	Captain A. M. Graham.
	Lieutenant A. A. Heyland.
	2/Lieut. E. H. Hunter.
	2/Lieut. A. S. Fletcher.
	Jemadar Budhibal Rana.
	22 other ranks.
Wounded	Captain A. N. Rolfe (twice).
	Major C. E. B. Champain.
	Captain H. T. Molloy.
	Captain W. G. Harington.
	Subadar Ramsing Thapa.
	Subadar Mansaram Pun.
	87 other ranks.

Mesopotamia, 1915-1918.

Killed	Major W. G. Harington.
	24 other ranks.
Accidentally killed	2 other ranks.
Died of wounds	4 other ranks.
Died of disease	7 other ranks.
Missing	1 other rank.
Wounded	Captain W. G. Harington (twice).
	Captain H. A. Wellesley.
	Captain R. M. Bruce.
	Captain J. F. Marindin.
	Subadar Pahalsing Rana (twice).
	Subadar Chintram Bura.
	96 other ranks.
Accidentally wounded	1 other rank.

Waziristan, 1920.

Killed	Major J. D. Crowdy.
	Captain G. A. Maconchy.
	Captain J. C. Marsh.
	Captain K. J. Macintosh.
	Lieutenant H. C. M. Davis.
	Subadar Bhawansing Thapa.
	52 other ranks.
Died of wounds	Jemadar Hastabal Thapa.
Wounded	Lieut.-Colonel D. M. Watt.
	Major C. P. Blackett.
	Captain J. M. Hobbs.
	Lieutenant P. R. Broadway

Waziristan, 1920—Wounded (continued). Lieutenant de L. R. Browne.
Subadar-Major Arjun Thapa.
Subadar Sahabir Gurung (twice).
Subadar Indrabir Khan.
Subadar Narbahadur Gurung.
Jemadar Chandrasing Gurung.
Jemadar Gangabir Thapa.
Jemadar Dhanbar Gurung.
Jemadar Tekbahadur Mal.
Jemadar Lalbahadur Rana.
158 other ranks.

Waziristan, 1923 (with 2/6th Gurkha Rifles).
  Killed ... ... 1 other rank.
  Died of disease ... ... 2 other ranks.
  Wounded ... ... 1 other rank.

3RD BATTALION.

Operations against Afghanistan, 1919.
  Killed ... ... 1 other rank.
  Died of wounds ... ... 1 other rank.
  Died in action of heat stroke ... 5 other ranks.
  Wounded ... ... Lieutenant T. R. Harrison.
  5 other ranks.

Operations in Mesopotamia, 1920.
  Died of wounds received in action ... 1 other rank.
  Accidentally shot and killed ... ... 1 other rank.
  Wounded ... ... 10 other ranks.

THE 5TH ROYAL GURKHA RIFLES (F.F.)

APPENDIX IV

LIST OF OFFICERS WHO SERVED WITH THE REGIMENT, 1858 TO PRESENT DAY.

Note.—After the raising of the 2nd Battalion figures preceding the name of an officer denote with which battalion or battalions he served.

Date of Appointment.	Name.	Remarks.
22/5/58	Lieut. C. J. Nicholson	Proceeded on fifteen months' leave to Europe from 9/1/58, and did not join the Regiment.
22/5/58	Captain H. F. M. Boisragon	Transferred to command the 4th Sikh Infantry on 31/12/60.
7/6/58	Surgeon H. B. Buckle	
5/7/58	Captain H. Close	Transferred to command 4th Punjab Infantry on 2/10/76.
9/7/58	Surgeon G. W. Clemenger	Left in 1864.
16/9/58	Lieut. P. W. Pawlett	Left in same year for Political Employ.
13/1/59	Lieut. H. L. C. Bernard	Resigned on 28/8/64.
28/2/60	Lieut. E. C. Codrington	Transferred to 3rd Sikh Infantry, 22/3/73.
22/12/60	Major O. E. Rothney	Commanded the Regiment until 1873. Appointed on leaving to the Brigade Staff of the Army with the rank of Brigadier.
31/12/60	Lieut H. G. Beacher	Struck off the strength in August, 1862.
16/1/63	Lieut. J. S. Oliphant	Died on 12/1/65 of wounds received at Ambela.
18/3/63	Major J. P. W. Campbell	Left in 1864.
18/4/63	Lieut. J. M. Sym	Retired in 1892 after completing command. Major-General, K.C.B.
23/11/63	Lieut. T. R. Taylor	Died in 1864.
23/11/63	Lieut. A. E. Bird	Died in 1864.
28/11/63	Lieut. E. G. Serle	
3/2/65	Lieut. H. J. Lawrence	Left for Political Employ, 1/8/66.
18/4/65	Assistant-Surgeon J. R. Johnson	Left in 1878. Died at Abbottabad 20/5/78.
27/7/65	Ensign J. B. Hutchinson	Left on 9/3/68 for service with the Foreign Department.
31/7/65	Lieut. W. H. Unwin	Retired when second-in-command on 1/8/84. Lieut.-Colonel.
18/4/66.	Surgeon-Major T. Maxwell	

THE 5TH ROYAL GURKHA RIFLES (F.F.)

Date of Appointment.	Name.	Remarks.
31/8/66	(1)Ensign L. R. Battye	Killed in the Black Mountain, 16/6/88.
6/1/68	Surgeon H. Tham	Left 1/5/68.
28/8/68	(1)(2)Lieut. E. Molloy	Raised 2nd Battalion. Retired 1894. Colonel, C.B.
14/5/68	Lieut. B. Hudleston	Left in 1870.
18/11/69	Assistant-Surgeon A. Skeen	
8/11/70	Captain W. G. Gowan	Proceeded on furlough on 29/11/75 and did not return to the Regiment.
10/11/70	Assistant-Surgeon J. Lloyd	
27/3/73	Captain J. Cook	Died of wounds received during the attack on the Takht-i-Shah Hill on 19/12/79. Major, V.C.
11/5/74	Colonel P. F. Gardiner	Retired on 29/9/78 after commanding the Regiment.
28/5/75	Captain C. F. Powell	Severely wounded at Mangior Defile and later died of wounds.
5/10/76	Major A. Fitzhugh	Retired on 27/9/86, after commanding the Regiment. Colonel C.B.
2/4/77	(1)Lieut. A. R. Martin	See Appendix VII.
9/11/77	(1)(2)Lieut. C. C. Chenevix-Trench.	Died in Simla, 1891.
21/6/78	Surgeon-Major G. Farrell	Left in 1886. P.M.O. Burma F.F. Brigade Surgeon.
17/11/78	Lieut. C. C. St. E. Lucas	Attached.
29/11/78	Lieut. J. C. B. Craster	Attached.
27/1/80	Lieut. W. R. Yielding	Attached.
6/5/81	(1)Lieut. A. A. Barrett	See Appendix VII.
18/5/81	Lieut. M. A. P. Taylor	
21/11/82	Surgeon D. B. Spencer	
10/10/84	(1)Lieut. J. O. S. Fayrer	Died in England. Major.
14/11/84	(1)Lieut. E. de. S. Smart	Retired 1897 through ill health. Captain.
20/2/85	(1)(2)Lieut. J. M. Stewart	See Appendix VII.
19/7/85	Surgeon G. H. Fink	Officiating.
8/2/86	(1)Lieut. J. M. Smith	To Political Department, 1889. Colonel, V.C.
30/8/86	(1)Surgeon J. A. Nelis	Handed over medical charge of the 1st Battalion in 1897.
10/11/86	(1)(2)Major A. Gaselee	Transferred to command 4th Sikh Infantry, 1890. Commanded 1st Battalion, 1893-1896. Promoted Colonel on the Staff. Retired after commanding Northern Army. General, G.C.

THE 5TH ROYAL GURKHA RIFLES (F.F.)

Date of Appointment	Name	Remarks
10/11/86	(2)(1)Major L. R. H. D. Campbell	Transferred to 2/3rd Gurkha Rifles.
10/11/86	(2)(1)Lieut. E. Vansittart	Transferred to command 8th Gurkha Rifles, 15/5/02.
10/11/86	(2)(1)Lieut. A. H. G. Kemball	See Appendix VII.
10/11/86	Lieut. A. S. Rooke	See Appendix VII
10/11/86	Lieut. C. M. Crawford	Died in Chitral, 1912. Lieut.-Colonel. Commanded 1/6th Gurkha Rifles and 2/6th Gurkha Rifles.
10/11/86	Lieut. W. Hudson	Transferred to 22nd Madras Infantry in 1894.
17/11/86	Surgeon G. Duncan.	
7/4/87	(1)Lieut. G. H. Boisragon	See Appendix VII.
21/6/87	(1)Lieut. C. H. Davies	Died in Chilas, 15/12/99.
8/8/88	(2)Lieut. N. E. Chesney	Retired in 1905. Major.
6/6/88	Lieut. F. F. Badcock	See Appendix VII.
1/8/88	(2)Lieut. F. G. Lucas	See Appendix VII.
18/8/88	(1)(2)Captain G. Hawkes	Retired in 1891 and died in England in 1927. Commanded 2nd Battalion.
28/8/88	(2)(1)Captain F. W. Evatt	Retired 6/5/09. Major. See Appendix VII.
9/5/89	(1)Colonel F. E. Hastings	Attached.
25/5/89	(2)Lieut. F. W. Lethbridge	Transferred to Cantonment Magistrate's Department in 1894.
3/6/89	(1)2/Lieut. the Hon. C. G. Bruce	See Appendix VII.
9/1/92	Lieut. E. B. C. Boddam	See Appendix VII.
11/2/92	(1)Lieut. S. D. B. Ketchen	Accidentally killed on the Safed Koh on 12/12/01.
7/4/92	(1)(2)Lieut. C. R. Johnson	Retired 1919 after commanding 2nd Battalion.
12/5/92	Surgeon-Captain W. Heeney	
14/4/93	(1)(2)2/Lieut. H. J. P. Browne	See Appendix VII.
18/2/94	(2)(1)Lieut. M. R. W. Nightingale	See Appendix VII.
11/12/94	(2)(1)Lieut. M. H. P. Barlow	Died at Fort Lockhart, 12/8/02.
29/11/95	(2)Lieut. R. F. Warburton	Died in England, 1906.
20/1/96	Surgeon-Major A. W. MacKenzie	
22/4/96	(2)Lieut. H. A. H. Thompson	Transferred to 2/1st Gurkha Rifles, 1897.
27/10/97	(1)Lieut. A. B. R. Battye	
25/7/98	(1)(2)Lieut. H. A. Holdich	Left in 1921 to command 1/1st Gurkha Rifles. See Appendix VII.

THE 5TH ROYAL GURKHA RIFLES (F.F.)

Date of Appointment.	Name.	Remarks.
25/7/98	(1)(2)Lieut. C. E. Bateman-Champain	Retired 1923 after commanding 2nd Battalion.
5/8/98	(1)(2)Lieut. F. H. Bridges	Died 1916. Major.
22/2/99	(2)(1)Lieut. D. M. Govan	See Appendix III.
31/3/99	Major C. E. L. Gilbert, I.M.S.	
10/5/99	Lieut. H. Bawlton, I.M.S.	
15/5/99	Brevet Lieut.-Colonel E. W. F. Martin	Died 1906 while commanding 2nd Battalion.
16/10/99	(2)(1)Lieut. H. M. Battye	See Appendix III.
24/1/00	(2)(1)Lieut. A. M. Graham	See Appendix III.
19/5/00	Captain F. R. Ozzard I.M.S.	
30/7/00	Captain N. R. J. Rainier, I.M.S.	
13/4/01	Lieut. T. G. N. Stokes I.M.S.	
26/7/02	Lieut. F. E. Wilson, I.M.S.	
16/4/03	2/Lieut. H. T. Molloy	Still serving.
7/4/03	(1)2/Lieut. E. C. de R. Martin	Transferred to British Service, 1914. See Appendix VII.
16/9/03	Captain I. L. MacInnes, I.M.S.	
24/9/03	Lieut. A. E. Johnson	2/1st Gurkha Rifles (attached).
9/5/04	(2)(1)Lieut. G. P. Sanders	Transferred to command 3/11th Gurkha Rifles, 27/4/21. Commanded 2/6th Gurkha Rifles.
27/9/04	(1)(2)Lieut. the Hon. A. C. Murray	Transferred to British Service, 1914. See Appendix VII.
9/12/04	Captain C. M. Goodbody, I.M.S.	
4/5/05	(2)Lieut. J. D. Crowdy	See Appendices III and VII.
30/7/05	(2)Lieut. W. K. P. Wilson	Transferred to 30th Punjab Infantry, 1906.
26/8/05	(1)2/Lieut. C. H. F. Nixon	Transferred to 91st Punjabis, 26/5/10.
19/10/05	(2)Lieut. T. Luck	Transferred to 67th Punjab Infantry, 1907.
28/12/05	(1)Captain J. K. S. Fleming, I.M.S.	Struck off in 1917 on the reorganization of the I.M.S.
3/5/06	(2)(3)(1)2/Lieut. H. R. C. Lane	Still serving.

THE 5TH ROYAL GURKHA RIFLES (F.F.)

Date of Appointment.	Name.	Remarks.
20/11/06	(2)2/Lieut. V. W. Brett	Transferred to Grass Farms Department.
28/1/07	(2)Lieut. R. C. Duncan	Still serving.
22/3/07	(1)2/Lieut. A. B. Hay-Webb	See Appendices III and VII.
28/3/07	(1)2/Lieut. W. K. Brown	See Appendix III.
21/6/07	(1)Lieut. O. E. Todd	Died 1916. Major.
25/9/07	(1)2/Lieut. G. Turner	See Appendix III.
1/11/07	(1)2/Lieut. D. I. B. Lloyd	See Appendix III.
14/11/07	Lieut. J. M. B. Taylor, I.M.S.	
24/11/07	(2)Captain F. Skipwith	See Appendix VII.
5/12/07	(2)2/Lieut. A. A. Heyland	See Appendices III and VII.
26/3/08	Lieut. W. G. Harington	See Appendix III.
24/11/08	(2)2/Lieut. A. N. Rolfe	See Appendix VII.
29/7/09	(1)2/Lieut. R. L. Beddy	See Appendix III.
16/11/09	(1)2/Lieut. K. C. S. Erskine	Still serving.
15/12/09	(2)2/Lieut. E. D. T. Metcalfe	See Appendix VII.
19/3/10	(1)2/Lieut. H. J. Cummins	See Appendix III.
11/4/10	(1)Lieut. H. C. G. Lemon	
12/6/10	(1)Lieut. F. R. M. Campbell	Transferred to 91st Punjabis, 30/11/11.
28/10/10	(2)Lieut.-Colonel M. A. Ker, I.M.S.	
22/4/11	(1)Major C. H. Bowle Evans, I.M.S.	
7/11/12	(1)(2)2/Lieut. H. A. Wellesley	Still serving.
15/11/13	Captain R. W. G. Hingston, I.M.S.	
18/8/14	(2)(1)2/Lieut. F. E. Le Marchand	Still serving.
17/3/14	(2)Lieut. C. A. Gouldsbury	Still serving.
8/10/14	(2)2/Lieut. R. M. Bruce	Still serving.
10/10/14	(1)2/Lieut. H. D. H. Y. Nepean	Still serving.
28/10/14	(2) Major W. C. Ross, I.M.S.	
16/10/14	Captain M. F. Reaney, I.M.S.	See Appendix III.
14/1/15	(1)2/Lieut. N. R. C. Cosby	Still serving
26/1/15	(2)2/Lieut. G. A. Maconchy	See Appendix III.
14/8/15	(1)2/Lieut. J. H. Stables	See Appendix III.
17/8/15	(2)2/Lieut. J. C. March	See Appendix III.
1/7/15	(2)Major W. T. McCowen, I.M.S.	
6/9/15	(1)Captain P. J. Veale, I.M.S.	
28/10/15	(2)2/Lieut. J. F. Marindin	Still serving.
19/11/15	(2)2/Lieut. J. C. Coates	Still serving.
25/4/16	(1)(2)2/Lieut. C. S. Baker	Still serving.

THE 5TH ROYAL GURKHA RIFLES (F.F.)

Date of Appointment.	Name.	Remarks.
25/4/16	(1)2/Lieut. W. B. O. Fox	Demobilised.
2/7/16	(1)(2)2/Lieut. K. J. Macintosh	See Appendix III.
2/7/16	(1)2/Lieut. A. P. Q. Thomson	Still serving.
2/7/16	(1)2/Lieut. J. F. Petrie	Demobilised.
24/11/16	(1)2/Lieut. F. A. B. Fisher	Demobilised.
24/11/16	(1)2/Lieut. J. D. H. Cook	See Appendix III.
29/11/16	(1)2/Lieut. J. E. Walker	Demobilised.
5/2/17	(2)Lieut. R. N. D. Broad	Demobilised.
5/11/17	(2)2/Lieut. M. A. Platts	Demobilised.
5/11/17	(2)2/Lieut. L. A. Alexander	Still serving.
12/11/17	(2)2/Lieut. K. C. Garvie	Demobilised.
1/12/17	(1)Lieut. R. A. Briggs	Still serving.
8/12/17	(1)Lieut. R. T. Cameron	Still serving.
11/12/17	(1)2/Lieut. P. R. Broadway	Still serving.
28/1/18	(2)Lieut. H. J. Silberbauer	Demobilised.
4/2/18	(2)2/Lieut. E. E. H. Green	Retired 1928.
16/8/18	(2)Lieut. R. D'Oyly Hughes	Still serving.
26/4/18	(2)Lieut. J. M. Hobbs	Still serving.
21/6/18	(1)Lieut. W. R. Watt	Demobilised.
5/9/18	(1)2/Lieut. H. R. S. Plunkett	Demobilised.
5/9/18	(2)2/Lieut. H. J. W. Diack	Demobilised.
7/10/18	(1)2/Lieut. F. H. A. Stables	Still serving.
22/11/18	(1)Captain R. M. S. Barton	Demobilised. I.A.R.O.
11/1/19	(1)Lieut. I. A. T. Edwards	Still serving.
19/1/19	(1)Lieut. N. A. Grinsted	Retired on 25/4/22.
80/8/19	(1)2/Lieut. E. H. Weigall	Demobilised.
15/4/19	(2)Lieut. H. A. St. E. French	Demobilised.
18/5/19	(1)2/Lieut. E. N. Warwick	Killed while flying in the Aerial Derby, 1928, after demobilisation.
1/2/20	(1)Captain E. L. Bartleman	Retired on 29/4/22.
6/2/20	(2)Lieut. A. T. Cornwall Jones	Still serving.
6/2/20	(1)Lieut. B. Woods-Ballard	Left for Political Department on 21/11/24.
13/2/22	(3)(2)Captain R. G. Leonard	Still serving.
4/2/22	(1)Lieut. T. L. M. Annesley	Retired on 25/4/22.
10/3/22	(2)2/Lieut. R. C. O. Hedley	Still serving.
12/4/22	(1)Lieut. W. G. S. Thompson	Still serving
80/11/22	(1)Brevet Lieut.-Colonel H. E. Weekes	Left in 1928 for Staff Employ after completing command of 1st Battalion.
19/3/23	(1)2/Lieut. R. H. Pease	Still serving.
1/7/23	(1)Captain T. R. Harrison	Still serving.
9/11/23	(1)Lieut. A. H. Woodhouse	Still serving

THE 5TH ROYAL GURKHA RIFLES (F.F.)

Date of Appointment.	Name.	Remarks.
10/11/23	(2)Brevet Lieut.-Colonel H. St. G. Scott	Left 1928, being appointed Colonel Commandant, S.A.S., India, after completing command of 2nd Bn.
23/3/24	(2)2/Lieut. A. MacE. Williams	
15/5/24	(1)(2)(1)Major F. S. Massy	Still serving.
6/7/24	(2)Captain J. L. Johanson	Still serving.
21/3/25	(2)2/Lieut. K. D. Outram	Still serving.
	(2)2/Lieut. O. R. Bethune	Still serving.
31/10/27	(1)2/Lieut. G. W. S. Burton	Still serving.

APPENDIX V

LIST OF OFFICERS ATTACHED DURING THE GREAT WAR, 1914-18.

1st BATTALION.

Lieut.-Colonel Firth	2/10th Gurkha Rifles
Major A. B. Tillard, D.S.O.	2/1st (K.G.O.) Gurkha Rifles.
Major W. J. Evans	1/1st (K.G.O.) Gurkha Rifles.
Major F. L. Y. Brett	7th Gurkha Rifles.
Captain D. S. Orchard	1/8th Gurkha Rifles.
Captain E. C. Mockler	1/1st (K.G.O.) Gurkha Rifles.
Captain M. P. Reaney	I.M.S.
Captain G. Tomes	53rd Sikhs.
Captain F. M. Bailey	32nd Pioneers.
Captain P. J. Veale	I.M.S.
Captain W. L. Hogg	3rd Brahmans.
Captain Bowman	R.A.M.C.
Captain W. R. Watt, M.C.	
Captain R. M. S. Barton	I.A.R.O.
Lieutenant R. D. McKenzie	I.A.R.O.
Lieutenant R. B. H. Whitby	I.A.R.O.
Lieutenant H. J. Macartney	
Lieutenant I. Easterbrook	
Lieutenant E. Birkbeck	128th Pioneers.
Lieutenant Shewan	27th Punjabis.
Lieutenant H. Greene	92nd Punjabis.
Lieutenant U. J. Bourke	
Lieutenant G. S. V. Paterson	
Lieutenant W. M. Ferguson	I.A.R.O.
Lieutenant F. E. C. Hughes	1/1st (K.G.O.) Gurkha Rifles.
Lieutenant P. E. Cayley	I.A.R.O.
Lieutenant L. A. Foster	1/1st (K.G.O.) Gurkha Rifles.
Lieutenant W. R. Ransford	I.A.R.O.
Lieutenant C. M. H. Wingfield	2/1st (K.G.O.) Gurkha Rifles.
Lieutenant G. A. Anderson	I.A.R.O.
Lieutenant R. F. D. Plunkett	2/1st (K.G.O.) Gurkha Rifles.
Lieutenant C. E. Simpson	I.A.R.O.
Lieutenant R. Maynard	1/4th Gurkha Rifles
Lieutenant E. D. Pryor	I.A.R.O.
Lieutenant W. R. Thomson	I.A.R.O.
Lieutenant C. W. Cousins	I.A.R.O.
2/Lieutenant H. E. Winn	I.A.R.O.
2/Lieutenant G. K. Knowles	I.A.R.O.
2/Lieutenant J. H. Stables	I.A.R.O.
2/Lieutenant R. M. Banks	I.A.R.O.
2/Lieutenant J. W. W. Tregale	I.A.R.O.
2/Lieutenant J. F. Petrie	
2/Lieutenant F. A. B. Fisher	
2/Lieutenant J. F. Walker	

2/Lieutenant F. J. A. Terrel ... ... I.A.R.O.
2/Lieutenant H. B. Edwards ... ... I.A.R.O.
2/Lieutenant H. J. L. Phillips
2/Lieutenant J. E. B. Roberts
2/Lieutenant E. H. Hunter ... ... I.A.R.O.
2/Lieutenant A. S. Fletcher ... ... I.A.R.O.
2/Lieutenant J. D. H. Cook ... ...
2/Lieutenant C. G. Toogood ... ... 11th Bn. Gloucestershire Regt.
2/Lieutenant A. C. Gladstone ... ... I.A.R.O.
2/Lieutenant J. S. Lloyd ... ... 2/3rd Q.A.O. Gurkha Rifles.
2/Lieutenant E. Johnson ... ... 40th Pathans.
2/Lieutenant H. J. Thomson ... ... I.A.R.O.

2ND BATTALION.

2/Lieutenant A. W. M. Spottiswood ...
2/Lieutenant R. N. D. Broad ... ... I.A.R.O.
2/Lieutenant G. A. Maconchy ... ...
2/Lieutenant G. E. B. Roberts ... ... I.A.R.O.
2/Lieutenant H. E. Winan ... ... I.A.R.O.
2/Lieutenant C. N. D. Inglis ... ... I.A.R.O.
Captain R. W. E. Hingston ... ... I.M.S.
2/Lieutenant H. J. L. Phillips ... ... I.A.R.O.
2/Lieutenant J. D. H. Cook ... ... I.A.R.O.
2/Lieutenant R. C. Bayldon ... ... I.A.R.O.
2/Lieutenant L. J. Hicks ... ... I.A.R.O.
2/Lieutenant J. C. March ... ... I.A.R.O.
2/Lieutenant F. E. E. Abrahale ... ...
2/Lieutenant H. B. Corfield ... ... I.A.R.O.
2/Lieutenant H. N. Loch ... ...
2/Lieutenant C. W. Cousins ... ... I.A.R.O.
2/Lieutenant E. H. Saunders ... ... I.A.R.O.
2/Lieutenant F. Dewar ... ... I.A.R.O.
2/Lieutenant F. B. Fisher ... ... I.A.R.O.
2/Lieutenant A. C. Gladstone ... ... I.A.R.O.
2/Lieutenant R. M. Banks ... ... I.A.R.O.
2/Lieutenant C. G. Crawford ... ... 2/3rd (Q.A.O.) Gurkha Rifles.
2/Lieutenant C. P. Gouldsbury ... ... I.A.R.O.
Lieutenant F. K. Bradford ... ... 1/4th Gurkha Rifles.
2/Lieutenant C. T. A. Tyndall ... ...
2/Lieutenant N. W. Lawrie ... ...
Lieutenant J. McGarry ... ... I.A.R.O.
2/Lieutenant R. B. H. Whitley ... ... I.A.R.O.
2/Lieutenant W. E. Legge ... ... I.A.R.O.
Lieutenant L. M. Goodall ... ... I.S.C.
Lieutenant G. F. Paterson ... ... 3rd.
2/Lieutenant R. H. McArdle ... ...
2/Lieutenant J. Thompson ... ... I.A.R.O.
Lieutenant H. P. Keary ... ...

APPENDIX VI

COMMANDANTS, 5TH ROYAL GURKHAS, F.F.

Appointment.	Name.	Tenure.
1858	Major H. F. M. Boisragon	1858-1860.
1860	Colonel O. E. Rothney, C.S.I.	1860-1873.
1874	Colonel P. F. Gardiner	1874-1878.
1876	Colonel A. Fitzhugh, C.B.	1878-1885.
1863	Colonel J. M. Sym, C.B.	1885-1892, 1st Battalion.
1886	Lieut.-Colonel E. Molloy	1886-1894, 2nd Battalion.
1886	Colonel A. Gaselee, C.B., A.D.C.	1892-1896, 1st Battalion.
1890	Lieut.-Colonel G. Hawkes	1894-1901, 2nd Battalion.
1877	Brevet Lieut.-Colonel A. R. Martin	1896-1899, 1st Battalion.
1881	Brevet Lieut.-Colonel A. A. Barrett, C.B.	1899-1905, 1st Battalion.
1899	Brevet Lieut.-Colonel E. W. F. Martin	1901-1906, 2nd Battalion.
1886	Colonel A. H. G. Kemball	1905-1910, 1st Battalion.
1897	Brevet Colonel J. M. Stewart, A.D.C.	1906-1911, 2nd Battalion.
1887	Colonel G. H. Boisragon, V.C.	1910-1917, 1st Battalion.
1888	Lieut.-Colonel F. G. Lucas, D.S.O.	1911-1916, 2nd Battalion.
1895	Lieut.-Colonel C. R. Johnson	1916-1919, 2nd Battalion.
1894	Colonel M. R. W. Nightingale, C.M.G., C.I.E., D.S.O.	1917-1921, 1st Battalion.
1893	Colonel H. J. P. Browne, C.B.	1919-1921, 2nd Battalion.
1896	Colonel W. D. Villiers-Stuart, C.B.E., D.S.O.	1921-1924, 1st Battalion.
1898	Colonel C. E. Bateman-Champain	1921-1923, 2nd Battalion.
1922	Colonel H. St. G. Scott, D.S.O.	1923-1927, 2nd Battalion.
1923	Brevet Colonel H. E. Weekes, O.B.E.	1924-1928, 1st Battalion
1928	Lieut.-Colonel F. S. Massy	1927, 2nd and 1st Battalion.
1904	Lieut.-Colonel H. T. Molloy, D.S.O.	1928, 2nd Battalion.

APPENDIX VII

BRIEF RECORDS OF SERVICES OF OFFICERS OF THE REGIMENT ON STAFF OR OTHER EXTRA-REGIMENTAL EMPLOYMENT AND OF RETIRED OFFICERS DURING THE GREAT WAR.

BADCOCK, F. F.

July, 1912, left 5th Gurkhas on appointment as Commandant 2/6th Gurkhas in Chitral. March, 1916, proceeded to Mesopotamia and remained in command till May, 1917, when invalided. Mentioned in despatches twice, and awarded the Order of St. Stanislaus, 3rd Class, with Swords. 1918, promoted Colonel, and retired in 1919 as Honorary Brigadier-General after a short period as Inspector of Depots and latterly in command of the Abbottabad Brigade. Died in England in July, 1926.

BARRETT, A. A.

Posted to 5th Gurkhas, 1881, having previously seen service in Afghan War, 1879-80; Hazara Expedition, 1888; Miranzai Expedition and Hunza Nagar Expedition, 1891. 1895, appointed A.A.G., Punjab Frontier Force. 1897, served in Tirah Expedition as D.A.Q.M.G., and subsequently as A.Q.M.G. Mentioned in despatches and received Brevet of Lieutenant-Colonel. 1902, received Brevet of Colonel. 1903, awarded C.B. 1905, after commanding 1/5th Gurkhas, appointed D.A.G. in India. 1906, promoted Major-General. 1907-8, commanded a Brigade in the Bazar Valley Operations and in the Mohmand Field Force. Mentioned in despatches and awarded K.C.B. 1909, appointed A.G. in India; awarded K.C.V.O. 1911, promoted Lieutenant-General. 1912, commanded Poona Division; 1914, commanded Mesopotamia Expeditionary Force; awarded K.C.S.I. 1916, commanded Northern Command, India. 1917, promoted General and appointed A.D.C. to H.M. the King; awarded G.C.B., 1918, and G.C.S.I., 1920. 1920, retired. 1921, promoted Field-Marshal. Died in United Kingdom in 1926.

BATEMAN-CHAMPAIN, C. E.

August, 1914, furlough in United Kingdom; appointed Second-in-Command 9th Bn. The Rifle Brigade. February, 1915, posted to 1/1st Gurkhas in France. March, 1915, severely wounded at Neuve Chapelle. December, 1915, passed fit for light duty; appointed Staff G.H.Q., Egypt. June, 1916, appointed Senior Supervising Officer with Nepalese Contingent at Kakul, India. July, 1916, appointed A.M.S., Northern Command, India. November, 1917, passed fit for active service and rejoined 2/5th Gurkhas in Mesopotamia.

BODDAM, E. B. C.

June, 1915, evacuated to United Kingdom from wounds received while Second-in-Command 1/5th Gurkhas in Gallipoli; Mentioned in Despatches,

June, 1916. August, 1915, appointed G.S.O.1., 57th West Lancs. Division, at Canterbury. October, 1916, G.S.O.1., 73rd Division, at Blackpool. February, 1917, officiated in command of 1/5th Gurkhas. March, 1917, raised and commanded 3/6th Gurkhas. April, 1918, appointed G.S.O.1. 5th Mhow Division. November, 1918, Brigadier-General i/c Administration, Southern Command. May, 1920, retired as Honorary Brigadier-General.

BOISRAGON, G. H.

June, 1915, wounded in Gallipoli while commanding 1/5th Gurkhas, and evacuated to United Kingdom; Mentioned in Despatches; Brevet of Colonel; Order of the Nile, 4th Class. Passed fit for service, June, 1917, and employed under the War Office in United Kingdom till termination of war. Retired April, 1920.

BROWNE, H. J. P.

August, 1914, employed on Staff, Bombay. October, 1914, appointed Brigade Major 33rd Brigade, Mesopotamia, and thereafter G.S.O.1. 12th Division and B.G.G.S. Tigris Corps. On reorganization under General Maude was appointed B.G.G.S. II Corps; Mentioned in Despatches four times; Brevets of Lieutenant-Colonel and Colonel; Order of the White Eagle, 3rd Class. 1918, appointed B.G.G.S. Southern Command, India. 1919, returned to command 2/5th Gurkhas and thereafter commanded successively the Abbottabad, Dardoni, Ferozepore and Ambala Brigades. 1921, awarded C.B. 1923, retired as Major-General.

BRUCE, HON. C. G.

Appointed Commandant 1/6th Gurkhas, March, 1914, 1915, Brevet of Colonel, Gallipoli. August, 1916, appointed to command Bannu Brigade. May, 1917, commanded North Waziristan Column in operations against Wazirs; Mentioned in Despatches and awarded C.B. 1919, Mentioned in Despatches (Afghan War). 1920, retired as Honorary Brigadier-General.

CROWDY, J. D.

November, 1914, appointed Brigade Major, Poona Brigade. December, 1915, appointed G.S.O.3, Tigris Corps; present in actions for the relief of Kut. July, 1916, Brigade Major 21st Infantry Brigade. From January, 1917, to December, 1918, held a series of appointments as G.S.O.2 in various formations in Mesopotamia. Rejoined 2/5th Gurkhas in 1919, and was killed in action in the Ahnai Tangi. Mentioned in Despatches three times. Awarded D.S.O., August, 1918.

EVATT, F. W.

May, 1909, retired as Major. August, 1914, posted to 9th Bn. The Rifle Brigade, at Aldershot. September, 1914, appointed Commandant 11th Bn. The West Yorkshire Regiment, and served in England and France. October, 1916, invalided. August, 1917, appointed Commandant 4th (Reserve) Bn. The East Lancashire Regiment, and served on Yorkshire Coast Defences. March, 1918, resigned on account of ill-health. June, 1919, promoted Honorary Colonel for valuable services during the war.

THE 5TH ROYAL GURKHA RIFLES (F.F.)

GRAHAM, A. M.

Posted to 2/2nd Gurkhas and killed in action at Givenchy, December, 1914. (*Vide* Part III.)

HAY-WEBB, A. B.

August, 1914, furlough in United Kingdom. Posted to 9th Bn. The Rifle Brigade, Aldershot. November, 1914, posted to 2/2nd Gurkhas in France and severely wounded, December, 1914. May, 1915, passed fit for service and posted to 1/1st Gurkhas in France. August, 1915, transferred to Gallipoli, rejoined 1/5th Gurkhas and died of wounds received in action on August 21st, 1915.

HEYLAND, A. A.

April, 1915, proceeded to France with draft for 1/1st Gurkhas and killed in action at Festubert, May, 1915. (*Vide* Part III.)

HOLDICH, H. A.

October, 1914, appointed Brigade Major, 16th Indian Infantry Brigade, and proceeded to Mesopotamia; wounded in action and invalided; Mentioned in Despatches four times; Brevet of Lieutenant-Colonel and D.S.O. June, 1916, Staff Tigris Army Corps. March, 1917, Staff A.H.Q., India. November, 1917, appointed Director of Movements and Quartering, India; temporary Brigadier-General. June, 1919, Brevet of Colonel. September, 1919, substantive Colonel. August, 1920, appointed temporary Commandant 1/1st Gurkhas. January, 1921, appointed Colonel Commandant 1st Indian Infantry Brigade. October, 1922, retired as Honorary Brigadier-General.

KEMBALL, A. H. G.

On completing command, retired in 1910 to British Columbia; awarded C.B. May, 1915, became Second-in-Command of the 54th Kootenay Battalion raised in Nelson, British Columbia. June, 1915, appointed Commandant and took the Battalion to England in November, 1915. August, 1916, proceeded to France and was killed in action at the Vimy Ridge in February, 1917. Awarded D.S.O., January, 1917, and Mentioned in Despatches, June, 1917.

NOTE.—*In recognition of the gallantry displayed by Colonel Kemball in the action in which he was killed, the Germans proposed a temporary cessation of hostilities to enable his body to be recovered. This was agreed to, and the body was brought to our lines with every mark of respect.*

LUCAS, F. G.

While commanding 2/5th Gurkhas in Mesopotamia in 1916, appointed to command 42nd Infantry Brigade; awarded C.B. After return to India in 1919 commanded Dardoni Brigade for a short period, and subsequently the 67th Brigade during the Mahsud operations in 1919. Awarded C.I.E. and C.S.I. Retired in 1920 as Brigadier-General, after commanding the Abbottabad Brigade. Died in United Kingdom in 1922.

MARTIN, A. R.

1899, while Commandant 1/5th Gurkhas, appointed D.A.G. in India. 1901, appointed Assistant Military Secretary for Indian Affairs. Awarded C.B., 1902. 1902, appointed D.A.G., Bengal. 1903, appointed to command Second Class District and promoted Major-General (1904). 1904, commanded Bareilly Brigade, 7th Division. 1906, appointed A.G. in India. 1908, commanded 2nd Division; awarded K.C.B. (1910). 1912, retired. Died in United Kingdom in 1926.

MARTIN, E. C. DE R.

October, 1914, transferred to 2nd Bn. K.O.Y.L.I., and proceeded to France, December, 1914. February, 1915, invalided to United Kingdom. August, 1915, rejoined Battalion on Somme. February, 1916, appointed Instructor, 4th Army School. July, 1916, appointed Brigade Major, 74th Infantry Brigade. February, 1917, appointed Commandant 11th Bn. Lancashire Fusiliers; wounded in action at Messines. April, 1918, captured and remained in Germany till Armistice, after which employed in repatriation of prisoners. February, 1919, appointed Staff, War Office. August, 1919, retired. Mentioned in Despatches, June, 1916. Awarded M.C., December, 1916. Brevet of Major, June, 1917. Awarded D.S.O., August, 1917. Awarded C.M.G., January, 1919.

METCALFE, E. T.

Transferred to S. and T. Corps in 1914. 1916, proceeded on service to Mesopotamia with 7th Division. 1918, proceeded to Palestine; Mentioned in Despatches and awarded M.C. 1921, appointed D.A.D.S., Rawalpindi District. 1922, appointed D.A.D.T. (M.T.), Army Headquarters. 1927, appointed D.A.D.S., Rawalpindi District. Awarded O.B.E., 1927.

MOLLOY, H. T.

August, 1914, on furlough in United Kingdom; posted to 8th Bn. The King's Royal Rifle Corps. November, 1914, posted to 2/2nd Gurkhas in France. November, 1914, invalided to United Kingdom; light duty as Instructor Junior Officers' School, Chatham. May, 1915, posted to 2/4th Gurkhas in France. August, 1915, transferred to Gallipoli and appointed to command 1/5th Gurkhas; severely wounded; D.S.O. (*vide* p. 460). Invalided to United Kingdom and employed on Staff at Harwich when fit for light duty. July, 1916, Instructor Machine Gun School, Grantham. October, 1916, returned to India and commanded Depot 2/5th Gurkhas. January, 1917, Company Commander, Cadet College, Quetta. September, 1917, commanded Depot 2/5th Gurkhas, and January, 1918, Depot 2/6th Gurkhas. November, 1918, Instructor Small Arms School, May, 1919, Staff, 4th Division (Afghan War). August, 1919, Instructor Small Arms School. January, 1920, Instructor Mountain Warfare School. October, 1920, rejoined 2/5th Gurkhas.

MURRAY, THE HON. A. C.

1907, transferred from 5th Gurkhas to King's Own Scottish Borderers. Resigned commission later and became Member of Parliament for Kincardineshire. August, 1914, raised and commanded a squadron of the 2nd King Edward's Horse, which formed part of the Canadian Cavalry Brigade. The Brigade went to France early in 1915 and served in the trenches dismounted. 1916, Mentioned in Despatches and awarded D.S.O. 1917-18, served as Assistant Military Attaché, Washington; awarded C.M.G.

NEVILLE ROLFE, A.

November, 1914, posted to 2/8th Gurkhas in France. March, 1915, wounded in action at Neuve Chapelle and invalided to United Kingdom. August, 1915, passed fit for light duty, returned to India and commanded the Depots of 1/5th and 2/5th Gurkhas. August, 1916, passed fit for active service and joined 2/5th Gurkhas in Mesopotamia in January, 1917; Mentioned in Despatches. 1919, appointed Brigade Major, Lahore, and afterwards Lucknow. In December, 1919, health broke down as a result of the wound received in France, necessitating retirement in September, 1922.

NIGHTINGALE, M. R. W.

December, 1917, appointed to command of 54th Indian Infantry Brigade, Mesopotamia. November, 1918, appointed Commandant Mosul Brigade Area. July, 1919, commanded column for operations in South Kurdistan. October, 1921, commanded Mosul District. June, 1922, commanded column operating against Kurds in Sulimaniya Area. October, 1922, unemployed in United Kingdom. August, 1923, appointed to command 5th Indian Infantry Brigade, Razani. May, 1924, promoted Major-General. October, 1924, unemployed in United Kingdom. February, 1925, appointed to command Allahabad Brigade Area. March, 1927, appointed to command Sind Brigade Area. Mentioned in Despatches seven times. Awarded D.S.O., 1915. Awarded C.M.G., 1917. Brevet of Colonel, 1918. Awarded C.I.E., 1920. Awarded C.B., 1923.

PHILLIPS, I.

May, 1903, retired and took up politics in United Kingdom. 1907 to 1913, commanded Pembroke Yeomanry with Honorary rank of Colonel. August, 1914, appointed Staff, War Office. October, 1914, raised and commanded 113th Infantry Brigade, temporary Brigadier-General. January, 1915, appointed to command 43rd Welch Division, afterwards re-numbered 38th; subsequently appointed Parliamentary Military Secretary in Ministry of Munitions. November, 1915, rejoined 38th Division and took it to France. July, 1916, retired and resumed Parliamentary work. 1918, awarded K.C.B.

ROOKE, A. S.

Retired, 1912. January, 1915, appointed Telegraph Censor. July, 1915, appointed Governor, 1st Class, British Military Prisons in the Field in France. 1917 to 1919, Deputy Director Military Prisons; Mentioned in Despatches four times. June, 1919, awarded O.B.E.

SKIPWITH, F. S.

October, 1914, appointed G.S.O.2, Meerut Divisional Area. May, 1917, proceeded to Mesopotamia as G.S.O.2, Line of Communications, Basra.

October, 1917, appointed G.S.O.2, G.H.Q., Baghdad. January, 1918, rejoined 1/5th Gurkhas; Mentioned in Despatches. October, 1919, invalided to United Kingdom. February, 1921, commanded 2/2nd Rajputs. October, 1921, Commandant 2/10th Gurkhas. August, 1926, retired.

STEWART, J. M.

August, 1914, commanded Force " C," British East Africa; received thanks of Government for successful defence of Colony. Commanded Northern Area in attack on German position at Bukeba, and specially promoted Major-General. Commanded 1st Division in operations against German East Africa. Returned to India on reorganization of forces in British East Africa, and appointed P.A. and G.O.C., Aden, where conducted operations against the Turks throughout remainder of the war; awarded K.C.M.G. and Legion of Honour (Commander). 1920, Mentioned in Despatches for services in connection with operations in Somaliland. Retired and awarded Distinguished Service Pension. 1923, appointed Chief Commissioner British Red Cross Society in Greece; received thanks of Greek Government. 1924, awarded K.C.B.

VANSITTART, E.

1902, left 5th Gurkhas to raise 2/8th Gurkhas in Burma. 1907, retired. September, 1914, raised 8th Bn. The Royal West Kent Regiment and took them to France, August, 1915. Commanded this Battalion at Loos, September, 1915; severely wounded and reported killed; captured by Germans and became a prisoner of war at Crefeld till 1916, when sent to Switzerland. Repatriated, 1917. Awarded D.S.O., 1919.

VILLIERS-STUART, W. D.

August, 1914, on furlough in United Kingdom; posted as Second-in-Command 9th Bn. The Rifle Brigade. May, 1915, appointed Commandant and proceeded to France. November, 1915, invalided to United Kingdom. January, 1916, rejoined 1/5th Gurkhas in Egypt. May, 1916, appointed Superintending Officer Nepalese Contingent, Kakul. March, 1917, organized and commanded Mountain Warfare School, Abbottabad. November, 1917, raised and commanded 3rd Bn. The Guides. March, 1918, Commandant Mountain Warfare School, Abbottabad. October, 1918, appointed Inspector of Infantry, Northern India, Temporary Brigadier-General. February, 1920, Commandant Mountain Warfare School, Abbottabad. November, 1920, rejoined 1/5th Gurkhas. Mentioned in Despatches four times. Brevets of Lieutenant-Colonel and Colonel. Awarded C.B.E., 1919. Awarded D.S.O., 1925. Order of the Star of Nepal, 2nd Class.

APPENDIX VIII

The Work of the Depots during the Great War.

A. DEPOT COMMANDERS.

1st Battalion.

Rank and Name.	From.	To.
Captain O. E. Todd	3/11/14	12/12/15
Lieutenant A. N. Rolfe	12/12/15	28/2/16
Lieutenant K. C. S. Erskine, M.C.	28/2/16	2/3/16
Captain W. H. Hogg	8/10/16	18/11/16
Major G. P. Sanders	18/11/16	21/1/17
Captain D. S. Orchard	21/1/17	19/2/17
Captain E. C. Mockler	12/3/17	1/10/18
Major G. P. Sanders	1/10/18	27/3/19

2nd Battalion.

Rank and Name.	From.	To.	Remarks.
Lieutenant A. Neville Rolfe	29/2/16	6/6/16	Campbellpore and Abbottabad.
Major C. E. Bateman-Champain	6/6/16	19/6/16	Abbottabad.
Captain A. Neville Rolfe	19/6/16	16/11/16	,,
Captain H. T. Molloy	16/11/16	22/1/17	,,
Major G. P. Sanders	22/1/17	14/10/17	,,
Major H. T. Molloy	14/10/17	12/3/18	,,
Lieut.-Colonel C. R. Johnson	12/3/18	20/8/19	Battalion was actually in Abbottabad from June 4th to 26th, 1919.
Captain H. L. Silberbauer	20/8/19	1/11/19	Abbottabad.
Lieutenant G. F. Paterson	1/11/19	18/11/19	,,
Lieut.-Colonel C. R. Johnson	18/11/19	18/12/19	,,
Lieutenant G. F. Paterson	18/12/19	16/4/20	,,
Captain H. N. Loch	16/4/20	25/5/20	,,

B. STATEMENT OF RECRUITS ENROLLED.
1st Battalion (Period 4/8/14 to 20/3/19).

	Thakurs.	Chettris.	Gurungs.	Ghales.	Magars.						Newar.	Limbu.	Rai.	Lama.	Sunwar.	Others.	Total.
					Ale.	Bura.	Gharti.	Pun.	Rana.	Thapa.							
4/8/14—31/12/14 ...	5	8	21	2	5	4	8	6	6	39	—	—	—	—	—	3	102
1915 ...	80	73	117	18	18	13	25	42	48	187	29	—	57	5	7	13	672
1916 ...	19	59	163	12	18	32	49	71	68	218	9	—	2	—	—	23	738
1917 ...	6	28	92	6	11	12	21	44	17	112	8	—	—	—	2	14	373
1918 ...	8	69	66	8	7	14	15	19	12	84	19	41	55	55	8	14	494
1/1/19—20/3/19 ...	1	3	5	—	1	—	1	1	3	2	—	—	—	—	—	1	18
Total ...	69	240	464	41	50	75	114	183	154	642	65	41	114	60	17	68	2397

2ND BATTALION (PERIOD 4/8/14 TO 25/5/20).

	Magars.	Gurungs.	Thakurs.	Chettris.	Rais.	Limbus.	Lamas.	Sarkis.	Other Jats.	Followers.
1914	59	15	2	6	—	—	—	1	5	3
1915	374	177	38	100	74	1	14	3	22	14
1916	364	161	22	60	—	1	1	—	33	54
1917	331	109	11	31	1	3	1	12	23	19
1918	88	53	8	14	5	—	13	—	16	17
1919	25	10	5	4	—	1	—	—	6	—
1920	124	73	5	2	—	—	—	—	5	—
TOTAL	1365	598	91	217	80	6	29	16	110	107

C. DRAFTS SENT BY DEPOTS.

1st Battalion.

Date.	B.Os.	G.Os.	G.O.Rs.	Followers.	Unit.	Destination.	Name of B.O.	Remarks.
8/11/14	—	—	—	—	—	—	—	Bn. proceeds on service.
29/1/15	—	1	48	—	1/5th G.R.	Egypt	—	
27/2/15	—	1	46	2	1/5th G.R.	Egypt	—	1 G.O. and 1 N.C.O. from 2/4th G.R.; remainder, Assam Military Police.
30/6/15	—	—	15	—	1/5th G.R.	Gallipoli	—	
9/7/15	1	—	83	—	1/5th G.R.	Gallipoli	2/Lt. H. D. H. Y. Nepean	
18/8/15	1	1	40	2	1/5th G.R.	Gallipoli	2/Lt. H. E. Winn	
18/9/15	—	—	200	—	1/5th G.R.	Gallipoli	—	
12/12/15	1	2	200	—	1/5th G.R.	Egypt	Capt. O. E. Todd	
2/8/16	—	—	108	2	2/5th G.R.	Mesopotamia	—	Includes 72 Assam. Mil. Police Depot joins Bn. at Peshawar.
23/5/16	1	—	—	—	1/8th G.R.	Mesopotamia	2/Lt. H. Trotter	
22/7/16	1	—	—	—	1/8th G.R.	Mesopotamia	2/Lt. J. H. Stables	
8/8/16	2	3	219	—	1st Gurkha Res. Bn.	Malakand	2/Lt. G. J. Knowles 2/Lt. H. J. Phillips	
25/9/16	—	—	5	—	1st Gurkha Res. Bn.	Malakand	—	
30/9/16	—	—	—	—	—	—	—	Bn. proceeds to Nowshera.
8/10/16	—	—	19	—	1st Gurkha Res. Bn.	—	—	
2/11/16	—	—	—	—	—	—	—	Bn. returns to Abbottabad. Bn. proceeds to Mesopotamia.
19/2/17	—	—	—	—	1/5th G.R.	Mesopotamia	—	
12/3/17	—	—	20	—	Force D.	Mesopotamia	—	
17/4/17	—	—	8	—	1/5th G.R.	Mesopotamia	—	
6/5/17	—	—	25	—	1st Gds. Inf.	Mesopotamia	—	
24/5/17	—	—	43	—	1/5th G.R.	Mesopotamia	—	Ward Orderlies.
27/6/17	—	—	25	—	Force D	Mesopotamia	—	Burma Military Police.
18/7/17	—	4	2	—	1/5th G.R.	Mesopotamia	—	
24/8/17	—	—	71	—	Force D	Mesopotamia	—	Ward Orderlies.
4/9/17	—	—	4	—	1/5th G.R.	Mesopotamia	—	
19/9/17	—	3	35	—	1/5th G.R.	Mesopotamia	—	Ward Orderlies.
22/10/17	—	—	183	—	1/5th G.R.	Mesopotamia	—	
29/10/17	—	—	8	—	Force D	Mesopotamia	—	Ward Orderlies.
10/11/17	—	—	48	—	1/5th G.R.	Mesopotamia	—	
22/11/17	—	—	14	—	1/5th G.R.	Mesopotamia	—	
17/12/17	1	—	—	—	1/5th G.R.	Mesopotamia	Lt. R. D. McKenzie	
28/5/18	2	—	97	2	1/5th G.R.	Mesopotamia	Lt. R. B. H. Whitby Lt. C. E. Simpson Lt. R. A. Briggs	
12/8/18	1	—	—	—	3/11th G.R.	Manmad	—	
25/8/18	1	2	32	—	1/11th G.R.	Manmad	Major E. C. Mockler	
5/10/18	—	—	—	—	—	Egypt	—	
27/8/19	—	—	—	—	—	—	—	Bn. returns to Abbottabad.
Total	**12**	**17**	**1388**	**8**				

2ND BATTALION.

Date.	Proceeded to.	Strength.				Remarks.
		B.Os.	G.Os.	G.O.Rs.	Followers.	
24/3/16	1st, to Battalion in Mesopotamia	1	—	67	1	Lieut. Cousins.
24/5/16	2nd, to Battalion in Mesopotamia	1	—	71	—	Lieut.-Colonel C. R. Johnson.
24/6/16	3rd, to Battalion in Mesopotamia	—	—	52	—	
30/9/16	4th, to Battalion in Mesopotamia	1	—	79	1	Capt. R. C. Duncan.
8/10/16	5th, to Battalion in Mesopotamia	—	—	50	6	
8/11/16	6th, to Battalion in Mesopotamia	—	—	—	—	
9/1/17	7th, to Battalion in Mesopotamia	1	1	25	1	Capt. A. Neville Rolfe.
17/4/17	8th, to Battalion in Mesopotamia	—	—	20	2	The Band.
21/5/17	9th, to Battalion in Mesopotamia	—	—	25	6	
24/8/17	10th, to Battalion in Mesopotamia	—	2	149	—	
11/9/17	11th, to Battalion in Mesopotamia	—	—	40	—	
15/9/17	12th, to Battalion in Mesopotamia	—	—	27	6	
25/9/17	13th, to Battalion in Mesopotamia	—	2	83	6	
22/10/17	14th, to Battalion in Mesopotamia	1	—	170	—	Lieut. F. B. Fisher.
28/5/18	To Battalion in Mesopotamia	3	—	176	7	Lieuts. Broad, Garvie and Alexander.
19/12/18	To Battalion in Waziristan	—	—	95	—	
8/1/20	To Battalion in Waziristan	—	—	70	—	
20/1/20	To Battalion in Waziristan	1	1	149	6	Capt. L. A. Alexander.
18/2/20	To Battalion in Waziristan	—	1	47	—	
12/4/20		9	7	1895	42	

THE 5TH ROYAL GURKHA RIFLES (F.F.)

OTHER DRAFTS PROVIDED BY THE DEPOT.

Date.	Proceeded to.	Strength.				Remarks.
		B.Os.	G.Os.	G.O.Rs.	Followers.	
29/1/17	Guides Infantry	1	1	200	3	2/Lieut. J. C. Coates.
1/9/17	Volunteers to 1st Battalion in Mesopotamia	—	—	75	—	
8/3/18	To 1st Battalion in Mesopotamia	—	—	50	—	
15/5/19	To 3/5th Battalion in Mesopotamia	—	2	196	—	
12/9/20	To 3/5th Battalion in Mesopotamia	—	—	81	—	
	Total	1	3	552	3	
24/9/14	No. 6 Indian General Hospital	—	—	3	—	
—/8/15	To 1/1st G.R., Indian Expeditionary Force "A"	1	1	104	3	Lieut. A. A. Heyland.
22/3/15	Instructors to Nepalese Contingent	—	—	16	—	
24/8/15	Improvised Signal Company, 1st Peshawar Division	—	—	8	—	
26/3/15	No. 4 Combined Field Ambulance	—	—	2	—	
1/6/15	Instructors to Nepalese Contingent	—	1	10	—	
30/6/15	To 1st Battalion in Gallipoli	3	4	196	—	No. 3 Double Coy., under Capt. W. G. Harington.
18/8/15	To 1st Battalion in Gallipoli	1	1	30	—	Lieut. J. D. Cook.
28/12/15	Instructors to Nepalese Contingent	—	1	10	—	
	Total	5	8	379	3	

INDEX

NOTES.—(1) For reasons of space the Appendices have not been indexed. The names of British Officers occurring in Appendices II and VII have, however, been included in the Index.
(2) Wherever 1/5th, 2/5th, and 3/5th occur in the Index "Gurkhas" is to be understood.

A

Abadan occupied by 16th I.I. Bde., 278
Abbott, F. B., good work in J13, Gallipoli, 237, 238; seriously wounded, 238
Abbott, James, his connection with Hazara, 5-7
Abbottabad, founded by Herbert Edwardes, 7; as home of 5th Gurkhas, 7
Abdel Rahman Bair, feature figuring in attack from Anzac, Gallipoli, 247, 250
Abdullah Khan of Dilbori, raids into Agror, 77; outlawed, 78
Abdullai, Mahsud Sept, opposition by, 391.
Abdur Rahman, chosen as Amir, 64; visit to Rawalpindi, 79
Abdur Rahman Khel, Mahsuds, 2/5th in operations against, 431, 432
Abu, on Black Mountain, bad weather at, 178
Abu Risha (village), feature of action at Khidhr, 367
Achakzai expedition, 72.
Achi Baba, Gallipoli, dominating southern area, 220
Afghan War, Second: Leading part played by 5th Gurkhas in, xvi; causes, 33; plan of campaign, 34; advance of Kurram Field Force, 35, 36; flank march and action at Spingawai Kotal, 37-40; activities of Kurram F.F., 40-42; occupation of Kandahar by Sir Donald Stewart, 43; occupation of Jalalabad and Gandamak by Sir Sam Browne, 43; peace with Afghanistan, 43
  Murder of Sir Louis Cavagnari and re-opening of campaign, 44; advance of Kabul F.F., 45, 46; Battle of Charasia, 46-49; Kabul occupied, 50; Sherpur threatened by Afghan confederation, 52; combined movement of Baker and Macpherson, 53-57; disaster at Kila Kazi, 56; attack on Takht-i-Shah, 58, 59; Field Force concentrates at Sherpur, 60; investment of Sherpur, 62, 63; Afghan concentration dispersed, 63; plans for future, 64; disaster at Maiwand, 65-67; evacuation of Kabul, 67; relief of Kandahar, 67-70; battle of Kandahar, 70, 71; end of war, 72
Afghan War, Third: Causes, 353; summary of events, 353, 354; 3/5th in, 354-359

Afghans, precipitate flight after Peiwar Kotal action; dispositions at Charasia, 46; confederation of, after occupation of Kabul, 52; dispersal of, before Sherpur, 63; accept Abdur Rahman, 65; tactics of, at Maiwand, 66; dispositions of, at Kandahar, 71; in Third Afghan War, 353, 354
Afridis, situation of territory of, 100; in Tirah campaign, 139, 143, 144, 150, 151
Aghil, mountain range crossed by exploring party, 94
Aghyl Dere (ravine), figures in attack from Anzac, Gallipoli, 247, 252, 253, 255
Agror, position in relation to Black Mountain, 24; occupied prior to Isazai expedition, 116; 1/5th detachments in, 386; 2/5th detachments in, 434-436
Agror, Khan of, feud with Dilbori Khan and consequences, 77
Ahmad Khan spur, feature of Battle of Kandahar, 70
Ahmed Khel, Sir D. Stewart's victory at, 64
Ahnai Tangi, taken without fighting, 1860, 11; topography of, 415; actions at, 416-419
  2/5th in final action at, 416-419: Flathead Left taken, 417; two platoons overwhelmed in attempt to reach Flathead Right, 417; bayonet charge against Mahsuds on Flathead Left, 417; "C" Company, vanguard, cut off and fights its way back, 417; companies forward of Flathead Left beat off six attacks, 418; completion of piquet and withdrawal to camp, 418
Aka Khel, on Tank Zam, 2/5th at, 423
Akazais, location on Black Mountain, 24; attack by, on Oghi, 25; operations against, 27, 89, 90; blockade of, 78; gathering of, dispersed by Lieut. Barrett, 78; responsible for L. R. Battye's death, 84; further operations against, 176-181
Alachi, Gen. Symons at, in 1897, 151
Alachi Pass and Hills, situation of, 191
Albu Muhar, on Euphrates, 3/5th in action at, 373
Alexandra Ridge, Waziristan, situation, 394; 1/5th find piquets on, 399
Alexandria, arrival of 1/5th at, from Gallipoli, 293

INDEX

Ali Khel, Regiment at, 40, 42
Ali Masjid, 3/5th at, 354; marches to, 355
Alisherzai, Orakzai section, 103
Alisherzai Kotal, leading from Khanki River to Kharmana River, crossed in second Miranzai Expedition, 104
Allaiwals, location north-east of Black Mountain, 25; operations against, 92, 93
Al Minar, post on Tigris garrisoned by 2/5th, 330
Alps, visits by men of 5th Gurkhas, 126
Alus, 2/5th at, after Khan Baghdadi, 340
Amanulla of Kabul, anti-British attitude in 1919, 353
Amar Sing Thapa, Rifleman, with Martin Conway expedition, 116; in Alps, 126
Amar Sing Thapa, Sub.-Major, admitted 2nd Class Order of Merit, 198; goes to England, 198; death of, 438
Amara, capture of, 279
Amb, Khan of, help against Black Mountain tribes, 25, 26
Ambela Campaign, 1863, 13-23; causes, 13, 14; plan of campaign, 14, 15; concentration of troops, 15, 16; defective arrangements, 16; topography of Ambela, 16; change of plans due to intervention of Bunerwals, 16, 17; action at Conical Hill, 17; enemy attack on Eagle's Nest, 17, 18; first loss and recapture of Crag Piquet, 18; attack on front of camp by Swatis repulsed by 5th Gurkhas, 18; altered dispositions, 19, 20; enemy attack on troops covering working parties, 19; second loss and recapture of Crag Piquet, 20; enemy irruption during change of dispositions, 20, 21; third loss and recapture of Crag Piquet, 21; Neville Chamberlain wounded, Gen. Garvock takes command 22; offensive action, 22, 23; destruction of Malka and end of campaign, 23
Amritsar, disturbances at, 351, 384
Ana, capture of, 300
Anafarta Sagir, feature of Suvla area, Gallipoli, 248, 258
Anderson, Brig.-Gen., commanding 1st Bde., Zakka Khel Expedition, 191
Annaberg, s.s., takes 1/5th to Gallipoli, 216, 218, 219
Ansaram Pun, good work at Ramadi, 292
Anzac, name given to Australian and New Zealand Army Corps. *See* under "Australian Forces," "New Zealand Forces"
Anzac, in Gallipoli, landing effected at, 218; topography of, 247; Turkish forces opposing at, 248; fighting at, 248, 249, 257
Arab Rising, general situation, 363, 364; 3/5th in, 363-378; relief of Samawa, 364-370; march dispositions, 364, 365; action at Khidhr, 366-368; Samawa occupied, 369; punitive operations, 368, 369, 370-374; further advance, 374; action at Imam Abdulla, 374-378; armistice, 378
Arabs, in Mesopotamia, 284-287, 293, 324, 325; in Arab Rising, 365-378
Arambi Valley, traversed by 5th Gurkhas in Achakzai Expedition, 72
Arankola, s.s., takes 1/5th from Egypt to India, 274; takes wing of 2/5th to Mesopotamia, 320
Argandab, River and Valley, feature of Battle of Kandahar, 70, 71
Arhanga Pass, capture of, 143
Ari Burnu, in Gallipoli, landing effected at, 218; position in Anzac defences, 220
Arjun Thapa, retirement from 2/5th and distinctions gained, 442
Armament of 5th Gurkhas, originally muskets and two-grooved rifles, 4; receipt of rifles, Short Enfield pattern, 29; replacement of bayonets by swords, 29; Martini-Henry rifle received, 87; Lee-Metford rifles received, 158, 188; Maxim guns received, 161, 188; Short Lee-Enfield rifles, 166; original of 2/5th, 175; H.V. rifles for Mark VII bullet, 287
Armistice with Germany, 300, 340
Arms, supporters for, of Lord Roberts, xviii.
Arsala Khan of Allai, operations against, 91, 93
Artaubari, on Euphrates, destroyed by 3/5th, 371, 372, 375-377
Asa Khan, camp in Tank Zam, 419
Asad Khel, new road passes, 391; 1/5th at, in 1922, 392, 393
Asmai Heights, position in relation to Kabul, 50; unsuccessful action by Gen. Baker, 60.
As Sahilan, Nasiriya, operations against Arabs, 324-325
Assault-at-Arms, success of 1/5th at Rawalpindi, 408
Ata Muhammad Khan of Agror, arrest of, 25; reinstatement, 28
Attock, floods at, 31
Auburn Village, Makin, 2/5th at destruction of, 427, 428
Australian Forces, in Suez Canal defence, 209; friendship with Gurkhas, 210; in Gallipoli, 220, 243, 249, 250, 251, 252, 256, 258, 260, 261, 263, 265
Avalanche, Mummery and two Gurkhas killed by, 125; danger of, at Lowarai Pass, 184
Awards of 5th Gurkhas, App. II, 450
Aylmer, Fenton, gains V.C. at Nilt, 109, 110; commanding Tigris Corps, 280
Ayub Khan, defeats Gen. Burrows at Maiwand, 65, 66
Aziziyeh Canal, feature of Battle of Ramadi, 289, 291, 331

B

Babawali Kotal, key of Afghan position at Battle of Kandahar, 70
Baber Shamsher Jang Bahadur Rana, letter from, 388
Babusar Pass, leading from Kagan to Cholas, 131, 132, 157
Baby 700; feature figuring in attack from Anzac, Gallipoli, 247
Badcock, F. F., in Hunza-Nagir Expedition, 104-105; gallantry at Nilt and award of D.S.O., 109, 110; wounded at Nilt, 111; wounded at Khorappa, 142; other services, 481; distinctions won, 453
Badder Toi, Waziristan, 428, 429
Bagh, Gurkha Scouts at, 144
Bagh Spring, Khyber, seized by Afghans, 353
Baghdad, operations leading to occupation, 281, 282; occupied, 282; 1/5th at, 283
Baghiari, Khyber, piquetting from, by 3/5th, 355
Bagrian, 1/5th at, in third Black Mountain Expedition, 89; both Battalions 5th Gurkhas at, 116
Bahadur Khel, 1/5th at, in 1922, 391
Baiji, Mesopotamia, 2/5th at, 242
Bailey, F. M., wounded in Battle of August 21st, 262
Baio, hostile gathering at, in fourth Black Mountain Expedition, 180
Bait Isa, on Tigris, failure to capture, 280
Baker, Brig.-Gen., commands 2nd Brigade, Kabul F.F., 45; conducts main attack at Charasia, 47-49; turning movement against Muhammad Jan, 53, 57; success at Takht-i-Shah, 59; unsuccessful at Asmai, 60; in command of Achakzai Expedition, 72
Baker, C. S., wounded at Battle of Ramadi, 292
Bakrai, bridge at, in 4th Black Mountain Expedition, 179
Bala Hissar occupied by 5th Gurkhas, 50; explosion at, 50
Baldwin, Brig.-Gen., with reinforcements in Anzac attack on August 9th, 250; killed in action, 250
Bali Hill, Khyber, piquet wiped out, 355
Baltit, capital of Hunza, occupied, 214
Baltoro Glacier, Upper, explored by Martin Conway Expedition, 116
Baluchistan Post in Suez sector of canal defences, 213
Band of 5th Gurkhas, 171, 438
Bandra, s.s., takes 3/5th to Basra, 362
Bankora, s.s., takes 2/5th from Basra to India, 343
Bannu, 1/5th at, in 1895, 136
Baquba, Mesopotamia, operations from, 284
Baradar, on Black Mountain, 24
Baraki Rajan, 5th Gurkhas at, 65
Barari Right Piquet, 2/5th engaged while establishing, 421
Barari Tangi, action at, in 1860, xv, 11; topography, 420; 2/5th in night operation at, to secure Tangi, 421
Baratoff, Russian General, co-operation with, 282
Bara Valley, situation, 99; heavy rear-guard fighting in 1897, 150
Barbuti Bridge over Euphrates, destroyed by Arabs, 370
Barchar, spur of Black Mountain, ascended by L. R. Battye, 84; by 2nd Column in expedition of 1888, 88; by Sir J. McQueen's Force in 1890. 98
Barkai, concentration of Tirah F.F. at, 150
Barlow, A. E., in Arab Rising, 371, 373
Barlow, C. P., commanding 3/5th in Arab Rising, 362, 371, 373, 376; distinctions won with 3/5th, 465
Barlow, M. H. P., appointed to Gurkha Scouts in 1898, 151; death at Kohat, 171
Barpeta, s.s., takes 1/5th to Egypt, 205; takes 1/5th from Basra to India, 302
Barrett, A. A., successful action against tribal gathering near Oghi, 78; in command of Hunza-Nagir Detachment, 106; frost-bitten at crossing of Burzil Pass, 107; Commandant, 1/5th, 157; leaves Regiment on promotion, 170; commanding 2nd Bde., Zakka Khel Expedition, 191, 194; commanding 6th Poona Division at outbreak of Great War, 279; in command of Force D, Mesopotamia, 279; return to India, 279; promoted Field-Marshal, 437; death in England, 409; tribute to, 410; other services and distinctions, 481
Barrow Cup, won by 2/5th, 442
Bar Spur impinging on Badder Toi near Kaniguram, 429
Basket Ball, 400
Basra, arrival of 1/5th at, 278; first occupation of, 279; arrival of 2/5th at, 281; 1/5th embarked at, 301; 2/5th embark at, 342; arrival of 3/5th at, 363; 3/5th embark at, 379
Bateman-Champain, C. E., in France, 306; wounded at Neuve Chapelle, 319; commanding 2/5th in Mesopotamia, 335, 336; appointed Commandant 2/5th, 437; retirement, 440; other services, 481; distinctions won, 462
Bath-houses, 171, 188
Bathing in Suez Canal, 216
Battakundi in Kagan, 1/5th at, 131
Battery, F.A., R.H.A., hard pressed at Kila Kazi, 56
Battle Honours of 5th Gurkhas for Afghanistan, 77; for the Great War, 409

496 INDEX

Battle of June 4th, Gallipoli, object of, 220, 221; bombardment and initial successes, 221, 222; Turkish counter-attacks and check, 222; part of 1/5th, 222-227; casualties, 227

Battle of June 28th-July 3rd, plan, 232; dispositions, 233; progress of brigades, 233, 234; action of Indian Bde., 234; part of 1/5th, 234-243; fighting in J13, 236-240; Turkish counter-attacks, 240-243; casualties of 1/5th, 244

Battle of August 6th-10th, object and plan, 246; description of terrain, 247, 248; distribution of Turkish forces, 248; progress of battle, 248-251; 1/5th in the battle, 251-256; casualties of 1/5th, 255

Battle of August 21st, object and plan, 258, 259; progress of several attacks, 259-261; 1/5th in the battle, 261-264; casualties of 1/5th, 264; description of ground to be traversed by 1/5th, 262

[*Note.*—Other actions are indexed under the names of the localities at which they were fought.]

Battleship Hill, feature figuring in attack from Anzac, Gallipoli, 247

Battye, H. M., climbs Mali-Ka-Sar, 126; in battle of June 4th, 224, 226; killed in action, 226; tribute to, 227; distinctions won, 456

Battye, L. R., death on Black Mountain, 84-86; tribute to, 86

Battye, R., killed in action at Thabai, 147

Bauchop's Hill, Gallipoli, feature figuring in attack from Anzac, 247, 249

Bazar Passi, situation of, 191; crossed by wing of 2/5th in 1908, 193

Bazar Valley, Gurkha Scouts in, 151; topography, 191; operations in, in 1908, 192-196; withdrawal from, 197

Beddy, R. L., killed in action, Gallipoli, 225; tribute to, 228; distinctions won, 456

Beersheba, Turks withdraw to, from canal, 212

Belgians, King and Queen of, visit Malakand, 441

Bemaru Ridge, northern boundary of Sherpur, 61

Bench Mark, post in Suez Canal defence, 207

Bengal Cavalry, 3rd, in Achakzai Expedition, 72

Bengal Cavalry, 6th, at Thabai; death of Richmond Battye, 147

Bengal Cavalry, 12th, pursuit by, after Peiwar Kotal action, 39; at Charasia, 47

Bengal Cavalry, 16th, with Regiment in affair at Khabbal Hill, 26

Bengal Infantry, 11th, in fourth Black Mountain Expedition, 179, 180

Bengal Infantry, 27th, in second Miranzai Expedition, 101

Bengal Infantry, 29th, on Samana, 100

Bengal Lancers, 14th, at Karez Mir, 53; gallantry of Squadron at Kila Kazi, 56

Besai Ridge, enemy detachments on, 355; overrun by 3/5th, 356, 357

Besal, in Kagan, 1/5th, at 132

Bet Badshah, frontier crossed near, on return from Marri Expedition, 75

Bhagiram Gurung, Subadar-Major, killed in Bala Hissar explosion, 50

Bhanbir Rana, gallantry in battle of August 6th-10th, 314

Bhogarmang, summer camp at, 189

Bikanir Camel Corps in Suez Canal defence, 209, 214

Biran, 1/5th at destruction of, in 1888, 90

Bird, R. E., violin-playing of, 168

Birdwood, Sir W. R., commanding Anzacs in Gallipoli, 220; responsible for evacuation arrangements, 273; message to 1/5th after evacuation, 274; visit to 1/5th, 312

Birkbeck, E., killed in battle of August 6th-10th, 255; distinctions won, 456

Birkhdhoj Khattri, gallantry at Thabai, 147

Bir Mabeiuk, Turks located at, 209

Bir Sing Gurung, gallantry at Thabai, 147

Bitter Lakes, in Suez Canal defences, 208

Biyuk Anafarta, Gallipoli, valley figuring in Suvla attack, 248

Blackett, C. P., wounded with 2/5th at Barari Tangi, 421

Black Mountain, description of, 24, 25; second expedition, 27, 28; third expedition, 87-93; promenade, 98, 99, 176; fourth expedition, 99, 177-181.

Blair, Lieut. R. E., life saved by three sepoys of Regiment at Ambala, 19

Blizzard in Gallipoli, 268, 269

Bluff Piquet at Barari Tangi, 2/5th engaged while establishing, 421

Boddam, E. B. C., in China, 154; enters Staff College, 187; wounded in battle of June 4th, 224; takes command of 1/5th on recovery from wounds, 277; transferred to command 3/6th Gurkhas, 277; other services, 481; distinctions, 456

Boer prisoners at Kakul, 161

Boghra Pass leading to Achakzai country from Charman, 72

Boisragon, G. H., strenuous march by, 103; replaces Barrett in command of 1/5th detachment, 107; gains V.C. at storming of Nilt, 109, 110; appointed Commandant, 1/5th, 170; commands Kubri Column in pursuit of Turks, 214; wounded in battle of June 4th, 224; other services, 482; distinctions won, 453, 455, 456

Boisragon, H. F. M., appointed first Commandant, 5th Gurkhas, 4; transferred to command 4th Sikhs, 12; distinctions won, 450

Bombs, shortage of, in Gallipoli, 228, 236, 237, 238

Boomerang Redoubt, captured by Border Regiment in battle of June 28th, 233

Border Regiment, 2nd Bn.: In Waziristan, 1895, 135; in Gallipoli, 230, 233

Bori Pass, situation of, 191

Boundary on Black Mountain Frontier, 24

Bowman, Capt., R.A.M.C., good work at Ramadi, 292

Brackenbury, Lieut.-Gen. H., visits Abbottabad, 132, 133, 183

Bradshaw, Capt., in Hunza-Nagir Expedition, 109, 111

Brett, F. L. S., attached to 1/5th in Mesopotamia, 287, 288, 295

Bridges, F. H., in China, 154

Bridging feat by 1/5th Havildar, 132

Brigade, Abbottabad, formed, 186

Brigade, Indian, in Gallipoli: In battle of June 4th, 222; in battle of June 28th, 233, 234, 235; in battle of August 6th-10th, 249; in battle of August 21st, 260, 261

Brigade, 42nd, in Mesopotamia: In operations of Lucas Column, 284-287; at Ramadi, 290-293; at Ramadi and Madhij after the battle, 295; at Uqbah, 296; in Battle of Khan Baghdadi, 297, 299, 338, 339; in operations against Arabs at As Sahilan, 324, 325

Bright, Major-Gen. R. O., commanding 1st Bde., second Black Mountain Expedition (as Brigadier-General), 26; commanding Khyber Division, 44; sends reinforcements to Sherpur, 62

British India, residents of, in enemy ranks, 93

British Officers, 5th Gurkhas, originally appointed to Regiment, 4; in Ambela campaign, 15; in Second Afghan War, 34; in second Miranzai Expedition, 101; at capture of Saragarhi, 103; in Hunza-Nagir Expedition, 106; in Mahsud-Waziri Expedition, 1894-95, 133; in campaign of 1897, 138; on active service between 1898 and 1908, 154, 187; in Zakka Khel Expedition, 190; with 1/5th to Egypt, 204; with 1/5th to Gallipoli, 218; with 1/5th to Mesopotamia, 278; serving in France, 274, 306-308, 309; with 2/5th to Mesopotamia, 320; with 3/5th to Mesopotamia, 362; with 2/5th to Waziristan, 415; mustering out after Great War, 437

2 K

Broadway, P. R., wounded with 2/5th at Ahnai Tangi, 417

Brompton Village, Makin, 2/5th at destruction of, 427, 428

Brooking, Major-Gen. H. T., commanding 15th Division in Mesopotamia, 323, 324, 329, 331, 336, 339, 340; his message at Battle of Ramadi, 293; after Khan Baghdadi, 300; his farewell order to 1/5th, 301; his farewell address to 2/5th, 341

Brown Tower, feature of action of February 20th, at Makin, 426

Brown, W. K., in battle of June 4th, 224, 225; killed in action, 225; tribute to, 228; distinctions won, 456

Browne, G. de la Rue, wounded with 2/5th in Waziristan, 425

Browne, H. J. P., success at Thabai, 149; appointed to Gurkha Scouts in 1898, 151; enters Staff College, 170; appointed Commandant, 2/5th, 434; officiating in command of Abbottabad Brigade during trouble in Agror, 434; awarded C.B., 436; other services, 482; distinctions won, 457, 458, 461

Brownlow, Col., killed in action at Kandahar while in command of 72nd Highlanders, 71

Bruce, the Hon. C. G., with Martin Conway Expedition, 116; institutes Hill Race, 122; his account of hill racing, 122-124; his account of mountain exploration, 125, 126; in Upper Garhwal, 125; with Gurkha Scouts in Tirah, 139; as trainer of scouts, 169; conducts first reservists' training, 169; in command of 1/6th Gurkhas in Gallipoli, 223; in battle of June 28th, 237, 238; other services, 482; distinctions won, 452, 453, 454

Bruce, R. M., wounded at As Sahilan, 325; distinctions won, 461, 462

Budh Sing Gurung, good work at Hill 60, 270

Budhiparsad, winner of Hill Race, 122

Buldar Rakiot Valley, Mummery's objective when killed, 125

Buner, influence on Ambela campaign, 14

Buner standard, capture of, 22; treasured in Mess, 128

Bunji, 1/5th detachment at, 107

Burawai, in Kagan, 1/5th at, 131

Burhan, 1/5th detachment at, during Punjab unrest, 384

Burrows, Brig.-Gen., sent to Girishk, 66; defeated at Maiwand, 66

Burzen Pass, traversed on return from Marri Expedition, 75

Burzil Pass, nature of, 106; crossed in blizzard, 106

C

Cameron, R. T., in Waziristan, 396
Campbell, J. P. W., transferred to command Regiment during Ambela campaign, 15; wounded at third recapture of Crag Piquet, 21
Campbell, Major, inspiring action at Imam Abdulla, 375
Casualties of 5th Gurkhas, App. III, 466
Cavagnari, Louis, murdered at Kabul, 44
Cayley, P. E., distinctions won in Waziristan, 464
Chagru Kotal, leading from Shinauri to Khanki, 141
Chailak Dere (Ravine), Gallipoli, feature in attack from Anzac, 247, 249
Chakdara, Swat Valley, 2/5th detachment at, 441, 442; outrages by tribesmen against 2/5th at, 432
Chalt, Kanjuti enterprise against, 106
Chaman, position in relation to Achakzai country, 72
Chamberlain, Sir Neville, his account of action at Mir Karez, xvii; in command in Ambela Campaign, 13-23; wounded at third recapture of Crag Piquet, 21; his mission to Kabul turned back, 34
Chamiari, Murree Hills, 3/5th at, 351
Chamkannis, location, 137; blockade of, 137, 138
Champain, C. E. Bateman. *See* under Bateman-Champain.
Chandra Shamsher Jang, Rana Bahadur, Maharajah and Prime Minister of Nepal, letter from, 440
Channer, V.C., Brig.-Gen. G. N., in command of 1st Bde., third Black Mountain expedition, 87
Chaprot, Kanjuti enterprise against, 106
Charasia, prominent part of 5th Gurkhas in Battle of, xvii; topography of, 46; action at, 46-49
Charkhel, boundary delimitation at, 135
Cheblat, River, fishing in, 120; railway bridge over, guarded by detachment 1/5th during Punjab unrest, 384
Chenevix-Trench, C. C., influence on efficiency of 5th Gurkhas, 80; good work for 2/5th, 174; distinctions won, 451
Chigharzais, location on Black Mountain, 24; attack by, on Oghi, 25; operations against, 27, 179; gathering of, dispersed by Lieut. Barrett, 78
Chihildukhtaran, on route of Gen. Baker's turning movement against Muhammad Jan, 53
Chilas, threat of trouble in, 131; march of 1/5th detachment, 157
China, destroyed, 1897, 151; situation of, 191; wing of 2/5th at, in 1908, 193; operations at, in 1908, 194, 195, 196

Chintram Bura, gallantry in battle of August 6th to 10th, 313; in battle of August 21st, 315
Chirmang, wing of 1/5th at, in 1888, 91
Chitral, campaign of 1895, 136; 1/5th in, 162-165; 2/5th in, 184; 2/5th with escort to, 188
Chitralis, in Hill races against Gurkhas, 123
Chittabat, situation on Black Mountain, 24; attack on, 27; occupied in 1888, 89
Chocolate Hill, feature of Suvla area, Gallipoli, 248
Cholera outbreaks, 5, 24, 115, 116, 175, 323
Chora, Gurkha scouts at, 151; 2/5th at, in 1908, 192, 197
Chora Pass, situation of, 191
Chotiali, 5th Gurkhas at, in Marri Expedition, 74
Chunuk Bair, feature figuring in attack from Anzac, Gallipoli, 247, 249, 250, 253, 254, 256; Turkish artillery on, 262
Climo, Major-Gen. S. H., commanding Waziristan Force, visits to 2/5th, 427, 430; his farewell address to 2/5th, 432
Clio, H.M.S., in Suez Canal defence, 209, 210, 211
Close, H., appointed to 5th Gurkhas, 4; mistakenly arrested after Regiment's action of October 30th, 1863, 19
Cloud End, piquet position upstream of Sorarogha: operations abandoned owing to bad weather, 422, 423; completed successfully, 423, 424
Coincidence, remarkable, of loss and recovery of notebook of Sasidhar Thapa, 294
Colony, Gurkha, inception of scheme, 8; land taken by Government, 162
Comforts for troops, in Great War, 205, 206, 274
Coningham, Brig.-Gen. F. S., commanding Samcol, 363; commanding 5th I.I. Bde., 390; commanding Abbottabad Bde., 440; his farewell message to 2/5th, 441
Connaught Rangers, 5th, in Gallipoli, 260, 261, 263, 265
Connaught, Duke of, review by, of troops at Rawalpindi, 387
Conway, Martin, exploration of Karakoram, 116; in Alps, 126
Cook, John, leads attack on barricade at Spingawai Kotal, 38; saves life of Major Galbraith, 38; awarded V.C., 38; gallantry and skilful handling of rearguard at Monghyr Defile, 41; leads attack at Karez Mir, 54; gallantry at Kafir Jan defile, 57; mortally wounded while gallantly leading assault on Takht-i-Shah, 59; order of the day by Sir F. Roberts, 61; tribute by Parsu Khattri, 62; distinctions won, 450, 451

Cook, J. D. H., killed at Battle of Ramadi, 292
Corrie, Capt., in first ascent of Mount Kolahoi, 125
Cosby, N. R. C., in battle of June 4th, 224, 226, 227; in battle of June 28th, 236, 237, 238; wounded, 237, 238; in battle of August 6th-10th, 253-255; in battle of August 21st, 263-264; in Waziristan, 396; distinctions won, 454, 455, 456, 458
Cousins, C. W., distinctions won, 462
Cox, Major-Gen. H. V., commanding 29th I.I. Bde. in Gallipoli, 218, 219; commanding mixed force in battle of August 21st, 258, 260, 263; conducts operations at final capture of Hill 60, 265
Crag Piquet, position in relation to camp at Ambela, 16; first loss and recapture, 18; second loss and recapture, 20; third loss and recapture, 21
Crawford, C. M., experiences in Russo-Japanese War, 154
Crest of 5th Gurkhas, modifications, 412
Cricket, 128
Crowdy, J. D., commanding 2/5th in Waziristan, 414; leads charge at action of Ahnai Tangi, 417; killed in action, 417; tribute to, 419; distinctions won, 461, 462; other services, 482
Crown Prince of Germany, visits Abbottabad, 171, 199
Ctesiphon, Battle of, 279
Cummins, H. J., killed in battle of August 21st, 262; tribute to, 264; distinctions won, 456

D

Dabbus, on Euphrates, operations at, 372-374
Dag, Cherat (Foothills), 1/5th training at, 275; 3/5th training at, 351
Daishi, Black Mountain tract, inhabited by Swatis, 24; operations against, 27
Dakka, operations at, in 1919, 354
Dalbir Ale, Subadar, endurance of, 177
Dalbir Chand, gallantry at Hill 60, 268
Damakjelik Bair, Gallipoli, feature of Anzac area, 247, 249; 1/5th at, 257, 261
Daradar Valley, situation, 103; visited in second Miranzai Expedition, 104
Darai, 1/5th at destruction of, in 1888, 90
Dara Poi, Waziristan, 428
Darbanai, on Indus, 2/5th in attack on, in fourth Black Mountain Expedition, 179
Darband, on Indus, position in relation to Black Mountain, 24; base of small column in second Black Mountain Expedition, 27; base of fourth column in third Black Mountain Expedition, 88; base of Hazara F.F. in fourth expedition, 99, 177; base of Isazai F.F., 117

Darband, at foot of Samana, 101
Dargai (Samana), actions at, 141, 142
Darsamand, Miranzai, 1/5th at, with Kohat-Kurram Force, 386
Dasram, S. A. S., good work at Ramadi, 292
Daudiya, on Tigris, occupied at time of arrival of 1/5th in Mesopotamia, 282; garrisoned by 2/5th, 330
Davies, C. H., death of, in Chilas, 158
Davis, H. C. M., killed in action at Giga Khel, 432
Deh-Mazang Gorge, position in relation to Kabul, 50; 5th Gurkhas in withdrawal through, 61
Delamain, Brig.-Gen. W. S., commanding 16th I.I. Bde. at start of campaign in Mesopotamia, 279
Delhi, manœuvres and Durbar at, 80, 82
De Lisle, takes over command of 29th Div., 232; plans of attack of August 21st, 258
Demobilization, after Great War, 383, 434
Deoram Thapa, wins Hill Race, 122
Depots, good work of, 385; App. VIII, 487
Dera Ismail Khan, 1/5th at, 133; 2/5th at, 414
Derajat Mountain Battery (22nd), in Achakzai Expedition, 72
Deraji, on Euphrates, 3/5th at, 365
Dervish Ali Kuyu, Gallipoli, objective of Indian Brigade in battle of August 21st, 250
Deserter, incident of, at Ismailia, 212
Designation, of 5th Gurkhas: original, 3; changes, 117; title of " Royal " conferred, 379, 388; change averted, 439; of private soldier changed from Sepoy to Rifleman, 117
Detachments, 156, 159, 166, 189
Dhan Bahadur Khattri, good work at Imam Abdulla, 378
Dhan Sing Gurung, escape from Turks, 227
Dharmjit Pun, wins Hill Race, 122
Dhibban, on Euphrates, operations at, 288
Dhuwairah, on Euphrates, destroyed by 3/5th, 369
Dickson, Lieut., murdered by Mahsuds, 391
Dilbori, Khan of, feud with Khan of Agror, and consequences, 77
Dilbori Village, Lieut. Barrett's successful action at, 78
Diliarai, on Indus, piquetted in fourth Black Mountain Expedition, 179
Dirigi, Marri Expeditionary Force broken up at, 75
Division, 10th, arrival for August offensive, Gallipoli, 246; non-success at Suvla, 251
Division, 11th, arrival for August offensive, Gallipoli, 246; non-success at Suvla, 251; in battle of August 21st, 258

Division, 13th, arrival for August offensive, Gallipoli, 246; in Anzac attack, 250; in Mesopotamia, 280
Division, 29th, in Gallipoli, 219, 221, 233, 248, 258, 259
Diyala, crossing of, 282
Djemal Pasha, in command of Turkish forces moving on Suez Canal, 208
Dobbs, Capt., in Arab Rising, 366, 373
Doda, on Black Mountain, attacked by Northumberland Fusiliers and 3rd Sikhs, 90
Dorset Regiment, 1/4th, in 42nd Bde., Mesopotamia, 283, 284-287, 289, 290, 292, 298, 299, 321, 324, 331, 332, 334, 339
Dotiwala, N. M., distinctions won with 2/5th, 463
Double-company system introduced, 158
Double Hill, feature of Battle of Ramadi, 290, 291, 333
Dran, towers destroyed in second Miranzai Expedition, 104
Dress of 5th Gurkhas when raised, 4; service uniform after Afghan War, 80; introduction of felt hat, 163, 188; shorts, 166; post-war changes, 407
Drosh, headquarters of 1/5th in Chitral, 163
Dujaila, Battle of, 280
Duncan, R. C., reconnaissance of desert route, 322; service on the Staff in Mesopotamia, 335; distinctions won, 461, 462, 463, 464
Duncan's Piquet, Razmak Narai, affair at, 402, 403
Durand, Lieut.-Col. A., in command of Hunza-Nagir Expedition, 107; wounded at Nilt, 109
Durand Boundary, delimitation and unrest resulting from, 133, 188
Durbi Khel Pass leading from Bagh to Kharmana, 146
Dwatoi (Tirah), Gurkha Scouts at, 145
Dwatoi (Waziristan), 2/5th engaged at, 424; topography, 428

E

Eagle's Nest, position in relation to camp at Ambela, 16; enemy attack on, 18
Edward VII, King, death of, 171
Egypt. *See* Suez Canal
Ekma, s.s., takes wing of 2/5th to Basra, 320
Elephanta, s.s., takes 1/5th to Basra, 278
Elephants, on Machai Peak, 27; at Peiwar Kotal, 38
El Fardan, in Suez Canal Defence Scheme, 207, 209; patrol near, shelled by naval guns, 209; Turkish attack on, 211
Ellis, Major-Gen. W. K., in command of fourth Black Mountain Expedition, 177
Equipment of 5th Gurkhas originally black, 4; Mackenzie pattern received, 115; bandolier, 166; aluminium water-bottle, 166; rucksack, waterproof capes, 166; Brown substituted for black, 166; Mills-Burrows, 166; aluminium cooking pots, 188
Ergatta, trying experience of troops at, during Kabul-Kandahar march, 69
Erskine, K. C. S., good work in battle of June 28th, 239, 240; in temporary command of 1/5th, 241; in battle of August 6th-10th, 255, 313; wounded, 255, 313; accidentally shot at Madhij, 289; at Khan Abu Rayat, 296; at Khan Baghdadi, 299; in charge of regimental guard of honour for Prince of Wales, 390; in Waziristan, 396; distinctions won, 454, 455, 456, 459
Escape Hill, feature of Battle of Ramadi, 290, 292
Eski Hissarlik, Gallipoli, position in relation to Helles defences, 220
Es-Sinn. *See* Kut
Establishment of 5th Gurkhas, original, 449; changes in, 12, 29, 83, 115
Euphrates, operations on, 279, 281, 282, 284-286, 288-294, 295-299, 324, 325, 364-378
Euphrates Valley Canal, feature of Battle of Ramadi, 289, 331
Evacuation of Gallipoli, 1/5th in, 269, 271, 316, 317; Special Order of the Day, 272, 273
Evatt, F. W., gets big bag of quail, 119; services after leaving 5th Gurkhas, 482
Exham, H., with 2/5th in Waziristan, 416, 425, 427; distinctions won with 2/5th, 463
Exploration, F. Younghusband's expedition, 94, 96; Martin Conway's Expedition, 116; Mountain exploration by 5th Gurkhas, 124-126

F

Falbah, feature of action at Imam Abdulla, 375, 376; Samcol concentration at, 378
Fallahiya trenches captured by 13th Division, 280
Faluja, on Euphrates, occupied at time of arrival of 1/5th in Mesopotamia, 282; 42nd Bde. at, 289, 331
Fao taken by 16th I.I. Bde., 279
Farrell, G., distinctions won, 450, 452
Fateh Jang, 3/5th in strenuous march from, 349
Ferozepore, 3/5th at, 347, 348; 1/5th detachment at, 384
Fever epidemics in Hazara, 29, 116, 133, 156, 318; in Miranzai, 386; in Swat Valley, 441
Filippo da Filippi Expedition, 125
Firth, Lieut.-Col., takes command of 1/5th, 244; illness and departure, 257, 314; distinctions won, 455

Fishermen's Huts, Gallipoli, left of Anzac position, 220
Fishing, 119, 120; in Suez Canal, 216
Fitzhugh, A., appointment to command 5th Gurkhas, 32; leads attack on barricade at Peiwar Kotal, 38; at action of Monghyr Defile, 41; prominent in Battle of Charasia, 48; wounded at Karez Mir, 55; Bt. Lieut.-Col., 64; awarded C.B., 77; relinquished command, 81; farewell order, 81; distinctions won, 450, 451
Flathead Left, feature of Ahnai Tangi action, 416-418
Flathead Right, feature of Ahnai Tangi action, 416-418
Fletcher, A. S., killed in battle of August 6th-10th, 255, 313; distinctions won, 456
Foot, 66th (2nd Bn. Royal Berkshire Regiment), at Maiwand, 66
Foot, 67th (2nd Hampshires), at Karez Mir, 53
Football, Rugby, tried, 118; Association started, 118; rise of, 120; tournaments, 120, 189, 198, 208, 405, 410, 411, 437, 441, 443
Forbes-Sempill, the Hon. D., killed in withdrawal from Halwai while commanding Seaforths, 196
Fort Lockhart, Samana, 1/5th at, 404
Fort Maud, Khyber, piquetting from, by 3/5th, 355
"Forty-One Years in India," by Lord Roberts, quoted, 123
Fox, W. B. O., wounded at Battle of Ramadi, 292
France, British Officers of 5th Gurkhas serving in, 274, 306-308, 309
French, in Gallipoli, 218, 221, 230, 232, 243
French, Lord, attitude to Gallipoli venture, 217
Frontier unrest, 188

G

Galbraith, Brig.-Gen. W., in command of 2nd Bde., third Black Mountain Expedition, 88
Gallipoli, 1/5th in, 217-271; summary of events leading up to situation at time of arrival of 1/5th, 217, 218; general situation at time of arrival of 1/5th, 220; description of terrain, 220; battle of June 4th, 220, 228; battle of June 28th-July 3rd, 232, 243; battle of August 6th-10th, 246-256; battle of August 21st, 258, 264; capture of Hill 60, 265; trench warfare, 265-268; The Blizzard, 268, 269; evacuation, 269-271; Special Order of the Day, 272, 273
Gandamak occupied by Sir Sam Browne, 43; treaty of, 43
Gandhi, his *Satyagraha* campaign causes unrest, 383

Gardiner, P. F., appointed to command 5th Gurkhas, 30; departure, 32
Garhi, Pariari village destroyed in 1888, 91
Garhwal, Upper, mountain exploration in, 125
Gaselee, A., appointed to command 1/5th, 116; made A.D.C. to Queen, 131; promoted, 137; commands 2nd Bde., Tirah F.F., 141, 151; distinctions won, 452, 453
George V, H.M. King, visit to India as Prince of Wales, 166; Coronation ceremonies and Durbar, 171; message after evacuation of Gallipoli, 273
Germany, Armistice with, 300, 340; influence in Kabul, 353
Ghanba, Regiment present at destruction of, 32
Ghanian, Lieut. Barrett's successful action at, 78
Ghazikot visited by 4th Column in third Black Mountain Expedition, 88
Ghorapher Pass, action at, 92
Giga Khel, village of Abdur Rahman Khel destroyed in 1920, 431
Gilgit, topography of, 105; visited by 1/5th detachment, 107
Gladstone, A. C., in evacuation of Gallipoli, 316; in Battle of Ramadi, 334; distinctions won, 461, 462
Godwin-Austen, Mount, picture in 5th Gurkha Mess, 116
Golf, 127; in Mesopotamia, 342
Gonala Peak near scene of Mummery's disaster, 125
Gorakhpur, accidents at, during first reservists' training, 169
Goria Rana, gallantry at Dwatoi, 145
Gorringe, Major-Gen. G. F., commanding 12th Division, Mesopotamia, 279; commanding Tigris Corps, 280
Gough, Brig.-Gen. Charles, with reinforcements to Sherpur, 62
Gouldsbury, C. A., distinctions won, 461, 462
Govan, D. M., in battle of June 4th, 224, 225; in command of 1/5th, 229; in battle of June 28th, 236, 237; killed in action, 237; tribute to, 237; distinctions won, 456
Graham, A. M., in N.E. Frontier Expedition, 154, 170; killed with 2/2nd Gurkhas in France, 307, 308
Great War of 1914-18, outbreak of, 203, 305, effect of outbreak on units at Abbottabad, 203; 1/5th in defence of Suez Canal, 206-216; 1/5th in Gallipoli, 217-271; 2/5th at Oghi, 308, 309; 2/5th in Mesopotamia, 320, 342; 1/5th in India, 274-278; 1/5th in Mohmand Blockade, 277; 1/5th in Mesopotamia, 278-302; war services of officers and ex-officers not present with the Regiment, 307, 308, 319, App. VII, 481

Greene, H., killed with 1/6th Gurkhas in battle of August 21st, 264
Greenfly, river monitor, sacked by Arabs, 368, 369
Green Patch Farm captured by 1/5th in battle of August 21st, 260, 261, 262, 263
Green Ridge, Waziristan, situation of, 395
Grombtchevsky, Russian explorer, meeting with, 94, 95 ; impressed by smartness of Gurkhas, 96
Guides, Corps of, drafts to 5th Gurkhas when raised, 3, App. I, 449 ; in action at Palosin, 10, 11 ; defence of Embassy at Kabul, 44 ; arrival at Kabul, 59 ; in attack on Takht-i-Shah, 59 ; exploring activities, 124 ; presentation to, by 3/5th, 361
Guides, Corps of, 3rd Bn., raised and commanded by W. D. Villiers-Stuart, 385 ; in Waziristan, 429
Gujranwala, disturbances at, 351
Gulistan, Samana, besieged in 1897, 140 ; 1/5th detachment at, in 1924, 404
Gully Ravine, Gallipoli, 1/5th at, 219
Gumal River, route used by 1st Bde. to Wana in 1895, 135
Guman Sing Gurung, killed with Mummery on Nanga Parbat, 125
Gundigan, village captured in Battle of Kandahar, 71
Gundi Mulla Sahibdad, village captured in Battle of Kandahar, 71
Gun Ridge, Waziristan, situation of, 399
Gurguri, 1/5th at, in 1922, 391
Gurkha, description of, by J. M. Stewart, 80 ; Younghusband's tribute to, 96 ; characteristics, xiv, 177, 178, 236, 352, 445
Gurkha Bluff, Gallipoli (named after 6th Gurkhas), 222, 223
Gurkhas, 1st, in attack on Chittabat, 27 ; at Wana, 133
Gurkhas, 2nd, in Kabul–Kandahar march, 67 ; prominent in Battle of Kandahar, 71 ; at Dargai, 142
Gurkhas, 4/3rd, 1/5th send company to, when raised, 276 ; presentation of cup by, to 1/5th, 276 ; in Waziristan, 425, 426, 432
Gurkhas, 4th, arrival at Ambela, 18 ; in Kabul–Kandahar march, 67 ; in Marri Expedition, 73 ; at Arhanga Pass, 143 ; at Thabai, 148 ; families of 3/5th accommodated by, 350
Gurkhas, 5th, leading part in second Afghan War, xvi ; conduct at Battle of Charasia, xvii ; at Mir Karez, xvii ; raised after Indian Mutiny, 3 ; original armament, 4 ; dress, 4 ; accoutrements, 4 ; lines, 5, 8 ; early recruitment, 8 ; Gurkha Colony, 8 ; in Mahsud-Wazir Expedition, 1860, 9-12 ; baptism of fire at Palosin, 10, 11.

In Ambela Campaign, 13-23 : Action of Conical Hill, 14 ; as reinforcements at Eagle's Nest, Ambela, 18 ; in occupation of Eagle's Nest piquet, 18 ; in charge to save guns, 18 ; gallantry of detachment in withdrawal of covering parties on November 6th, 19 ; in second capture of Crag Piquet, 20 ; successful action during change of dispositions, 20, 21 ; in third recapture of Crag Piquet, 21 ; successful charges during offensive and capture of standard, 22.

Forced march to Oghi, 25 ; harassing duties in Agror, 25, 26 ; in second Black Mountain Expedition, 26-28 ; in attacks on Chittabat and Machai, 27 ; in Jowaki-Afridi Expedition, 30-32.

In Second Afghan War, 34-73 : Join Kurram F.F. under Gen. Roberts, 34 ; advance to Peiwar Kotal, 35, 36 ; action at Spingawai Kotal, 37-40 ; in rearguard action at Monghyr Defile, 41, 42 ; escort to Major Cavagnari, 44 ; occupation of Shutargardan Pass, 45 ; advance towards Kabul, 45 ; action at Charasia, 46-49 ; occupy Bala Hissar and sustain casualties in explosion, 50 ; reach Sherpur, 51 ; with Gen. Macpherson against Kohistanis, 53 ; in action at Karez Mir, 53, 55 ; in action against Muhammad Jan's *lashkar*, 56 ; in assault on Takht-i-Shah, 58, 59 ; holding Takht-i-Shah against enemy attack, 60 ; spirited action in withdrawal from Takht-i-Shah, 60, 61 ; in investment of Sherpur, 62 ; with Gen. Baker to Maidan via Logar Valley, 65 ; in Kabul–Kandahar march, 67-70 ; in Battle of Kandahar, 70, 71 ; in Achakzai Expedition, 72 ; farewell to 72nd Highlanders, 72.

In Marri Expedition, hardships and sickness, 73-75 ; present shield to 72nd Highlanders, 76 ; detachment with Lieut. Barrett in action near Oghi, 78 ; at Rawalpindi and Delhi, 79

Gurkhas, 5th, 1st Battalion : Drafts to 2nd Battalion when raised, 83 ; detachment with Major L. R. Battye on occasion of his death on Black Mountain, 84, 86 ; in third Black Mountain Expedition, 87, 93 ; detachment with Sir F. Younghusband, 94-96 ; at Rawalpindi, 96 ; in Black Mountain promenade, 98 ; in 2nd Miranzai Expedition, 99-104 ; in brilliant attack on Saragarhi, 102 ; detachment in Hunza-Nagir Expedition, 104-115 ; storming of Nilt, 108-111 ; in Isazai Expedition, 117 ; in Kagan, 131 ; in Mahsud-Waziri Expedition of 1894-95, 133-136 ; in Chamkanni Blockade, 137, 138 ; in attack on Sadda, 140 ; in action at Thabai, 145-149 ;

provide contingent of Gurkha Scouts, 139, 142-145, 150-153 ; during peace, 1899-1914, 154-172

IN GREAT WAR, 203-302 :

Embark for Egypt, 204

In Egypt, 206-216 : In Ismailia section of Canal defences, 206-213 ; Turkish attack, 211 ; in Suez Sector, 213-216 ; pursuit of Turkish Column, 214, 215 ; at Shaloufa, 216 ; embark for Gallipoli, 216.

In Gallipoli, 217-271 : arrival, 219

Battle of June 4th, 220-227 : Trench routine, 229, 230 ; good work recognized, 231.

Battle of June 28th, 232-243 : Fighting in J13, 236-240 ; repulse of Turkish counter-attacks, 240-243 ; recognition of good work, 242 ; rest at Imbros, 243-245

Battle of August 6th-10th. 246-256 : Night advance to objective, 251, 252 ; disorganization due to haste, 252 ; progress of attacks in scrub, 252, 253 ; isolation of 3rd D.C., 253-255 ; casualties 255 ; repulse of counter-attacks, 255, 256

Move to Damakjelik Bair, 257 ; trench routine, 257.

Battle of August 21st, 258-264 : Capture and consolidation of Green Patch Farm position, 261-264

Trench warfare at Hill 60, 265-268 ; the Blizzard, 268, 269 ; evacuation, 269, 271

Egypt again, 273, 274 ; return to India, 274 ; reorganization, 275, 276 ; Mohmand Blockade, 277

Arrival in Mesopotamia, 278

In Campaign in Mesopotamia, 283-302 : Meeting with 2/5th, 283 ; join 42nd Bde., 283 ; in operations of Lucas Column, 284-287

Battle of Ramadi, 288-294 : Capture of Middle Hill, 290 ; attack on Ramadi Ridge, 291, 292 ; surrender of Turks, 293 ; good work recognized, 293, 294 ; casualties, 294.

At Ramadi, Madhij and Khan Abu Rayat, 295, 296

Battle of Khan Baghdadi, 297-299 ; capture of Turkish guns, 299

Garrison duty at Ramadi, Jift and Shergat, 300, 301 ; return to India, 302

On internal security duty, 383-385 ; with Kohat-Kurram Force, 386 ; detachments in Agror, 386 ; at Parachinar, 390-391 ; on active service in Waziristan, 391-403 ; on Samana, 404-406 ; Abbottabad, 406-412 ; move to Malakand, 412

Gurkhas, 5th, 2nd Battalion : Raising of, 173, 174 ; efficiency quickly attained, 174, 175 ; detachment in third Black Mountain Expedition, 175 ; in Black Mountain Promenade, 176 ; in fourth Black Mountain Expedition, 177-181 ; in Isazai Expedition, 182 ; detachment in Mahsud Expedition of 1894-95, 183 ; provide contingent of Gurkha scouts in Tirah, 184 ; in Zakka Khel Expedition, 190-198

IN GREAT WAR, 305-343 :

" *C* " *Company with 1/5th in Gallipoli,* 310-317 ; arrival at Imbros, 244, 311; landing at Anzac, 312 ; in battle of August 6th-10th, charge up hillside from Aghyl Dere, 313 ; further advance, 313 ; resistance to Turkish counter-attacks, 314 ; at Damakjelik Bair, 314 ; in Battle of August 21st : advance to forward slopes of Hill 60, 314 ; action in Turkish counter-attack, 315 ; trench warfare at Hill 60, 316 ; the Blizzard, 316 ; provide rearguard in evacuation, 316-317 ; transferred to Mesopotamia, 317

Detachment from Battalion at Oghi in 1915, 319 ; Battalion move to Mohmand Border, 319 ; embark for Mesopotamia, 320

In Campaign in Mesopotamia : Join 42nd Bde., 321 ; work at Basra, 322 ; move to Nasiriya, 322 ; destruction of Abdul Hussein, 323 ; operations against Arabs at As Sahilan, 324, 325 ; move to Baghdad, 328 ; meeting with 1st Battalion, 328 ; furnish garrisons of Tigris posts, 330 ; at Hinaidi and Karada, 330 ; advance to Ramadi, 331.

In Battle of Ramadi, 332-335 ; occupation of Lower Knoll and Dam, 332 ; capture of Mushaid Ridge, 333 ; capture of Double Hill, 333 ; attack on Ramadi Ridge, 333 ; surrender of Turks, 334 ; after the battle at Ramadi and Madhij, 335, 336 ; Khan Abu Rayat and Uqbah, 336, 337 ; night advance to Sahaliya, 338

In Battle of Khan Baghdadi, 338, 339

At Alus, Khan Baghdadi and Ramadi after the battle, 340, 341 ; furnish proclamation Guard of Honour, 340 ; move to Baiji, 341 ; return to India, 342

Garrison duty at Rawalpindi, 413

In Waziristan, 414-433 : Join 67th Bde. under Gen. Lucas, 415 ; arrival at Kotkai, 415 ; capture of Ahnai Tangi Gorge, 416

Action at Ahnai Tangi, 416-418

Operations to cover construction of permanent piquets, 419, 420 ; advance to Sorarogha, 420 ; night operations to secure covering positions for construction of Bluff Piquet, 421; permanent piquet established at Barari Right, 421; operation to establish piquet at Cloud End abandoned owing to bad weather, 422; Cloud End piquet established, 423; advance to Makin, 424; operations round Makin, 425-428; advance to Kaniguram, 429; punishment of Abdur Rahman Khel 431, 432; at Ladha, 432; move to Kotkai, 433; return to Abbottabad, 433; one company to Agror, 434; attack on camp by tribesmen, 435; one company to Waziristan with 2/6th Gurkhas, 439; in the Malakand, 440-443; return to Abbottabad, 443

Gurkhas, 5th, 3rd Battalion: Origin, 347; composition, 347; at Ferozepore, 349; at Rawalpindi, 349; good marching performance, 349, 350; detachment in Marri Expedition of 1918, 350; at Peshawar, 350, 351; in Murree Hills, 351, 352

In Third Afghan War, 353-359: Causes and summary of events, 353, 354; safeguarding the Khyber, 355; operations from Kacha Garhi, 355-358

Peshawar again, 359; at Mardan, 360, 361; mobilization for Mesopotamia, 361

In Arab Rising, Mesopotamia, 362, 379; General situation, 363, 364; advance across desert, 264-366; action at Khidhr, 366-368; punitive measures near Khidhr, 368, 369; relief of Samawa, 369; punitive operations from Samawa, 370-374; action of Imam Abdulla, 374-378; armistice, 378

Garrison duty in Iraq, 378-379; return to India, 379; disbandment, 379, 380

Gurkhas, 1/6th (previously 42nd), arrival in Abbottabad, 160; friendly rivalry, 160, 161; draft to 2/5th when raised, 173; strong detachment of 2nd Battalion in Zakka Khel Expedition, 190

In Gallipoli, 218-271: Arrival, 218; in battle of June 4th, 221, 222, 223, 225; in battle of June 28th, 234, 238-240; in battle of August 6th-10th, 250, 251, 252, 256; with 6th South Lancs. only unit to gain position overlooking Narrows, 250; at Damakjelik, 257; in battle of August 21st, 261, 263

Gurkhas, 2/6th, in Mesopotamia: In 42nd Bde., 283, 321; in Karud Arab Operations, 285; in Battle of Ramadi, 290, 292, 298, 332; in Battle of Khan Baghdadi, 298, 339; at Oghi, 436

Gurkhas, 2/8th, in Waziristan, 1923, 393

Gurkhas, 3/8th, in Arab rising, 366

Gurkhas, 2/9th, in Waziristan, 418, 425, 426, 432

Gurkhas, 2/10th, in Gallipoli, 218-271, 234, 251, 252, 253, 254, 255, 257, 261, 263

Gurkhas, 1/11th, draft from 1/5th when raised, 300; also from 2/5th, 340; in Arab rising, 365, 369, 376

Gurkhas, 3/11th, in Waziristan, 425

Gurlamah Kach, 2/5th bivouac at, before Ahnai Tangi action, 416

Gwada, in Khanki Valley, 101, 104

H

Habbaniyeh Lake, feature of Battle of Ramadi, 289, 291, 331

Habibulla, Amir, murdered, in 1919, 353

Halwai, in Bazar Valley, attack on, destruction of, withdrawal from, in 1908, 195, 196

Hamilton, Vereker, history of his painting, "Storming of Spingawai Kotal," xvi

Hamilton, Gen. Sir Ian, author of foreword to this volume, xv-xx; his connection with Frontier Force and 5th Gurkhas, xv-xvii; his appreciation of Lord Roberts, xviii; his demand for Gurkhas at Gallipoli, xix; as C.-in-C. at Gallipoli, 217, 218, 230, 251, 265, 271

Hammond, V.C., Brig.-Gen., commands Tilli Column in 1891, 177

Hangu, base of 2nd Miranzai Expedition, 100; 1/5th at, in 1924, 404

Hanna, Battle of, 280

Haricot Redoubt, Gallipoli, captured and lost by French, 221, 222; captured and held, 230

Harington, W. G., in battle of August 6th-10th, 255, 313; wounded, 255, 313; commanding 2/5th at As Sahilan, twice wounded, 324; immediate award of D.S.O., 325; in Battle of Ramadi, 332, 333; killed in attack on Ramadi Ridge, 333; tribute to, 334, 335; distinctions won, 461

Harkbahadur Thapa, gallantry at Hill 60, 267

Harkbir Thapa, with Martin Conway Expedition, 116; gallantry at Thol Cliffs, 114; great running feat in Skye, 124; in Alps, 126; ambushes Turkish patrol, 210

Harnai Railway, raided by Marri tribesmen, 78

Haro, River, in Northern Command manœuvres of 1925, 408

Harrison, T. R., gallantry in pursuit of raiders, 357, 358; distinctions won, 465

Hart, V.C., Brig.-Gen., in Tirah, 1897, 141

Hasan Abdal, forced march to, by 2/5th, in 1908, 190; 1/5th detachment at, during Punjab unrest, 384

Hashim Ali, chief of Hassanzai, 116, 178, 181

Hassanzais, location on Black Mountain, 24; attack by, on Oghi, 25; operations against, 27, 89, 90, 177-181

Hatala, 2/5th at, 414

Havelian, 1/5th detachment at, during Punjab unrest, 384
Hawkes, G., commands 2/5th, 183
Hay-Webb, A. B., in Abor Expedition, 154, 170; mortally wounded in battle of August 21st, 262; tribute to, 264; distinctions won, 456
Hazara District, transfer from Kashmir, 5; during Second Sikh War, 6, 7; annexed and James Abbott appointed Deputy Commissioner, 7
Hazara Goorkha Battalion, original alternative title of 5th Gurkhas, 3
Hazara Mountain Battery (24th), at Conical Hill and Eagle's Nest, Ambela, 17; in third Black Mountain Expedition, 88; in Hunza-Nagir Expedition, 106.
Hazara Singh, gallantry at Nilt, 109, 110
Hazro, 1/5th at, in Northern Command manœuvres of 1925, 408
Heat, on N.W. Frontier and in Afghanistan, 25, 68, 69, 103, 355, 356; in Gallipoli, 251, 254; in Mesopotamia, 286, 287, 323, 330, 365
Helles, in Gallipoli, landing effected at, 218; topography, 220; fighting at, 220-230, 232-243, 248
Helmand River, connection with Maiwand disaster, 66
Hetman Chair, Gallipoli, objective of 11th Div. in battle of August 21st, 258, 260
Heyland, A. A., with 1/1st Gurkhas in France, 309; killed at Festubert, 309
Highland Light Infantry (71st), in action at Conical Hill, Ambela, 17; in third recapture of Crag Piquet, Ambela, 21
Highlanders, 72nd (Seaforths), in attack on Spingawai Kotal, 38; at Monghyr defile, 41; at Charasia, 47, 48; kindness to 5th Gurkhas after Bala Hissar explosion, 51; in assault on Takht-i-Shah, 58, 59; brigaded with 5th Gurkhas in Kabul-Kandahar march, 67; prominent in Battle of Kandahar, 71; in Achakzai Expedition, 72; friendship with 5th Gurkhas, 51, 72, 76; in Zakka Khel Expedition, 191, 194, 195, 197; entertain 2/5th at Nowshera, 198
Highlanders, 92nd (Gordons), at Charasia, 49; in attack on Takht-i-Shah, 59; in Battle of Kandahar, 71; at Dargai, 142
Hijrat, cause of unrest, 386, 434
Hill, Col., commanding in Kurram, 145, 146
Hill Q, feature figuring in attack from Anzac, 247, 249, 250, 252, 253, 254, 255, 256
Hill race, 121, 124, 165, 171, 198
Hill 60. See Kaiajik Aghala
Hill 70. See Scimitar Hill.
Himlal Khattri, good work at Imam Abdulla, 377

Hinaidi, Mesopotamia, 42nd Bde. at, 283-287; operations from, 284-287
Hindustani Fanatics, history of, 13, 14; outrages by, lead to Ambela Campaign, 14; operations against, 88, 117, 178; activity in 1915, 318
Hisarak, visited by 5th Gurkhas, 65; on route of Kabul-Kandahar march, 68.
Hispar Glacier, exploration of, 116
Hit, Turkish L. of C. to, from Ramadi, 289, 290; Turks at, after Ramadi, 296; Turkish withdrawal from, 296, 297; occupied by 50th Bde., 297, 337; 15th Div. at, 297, 337
Hobbs, J. M., wounded at Makin, 426; distinctions won after joining 2/5th, 463
Holdich, H. A., enters Staff College, 170; wounded in Mesopotamia, 1915, 319; awarded D.S.O. for distinguished service on the Staff, 326; distinctions won, 460, 461; other services, 483
Honours of 5th Gurkhas, Appendix II, 450
Hunter, E. H., killed in battle of August 6th-10th, 255, 313; distinctions won, 456
Hunter Weston, Sir A., commanding VIII Corps in Gallipoli, 232
Hunza Valley, visited by exploring party, 94; topography, 105
Hussars, 14th, in Mesopotamia, 284, 285

I

Imam Abdulla, reconnaissance of, 371, 372; action at, 374-378
Imam Hamza, Mesopotamia, visited in operations of Lucas Column, 285
Imam Jaubah, 3/5th at, 372
Imbros, 1/5th at, in 1915, 244, 245
Influenza, in Mesopotamia, 300; in Abbottabad, 385
Inspections, by Col. Wilde, in 1861, 12; by Brig.-Gen. Keyes, 1874, 29; by Brig.-Gen. Roberts, 31; others, 155, 156; of 2/5th, 175, 176, 185; of 3/5th by Gen. Sir C. Monro, 361; by Lord Rawlinson, 380
Isazai Expedition, 117, 182
Ismail Oglu Tepe, feature of Suvla area, Gallipoli, 243, 258, 259, 260
Ismailia, 1/5th at, in 1914, 206-213

J

J9, J10, J11 trenches captured by 87th Bde. in battle of June 28th, 233
J11a trench, cleared by 86th Bde. in battle of June 28th, 234
J12 trench, lodgment effected in, 234
J13 trench, lodgment effected in, 234; occupied by 1/6th Gurkhas, 234; hard fighting in, by 1/5th and 1/6th Gurkhas, 236-240

Jacob, Major-Gen. A. le G., commanding Kohat District, 405 ; farewell message, to 1/5th, 406
Jaliran Spur, feature of Battle of Kandahar, 70
Jal Pass, roadmaking at, by 1/5th in 1888, 89
Jamrud, 2/5th at, in 1908, 191, 197 ; 3/5th at, in 1919, 355
Jamu Valley, visited by Regiment, 31
Jandola, 1/5th at, 133, 135
Jangbir Thapa, Sepoy, 5th Gurkhas, gallantry of, in action at Ambela, 19
Jangia Thapa, Lord Roberts' orderly and nicknamed "Bullets," 137 ; visits Australia, 158
Janjal, on Tank Zam, 2/5th at, 423
Jebel Hamrin (Mountains), Turkish position on, 288
Jift, 1/5th join 55th Bde. at, 301
Johnson, C. R., arrival in Mesopotamia to command 2/5th, 323
Johnson, Col. Frank, Administrator of Martial Law in Lahore, 384
Joke, of soft stones, 95 ; of bleached bone, 97 ; of Mr. B's stories, 97 ; of C.O.'s charger, 97 ; of Japanese Attaché, 189
Jourdain, Col., commanding 5th Connaught Rangers in Gallipoli, 263
Jowaki-Afridis, Regiment in expedition against, 30-32
Jubbah, 42nd Bde. at, after Khan Baghdadi, 300, 339
Jubilee of 5th Gurkhas, 171, 196
Juthe Gurung, Subadar, gallantry and death in battle of June 4th, 226

K

Kabak Kuyu, feature north of Anzac position, Gallipoli, 257 ; captured in battle of August 21st, 258, 260, 261, 262, 263
Kabir Thapa, good work at Imam Abdulla, 377, 378
Kabul, murder of British envoy at, 44 ; occupied by Sir F. Roberts, 60 ; temporarily abandoned, 60 ; re-occupied, 63 ; fighting around, 52-63
Kabul F.F., composition, 45 ; operations by, 45-64
Kabul–Kandahar F.F., composition, 67 ; march of, 67-70 ; in Battle of Kandahar, 70, 71
Kacha Garhi, 3/5th at, 354
Kafir Jan Defile, Afghan attack on convoy at, 57
Kagan, mountain climbing in, 126 ; expedition to, 131, 132 ; summer camps in, 155, 189
Kagan Village, 1/5th at, 131
Kage Oba, 1/5th at, in 1888, 92

Kahan, halt at, amid fine surroundings in Marri Expedition, 75
Kaiajik Aghala (Hill 60), feature figuring in attack from Anzac, 247 ; objective of Gen. Cox's Column on August 21st, 258, 259, 260, 261, 262, 263 ; final capture of, 265 ; 1/5th at, 265-270
Kaj Nag, good shooting in, 118
Kajuri Plain, inhabited by Afridis, 100 ; 3/5th at, 354
Kakul, Boer prisoners at, 161 ; Nepalese contingent at, 276 ; 3/5th mobilize at, 361
Kalabagh, Murree Hills, war-time camp at, 350
Kalat-i-Ghilzai, garrison of, evacuated, 69
Kale Gurung, enterprise in battle of August 6th-10th, 313
Kaman Sing Burathoki, enterprise at Sampagha Pass, 143 ; gallantry at Dwatoi, 145
Kandahar occupied by Sir D. Stewart, 43 ; investment of, after Maiwand, 67 ; relief of, 70 ; battle of, 70, 71
Kaniguram, visited by expedition of 1860, 11 ; advance to, in 1920, 429 ; 2/5th at, 429, 430, 432
Kanjut, topography of country, 105
Kanjutis, inhabitants of Hunza and Nagir: characteristics, 105 ; in expedition of 1891, 108, 114
Kantara, in Suez Canal defences, 208 ; attacked by Turks, 209 ; skirmishes at, 210
Kapurthala Infantry, disaster in Kharmana Defile, 145, 146
Karachi, embarkation and disembarkation at, 205, 274, 278, 302, 310, 320, 362, 379
Karada, Mesopotamia, 42nd Bde. at, 287, 288
Karakol Dagh, Gallipoli, feature of Suvla area, 251
Karakoram Mountains, exploration of, 94
Karakoram Pass, crossed by exploring party, 94
Karbir Burathoki, with Martin Conway Expedition, 116 ; with Mumm in Garhwal, 125 ; in Alps, 126 ; brilliant coup at Maidan (Tirah), 144
Karez Hill, feature of Battle of Kandahar, 70, 71
Karud Arabs, operations against, by Lucas Column, 284-287
Kashmir, scene of mountain exploration, 125
Kashmir Infantry, in Hunza-Nagir Expedition, 107
Kasirin, post on Tigris garrisoned by 2/5th, 330
Kazlar Chair, feature north of Anzac position, Gallipoli, 257
Kemball, A. H. G., in Gilgit, 106, 115 ; characteristic action when commanding 1/5th, 168 ; retirement, 170 ; distinctions won, 460 ; other services and distinctions, 483

Kempster, Col. F. J., in Tirah, 1897, 141
Kenny's Peak, near Makin, feature of operation, February 25th, 1920, 428
Keshan, Turkish forces at, 248
Ketchen, S. D. B., death on Safed Koh, 161
Keyes, Sir Charles, commanding P.F.F., 1874, xv; his action at Barari Gorge in 1860, xv; in command of 1st P.I. at action of Conical Hill, 17; in command of Jowaki-Afridi Expedition, 31, 32
Khabal, on Indus, 5th Gurkhas at destruction of, 23
Khabbal Hill, Agror, affair at, 26
Khaisara Nullah, 1/5th at, in 1895, 135
Khaisora River, 5th Gurkhas at, in 1860, 11; new road up, 391
Khan Abu Rayat, part of 42nd Bde. at, after Ramadi, 296, 366; 1/5th detachments at, after Khan Baghdadi, 300
Khan Baghdadi, battle of, secrecy, 297; plan, 297; progress of attack, 297, 298; 42nd Bde. in the battle, 298, 299, 338, 339
Khan Maqdam, operations of Lucas Column at, 285
Khan Nuktah, 42nd Bde. at, in advance to Ramadi, 289, 331
Khandi Mishti, towers destroyed in second Miranzai Expedition, 104
Khanki River, topographical situation, 99; inhabited by Orakzais, 100
Kharai Pass, situation, 103; heavy rain at, 104
Khar Ghundai, in Bazar Valley, 194
Kharki Jheel, good shooting at, 118, 119
Kharmana Valley, entered in second Miranzai Expedition, 104; reconnaissance of, 145, 146
Khidhr, position on railway, 364; action at, 366-368
Khirgi, 2/5th at, in 1920, 415
Khojak Pass, seized by Achakzais, 72.
Khora Bort Pass, crossed by J. M. Stewart, 125
Khorappa, Tirah F.F. at, F. F. Badcock wounded at, 142
Khor Tarmiya, Lucas Column at, 286
Khost, Sir F. Roberts's visit to, 42; proximity to British frontier, 386
Khudhaira Bend, on Tigris, gains extended to, 281
Khunainiyah, on Euphrates, 3/5th in action at, 374
Khwaja Khidr, boundary delimitation at, 135
Khyber Pass, held in 1878-80, 34, 43; inhabited by Afridis, 100; Afridi attack on, 139; 3/5th in, 354, 355
Khyber Rifles, in third Black Mountain Expedition, 88, 92; in fourth expedition, 177, 179, 180; in Zakka Khel Expedition, 191

Kila Abdulla, 5th Gurkhas at, in Achakzai Expedition, 72
Kila Kazi, Gen. Massy's unsuccessful action at, 56
Kilmarnock caps, introduction of, 24
King's Own Yorkshire Light Infantry, 1st Bn., in Arab Rising, 370
Kiritch Tepe Sirt, feature of Suvla area, Gallipoli, 248
Kirman Nullah, 1/5th at, in 1897, 138
Kishanbir Nagarkoti, first award of Order of Merit, 42; promotion from 3rd to 2nd Class and 2nd to 1st Class Order of Merit, 64; extreme gallantry on occasion of Major Battye's death, and special award of gold bar for wear on ribbon of Order of Merit, 84-86; granted special pension, 115
Kitchener, Lord, his reforms of Indian Army, 167; visits to Abbottabad, 186
Kitchener tests, 167, 188
Knight Templar, s.s., takes 1/5th from Mudros to Egypt, 273
Knowles, I. G., in battle of June 4th, 224; wounded in battle of August 21st, 264
Kohat, 5th Gurkhas at, in 1878, 34; 1/5th at, in 1891, 100; 2/5th at, in 1902, 188; 1/5th at, in 1920, 386; football and shooting successes at, in 1924, 405; F.F. War Memorial at, 406
Kohat Mountain Battery (21st), in Agror, 116; in Kagan, 131; at Thabai, 148; in Gallipoli, 249, 251; in Mesopotamia, 324
Kohat Toi, course of, in relation to Miranzai Plain, 99
Kohistanis, advance on Kabul from north, 53; stand at Mir Karez, 53; possibility of trouble with, 131
Koja Chemen Tepe, highest point of Sari Bair, 220, 247, 249, 251
Kolahoi, first ascent of, 125
Kolu Plateau, traversed in Marri Expedition, 74
Kopra, Pariari Village destroyed, in 1888, 91
Kot Najibullah, manœuvres at, 407
Kotal-i-Takht, visited by 5th Gurkhas, 65
Kotkai, Waziristan, 2/5th at, 415, 433
Kress von Kressenstein, Chief of Staff with Turkish forces moving on Suez Canal, 208
Krithia, Gallipoli, 220; third battle of, 220-228; Turkish forces opposing at, 248
Kubra, on Suez Canal, skirmish at, 210
Kubri, in Suez section of Canal defence, 213; approach of Turkish column to, 213; 1/5th in pursuit of Turkish column from, 214, 215; 1/5th at, after Gallipoli, 274
Kulbahadur Gurung, in first ascent of Mount Kolahoi, 125; selected for special duty in Gallipoli, 245; retires and becomes Hon. Captain, 402
Kulbahadur Rai, gallantry at Makin, 440

Kulu, scenes of mountain exploration, 125
Kundiwam, in Southern Waziristan, 135
Kunhar, on Indus, visited by 4th Column in Black Mountain Expedition, 1888, 88
Kupiri Algad, Waziristan, difficult track up, 393
Kurram Field Force, 1878, composition, 35; operations, 35-44
Kurram Fort, occupation by Field Force, 36
Kurram River, route up, in 1878, 35, 36
Kurram Valley, events in 1847, 140, 145-149
Kushk-i-Nakhud, connection with Maiwand disaster, 66
Kut (Kut-al-Amara), Turks defeated at, 279; operations for relief of, 280; fall of, 280
Kwar, in Bazar Valley, destroyed in 1908, 195

L

Ladha, Waziristan, 2/5th at, 429, 432, 433
Lagardara Valley, situation, 103; visited in second Miranzai Expedition, 104
Lahore, 1/5th at, on way to Egypt, 205; disturbances at, 351; 1/5th detachment at, 384
Lahoul, mountain exploration in, 125
Lake, Sir P., in chief command in Mesopotamia, 280, 281
Lakka, on Samana, 1/5th lead advance to, 101
Lala Baba, Gallipoli, feature north of Anzac position, 259
Lala China, in Khyber, 2/5th at, in 1908, 191, 197
Lalitbahadur Mal, good work at Imam Abdulla, 377
Lancashire Fusiliers, in Gallipoli, 221
Lancers, 9th, gallantry at Kila Kazi, 56
Lancers, 37th, in Arab Rising, 372, 375
Landi Kotal, Gurkha scouts at, 151; wing of 2/5th at, in 1908, 191
Lane, H. R. C., in charge of Kalabagh Camp, 350; commanding 3/5th at Shamgakki, 356; in Arab Rising, 371, 373, 376; in temporary command of 1/5th at Parachinar, 390; in temporary command of 1/5th in operations in Waziristan, 395; distinctions won, 458, 459, 460, 465
Laram, boundary delimitation at, 135
Lataband Pass, communication opened through, to Khyber, 52
Latamber, 1/5th at, in 1922, 391
Lawrencepur, 1/5th guarding railway from and to, 384
Leh, visited by exploring party, 94
Lemnos, aspect of harbour during Gallipoli Campaign, 219, 311
Lines, earliest occupied by 5th Gurkhas, 5; new built, 8; at Oghi, 29; building of new, for 1/5th, 83; for 2/5th, 174

Lloyd, D. I. B., wounded in battle of June 28th, 241; killed in action, 256; tribute to, 264; distinctions won, 456
Loch, H. N., in Arab Rising, 366, 371
Lockhart, Sir William, in command of second Miranzai Expedition, 100; in command of Isazai Expedition, 117; of Mahsud–Waziri Expedition, 1894-95, 135; of Tirah Expedition, 139
Logar River, advance of Kabul F.F., 45; abandoned as line of communication, 52
Lone Pine, feature figuring in attack from Anzac, Gallipoli, 247, 249
Longstaff, Dr., in exploration of Upper Garhwal peaks, 125
Lora, Pariari village destroyed in 1888, 91
Lowarai Pass, good work by 2/5th at, 184
Lucas, C. C. St. E., distinctions won, 450, 451
Lucas, F. G., responsible for development of football, 120; commands Gurkha Scouts in Tirah, 139; brilliant success at Thabai, 148; in Waziristan Blockade, 160; Brevet Majority and D.S.O. for work with Gurkha Scouts, 184; in Bazar Valley Expedition of 1908, 191, 193, 197; appointed Commandant, 2/5th, 199; in command of 42nd Bde., 282, 283, 284-287, 296, 322, 328, 336; commanding 67th Bde. in Waziristan, 1919-20, 415-433; death in England, 438; tribute to, 438; distinctions won, 460, 461; other services and distinctions, 483
Lumsden, Col. H., in command at Palosin, 10; his commendation of 5th Gurkhas, 11

M

Macgregor, Brig.-Gen., in command of Marri Expedition, 73
Machai, highest point of Black Mountain, 24; climbed by elephants, 27; bad weather at, 28; 1/5th at, in 1888, 91
Machi Khel, 1/5th in punishment of, 135
Machine guns, competition shooting, 1/5th, 411; 2/5th, 443
Mackenzie, Colin, in Hunza-Nagir Expedition, 108, 110, 112
Mackintosh, K. J., wounded at Ramadi, 291; mortally wounded at Ahnai Tangi, 418
Maconchy, G. A., killed in action at Ahnai Tangi, 417
Macpherson, Brig.-Gen., commands 1st Bde., Kabul F.F., 45; move against Kohistanis, success at Karez Mir, 53-55; action against Muhammad Jan's *lashkar*, 56; withdrawal to Sherpur, 60
McQueen, Major-Gen. J. W., in command of third Black Mountain Expedition, 87; visit to Black Mountain, 98
Madaglasht, Chitral, 1/5th camps at, 164

Madhij, 1/5th on outposts at, before Ramadi, 289; 42nd Bde. at, after Ramadi, 295, 335; 2/5th on outposts at, before Ramadi, 331

Magil, Mesopotamia, 1/5th at, 1917, 278; 2/5th at, 1916, 321

Magniac, Lieut.-Col., murdered by Arabs, 284

Mahsud Wazirs, expedition of 1860, 9-12; of 1894-95, 133-136; outrages by, near Makin, 391; in operations of 1922-23, 393, 394, 396, 397; in 1919-20 operations, 415-433. *See also under* Waziristan

Maidan (Afghanistan), advance of Muhammad Jan from, 53; 5th Gurkhas at, 65

Maidan, Hindustani settlement on Indus, destroyed 1888, 89

Maidan (Tirah), inhabited by Afridis, 100; Tirah F.F. at, 144

Maidhar Gharti, gallant action in advance to Walai, 193

Maion, position of, 108

Maiwand, disaster at, 65-67

Maizar, treachery of Mada Khel at, 138

Makin, destroyed in 1860, 11; 1/5th at, in 1894-95, 134; 7th and 9th Bdes. in punitive operations at, 394; 2/5th in operations at, 424-428

Makranai, 2/5th at, in 1891, 179

Mali-Ka-Sar, ascent of, 126

Malakand, outbreak at, 138; 1/5th at, 412; 2/5th at, 440-443

Malka, stronghold of Hindustani Fanatics, 14; destroyed by Bunerwals, 23

Mamand, 5th Gurkhas at, in Marri Expedition, 74

Mamuzai, section of Orakzais, 103

Mana-ka-Dana occupied in second Black Mountain Expedition, 27; in third expedition, 89

Manchester Bde., in third Battle of Krithia, 221, 222

Mandai, 5th Gurkhas at, in Marri Expedition of 1880, 24

Mandi, 5th Gurkhas at destruction of, 23

Maniraj Gharti, winner of Hill Race, 123

Maniram Pun, gallantry at Dwatoi, 145

Manners-Smith, J., in Hunza-Nagir Expedition, 108, 110; gains V.C. at storming of Thol Cliffs, 112-114

Manœuvres, at Hasan Abdal, 29; at Delhi, 79; at Rawalpindi, 96; at Attock, 157, 176; in Yusafzai, 188; at Kot Majibullah, 407; between Hatti and Attock, 408, 409; between Gujrat and Jhelum, 412

Mansaram Pun, gallantry in battle of August 6th-10th, 313; wounded in explosion of Turkish mine, 316

Mansehra, unrest at, 434

Marble Arch, feature of Ahnai Tangi action, 416; piquet established on, 419

March, J. C., killed in action at Ahnai Tangi, 417

March Past of 5th Gurkhas, 171

Marches, noteworthy, to Oghi, 25; Karez Mir-Sherpur, Takht-i-Shah-Sherpur, 53, 56, 58, 60, 61; Kabul-Kandahar, 68-70; in Marri country, 74; Delhi-Abbottabad, 80; Mazrai-Kage Oba, 92; Sangar-Chikar Kot-Hangu, 103; Parachinar-Sadda, 140; Abbottabad-Hasan Abdal, 190; in pursuit of Turks from Kubri, 214; against Samaikcheh Arabs, 286; Fateh Jang-Rawalpindi, 349; in Khyber, 355; Kacha Garhi-Shamgakki-Besai, 355, 357

Mardan, 3/5th at, 360

Margalla Pass, camp at, in 1908, 168, 198; 1/5th guarding railway from and to Lawrencepur, 384

Marindin, J. F., wounded at Battle of Ramadi, 333

Markhor, variations of type, 164

Marobi, 1/5th at destruction of, 134; 2/5th engaged during advance to, 424

Marri Expedition of 1880, 73-75; of 1918, 350

Martin, A. R., prominent in Battle of Charasia, 48; in command of 1/5th on Samana, 1891, 100; directs brilliant attack on Saragarhi, 102; A.A.G. in Mahsud Expedition of 1894-95, 137; appointed commandant 1/5th, 137; appointed D.A.G., 157; appointed Colonel, 5th Gurkhas, 389; death in England, 409; tribute to, 410; distinctions won, 450, 451, 452, 453; other services, 484

Martin, E. C. de R., services after leaving 5th Gurkhas, 484

Martin, E. W. F., commandant 2/5th, 185; death at Abbottabad, 187

Massy, Brig.-Gen., commands Cavalry Bde., Kabul F.F., 45; unsuccessful action at Kila Kazi, 56

Massy, F. S., appointed Commandant of 2/5th, 443; of 1/5th, 412

Mastan, part of Samana, capture of, 101

Mastura River, topographical situation, 99; inhabited by Orakzais, 100; march of 2nd Div., Tirah F.F., 150

Matheson, Major-Gen. Sir T., commanding in Waziristan, 394; his farewell message to 1/5th, 404

Maton, visited by Gen. Roberts, 42

Maude, Lieut.-Gen. Sir F. S., in chief command in Mesopotamia, 281, 304, 323, 335; death from cholera, 335

Maxim gun, first used on service in Isazai Expedition, 117; issued to 1/5th, 161; to 2/5th, 188

Mazrai Pass, crossed on way to Allai in 1888 expedition, 92

Meerut, individual shooting championships at, 408, 411
Mendali, on Persian Frontier, occupation of, 331
Mesopotamia, campaign in, 278-343; summary of events up to arrival of 1/5th, 278-282; situation at time of arrival of 1/5th, 282; 2/5th in, 280, 320-42; 1/5th in, 278, 283-302; events leading up to Arab Rising, 363, 364; 3/5th in, 362-379
Mess, of 5th Gurkhas, 128, 129
Metcalfe, E. D. T., services after leaving 5th Gurkhas, 484
Middle Hill, feature of Battle of Ramadi, 290, 291, 292, 293
Mine, explosion of Turkish, at Hill 60, 270
Minerva, H.M.S., in Suez Canal Defence, 209
Mines, use of, by Turks against warships, 217
Mintaka Pass, crossed by exploring party, 94
Miranzai, second expedition, 99-104
Mirian, on Tochi, 134, 135
Mir Muhammad (styled Mushk-i-Alam) rouses Afghans after occupation of Kabul, 52
Mirpur Jheel, snipe shooting at, 119
Mirzail, concentration at, in 1895, 136
Mizaihar-al-Jarudh-al-Shinabirah, feature of action at Imam Abdulla, 375, 377
Mohmand Expedition, of 1908, 168; blockade of 1916, 1/5th in, 277
Moia Harab, occupied by Turks, 209
Molloy, E., promoted Brevet Major, 77; raises and commands 2/5th, 173, 174; in fourth Black Mountain Expedition, 177, 178; delicate mission entrusted to, 181; departure owing to ill health, 182; death at Lugano, 187; distinctions won, 451, 452, 460
Molloy, H. T., good work in Gorakhpur accident, 169; in battle of August 21st, 262, 263, 315; exceptional services earn belated award of D.S.O., 263; wounded, 266; with 2/2nd Gurkhas in France, 306, 307, 308; appointed Commandant 2/5th, 443; other services, 484; distinctions won, 454, 460
Mountain Battery, No. 1, at Peiwar Kotal, 37; at Monghyr Defile, 41; at Karez Mir, 53, 54
Mountain Battery, No. 2, at Charasia, 47, 48
Mountain Battery, No. 3, in second Miranzai Expedition, 101; in Zakka Khel Expedition, 195
Mountain Battery, No. 9, in fourth Black Mountain Expedition, 177, 179
Mountain Battery, 27th, in Waziristan, 428
Mountain Warfare School, W. D. Villiers-Stuart in charge, 385; 1/5th provide demonstration troops, 387

Mudros, 1/5th leave, for Egypt, 273
Mufraz, on Euphrates, Lucas Column at, 284, 285, 286
Muhammad Akram Khan. *See* Amb, Khan of
Muhammad Aslam Khan, in command of Khyber Rifles, 88, 178; injured at Abu, 178
Muhammad Jan, leads gathering from Maidan and Ghazni, 53
Mulla Powindah, causes unrest, 133
Multan, 1/5th detachment at, 384
Mumm, in exploration of Upper Garhwal peaks, 125
Mummery, killed on Nanga Parbat, 125
Murray, the Hon. A. C., services after leaving 5th Gurkhas, 484
Mushaid Ridge, Turkish position at Battle of Ramadi, 289, 290, 331, 332
Mushk-i-Alam. *See* Mir Muhammad

N

Nadir Khan, Afghan Commander-in-Chief in 1919, 353; advance to Thal, 354
Nafata, Turkish patrols at, after Ramadi, 296
Nagdu, Sepoy, daring and resource at Thol Cliffs, 112, 113
Nagir, topography, 105
Nagoman, on Mohmand border, 2/5th at, 319
Nahr-al-Gulaidh, feature of action at Khidhr, 366
Nahr-as-Suwaili, feature of action at Khidhr, 366
Naine Bura, gallantry at Makin, 427
Nakatu Pass, at head of Daradar Valley, crossed in second Miranzai Expedition, 104
Nandabahadur Thapa, notable shooting achievements at Meerut, 411
Nandiharis, location on Black Mountain, 24; visited in second Black Mountain Expedition, 28
Nanga Parbat, Mummery and two Gurkha orderlies, killed on, 125
Naran, in Kagan, 131
Narbahadur Gurung, gallantry in battle of August 6th-10th, 314
Nasiriya, Turkish resistance at, overcome, 279; 15th Div. at, 282; 2/5th at, 322-327; 3/5th at, 364
Nasrulla, becomes Amir after murder of Habibulla, 353
Native Infantry, 14th, in Ambela Campaign, 21; in Mahsud Expedition of 1894-95, 135; in Gallipoli, 218, 221, 240, 251, 257, 261, 263
Naval Division, in Gallipoli, 220, 221
Navy, in Suez Canal defence, 209, 210, 211; in Dardanelles, 217, 232, 233, 241, 250, 254
Neave, Dr., in first ascent of Mount Kolahoi, 125
Nejef, religious centre of Iraq, 368

INDEX 511

Nepal, war contribution of, 276, 319, 383
Nepean, H. D. H. Y., in battle of August 21st, 263; wounded, 264; saves a drowning man, 284; wounded at Ramadi, 292; at Khan Baghdadi, 298; distinctions won, 457, 458
New Zealand Forces, in Suez Canal defence, 209; friendship with Gurkhas, 210, 276; in Gallipoli, 220, 232, 243, 249, 250, 251, 253, 254, 257, 258, 260, 261, 265
Nibruncsi Point, southern promontory of Suvla Bay, Gallipoli, 248
Nicholson, C. J., appointed 5th Gurkhas, 4
Nightingale, M. R. W., appointed to Gurkha scouts in 1898, 151; in China, 154; in battle of June 4th, 224; wounded and awarded D.S.O., 226; assumes command of 1/5th on recovery from wounds, 275; commanding 1/5th in Mesopotamia, 287, 292, 295, 333; commanding 54th Bde., 295; farewell message from, 389; commanding 5th Bde. in Waziristan, 402; other services, 485; distinctions won, 454, 455, 456, 457, 458
Nilt, topography of, 108; storming of, 108-111
Nimbal, summer camp at, 437
Nixon, Sir J., commanding in Mesopotamia, 279, 280
Northamptonshire Regiment, disaster at Saran Sar, 144
Northumberland Fusiliers (1st Bn.), in third Black Mountain Expedition, 88, 89, 92; friendship with 5th Gurkhas, 169; presentation of football cup by, 121, 198
Nowshera, 1/5th at, in 1916, 277
Nukhailah, on Euphrates, 3/5th in action at, 373, 374
Nushik La, first traversed by Martin Conway Expedition, 116

O

Ocean, H.M.S., in Suez Canal defence, 209
Oghi, position in relation to Black Mountain, 24; attacked by tribesmen, 25, 435, 436; forced march to, by 5th Gurkhas, 25; building lines at, 29; Lieut. Barrett's successful action from, 78; force stormbound at, 98; small column at, in fourth Black Mountain Expedition, 177; unrest at, in 1915, 319, 386, 434; post war occupation, 386, 434-436
Ogilvy, J. D., in temporary command of 2/5th, 432
Oliphant, J. S., 5th Gurkhas, death from wounds in action, Ambela, 19
Oprang Valley, traversed by exploring party, 94
Orakzais, situation of territory of, 100; in second Miranzai Expedition, 100-104; in Tirah Expedition, 141-143

Organization, of 5th Gurkhas, originally wing system, 23, 118; double company system introduced, 158; Headquarter Wing instituted, 389; Training Company instituted, 409

P

Pala visited by Regiment, 31
Palin, Lieut.-Col., commanding Indian Bde. in battle of August 21st, 260
Palosi-on-Indus occupied in fourth Black Mountain Expedition, 178, 179
Palosin, 5th Gurkhas in action at, 1860, xvi, 10, 11; 2/5th at, 415
Pamirs, exploration of passes, 94
Pani Patiya, Hindu ceremony of purification, 379, 383
Panjdeh, Russian act of aggression at, and consequences, 80, 81
Parachinar, 1/5th at, in 1897, 138, 140; 1/5th at, in 1922, 390
Parbal Gurung, Subadar-Major, responsible for tree planting, 8
Parbir Thapa, with Martin Conway Expedition, 116; in Alps, 126
Pariari Saiyads, location on Black Mountain, 25; attack by, on Oghi, 25; operations against, 27, 91; blockade of, 78
Parsu Khattri, awarded Order of Merit at Peiwar Kotal, 40; gallantry at Thabai and promotion to 2nd Class of Order, 147; retires, 158
Partiman Rana, good work at Hill 60, 270
Paterson, G. S. V., wounded at Battle of Ramadi, 292
Pathans, in hill races against Gurkhas, 123, 135, 151, 196
Peiwar Kotal, picture by Vereker Hamilton, xvi; reconnaissance, 36; action at, 37-40
Peshawar, 1/5th pass through, in 1895, 136; 1/5th at, in 1908, 167; 1/5th at, in 1916, 274, 275; 3/5th at, 350, 359
Peshawar Mountain Battery (23rd), with Regiment at Oghi, 25; at capture of Saragarhi, 102
Pezu, 1/5th at, in 1895, recovery of Mess property, 135, 184
Philipps, I., distinctions gained with 5th Gurkhas, 453; other services and distinctions, 485
Piaza Raghza, 2/5th at, 424
Pioneer Peak climbed by Martin Conway Expedition, 110
Pioneers, 23rd, at Peiwar Kotal, 39; at Monghyr Defile, 41; at Charasia, 47, 48, 49; in Kagan, 131 *et seq.*
Pioneers, 32nd, in fourth Black Mountain Expedition, 177
Pipe Band of 2/5th, 198, 443

Piquets on N.W. Frontier, 10, 18, 20, 21, 25, 140, 145, 194, 195, 392, 393, 394, 398, 399-403, 416-418, 419-424
Pir Ghal Mountain in Waziristan, 134
Pir Gumat Shah, 1/5th at, in Northern Command manœuvres of 1925, 408
Pir Paimal Spur, feature of Battle of Kandahar, 70
Pisan, in Hunza Valley, 114
Plunkett, R. F. D., drowned in Mesopotamia, 300
Pokal, arduous march to, in 1888, 93; action at and destruction of, 93
Policy, Frontier, 390
Polo, 126, 127, 437, 439
Port Said, 1/5th embark at, 216
Potah, 2/5th at, 414
Potwala Ravine, 1/5th at, in 1894, 134
Powell, C. F., mortally wounded at Monghyr Defile, 43; distinctions won, 450
Powlett, P. W., first Adjutant, 5th Gurkhas, 4
Poynder, Lieut., good work in J13, Gallipoli, 239
Presentation of Shield by 5th Gurkhas to 72nd Highlanders, 76; of drum-major's staff by 72nd to 5th Gurkhas, 76
Primrose, Lieut.-Gen., succeeds Sir D. Stewart at Kandahar, 65; invested after Maiwand, 67
Prisoners, treatment of Turkish, by Gurkhas, 215
Punaram Khattri, good work at Imam Abdulla, 378
Punch cartoon, "Willcocks's Week-end War," 168
Puniali Levy, in Hunza-Nagir Expedition, 107, 108
Punjab Cavalry, 3rd, in Marri Expedition, 73
Punjab Cavalry, 5th, in sortie from Sherpur, 63
Punjab Infantry, 1st (55th Coke's Rifles), success at Barari Tangi, 11; under Keyes in action of Conical Hill, Ambela, 17; in first recapture of Crag Piquet, Ambela, 18; in second Miranzai Expedition, 107; in Waziristan, 426, 430, 431
Punjab Infantry, 2nd (56th Punjab Rifles), at Peiwar Kotal, 39; at capture of Saragarhi, 102; on Suez Canal, 210, 211, 213, 214; in Waziristan, 393, 395
Punjab Infantry, 3rd (57th Wilde's Rifles), with Regiment at destruction of Shahtut, 28
Punjab Infantry, 5th (58th Vaughan's Rifles), at Eagle's Nest, Ambela, 17; in third recapture of Crag Piquet, Ambela, 21; at Charasia, 47, 48, 49; at Sadda in 1897, 140
Punjab Infantry, 6th (59th Scinde Rifles), at Eagle's Nest, Ambela, 17; in Zakka Khel Expedition, 191

Punjab Infantry, 20th, small party in Hunza-Nagir Expedition, 109; in Waziristan, 1895, 135
Punjab Infantry, 25th Regiment of, original title of 5th Gurkhas, 3
Punjab Infantry, 29th, at Peiwar Kotal, 36, 37
Punjab Irregular Force (later Punjab Frontier Force), 5th Gurkhas raised as part of, 3; change of designation, 24; control transferred to G. of I., 83; eulogy of, by Gen. Brackenbury, 132, 133; dissolution of, 186
Punjab Native Infantry, 20th, hard pressed at Eagle's Nest, Ambela, 18; in first recapture of Crag Piquet, Ambela, 18; with Regiment in attack on Machai, 27
Punjab Police Battalions, drafts to 5th Gurkhas when raised, 3, App. I, 449
Punjabis, 28th, in Zakka Khel Expedition, 191, 193, 195
Punjabis, 2/76th, in Waziristan, 418
Purnea, s.s., takes 3/5th from Basra to India, 379
Pustawani Valley visited by Regiment, 32

Q

Quadrilateral Redoubt, in Gallipoli, captured by French, 243
Queen's Regiment, at Arhanga Pass, 143; at Thabai, 148; camaraderie, 158
Quetta, 5th Gurkhas at, 72; 5th Gurkhas leave, 73
Qurna, first occupation of, 279

R

Racquets, 127, 198
Radwaniya Canal, operations by Lucas Column towards, 285
Ragobir Nagarkoti, awarded Order of Merit at Peiwar Kotal, 40; killed in withdrawal from Takht-i-Shah, 61
Ragobir Thapa, killed with Mummery on Nanga Parbat, 125
Raising of 5th Gurkhas, 3, App. I, 449; of 2/5th, 83, 173; of 3/5th, 347
Rajgal Valley visited in 1897, 150
Ramadi, message from Army Commander, 294
Ramadi, Battle of, preparations, 288, 289, 331, 332; description of terrain, 289, 290; 1/5th in the battle, 291-294; 2/5th in the battle, 332-335
Ramadi Ridge, feature of Battle of Ramadi, 290, 291, 293, 333, 334
Ramadi, Turkish position at, 288; first attack on, 288; 1/5th and 2/5th at, after the battle, 295, 335; 1/5th return to, 300; 2/5th return, 340

INDEX 513

Ram Sing Thapa with 1/1st Gurkhas in France, 309

Ranbir Gurung, good work in Gallipoli, 230

Rations for Kabul–Kandahar march, 68

Rawalpindi, reception of Amir at, 79; camp of exercise, 96, 137; standing camp at, 168; 3/5th at, 349; march of 3/5th to, from Chamiari, 352; 1/5th at, for Duke of Connaught's visit, 387; 2/5th on garrison duty at, 413; 2/5th at, for Duke of Connaught's review, 437

Razani, visited by expedition of 1860, 11; on new frontier road, 391; 1/5th at, in 1923, 393, 399-403

Razmak, visited by expedition of 1860, 11; of 1894, 134; 1/5th at, in 1923, 394-399; 1/5th in operations conducted from, 395-398; camel raiders ambushed by 2/5th, 398

Razmak Narai Pass on new frontier road, 391; secured by 7th Bde. in 1923, 393

Reaney, M. F., Capt., I.M.S., killed in action in Gallipoli, 241; distinctions won, 456

Recruiting, first party in 1858 to Kumaon, 8; for Second Afghan War, 34

Reservists, response on outbreak of Great War, 203, 305

Rhododendron Spur, feature figuring in attack from Anzac, Gallipoli, 247, 249

Richardson, Col., commanding in Kurram, 1897, 140

Rifles, 60th, 1st Bn., in second Miranzai Expedition, 101, 102

Rifles, 60th, 2nd Bn., in Marri Expedition, 73

Ril occupied in fourth Black Mountain Expedition, 178

River Clyde, 1/5th land near, 219

Road, as feature of policy, 390; in Waziristan, 391

Roberts, Countess, D.B.E., volume dedicated to, v; visits Abbottabad, 440; presentation by, 440

Roberts, Frederick Slade, Field-Marshal Earl, choice of supporters for arms, xviii; first inspection of 5th Gurkhas, 32; in command of Kurram F.F., 34; victory of Peiwar Kotal, 36-40; his appreciation of conduct of 5th Gurkhas at Monghyr Defile, 42; visit to Khost, 42; commands Kabul F.F., 44; advance towards Kabul, 45; victory at Charasia, 46-49; occupies Kabul, 50; in command of all troops Eastern Afghanistan, 52; plan for dealing with Afghan concentration, 52, 53; action to cover Massy's defeat by Muhammad Jan, 56; decision to concentrate at Sherpur, 60; disperses Afghan concentration, 63; transfer of command to Sir D. Stewart, 64; selected to command Kabul-Kandahar F.F., 67; arrangements for march, 67; victory of Kandahar, 70, 71; farewell to 5th Gurkhas, 72; appointed Colonel of 5th Gurkhas, 165, 186; presentation of shooting trophy, 172; death in France, 205, 307

Roberts, G. E. V., mortally wounded at Hill 60, 267; distinctions won, 456

Roe, C. D., with 2/5th in Waziristan, 419

Rolfe, A. N., with 2/8th Gurkhas in France, 308; wounded at Givenchy, 308; distinctions won, 462; other services, 485

Rombulow-Pearse, A. B., with 3/5th, 359

Rooke, A. S., services after leaving 5th Gurkhas, 485

Roosmale Cocq, C. A., raises and commands 3/5th, 347; transfer to 1/8th Gurkhas, 349

Rothney, O. E., appointment to 5th Gurkhas, 10; in command of Regiment at Palosin, 10, 11; in command at Oghi, 25; in command of reserve column, second Black Mountain Expedition, 27; promotion and departure, 29; distinctions won, 450

Royal Bengal Fusiliers (101st), in action at Conical Hill, Ambela, 17; in second recapture of Crag Piquet, 20

Royal Cord, introduction and significance 405,

Royal, title of, conferred on 5th Gurkhas, 379, 388, 437

Rumaitha, on Euphrates, 3/5th at, 378

Russell, Brig.-Gen., in battle of August 21st, 260, 261

Russians, relations with Afghanistan, 33, 34; high-handedness at Panjdeh, 80, 81; activity in Pamirs, 94, 95, 105; co-operation in Mesopotamia, 282

S

Saadat Khan, Ressaldar, his exploit near Tank, 1860, 9

Sadda, 1/5th at, in 1897, 138; attack on, 140

Safah, 2/5th detachment at, 325;

Safed Koh, topographical situation, 100, 191

Saghir Dere, ravine in Gallipoli, 232, 233

Sahaliya, abandoned by Turks, 297; 15th Division at, 297, 337

Saidra, 1/5th at destruction of, in 1888, 90

Saiyid Ahmed Shah, founder of colony of Hindustani Fanatics, 12, 13

Saiyid Akbar, succeeds Saiyid Ahmed Shah as leader of Hindustani Fanatics, 14

Salt Lake, feature of Suvla area, Gallipoli, 248

Saltow Pass, search for, 95

Samaikcheh, Arab district north of Baghdad, operations of Lucas Column, 286, 287

Samana, position of, 99; capture of, 101, 102; 1/5th provide garrison, 159; 2/5th provide garrison, 185; 1/5th at, in 1924, 404

Samarra, Turks driven north of, 288

Samawa, Turkish detachment at, in 1916, 324; operations for relief of, in 1920, 364, 370; occupied by Samcol, 370

Sambalbat, spur of Black Mountain ascended by 3rd Column in third expedition, 88; by Sir J. McQueen's Force in 1890, 98
Samcol, column for relief of Samawa, operations, 364-378
Sampagha Pass, capture of, 143
Sanders, G. P., in Tibet, 154; in temporary command of 2/5th, 322, 335; in temporary command of 1/5th, 385; transfer to command 3/11th Gurkhas, 389; commanding 2/6th Gurkhas in Waziristan, 439; distinctions won, 458
Sandstorms, in Egypt, 207, 211, 215; in Mesopotamia, 288, 293; at Parachinar, 391
Sangar, on Samana, 101; 1/5th detachment at, in 1924, 404
Sang-i-Nawishta, held by Afghans in Charasia Battle, 46, 47, 49
Sanman Sunwar, good work at Imam Abdulla, 378
Sannaiyat, on Tigris, successive failures to capture, 280, 281; captured 281
Santbir Thapa, winner of Hill Race, 123
Sappers and Miners: No. 2 Company, in Waziristan, 135; No. 3 Company, in third Black Mountain Expedition, 88; No. 7 Company, at Charasia, 47
Saragarhi, brilliantly captured by 1/5th in 1891, 101; resistance of 36th Sikhs at, in 1897, 140
Saran Sar, disaster to Northamptons at, 144; Gurkha Scouts at, 152
Sara Paial, in Bazar Valley, 194
Sari Bair, Gallipoli, position overlooking Anzac, 220, 247, 250; 1/6th Gurkhas gain position on, overlooking Narrows, 250
Sarkai Ghar, ridge cut through by Tank Zam, operations at, 320, 321
Sarmando, in Bazar Valley, destroyed, 1908, 195
Sartop, on Samana, 101
Sarwakai Pass, 2/5th at, in 1908, 195
Sazli Beit Dere (Ravine), figures in attack from Anzac, Gallipoli, 247. 249
Scimitar Hill (Hill 70), feature of Suvla area, 248; objective of 29th Division on August 21st, 258, 259
Scorpion, H.M.S., in battle of June 28th, 233, 241
Scott, H. St. G., appointed Commandant, 2/5th Gurkhas, 440; leaves 2/5th, 443
Scouts, employment at Makin, 134
Scouts, Gurkha, in 1897, 139, 141-153; in first action at Dargai, 142; of 3rd Gurkhas only in second attack on Dargai, 142; at Sampagha Pass, 143; at Arhanga Pass, 143; in Maidan, 144; at Bagh, 144; at Dwatoi, 145; in advance to Kharmana, 146; at Thabai, 146-149; in Bara Valley,

150; in Bazar Valley, 151; strength increased, 151; C. G. Bruce's account of, 152; Sir W. Lockhart's tribute, 153
Seaforth Highlanders, 2nd Bn., in third Black Mountain Expedition, 88, 91
Security, internal, 1/5th employed on, 384, 385
Sembar Pass, transport in difficulties at, in Marri Expedition, 74
Serai Kala. *See* Taxila
Serapeum, in Suez Canal defences, 207
Seri, 2/5th at destruction of, in 1891
Shabkadr, threatened by Mohmands in 1916, 277
Shagai, Khyber, piquetting from, by 3/5th, 355
Shahidula, scene of Hunza raid, 94
Shah Jahan Khan, proclaimed Nawab of Dir, 441
Shahraban, operations at, at time of arrival of 1/5th in Mesopotamia, 282
Shahtut, Black Mountain, destruction of, 28
Shahur, 1/5th via, to Kundiwam, in 1895, 155
Shaiba, Battle of, 279
Shaikh Saad, Battle of, 280
Shaktu, visited in Mahsud Expedition of 1894-95, 135
Shal Nullah, Black Mountain, topography, 179
Shaloufa, post in Suez Canal defences, 216
Shamgakki Pass, situation of, 355; affair at, in 1919, 355-357
Shamsher Gurung, good work at Imam Abdulla, 377
Shankargarh, looted by Mohmands, 139
Sharpshooters, employment of, in Ambela campaign, 17; in operations against Allai, 92
Shatt-Abu-Shuraish, arm of Euphrates, 371, 374, 375
Shatt-el-Hai, possibility of Turkish advance by, 281; control extended to, 281
Shatt, in Suez sector of canal defences, 213
Sheikhan, situation of, 103
Sheikh Farajah, feature of Battle of Ramadi, 290
Shekhabad, visited by 5th Gurkhas, 65
Shells, shortage of, in Gallipoli, 228
Sher Darwaza Heights, position in relation to Kabul, 50
Shere Ali, partiality for Russia, 33; flight and death in Turkestan, 43
Shergat, on Tigris, 1/5th at, 301
Sherpur Cantonment, position in relation to Kabul, 50; occupation of, 51; threatened by confederation, 53; withdrawal of Field Force to, 60; investment of, 62, 63
Sheranni, 1/5th at, in 1895, 136
Shimshal Pass, exploration of, 94

INDEX

Shinauri, starting point for invasion of Tirah, 141
Shindih, visited by Regiment, 31
Shooting, big and small game, 119, 164; on range, special course, 157, 169; Roberts Cup Competition, 172, 189; A.R.A.I. competitions, 405, 407, 410
Shuidar, mountain in Waziristan, 394
Shutargardan Pass, reconnaissance of, 40
Siah-Sang Hill, position in relation to Kabul, 50
Sialkot, 2/5th detachment at, 413
Sikh Infantry, 1st (51st Sikhs F.F.), drafts to 5th Gurkhas when raised, 3, Appendix I, 449; in Egypt, 211, 213, 214, 216
Sikh Infantry, 2nd (52nd Sikhs F.F.), drafts to 5th Gurkhas when raised, 3, Appendix I, 449; with 5th Gurkhas in Kabul-Kandahar march, 67; in Battle of Kandahar, 71; in Achakzai and Marri Expeditions, 72, 73
Sikh Infantry, 3rd (53rd Sikhs F.F.), drafts to 5th Gurkhas when raised, 3, Appendix I, 449; with 5th Gurkhas in Kabul-Kandahar march, 67; in Marri Expedition, 73; in third Black Mountain Expedition, 88, 90; at Sampagha Pass, 143; at Arhanga Pass, 143; at Thabai, 148; in Zakka Khel Expedition, 191; in Egypt, 214, 216
Sikh Infantry, 4th (54th Sikhs F.F.), drafts to 5th Gurkhas when raised, 3, Appendix I, 449; in Zakka Khel Expedition, 191, 195
Sikhs, 14th. *See* Native Infantry, 14th
Sikhs, 3/23rd, in Arab Rising, 366, 371, 373, 375, 376
Sikhs, 45th, in Zakka Khel Expedition, 191
Sind Valley (Kashmir), traversed by Younghusband's party, 94
Siran River, fishing in, 120
Sitana, settlement of Hindustani fanatics at, 14; 5th Gurkhas at destruction of, 23
Siyaah, on Euphrates, destroyed by 3/5th, 371
Skeen, Major-Gen. A., commanding Derajat Column, Waziristan, 415; visit to 2/5th, 432
Skipwith, F., commanding 1/5th in Mesopotamia, 295; transferred to command 2/10th Gurkhas, 385; other services, 485; distinctions won, 458
Slavery, abolition of, in Nepal, 407
"Small Wars: Their Principles and Practice" by C. E. Calwell, quoted, 148
Sniper's Nest, near Makin, feature of operation of February 25th, 1920, 428
Sniping, at Khorappa, 142; at Maidan, 144; in Bara Valley, 115; at Walai, 194; in Mesopotamia, 325; in Waziristan, 399
Snow, at Sherpur, 63; on Burzil Pass, 106; on Black Mountain, 177; in Hazara, 183; at Lowarai Pass, 184; in Waziristan, 393, 394, 395, 397, 421, 430
Sorarogha, 2/5th engaged at, during piquet construction, 420; halt at, 420
South Lancashire Regiment, 6th, great feat in battle of August 6th-10th, 250
South Wales Borderers, in Gallipoli, 230
Sowabi, Arab tribe, concentration near Khidhr, 366
Spedding & Co., assistance in Hunza-Nagir Expedition, 106, 107
Spin Kach, road difficulties at, in Marri Expedition, 74
Spin Kamar, reverse at, in 1898, 151
Spingawai Kotal, action at, 37-40
Split Hill, feature of action of February 20th, at Makin, 426
Stables, J. H., murdered by Arabs, 286
Star Kili, in Daradar Valley, 1/5th at, 104
Stewart, Sir Donald, commands Kandahar F.F., 43, 44; advance to Kabul and victory at Ahmed Khel, 64; assumes command at Kabul, 64
Stewart, J. M., his memoranda of post-Afghan War period, 79, 118; visit to Pamirs, 105; in China and Tibet, 154; Brevet Majority for China, 187; transferred to command 1/9th Gurkhas, 187; returns to command 2/5th, 187; in Zakka Khel Expedition, 192, 193, 197; A.D.C. to King, 198; appointed to Staff, 199; appointed Colonel of 5th Gurkhas, 410; distinctions won, 460; other services and distinctions, 486
Stony Jheel, snipe shooting at, 119
Stories, of soft stones, 95; of Surbir Thapa and Grombtchevsky, 96; of bleached bone, 97; of silencing of Mr. B——, 97; of metamorphosis of Colonel's horse, 97; of loot, 152; of Mr. Lionel James, 152; of excited Staff officer, 166; of terse appreciation, 167; of fly catching, 168; of Japanese attaché, 189; of the Force Commander as postman, 196; of nerves at Jamrud, 358; of the strong Lama, 359; of the acquisitive Q.M., 359; of the nightmare, 359; of the artist cook, 392
Strahan, G. C., in temporary command of 2/5th in Waziristan, 425, 427, 428; distinctions won with 2/5th, 463
Submarines, danger of, on voyage to Gallipoli, 219
Suez, 1/5th disembark at, 206; 1/5th at, after Gallipoli, 274
Suez Canal, situation on, in 1914, 206, 207; dispositions on, 207; traffic through, 210; Turkish attack on, 211; southern sector of defences, 213-216; 1/5th in pursuit of Turkish column, 214, 215; second visit of 1/5th, 273, 274

Suji Kach, visited on return from Marri Expedition, 75
Summer camps, 155, 189, 437
Surbir Thapa, with Francis Younghusband in exploration, 94; his message to Grombtchevsky, 96
Sur Ghar Hills, situation of, 191
Surkh Kotal, held by Macpherson during Karez Mir action, 54
Surmal, attack on, in fourth Black Mountain Expedition, 179, 180
Surrender, final, of Turks, 300
Suru, scene of mountain exploration, 125
Susak Kuyu, captured in battle of August 21st, 258, 260
Sutton, Colonel, commanding 2/10th Gurkhas in Gallipoli, 253, 355
Suvla Bay, Gallipoli, 247; topography, 247, 248; landing at, 251; fighting by IX Corps from, 251
Suvla Point, Gallipoli, northern promontory of Suvla Bay, 248
Swatis, attack by, at Ambela, 18; locations on Black Mountain, 24
Swiftsure, H.M.S., in Suez Canal defence, 209
Sym, J. M., officiates as Adjutant, 24; with reinforcements to Gen. Baker, 50; in command at capture of Takht-i-Shah, 58; prompt action in withdrawal from Takht-i-Shah, promoted Brevet Lieut.-Colonel, 77; improvement effected by, in marching, 80; in command of first column in third Black Mountain Expedition, 88; reconnoitres Ghorapher Pass, 92; awarded C.B., 96; in command of first column, second Miranzai Expedition, 100; helpful attitude when 2/5th was raised, 174; appointed Colonel 5th Gurkhas, 205; death of, 389; distinctions won, 451, 452
Symons, Brig.-Gen. W. P., in command of 2nd Bde., Waziristan F.F., 134; of 1st Div., Tirah F.F., 141

T

Table Top, feature figuring in attack from Anzac, Gallipoli, 247, 249
Takht-i-Shah Hill, position in relation to Kabul, 50
Takhtak Village, tower destroyed, second Miranzai Expedition, 104
Talbot, H.M.S., in battle of June 28th, 233
Tamre Oba, on Khaisora, new road passes, 391
Tanaolis, help against Black Mountain tribes, 25
Tangi Wardak, visited by 5th Gurkhas, 65
Tank, scene of Saadat Khan's exploit, 9; 1/5th at, 135; 2/5th at, 414

Tank Zam, 1/5th in, 9, 133; 2/5th in operations on, 415-424
Tauda China, Waziristan, alignment of new frontier road along, 391; topography of, 394; camp on, near Makin, in 1920, 424-428
Taxila (Serai Kala), 1/5th detachment at, during Punjab unrest, 384
Taylor, Lieut., at storming of Thol Cliffs, 112
Tel-al-Rayan, 42nd Bde. Headquarters at Battle of Ramadi, 333
Tel-Sina-Dhibban, 42nd Bde. at, in advance to Ramadi, 289, 331
Telephone, early use of, 168
Tennis, Lawn, 127; in Mesopotamia, 342
Thabai, actions at, 146-149
Thabai Pass, situation of, 191
Thakot, position in relation to Black Mountain, 24; visited in third expedition, 91
Thal (Chotiali), 5th Gurkhas at, in Marri Expedition, 74
Thal (in Kurram), concentration of Kurram F.F., 34; arrival of 5th Gurkhas, 34; 1/5th at, in 1922, 390, 391; 1/5th detachment at, in 1924, 404
Thal (in Tochi), road from, 391
Thams, rulers of Hunza and Nagir, 106
"The Campaign in Tirah, 1897-98," by Col. H. D. Hutchinson, quoted, 139, 143, 144
"The Risings on the North-West Frontier, 1897-98," Pioneer Press, quoted, 140, 142, 144, 147
"The Second Afghan War: Official Account" quoted, 68
Thol, situation of, 108
Tigris, operations on, 279-282, 286, 287
Tikari, Black Mountain tract inhabited by Swatis, 24; visited in second Black Mountain Expedition, 28
Tilchand Thapa, gallantry at Makin, 425
Tillard, with Gurkha scouts in Tirah, 139; takes command of 1/5th, 266; leaves, 1/5th, 274; distinctions won, 456
Tilli, 2/5th at, in 1891, 177, 178
Timsah, Lake, in Suez Canal defence, 208, 211
Toba Plateau, 5th Gurkhas at, in Achakzai Expedition, 72
Tochi River, 136
Tomes, Capt., 53rd Sikhs, killed in Gallipoli, 256
Torbela, fishing at, 120
Towara, action at, in second Black Mountain Expedition, 88
Townshend, Major-Gen. C. V., captures Amara, 279; victory at Es-Sinn, 279; at Battle of Ctesiphon, 279; in Kut, 280
Tragbal Pass, nature of, 106
Training, 155, 163, 164, 165, 169, 360

Transport, difficulties with, at Ambela, 14; for Kabul-Kandahar march, 68; 70, footnote; difficulties of, at Sembar Pass in Marri Expedition, 74; at Ghorapher Pass in 1888, 92; scarcity of, when 1/5th ordered to Miranzai, 100; regimental establishment reduced, 115; trouble with mules at Khirgi, 415

Tree Hill, feature of affair of February 19th, 1920, at Makin, 425

Tree-planting, at Abbottabad, 8, 175; on Samana, 158

Trench warfare, experiences of 1/5th in, 229, 230, 257, 265-268

Trissul, Mount, ascent of, 125

Trommer, Col. von, in command of Turkish column near Kubri, 215

Trout fishing, 120

Tsalai, on Samana, affair at, 101

Tsapara, capture of, by 2/5th in 1908, 192

Tsatsobi Pass, situation of, 191; reconnaissance of, in 1908, 195

Tulbir Gurung, winner of Hill Race, 122

Turis, dislike of Afghan rule, 34; transfer to British rule, 35

Turkey, war with, declared, 279; capitulation of, 300, 340; influence in Kabul, 353

Turks, advance on Suez Canal, 210, 211; attack on canal, 211; operations of column under von Trommer, 213-215; in Gallipoli, 218-271; extraordinary bravery of, in counter-attacks, 240-243; forces available, 218, 248; in Mesopotamia, 279, 280, 281, 282, 288-294, 296, 297, 298, 299, 300, 331-334

Turner, G., in battle of June 4th, 224, 225; killed in action, 225; tribute to, 227; distinctions won, 456

Twigg, Capt., in Hunza-Nagir Expedition, 108, 110

U

Ujir Sing Gurung, good work in Gallipoli, 230

Unhar River, course in relation to Black Mountain, 177

Unrest, internal, in India, 351, 352, 353, 384; 1/5th on security duty during, 384; in Hazara and Agror, 386

Uqbah, Turkish patrols at, after Ramadi, 296; occupied by 59th Bde., 296; 42nd Bde. advances to, 296, 336; 1/5th detachments at, after Khan Baghdadi, 300

Ur of the Chaldees, railway junction, Iraq, 364; 3/5th at, 365

Urmston, H. B., 6th P.I., death on Black Mountain, 84-86

V

Vansittart, E., commanding wing of 1/5th at Sadda, 140; commanding wing at Thabai, wounded, 149; transfer, 161; first Adjutant, 2/5th, 174; good work recruiting, 174; services after leaving 5th Gurkhas, 486

" V " Beach, Gallipoli, 1/5th land at, 219

Victoria, Queen, death of, 159; solicitude for soldiers, 160

Villiers-Stuart, W. D., wounded at Thabai, 147; march to Chilas, 157; in Waziristan Blockade, 160; arrival in Egypt from France to command 1/5th, 274; supervising officer, Nepalese Contingent, 276; raises and commands 3rd Guides, 385; in charge of mountain warfare school, 385; Commandant, 1/5th, 387; commanding 5th Bde. column in operations, Waziristan, 395; retirement, 405; other services, 486; distinctions won, 458, 459, 460

W

Wadi, Battle of the, 280

Wadi Hauran, floods in, hold up 2/5th, 339

Wadi-um-Muksheib, occupied by Turks, 209

Walai, situation of, 191; advance of 2/5th to, in 1908, 193; standing camp at, 193; Hill Race at, against Pathans, 196

Wales, Prince of, visit to Rawalpindi, 390; guard of honour from both battalions 5th Gurkhas, 390, 439

Wall, A. C., commanding 3/5th, 349

Wana, attack on camp, 133; Hill Race against Pathans at, 123; 1/5th at, 135

Wana Valley, view of, from Badder Toi, 431

Waran Valley, Dorsets lose heavily during withdrawal from, 144

War memorials, on Ramadi Ridge, 340; of Frontier Force regiments at Kohat, 406; of 5th and 6th Gurkhas at Abbottabad, 438, 439

Warwickshire Regiment, in Zakka Khel Expedition, 191

Water supply, in Abbottabad, 130

Watson, H. D., compiler of excellent gazetteer, 26

Watt, D. M., commanding 2/5th in Waziristan, 421, 422, 428, 431, 433; distinctions won with 2/5th, 463, 464

Watt, W. R., good work at Depot, 385

Wawiyah, 3/5th holding blockhouse line from, to Deraji, 379

Waziristan, 1/5th in, in 1922-23, 391-403; situation at time of arrival, 391, 392; securing route, Asad Khel to Razani, 392-393; forward move of 7th Bde., 393; advance to Razani and Razmak, 393, 394; description of terrain, 394-395; operations from Razmak, 395-399; road protection from Razani, 399-403; departure, 403

2/5th in, in 1919-1920, 414-433 : join 67th Bde., 415 ; preliminary operations at Ahnai, 416 ; action at Ahnai Tangi, 416-418 ; gradual advance to Makin against opposition, 419-424 ; operations round Makin, 425-428 ; advance to Kaniguram, 429 ; punishment of Abdur Rahman Khel, 431, 432 ; at Ladha, 432 ; move to Kotkai, 433 ; official summary of campaign, 433, 434 ; " B " Company attached to 2/6th Gurkhas in operations of 1923, 440

NOTE.—*See also under* "Mahsud Wazirs."

Webb, A. B. H. *See* Hay-Webb.

Weekes, H. E., appointed commandant 1/5th, 405 ; leaves Battalion on appointment to Staff, 412 ; responsible for levelling recruits' parade ground, 412 ; distinctions won, 459, 460

Welch Fusiliers, in fourth Black Mountain Expedition, 177, 179, 180

Wellesley, H. A., wounded at As Sahilan, 325 ; in Battle of Ramadi, 332, 333 ; distinctions won, 461, 462

White Tower, feature of action of February 20th, 1920, at Makin, 426

Willcocks, Major-Gen. Sir J., in command of Zakka Khel Expedition, 190

Wilson, Major-Gen., in command of Canal Defence Force, 207

Windy Corner, near Jamrud, resort of raiders, 357

Wing system, suitable when British officers few, 118

Winn, H. E., distinctions won, 455

Wolverine, H.M.S., in battle of June 28th, 283

" Wonders of Himalaya," book by Sir Francis Younghusband, quoted, 95, 96

Wood-cutting, 156

Woodyatt, Major-Gen. N., commanding 3rd Bde., in Mohmand blockade, 1916, 277 ; defeats tribesmen at Rustam, 318

Woon, Major-Gen. J. B., commanding Abbottabad Bde., 167

Y

Yahoudie, post on Tigris garrisoned by 2/5th, 330

Yakub Khan, succeeds Shere Ali as Amir, 43 ; makes peace with British, 43 ; his attitude after Cavagnari's murder, 44, 45 ; abdication and exile to India, 52

Yarkand River, visited by exploring party, 94

Yeatman-Biggs, Major-Gen., in command of flying column, 140

Yeomanry Div. (2nd), in battle of August 21st, 258, 259

Yilghin Burnu, feature of Suvla area, Gallipoli, 248, 251, 259

Yorkshire Regiment, at capture of Sampagha, 143 ; at Arhanga Pass, 143

Younghusband, Francis, exploration with men of 5th Gurkhas, 94-96

Yusafzai, sections of tribe inhabiting Black Mountain, 24

Z

Zakka Khel, in Tirah Campaign, 144, 151 ; Expedition of 1908, 190-198

Zamburak Kotal, trying experience of 5th Gurkhas at, in Kabul–Kandahar march, 69

Zaskar, scene of mountain exploration, 125

Zemu Glacier, survey of, 125

Zeriwam, camp at, below Ahnai Tangi, 416

Ziachen Glacier, survey of, 125

Zir Ghundai, in Bazar Valley, 194

Zoji La (Pass), traversed by exploring party, 94

MAP OF KABUL AND S[

URROUNDING COUNTRY.

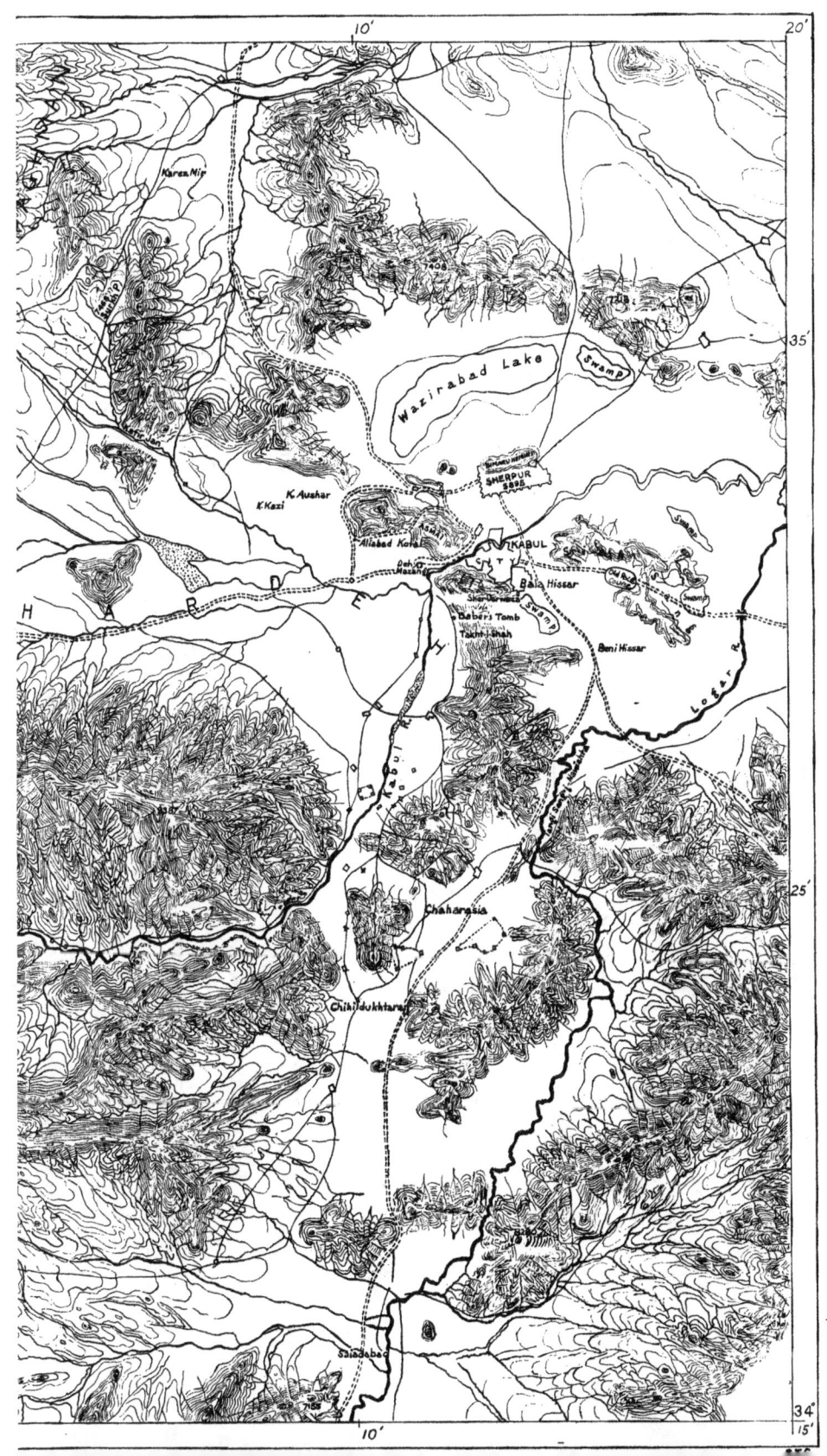

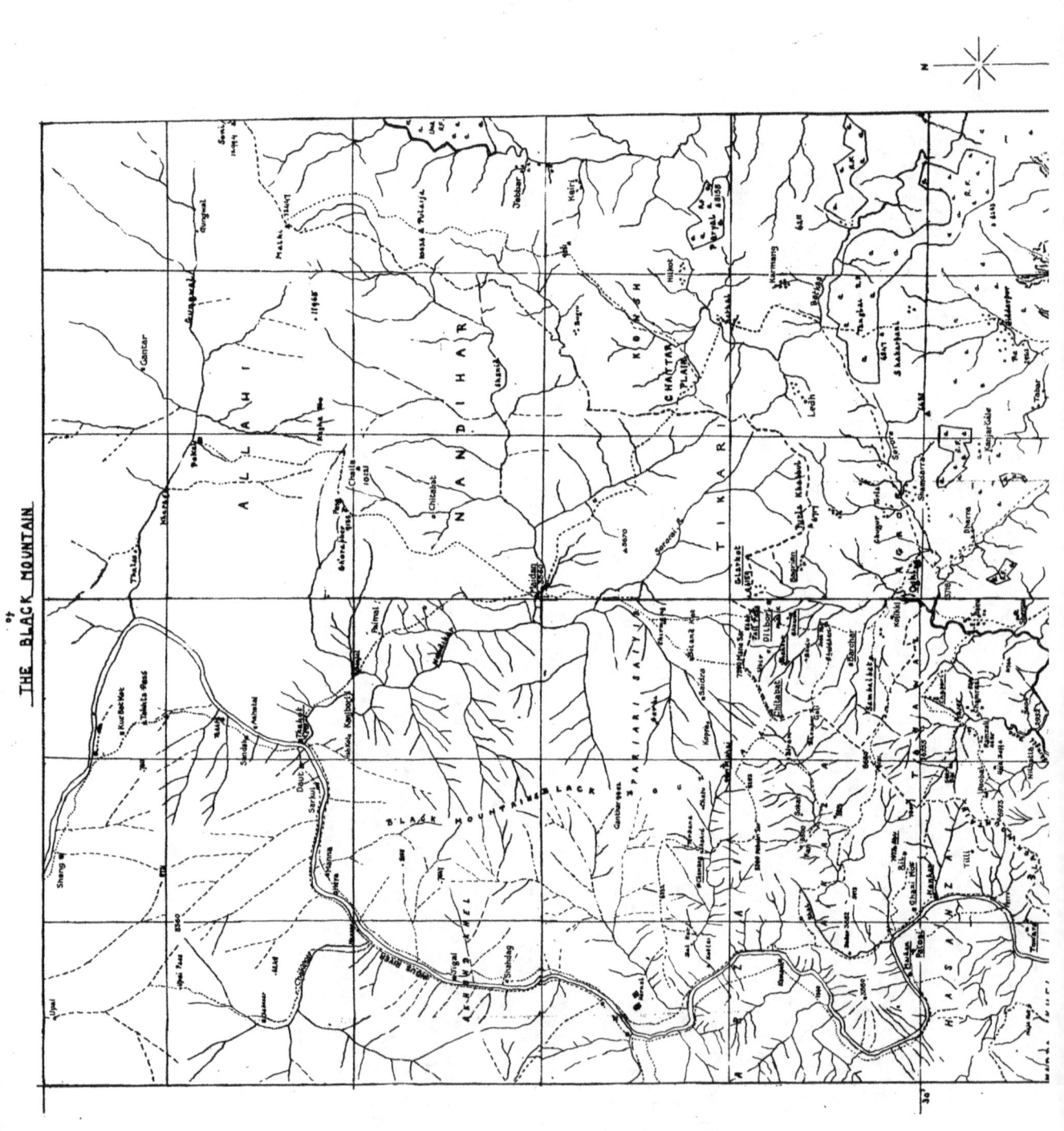

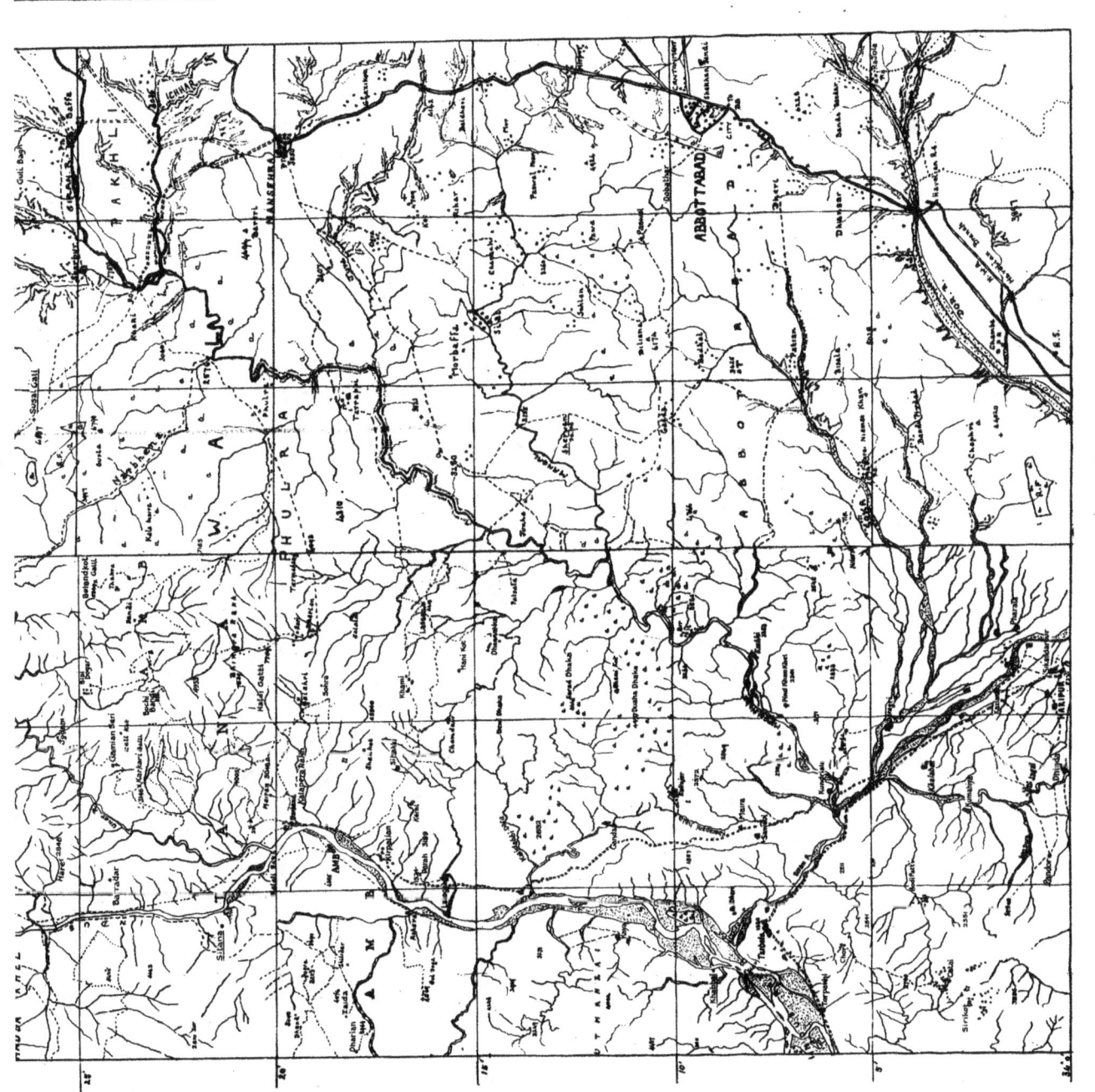

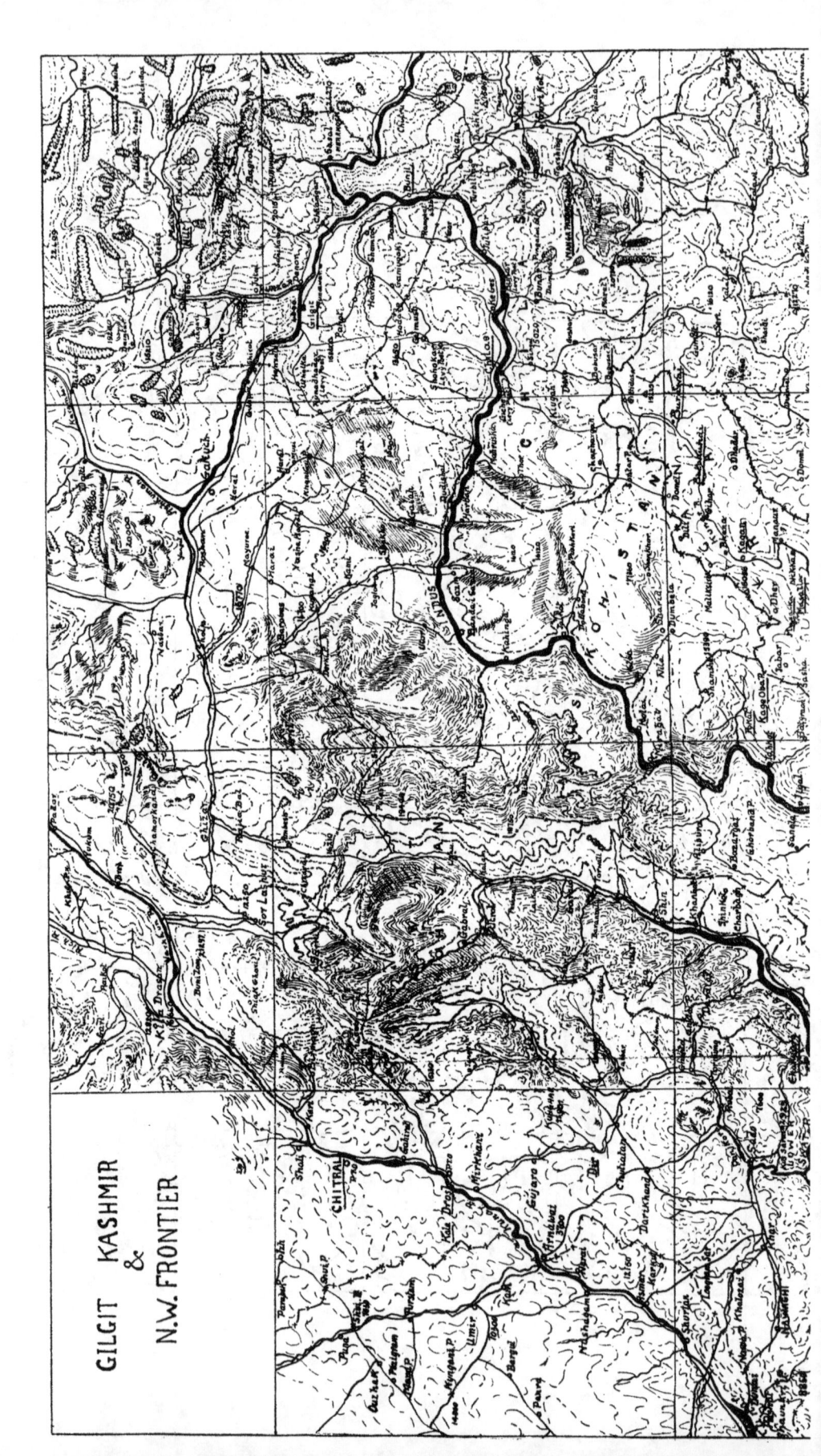

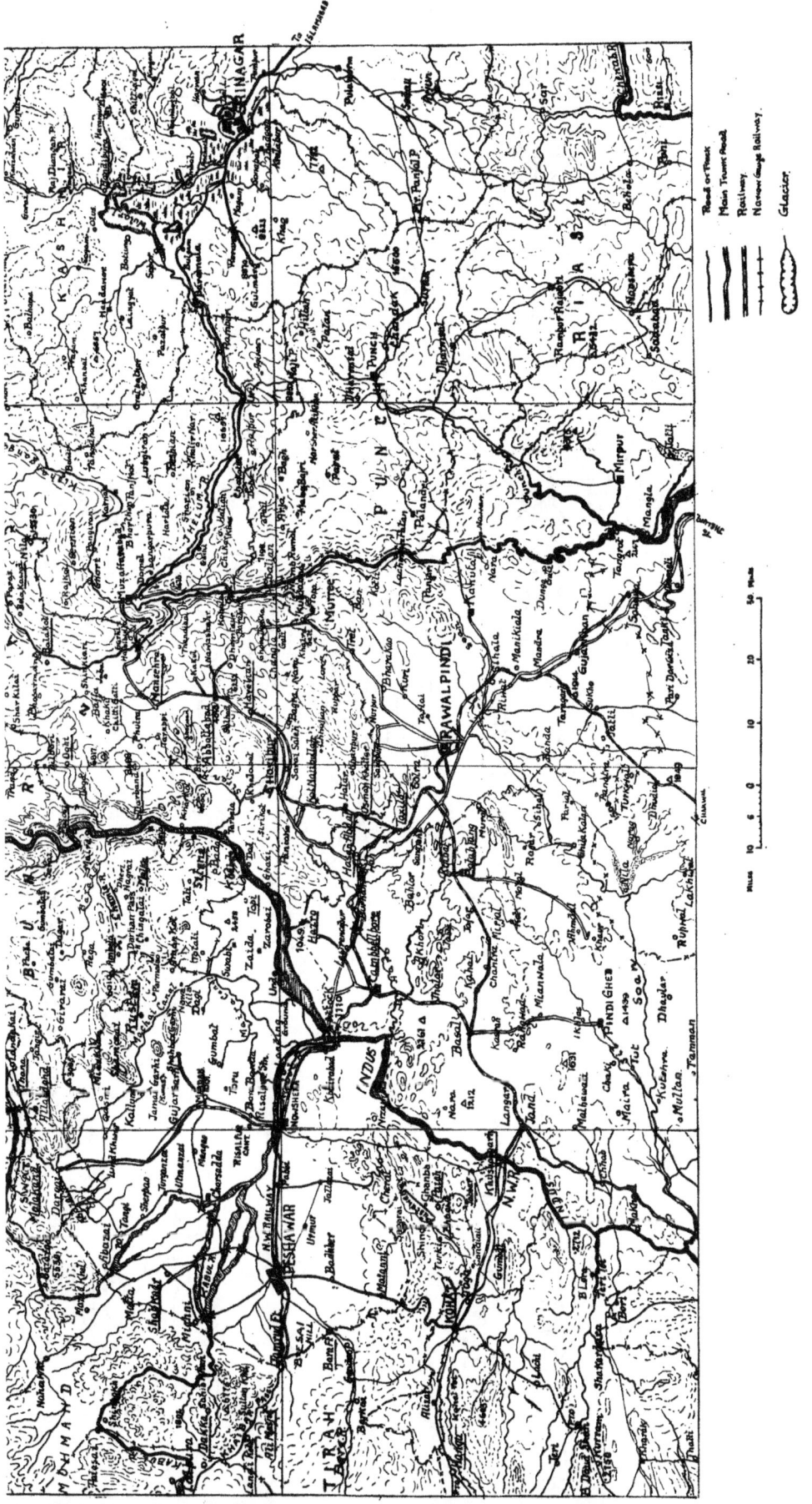

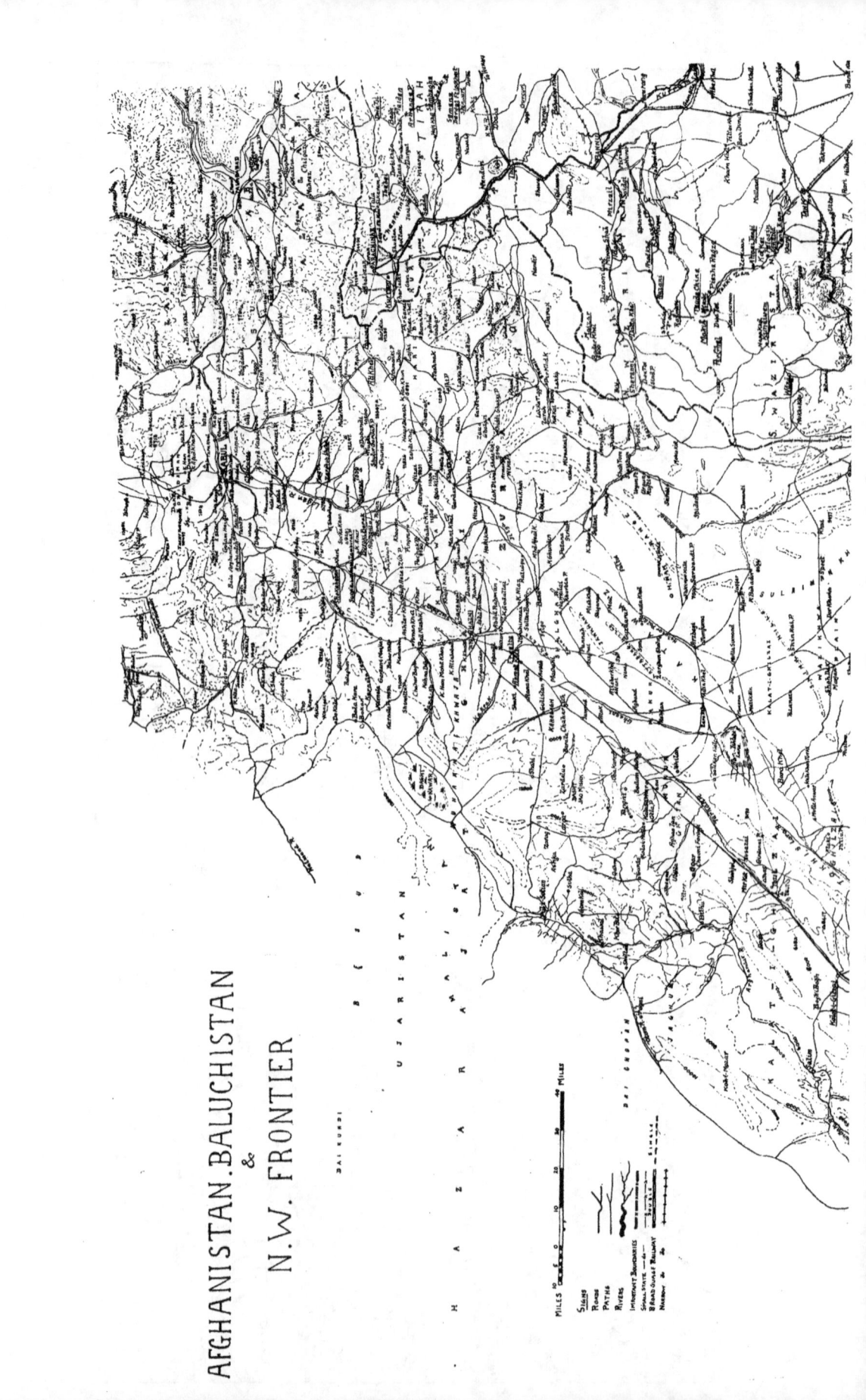

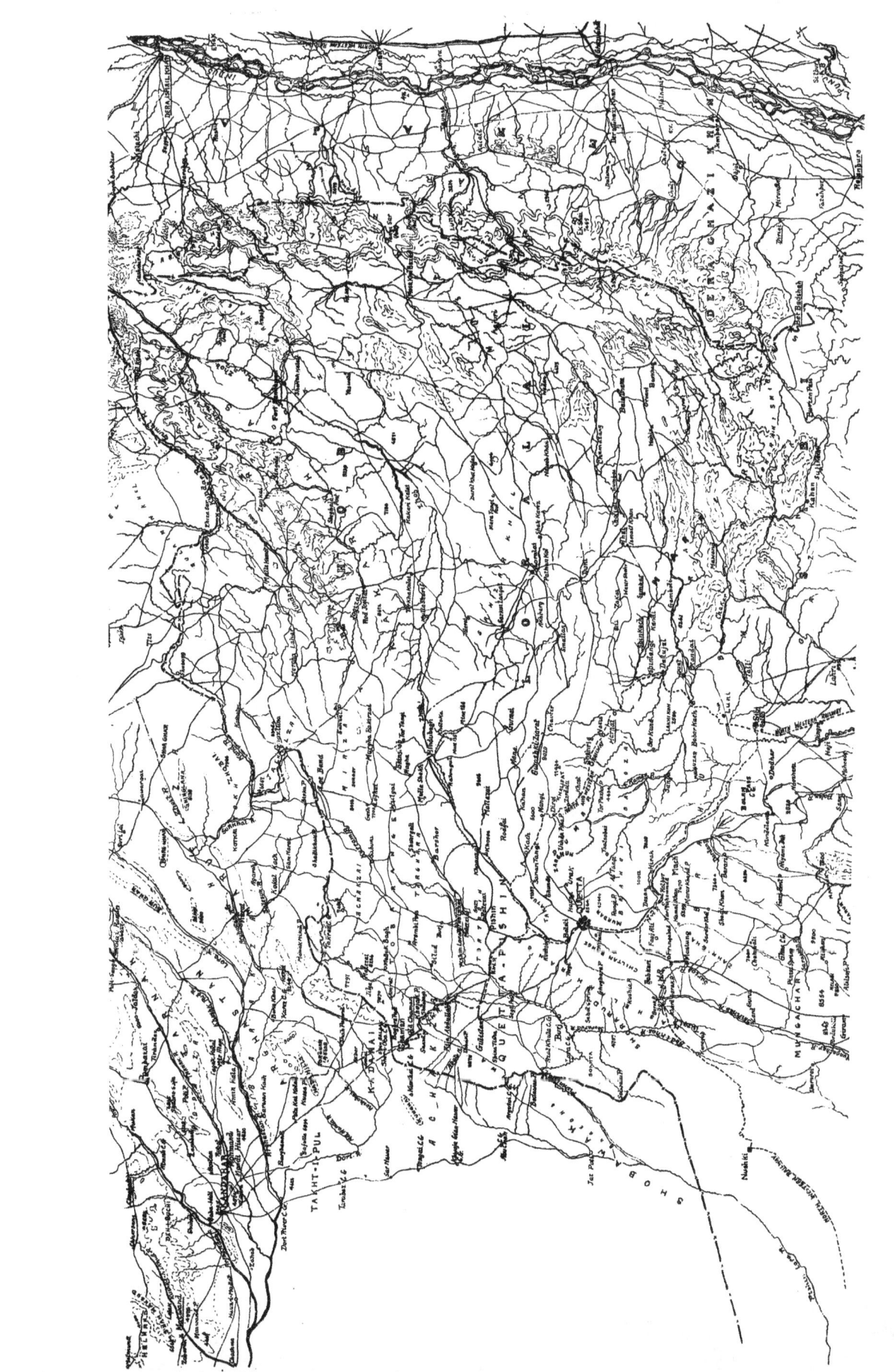

www.ingramcontent.com/pod-product-compliance
Lightning Source LLC
Chambersburg PA
CBHW080536230426
43663CB00015B/2616